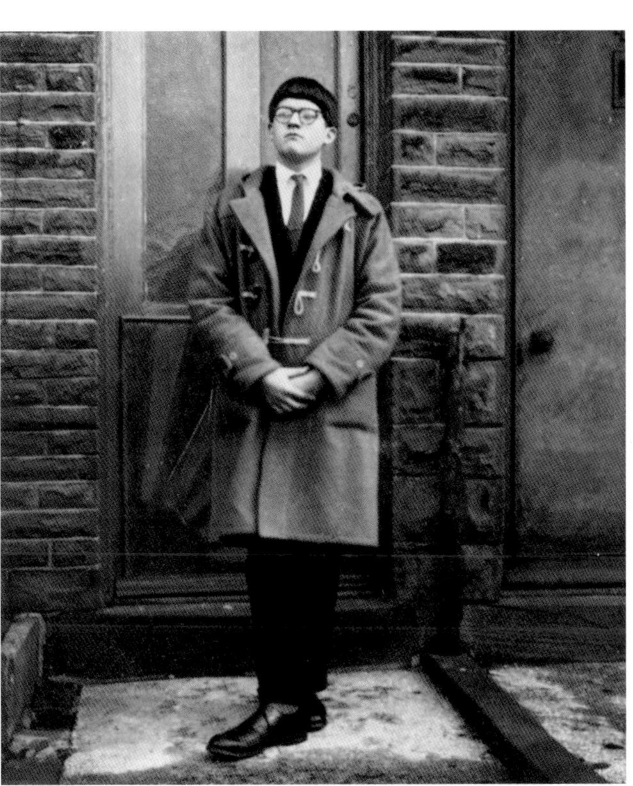

DAVID HOCKNEY

A CHRONOLOGY

TASCHEN

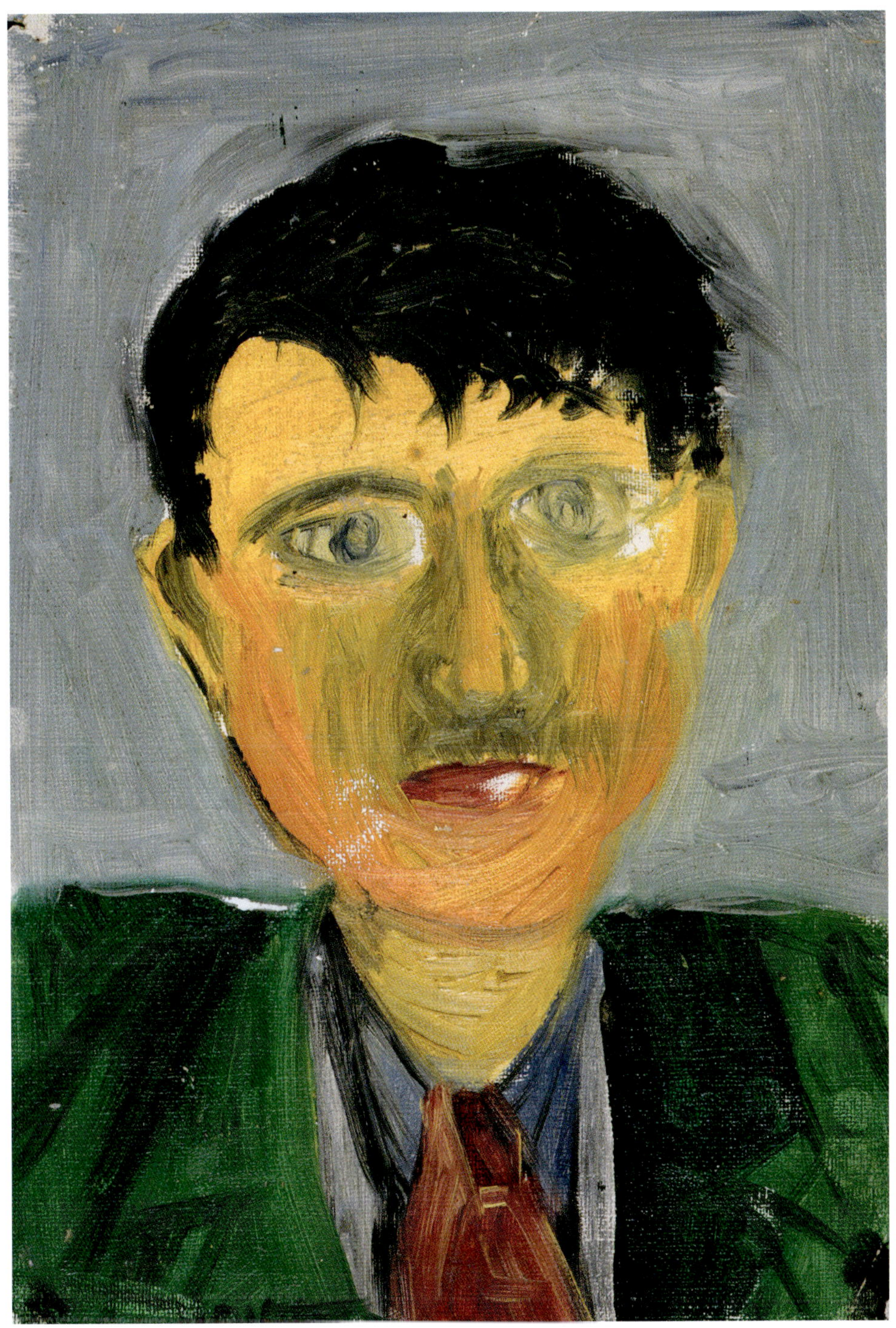

1937–1952

David Hockney is born on July 9, 1937, in the city of Bradford in Yorkshire, England, as the fourth of five children. His father Kenneth is an accountant's clerk, a proselytizing non-smoker, and a pacifist even in times of war; his mother Laura is a Methodist and vegetarian. They live in simple circumstances.

During elementary school Hockney proves a good student, already showing promise in art. Early formative experiences include visits to the opera with his father to see *La Bohème* by Puccini, which leaves a lasting impression both for the music and for its theme of an artistic lifestyle, and especially to the cinema, where they share a fondness for Laurel and Hardy movies: "When I was young I used to go to the cinema at least once a week—my father loved the cinema… Somehow, there was an excitement on that screen. The screen, as if by magic, was opening up the wall to you, it showed you another world even in the dingiest little cinema of suburban Bradford. I would always be sitting near the front row, looking up, looking at grainy pictures." His father is an occasional painter, but mostly he repaints things to make ends meet. "Just after the war you couldn't buy new bicycles—they were all exported—so my father used to buy old ones and paint them up to look like new. I used to watch him do it. The fascination of the brush dipping in the paint, putting it on, I love that… even now, I could spend the whole day painting a door just one flat color," Hockney later remembers.

He enters Bradford Grammar School on a scholarship in 1948. There he finds it preferable to be a mediocre student: "We had just an hour and a half of art classes a week in the first year; after that you went in either for classics or science or modern languages and you did not study art. I thought that was terrible. You could only study art if you were in the bottom form and did a general course. So I said, 'Well, I'll be in the general form, if you don't mind.' It was quite easy to arrange, because if you did less work you were automatically put in that section."

It is also the time that Hockney becomes aware of what he wants to do in life: "At the age of eleven, I decided, in my mind, that I wanted to be an artist, but the meaning of the word 'artist' to me then was very vague—the man who made Christmas cards was an artist, the man who painted posters was an artist, the man who just did lettering for posters was an artist. Anyone was an artist who in his job had to pick up a brush and paint something…The idea of an artist just spending his time painting pictures, for himself, didn't really occur to me.

Of course I knew there were paintings you saw in books and in galleries, but I thought they were done in the evenings, when the artist had finished painting the signs or the Christmas cards or whatever they made their living from."

His drawings are published in the school magazine, and he designs posters for events at school and in the city. In 1950, he applies for permission to enter Junior Art School and his teachers give him the necessary recommendations, but the Education Office rules he should finish grammar school first. As Hockney's performances in class become weaker, his parents arrange for private calligraphy lessons from a teacher at the Bradford School of Art, after which his grades improve again.

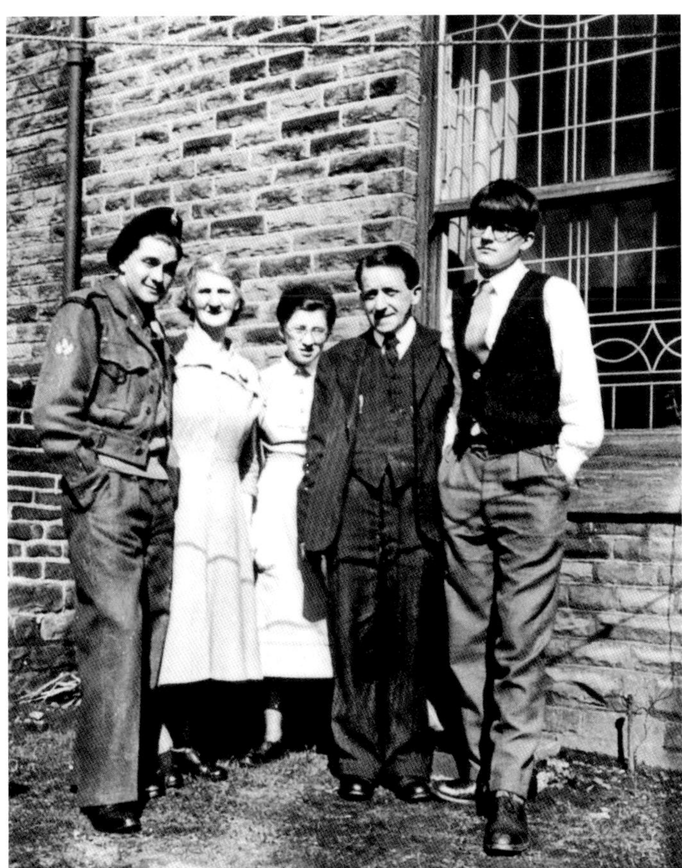

David Hockney with his brother, mother, sister, and father, Bradford, May 1954

Page 1: David Hockney standing by the front door painted by his father, Bradford, December 1954

Page 5: *Self Portrait*, 1951, oil on paper, 12 ³⁄₈ x 8 ¹⁄₂ in. / 31.5 x 21.6 cm

1953–1958

Hockney enters Bradford School of Art. He begins studying commercial art for pragmatic reasons, but soon switches to the painting department, even though he has to pretend he wants to become a teacher. The training he receives is purely academic, but he enjoys it: "I was interested in everything at first. I was an innocent boy of 16 and I believed everything they told me, everything. If they said, 'You have to study perspective,' I'd study perspective; if they told me to study anatomy, I'd study anatomy. It was thrilling, after being at the grammar school, to be at a school where I knew I would enjoy everything they asked me to do. I loved it all and I used to spend twelve hours a day in the art school." Progress comes soon: "What I was quick to notice, was that the teachers were seeing more than I was seeing. I hadn't looked hard enough, and I quickly saw that, and so I began to look harder myself. And if you are strict with yourself, after a few weeks you begin to get better and better." The course is small, with five other students, including Dave Oxtoby and Norman Stevens, who would become proficient artists themselves.

Hockney starts painting the city outdoors: "I did a number of little pictures of semi-detached houses, Bradford suburbs. I put all the paints on a little cart made from a pram, wheeled it out and painted on the spot." In 1955, he paints a portrait of his father: "My father, who'd bought the canvas, set up the easel and then set the chair up for himself, and he set mirrors round so he could watch the progress of the painting and give a commentary. And he would say, 'Oooh, that's too muddy, is that for my cheek? No, no, it's not that color.' I had this commentary all the time, and I'd say, 'Oh, no, you're wrong, this is how you have to do it, this is how they paint at the art school,' and I carried on. You aimed at likeness, but what you were really concerned about were tonal values—making sure you'd get the right tone. This meant you ignored color. Color was not a subject of painting in the art school." Much to Hockney's surprise, *Portrait of My Father* (p. 11) becomes the first painting he ever sells, during the *Yorkshire Artists Exhibition* at Leeds Art Gallery.

He grows more dissatisfied with the limited education he receives: "In my last year, when we'd already done a lot of drawing, I realized how academic the art school was, and I began to think, 'The whole problem is, I don't know anything about modern art.' They liked Sickert; Sickert was the great god and the whole

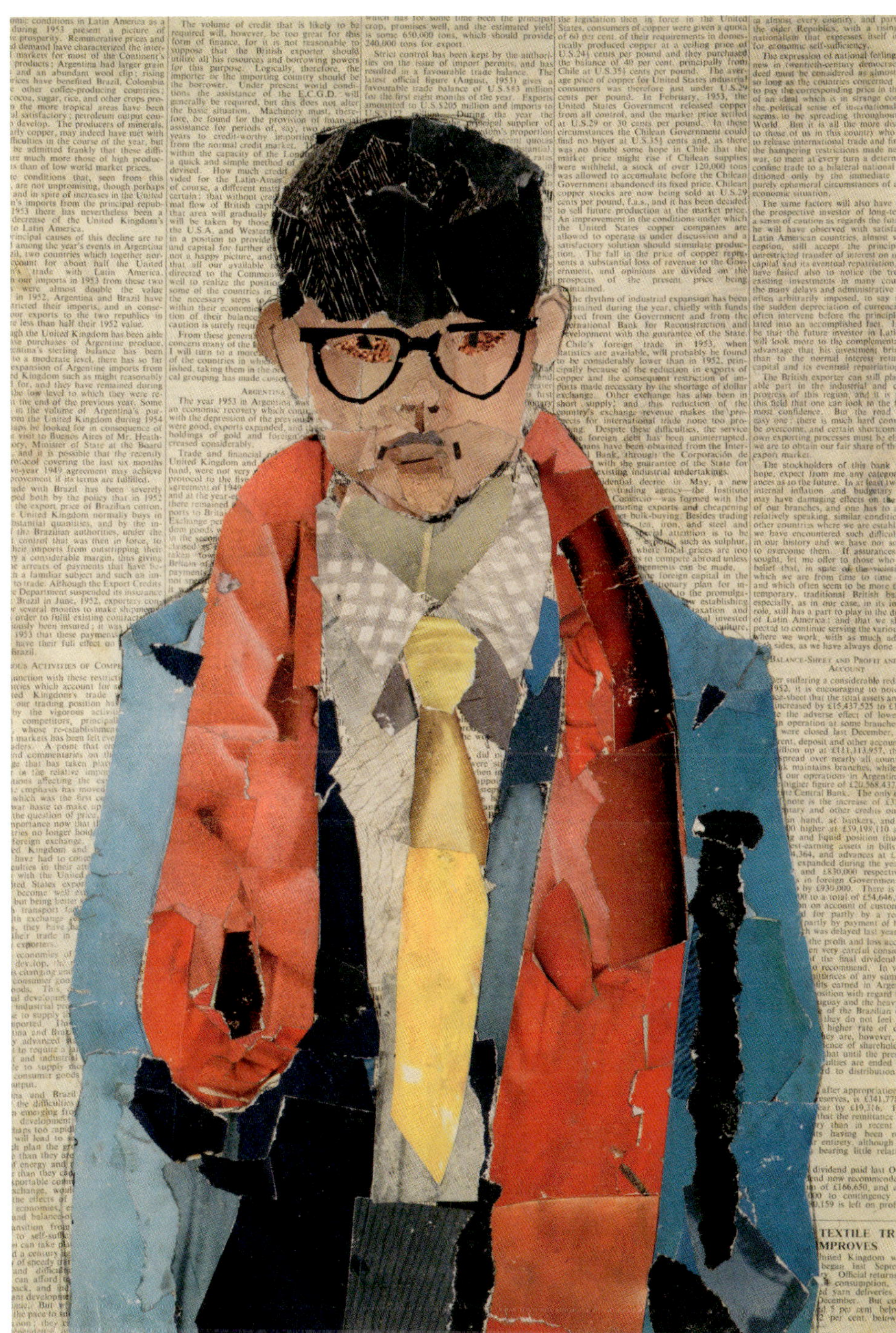

style of painting in that art school—and in every other art school in England—was a cross between Sickert and the Euston Road School...On the other hand, if you're a twenty-year-old, what does it matter?"

At the beginning of 1957, Hockney takes the entrance exams of the Royal College of Art and Slade School of Fine Art and passes both. First, though, he has to fulfill National Service as a conscientious objector, and through 1958 works as a hospital orderly with no time for painting. He sees exhibitions by Jackson Pollock at the Whitechapel Gallery in London and Scottish artist Alan Davie at Wakefield City Art Gallery: "I was very impressed with the works. That was the first abstraction; it confused me at first, but I could cope with it—I wasn't thrown into complete disarray."

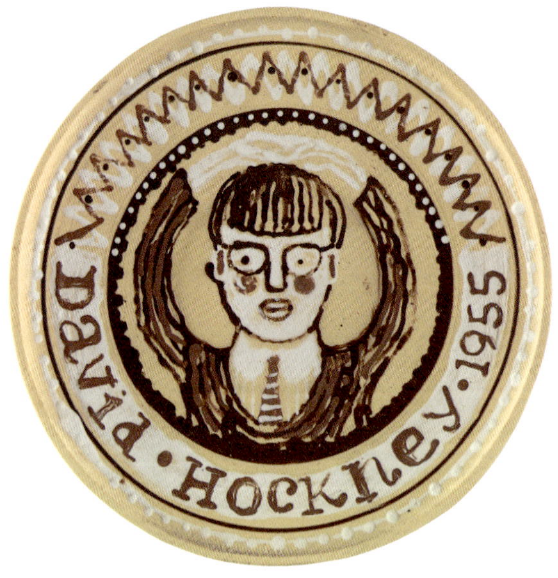

Self Portrait, 1955, ceramic,
9 ⅞ in. / 25 cm diameter

Right page: *Portrait of My Father,*
1955, oil on canvas, 20 x 16 in. /
50.8 x 40.6 cm

Page 9: *Self Portrait,* 1954, collage
on newsprint, 16 ½ x 11 ¾ in. /
42 x 29.8 cm

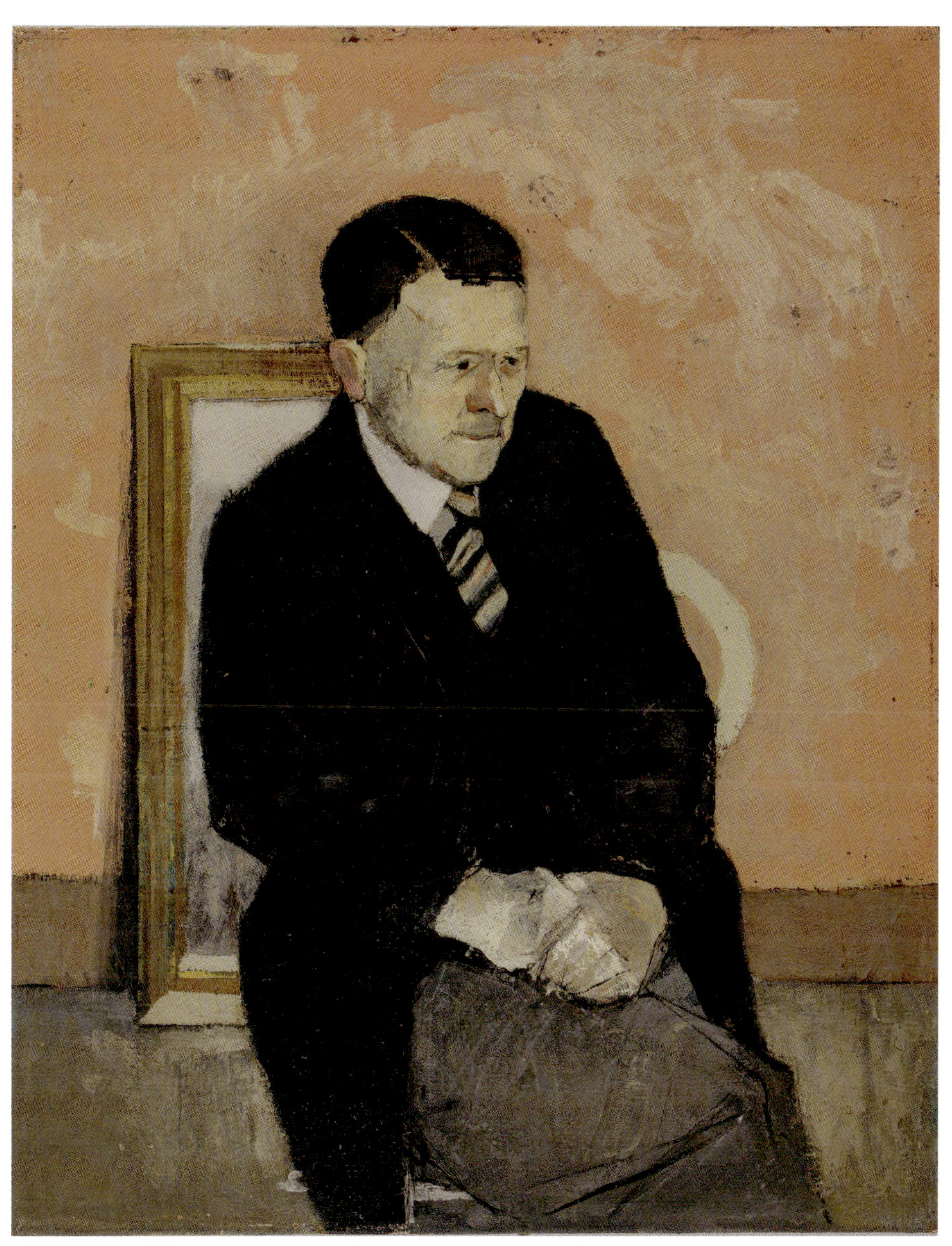

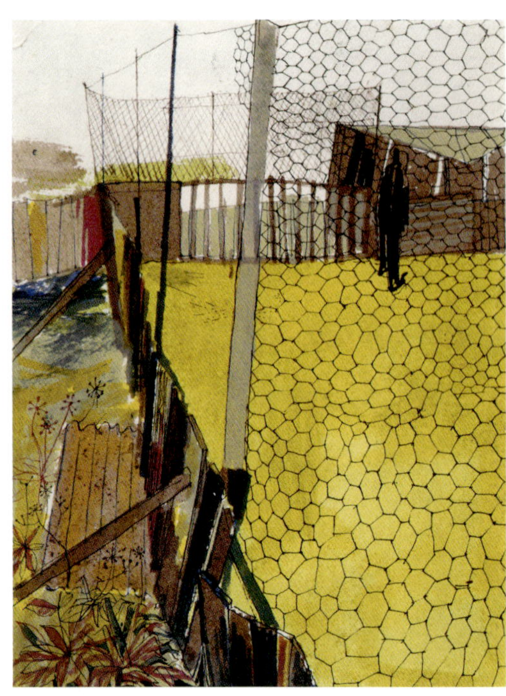

Gardens with Wire-Mesh Fencing, c. 1954–1955, pen, ink, and watercolor on paper, 10 $\frac{1}{2}$ x 8 in. / 26.5 x 20.3 cm

Street Scene, c. 1954, ink and wash on paper, 11 $\frac{7}{8}$ x 17 in. / 30.2 x 43 cm

Right page: *Roadmenders, Eccleshill,* c. 1957, oil on canvas stretched over board, 48 x 33 $\frac{1}{4}$ in. / 121.9 x 84.5 cm

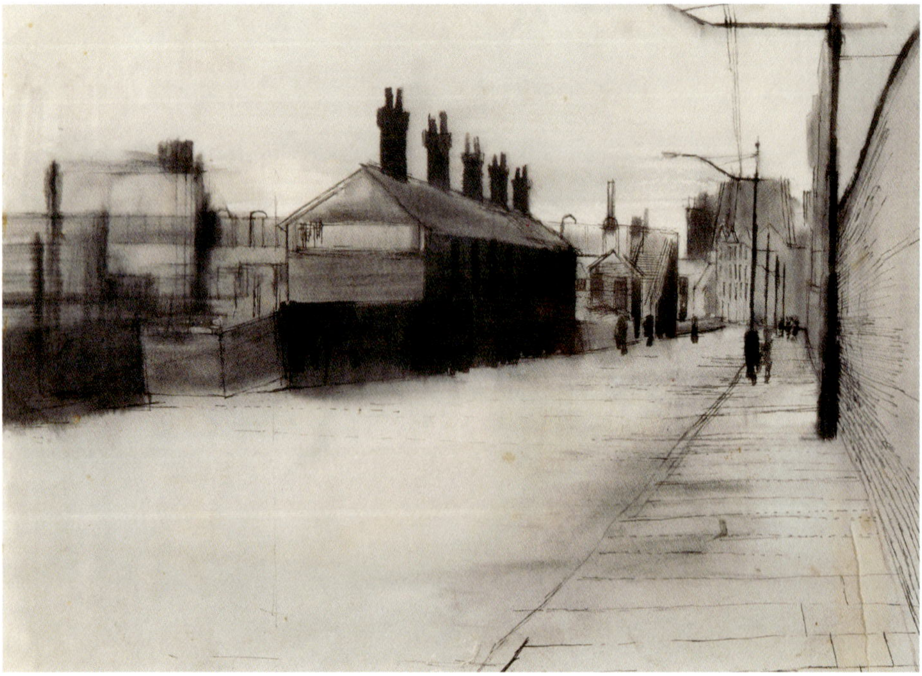

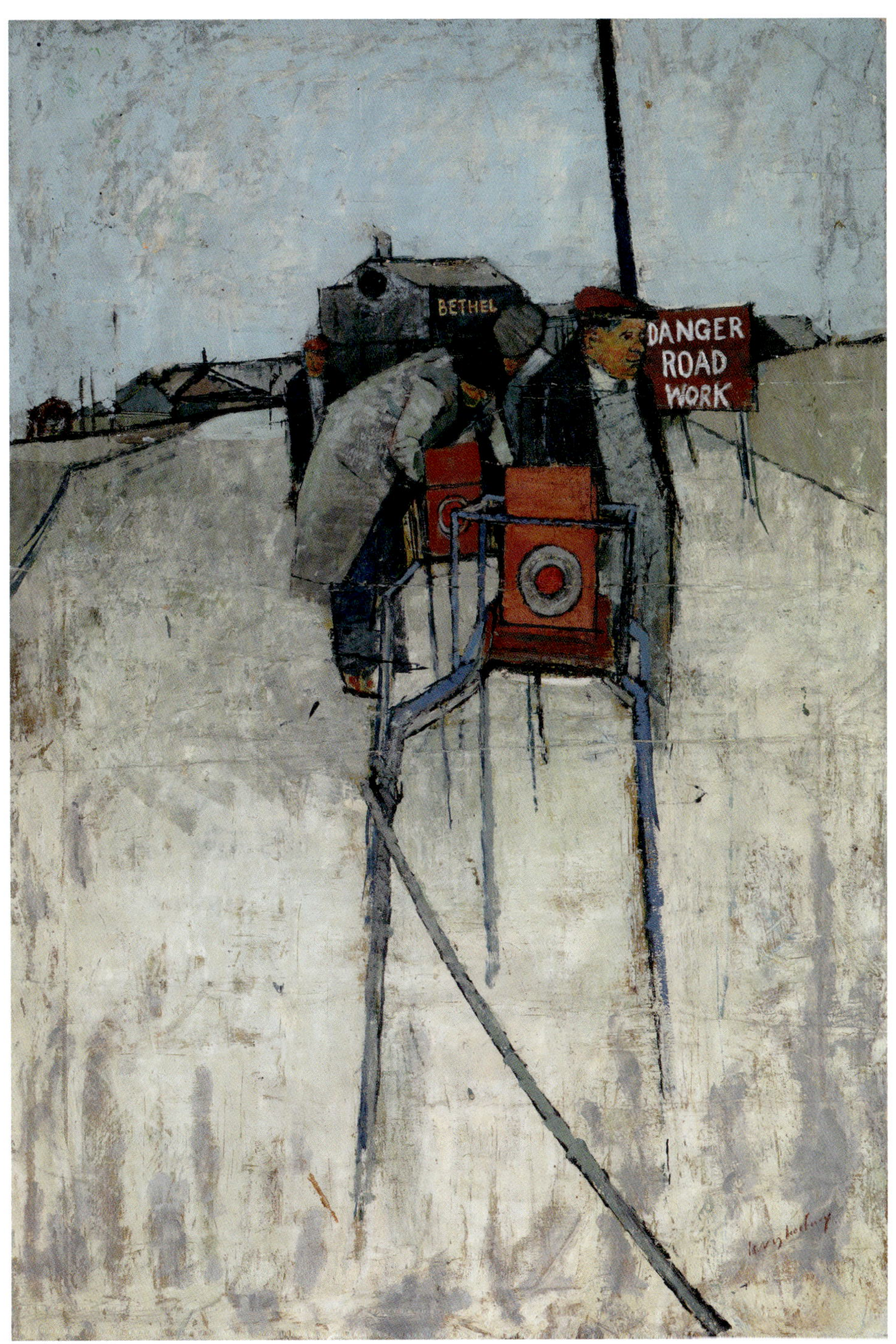
BETHEL
DANGER
ROAD
WORK

1959–1960

Hockney begins his studies at the Royal College of Art in London in September 1959. Among his tutors are Roger de Grey, Ruskin Spear, and Carel Weight, figurative painters whose outlook is not dissimilar to the academic values Hockney knows from Bradford. At first he feels insecure, a boy from Yorkshire who has rarely even visited London before, and remains unsure about what he is supposed to paint: "So I began at the Royal College and I thought, 'Well, I haven't done any drawing for two years, or very little, I'll make a drawing, a long drawing, to find out what I'll do in the meantime.' And I made two drawings of a skeleton (p. 17). Each one took about three or four weeks to do: two very academic, very accurate drawings of a whole skeleton, half-life-size." These drawings attract the notice of fellow student R. B. Kitaj, who will remain a lifelong friend. Kitaj remembers: "During our first days at the Royal College I spotted this boy with short black hair and huge glasses, wearing a boilersuit, making the most beautiful drawing I'd ever seen in an art school. It was of a skeleton. I told him I'd give him five quid for it. He thought I was a rich American. I was—I had $150 a month GI Bill money to support my wife and son. I kept buying drawings from him."

Hockney soon gets to know his fellow students: "I realized there were two groups of students there: a traditional group who simply carried on as they had done in art school, doing still life, life painting, and figure compositions; and then what I thought of as the more adventurous lively students, the brightest ones, who were more involved in the art of their time. They were doing big abstract expressionist paintings on hardboard." Hockney finds himself part of a very promising generation of painters, including Kitaj, Derek Boshier, Patrick Caulfield, Allen Jones, and Peter Phillips.

During the winter, Hockney experiments with abstract expressionism himself: "Young students had realized that American painting was more interesting than French painting. The idea of French painting disappeared really, and American abstract expressionism was the great influence. So I tried my hand at it, I did a few pictures, about 20 on three feet by four feet pieces of hardboard that were based on a kind of mixture of Alan Davie cum Jackson Pollock cum Roger Hilton. And I did them for a while, and then I couldn't. It was too barren for me." Most of the canvases are subsequently painted over or destroyed by the artist, who is looking for a way to make contemporary paintings outside of ab-

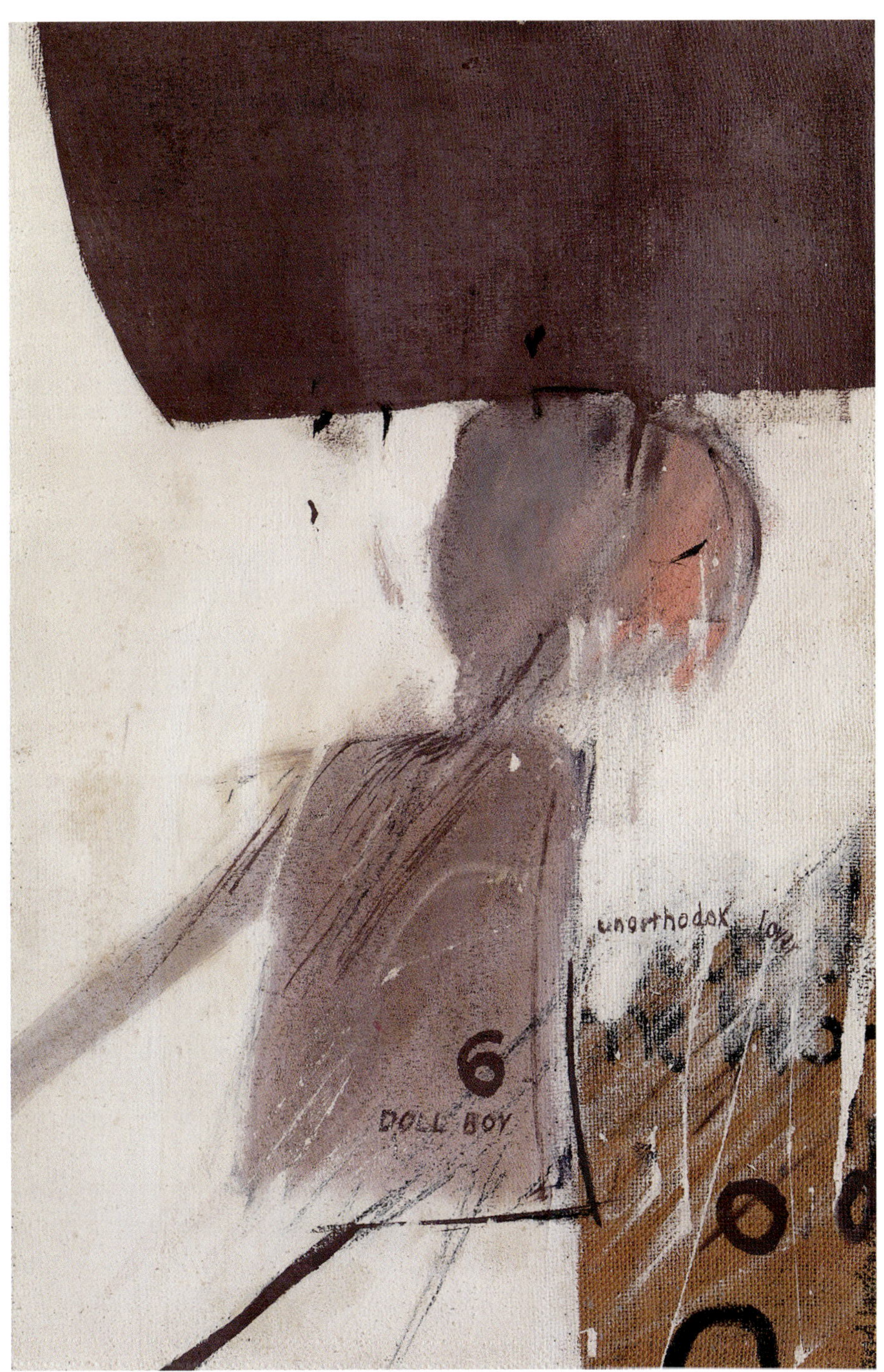

unorthodox love
6
DOLL BOY

straction: "Meanwhile I was drawing all the time. The one student I kept talking to a lot was Ron Kitaj. Ron was slowly doing these strange pictures, and I talked to him about them and about my work. And I said, 'Well, I don't know, it seems pointless doing it.' I'd talk to him about my interests; I was a keen vegetarian then, and interested in politics a bit, and he'd say to me, 'Why don't you paint those subjects?' And I thought, it's quite right…"

Early in 1960, Hockney participates in the *Young Contemporaries* group exhibition at RBA Galleries in London, organized by students and overseen by critic and curator Lawrence Alloway. In the *Times,* the reviewer favorably mentions Hockney's work and describes it as "indebted to Alan Davie."

In summer, Hockney sees a major Picasso exhibition at Tate Gallery, the first show of modern art to reach a broader public in England. He also reads "everything by Walt Whitman. I'd known his poetry before, but I'd never realized he was that good. There are quite a few of my paintings based on his work." One of those is *Adhesiveness* (p. 19), later described by the artist as "the first really serious painting I'd done; it is my first painting that begins to have precision." The title comes from an expression with which Whitman describes friendship, and the two sketchy figures, who seem to penetrate each other, are identified through a numbers code the poet used: 4.8. stands for the letters D and H and 23.23. for Whitman's initials.

Hockney's canvases of the time are still mainly abstract, an influence he struggles to overcome: "In 1960, for a young art student trying to think of modern art, the art of his time, obviously wanting to be involved in it, the opposition to the figure as a subject was very strong. I opposed it too; I thought, this is not the way to go. Yet obviously I was dying to do it, to come to some terms with the figure. Hence the use of words to make the feeling you get from the picture more specific." Thus *The Third Love Painting* (p. 20) contains several words and sentences, including a line by Whitman—"I am he that aches with amorous love"—which here carries homosexual connotations. "There are lots of ways you can read the title," Hockney says. "But the painting itself is just an abstraction. It's very close to abstract expressionism, in a way; there are one or two shapes that rather dominate it and can be interpreted in, I suppose, an ordinary way. But you are forced to look at the painting quite closely because it is covered with lots of graffiti, which makes you go up to it…If you see a little poem written in

Study of a Skeleton from Above,
1959, pencil on paper, 22 x 15 in. /
56 x 38 cm

Skeleton, 1959, charcoal and gouache
on paper, 15 ⅝ x 22 in. / 39.7 x 56 cm

Page 15: *Study for Doll Boy,* 1960, oil
on canvas, 24 x 16 in. / 61 x 40.6 cm

Page 19: *Adhesiveness,* 1960, oil on
board, 50 x 40 in. / 127 x 101.6 cm

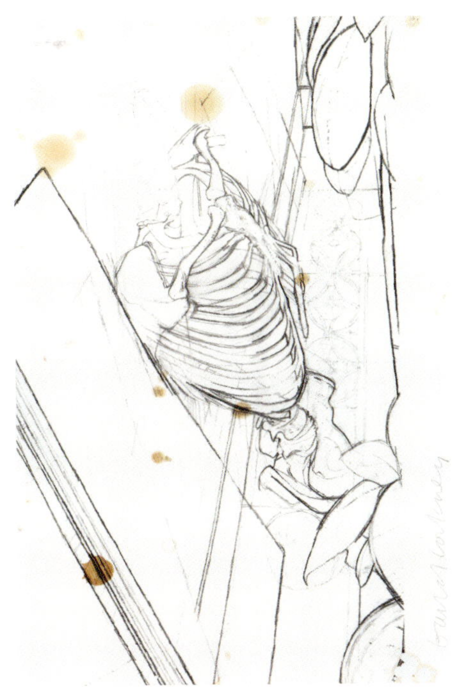

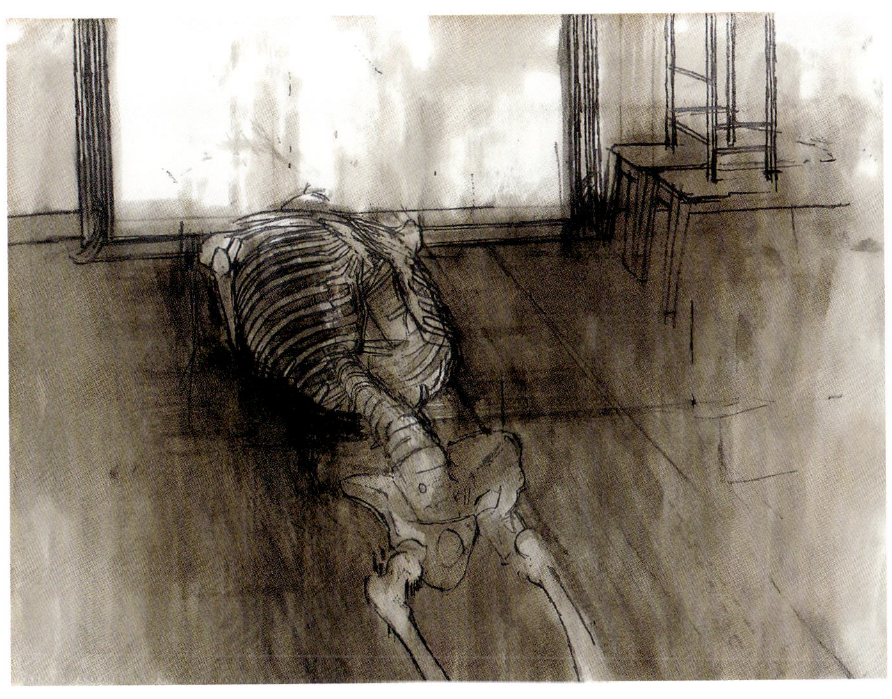

the corner of a painting it will force you to go up and look at it. And then the painting becomes something a little different; it's not just, as Whistler would say, an arrangement in browns, pinks, and blacks."

Hockney starts on *Doll Boy* (p. 21), an homage to pop singer Cliff Richard showing a figure in a white shirt with musical notes falling out of his bent neck and the word "queen" written over his crotch: "I used to cut out photographs of him from newspapers and magazines and stick them up around my little cubicle in the Royal College of Art, partly because other people used to stick up girl pin-ups … He had a song in which the words were, 'She's a real live walking talking living doll,' and he sang it rather sexily. The title of the painting is based on that line. He's referring to some girl, so I changed it to a boy."

As Hockney's friends at the Royal College—such as Kitaj, Phillips, and Boshier—are drawn toward Pop art, the teaching staff view them with suspicion; Allen Jones is even dismissed from the college at the end of the term. First recognition comes when Richard Hamilton visits the academy on invitation of the students to discuss their work and give out a few prizes. Two of those go to Hockney and Kitaj, which considerably raises their standing.

Group: *Annual Exhibition,* RBA Galleries, London (Jan 15–Feb 5); catalog. *Young Contemporaries,* RBA Galleries, London (Mar–Apr); catalog with a text by Peter Cresswell.

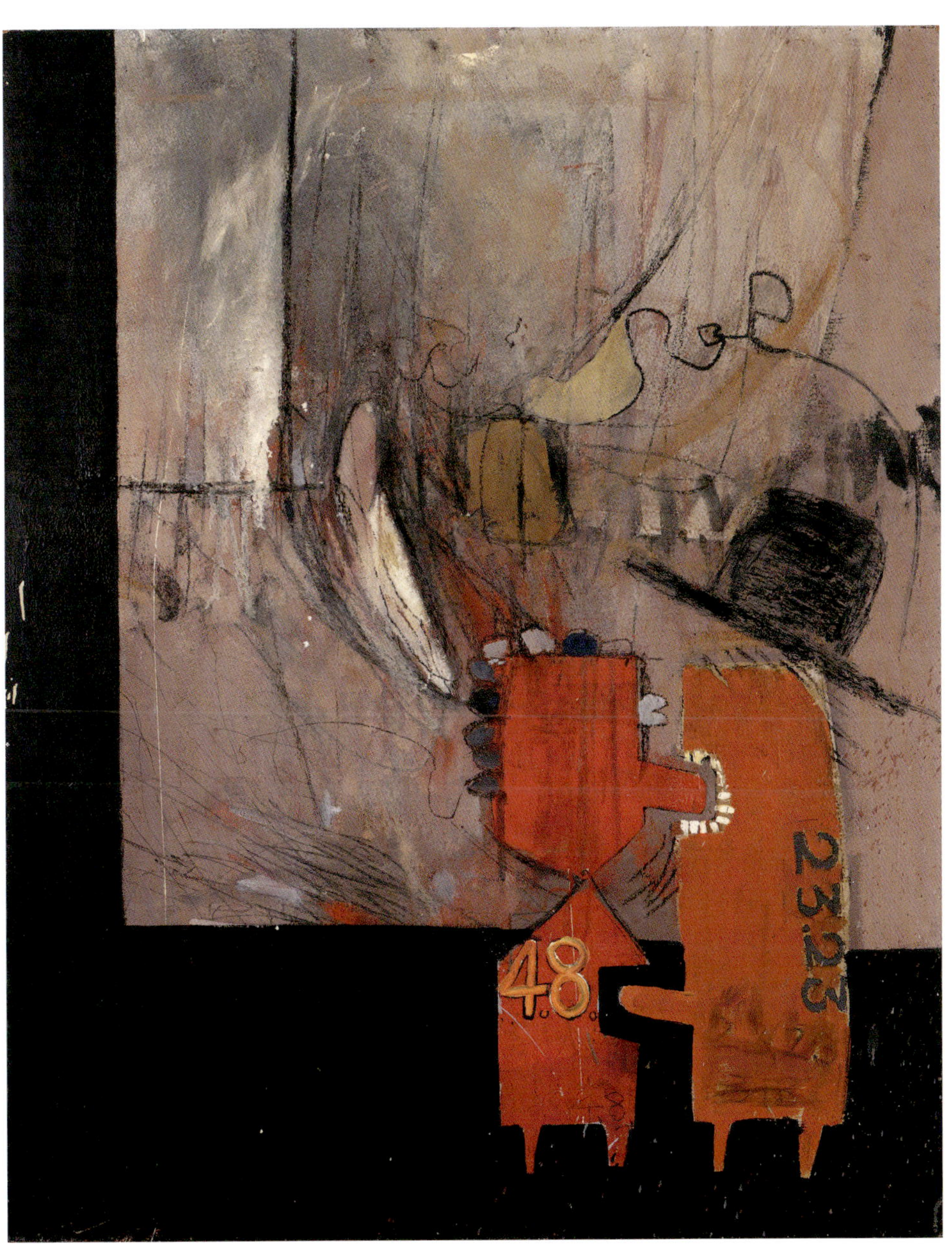

48
23.23

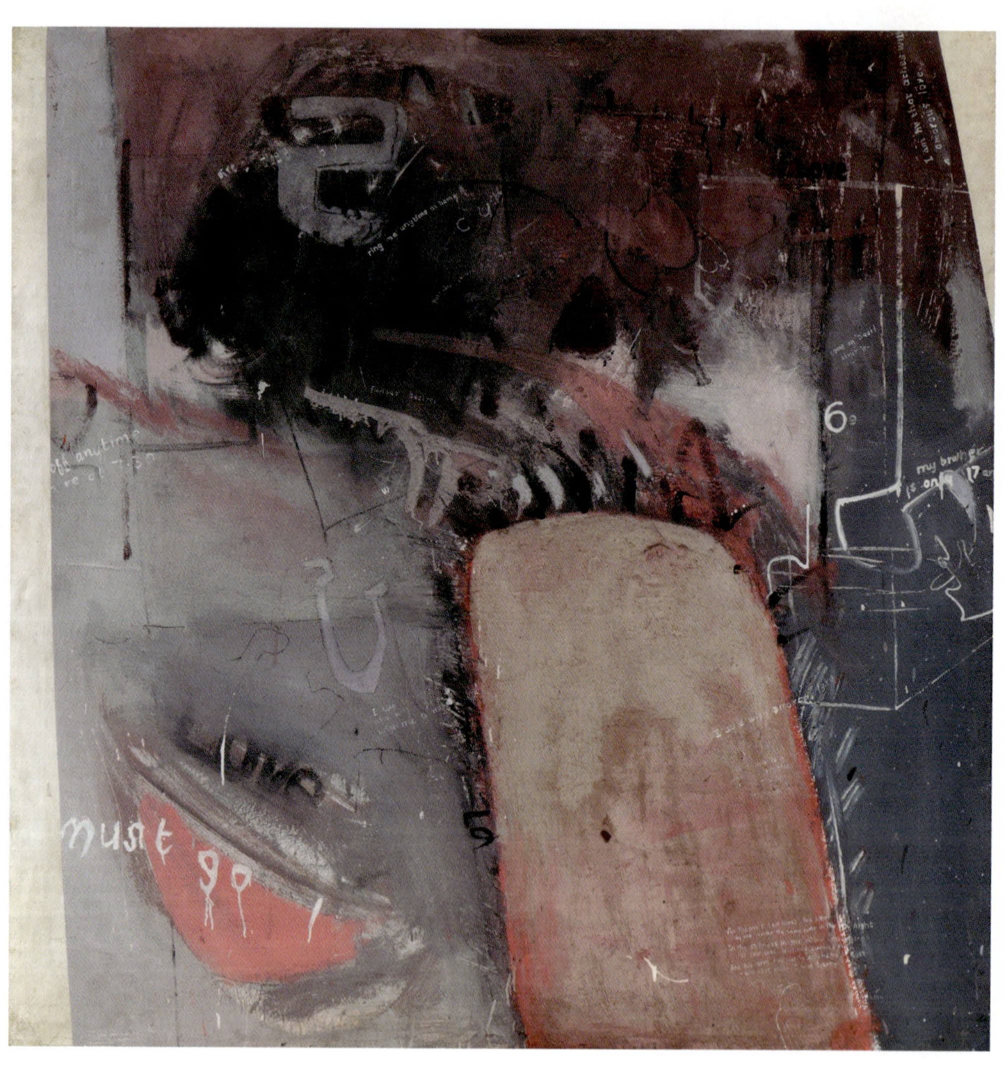

The Third Love Painting, 1960,
oil on board, 46 ^{3}/$_4$ x 46 ^{3}/$_4$ in. /
119 x 119 cm

Right page: *Doll Boy*, 1960–1961,
oil on canvas, 48 x 39 in. /
121.9 x 99.1 cm

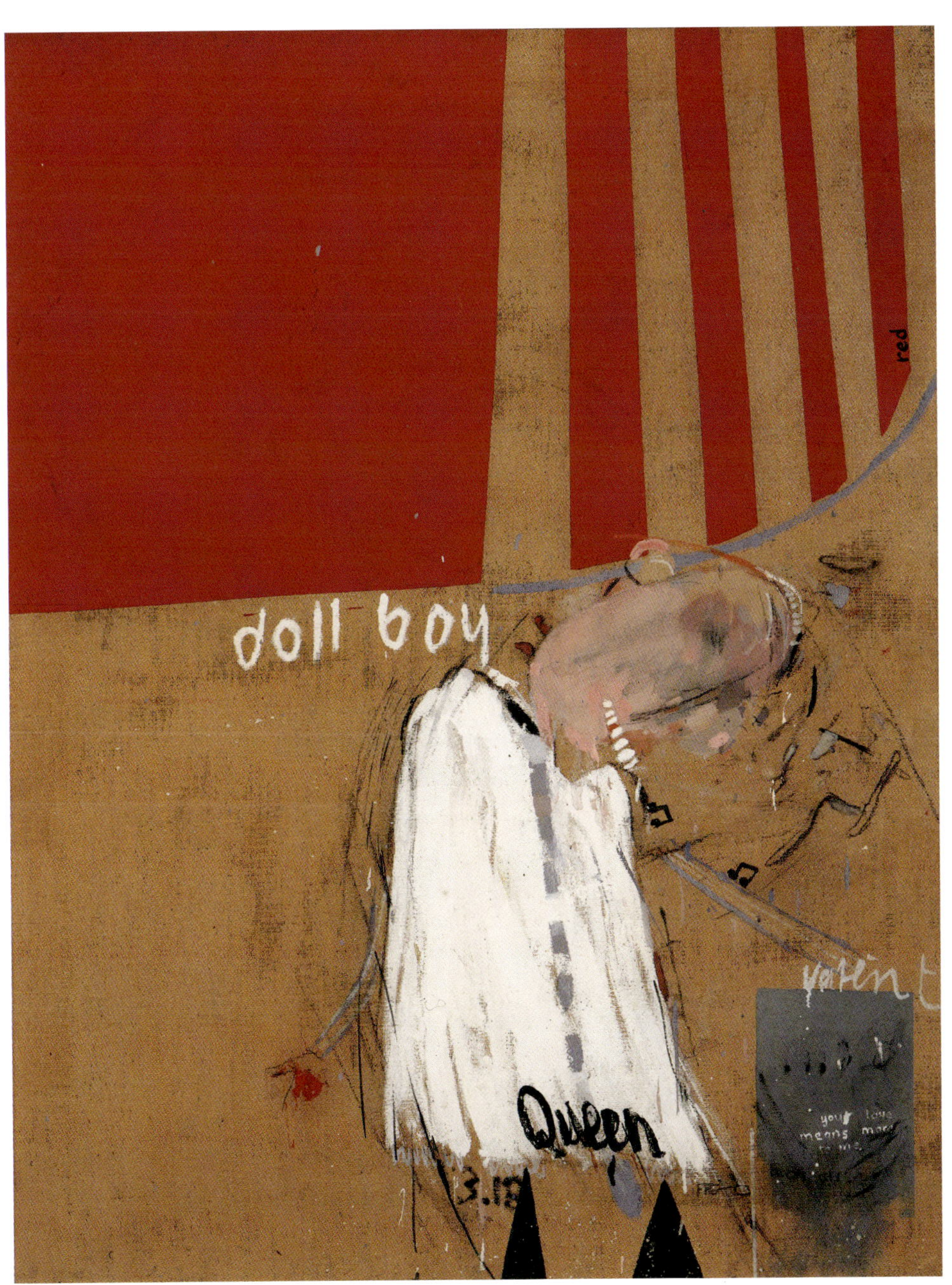
doll boy
red
Queen

1961

In February, Hockney makes his second appearance in the *Young Contemporaries* exhibition at RBA Galleries in London. This year, chief organizer is his friend Peter Phillips, who hangs works from the circle of the Royal College students to best effect. The exhibition stirs up wider attention: here appears to be a new generation of artists with its own spirit. "It was probably the first time that there'd be a student movement in painting that was uninfluenced by older artists in this country, which made it unusual," Hockney remembers. The *Times'* art critic is quick to identify that movement: "Among the paintings it is noticeable that abstraction, and particularly the improvised, American-style abstraction, is 'out,' and that a new manner, sharply flavoured with the signs, slogans, and mordant humour of metropolitan life, and emanating mostly from the Royal College of Art, is 'in.' Mr. Phillips, with his colourful, heraldic evocations of press-button machines and amusement arcades, is its chief representative, aided and abetted by Allen C. Jones, Barrie Bates, David Hockney, and Peter Kaye (the last three of whom introduce a weird, satirical element)."

In the aftermath of the show, Hockney meets the young art dealer John Kasmin, who works for Marlborough Gallery and privately buys *Doll Boy* from the artist for 40 pounds. As a consequence of the success and media coverage of the exhibition, people start coming to the Royal College—where Hockney is one of the few students to actually have a studio—curious about the art: "Every day there'd be somebody coming in and I knew this, so, in a way, I was painting for an audience all the time. The pictures were seen as I was painting them…Also I'd become conscious, not of the shock value of homosexuality—you can't shock students, you couldn't then and I don't think you could now; they're not shockable that way—but that I was being cheeky and bold, and that's what one should do, I thought, be slightly cheeky, although I'm a bit shy."

Hockney paints key pictures such as *The Cha-Cha That Was Danced in the Early Hours of 24th March 1961* (p. 29) and *We Two Boys Together Clinging* (pp. 30/31), which again is titled after a line of Walt Whitman's. His *Tea Painting in an Illusionistic Style* (p. 25) takes Hockney "as close to Pop art as I ever came…To make a painting of a packet of tea more illusionistic, I hit on the idea of 'drawing' it with the shape of the canvas. The stretcher is made up from sections and I made the stretchers myself. It was quite difficult stretching them all up—the back is almost as complicated as the front; it took me five days. I don't

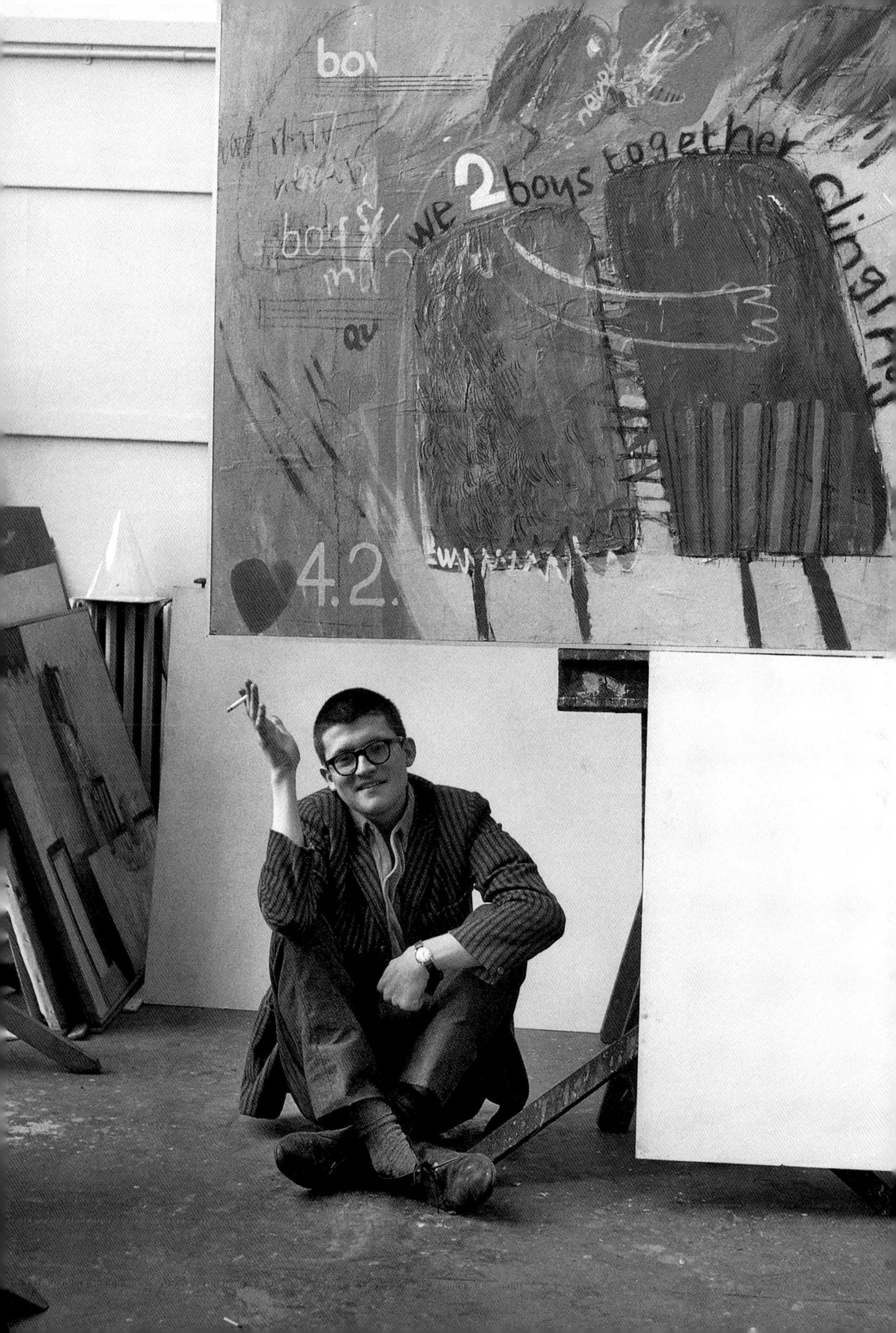

boy
never
we 2 boys together
clinging
2 boys
4.2.

think anybody had done shapes before…It's interesting, I spelt the word 'tea' wrong on the left hand section; I am a bad speller, but to spell a three-letter word wrong! But it's drawing in perspective and it was quite difficult to do. I took so long planning it that in my concern for flatness or abstraction I spelt it wrong."

Since free materials are offered for students at the Royal College's graphics department, Hockney tries his hand at etching to save on money for canvases. *Myself and My Heroes* (p. 27) shows him beside Walt Whitman and Mahatma Gandhi, who wear halos, while Hockney sports an army cap and is characterized through the simple words: "I am 23 years old and wear glasses." Hockney wins a Guinness Award for his etchings as well as a small prize in the *John Moores Exhibition* at Walker Art Gallery in Liverpool for his painting.

In summer, several artists from the Royal College decorate the new ship S.S. Canberra, awaiting its maiden voyage in London harbor. Hockney is given a room for teenagers called the "Pop Inn" (p. 27), which over five days he covers with graffiti and drawings. The fee along with the sale of some paintings and the prize money from his two awards allows him to travel, and as an affordable occasion presents itself, Hockney flies to New York for the first time in July.

He greatly enjoys his experience in New York: "The life of the city was very stimulating, the gay bars—there weren't many in those days; it was a marvelously lively society. I was utterly thrilled by it, all the time I was excited by it. The fact that you could watch television at three in the morning, and go out and the bars would still be open, I thought it was marvelous." Hockney buys an American suit and bleaches his hair platinum blonde inspired by an ad which asserts that "blondes have more fun." In September he returns to London and starts on a series of etchings, *A Rake's Progress,* developed loosely after the model of William Hogarth and describing his own recent experiences in New York.

He also paints *A Grand Procession of Dignitaries in the Semi-Egyptian Style* (p. 28), inspired by the Greek poet Constantin Cavafy's poem "Waiting for the Barbarians." It shows three flat figures, the first looking ecclesiastic, the second like a highly decorated Egyptian soldier, and the third containing a body of smaller figures: "The Egyptian style of painting of course is flat, and since I was breaking the rules of flatness, it was the semi-Egyptian style. The curtain at the top is the first time I used the curtain motif; I wanted it to look theatrical, be-

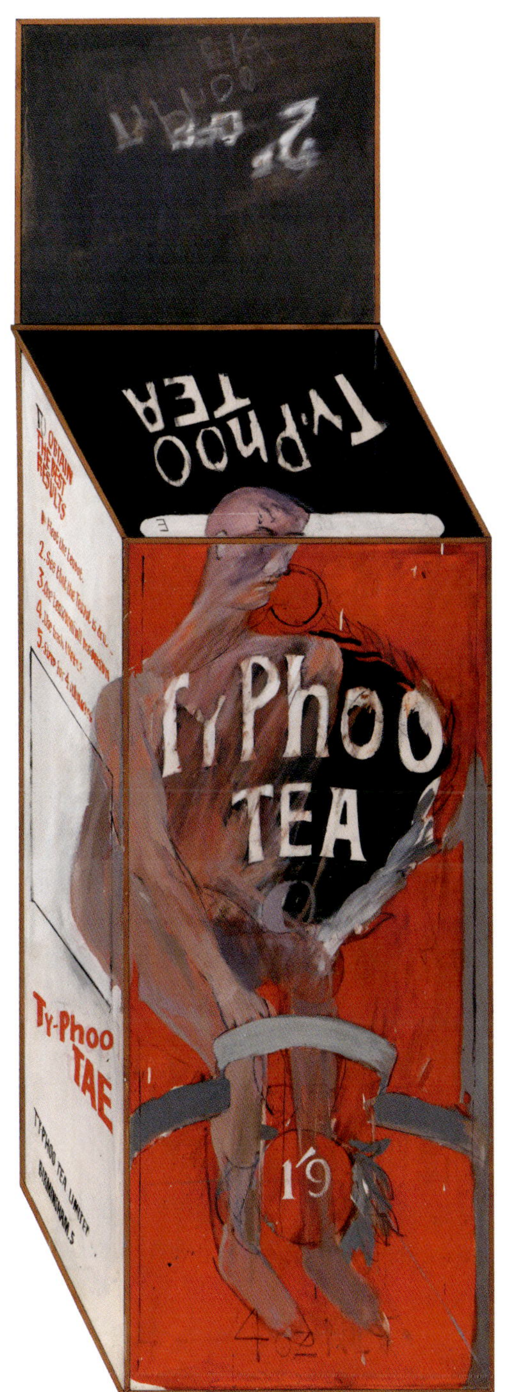

Tea Painting in an Illusionistic Style, 1961, oil on 4 canvases, 91 x 32 in. / 231.2 x 81.3 cm

Page 23: David Hockney with the larger version of *We Two Boys Together Clinging*, London 1961. Photo: Geoffrey Reeve

Page 27: *Myself and My Heroes*, 1961, etching in black with aquatint, edition of approx. 50, 10 1/4 x 19 3/4 in. / 26 x 50.2 cm

The "Pop Inn" teenage room on board the ocean liner SS Canberra with wall design by David Hockney, 1961

cause I felt the whole event was theatrical—the idea of people putting on a show for the barbarians."

In December Hockney goes on his first trip to Italy, crossing the Alps in the closed back of a van without a view of the scenery. "I love Gothic gloom almost as much as Mediterranean or Californian sun, and I thought the misty alps in winter would be a great thrill. But unfortunately I didn't see them…Afterwards when I came back I thought, it's such a shame when I could have painted a mountain picture; and then I thought, well I can, I can just make it up. And so I painted *Flight into Italy – Swiss Landscape* (p. 28)." After crossing the Alps, he drives on to Florence to visit the Uffizi, where he especially admires a large crucifixion on a cross-shaped wood panel by the Sienese Gothic painter Duccio.

Group: *Young Contemporaries*, RBA Galleries, London (Feb–Mar); catalog with a text by Lawrence Alloway. *New Painting 1958–1961*, Walker Art Gallery, Liverpool (Jul–Aug); touring exhibition organized by the Arts Council of Great Britain. *Deuxième Biennale de Paris: Manifestation biennale et internationale des jeunes artistes*, Musée d'art moderne de la Ville de Paris (Sep 29–Nov 5); catalog. *John Moores Exhibition*, Walker Art Gallery, Liverpool (Nov 16, 1961–Jan 14, 1962); catalog; Hockney wins the Junior Section Prize.

Award: First Prize of the *Guinness Award for Etching*, Royal College of Art, London.

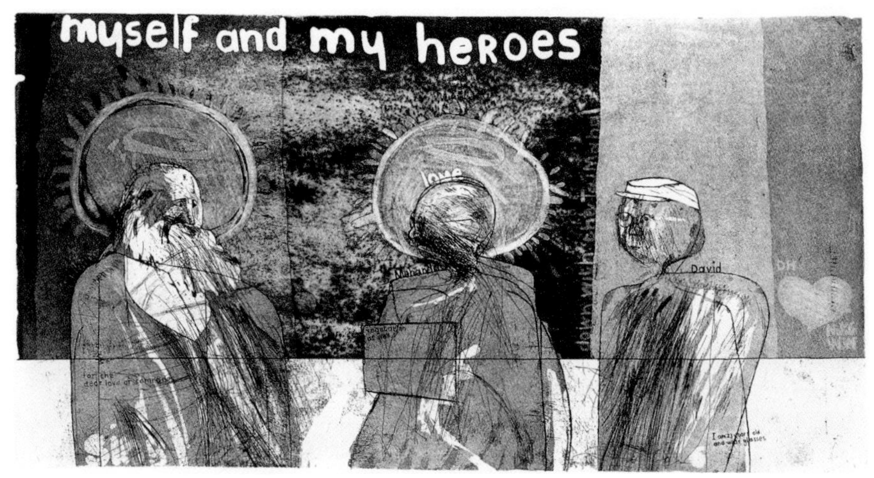

myself and my heroes
love
Mahatma
David
DH

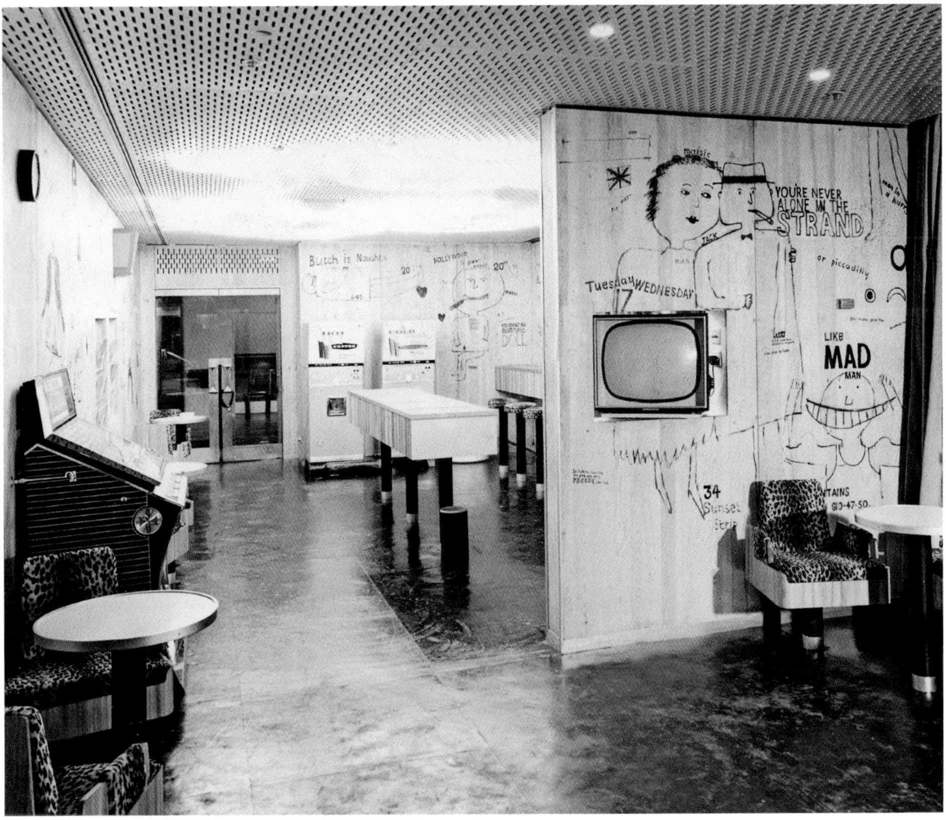

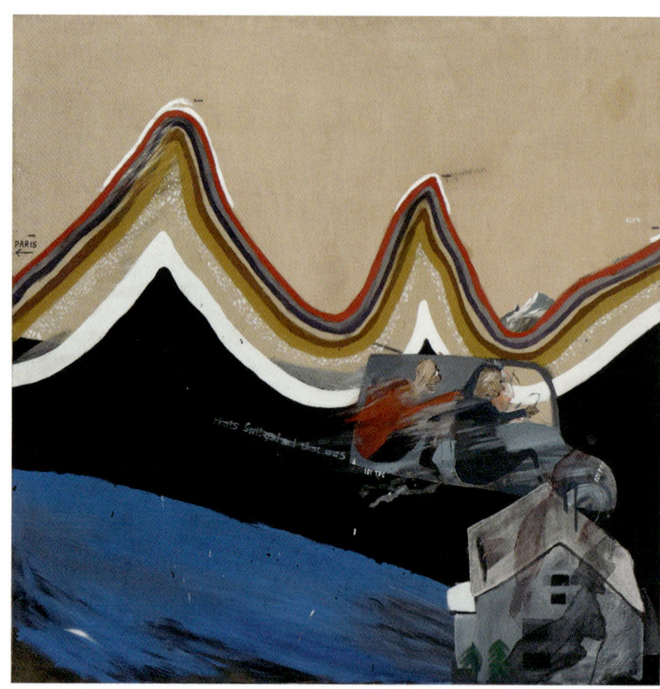

Flight into Italy – Swiss Land-scape, 1962, oil on canvas, 72 x 72 in. / 182.9 x 182.9 cm

A Grand Procession of Dignitaries in the Semi-Egyptian Style, 1961, oil on canvas, 84 x 144 in. / 213.4 x 365.8 cm

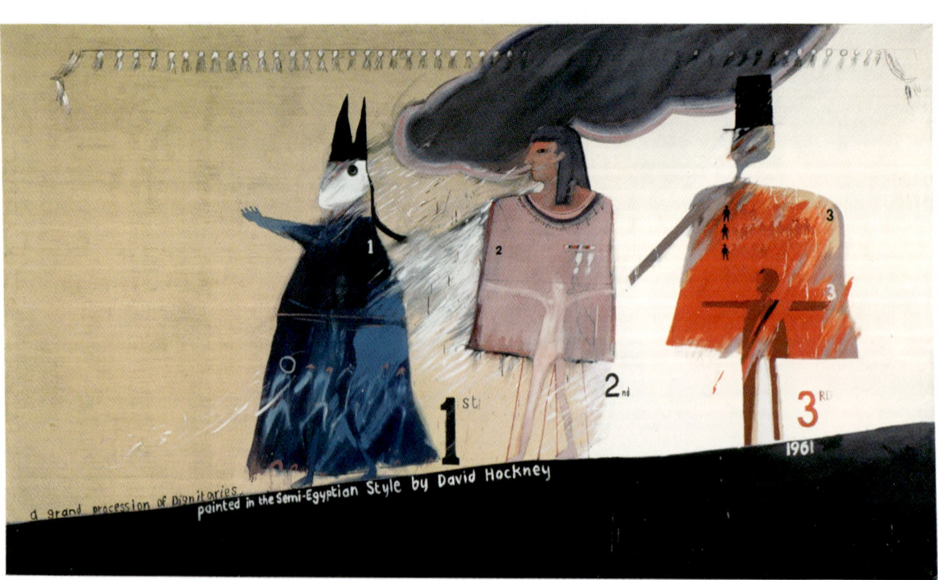

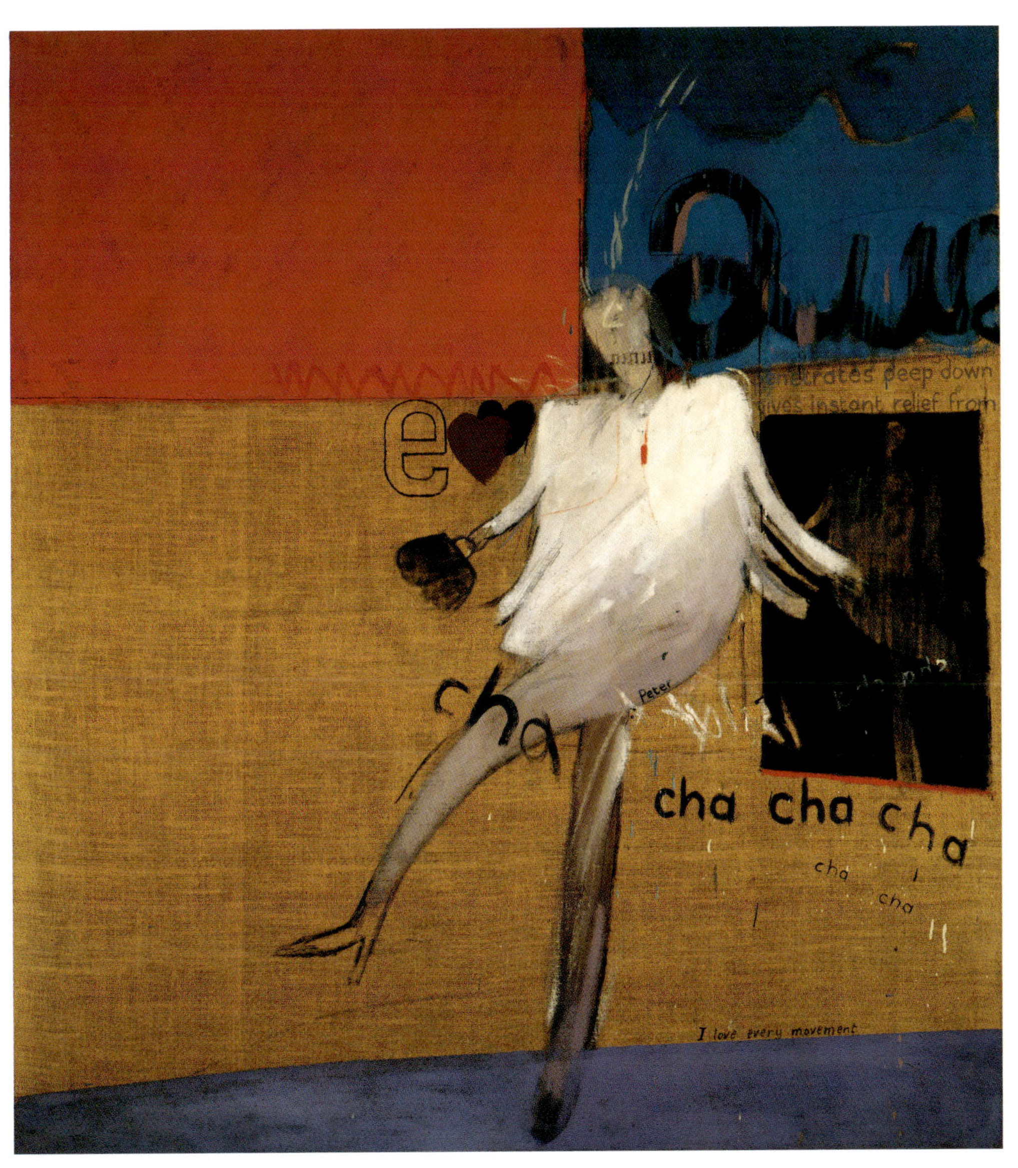

*The Cha-Cha That Was Danced in the
Early Hours of 24th March 1961,* oil on
canvas, 68 ¹/₈ x 62 ¹/₈ in. / 173 x 158 cm

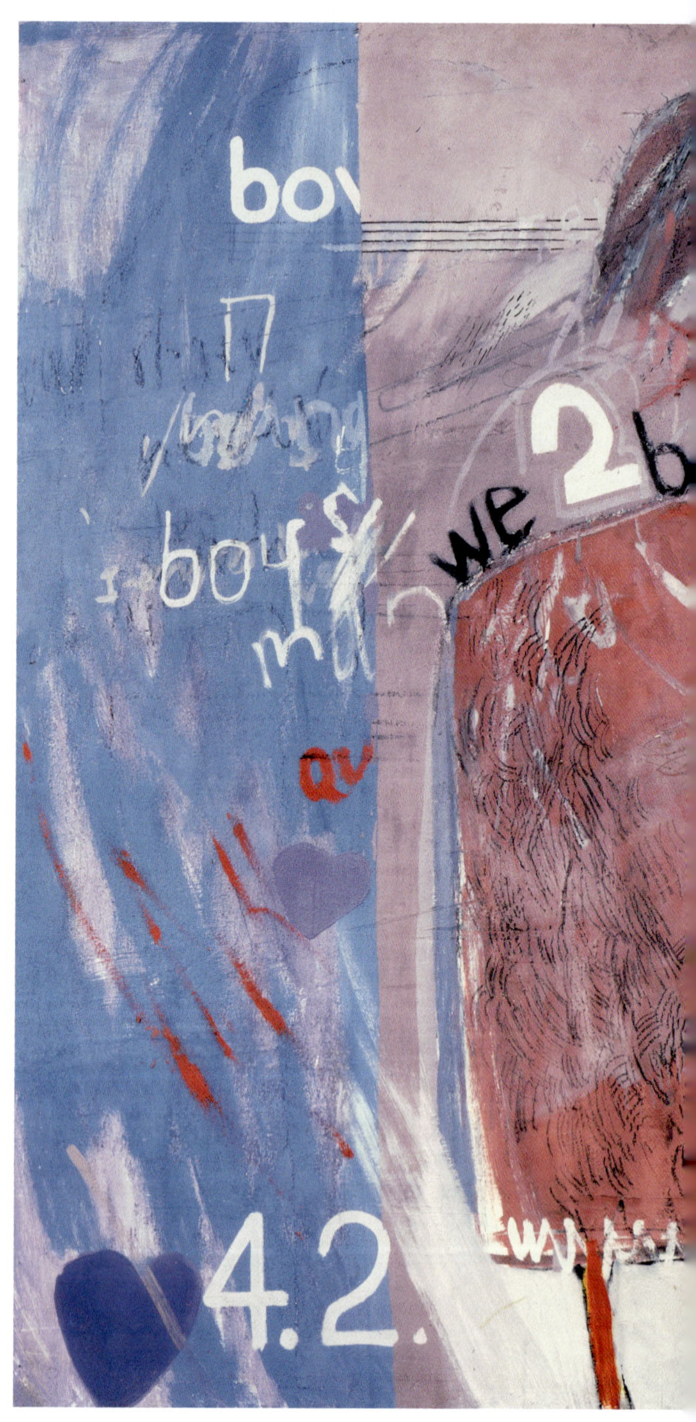

We Two Boys Together Clinging,
1961, oil on board, 48 x 60 in. /
121.9 x 152.4 cm

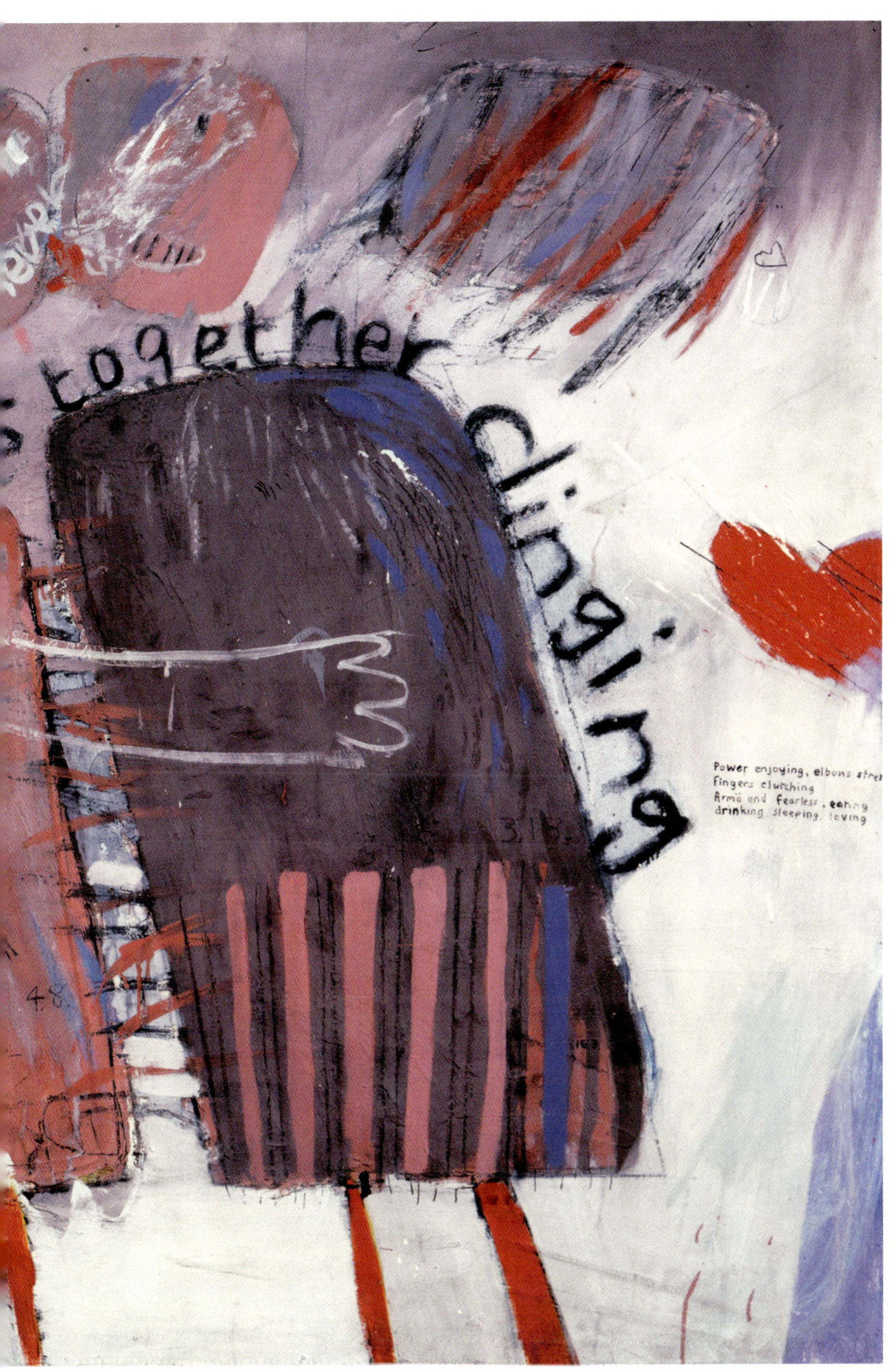
together clinging
Power enjoying, elbons stret
fingers clutching
Arms and fearless, eating
drinking sleeping, loving

1962 After his return from Italy, Hockney again shows his work at the *Young Contemporaries* exhibition, for which he also designs a poster. His four recent canvases are labeled *Demonstrations of Versatility,* presumably all painted in different styles: *Grand Procession of Dignitaries in the Semi-Egyptian Manner, Tea Painting in an Illusionistic Style, Flight into Italy – Swiss Landscape,* painted in a "scenic style," as well as *Figure in a Flat Style* (p. 35). "I realized you could play with style in a painting to make a 'collage' without using different materials," Hockney later describes his strategy. "The idea had been suggested to me by the work and ideas of Ron Kitaj, who's kept me fascinated by style ever since. I thought, this is an interesting thing you can play with, style as a subject." The idea of not letting himself be pinned down to a single stylistic manner will remain important to the artist throughout his career.

Hockney is now perceived as part of a new generation of artists, often associated with Pop art, although not all of its protagonists fit the term. The art critic of the *Times* evaluates the situation in a review of the exhibition *Four Young Artists* at the ICA: "It is too late now to abandon the term 'Pop art' for the type of painting that recently came out of the Royal College of Art and now has adherents all over the place. The phrase is useful and has stuck, and a better one like 'the new figurative painting' sounds colourless. The danger of it, like that of any catch phrase (and the reason Mr. David Hockney, one of its leading lights, feels impelled to declare, 'I am not a pop-painter'), is that of over simplification. Painters hate being pigeon holed in 'schools' and 'movements,' even when there is reasonable justification for it, and these particular painters are already showing that 'Pop art' is an idiom, or an attitude to source material, capable of very different types of individual interpretation … Mr. David Hockney [is] a fantasist with an entrancingly original imagination in which quaintness and caricature are combined. He does not reflect the outer world so much as project an inner one, the wry poetry of which is translated in a technique which can be extraordinarily exquisite and sensitive. But his performance is as precarious as a tightrope act: the balance is perfectly held, but pretentiousness and whimsicality seem to yawn on either side, making his achievement much the most interesting, but also the most dangerously fragile, of the four artists here."

John Kasmin is opening his own gallery, and Hockney sells him the exclusive rights to his work for three years, which secures a regular income for Hockney

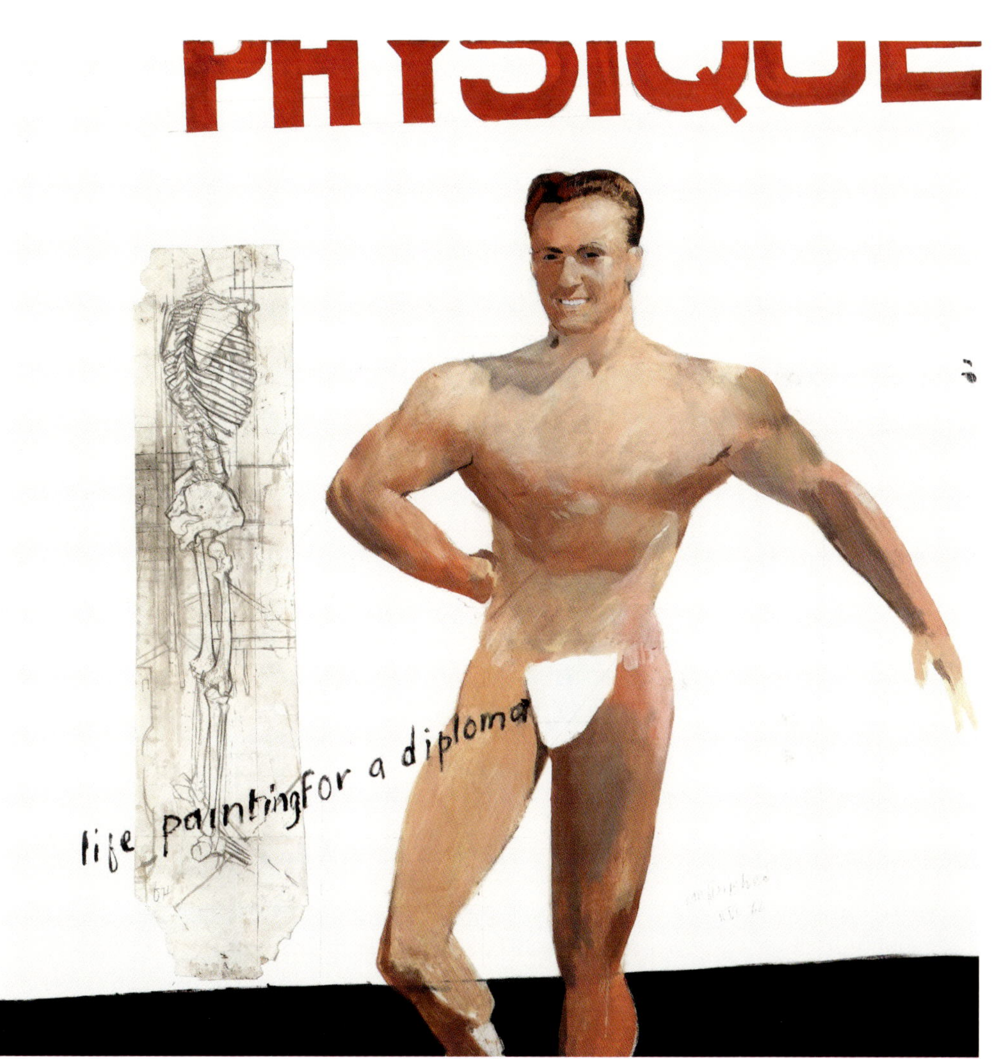

Life Painting for a Diploma, 1962, oil on
canvas with charcoal on paper, collage,
70 7/8 x 70 7/8 in. / 180 x 180 cm

even before he has finished his studies. Meanwhile, at the Royal College, the curriculum of the final year requires that students make paintings after life, and Hockney is not happy with the mostly female models on offer. In his *Life Painting for a Diploma* (p. 33), he circumvents requirements: "I got a copy of one of those American physique magazines and copied the cover; and just to show them that even if the painting isn't anatomically correct I could do an anatomically correct thing, I stuck on one of my early drawings of a skeleton." Finally he gets his friend Mo McDermott hired as an official model and uses him to paint a *Life Painting for Myself* (p. 35).

Hockney graduates from the Royal College of Art. Although it is felt that as one of the best students of recent years he deserves a gold medal, his quickly written thesis on fauvism has not received the required grade for a medal. The faculty have to review the paper and upgrade it before honoring their student. A gold medal is a relatively rare achievement and brings more public attention to the artist. Hockney is portrayed in *Town Magazine*: "His hair is an improbable buttercup yellow and his heavy spectacles give an air of ridiculous seriousness to his face—he looks in fact distinctly like the characters in his paintings which have a quality reminiscent of Dubuffet. 'I have my melancholic days mind you,' he says, but looks imperturbable...This odd Harpo-Marxist swivels his rainbow body in the chair...'I've got to go to Cecil Gee's now to buy a gold lamé coat. I'm going to wear it when they present me with the gold medal.'" Increasingly, Hockney is associated with Swinging London. He makes friends with the young fashion designer Ossie Clark, a stalwart of the scene.

After graduation, Hockney travels to visit Florence, Rome, and Berlin in the company of the American Jeff Goodman and on his return to London searches for a studio. He takes up a teaching post at Maidstone School of Art and in autumn moves into premises at Powis Terrace in the Notting Hill district, which is the first time he can live and work in the same space. He paints *The First Marriage (A Marriage of Styles I)* (p. 39), again trying out different stylistic approaches in a single painting, and *Picture Emphasizing Stillness* (p. 37), which on first view seems to show two men in conversation being attacked by a leopard in mid-jump...until the viewer detects the words "They are perfectly safe—this is a still," pointing to an inherent contradiction in painting. "It's robbed you of what you were thinking before, and you've to look at it another way," Hockney

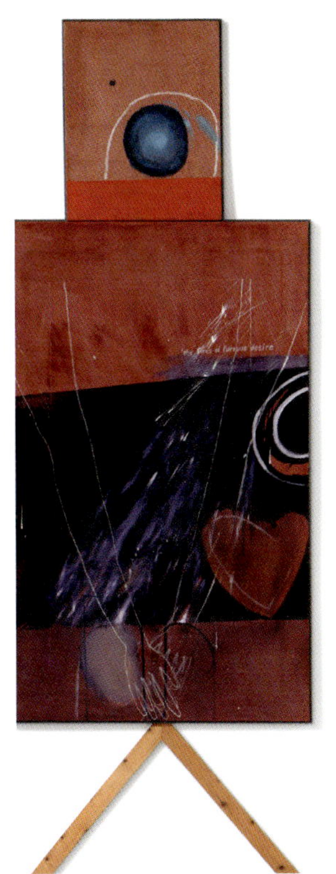

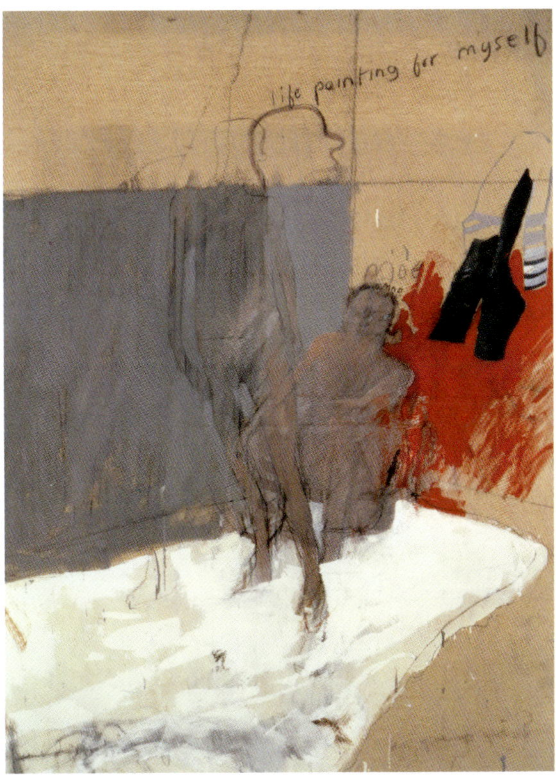

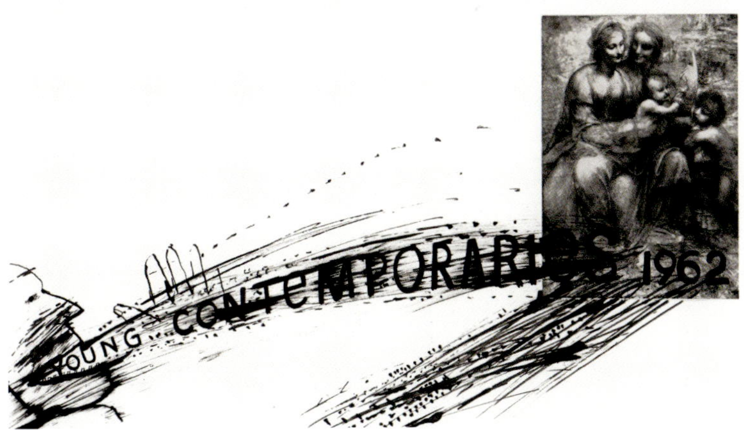

Figure in a Flat Style, 1961, oil on
2 canvases with wood, 88 ⅝ x 34 ⅛ in. /
225 x 86.7 cm overall

Life Painting for Myself, 1962,
oil on canvas, 48 x 36 in. /
121.9 x 91.4 cm

Young Contemporaries, 1962, ink
and collage on paper, 8 ¾ x 11 in. /
22.2 x 27.9 cm

says. "I began the painting without actually knowing its complete subject. Then I realized that what was odd and attractive about it was that, although it looks as though it's full of action, it's a still; a painting cannot have any action."

To the catalog for the group exhibition *Image in Progress* at Grabowski Gallery, Hockney contributes a short programmatic statement: "I paint what I like, when I like, and where I like, with occasional nostalgic journeys. When asked to write on 'the strange possibilities of inspiration' it did occur to me that my own sources of inspiration were wide—but acceptable. In fact, I am sure my inspirations are classic, or even epic themes. Landscapes of foreign lands, beautiful people, love propaganda, and major incidents (of my own life). These seem to me to be reasonably traditional."

Group: *Young Contemporaries*, RBA Galleries, London (Jan); catalog with a text by Andrew Forge. *Diploma Exhibition*, Royal College of Art, London. *Four Young Artists: Maurice Agis, John Bowstead, David Hockney, Peter Phillips*, Institute of Contemporary Arts, London (Jul). *Third International Biennale of Prints*, National Museum of Art, Tokyo (Oct 6–Nov 11); catalog. *Kompas II: Hedendaagse schilderkunst uit Londen*, Stedelijk van Abbemuseum, Eindhoven (Oct 21–Dec 9). *Towards Art? The Contribution of the RCA to the Fine Arts 1952–1962*, Royal College of Art, London (Nov 7–Dec 1); catalog.

Award: *Gold Medal*, Royal College of Art, London.

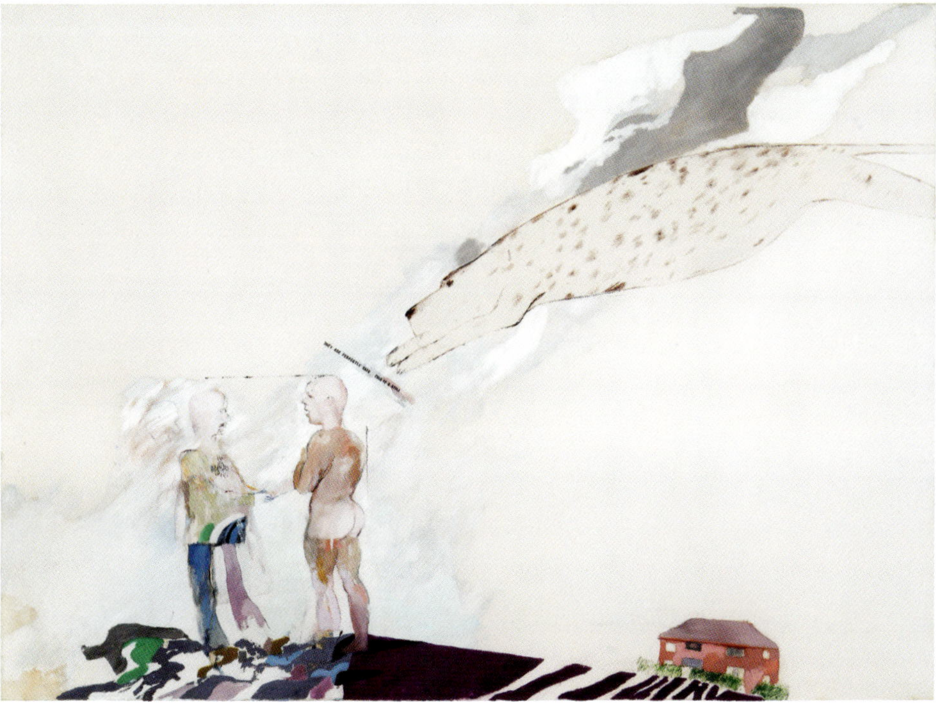

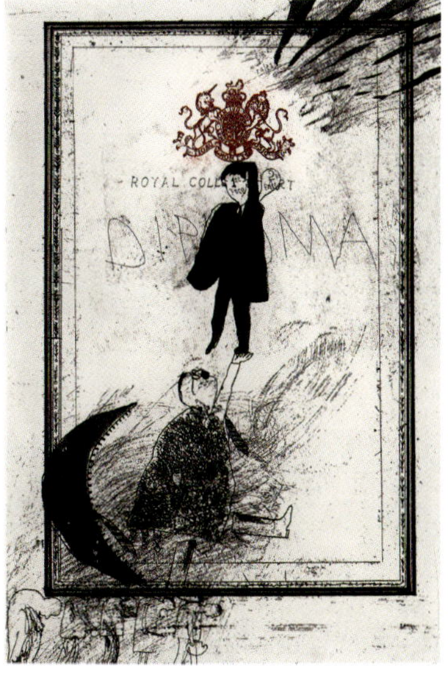

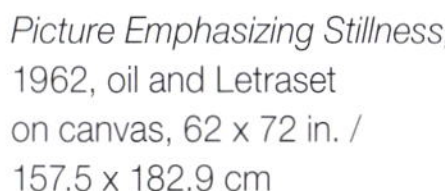
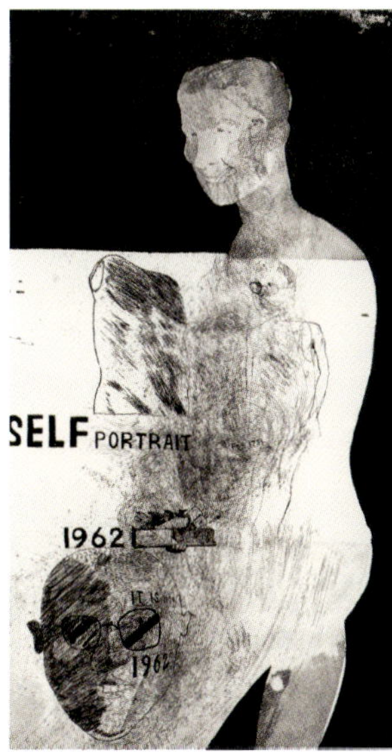

Picture Emphasizing Stillness,
1962, oil and Letraset
on canvas, 62 x 72 in. /
157.5 x 182.9 cm

Self Portrait, 1962,
etching, 27 ¹/₂ x 19 ³/₄ in. /
70 x 50.2 cm

The Diploma, 1962, two-
color etching with aquatint,
edition of approx. 50,
15 ³/₄ x 11 in. / 40 x 27.9 cm

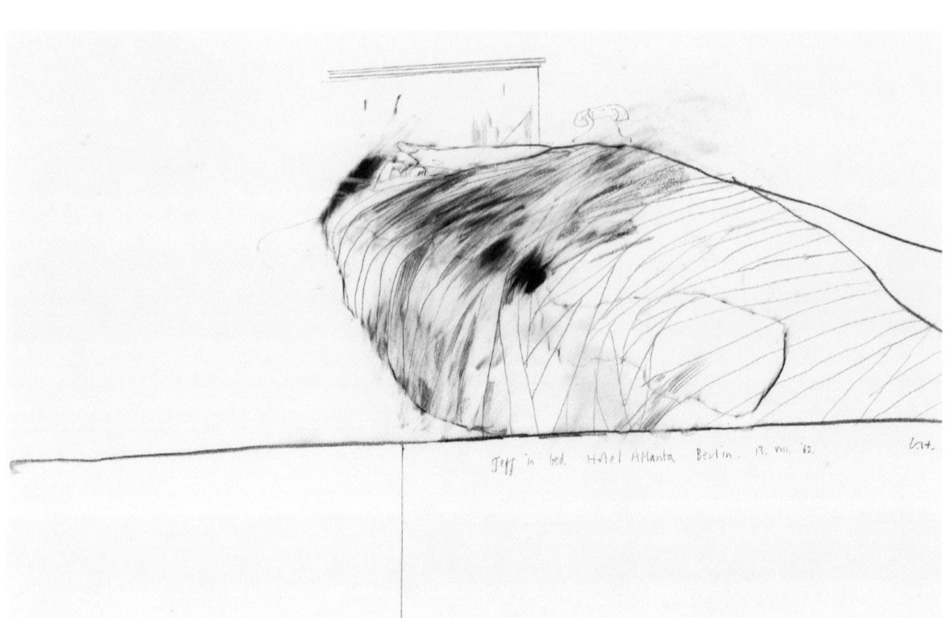

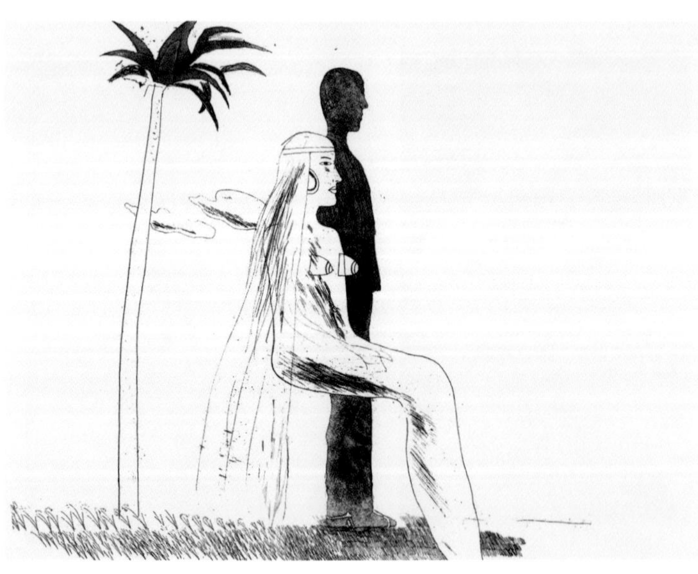

Jeff in Bed, Hotel Atlanta, Berlin, August 13th, 1962, pencil and black crayon on paper, 13 ¹/₂ x 19 ¹/₂ in. / 34.3 x 49.5 cm

The Marriage, 1962, etching and aquatint in black, edition of 75, 12 x 16 in. / 30.5 x 40.6 cm

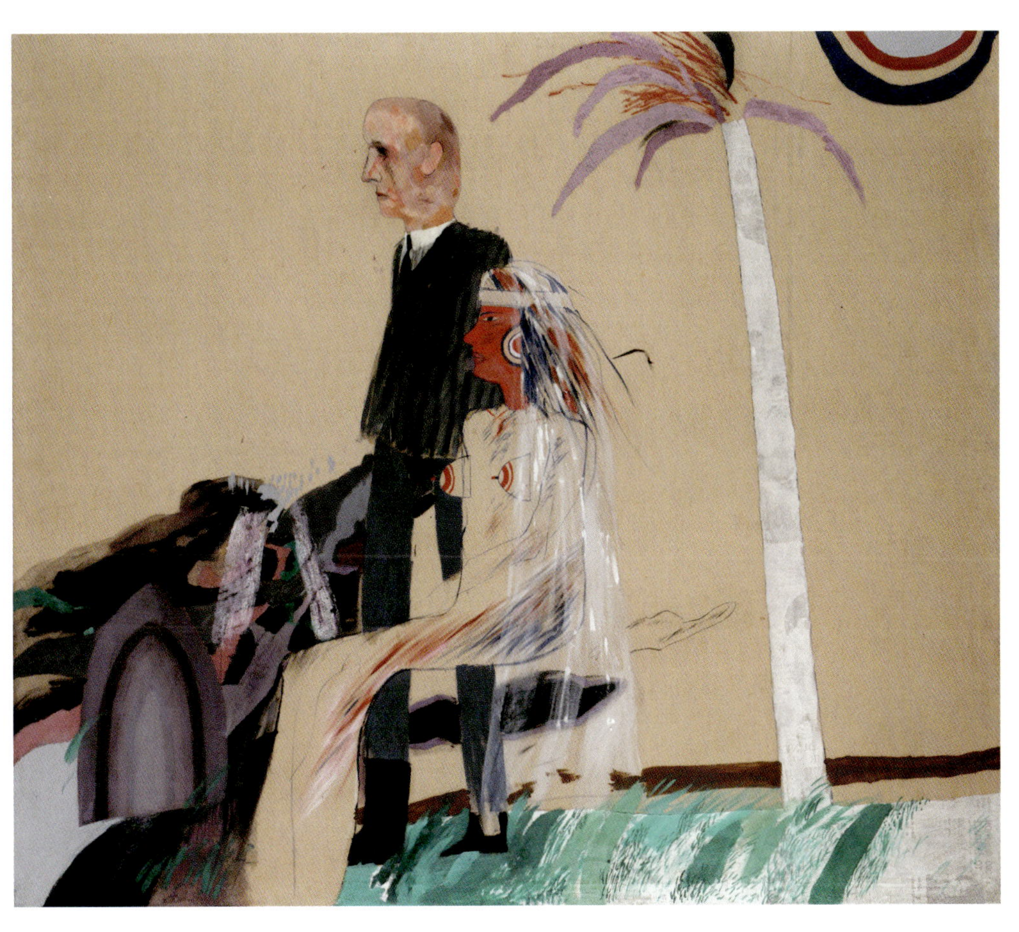

*The First Marriage (A Marriage of
Styles I),* 1962, oil on canvas,
72 x 84 ¼ in. / 182.9 x 213.9 cm

1963

Hockney continues painting in his new studio at Powis Terrace. *Play within a Play* (p. 43) is inspired by Baroque artist Domenichino, who made his canvases look like tapestries. They suggest the "idea of a very shallow space with a picture on a tapestry that has illusion and you don't know whether the illusion is real or not," Hockney says, "you're playing so many games, and they are visual…The figure is a portrait of John Kasmin. Kas had always wanted me to paint him but I'd never got round to it as I couldn't really decide how to do it. Now it seemed appropriate to trap him in this small space between art and life." *Domestic Scene, Notting Hill* (p. 45) is painted from life, the models being Ossie Clark and Hockney's friend and assistant Mo McDermott. *Domestic Scene, Los Angeles* (p. 45), which depicts two men under the shower, is painted from a photograph in the magazine *Physique Pictorial,* before the artist has ever been to the city: "It was only when I went to live in Los Angeles six months later that I realized my picture was quite close to life."

In May, Hockney finally finishes the print cycle *A Rake's Progress* (pp. 46–47). Paul Cornwall-Jones offers to publish it through Editions Alecto in an edition of 50: "They sold the sets for 250 pounds each, and I didn't dare tell people the price because it was so outrageous I was ashamed of it; I thought etchings should cost two or three pounds each; 250 pounds—madness! But with the money I realized I could go and live in California for a year."

In October, Hockney visits Egypt on invitation of the *Sunday Times,* who have launched a series sending artists to places that hold a special meaning for them. He produces 40 colored crayon drawings, starting with a view from his room at the new Hilton hotel in Cairo. His contribution is to run on November 24, but is cancelled after the assassination of President Kennedy two days prior. From his drawings Hockney paints the *Great Pyramid at Giza* (p. 44) in time for his upcoming first solo exhibition at John Kasmin's gallery.

Pictures with People In proves a huge success, and sells out completely. "One thing is certain," Nigel Gosling notes in the *Observer,* "Hockney's paintings are top of the hip parade, as crisply geared to our date as a 1963 scooter. There is something irresistibly fresh-faced about them. They wear an expression simultaneously innocent and cheeky, suggesting one of those elaborate leg-pulls which are so serious to the young…What is new and striking is the way he lets space blow through these pictures. He is a most musical performer." At the same time,

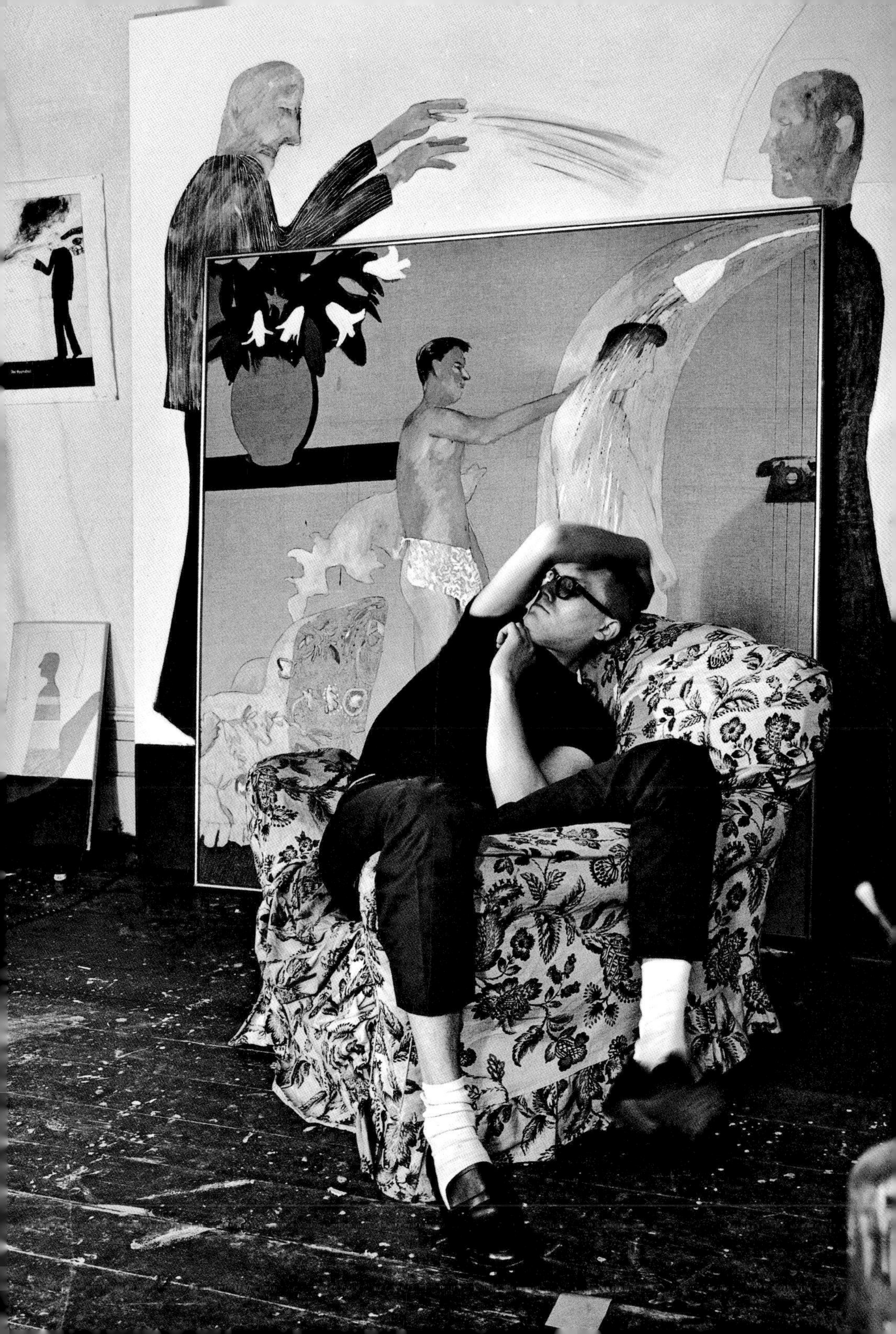

Editions Alecto exhibits *A Rake's Progress,* and the few critics not sold on the paintings find much to admire. Bryan Robertson in the *Times*: "The sequence of prints, happily, is a total success: edgy placing of images, a fastidiously dry sense of the juxtaposition of black and white and a highly individual formal sense, wiry but not untender, drive home at a spanking pace the up-to-date whimsically autobiographical version of the *Rake's Progress* morality tale, based here on the artist's own escapades in America."

In late December, Hockney takes a ship to New York, where he meets Andy Warhol, Dennis Hopper, and Henry Geldzahler, curator of twentieth-century art at the Metropolitan Museum of Art, who will remain a close friend over many years.

Solo: *David Hockney,* Bear Lane Gallery, Oxford (Jan–Feb). *A Rake's Progress and Other Etchings,* Editions Alecto Gallery, The Print Centre, London (Dec 3–24); travels to Lane Gallery, Bradford; Heffer Gallery, Cambridge; and Prestons Art Gallery, Bolton (through 1964); catalog. *Pictures with People In,* Kasmin Limited, London (opens Dec 6).

Group: *British Painting in the Sixties,* Whitechapel Art Gallery, London (Jun 1–30); travels to Zürich, Glasgow, and Hull; catalog. *Fifth International Exhibition of Graphic Art,* Moderna Galerija, Ljubljana (Jun 9–Sep 15); catalog. *Troisième Biennale de Paris: Manifestation biennale et internationale des jeunes artistes,* Musée d'art moderne de la Ville de Paris (Sep 28–Nov 3); catalog; Hockney wins the Graphics Prize. *John Moores Exhibition,* Walker Art Gallery, Liverpool (Nov 14, 1963–Jan 12, 1964); catalog.

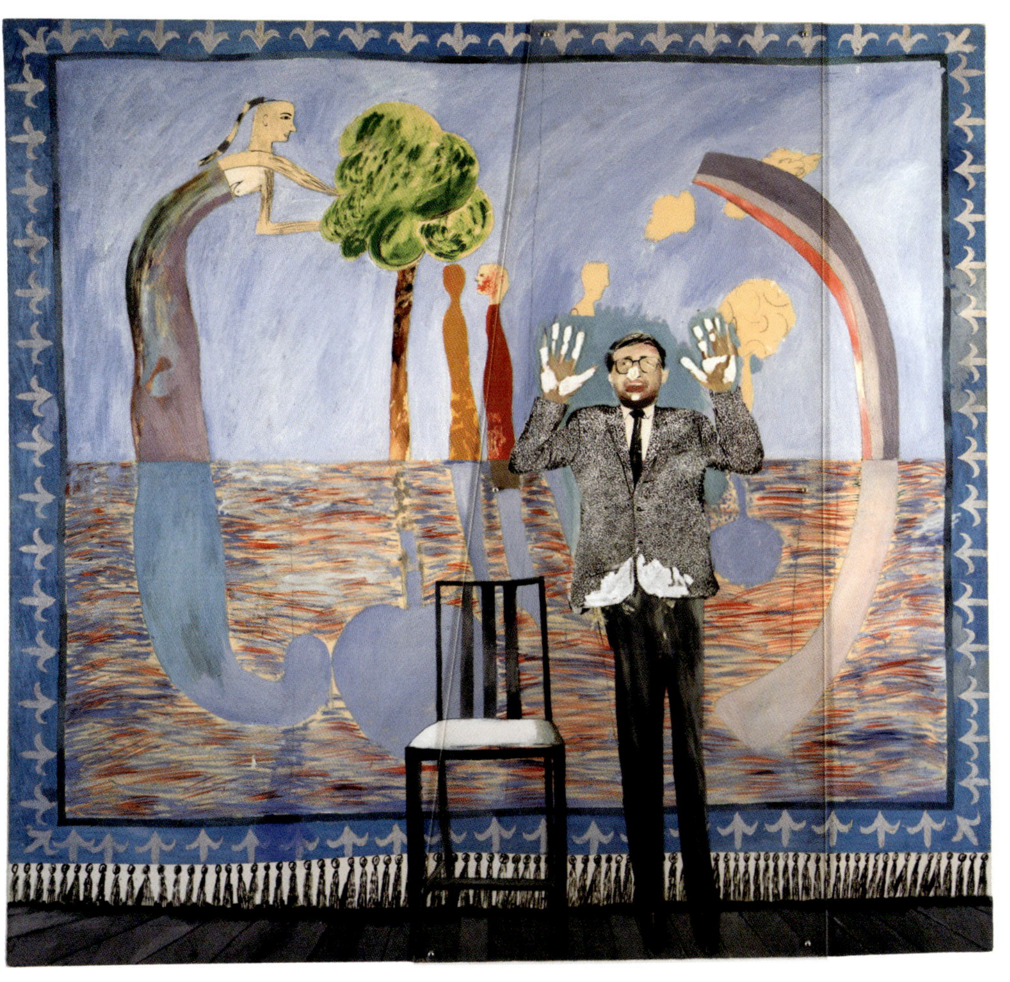

Play within a Play, 1963, oil on
canvas and Plexiglas, 72 x 78 in. /
182.9 x 198 cm

Page 41: David Hockney in front
of *Domestic Scene, Los Angeles*
and *The Hypnotist,* London 1963.
Photo: Jorge Lewinski

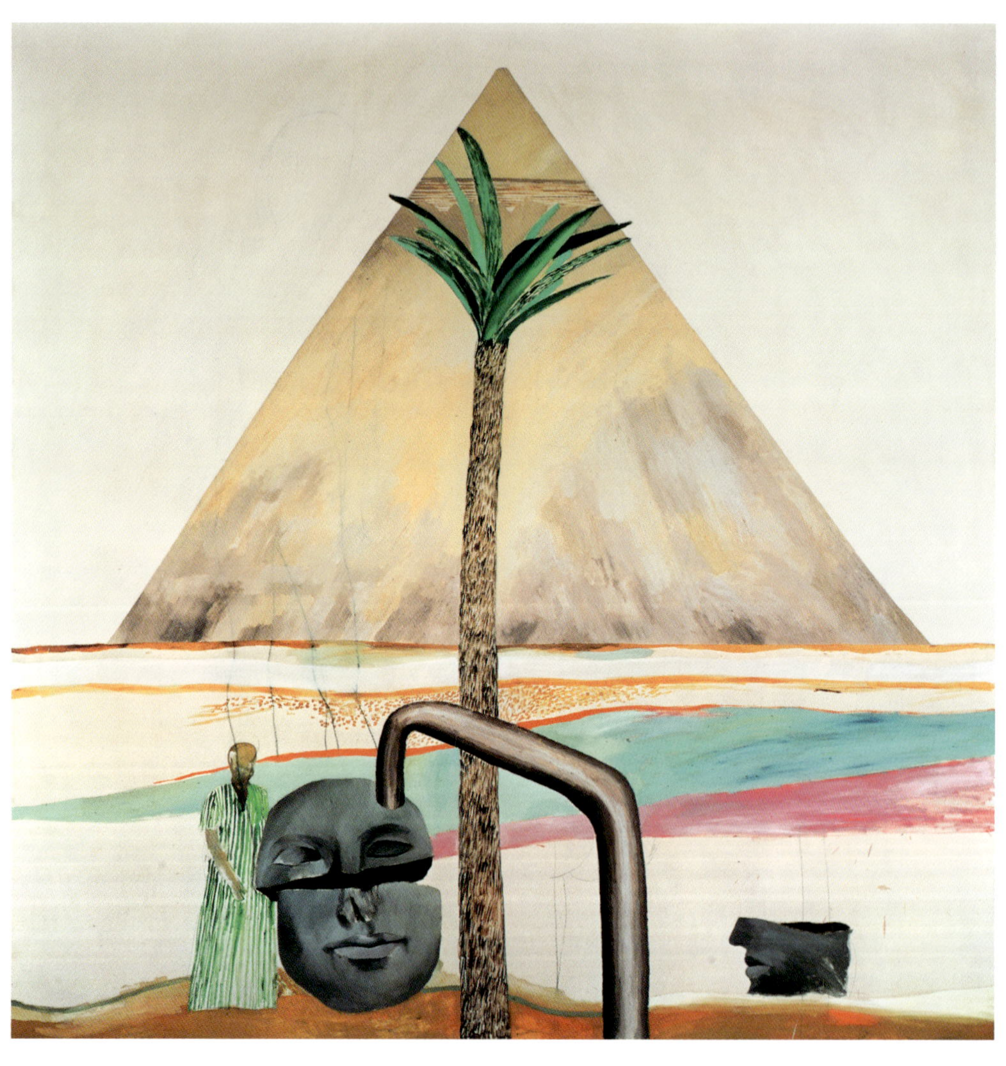

Great Pyramid at Giza with Broken Head from Thebes, 1963, oil on canvas, 72 x 72 in. / 182.9 x 182.9 cm

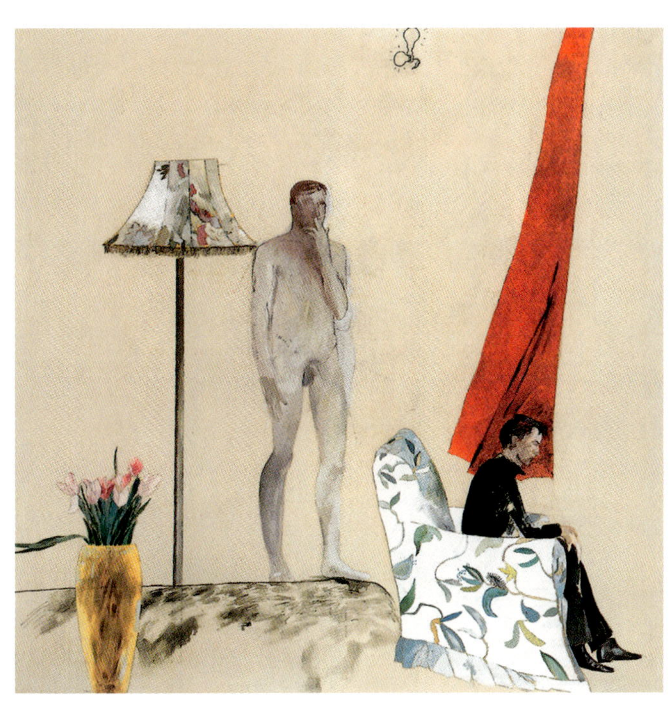

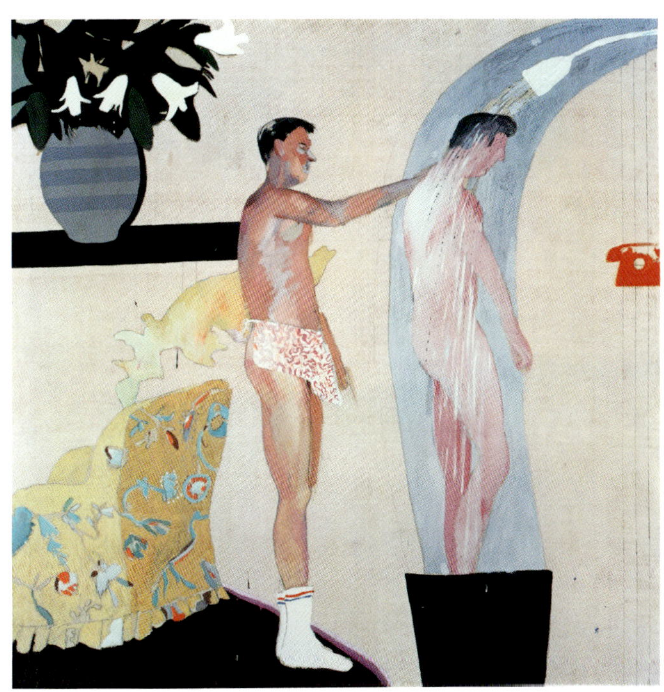

Domestic Scene, Notting Hill,
1963, oil on canvas, 72 x 72 in. /
182.9 x 182.9 cm

Domestic Scene, Los Angeles,
1963, oil on canvas, 60 x 60 in. /
152.4 x 152.4 cm

Pages 46–47: *A Rake's Progress,*
1961–1963, series of 16 etchings
with aquatint, edition of 50,
sheet size each 19 $^{1}/_{2}$ x 24 $^{1}/_{2}$ in. /
49.5 x 62.2 cm

Page 46: *The Arrival; Receiving
the Inheritance*

Page 47: *Meeting the Good
People (Washington); The Gospel
Singing (Good People) Madison
Squarc Gardcn*

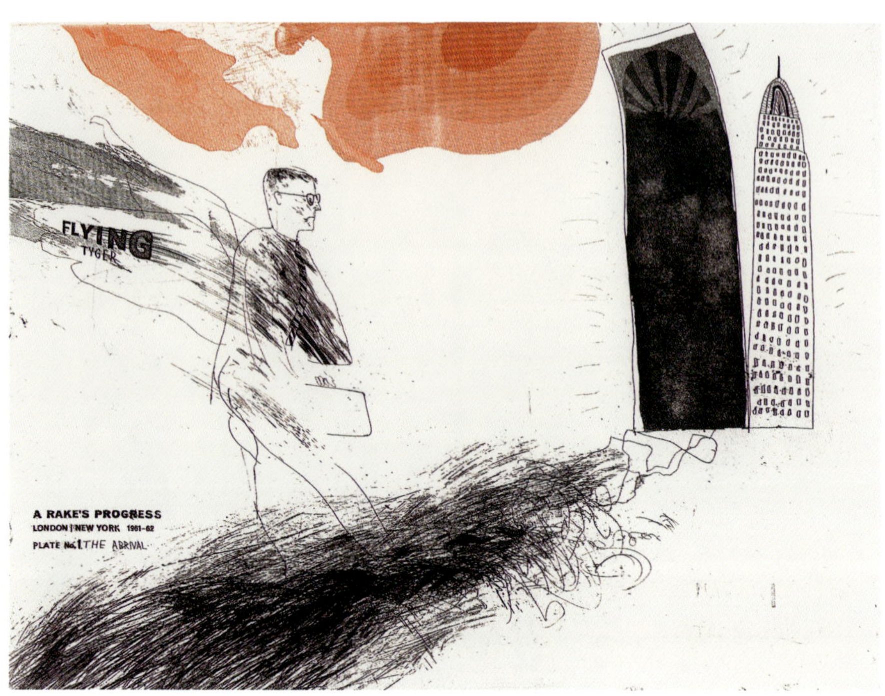
FLYING
TYGER
A RAKE'S PROGRESS
LONDON | NEW YORK 1961-62
PLATE No.1 THE ARRIVAL

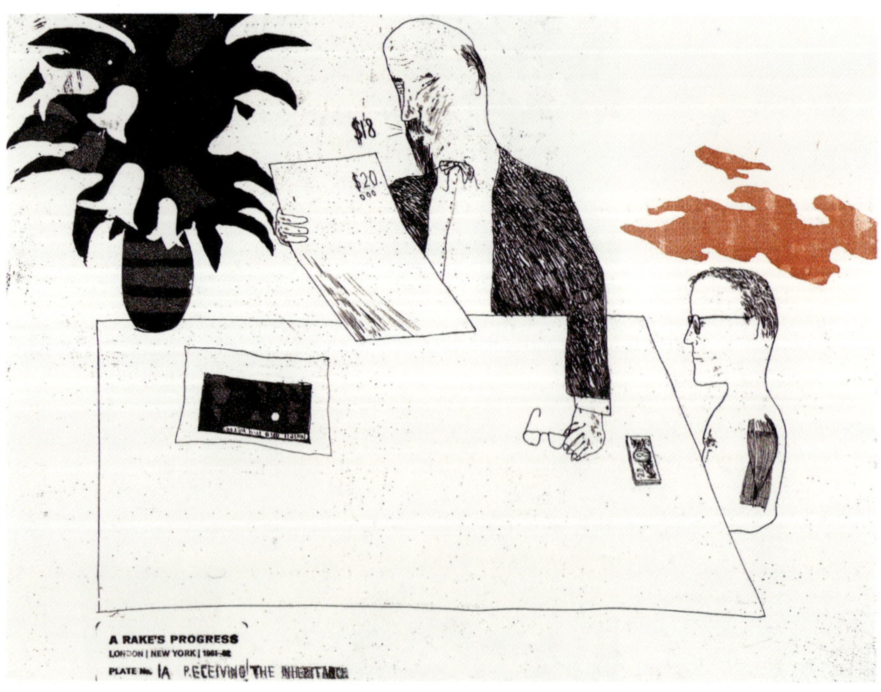
$18
$20.
000
A RAKE'S PROGRESS
LONDON | NEW YORK 1961-62
PLATE No. 1A RECEIVING THE INHERITANCE

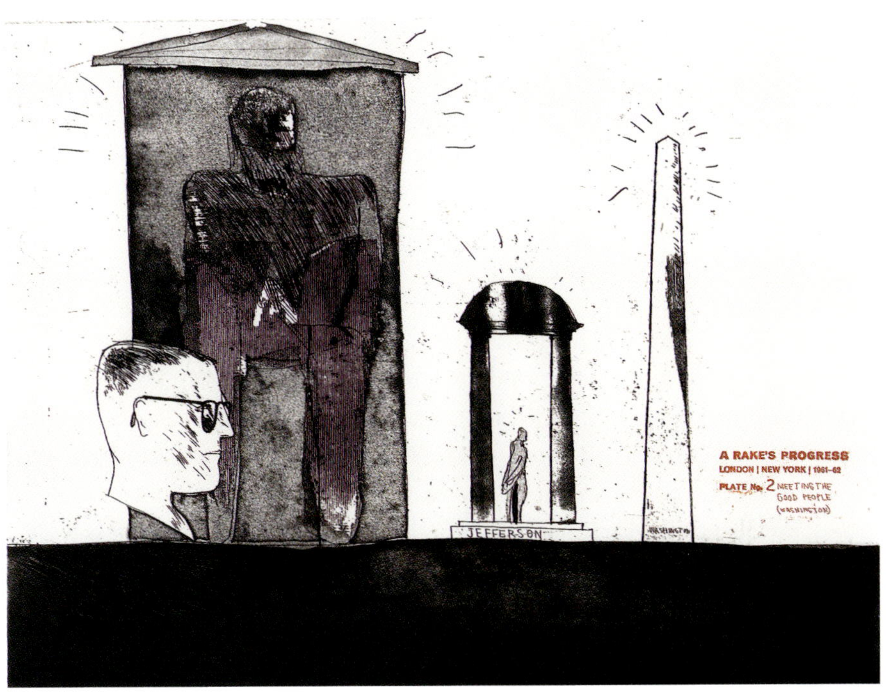

JEFFERSON
WASHINGTON
A RAKE'S PROGRESS
LONDON | NEW YORK | 1961–62
PLATE No. 2 MEETING THE GOOD PEOPLE (WASHINGTON)

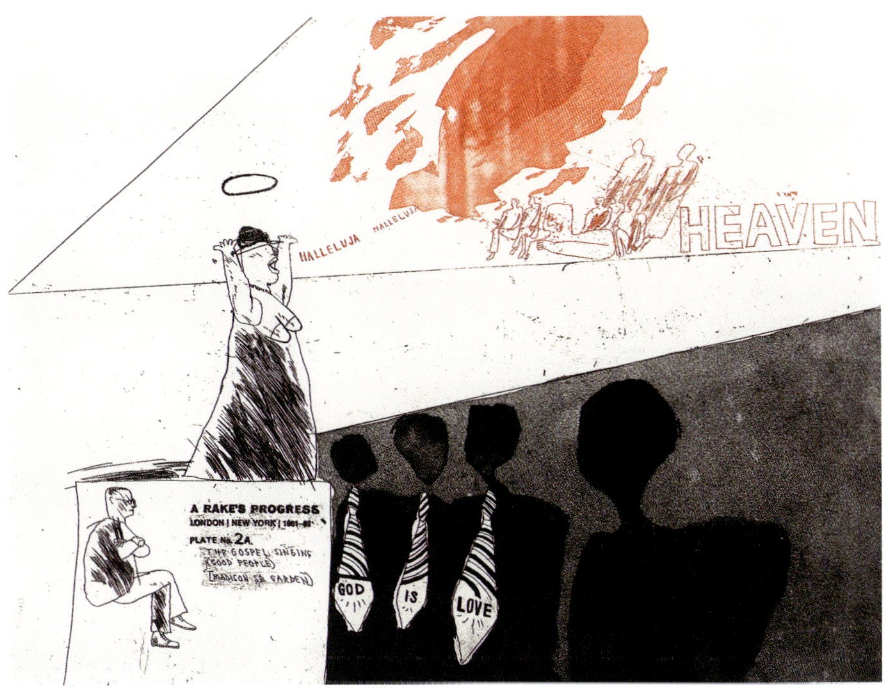

HALLELUJA   HALLELUJA
HEAVEN
A RAKE'S PROGRESS
LONDON | NEW YORK | 1961–62
PLATE No. 2A.
THE GOSPEL SINGING (GOOD PEOPLE) [MADISON SQ GARDEN]
GOD IS LOVE

1964

In January, Hockney moves to Los Angeles without much of a plan, checks into a motel at night, and tries walking to the city, only to discover that what he has taken for city lights is merely a brightly lit gas station. He buys a bicycle the next morning and makes a new attempt: "I had read John Rechy's *City of Night*... it was one of the first novels covering that kind of sleazy sexy hot nightlife in Pershing Square. I looked on the map and saw that Wilshire Boulevard, which begins by the sea in Santa Monica, goes all the way to Pershing Square; all you have to do is stay on that boulevard. But of course, it's about 18 miles, which I didn't realize. I started cycling. I got to Pershing Square and it was deserted; about nine in the evening, just got dark, not a soul there... I had a glass of beer and thought, it's going to take me an hour or more to get back; so I just cycled back and I thought, this just won't do, this bicycle is useless. I shall have to get a car tomorrow." Shortly after, with hardly any practice, he passes the very easy tests for a driving license, and is now allowed to drive a car. He finds a small studio in Santa Monica and starts painting.

Hockney begins using acrylic paint, first on *Man in Shower in Beverly Hills* (p. 53). He paints Southern California landscapes and city views and his first swimming pool painting, *California Art Collector* (pp. 54/55): "It's a Lady sitting in a garden with some art; there was a Turnbull sculpture. There was a lot of sculpture by Bill Turnbull; somebody'd been and sold them there a few years before. The picture is a complete invention. The only specific thing is the swimming pool, painted from an advertisement for swimming pools in the Sunday edition of the *Los Angeles Times*... As the climate and the openness of the houses reminded me of Italy, I borrowed a few notions from Fra Angelico and Piero della Francesca."

As Hockney gets around, he makes friends with neighbors such as writer Christopher Isherwood and artist Don Bachardy, actor and writer Jack Larson and screenwriter and director Jim Bridges, dealer Nicholas Wilder and master printer Ken Tyler. In the summer of 1964, he takes a six-week job teaching at the University of Iowa. Afterward, he visits the Grand Canyon with Ossie Clark and Derek Boshier.

In autumn, Hockney has his first US solo exhibition at the Alan Gallery in New York, while his etching cycle *A Rake's Progress* is exhibited at the Museum of Modern Art. Stuart Preston in the *New York Times*: "Like Picasso (although

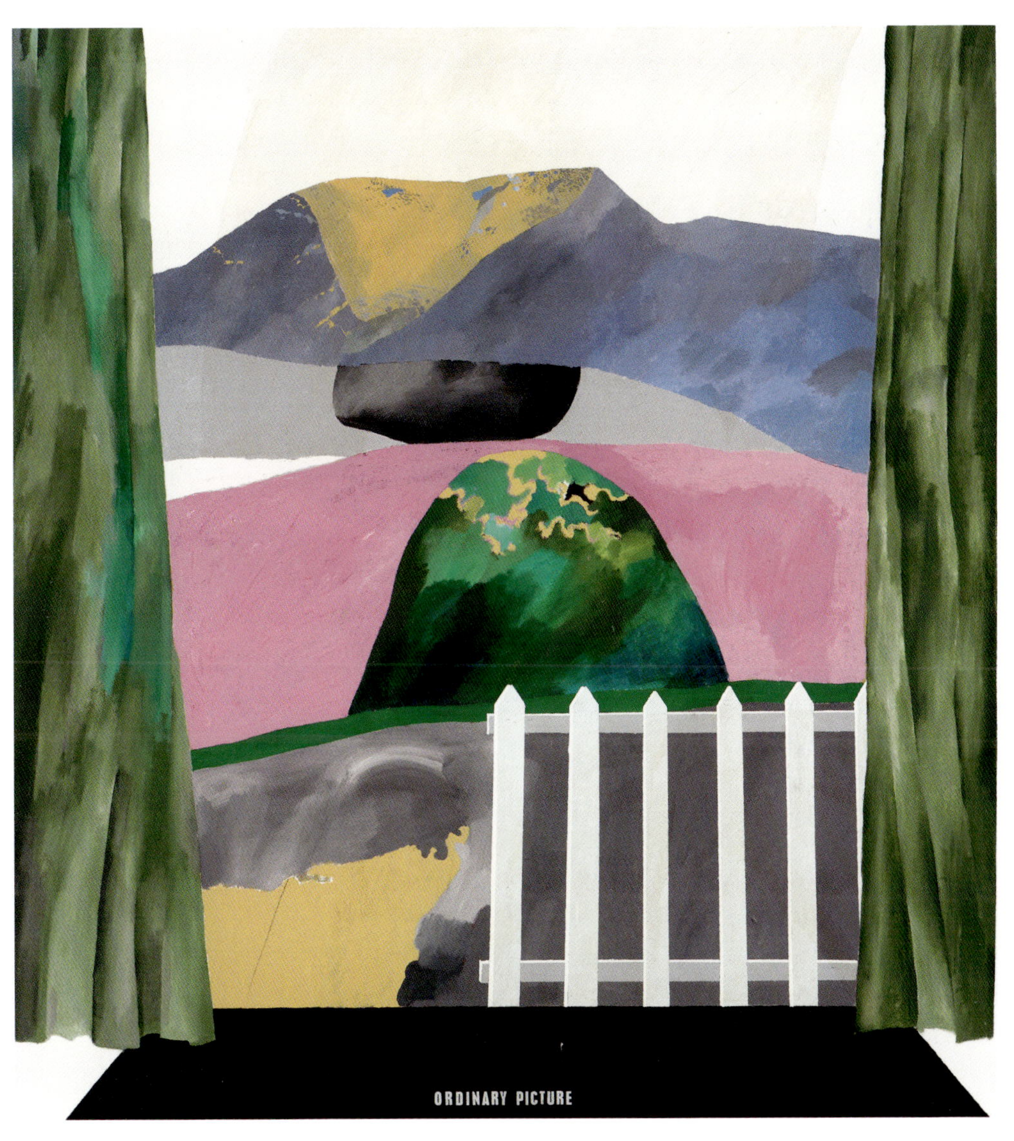

Ordinary Picture, 1964, acrylic on canvas, 72 x 72 in. / 182.9 x 182.9 cm

unlike him in every other respect), Hockney is primarily not a painter but an image maker, both fun and funny in his deadpan, zanily satirical interpretations of modern life. Paint (or lithography) is just a way of putting his comments across. For they are intensely literary, meant to be 'read' like little stories, and very good ones they are. Hockney gets sizzling results in his new version of Hogarth's *Rake's Progress,* a series of prints which wickedly recount his misadventures in the USA, situations that only savage innocence and a wild sense of humor could lead to. This may not be ART but it's artful and cunning. And solemnity is OUT."

Solo: *David Hockney,* Alan Gallery, New York (Sep 29–Oct 17).

Group: *Six Young Painters: Peter Blake, William Crozier, David Hockney, Dorothy Mead, Bridget Riley, Euan Uglow,* Blackburn Art Gallery, Blackburn (Jan); touring exhibition organized by the Arts Council of Great Britain. *VIII Mostra internationale di bianco e nero,* Villa Ciani, Lugano (Mar 27–May 31); Hockney wins the First Prize. *The New Generation,* Whitechapel Art Gallery, London (Mar–May); catalog. *Englische Kunst der Gegenwart,* Städtische Kunstgalerie, Bochum (Apr 19–Jun 7); catalog. *Britische Maler der Gegenwart,* Kunstverein für die Rheinlande und Westfalen, Düsseldorf (May 25–July 5); travels to Munich, Stuttgart, Frankfurt am Main, Berlin, and Bremen; catalog. *Figuratie defiguratie: De menselijke figuur sedert Picasso,* Museum voor Schone Kunsten, Ghent (Jul 10–Oct 4); catalog. *Contemporary Painters and Sculptors as Print Makers,* Museum of Modern Art, New York (Sep 15–Oct 24); catalog. *Pop, etc...,* Museum des 20. Jahrhunderts, Vienna (Sep 19–Oct 31); catalog.

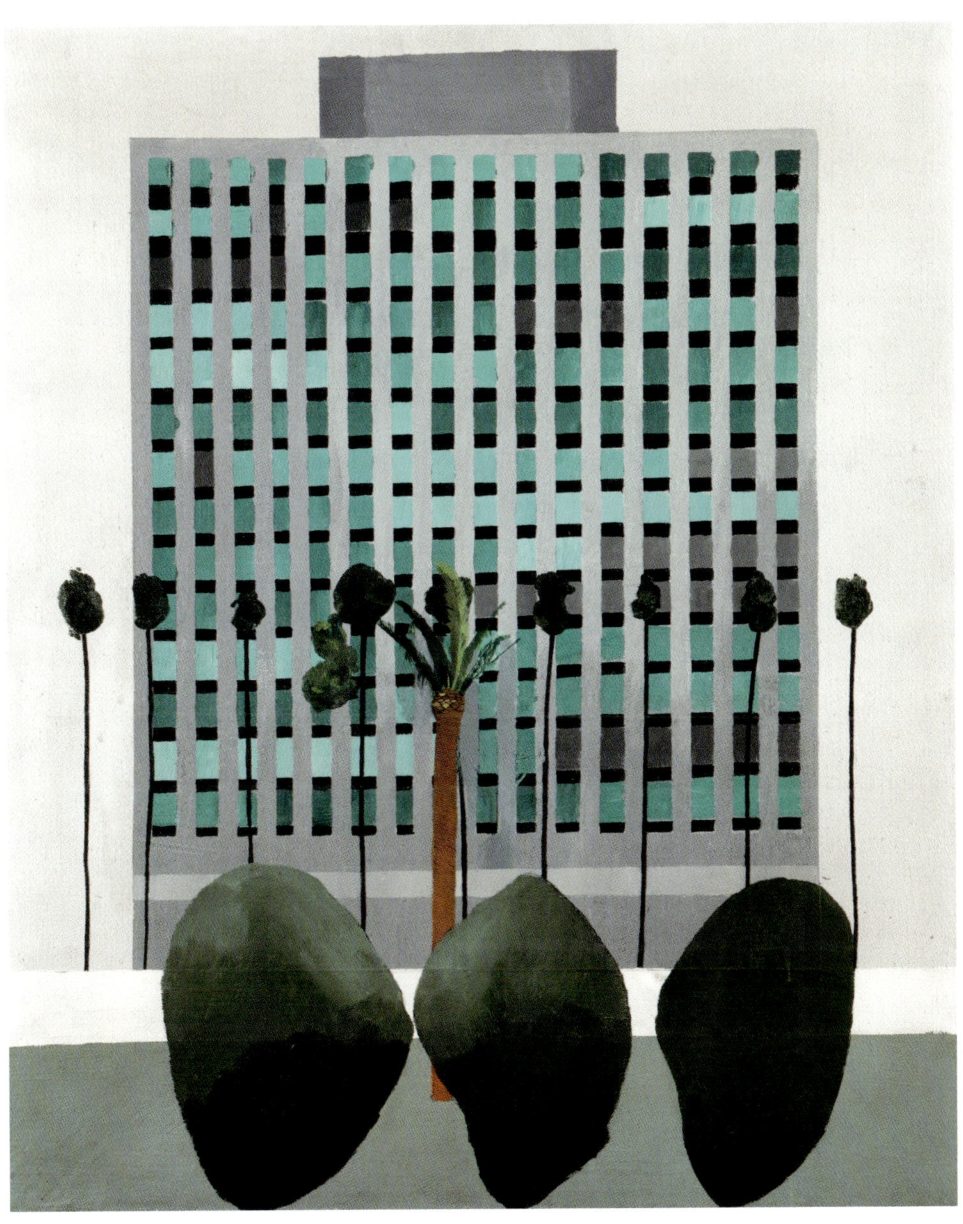

California Bank, 1964, acrylic on
canvas, 30 x 25 in. / 76 x 63.5 cm

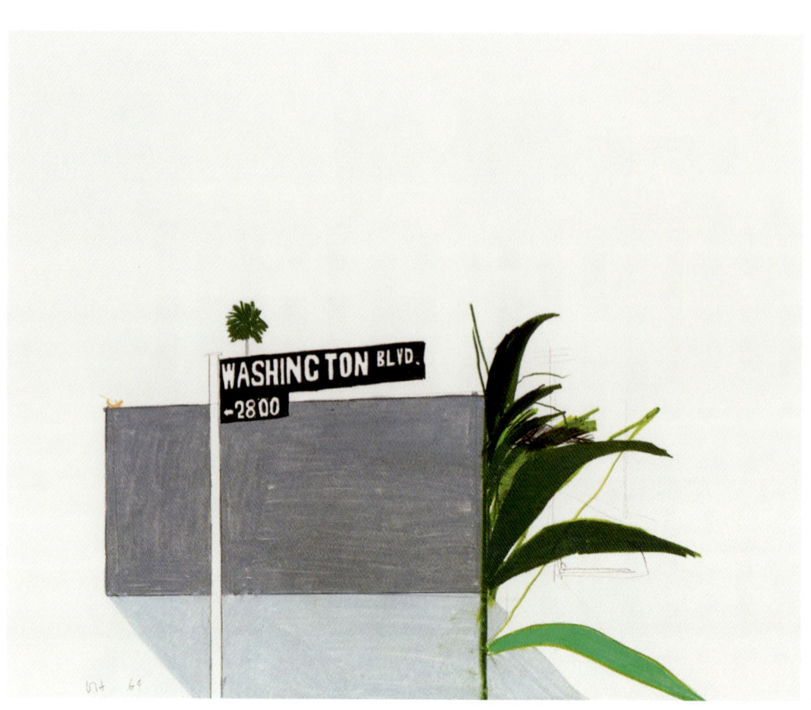

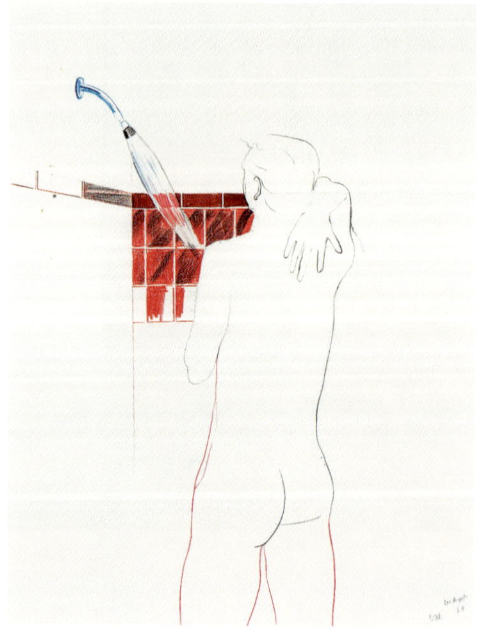

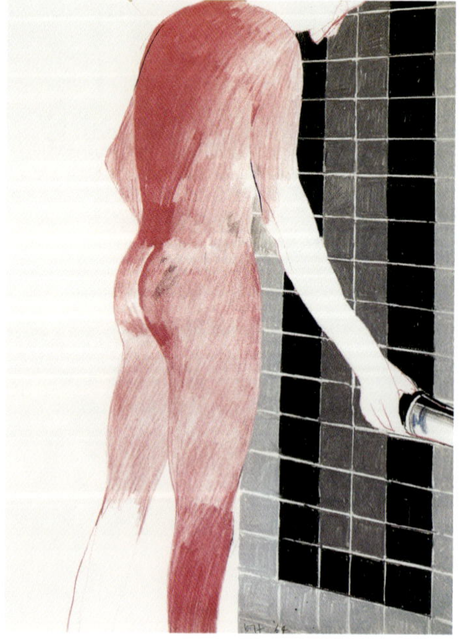

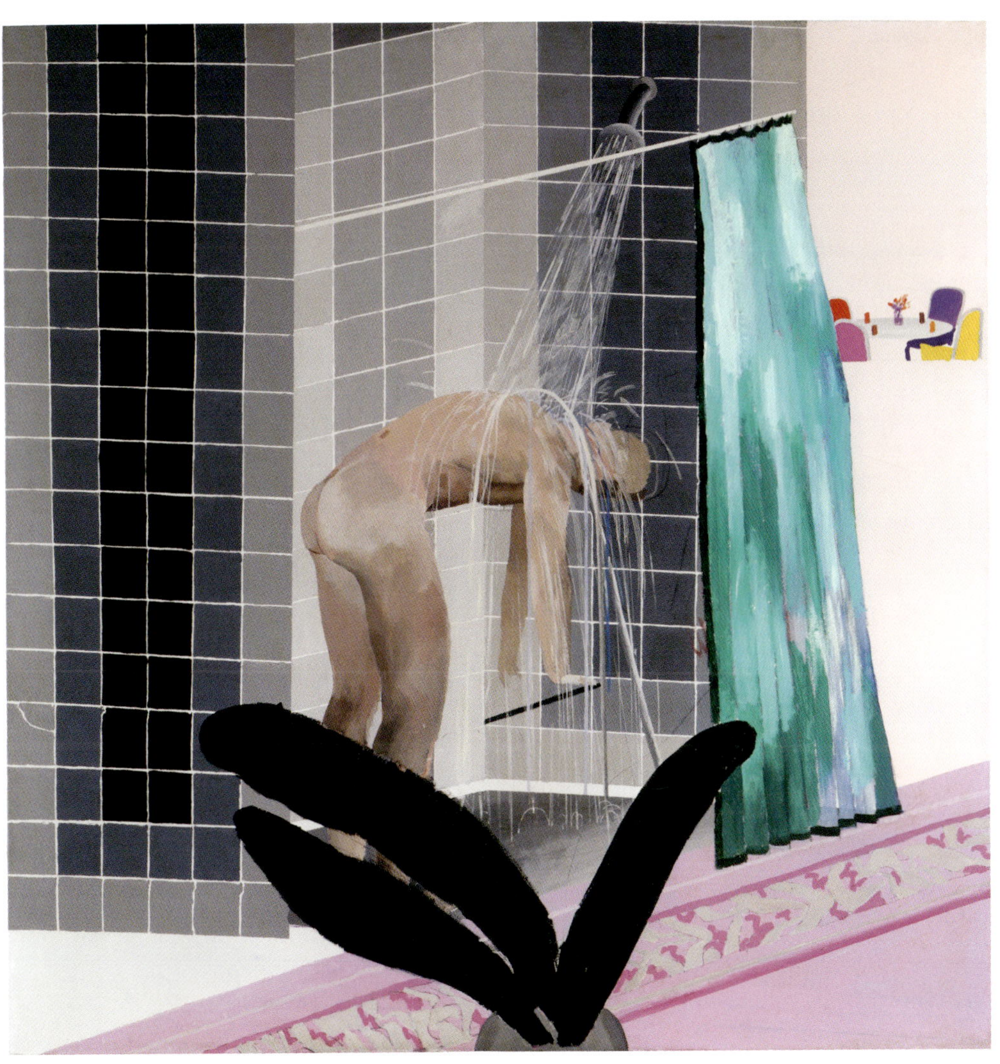

Above: *Man in Shower in Beverly Hills,* 1964, acrylic on canvas, 65 ¹/₂ x 65 ¹/₂ in. / 167.5 x 167.5 cm

Left page: *Washington Boulevard,* 1964, crayon on paper, 10 ¹/₂ x 13 ¹/₂ in. / 26.7 x 34.3 cm

Nude Boy, Los Angeles, 1964, pencil and colored pencil on paper, 12 ¹/₄ x 10 in. / 31.1 x 25.4 cm

Boy about to Take a Shower, 1964, colored pencil on paper, 13 ¹/₂ x 10 in. / 34.3 x 25.4 cm

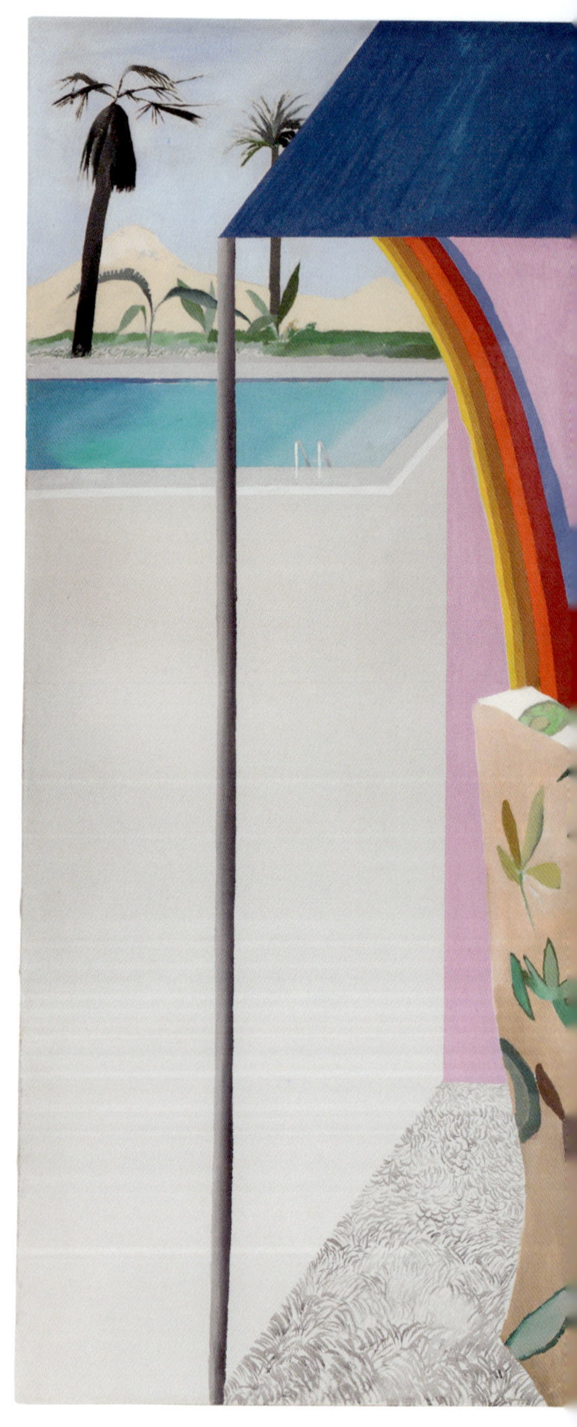

California Art Collector, 1964,
acrylic on canvas, 60 x 72 in. /
152.4 x 182.9 cm

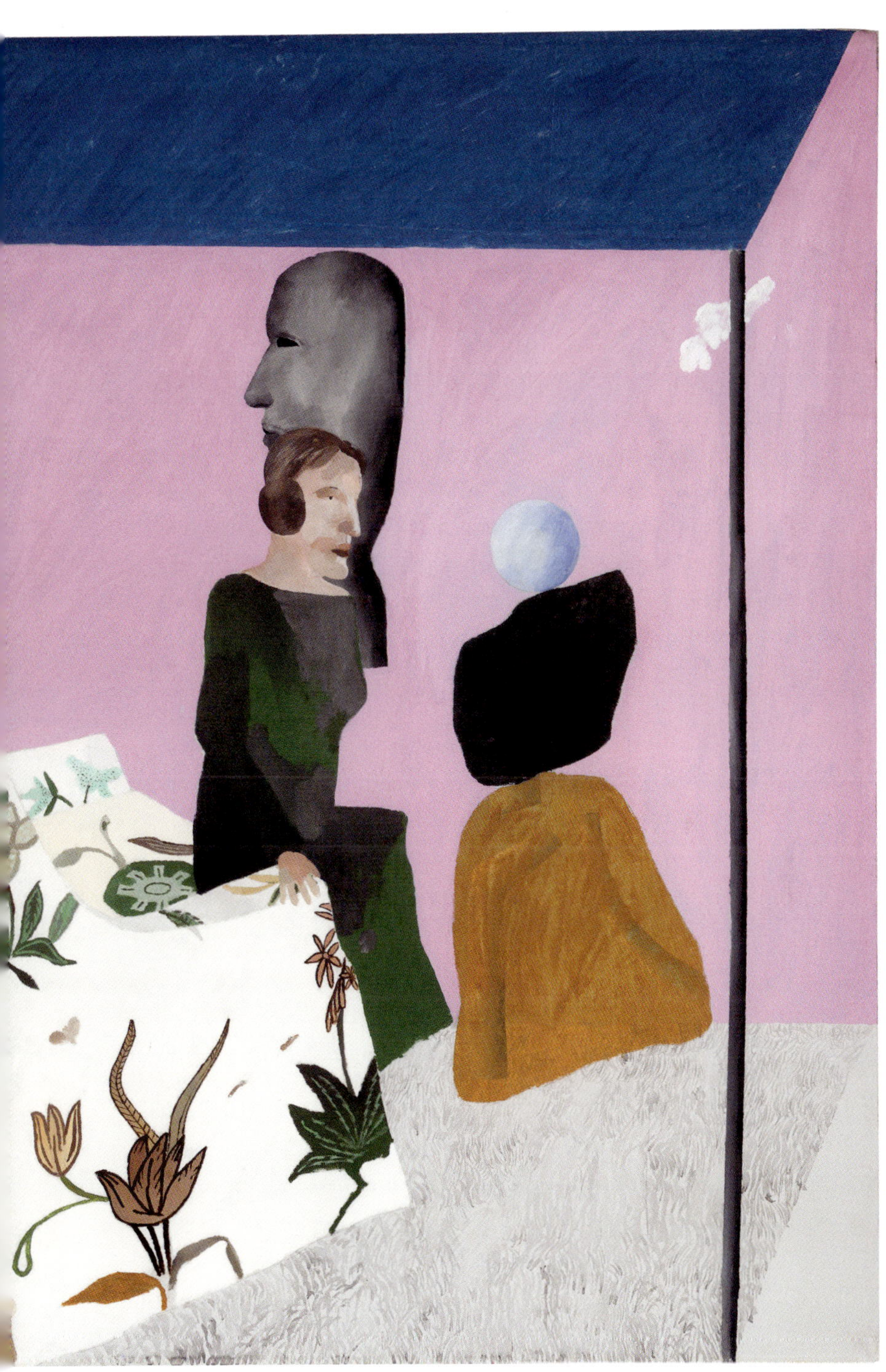

1965

Back in London, Hockney finishes several pool paintings from sketches, trying out different effects: "I had become interested in the more general problem of painting the water, finding a way to do it. It is an interesting formal problem, really, apart from its subject matter; it is a formal problem to represent water, to describe water, because it can be anything—it can be any color, it's movable, it has no set visual description. I just used my drawings for these paintings and my head invented."

In summer, he teaches at the University of Colorado in Boulder, surrounded by the beautiful scenery of the Rocky Mountains. "I go in the studio—no window! And all I need is a couple of little windows," he remembers. "So I painted *Rocky Mountains and Tired Indians* (pp. 62/63). The whole picture is an invention from geological magazines and romantic ideas (the nearest Indians are at least 300 miles from Boulder). The chair was just put in for compositional purposes, and to explain its being there I called the Indians 'tired.'" He also paints *More* and *Less Realistic Still Lifes* (p. 60) as well as a *Portrait Surrounded by Artistic Devices* (p. 61) depicting arrangements of abstract elements: "The idea grew from the curtain motif of previous pictures. The reasoning went something like this: curtains are associated with theatricality; visually the theater is an arrangement on a stage of figures and objects; the traditional still-life painting in art schools (based on Cézanne) is usually an arrangement of apples and vases or wine bottles on a table cloth, perhaps a curtain in repose. Remembering that Cézanne had said everything can be reduced to a cone, I conceived the idea of inventing some still lifes…I must admit that the dubious acrobatics of the reasoning were of great appeal at the time."

He is approached by printer Ken Tyler to create a series of lithographs on a Los Angeles theme. Titled *A Hollywood Collection* (p. 59), it is an imaginary art collection for a Hollywood star: six different types of valuable work complete with frame, including a landscape, a nude, and a "pointless abstraction."

In October, Hockney crosses the Atlantic back to London, where he has his second solo exhibition at Kasmin Limited, *Pictures with Frames and Still Life Pictures* (pp. 64/65). Again the show sells out and is a big critical success. The *Times* review states: "Most of David Hockney's latest paintings are the outcome of a trip to California. They are certainly among his best so far. In these, as in previous ones, his light touch is an antidote to the over-solemnity of some

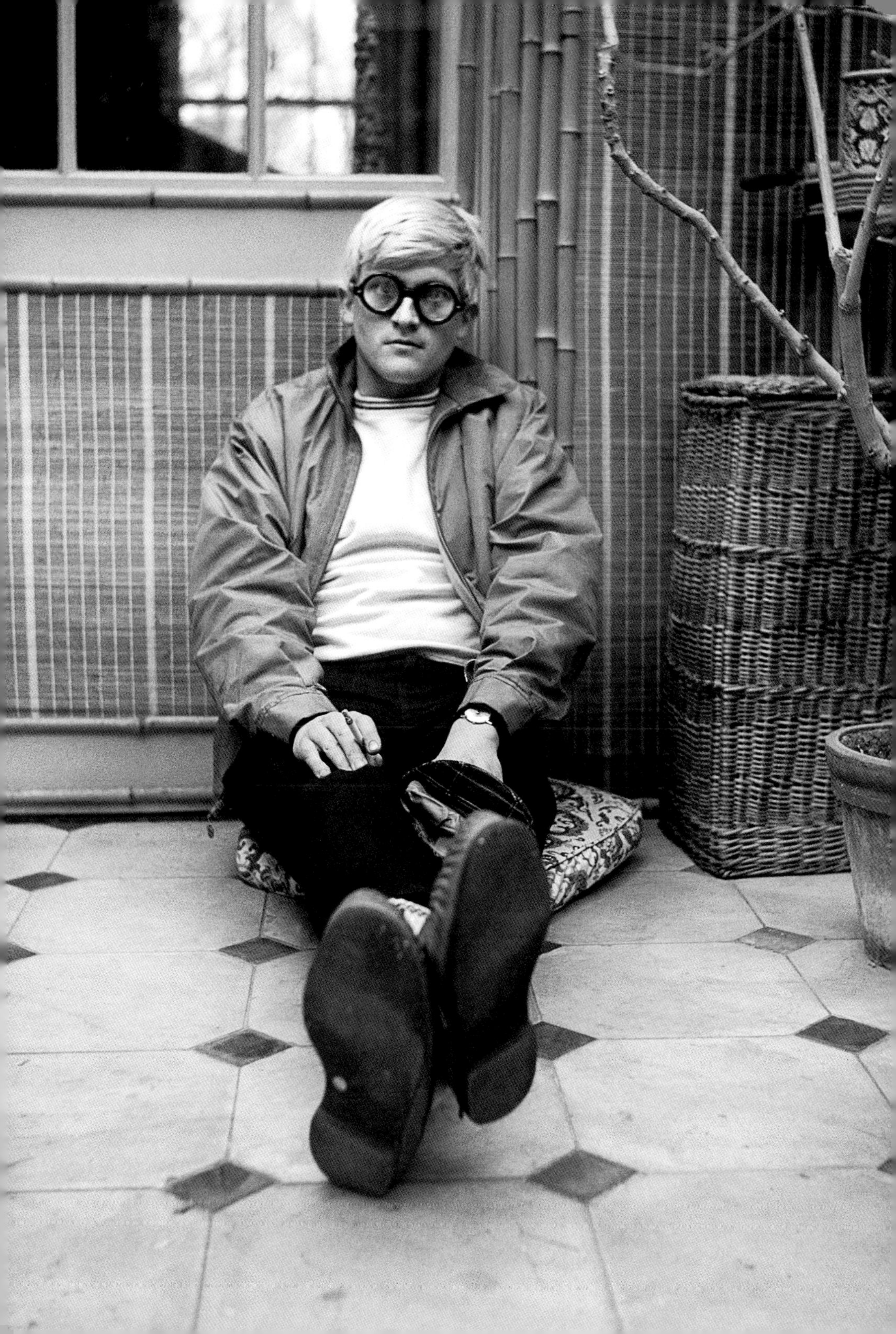

English painting. More than this, though, Mr. Hockney has taken one of the few fruitful courses for a figurative painter at a time when virtually all the devices of figurative painting have been found worn out and stale. He uses as his weapons exactly these illusionistic devices, relying on an extremely subtle formal sense to bring them into unexpected relationships, and thus create fresh images. His latest paintings revolve round the idea of the 'frame,' and by including the representation of a frame within the painting itself he gives the work another layer of meaning which causes us to ask exactly where reality lies."

Solo: *Pictures with Frames and Still Life Pictures,* Kasmin Limited, London (opens Dec 3).

Group: *Pop Art, Nouveau Réalisme, etc.,* Palais des Beaux-Arts, Brussels (Feb 5–Mar 1); catalog. *London: The New Scene,* Walker Art Center, Minneapolis (Feb 6–Mar 14); travels to Washington, D.C.; Boston; Seattle; Vancouver; and Toronto; catalog. *Industry and the Artist,* Walker Art Gallery, Liverpool (Feb 28–Mar 28). *Trends in Contemporary British Painting,* Bear Lane Gallery, Oxford (Jun–Jul); catalog. *Sixth International Exhibition of Graphic Art,* Moderna Galerija, Ljubljana (Jun); catalog; Hockney wins a Purchase Prize. *Impressions on Paper,* Arnolfini Gallery, Bristol (Oct–Nov).

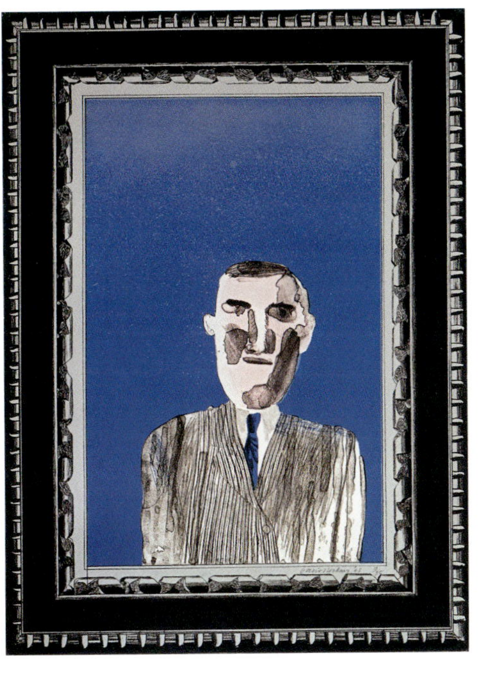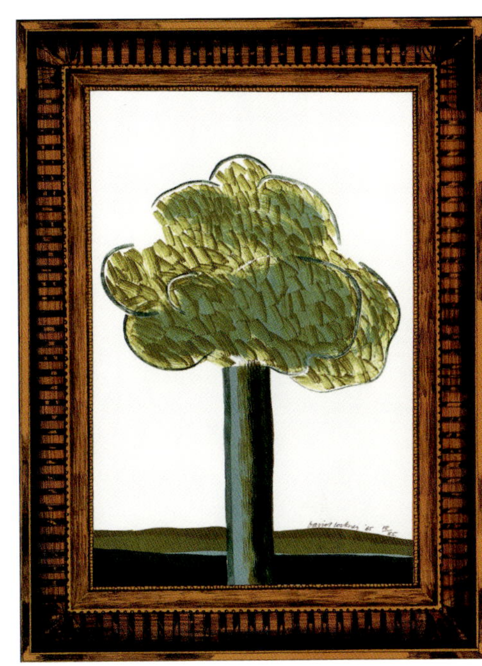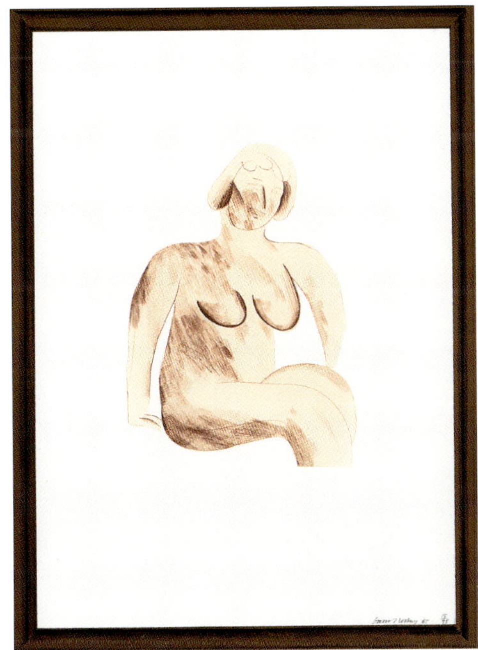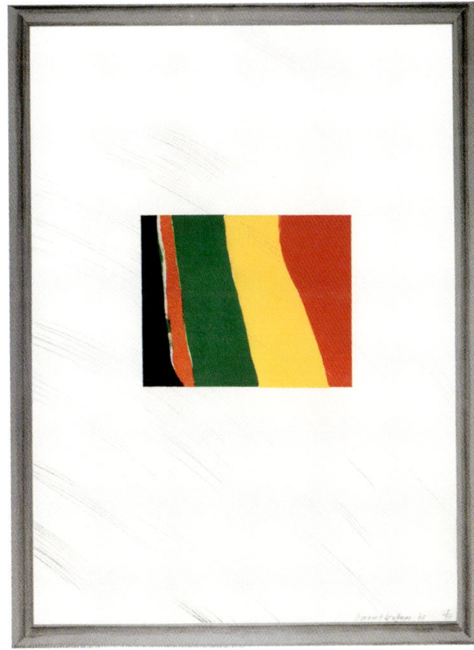

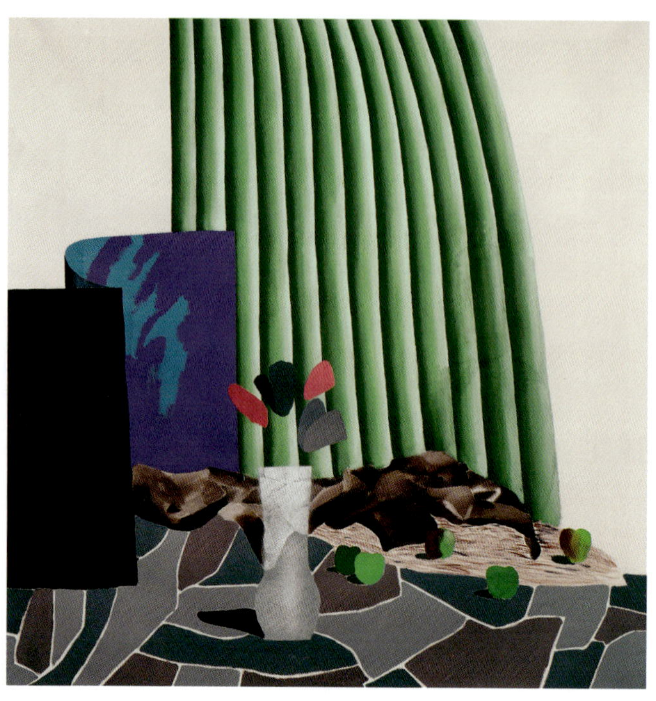

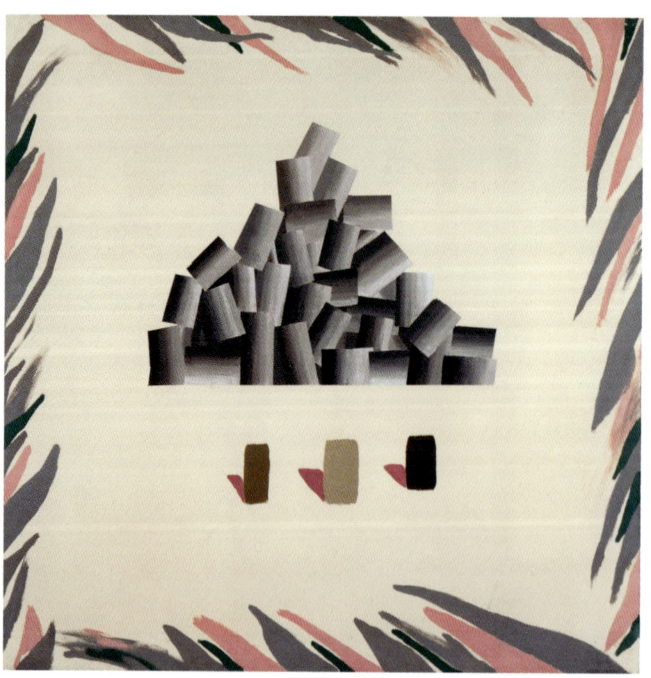

A More Realistic Still Life, 1965, acrylic on canvas, 60 x 58 ³/₄ in. / 152.4 x 149.4 cm

A Less Realistic Still Life, 1965, acrylic on canvas, 48 x 48 in. / 121.9 x 121.9 cm

Page 57: David Hockney at Reddish House in Broad Chalke, Wiltshire, 1965. Photo: Cecil Beaton

Page 59: *A Hollywood Collection,* series of 6 lithographs in an edition of 85, 1965

Picture of a Portrait in a Silver Frame; Picture of a Landscape in an Elaborate Gold Frame; Picture of a Simple Framed Traditional Nude; Picture of a Pointless Abstraction Framed under Glass, four- to six-color lithographs, each 30 ¹/₄ x 22 ¹/₄ in. / 76.8 x 56.5 cm

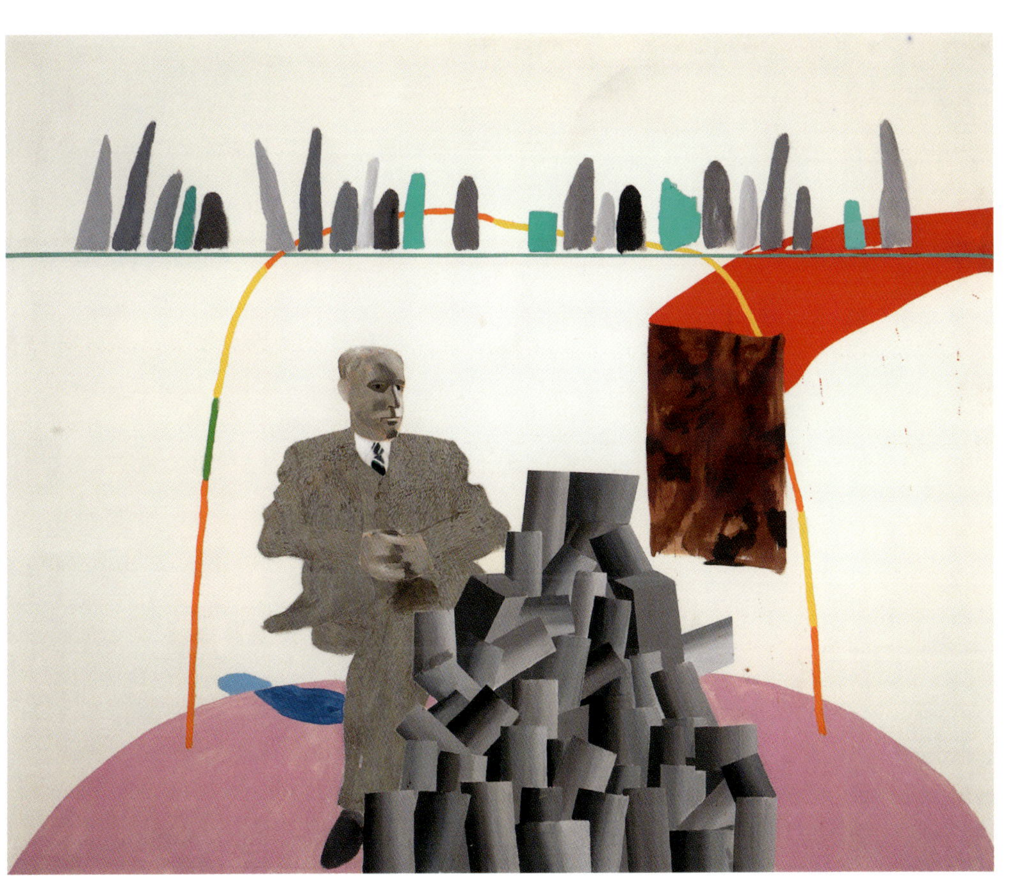

Portrait Surrounded by Artistic Devices, 1965, acrylic on canvas, 60 x 72 in. / 152.4 x 182.9 cm

Pages 62/63: *Rocky Mountains and Tired Indians,* 1965, acrylic on canvas, 67 x 99 ½ in. / 170.2 x 252.7 cm

Pages 64/65: *David Hockney: Pictures with Frames and Still Life Pictures,* exhibition view, Kasmin Limited, London 1965

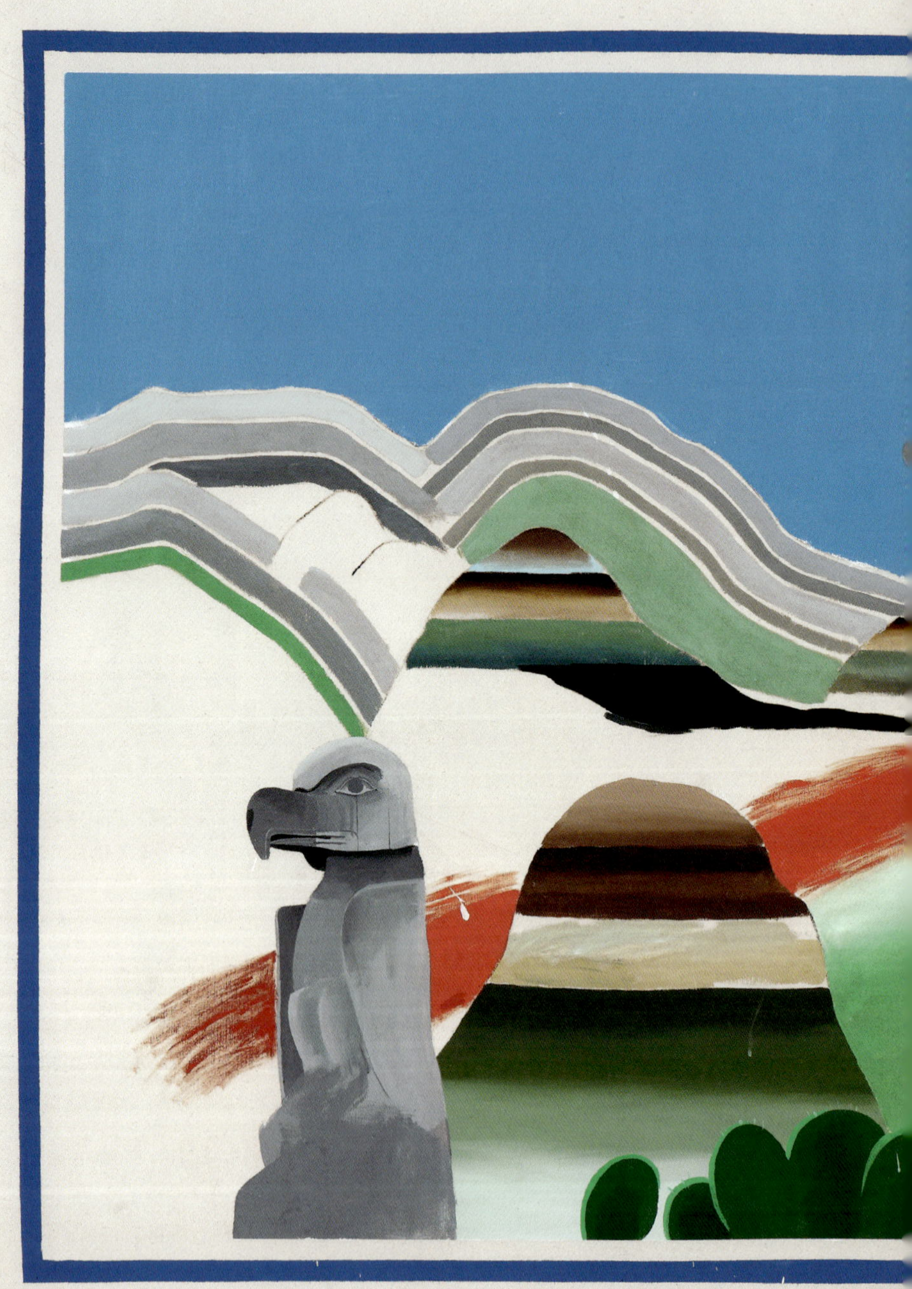

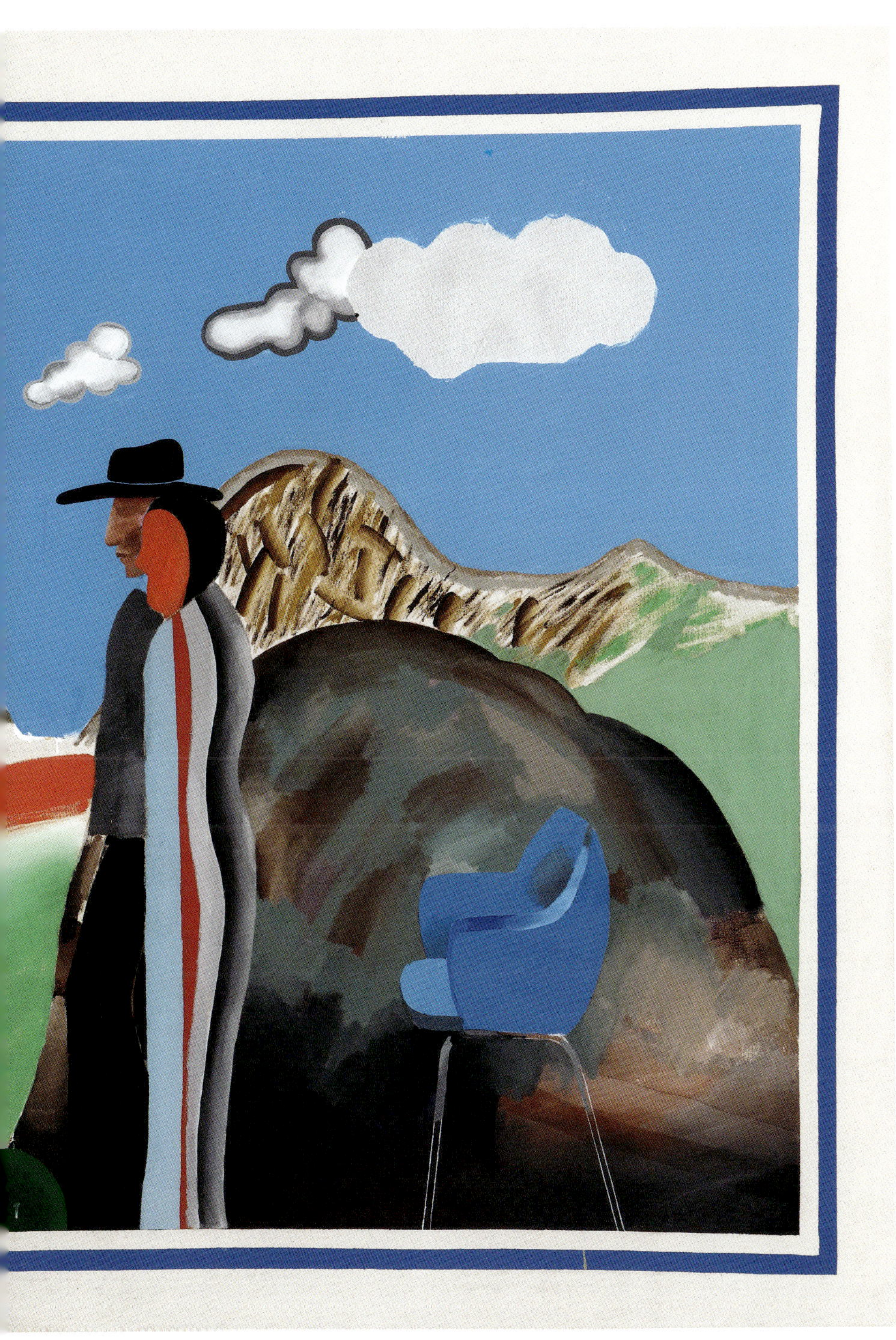

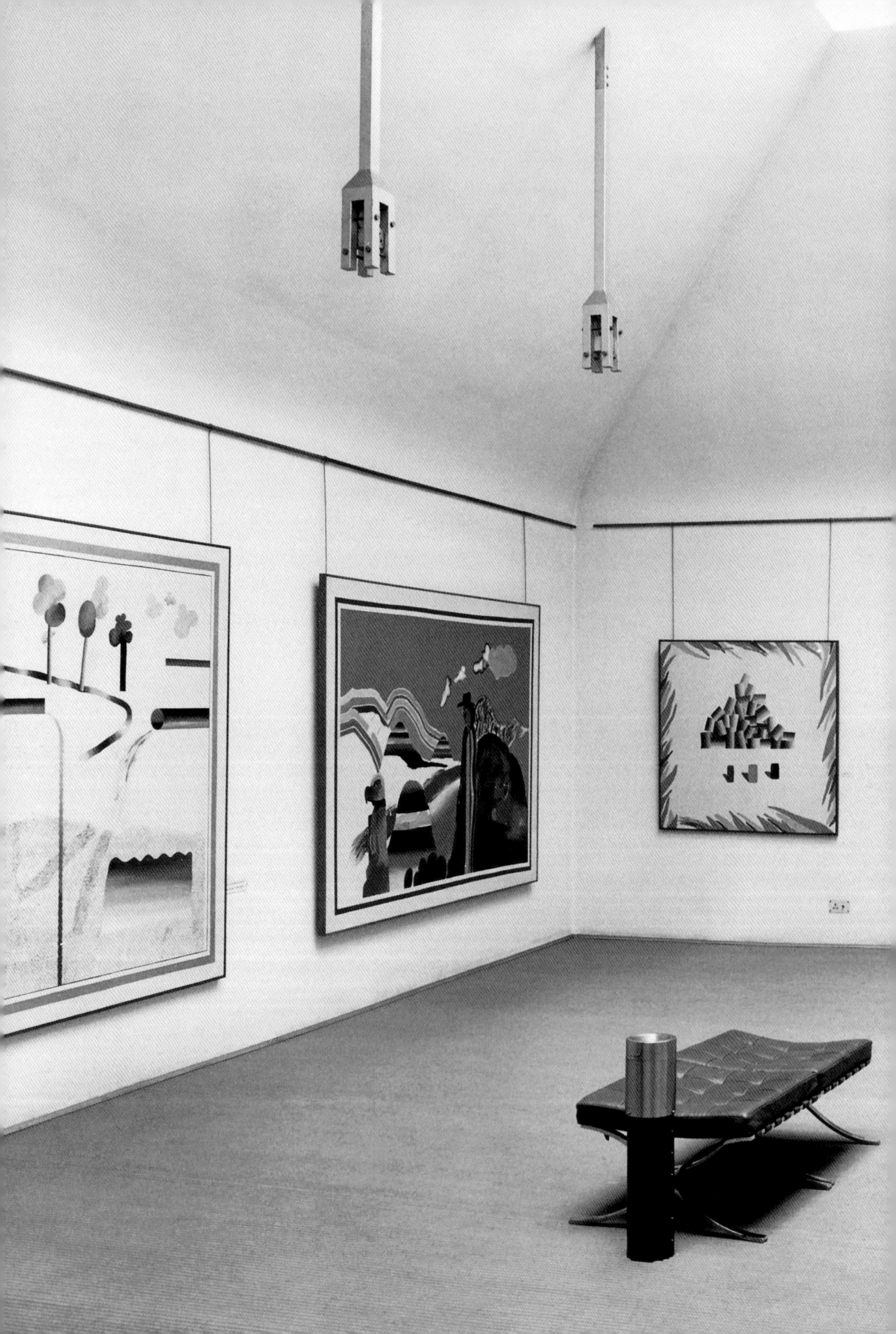

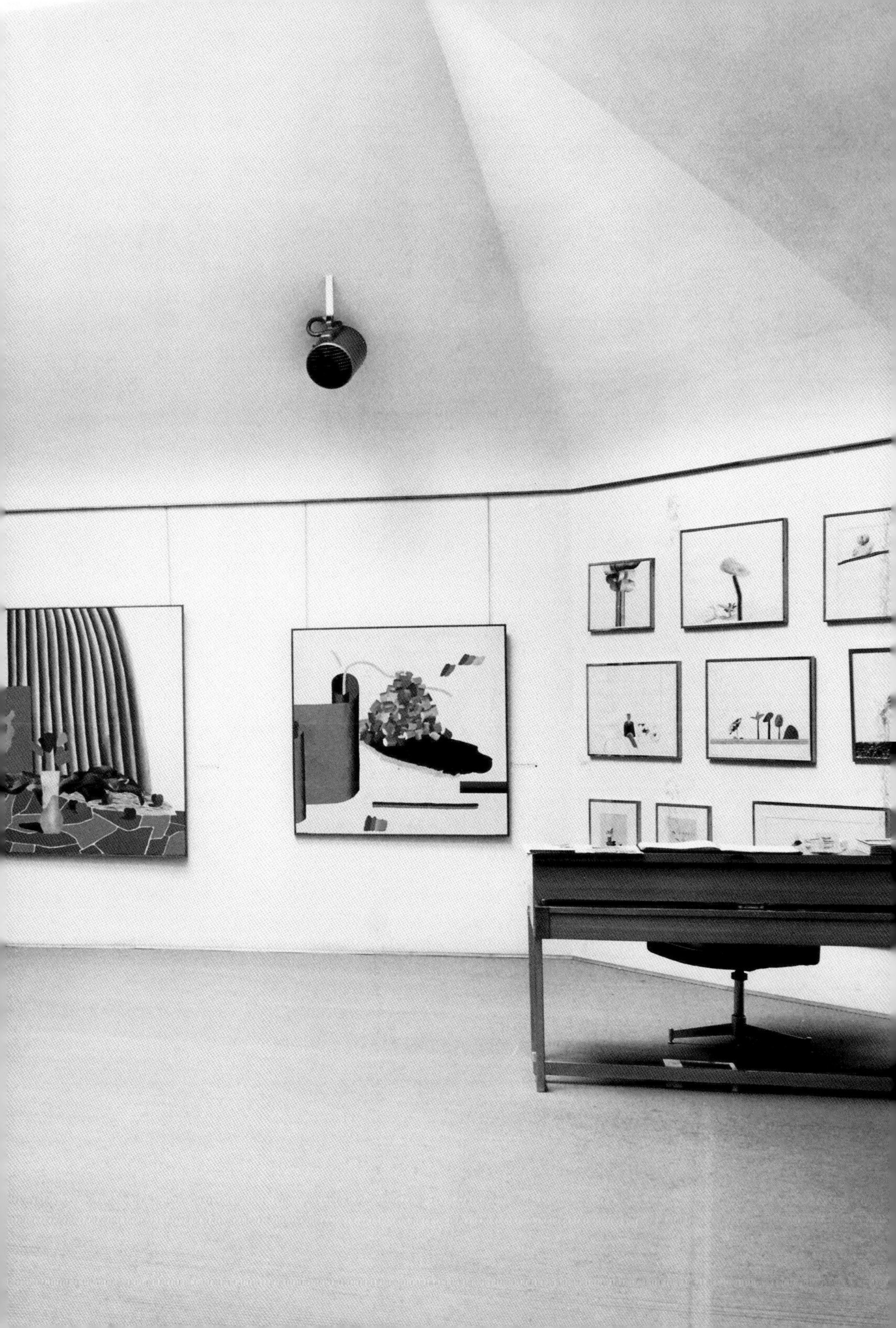

1966

In January, Hockney travels to Beirut to make sketches for a selection of poems by Constantin Cavafy, a favorite since his student days. His illustrations to 14 poems are exhibited and published by Editions Alecto (pp. 70/71). Paul Overy in *The Listener*: "Hockney has not attempted to capture the seamy Alexandria of Cavafy's youth. What he gives, apart from one or two etchings based on a visit to Beirut, is a direct observation of homosexual life in London. Probably homosexuality is less frowned on in Hockney's world than it was in Cavafy's Alexandria, despite its reputation. In Cavafy's poems there is always a sense of half-guilt, the thrill of the forbidden: 'With ideal limbs made for these beds / that current morality would call shameless.' Rather than attempt what would probably be impossible to express in visual terms anyway—Cavafy's concern with the intensity of physical experience and its importance in creating the future by means of memory—Hockney concentrates on presenting homosexual liaisons as something completely normal and acceptable."

Hockney is invited to design Alfred Jarry's *Ubu Roi* for the Royal Court Theatre of London (p. 69). After some misgivings, he accepts the challenge: "In paintings before that I had been interested in what you might call theatrical devices, and I thought that in the theater, the home of theatrical devices, they would be contradictory...So I agreed to do it without knowing how to do it. I took each scene and made a drawing of it. The concept was basically very simple: little painted backdrops, much smaller than the stage. They were like big paintings, about twelve feet by eight feet. They dropped down with big ropes on them, like a joke toy theater." Reviews of the performance are mixed. David Thompson in the *New York Times*: "It was always expected that Hockney would design for the theater sooner or later, and certainly his sets and costumes are among the most visually rewarding and entertaining things on a London stage at the moment. They won't revolutionize West End theater design (which is what one is always secretly hoping for on those rare occasions when 'real' artists venture into this domain), but at least they indicate standards of visual literacy in the theater that should be the norm instead of the exception. It just seems a pity that the occasion should be *Ubu*. The play is essentially crude and violent, and Hockney isn't." Hockney will not design for the theater again for a decade.

In summer, he returns to Los Angeles to teach drawing at the University of California. He holds the post for only six weeks, but during that time meets

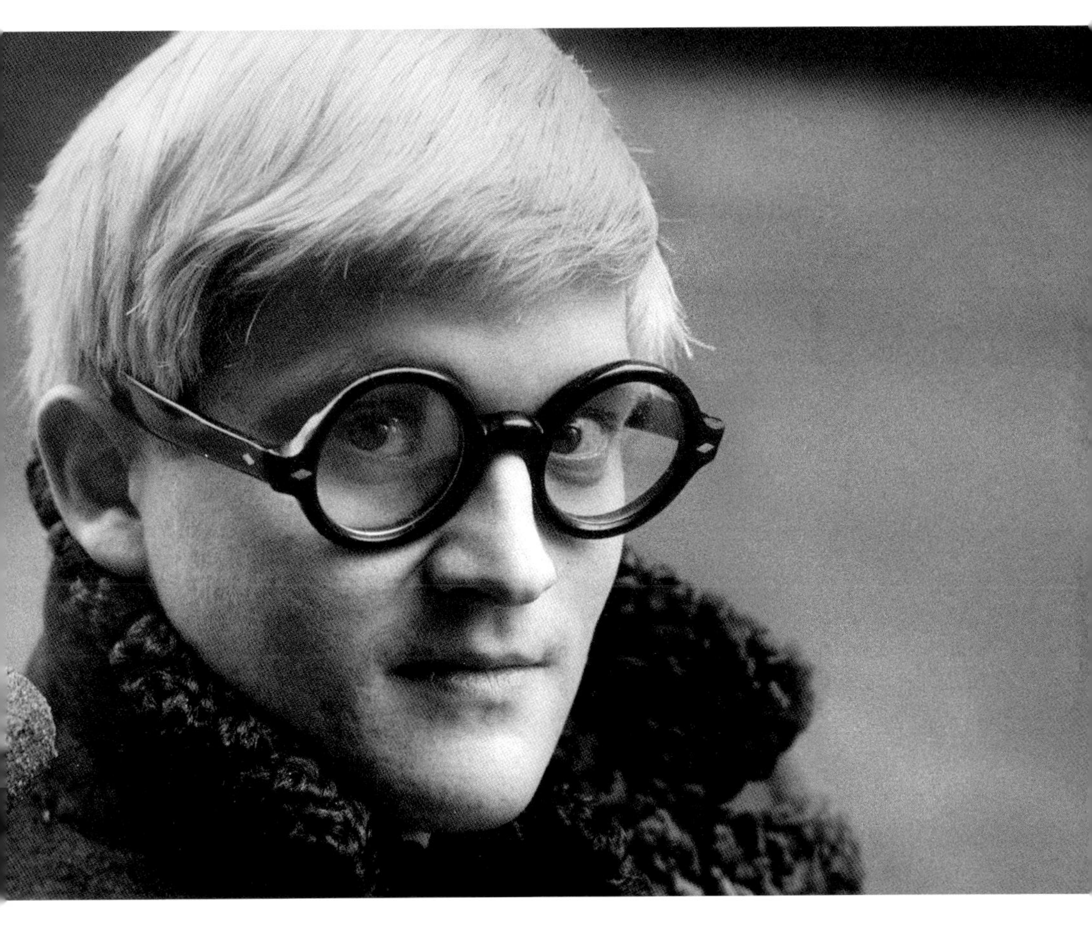

David Hockney, London 1966.
Photo: Jane Bown

Page 69: Stage design for Alfred
Jarry's *Ubu Roi,* 1966

Père and Mère Ubu, pencil and
crayon on paper, 14 $^1/_2$ x 19 $^1/_2$ in. /
36.8 x 49.5 cm

Mr. and Mrs. Ubu, pencil and crayon
on paper, 11 $^3/_4$ x 15 $^3/_4$ in. /
29.8 x 40 cm

the student Peter Schlesinger, who soon becomes his lover and favorite model. Hockney moves into a cheap studio on Pico Boulevard: "Every time you put the gas on, cockroaches sped away from the oven, but I didn't mind. I never had a phone put in, because right outside the door was a phone booth and I kept quarters and dimes to make calls." He starts painting *Beverly Hills Housewife* (pp. 74/75) on two canvases as the format won't fit the studio; it is the first painting for which he uses photographs as studies. In pool paintings such as *Peter Getting Out of Nick's Pool* and *Sunbather* (pp. 72, 73), he further explores depictions of water and the California lifestyle.

Solo: *Tekeningen en etsen,* Stedelijk Museum, Amsterdam (Apr 1–May 8). *David Hockney,* Palais des Beaux-Arts, Brussels. *David Hockney,* Galleria dell'Ariete, Milan (opens Mar 8); catalog with a text by Patrick Procktor. *Preparatory Drawings of the Sets for the Production of Ubu Roi; Twelve Etchings Inspired by the Poems of C. P. Cavafy,* Kasmin Limited, London (opens Jul 22). *David Hockney,* Studio Marconi, Milan.

Group: *British Prints in the Sixties,* Arnolfini Gallery, Bristol (May–Jun). *The Harry N. Abrams Family Collection,* The Jewish Museum, New York (Jun 29–Sep 5); catalog. *The Rake's Progress: William Hogarth and David Hockney,* touring exhibition organized by the British Council (through 1993). *The Marzotto Prize: Metropolitan Scene, Images and Objects,* Valdagno (Sep); travels to Baden-Baden, Humlebæk, Amsterdam, London, and Paris; catalog. *First International Print Biennale,* Cracow.

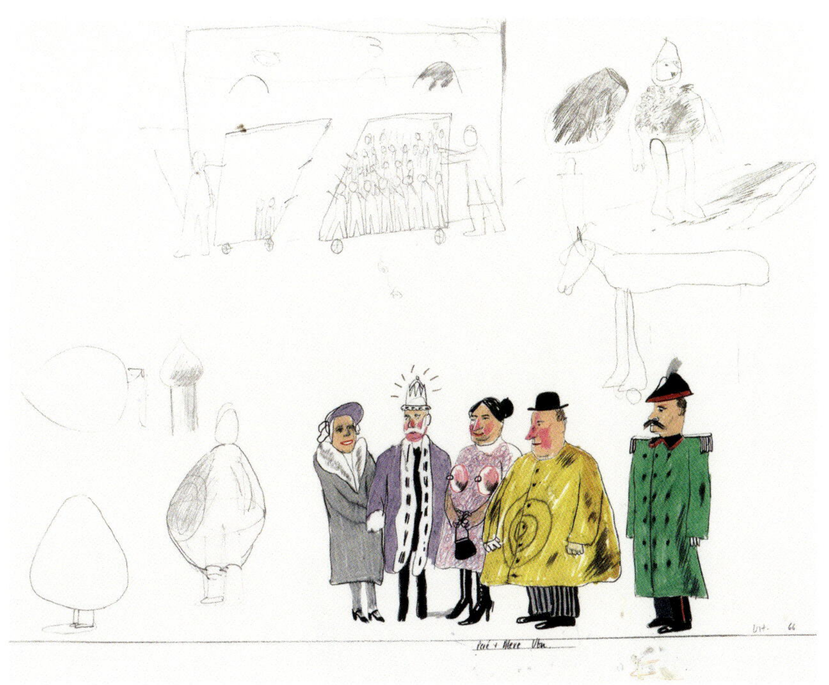
Père + Mère Ubu.

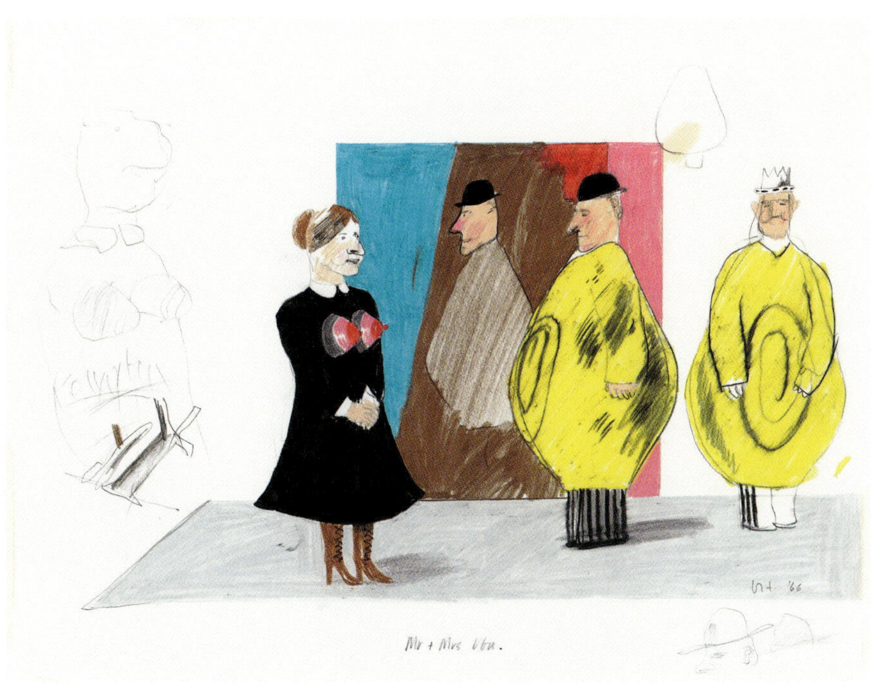
Mr + Mrs Ubu.

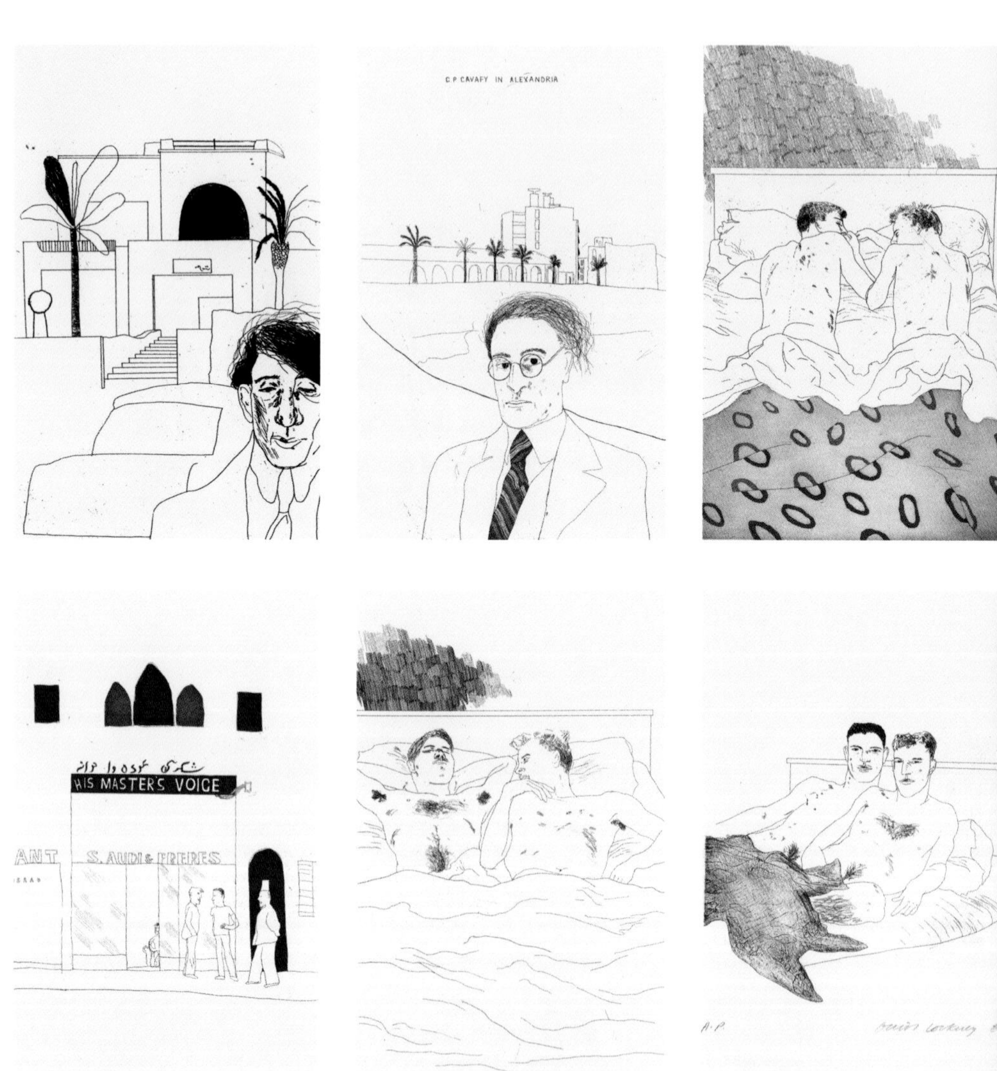

*Illustrations for Fourteen Poems from
C.P. Cavafy*, 1966–1967, editioned
series of 13 etchings, sheet size each
22 ¹⁄₂ x 15 ¹⁄₂ in. / 57.2 x 39.4 cm

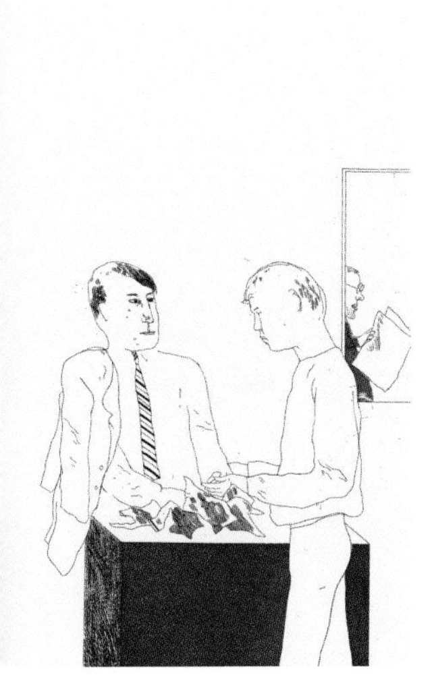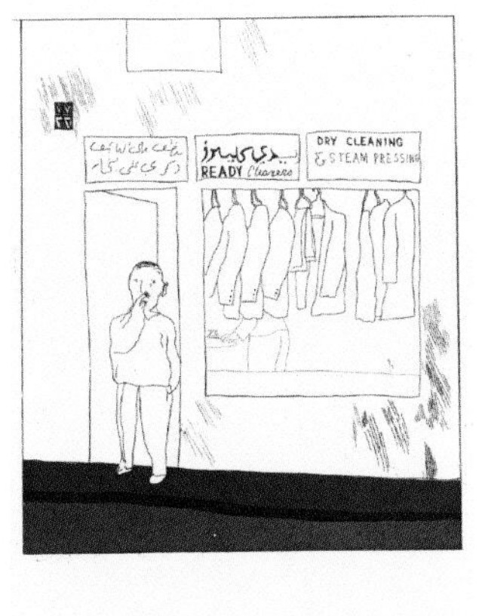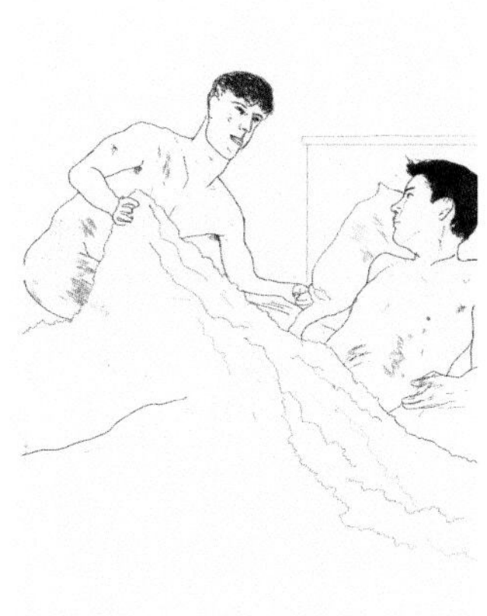

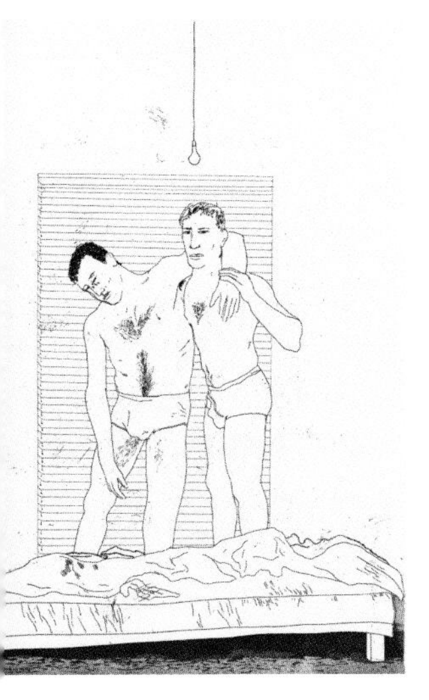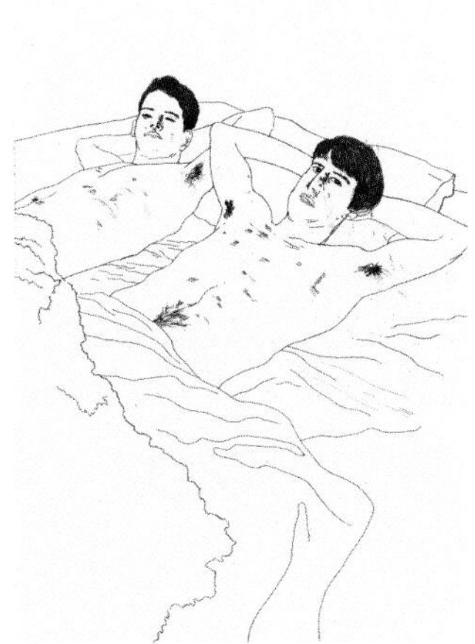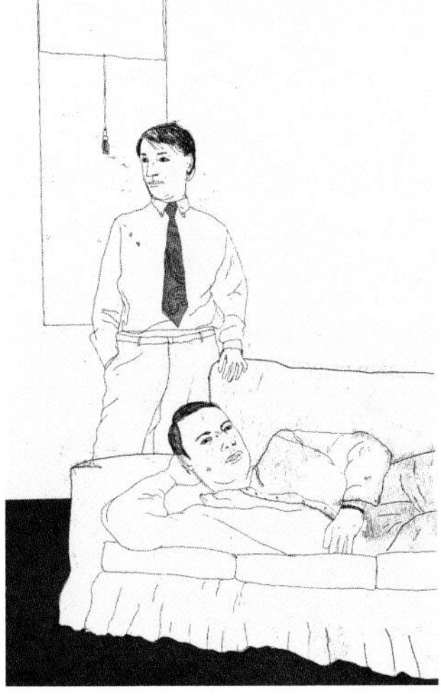

Top, left to right: *Portrait of Cavafy II; Portrait of Cavafy in Alexandria; Two Boys Aged 23 or 24; He Enquired after the Quality; To Remain; According to the Prescriptions of Ancient Magicians*

Bottom, left to right: *The Shop Window of a Tobacco Store; In the Dull Village; The Beginning; One Night; In Despair; Beautiful and White Flowers*

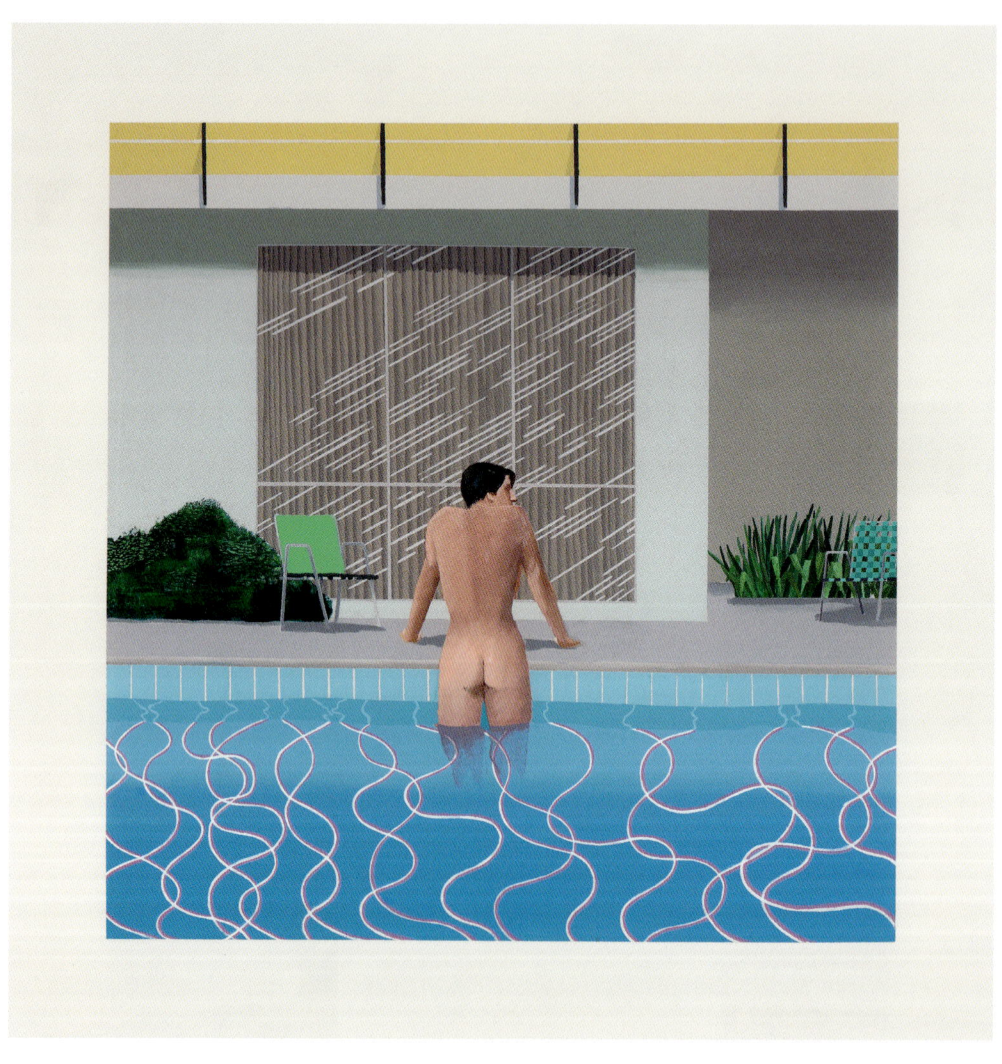

Peter Getting Out of Nick's Pool, 1966,
acrylic on canvas, 84 x 84 in. /
213.4 x 213.4 cm

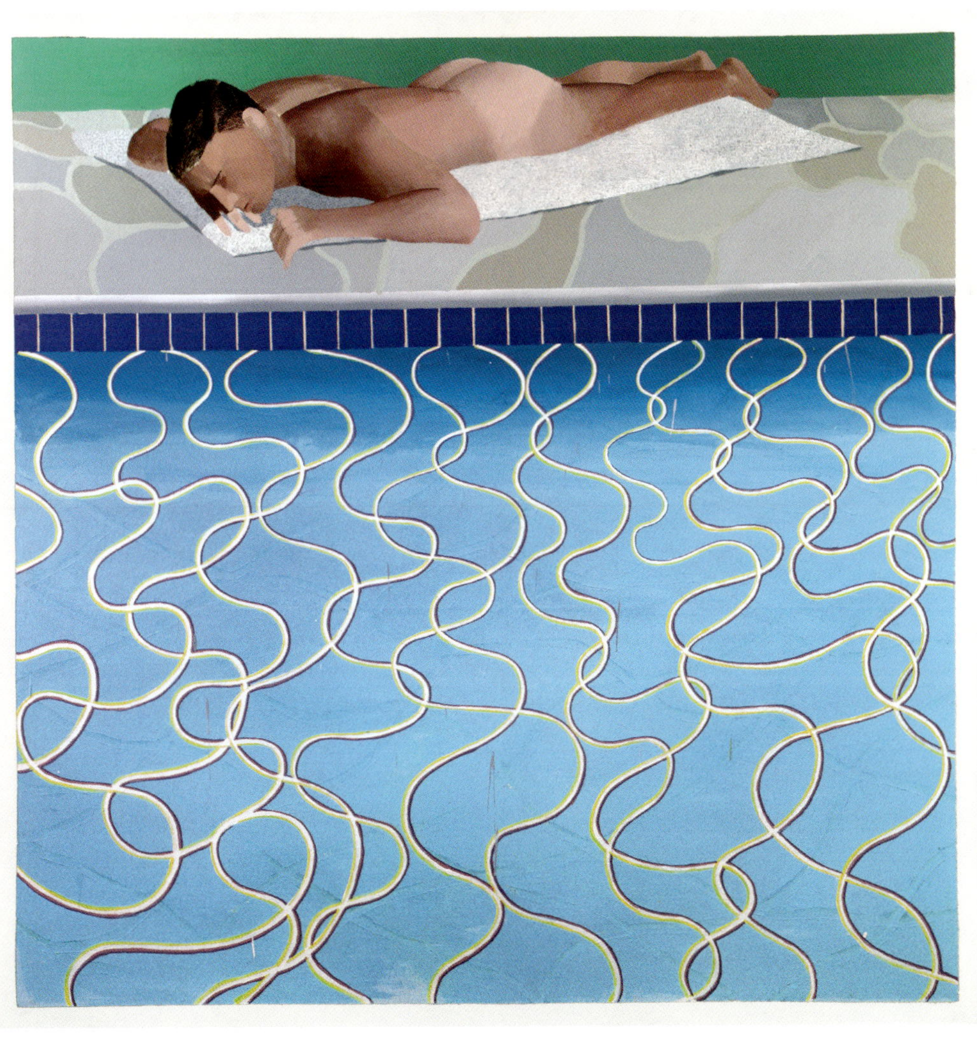

Sunbather, 1966, acrylic on canvas,
72 x 72 in. / 182.9 x 182.9 cm

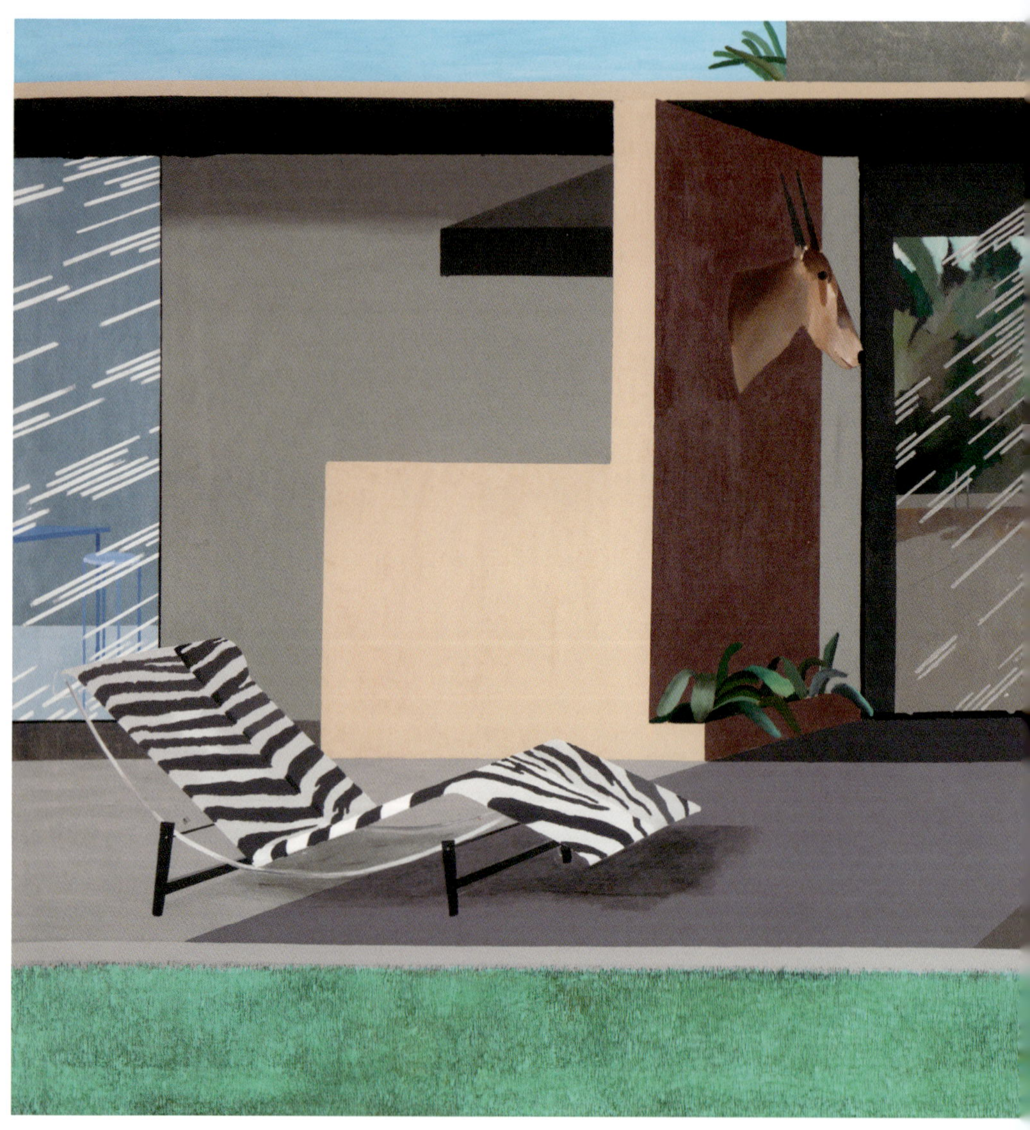

Beverly Hills Housewife, 1966–1967,
acrylic on 2 canvases, 72 x 144 in. /
182.9 x 365.8 cm

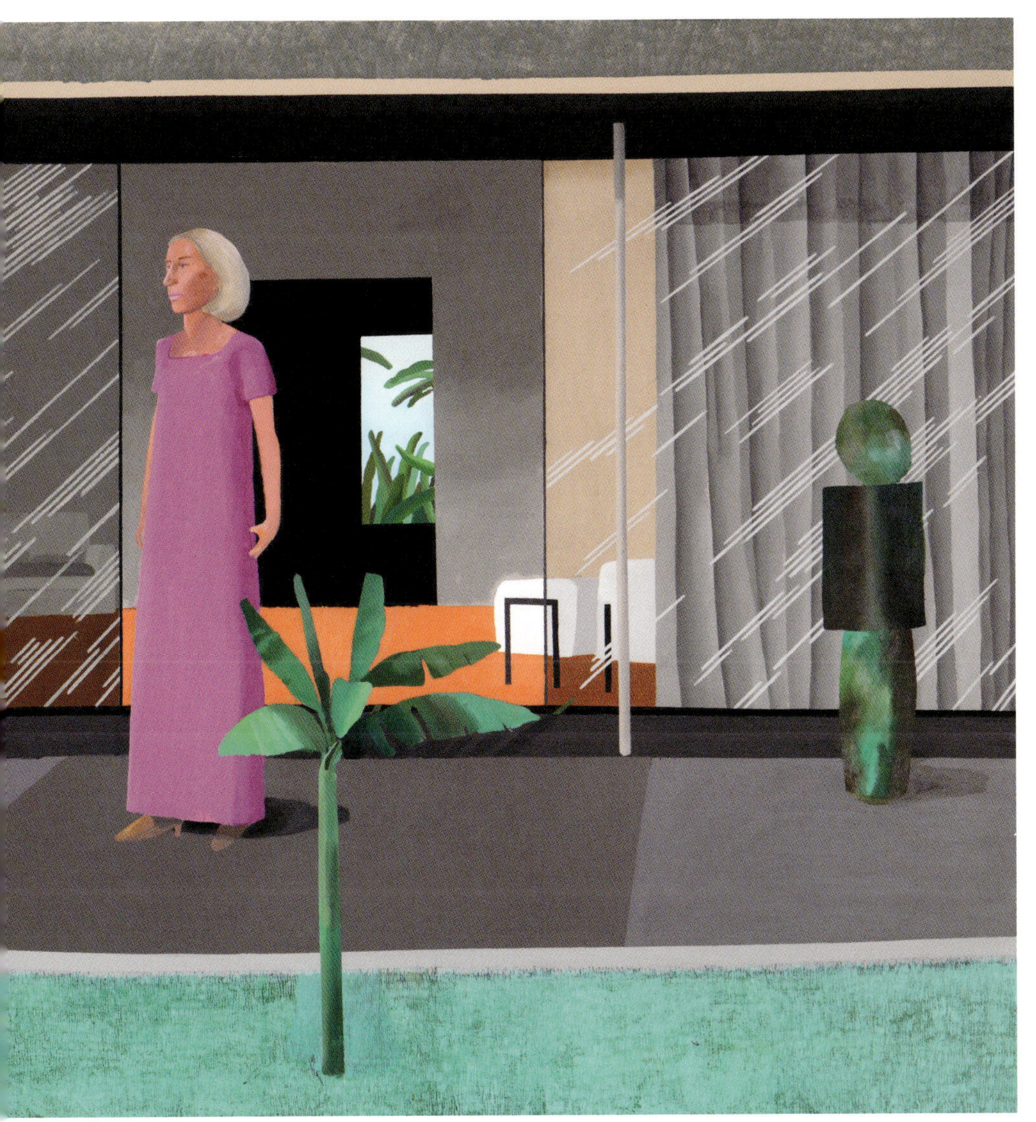

1967

Peter Schlesinger moves in with Hockney, and they happily share home life: "During the day Peter was out at school, and I painted, and in the evenings we'd go out and eat something. I don't think I ever cooked there at all. We used to go to the cinema a lot, then go back and read, just sit in bed and read. Because there was no phone, life was quiet and I think that year I painted more pictures than I'd ever done before…We saw Nick Wilder a lot, and Nick's friends, who were always rather young and beautiful boys. We'd go swimming at Nick's…I saw a lot of Christopher Isherwood and Don Bachardy…Looking back on it, it was certainly the happiest year I spent in California, and it was the worst place we lived in."

In spring, Hockney leaves for Berkeley to teach at the University of California. There he completes *A Bigger Splash* (p. 79), his most famous pool painting and possibly the most iconic of all his pictures: "It took me about two weeks to paint the splash," he later reflects. "It takes me two weeks to paint this event that lasts for two seconds. The effect of it as it got bigger was more stunning—everybody knows a splash can't be frozen in time, it doesn't exist, so when you see it like that in a painting it's even more striking than in a photograph, because you know a photograph took a second to take, or less. In fact if it's a splash and there's no blur in it, you know it took a sixtieth of a second, less time than the splash existed for. The painting took much longer to make than the splash existed for, so it has a very different effect on the viewer."

He also paints *The Room, Tarzana* (p. 80), using the color advertisement of a room with a single bed for a department store as his source, then adding a bare-bottomed figure to the bed. He places Schlesinger on the kitchen table in the appropriate pose. For Hockney it is a step toward greater naturalism: "Because of this light dancing around, I realized the light in the room was a subject and for the first time it became an interesting thing for me…Consequently I had to arrange Peter so the light was coming from the direction of the window. Before, I wouldn't have bothered to think of things like that, I'd just have laid him on the table and drawn him, and it wouldn't have mattered to me whether the shadows went this way or that."

In summer Hockney and Schlesinger travel to London, where they stay at Powis Terrace, exploring the city and meeting Hockney's friends. Then they travel to France and Italy in the company of painter Patrick Procktor. Hockney buys

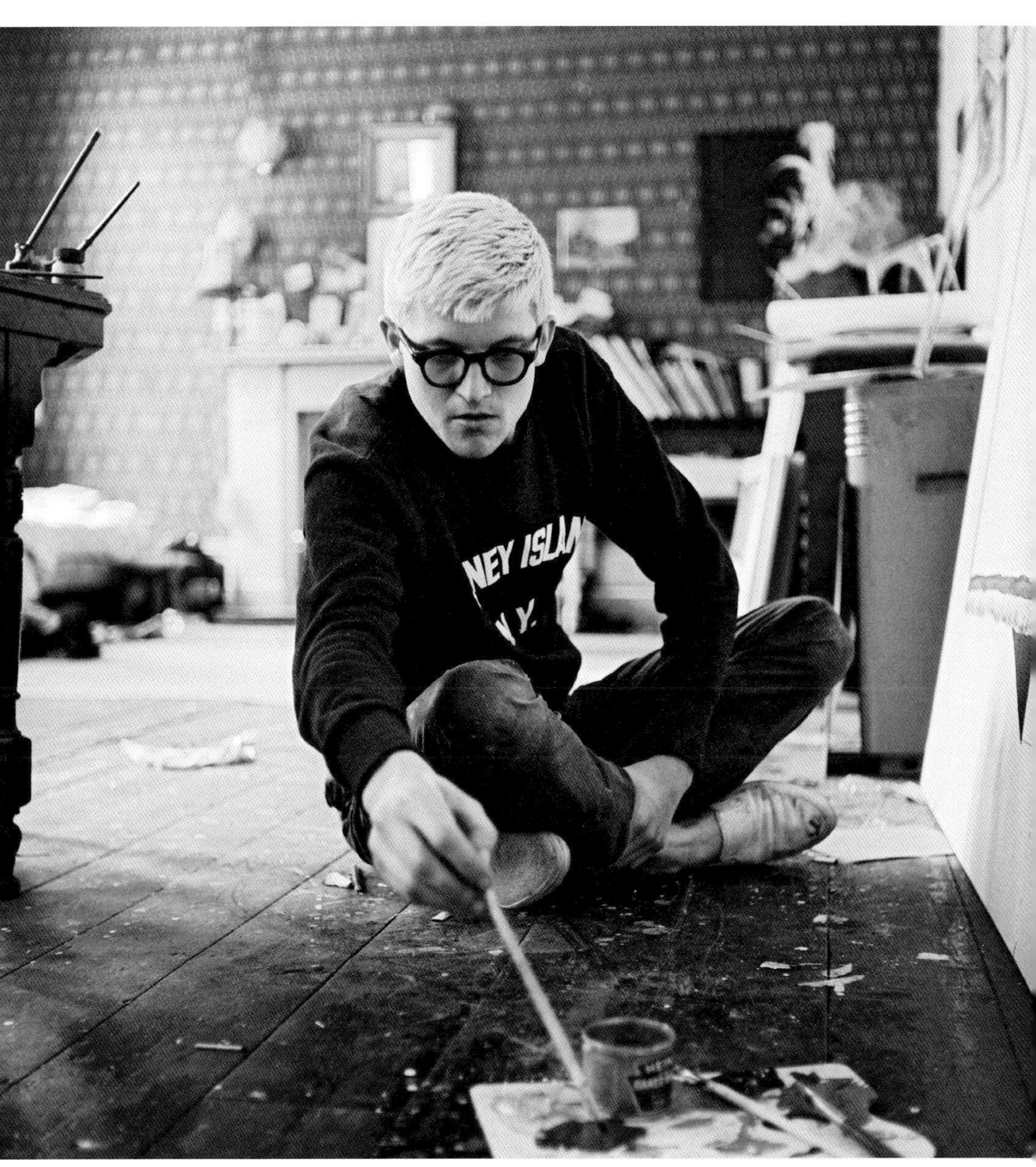

David Hockney in his studio, c. 1967.
Photo: Tony Evans

a 35 mm camera, more and more taking photographs as references for his paintings. When in autumn Schlesinger travels back to California to continue his studies, Hockney remains in London to work for his upcoming solo exhibition at the Kasmin Limited. He paints *The Room, Manchester Street* (p. 83), a portrait of Procktor in his studio, in continuance of his growingly naturalist work, with subtle backlighting and careful preparatory studies of the surroundings. "In 1967 Patrick's studio looked clean, neat and office-like. The next year it looked like a den in the Casbah—it seemed to change as often as Auntie Mame's. I recorded the changes in photographs, and this painting was made from drawings, life, and photographs."

Solo: *New Paintings and Drawings,* Landau-Alan Gallery, New York (Mar 14–Apr 8). *David Hockney,* Mala Galerija, Ljubljana (Jul); catalog with a text by Gene Baro.

Group: *Drawing towards Painting 2,* Arts Council of Great Britain Gallery, London (Apr 14–May 20); travels to Stoke-on-Trent, Northhampton, Oldham, Cardiff, St. Ives, Reading, Liverpool, Bradford, Norwich, Scarborough, and Glasgow; catalog. *Seventh International Exhibition of Graphic Art,* Moderna Galerija, Ljubljana (Jun 3–Aug 31); catalog. *Jeunes peintres anglais,* Palais des Beaux-Arts, Brussels (Oct 1–22); catalog. *Pittsburgh International Exhibition of Contemporary Painting and Sculpture,* Carnegie Institute, Pittsburgh (Oct 27, 1967–Jan 7, 1968); catalog. *Recent British Painting: Peter Stuyvesant Foundation Collection,* Tate Gallery, London (Nov 15–Dec 22); catalog. *John Moores Exhibition,* Walker Art Gallery, Liverpool (Nov 23, 1967–Jan 21, 1968); catalog; Hockney wins the First Prize.

Publication: David Hockney, *A Rake's Progress: A Poem in Five Sections,* text by Donald Posner, London: Lion and Unicorn Press.

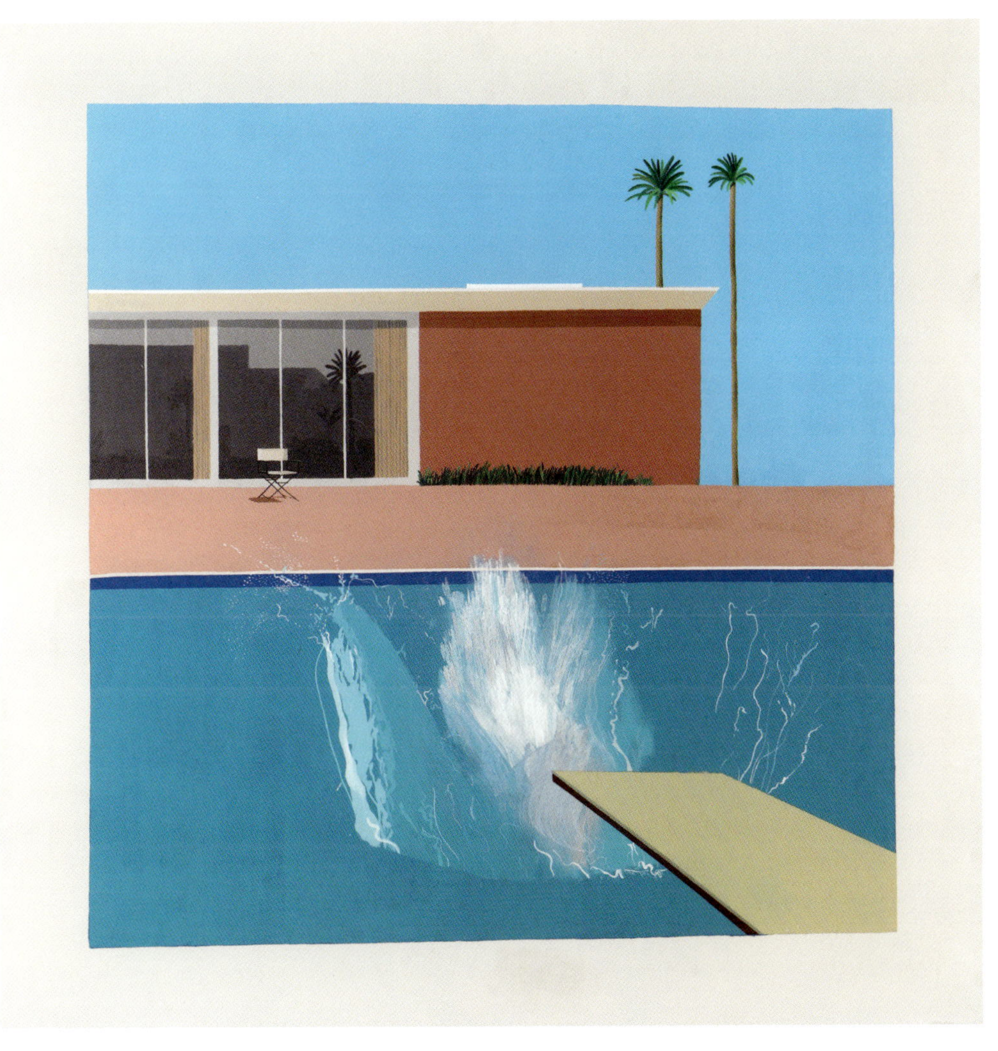

A Bigger Splash, 1967,
acrylic on canvas, 96 x 96 in. /
243.8 x 243.8 cm

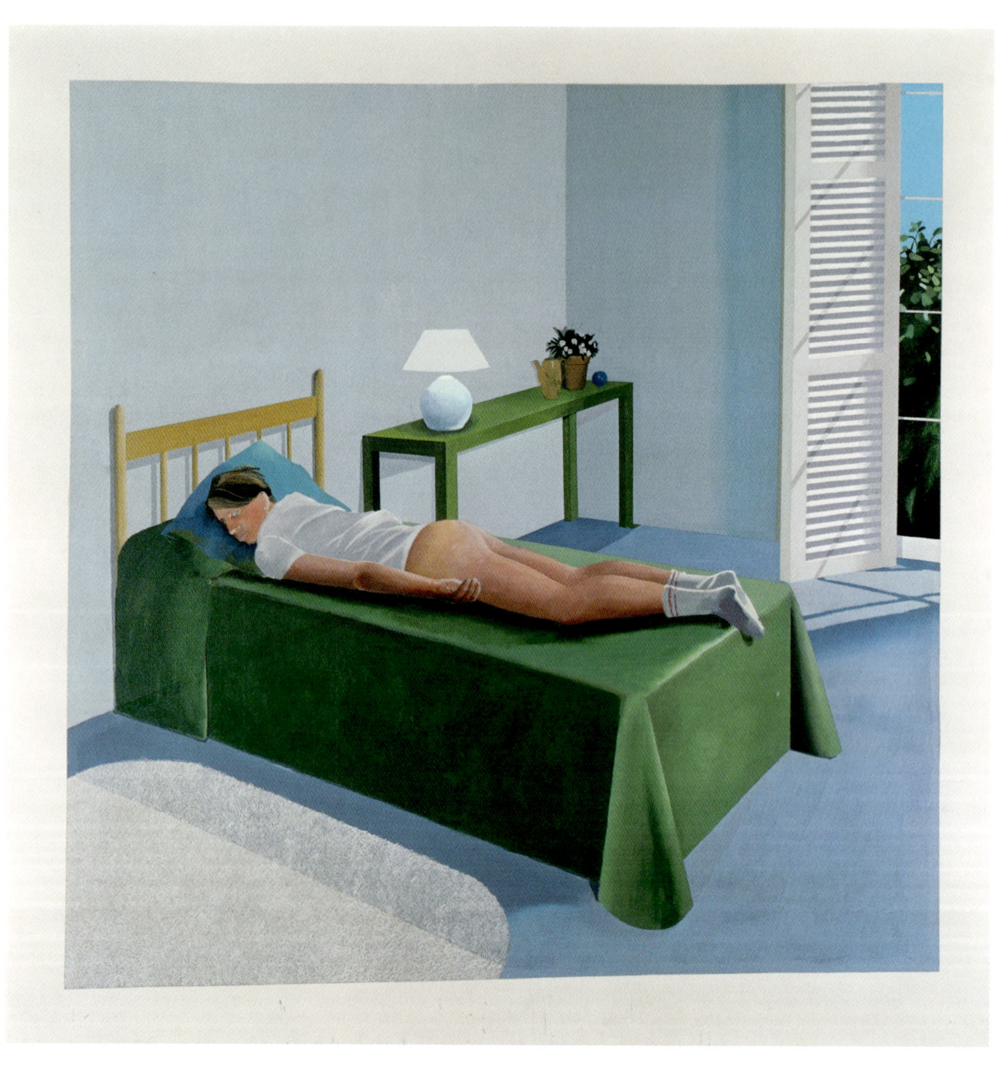

The Room, Tarzana, 1967,
acrylic on canvas, 96 x 96 in. /
243.8 x 243.8 cm

Right page: *Peter, Albergo La
Flora, Rome,* 1967, pen on paper,
14 x 17 in. / 35.6 x 43.2 cm

Peter, Carennac, 1967,
ink on paper, 14 x 17 in. /
35.6 x 43.2 cm

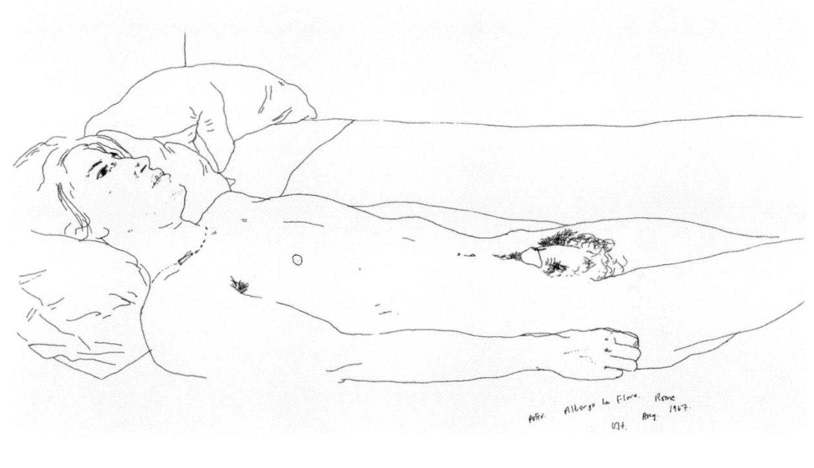

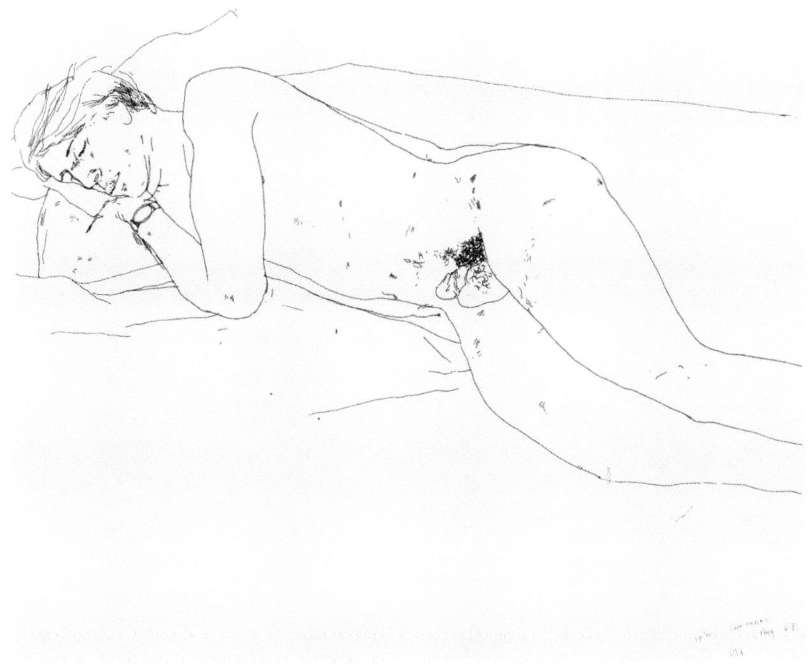

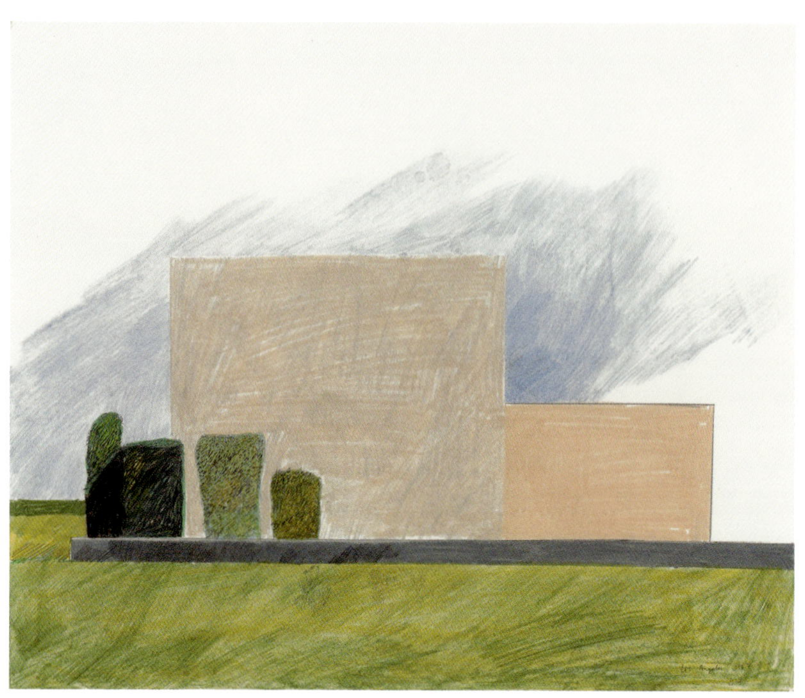

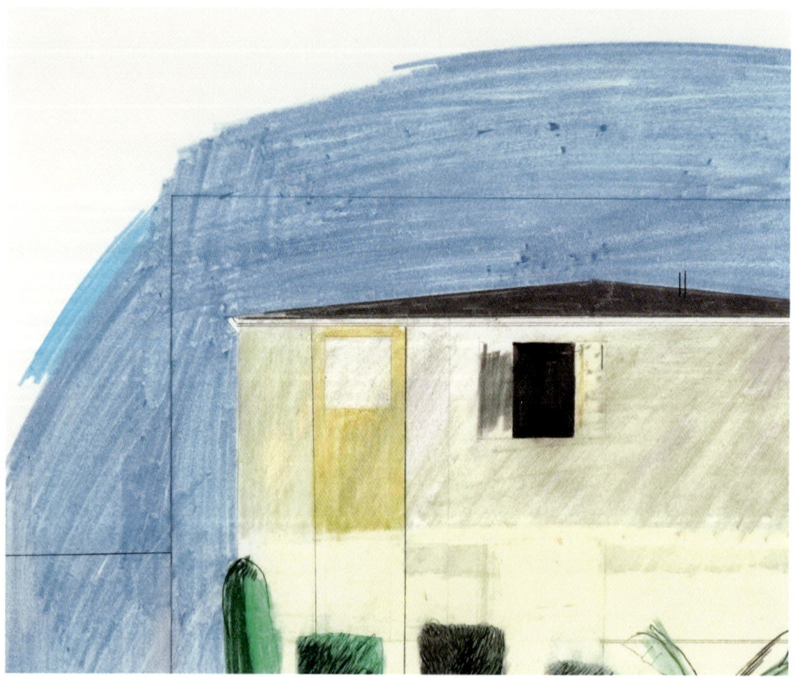

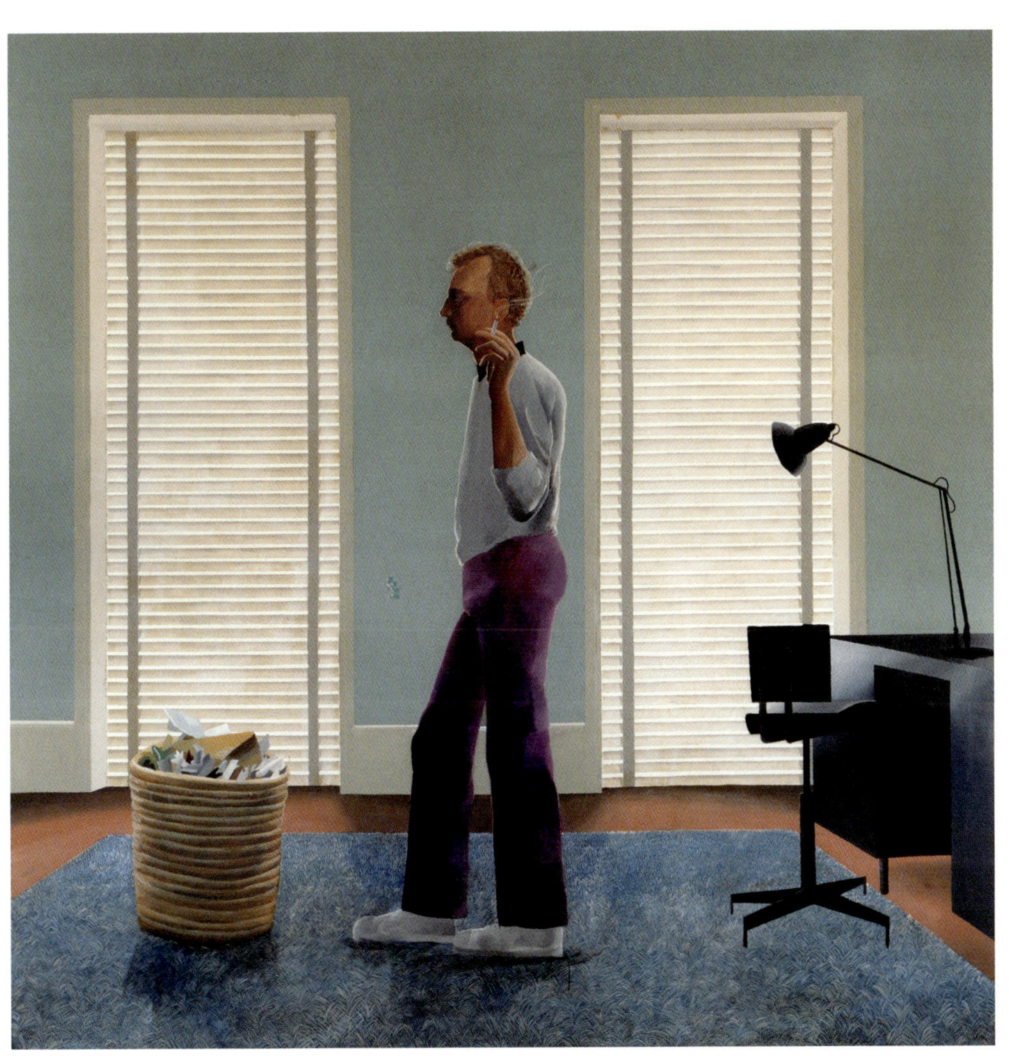

The Room, Manchester Street, 1967, acrylic on canvas, 96 x 96 in. / 243.8 x 243.8 cm

Left page: *Los Angeles,* 1967, pencil, colored pencil, and crayon on paper, 14 x 17 in. / 35.6 x 43.2 cm

House, Olympic Boulevard, 1967, crayon on paper, 14 x 17 in. / 35.6 x 43.2 cm

1968

The year begins with a solo exhibition at Kasmin Limited in London, titled *A Splash, a Lawn, Two Rooms, Two Stains, Some Neat Cushions and a Table…Painted* (p. 89). Guy Brett in the *Times*: "These new paintings are sharper and neater and broader in scale than earlier ones; the brittle subject matter and Hockney's dry shallow paint surface are very elegantly matched…Hockney has always liked this play between illusionism and the facts of flat painting; often he hasn't taken it farther than a trick, but in these Californian paintings the tricks seem to have become tied up with his feelings as well."

Hockney lives with Schlesinger in Santa Monica: "I rented a tiny little penthouse, old-fashioned, built in 1934, which for California is very old. It was like being on the Queen Mary, with the mist in the morning, in Winter, and it was very nice. They were very happy times; once we were in the house, I didn't care if I went out to see anybody or not." He starts on a large double portrait of his friends Christopher Isherwood and Don Bachardy (p. 87), sketching them in their house to find a composition: "Whenever I said, 'Relax,' Christopher always sat with his foot across his knee, and he always looked at Don. Don never looked that way; he was always looking at me. So I thought, that's the pose it should be." The painting progresses slowly, so he takes a different approach for the painting *American Collectors (Fred and Marcia Weisman)* (pp. 90/91): "There's a Turnbull sculpture, a Henry Moore sculpture, other things, all part of them. The portrait wasn't just in the faces, it was the whole setting…There's a totem pole in the picture that looks rather like Marcia. So it's a slightly different kind of portrait in that the objects round the figures are a part of them."

Hockney travels with friends around France and down the Rhine through the summer. Schlesinger joins him in London in autumn to take up his own studies at the Slade School of Fine Art. In December, Hockney visits New York to make drawings for another double portrait, which depicts Henry Geldzahler seated on a sofa facing the viewer and Christopher Scott standing beside him in profile. When the artist returns from the United States carrying a number of male physique magazines, they are seized by a British customs officer at the airport. Hockney threatens legal action and starts phoning the head offices at HM Customs and Excise: "So finally I got to the top guy, and he said, 'Yes, we're seizing them, they're pornographic.' So I said, 'Come on, I'm giving you

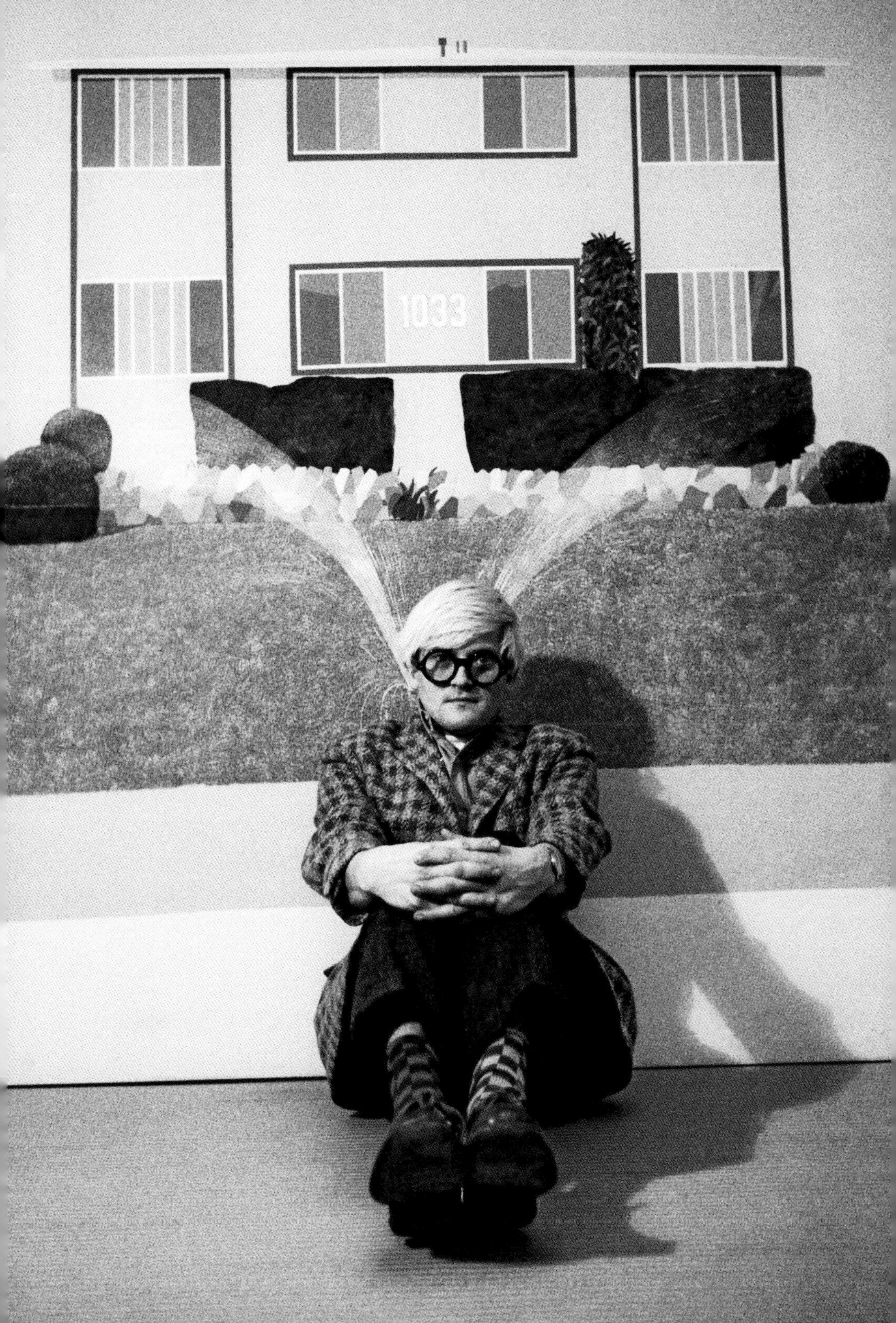

1033

one last chance. Why are they pornographic?' And he said, 'Why, in one of the pictures the boys have painted their genitals with psychedelic colors.' I cracked up laughing on the phone and thought, if he doesn't think it's funny, I can't communicate with him at all." Hockney gets Norman Reid of the Tate to send a letter to customs and popular art broadcaster Kenneth Clark to agree to testify should the case be taken to court. When customs give in and the magazines are finally delivered back, Hockney's victory against censorship is widely reported on both sides of the Atlantic.

Solo: *A Splash, a Lawn, Two Rooms, Two Stains, Some Neat Cushions and a Table…Painted,* Kasmin Limited, London (opens Jan 19). *David Hockney,* Editions Alecto Gallery, London (Jan). *Personal Drawings,* Kasmin Limited, London (opens Sep 18). *Oeuvrekatalog-Graphik,* Galerie Mikro, Berlin (Nov 9– Dec 28); catalog with a text by Wibke von Bonin, London: Petersburg Press.

Group: *Junge Generation Großbritannien,* Akademie der Künste, Berlin (Apr 28–Jun 9); catalog. *New Generation 1968: Interim,* Whitechapel Art Gallery, London (Apr–May); catalog. *From Kitaj to Blake: Non-Abstract Artists in Britain,* Bear Lane Gallery, Oxford (Jun 8–29). *34th International Art Exhibition La Biennale di Venezia,* Venice (Jun 22–Oct 20); catalog. *Documenta 4,* Kassel (Jun 27–Oct 6); catalog. *Menschenbilder,* Kunsthalle Darmstadt (Sep 14–Nov 17); catalog. *European Painters of Today,* Musée des Arts Décoratifs, Paris (Sep 27–Nov 17); travels to New York; Washington, D.C.; Chicago; Atlanta; and Dayton (through 1969); catalog.

Christopher Isherwood at 824 Third Street, Santa Monica, 1968, ink on paper, 17 x 14 in. / 43.2 x 35.6 cm

Christopher Isherwood and Don Bachardy, 1968, acrylic on canvas, 83 ¹⁄₂ x 119 ¹⁄₂ in. / 212 x 303.4 cm

Page 85: David Hockney in front of *A Neat Lawn* (1967) in his studio, London 1968. Photo: Jorge Lewinski

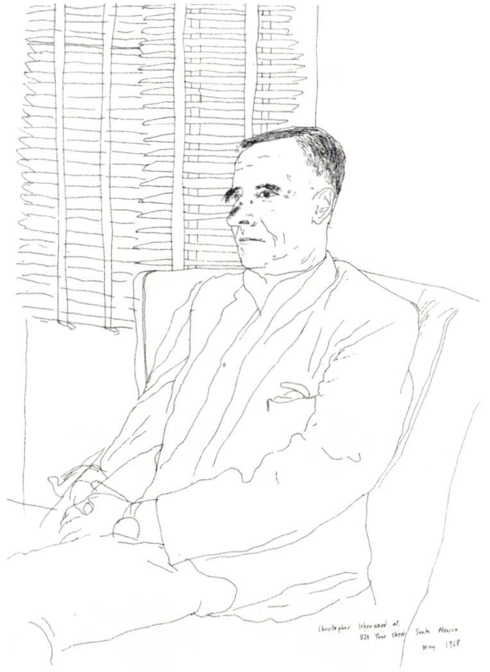

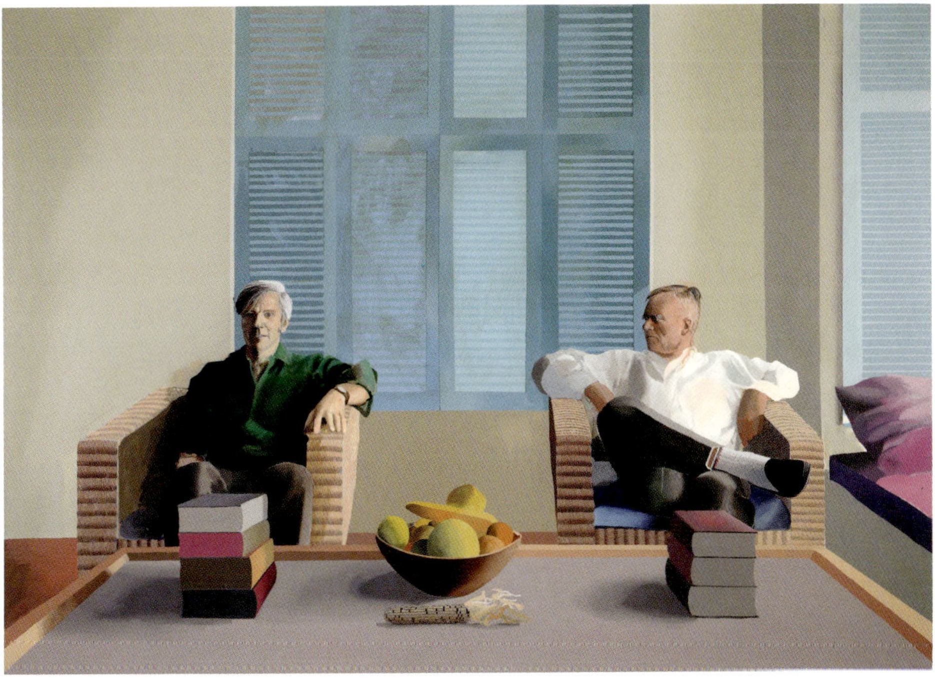

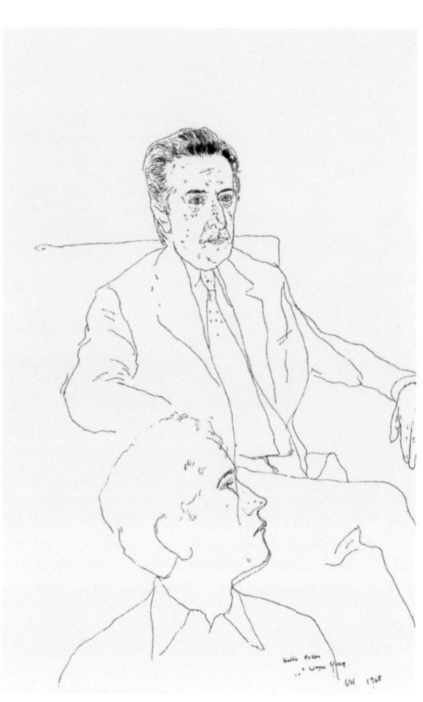

Freddie Ashton and Wayne Sleep,
1968, ink on paper, 20 x 12 ½ in. /
50.8 x 31.8 cm

*Henry Geldzahler and Christopher
Scott,* 1968, ink on paper, 11 x 14 in. /
27.9 x 35.6 cm

Right page: *David Hockney:
A Splash, a Lawn, Two Rooms, Two
Stains, Some Neat Cushions and a
Table…Painted,* exhibition views,
Kasmin Limited, London 1968

Pages 90/91: *American Collectors
(Fred & Marcia Weisman),* 1968,
acrylic on canvas, 84 x 120 in. /
213.4 x 304.8 cm

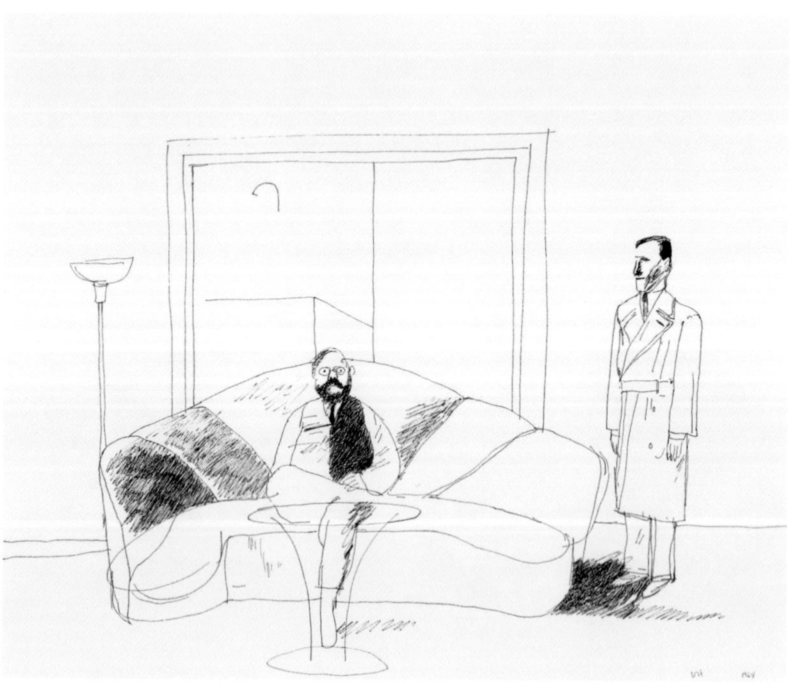

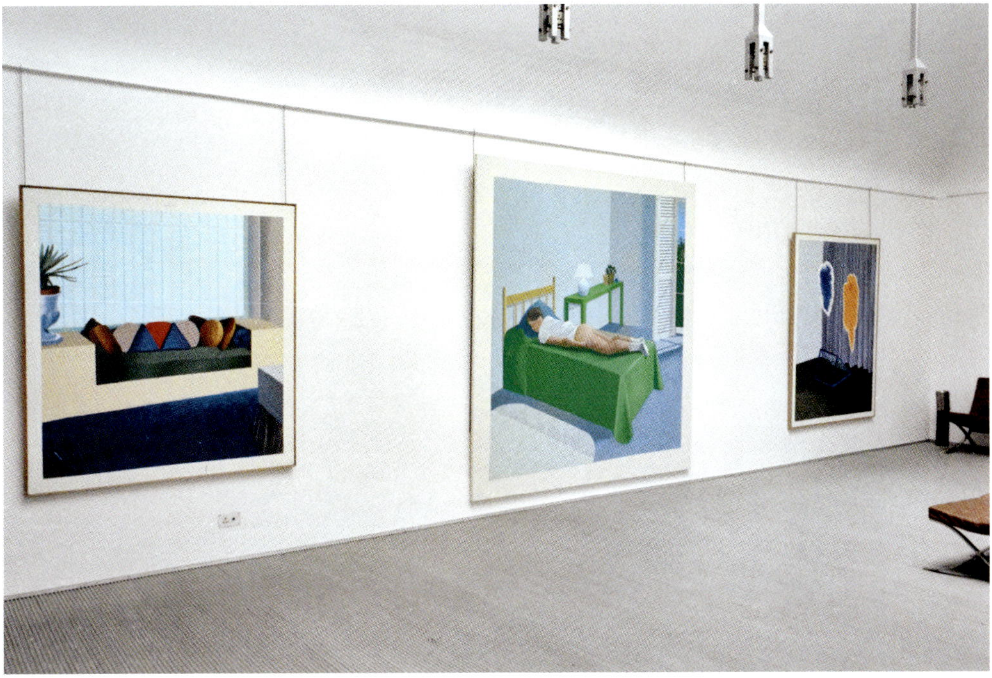

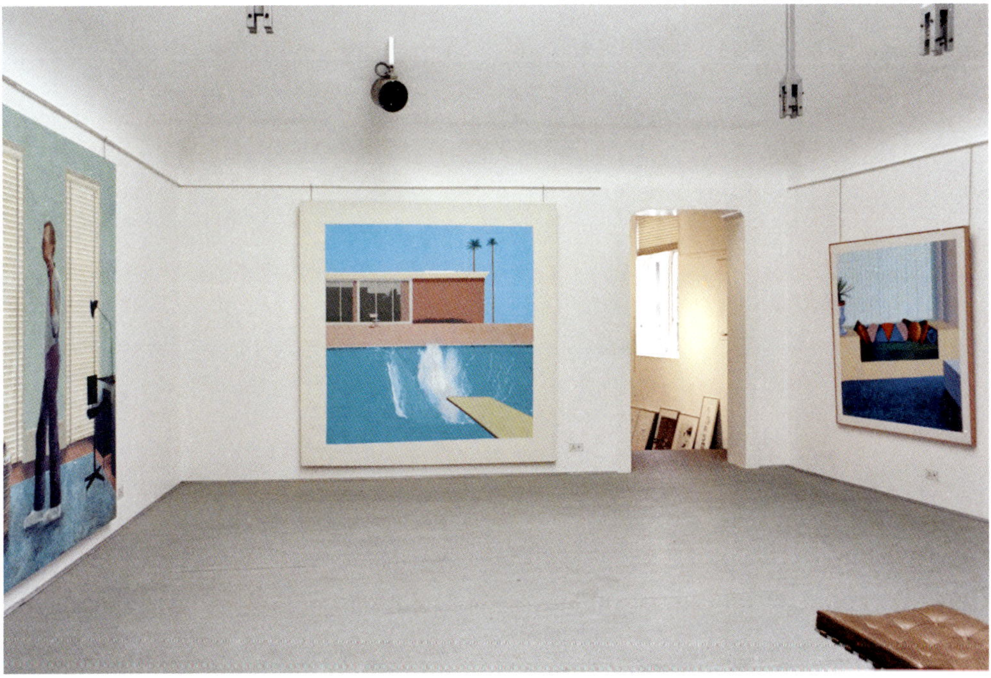

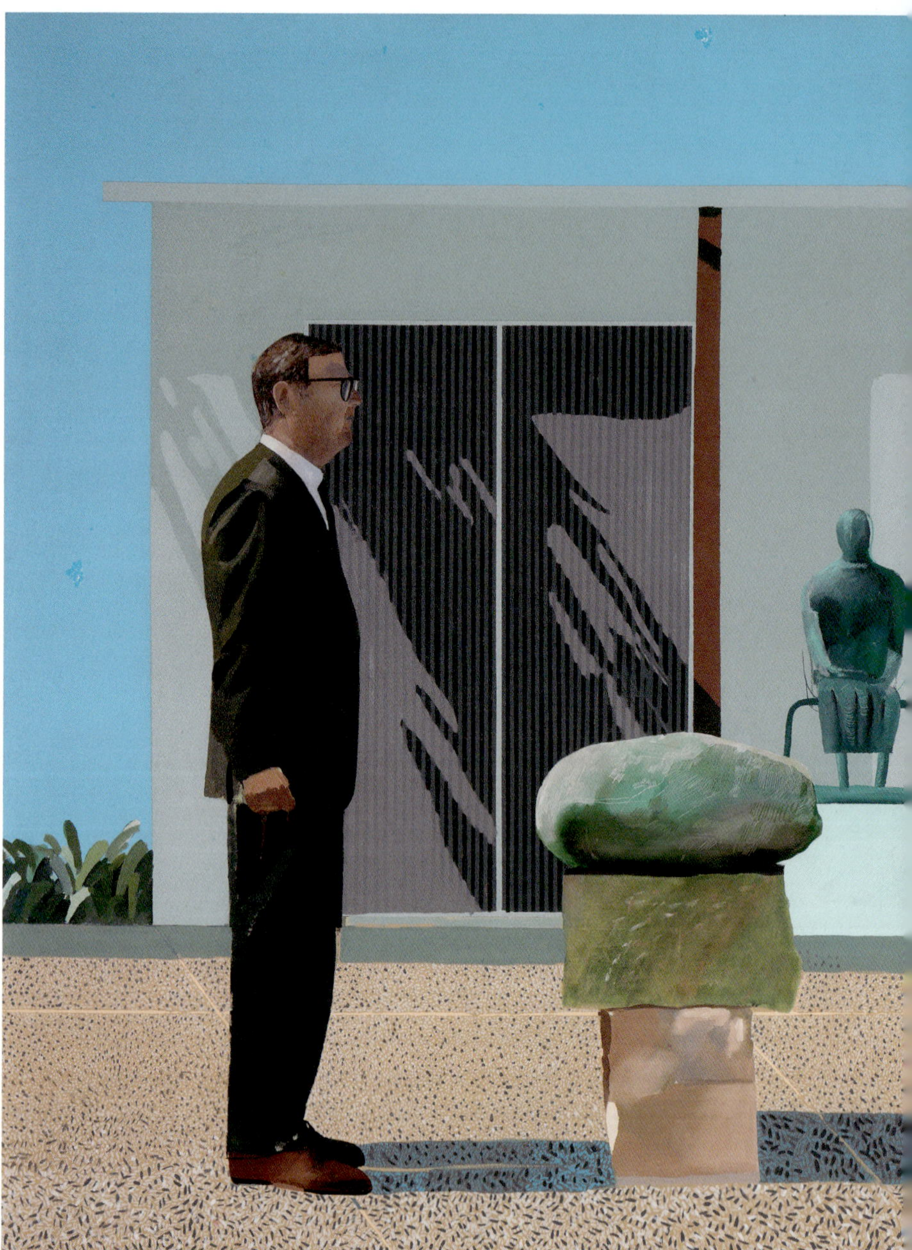

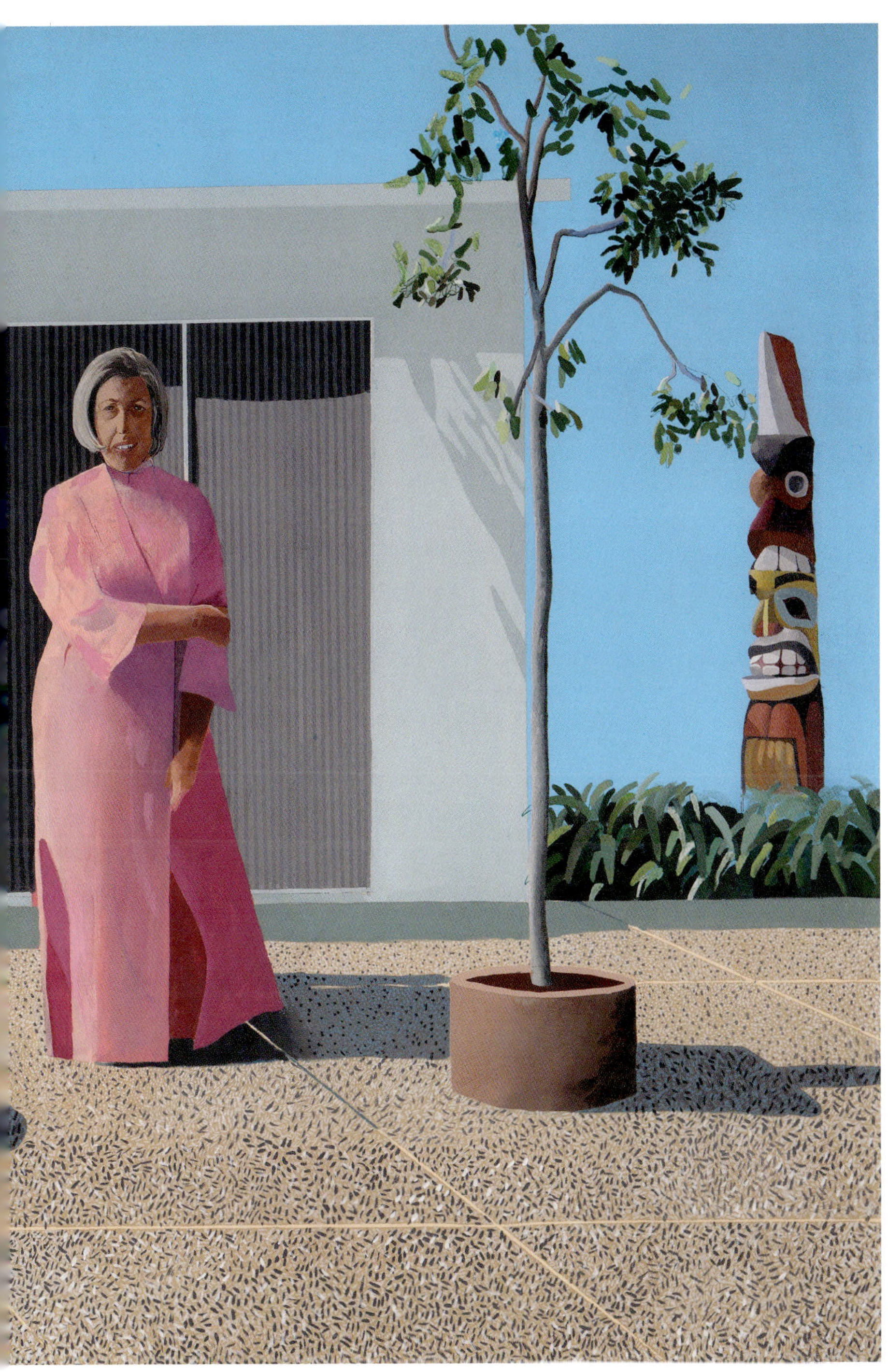

1969

Hockney finishes the double portrait *Henry Geldzahler and Christopher Scott* (pp. 98/99). His three big double portraits are among the exhibits in a solo show at André Emmerich Gallery in New York. Hilton Kramer in the *New York Times*: "Mr. Hockney offers us pictorial sociabilities of a high order, at once amused and disabused, very much part of the milieu they depict and yet detached enough to be witty, precise, and even, on occasion, a little cruel…No doubt the art of Painting has higher tasks to perform than those Mr. Hockney has undertaken in these three large pictures. Yet they remind us of certain resources that painting may still avail itself of, certain powers that it has long surrendered to photography, literature, and the movies that it may now want to recover, or at least reconsider. Perhaps the comedy of manners, insofar as it enters into pictorial art, will always be a form of illustration, and thus always dependent upon a realm of association that the painter can rely on without reconstituting in his own terms. But this is the risk of sociable art, and one of its pleasures."

In March Hockney abandons painting for the rest of the year to concentrate on a series of etchings illustrating fairy tales by the Brothers Grimm (pp. 96/97): "They're fascinating, the little stories, told in a very simple, direct, straightforward language and style; it was this simplicity that attracted me. They cover quite a strange range of experience, from the magical to the moral. My choice of stories was occasionally influenced by how I might illustrate them. For example, *Old Rinkrank* was included because the story begins with the sentence, 'A King built a glass mountain.' I loved the idea of finding how you draw a glass mountain; it was a little graphic problem. I included other stories simply because they were strange." Hockney works at Powis Terrace with Maurice Payne, and the printing is done by Paul Cornwall-Jones, who has separated from Editions Alecto and is now setting up Petersburg Press. The works are shown at Kasmin Limited at the end of the year. Nigel Gosling in the *Observer*: "The stories, with their dry grotesque poetry, seem tailor-made for the Hockney treatment. Abandoning here the deadpan realism he brought to his Cavafy drawings, he has reverted to the free imagination of his earlier work, and found in these nordic tales a marvelous equivalent to his particular blend of sharp detail and airborne fancy. The images are odd and touching at the same time…We are in the world of Rumpelstiltskin, of proud princesses in lonely towers, of fish who talk and knives which catch fire. Hockney

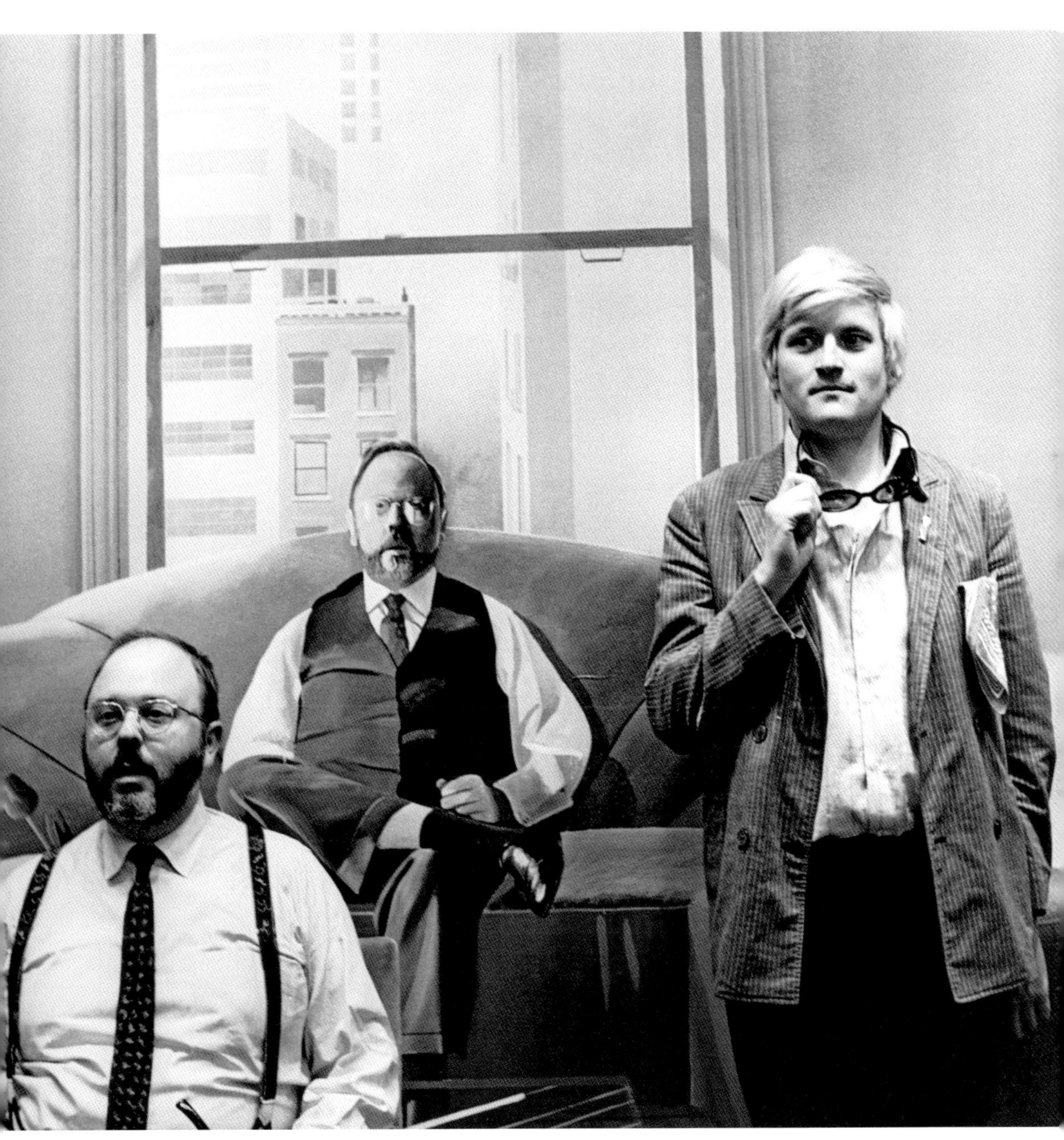

David Hockney and Henry Geldzahler in front of the painting *Henry
Geldzahler and Christopher Scott*,
1969. Photo: Cecil Beaton

Page 95: *Peter,* 1969, etching, edition
of 75, 37 x 28 ¼ in. / 94 x 71.8 cm

Self Portrait with Pen, 1969, ink on
paper, 17 x 14 in. / 43.2 x 35.6 cm

Glass Table with Objects, 1969,
five-color lithograph, edition of 75,
18 ¼ x 22 ¼ in. / 46.4 x 56.5 cm

catches the note exactly, steering without effort between the whimsical and the wonderstruck. Anybody (particularly if he also appreciates fine engraving) who sighs for the hard innocence of childhood and the weightless flight of its dreams should get a look at these little visions."

In the summer Hockney and Schlesinger again spend holidays in the south of France with Patrick Procktor, eventually joining Ossie Clark and Celia Birtwell, John Kasmin, and Henry Geldzahler. Hockney is the best man at the wedding of Ossie and Celia and begins preparatory drawings for a double portrait of the couple as a possible wedding gift.

Solo: *Paintings and Prints by David Hockney*, Whitworth Art Gallery, Manchester (Feb 21–Mar 15); catalog with a text by Mario Amaya. *Graphics*, Rodman Hall Arts Centre, St. Catherine's, Ontario (Nov 7–30). *David Hockney*, André Emmerich Gallery, New York (Apr 26–May 15). *Etchings*, Kasmin Limited, London (opens Dec 10).

Group: *Ars 69 Helsinki*, Ateneumin Taidemuseo, Helsinki (Mar 8–Apr 13); travels to Tampereen Nykytaiteen Museo, Tampere; catalog. *Marks on a Canvas*, Museum am Ostwall, Dortmund (May 18–Jul 13); travels to Hanover and Vienna; catalog. *Pop Art Redefined*, Hayward Gallery, London (Jul 9–Sep 3); catalog. *Artists from the Kasmin Gallery*, Arts Council Gallery, Ulster Museum, Belfast (Aug 1–30); catalog. *12 britische Artisten: Graphik und Objekte*, Künstlerhaus Wien, Vienna (Sep 18–Oct 19); catalog. *Englische Grafik Heute*, Schloss Wolfsburg (Nov 16–Dec 14); catalog. *The Rake's Progress: William Hogarth, David Hockney*, Akademie der Künste, Berlin (Dec 13, 1969–Jan 25, 1970).

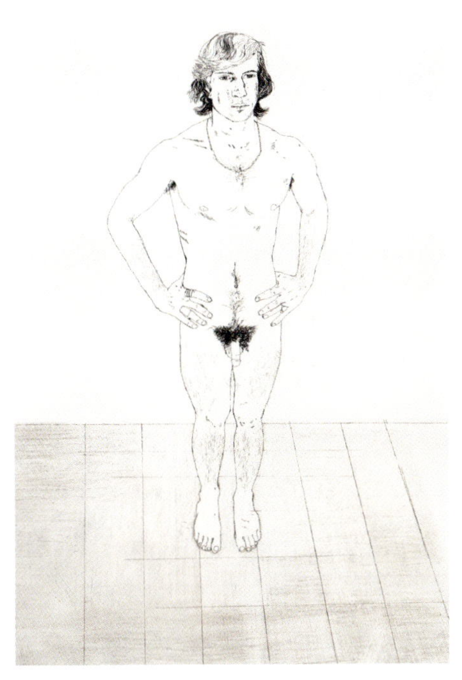

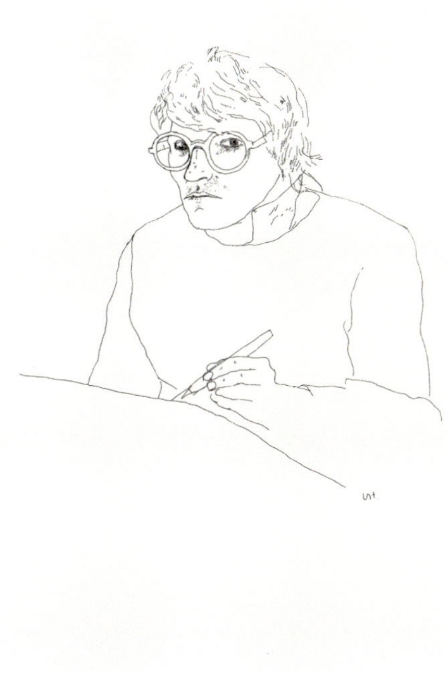

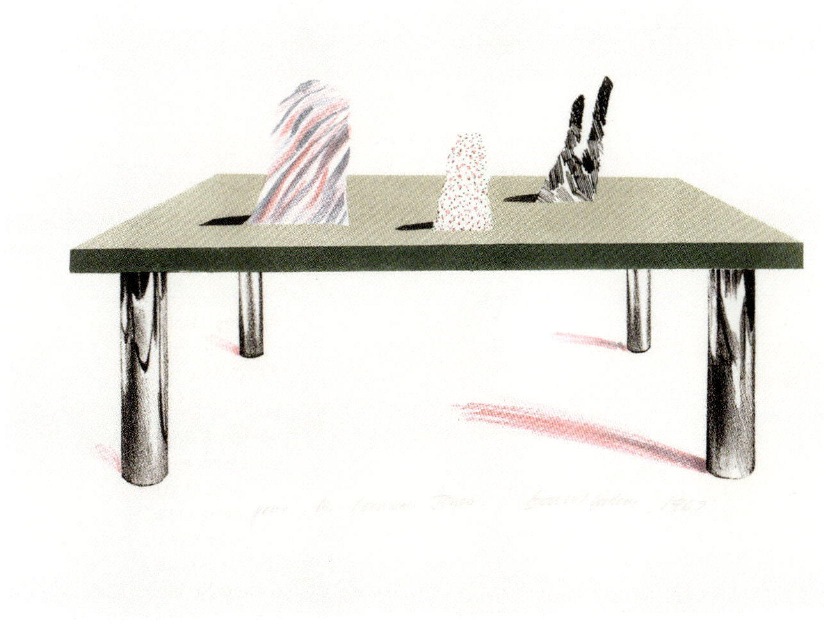

warned him, 'but if you can't do any better than that, you're finished.'

Next morning the boy went to the lake and called to the fish: 'I let you live, now tell me where I can hide so the Princess can't see me.' The fish thought about it for a long time. At last he cried: 'I've got it, I'll hide you in my belly.' So he swallowed the boy and dived to the bottom of the lake. The Princess looked through her windows, but when she couldn't see him even from the eleventh she was terrified; then from the last window she spotted him. The fish was caught and killed; and you can imagine how the boy felt when its belly was slit open. The Princess smiled as he lay on the ground gasping for breath; 'I won't kill you yet, but I'm quite sure that by tomorrow evening your head will be up there on the hundredth post.'

On the last day, downcast and walking in a field, he met the fox. 'You know every hole around here', he said. 'I let you live, now tell me where I can hide so the Princess won't see me.' 'That's not so easy,' the fox answered with a worried look, 'let me think.' Then he chuckled: 'I've got it!' He took the boy to a spring and they both jumped in. They came out together as a pedlar and a little sea hare. When the pedlar showed the pretty animal in the market place, such a crowd gathered around them that the Princess sent a servant to find out what was going on. When she saw the little sea hare she liked it and bought it for herself; but as the pedlar handed him over he whispered: 'When the Princess looks through her windows, crawl under her hair.'

It was now time to look for the boy. The Princess ran from window to window searching for him, and when she couldn't see him even from the twelfth window she lost her temper; she slammed it down so hard that the glass in it and all the others broke into a thousand pieces, and the castle shook to its foundations.

Suddenly the Princess felt the little creature behind her ear. She grabbed at it, and threw it to the floor screaming: 'Get out of here; be off with you.'

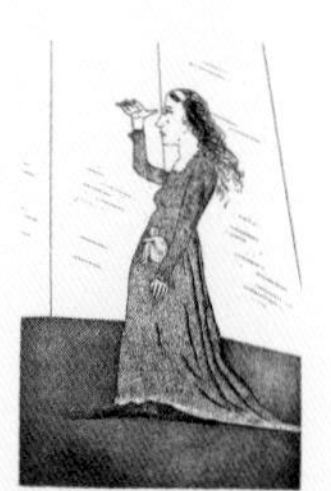

Then the little sea hare ran to the pedlar and they both rushed to the spring and dived in. As they parted, the boy thanked the fox: 'Compared to you, the raven and the fish were very stupid. You know all the tricks.'

The Princess accepted her fate. After the wedding the boy became ruler of the entire kingdom, but he never told her where he had hidden the third time or who had helped him. She admired him and thought to herself: 'He is cleverer than I am.'

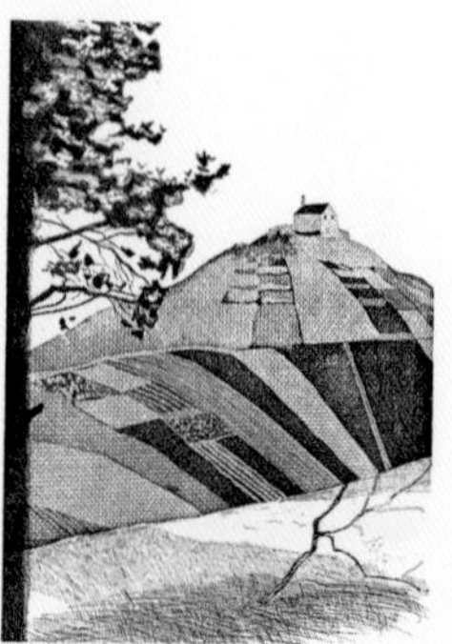

Fundevogel

A forester was out hunting in the woods one day when suddenly he heard the sound of crying. He followed the noise until he came to a clearing where he saw a child high up on a branch of a great tree; for a giant bird had snatched it from its mother's arms as she slept. He climbed up to get the child, thinking: 'I'll take it home and raise it with my little Liz.' and since it was a bird that had stolen the little boy he named him Fundevogel.

The two children grew up together; they loved each other so much that one was sad when the other was away.

The forester had an old cook. One evening she went out with two

leave me, I'll never leave you'; and Fundevogel answered: 'Not now nor ever.' So Liz begged him, 'Turn into a tower and I'll be in clock'; and as the three servants came near they saw only a tower with a clock near the top. 'We can do nothing here, let's go home.' When they got back the cook asked them if they had found anything. 'No, we saw nothing but a tower with a clock near the top.' 'Oh, you fools,' she screamed, 'why didn't you tear down the tower and bring back the clock?'

This time she went with them herself to catch the children; but they saw the servants coming from a distance, with the old cook waddling behind. Liz said to Fundevogel: 'If you'll never leave me, I'll never leave you'; and Fundevogel answered: 'Not now nor ever.' So Liz begged him: 'Turn into a lake, and I'll be a duck swimming on it.' When the cook saw the lake she lay down on her belly and started to drink it dry. Quickly, the duck swam over, grabbed her nose in its beak and pulled her into the water. The old cook drowned; and the children were home before the forester came back from the woods.

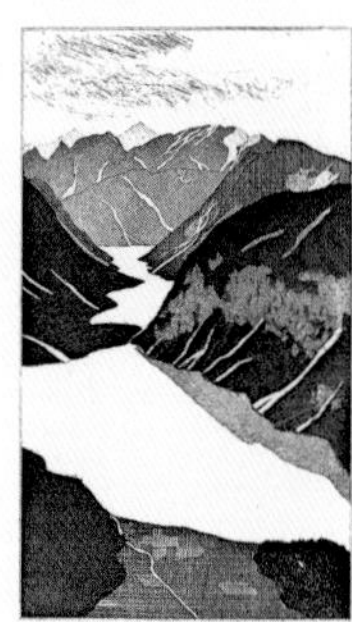

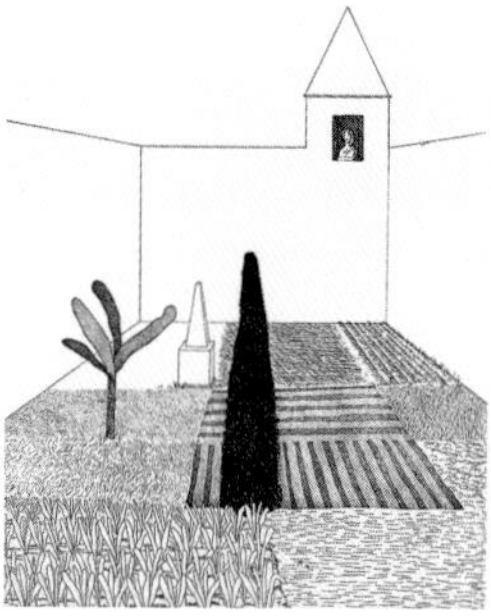

Rapunzel

A man and a woman had long wanted a child, and they believed that at last their wish would come true. The house in which they lived had a small window at the back which looked out on a wonderful garden with lovely flowers and herbs. But it was surrounded by a high wall, and nobody dared go in for it belonged to a powerful Enchantress.

One day the woman was standing at the window looking into the garden when she noticed a flower bed. Planted with the most luscious rapunzels, it looked so fresh and green that she couldn't leave the window. 'I must have some,' she thought, but since she knew it was forbidden, she grew pale and miserable. Her husband was worried and asked: 'What's wrong with you?' 'Oh, I saw some wonderful rapunzels in the garden behind the house, and if I can't have some I shall die.' The man loved his wife and wanted to help: 'I can't let her die,' he thought, 'I must get her some rapunzels whatever the cost.'

As it grew dark he sneaked into the garden, snatched a handful of the plants and took them to his wife, who quickly made herself a salad. It was so delicious that the next day she longed for more; and to calm her, her husband climbed into the garden once again. He was given a terrible fright when the Enchantress crept up behind him. 'How dare you,' she cried out in a rage, 'how dare you climb into my garden and steal my rapunzels?' 'I know I've done wrong,' he pleaded, 'but pity me. I was forced to do it; my wife saw your rapunzels from the window and she wanted them so much that she certainly would have died if I hadn't

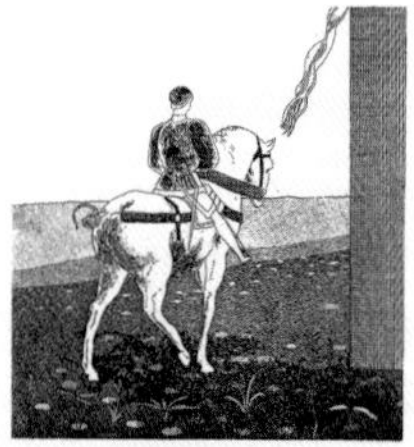

that's the ladder,' he thought, 'then I can climb up as well.' And when it was dark he went to the tower and called:

Rapunzel, Rapunzel
Let down your hair.

Her hair fell down and he climbed up. Rapunzel was very frightened for she had never seen a man; but the Prince was kind and told her how the song had moved him. When Rapunzel saw how young and handsome he

was, she thought: 'He will love me better than the old woman.' She put her hands in his and said: 'I wish I could go with you, but I can't get out. Each time you come bring a roll of silk and I will weave a ladder. When it's finished we'll escape together on your horse.' And to keep out of the old woman's way they agreed he should come only at night.

The Enchantress didn't suspect anything until one day Rapunzel said to her: 'Tell me, why are you so much harder to lift up than the young Prince who comes every night?' 'What's that you're saying? You horrid girl!' the old woman screamed. 'I thought I had hidden you from every-one; but you have cheated me!' She was so angry that she grabbed Rapunzel's hair and cut it off with a pair of scissors; the lovely blond hair fell to the floor. Then the cruel Enchantress carried the girl off to an endless desert and left her to look after herself.

The day she cast out Rapunzel the old woman fastened the long blond hair to the window-hook. When the Prince came and called:

Rapunzel, Rapunzel
Let down your hair,

she let it down and he climbed up; but instead of Rapunzel he found the Enchantress. 'The bird has flown,' she sneered, 'the cat has got it and will scratch out your eyes as well. Forget Rapunzel, you will never see her again.' In his sorrow the Prince threw himself from the window. He wasn't killed, but his eyes were pierced by thorns, and blinded, he staggered away. Roaming through the forest, helpless and in great pain, he ate nothing but roots and berries, and wept and mourned the loss of his lovely Rapunzel.

Years later he reached the desert where Rapunzel lived sadly with the twins she had born. When at last she saw him coming she called his name and he knew it was her voice; and as they embraced and wept, two of her tears fell on his eyes and he saw again. So he took her with the children to his kingdom, where they lived happily for many years.

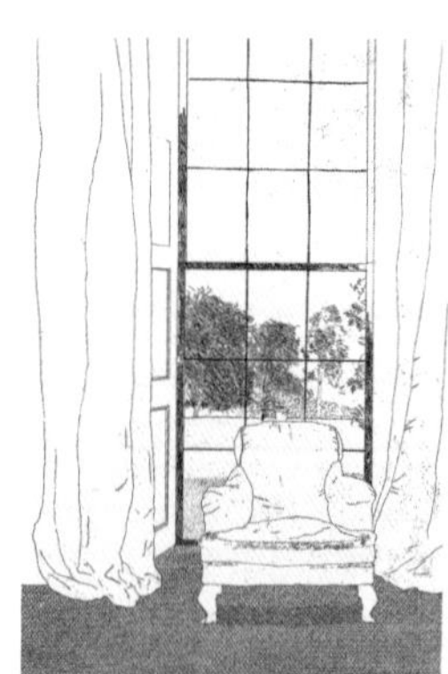

The Boy who left home to learn fear

A farmer had two sons. The elder was clever and knew his way around, but the younger one was stupid and good for nothing. When people saw him they said: 'That boy will give his father trouble.' It was always the elder boy who had to help his father; but if he was sent on an errand late at night and on the way he had to cross the churchyard or some other dismal place, he would plead: 'No father, I'd rather not go, it makes me shudder.'

When the younger brother sat in a corner and heard people telling ghost stories by the fire, he couldn't understand them when they said: 'Oh, that makes me shudder!' 'Why do they always say it makes me shudder, it makes me shudder,' he asked himself, 'I can't shudder—that must be something I have to learn.'

One day his father spoke to him: 'Listen my boy, you're getting older. It's about time you started to work. Look at your brother, he earns his keep; but what do you have to offer?' 'Father, I'd like to learn something,' he answered, 'if I had my choice I'd learn to shudder; I don't know the first thing about it.' His brother grinned and thought: 'Heavens, what a fool he is! He'll never get anywhere.' The father sighed: 'You'll learn soon enough what it is to be afraid; but you won't earn a living that way.'

Six Fairy Tales from the Brothers Grimm with Original Etchings by David Hockney, created in 1969, published by Petersburg Press in association with Kasmin Limited, London 1970

buckets to fetch water; after she had done this several times, little Liz became curious and asked her: 'Old Sanne, what is all this water for?' 'If you can keep a secret,' the cook whispered, 'I'll tell you!' When Liz promised, she told her: 'Tomorrow morning when your father is out

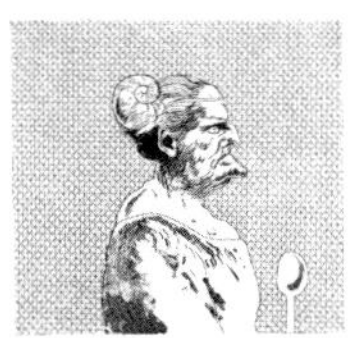

hunting I'll heat up this water, and when it's boiling in the pot I'll throw in Fundevogel and cook him.'

Very early the next morning, as the forester left to hunt, Liz woke Fundevogel and said: 'If you'll never leave me, I'll never leave you'; and Fundevogel answered: 'Not now nor ever.' 'Then I'll tell you why Old Sanne brought in so many buckets of water last night. I was curious and

asked her what she was going to do; she told me she would wait until father had gone out hunting then boil the water and throw you in. Hurry now, let's get dressed and escape.' So the children got up quickly and left the house.

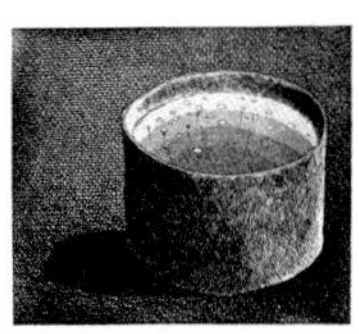

As soon as the water was boiling in the pot the cook went into the bedroom to grab Fundevogel, but both beds were empty. She was terribly worried now and thought to herself: 'What can I say to the forester when he comes home and sees the children are gone? I must get them back quickly!'

The cook sent three servants off on the run to catch up with the children.

They were sitting at the edge of the forest when they saw the servants coming, and Liz said to Fundevogel: 'If you'll never leave me, I'll never leave you'; and Fundevogel answered: 'Not now nor ever.' So Liz begged

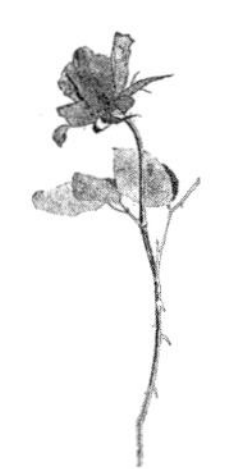

him, 'Turn into a rosebush, and I'll be a rose.' When the three servants reached the edge of the forest, they saw nothing but a rosebush with a single rose. 'Nobody here,' they called to each other, and told the old

cook: 'We couldn't find the children; we saw nothing but a rosebush with a single rose.'

The cook was angry. 'You fools!' she shouted. 'Why didn't you split

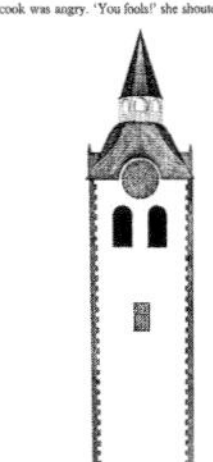

the rosebush in two, break off the rose and bring it back with you? Quick, go back at once and do it!' So they ran back to look for the spot. But the children saw them coming and Liz said to Fundevogel: 'If you'll never

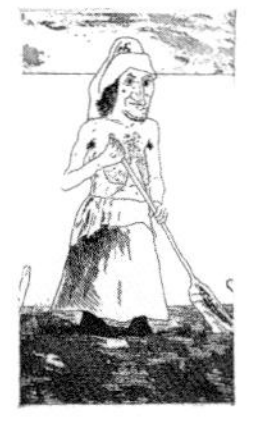

stolen her a few.' The Enchantress was cunning: 'If that's the truth,' she replied, 'I'll let you take all the rapunzels you want. But there is one condition; you must give me your child as soon as it is born. It will have a good life and I'll care for it like a mother.' In his terror the man agreed, and when the child was born the Enchantress took it away and named it Rapunzel.

Rapunzel was the most beautiful girl under the sun. When she was twelve years old the Enchantress led her deep into the forest and locked

her up in a small room high up in a tower, which had neither doors nor steps but only one window at the very top. When the Enchantress wanted to enter she stood under the window and called:

Rapunzel, Rapunzel
Let down your hair.

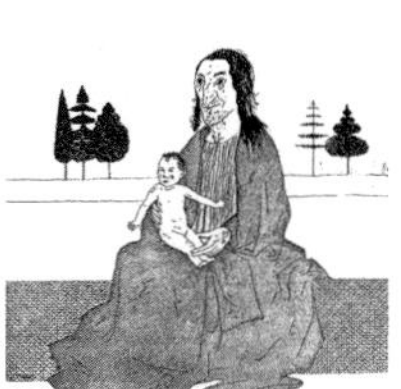

Rapunzel had long blond hair. When she heard the Enchantress calling she would wind it round a window-hook and let it down to the ground, so the old woman could climb up.

A few years later a Prince was riding through the forest and, as he

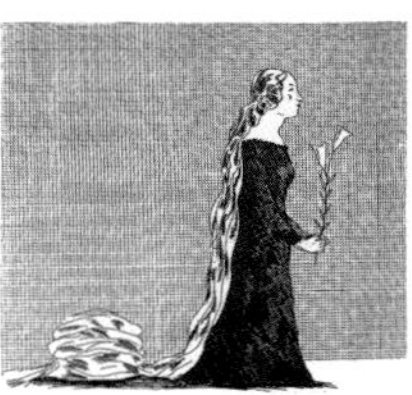

passed by the tower, he heard a beautiful voice and stopped to listen: Rapunzel was singing. The Prince longed to see her and searched for a door but the tower had none. He couldn't forget her voice and came to listen every day. Then one afternoon he heard the Enchantress calling:

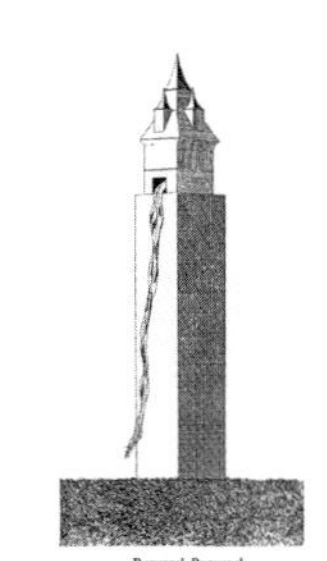

Rapunzel, Rapunzel
Let down your hair.

Rapunzel let down her hair and the Enchantress climbed up. 'Oh! If

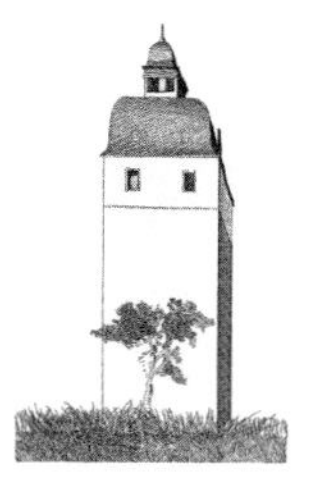

A few days later the father was telling the sexton his problems: 'The boy's so stupid; he won't work and can't grasp the simplest thing. Just think, when I asked him what he wanted to do, he said he was going to learn to shudder.' 'If that's all he wants,' the sexton grinned, 'I'll teach him. Leave it to me; I'll straighten him out.'

So he took the boy on and gave him the job of bell-ringer. Some days

later he woke him at midnight and told him to go to the church to ring the bell. 'I'll teach him what fear is', he thought, as he took a short cut to the tower. As the boy was about to ring the bell, he turned and saw a white shape on the stairs. 'Who's there?' he called, but the figure was silent. 'Speak up or get out. What do you want here anyway?' Expecting the boy to take him for a ghost, the sexton didn't move. So the boy shouted again: 'What do you want here? Answer me, or I'll throw you down the stairs!' But the sexton didn't take the threat seriously and stood perfectly still. The boy gave him one more chance but when he got no answer he

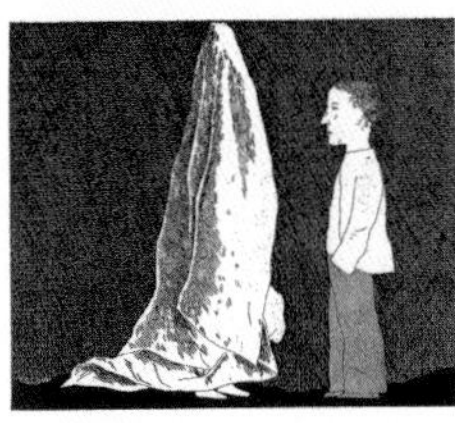

jumped on the startled ghost and kicked him down the stairs. Then he rang the bell and went home to bed.

The sexton's wife waited patiently for her husband. After a few hours she began to worry, so she woke the boy and asked him: 'Do you know where my husband could be? He left for the church before you.' 'I don't know,' he replied, 'but a figure in white was standing at the top of the stairs, and since he wouldn't answer me or get out of my way, I took him for a rogue and threw him to the bottom. Go and see if it's your husband, I'd be very sorry if it was. That would be bad luck.' The woman rushed to the tower and found the sexton moaning in a corner with a broken leg.

She carried him back to the house and ran screaming to the boy's father: 'Your son has kicked my husband down the stairs and broke his leg! Get him out of our house immediately!' The father was horrified and went to get the boy: 'Damn you!' he cursed. 'What mad tricks have you been up to? Are you completely off your head? 'Listen to me father,' he answered, 'I've done nothing wrong. It was midnight; a figure was standing there and he looked as if he were up to no good! I didn't know who it was and asked him three times either to speak up or be off.' 'Oh! my God,' his father groaned, 'you bring me nothing but trouble. Get out of my sight.' 'Well father, I don't mind. Just let me stay until morning, then I'll go off and learn to shudder. At least that way I can earn some money.' 'Do whatever you want, I don't care. I'll give you ten pennies, then go away, the further the better. Don't tell anyone where you're from or mention my name. I'm ashamed of you.' 'Whatever you wish, father—if that's all you ask it's easy enough.'

At dawn the boy took his money and walked down to the highway, mumbling to himself: 'If only I could learn to shudder.' He passed a man who heard him talking. They walked together for a while, and when they came to a gallows, the fellow said: 'Look, this is the tree where seven men married the ropemaker's daughter; now they're learning to fly. Just

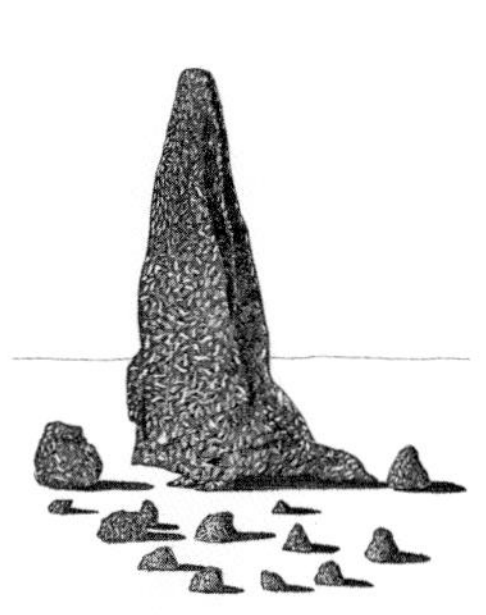

Pages 98/99: Henry Geldzahler and Christopher Scott, 1969, acrylic on canvas, 84 x 120 in. / 213.4 x 304.8 cm

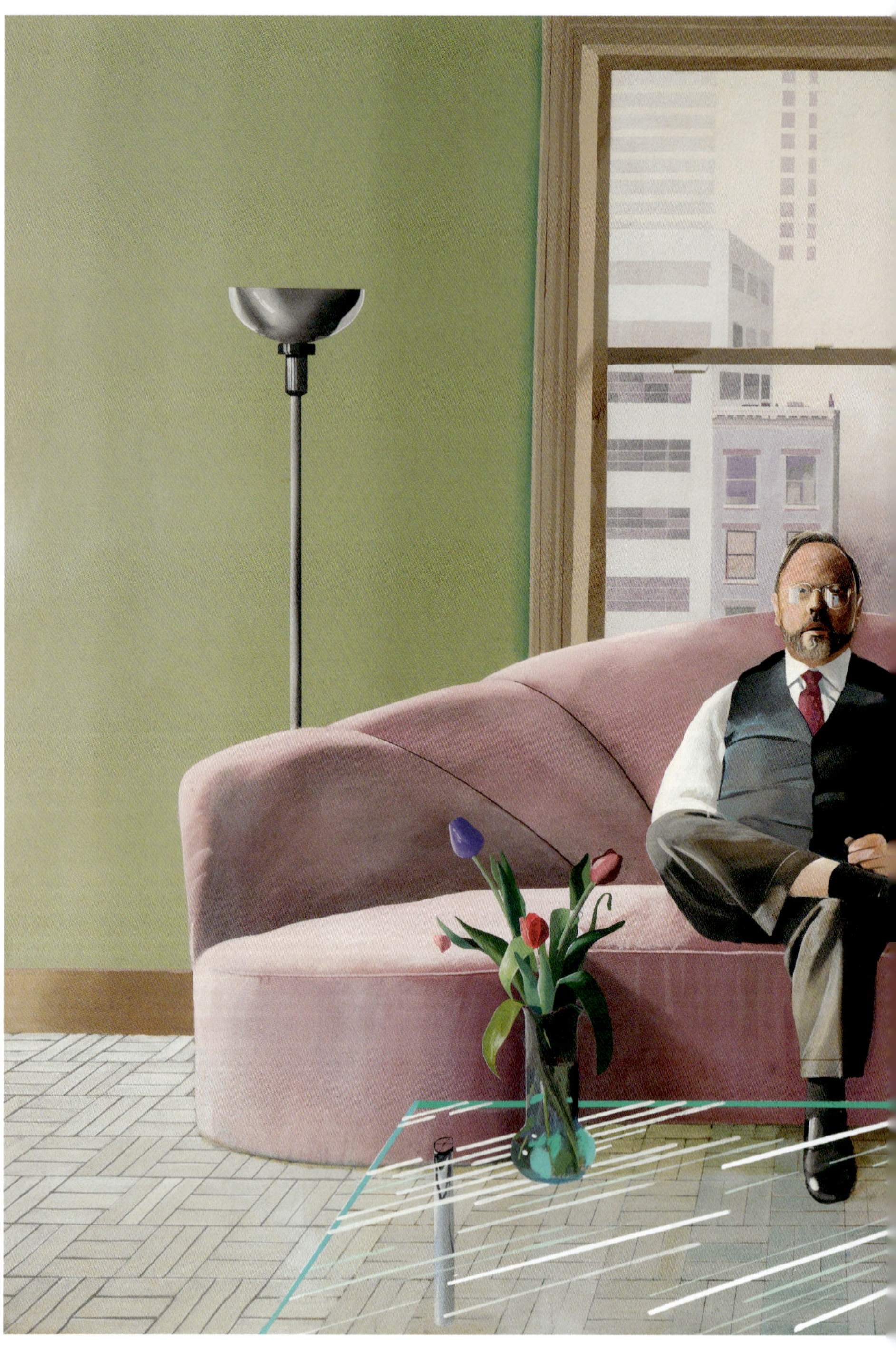

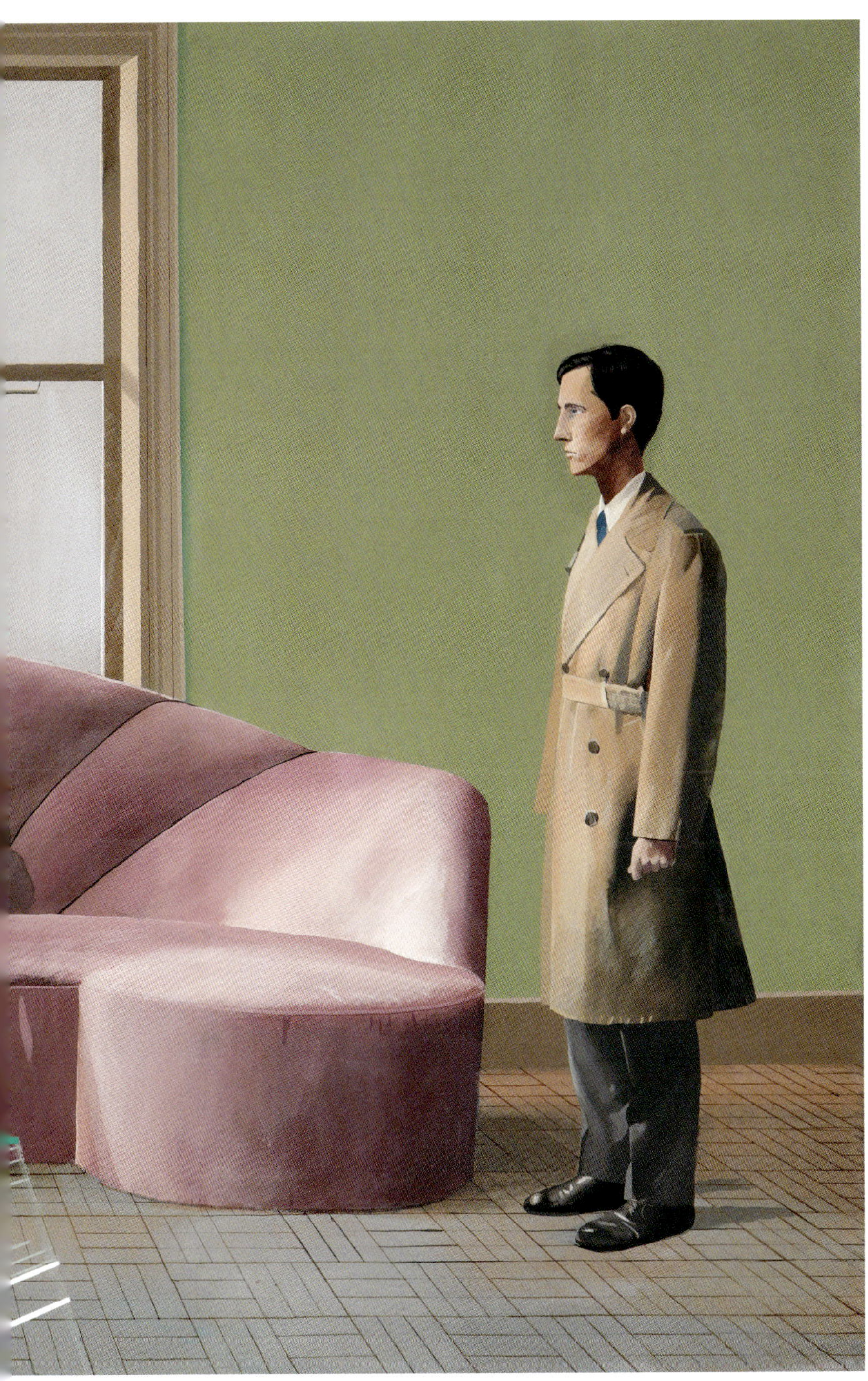

1970

Hockney starts painting *Le Parc des Sources, Vichy* (p. 103) from photographs and sketches he has made on location the previous year. Peter Schlesinger and Ossie Clark are seen as back figures sitting on plastic chairs and looking at a park, with an empty third chair beside them that the artist might just have left to make the picture. It is one of Hockney's first works to deal with the question of perspective and illusionist space: "Vichy is a very pretty town with a park in the middle, a kind of formal garden, and they use this false perspective of trees to make it look longer than it really is. And I thought, it's marvelous, the whole thing is like a sculpture." In contrast to later works, in which he seeks painterly alternatives to one-point perspective, the picture is a naturalist rendering of a found situation: "There's a strong surrealist element in the painting because of the use of the false perspective, which is really what interested me. The actual trees there form a triangle, not an alley just disappearing into the distance."

In April, Hockney's first big retrospective of *Paintings, Prints and Drawings, 1960–1970* opens at the Whitechapel Art Gallery in London (p. 105), showing 45 paintings, the complete graphic work, and numerous drawings, and set to travel to various European museums afterward. Hockney selects the paintings for the show and then leaves to travel, delegating the hanging to curator Mark Glazebrook. The idea of a retrospective starts worrying him: "I was away in France, with Christopher Isherwood, and we came back the day before the exhibition opened and went to the opening like everybody else; so it was a surprise to me. I must admit, just a few days before we came back, I began to think, 'Oh my God, all those early pictures which I haven't seen in ten years are going to look terrible; I'm going to be really embarrassed by them' ... When I saw them, though, I thought, they do stand up; they're not that bad. I began to see for the first time the way things worked, the way my mind was working. I'd never been able to stand outside it before. I could see the way things progressed, how I'd taken one aspect of a painting and developed it in other pictures so that it changed quite visibly; it was the consistency that surprised me ... It's a shock and you see all the faults, but you see the virtues too. Usually all you ever have in your studio is, at the very most, perhaps a year's work."

The reviews are positive; Norbert Lynton writes in the *Guardian*: "The exhibition needs looking at—and for longer than a critic can allow himself if he is to

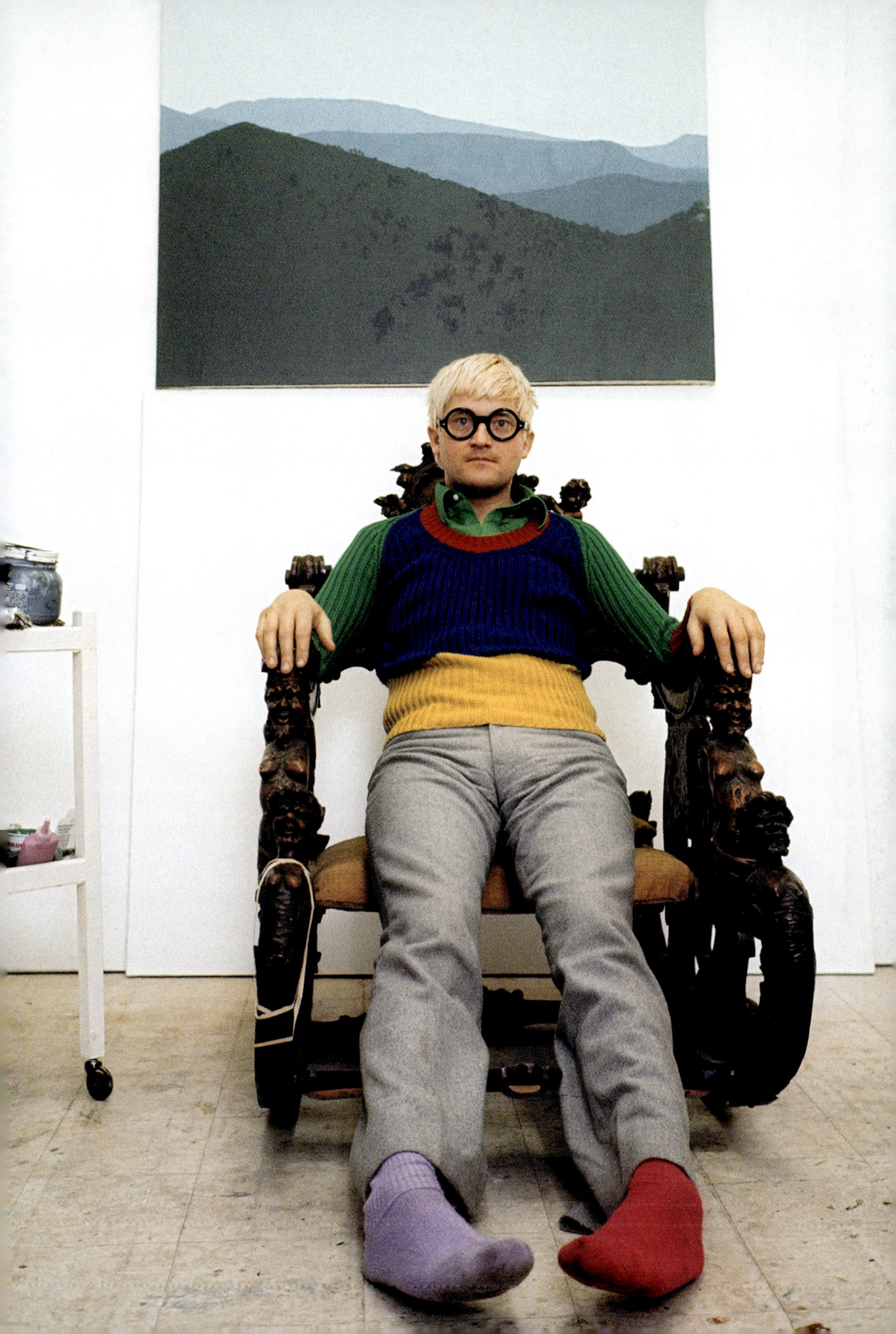

get his piece in. It needs thinking about too, and I should like to suggest some questions and offer a few partial answers. How much, and how, has Hockney's work changed over the years? Clever, subtle, and witty in 1962, it has become a great deal more refined, economical, and serious. Economy has meant greater decision and less playfulness. It has taken him a few years to recognize himself. How avant-garde is it? Not particularly. In 1962 he was hailed as a Pop artist but his interest was more in the art of the museums and in graffiti. Pop elements still occur from time to time, the graffiti influence has largely disappeared, and his interest in past art, as in poetry, persists. But Hockney's vision has become more and more straightforward." James Burr in *Apollo* poses the question where Hockney's artistic development might possibly lead him: "It seems to have reached a point of development that looks ominously like a cul-de-sac, but no doubt by some unusual act of visual agility he will extract himself and continue his distinctively eccentric painting progress without which English painting would be markedly the poorer."

In the catalog to the exhibition, which includes a catalogue raisonné of Hockney's work to date, the artist himself takes stock of his development toward a more realistic, more visual style. In the earlier work, he says, the motifs were invented, even if they looked taken from nature: "It wasn't how they appeared. It was how I thought they might appear... The ideas were really still artistic in that way... and instead of being inward I just wanted them to come outward a bit, and become more about life as it was. That's when I started doing the portraits and the paintings began to get more realistic, I began to be interested in light and things like that. Since then in many ways they have got more ordinary, I mean more conventional."

Around May Hockney finally begins the double portrait of Ossie Clark and Celia Birtwell, *Mr. and Mrs. Clark and Percy* (pp. 106/107)—the latter being their cat—which he has planned since the couple's wedding the year before. It is a painting that for him will mark the point closest to a naturalist ideal in his work, and its many details and technical problems will occupy him for a year: "The figures are nearly life-size; it's difficult painting figures like that, and it was quite a struggle. They posed for a long time, both Ossie and Celia. Ossie was painted many, many times; I took it out and put it in, out and in. I probably painted the head alone twelve times; drawn and painted and then completely

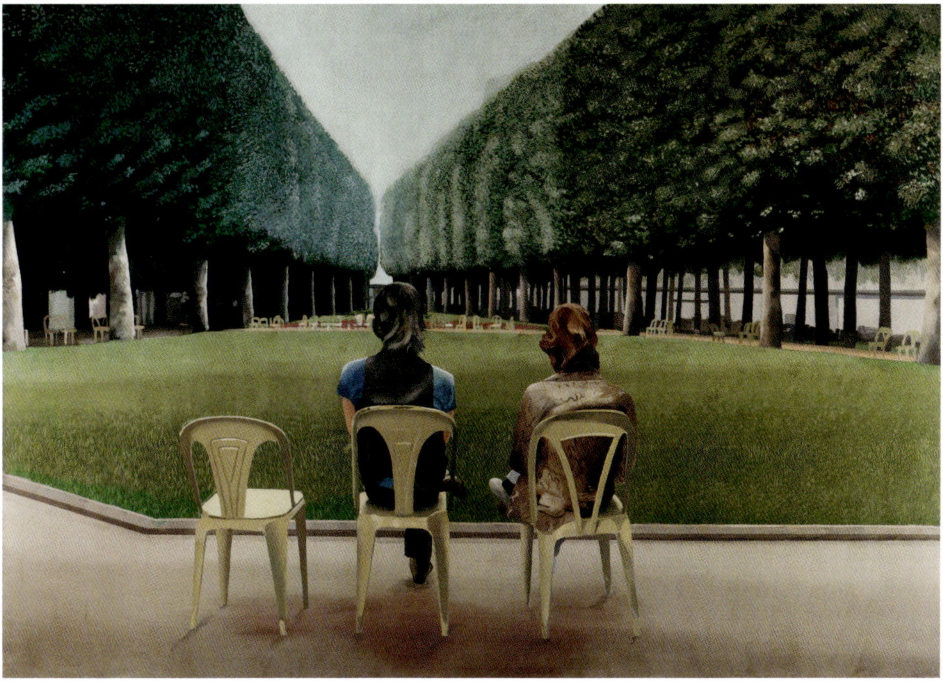

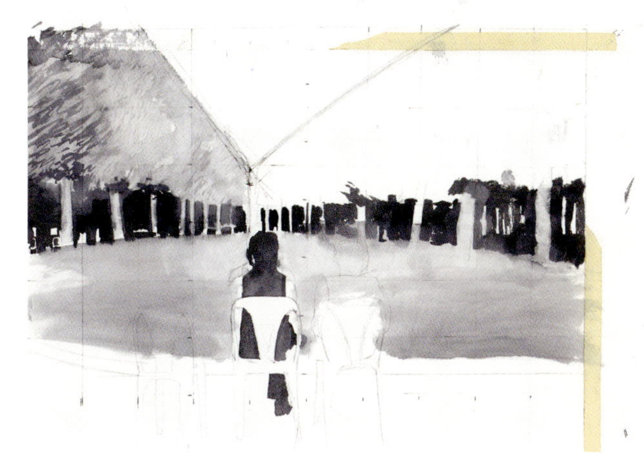

Le Parc des Sources, Vichy, 1970, acrylic on canvas, 84 x 120 in. / 213.4 x 304.8 cm

Squared-up drawing for *Le Parc des Sources, Vichy,* 1970, ink and pencil on paper, 21 ½ x 29 ½ in. / 54.6 x 74.9 cm

Page 101: David Hockney, 1970. Photo: Jack Garofalo

Page 105: *David Hockney: Paintings, Prints and Drawings, 1960–1970,* exhibition views, Whitechapel Gallery, London 1970

Pages 106/107: *Mr. and Mrs. Clark and Percy,* 1970–1971, acrylic on canvas, 84 x 120 in. / 213.4 x 304.8 cm

removed, and then put in again, and again. You can see that the paint gets thicker and thicker there…The one great technical problem in it is that the source of light is from the middle of the painting…It's easier if the source of light is from the side and you can't see it, because if you can see it, it has to be the lightest thing in the painting, and it creates problems about tone…To come to terms with tone, you have literally to be in front of something, and really look and see carefully what tonal values really are; you have to look and look. Well, this painting wasn't painted like that. Although the figures were painted from life a great deal they were posed in my studio because the painting is very big. What I wanted to achieve by such a big painting was the presence of two people in this room. All the technical problems were caused because my main aim was to paint the relationship of these two people."

Around this time, looking for better ways to record details in his photographic studies and avoid wide-angle distortion, Hockney starts pasting different shots of a scene from various angles together, the earliest use of the photo assemblages that he will come to call "joiners."

Solo: *Paintings, Prints and Drawings, 1960–1970,* Whitechapel Gallery, London (Apr 2–May 3); travels to Kestner-Gesellschaft, Hanover (May 22–Jun 21); Museum Boymans-van Beuningen, Rotterdam (Jul 25–Aug 29); and Muzej Savremene Umetnosti, Belgrade (Sep 18–Oct 15); catalog with a text by Mark Glazebrook and an interview with the artist, London: Lund Humphries; German edition ed. by Wieland Schmied, texts by Günther Gercken and Heiner Bastian. *Six Fairy Tales from the Brothers Grimm and Other New Etchings,* André Emmerich Gallery, New York (Oct 31–Dec 3). *Das graphische Werk,* Galerie Der Spiegel, Cologne (Nov–Dec 1970). *Recent Drawings,* Kasmin Limited, London (opens Dec 9). *Six Fairy Tales,* Galleria Milano, Milan (opens Dec 11). *David Hockney,* Lane Gallery, Bradford.

Group: *Image/Dessin: Animation, Recherché, Confrontation,* Musee d'art moderne de la Ville de Paris (Jan 16–Feb 15); catalog. *Narrative Painting in Britain in the 20th Century,* Camden Arts Centre, London (Feb 10–Mar 8); catalog. *Contemporary British Art,* National Museum of Modern Art, Tokyo (Sep 9–Oct 25); catalog. *British Painting and Sculpture, 1960–1970,* National Gallery of Art, Washington, D.C. (Nov 12, 1970–Jan 3, 1971); catalog.

Publication: *Six Fairy Tales from the Brothers Grimm with Original Etchings by David Hockney,* London: Petersburg Press in association with Kasmin Limited.

Film: *David Hockney's Diaries,* GB, 28 min., dir. by Christian and Michael Blackwood.

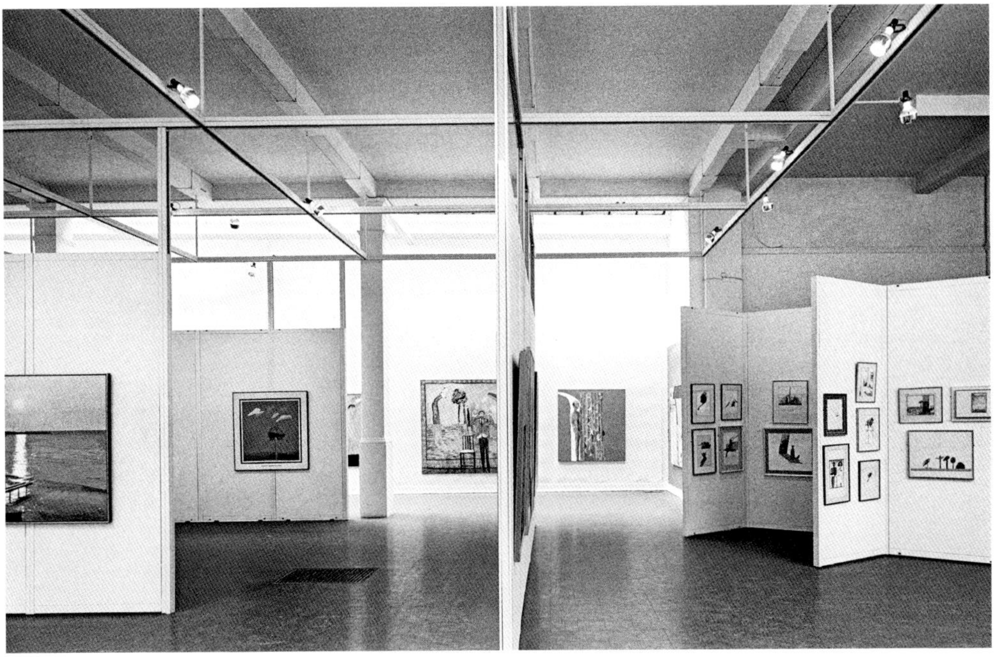

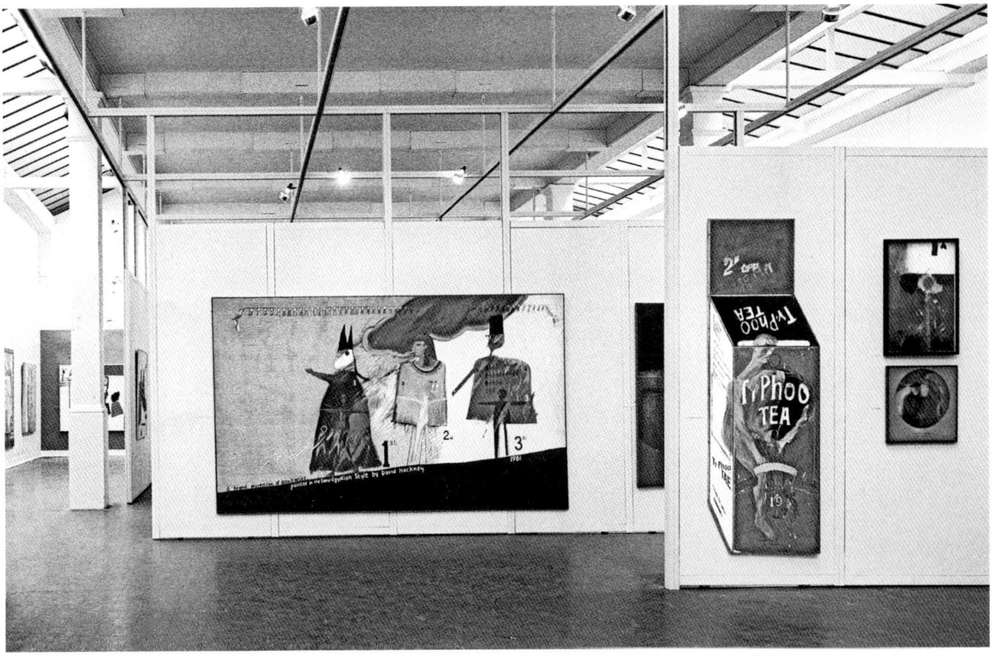
1st
2d
3rd
1961
Style by David Hockney
TyPhoo TEA
2d OFF

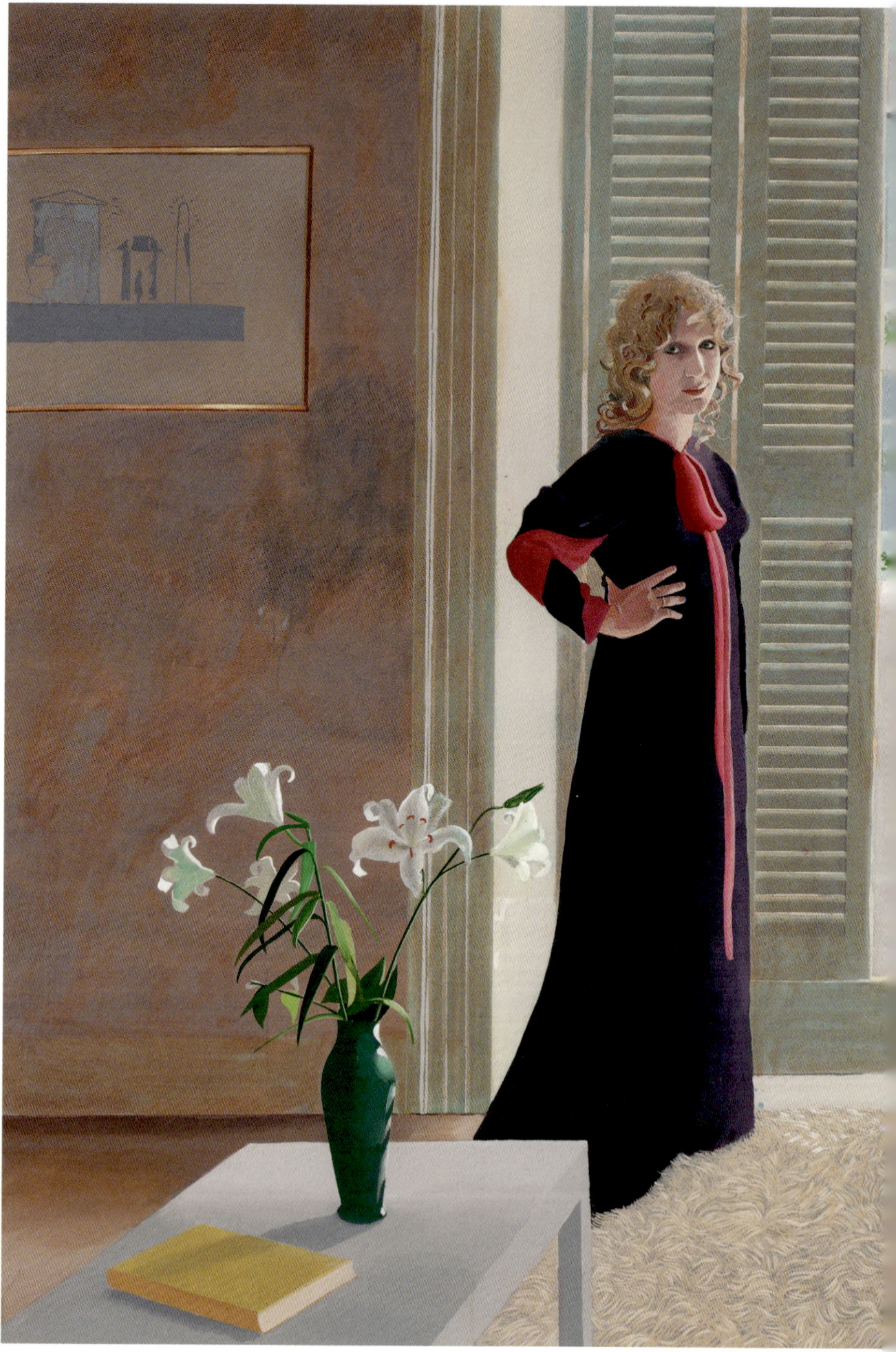

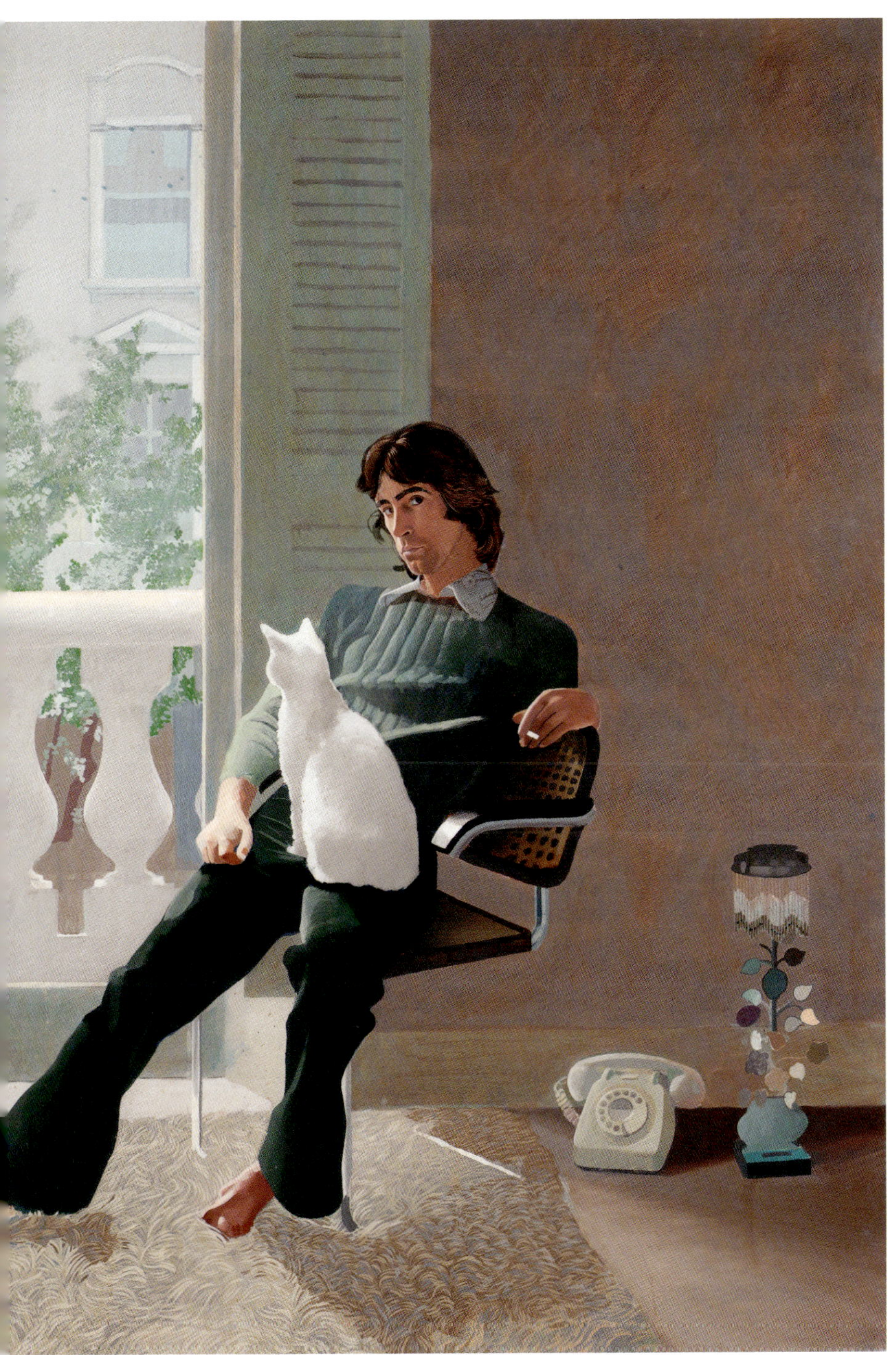

1971

After working on it for a year, Hockney completes his double portrait of Celia Birtwell and Ossie Clark. It is shown at the National Portrait Gallery in London in a group show reviewed by Peter Quennell in the *New York Times*: "David Hockney's huge picture of Mr. and Mrs. Clark and their charming white cat, Percy, does make some genuine additions to our knowledge of a portrait-painter's methods. Like Hockney's other works, it is pallid, spacious, calm. From their quiet, agreeably furnished surroundings—Ossie Clark, by the way, is a well-known London dress designer—the Clarks gaze out with expressions of reflective dignity. The picture is beautifully balanced; every detail is exactly spaced. David Hockney, we learn, painted one face no less than 16 times, while a dozen separate re-paintings eventually fixed the view beyond the window."

Hockney, after much hesitation, takes on his only ever commission for a portrait painting; the subject is to be Sir David Webster, director of the Royal Opera House, London. The task proves difficult as Hockney, aside from his love of opera, feels he has no personal relation to the sitter: "Even before I began the painting, I didn't know how to do it and what setting to do it in. I went to visit Webster many times…but it took me a long time to find the subject…Then they began to natter me, when will it be ready, he's retiring on this date, and so on. And in the end I thought, all I can do is paint him in my studio. So that's the setting; the table and chair and flowers are in my studio." While sitter and commissioner are delighted with the work, Hockney will not accept a portrait commission again.

He travels to Morocco with Peter Schlesinger and Celia Birtwell and on his return paints *Sur la Terrasse* (p. 111), a portrait of Schlesinger seen from behind on the terrace in Marrakesh. Their relationship is breaking up, though, and after the summer Schlesinger is moving out of Powis Terrace to settle in his own studio. Hockney is downcast: "It was very traumatic for me, I'd never been through anything like that. I was miserable, very, very unhappy." During these stressful times, filmmaker Jack Hazan starts a documentary on Hockney, whom he will film on many occasions over the next three years. Unknown to the artist, he decides to include the story of the break-up in the film.

Meanwhile Hockney seeks solace in his work, completing seven paintings in two months. *Rubber Ring Floating in a Swimming Pool* (p. 114) is based on a photograph taken in Cadaqués: "I was so struck by the photograph's looking like

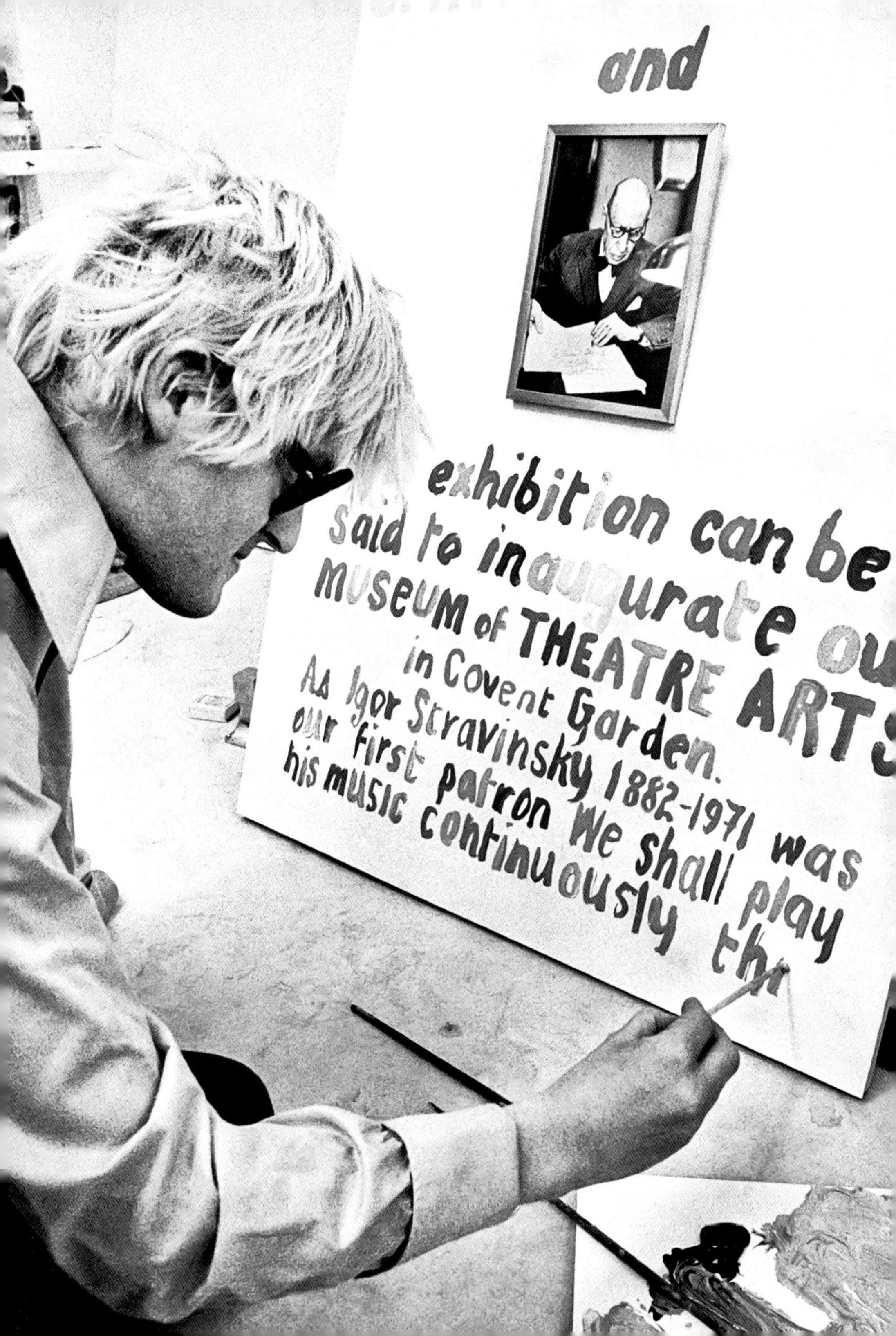

and

exhibition can be
said to inaugurate our
museum of THEATRE ARTS
in Covent Garden.
As Igor Stravinsky 1882-1971 was
our first patron We shall play
his music continuously th

a Max Ernst abstract painting, that I thought, it's marvelous, I could just paint it." In the Musée d'art moderne in Paris, Hockney finds a sculpture by Julio González casting strong shadows on the wall (p. 114): "These shadows with their completely flattened forms seemed to contradict the idea of cubist sculpture. They amused me because somehow I'd accepted the intellectual and conceptual idea of cubist sculpture and thought the shadows should accept those ideas as well." And *The Island* (p. 113) is painted after a postcard from Japan, the artist trying to see if he could predict what the country would be like before traveling there: in autumn, Hockney goes on a two-month trip with Mark Lancaster, taking in Hawaii, Japan, and Southeast Asia.

Solo: *Zeichnungen, Grafik, Gemälde,* Kunsthalle Bielefeld (Apr 25–May 30); catalog ed. by Gerhard Schack and Ulrich Weisner, text by Günther Gercken. *Illustrationen zu sechs Märchen der Brüder Grimm,* Frankfurter Kunstkabinett Hanna Bekker vom Rath, Frankfurt am Main (Jan 12–Feb 6); catalog. *Etchings Illustrating Six Fairy Tales after the Brothers Grimm,* Margo Leavin Gallery, Los Angeles (Mar 8–31). *Illustrationen zu Grimm's Fairy Tales,* Ziegler Editionen und Grafik, Zürich (Oct 19–Nov 27).

Group: *Snap! An Exhibition Exploring the Ideas and Motives behind Portraiture,* National Portrait Gallery, London (Mar–Apr); catalog. *Drawing and Paintings by David Hockney and Alan Davie,* University of Lancaster (Oct 15–30); travels to Jarrow, Newcastle, Carlisle, Alnwick, and Whitehaven; catalog with a text by Helen Kapp.

Publication: *72 Drawings by David Hockney, Chosen by the Artist,* New York: Viking; London: Jonathan Cape.

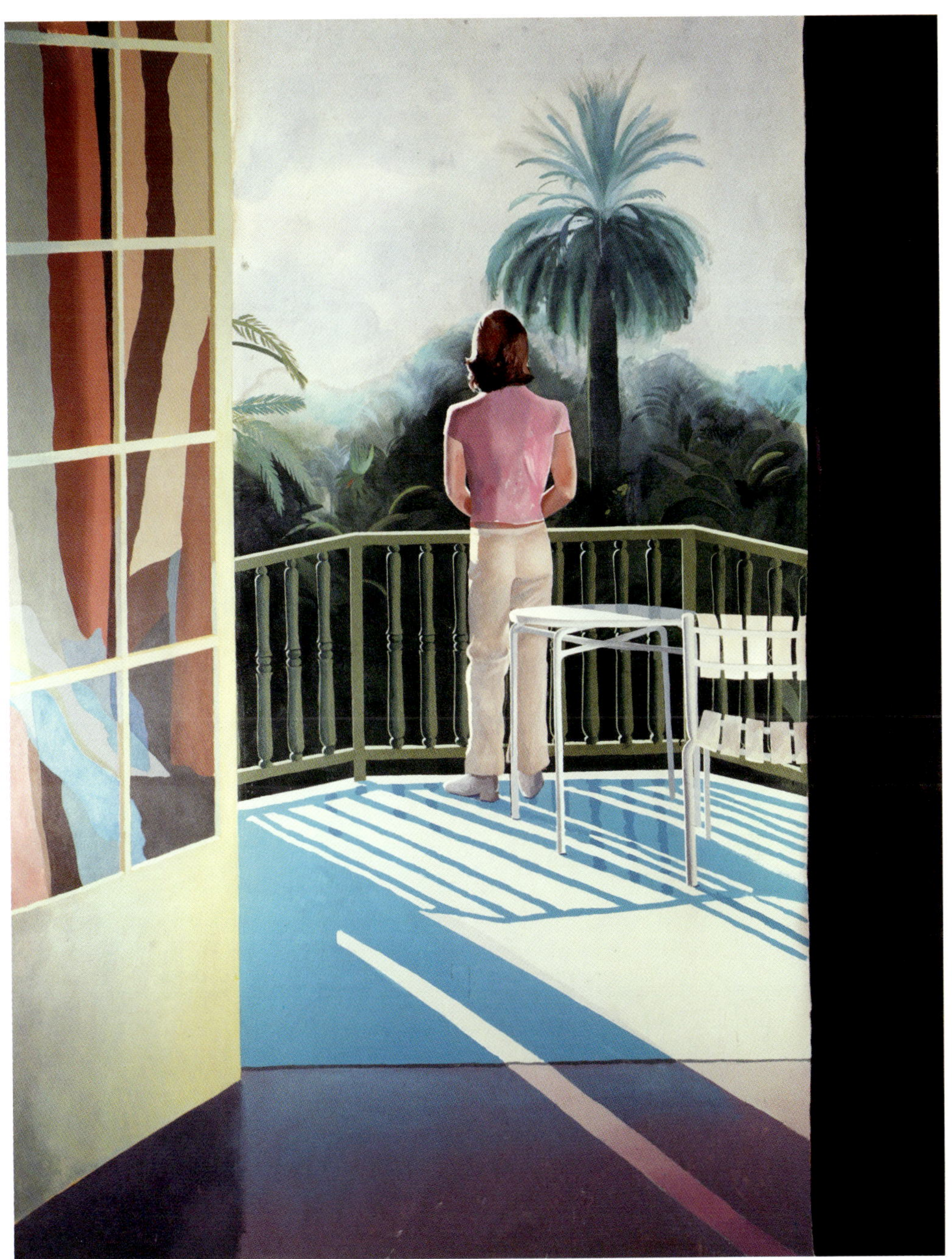

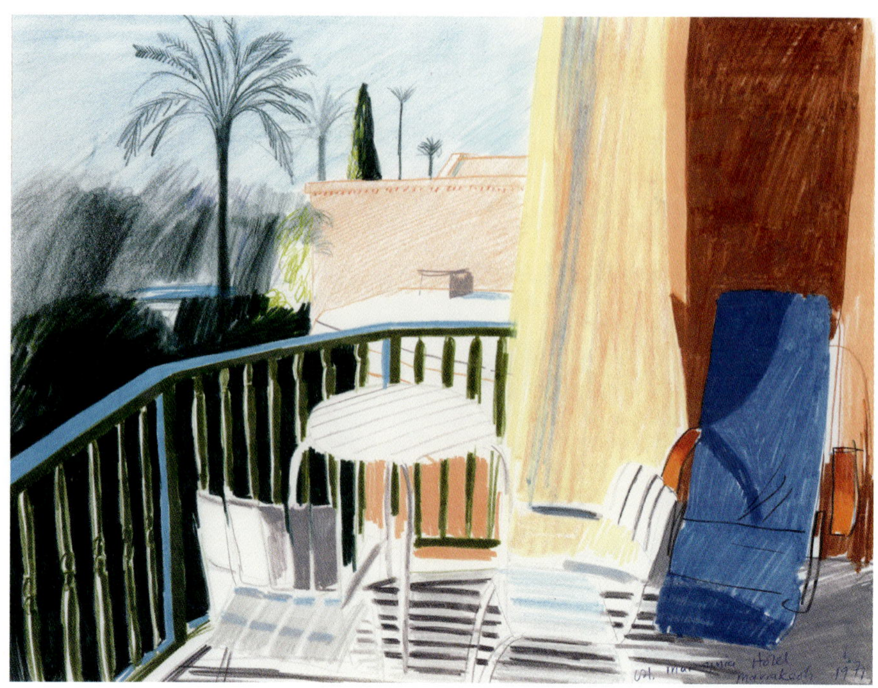

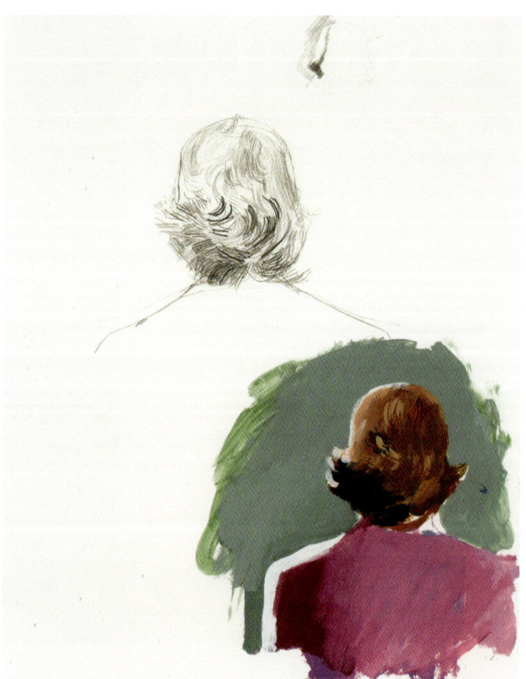

Balcony, Mamounia Hotel, Marrakesh,
1971, crayon on paper, 14 x 17 in. /
35.6 x 43.2 cm

Study for *Sur la Terrasse,* 1971,
oil, watercolor, and pencil on paper,
17 x 14 in. / 43.2 x 35.6 cm

Right page: *Inland Sea, Japan,*
1971, crayon on paper, 14 x 17 in. /
35.6 x 43.2 cm

The Island, 1971, acrylic on canvas,
60 x 72 in. / 152.4 x 182.9 cm

Page 109: David Hockney painting
a poster for a commemorative event
in Covent Garden on the death of
composer Igor Stravinsky, London
1971. Photo: Michael Ward

Page 111: *Sur la Terrasse,* 1971,
acrylic on canvas, 108 x 84 in. /
274.3 x 213.4 cm

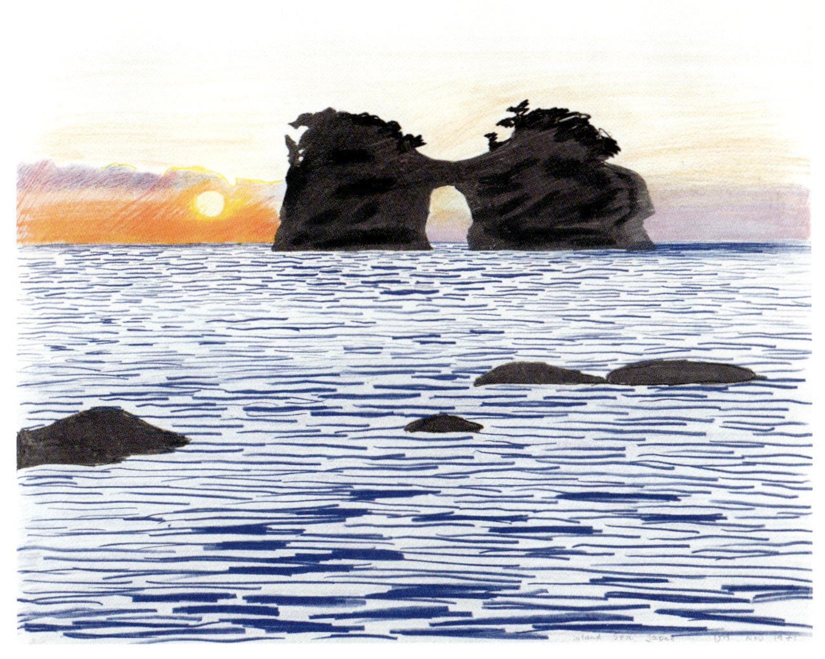

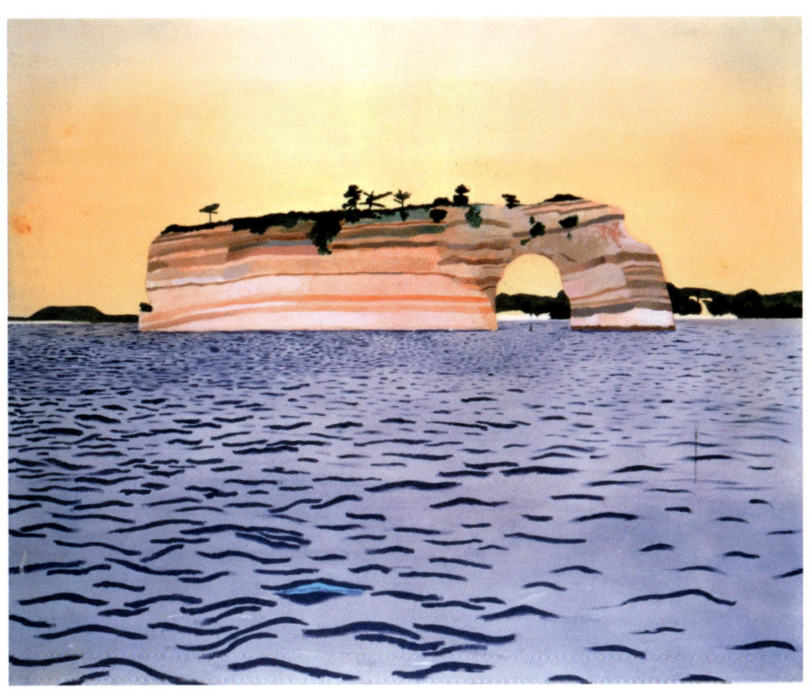

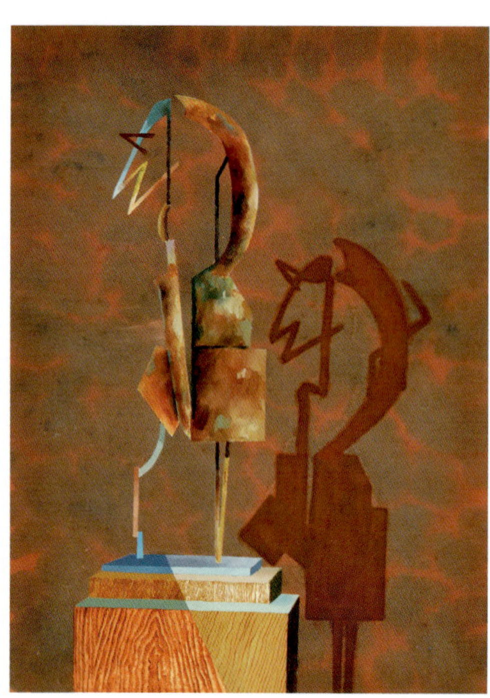

Gonzalez and Shadow, 1971,
acrylic on canvas, 48 x 36 in. /
121.9 x 91.4 cm

*Rubber Ring Floating in a Swimming
Pool,* 1971, acrylic on canvas,
36 x 48 in. / 91.4 x 121.9 cm

Right page: *Celia, Carennac,
August 1971,* pencil and colored
pencil on paper, 17 x 14 in. /
43.2 x 35.6 cm

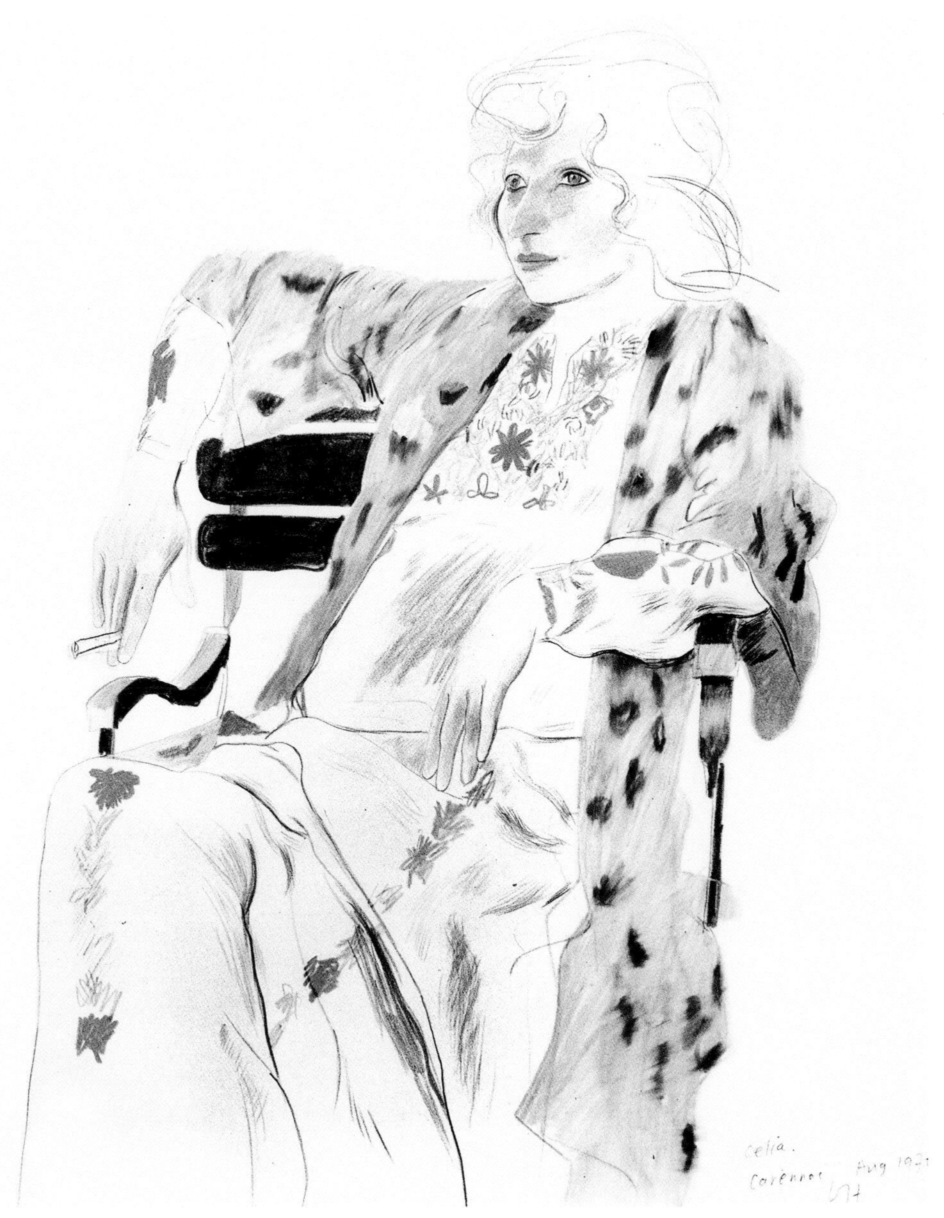

celia.
Carennac Aug 1971

1972

Hockney works on *Portrait of an Artist (Pool with Two Figures)* (pp. 124/125), a painting that shows Peter Schlesinger at the edge of a pool looking down at a figure diving in the water. Begun in the previous year, after their separation, the picture doesn't come easy: "After about four months, it dawned on me what was wrong: it was the angle of the pool which was causing me all the problems. I couldn't alter the water section and it was impossible to adjust it, so I decided to repaint the picture completely." The decision comes late in March, less than two months before Hockney's exhibition at André Emmerich in New York, so he has to act quickly. He travels to Le Nid du Duc to photograph the pool with Mo McDermott as a stand-in for Schlesinger. Back in London, he makes a composite photograph of Schlesinger in a park. Filmmaker Jack Hazan offers the use of his lights so Hockney can paint at night, in exchange for being allowed to film on occasion. He works for 18 hours each day over two weeks: "I literally finished the painting the night before it had to be sent off to the exhibition. I varnished it, and the next morning we got up at six o'clock to begin rolling it. At eight-thirty the men came to collect it to send it off on a plane to New York, and it got there just in time."

At André Emmerich Gallery, Hockney exhibits paintings created since last summer. James Mellow in the *New York Times*: "His current show, like most of his recent shows, is distinctly a performance. He is an artist with a keen eye, both for the social scene in which Pop art made its stand—that is, the world of fashionable and eclectic modern taste—and for the stylistic vagaries of the art world in general." This exploration of style the critic sees best exemplified in *Still Life on a Glass Table* (p. 120): "Looking at its oversimplified bunch of tulips and its single iris in another vase, one also begins to think about the way nature is regularly overhauled to fit some prescribed artistic style."

Hockney begins a double portrait of his friends George Lawson and Wayne Sleep (p. 119), which again proves difficult to finish. It marks the end of his interest in naturalism: "Actually it was only a relatively short period, from 1969 to 1972 or so, where I did a number of paintings in a naturalistic style with a very clear one-point perspective. In fact, it was so clear that the vanishing point was bang in the middle of the canvas…What I was struggling to do, was to make a very clear space. That is what deeply attracts me to Piero, why he interests me so much more than Caravaggio: this clarity in his space that seems so real. Well,

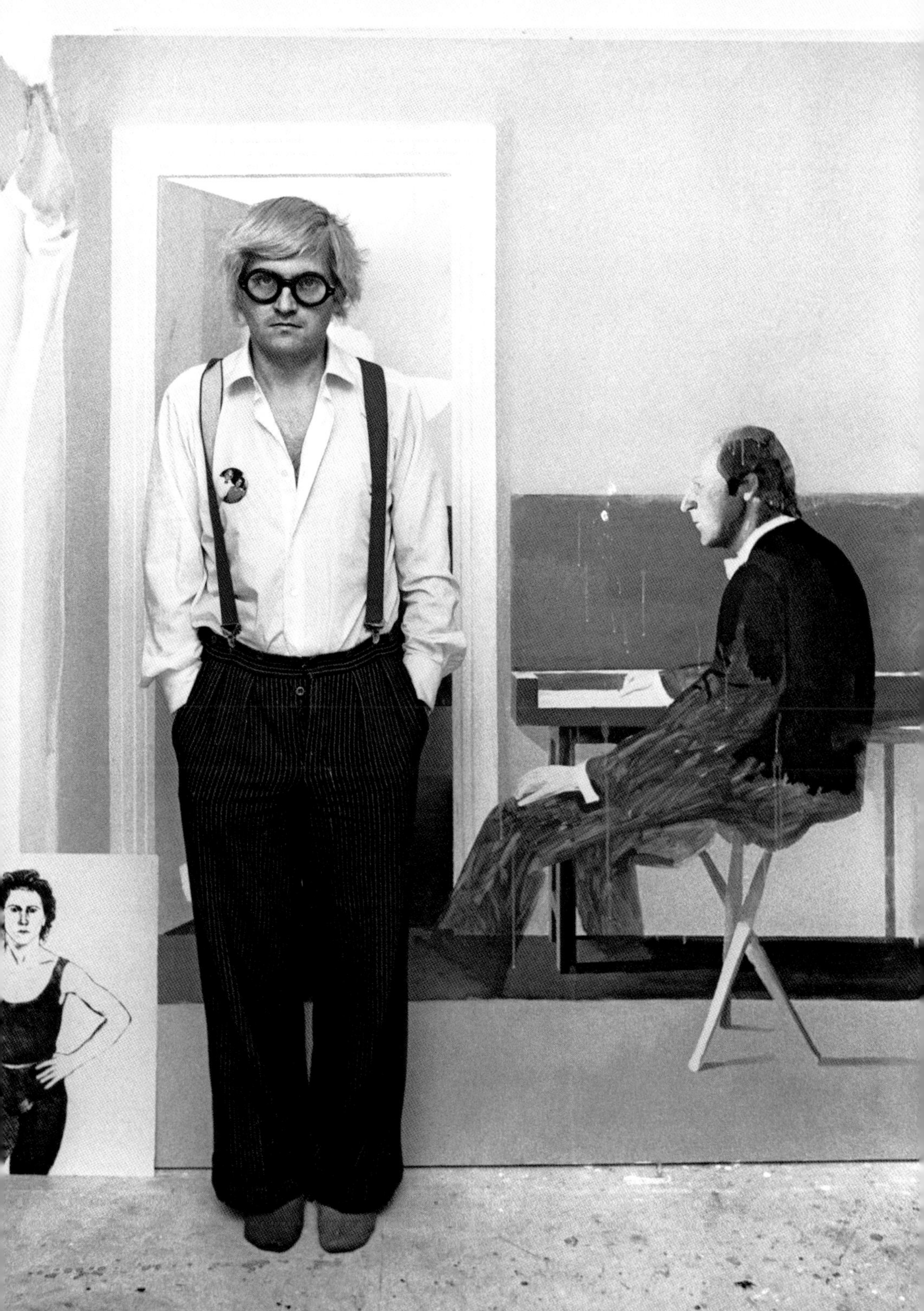

I just couldn't achieve that clarity, frankly; it was a hopeless struggle, and the painting I eventually gave up on was the double portrait of George Lawson and Wayne Sleep, which I never exhibited, though it has been reproduced; it's a very dull picture." As the painting was the planned centerpiece for the closing exhibition of John Kasmin's gallery in London, this ends up looking "rather a wishy-washy show," in the artist's words. Pictures on display include *Japanese Rain on Canvas* (p. 121), for which Hockney has dripped actual water over the painted canvas, and *Mount Fuji and Flowers* (p. 123), where the artist compensates a slight disappointment with the Japanese landscape, encountered on a trip in the previous autumn, through a postcard motif.

Solo: *Grimm's Fairy Tales, Suite of Etchings,* Victoria and Albert Museum, London (Sep 6–Oct 15); catalog with statements by David Hockney. *David Hockney,* Kinsman Morrison Gallery, London (Jan). *David Hockney,* D.M. Gallery, London (Mar). *Paintings and Drawings,* André Emmerich Gallery, New York (May 13–31); catalog. *David Hockney,* Fieldborne Galleries, London (Nov 3–26). *David Hockney,* Kasmin Limited, London (opens Dec 6).

Group: *Reflections,* Mappin Art Gallery, Sheffield (Apr 1–May 7); catalog. *Contemporary Prints,* Ulster Museum, Belfast (Jul 5–Sep 10); catalog.

Film: *Portrait of David Hockney,* GB, 13 min., dir. by David Pearce.

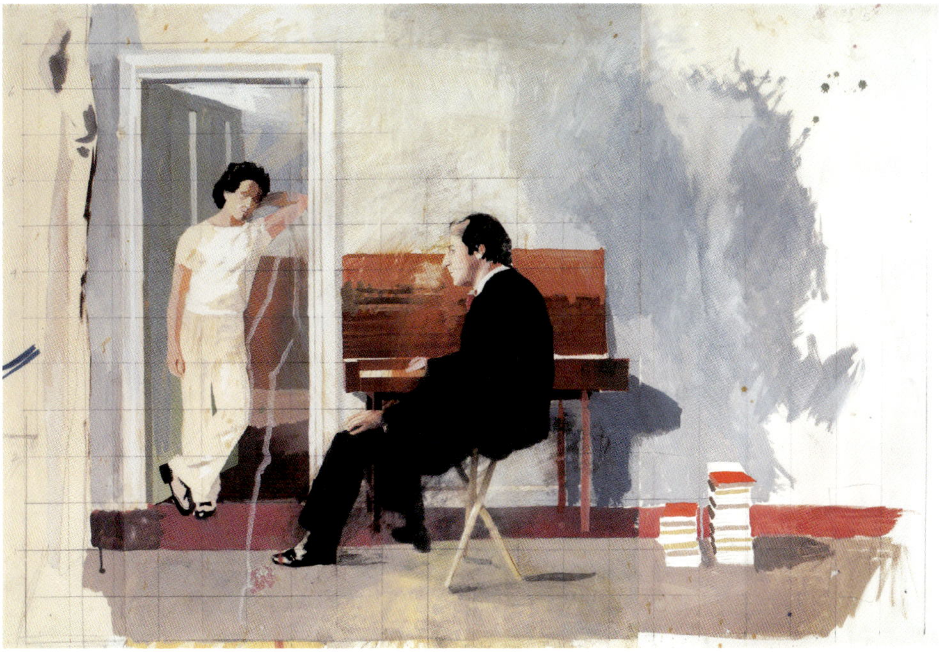

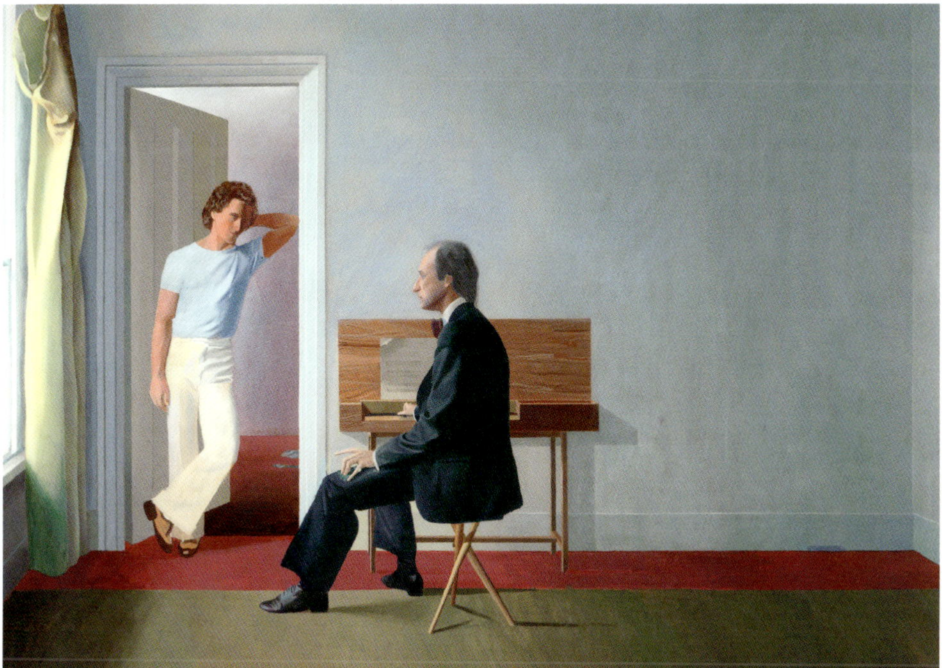

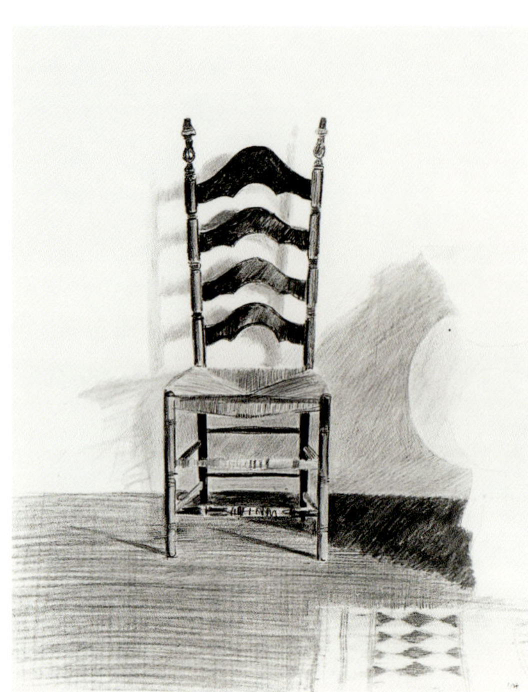

Chair, 1972, crayon on paper,
17 x 14 in. / 43.2 x 35.6 cm

Still Life on a Glass Table, 1971,
acrylic on canvas, 72 x 108 in. /
182.9 x 274.3 cm

Right page: *Japanese Rain on
Canvas,* 1972, acrylic on canvas,
48 x 48 in. / 121.9 x 121.9 cm

Page 117: David Hockney in
front of his unfinished portrait of
George Lawson and Wayne Sleep
in his studio on 17 Powis Terrace,
London 1972. Photo: Bob Collins

Page 119: *Study for George
Lawson and Wayne Sleep,* 1972,
pencil, watercolor, and gouache
on paper, 35 x 52 ½ in. /
88.9 x 133.4 cm

*George Lawson and Wayne
Sleep,* 1972–1975, acrylic on
canvas, 80 x 120 in. /
203.2 x 304.8 cm

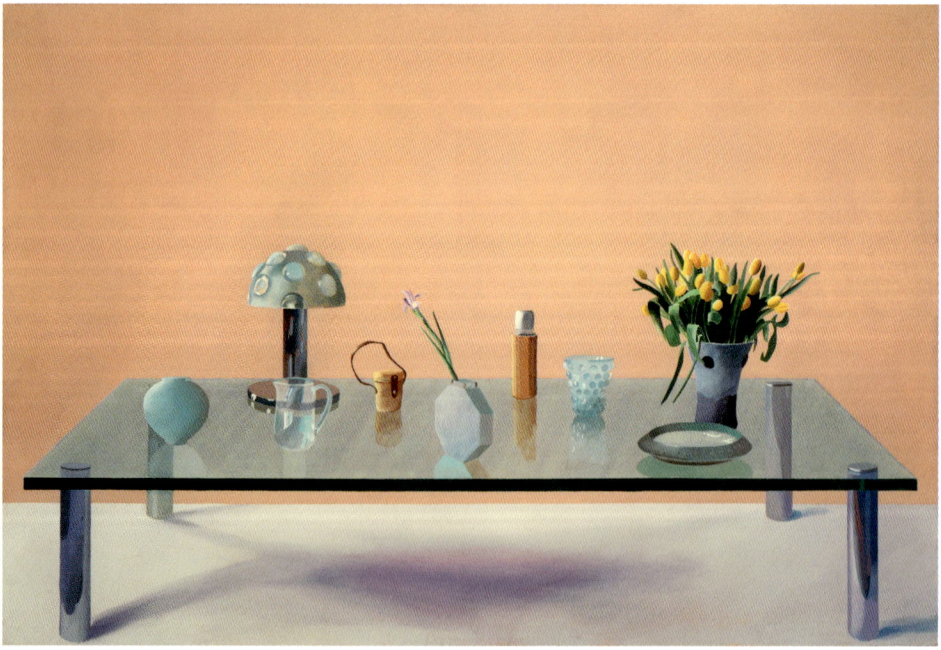

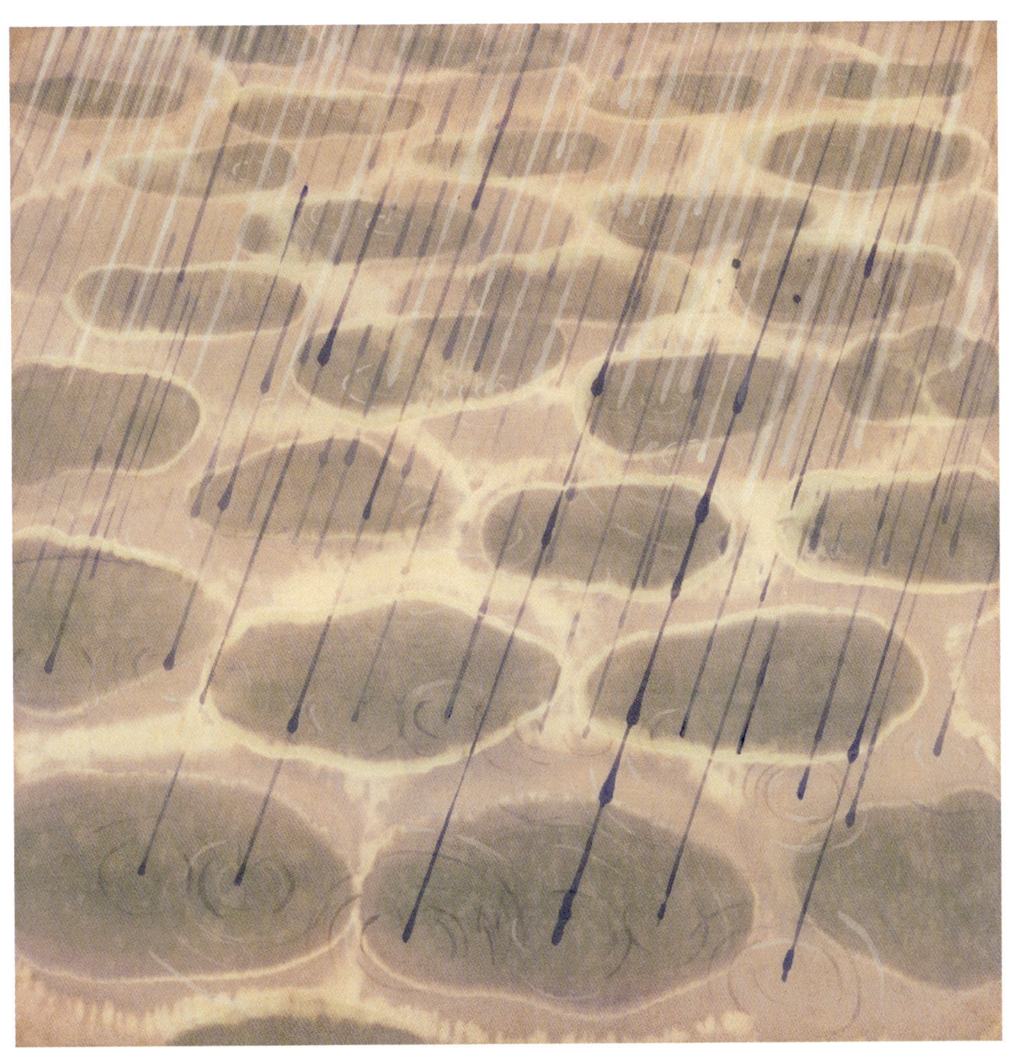

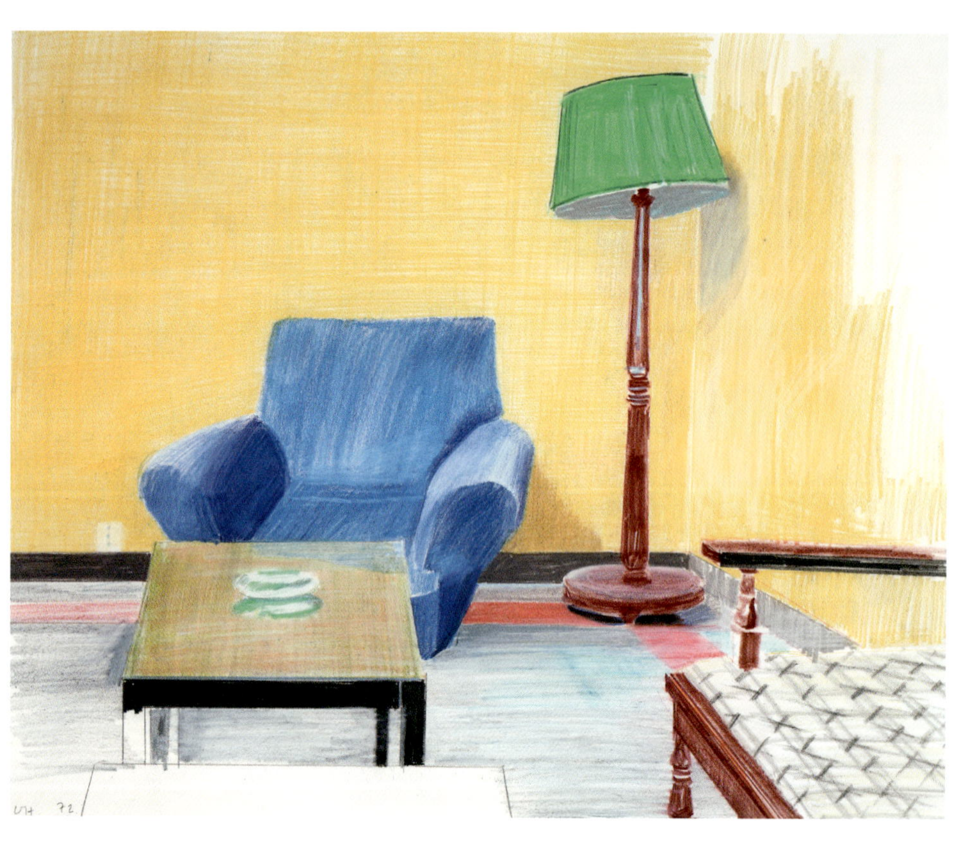

Armchair, Table and Lamp, 1972,
crayon on paper, 14 x 17 in. /
35.6 x 43.2 cm

Right page: *Mt. Fuji and
Flowers,* 1972, acrylic on canvas,
60 x 48 in. / 152.4 x 121.9 cm

Pages 124/125: *Portrait of an
Artist (Pool with Two Figures),*
1972, acrylic on canvas,
84 x 120 in. / 213.4 x 304.8 cm

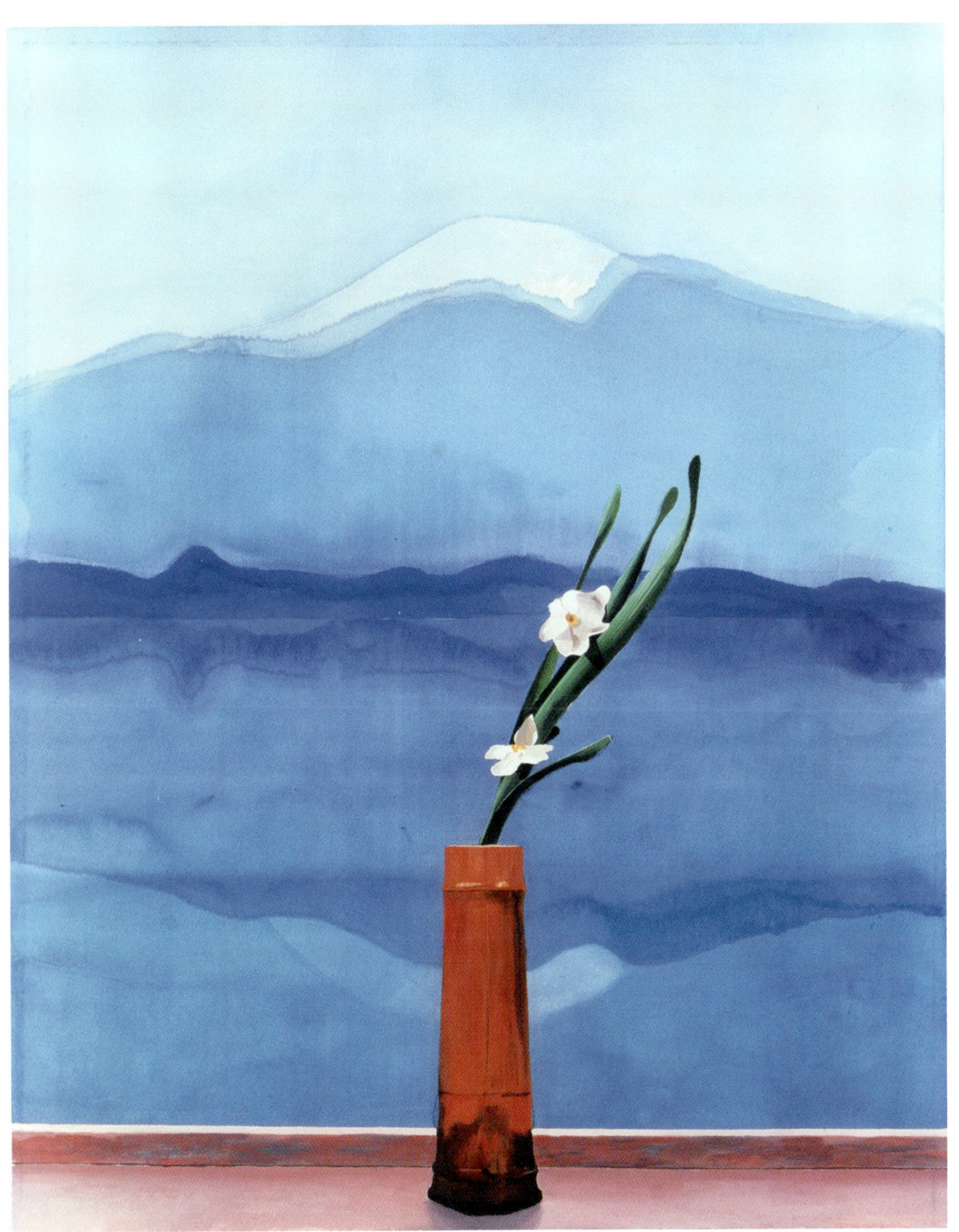

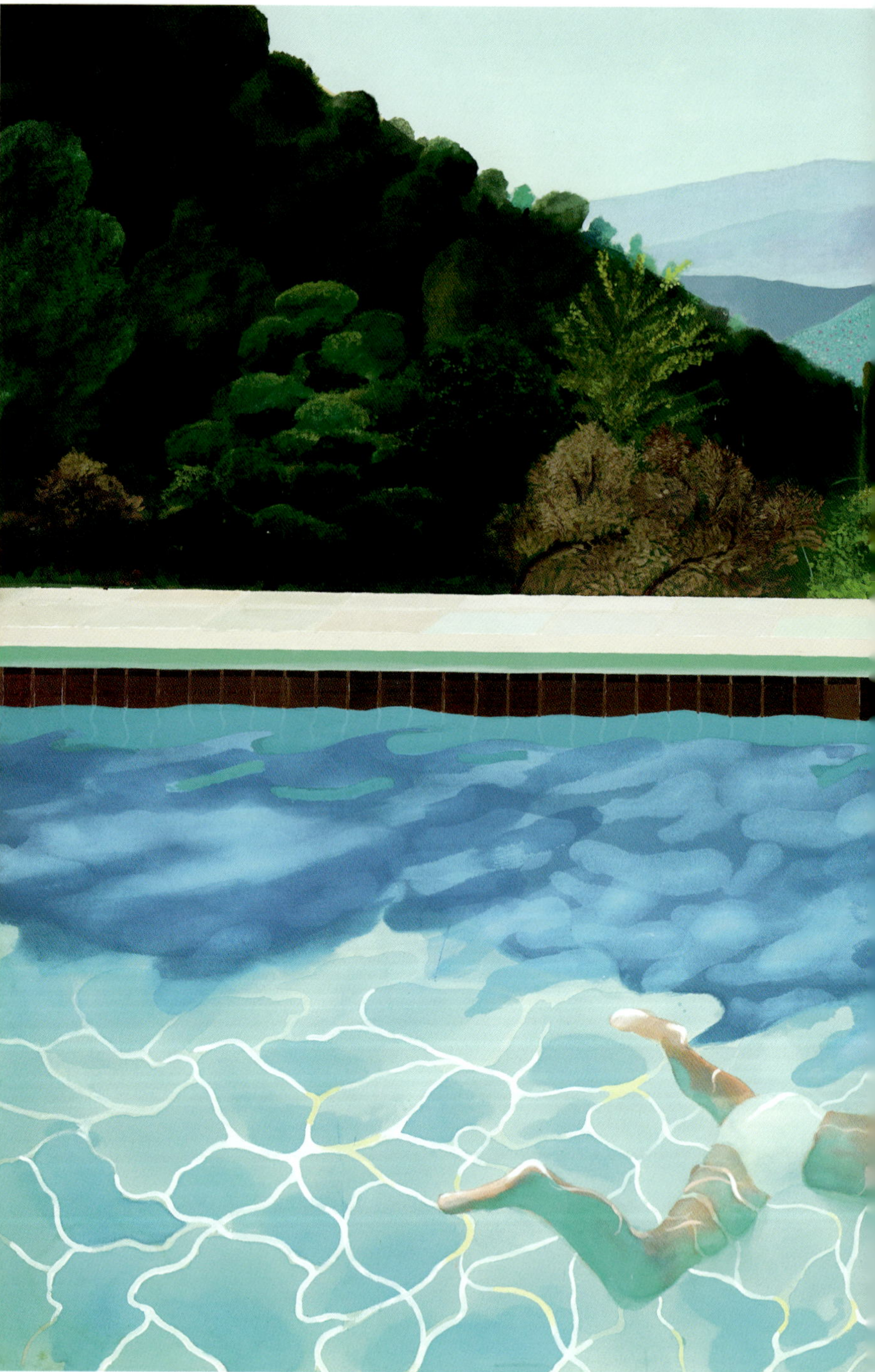

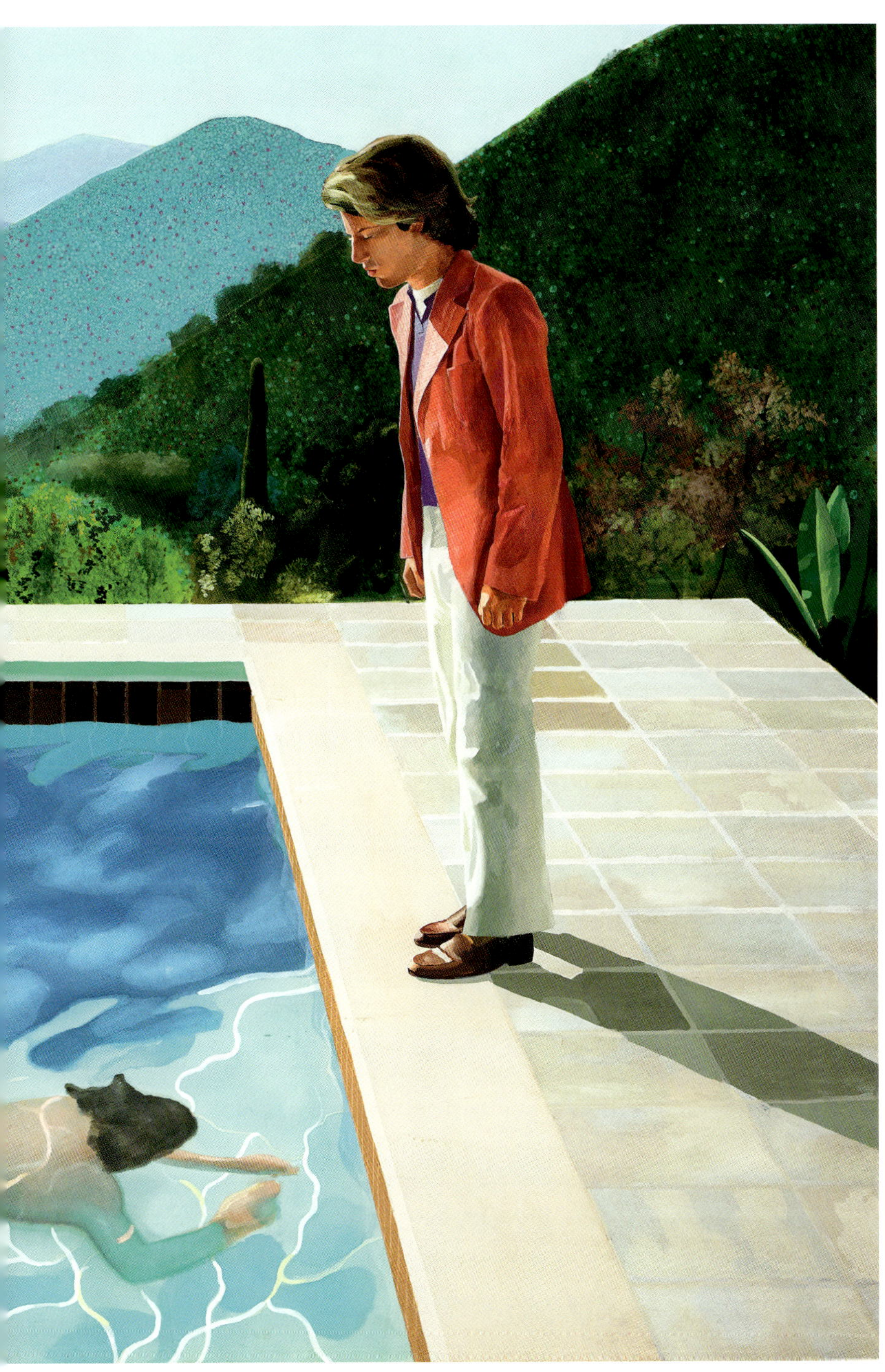

1973

Hockney begins the year in California, producing prints with Ken Tyler at the Gemini workshop in Los Angeles. They experiment with new color lithography techniques to create *The Weather Series* (pp.132–133), influenced by the stylized depiction of weather phenomena in Japanese art. In homage to Tyler, Hockney also portrays him in the lithograph *The Master Printer of Los Angeles* (p. 129). Celia Birtwell comes to visit him with her two young sons, aged three and one and a half, and their nanny, and they live together in a beach house in Malibu. Birtwell and Hockney develop a deep friendship.

When her husband Ossie Clark comes to collect his family, Hockney decides to travel to Paris for a change of air. On the day of his departure he hears that Picasso has died. In Paris, he produces the prints *The Student – Homage to Picasso* and *Artist and Model* (pp. 130, 131) that show him with his hero. For these he has the opportunity to work with Aldo Crommelynck, Picasso's own printer for etchings, who teaches him some technical secrets, like perfecting a technique called the sugar lift and a form of color etching that still allows the artist to work with full spontaneity.

During the summer, Hockney and Henry Geldzahler rent a house near Lucca to write a book on the artist. The project is interrupted when friends and new acquaintances start inviting themselves, including John Kasmin, Mo McDermott, and Eugene Lamb.

After a short time back in London, Hockney moves to Paris for good: "I simply locked up Powis Terrace and went off. I was in a state of confusion and I felt I had to get away from London. That period was very disturbing for me, I had been struggling with the paintings, like the one of George Lawson and Wayne Sleep, which I eventually abandoned. There was something wrong in what I was doing and I had to find out what it was and I needed peace and quiet. It was always hard to get peace and quiet in London. There were always people asking, would you do this, would you talk on that, would you do a television program, would you do the other? I am probably too amiable a person to say no. My way of getting out of it was to go off to Paris."

In Paris, he works on highly finished drawings of new and old friends including Celia Birtwell, the young designer Jean Léger, fashion student Gregory Evans, and Yves-Marie Hervé, a student at the École du Louvre with whom he develops a close relationship. "I spent a lot of time doing quite big portrait

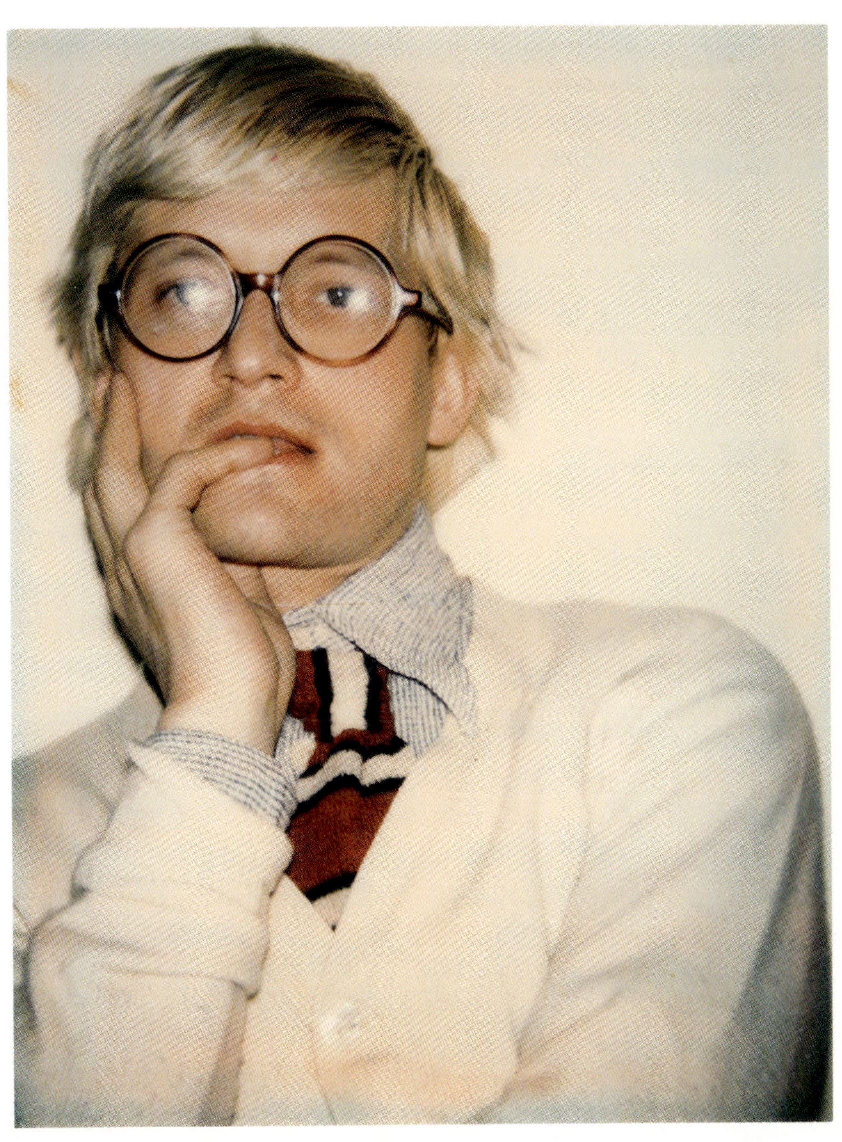

David Hockney, 1973. Photo: Andy Warhol

Page 129: *The Master Printer of Los Angeles,* 1973, lithograph, edition of 27, 47 $^5/_8$ x 31 $^3/_4$ in. / 120.7 x 80.6 cm

drawings," he remembers. "I did them slowly. I would spend two or three days drawing the person slowly, rather academically, sort of 'accurately' in an ordinary sense." Mostly, though, he enjoys the slowed-down mood of his life: "I used to have my breakfast out at the Café de Flore and read the papers, and then after that I'd come back to the flat and paint. I might go out to lunch at one of the little places on the corner—there were loads of places—and then I'd work in the afternoon, and about five or six o'clock I'd walk down to the Café de Flore or Les Deux Magots. At first I thought that old bohemian Paris had gone and then I realized that in fact I was living in the last bit of it."

Solo: *Prints,* Holburne Museum, Bath (Feb 3–Mar 10). *The Weather and Other Lithographs,* André Emmerich Gallery, New York (May 19–Jun 15). *David Hockney,* Jordan Gallery, London (Jul). *David Hockney,* Galerie Herbert Meyer-Ellinger, Frankfurt am Main (Aug–Oct). *Print Retrospective,* M. Knoedler & Co., New York (Oct 18–Nov 28); catalog with a text by Barbara Mathes.

Group: *La peinture anglaise aujourd'hui,* Musée d'art moderne de la Ville de Paris (Feb 7–Mar 11); catalog. *British Artists' Prints of the Sixties: A British Council Exhibition,* Aarhus Kunstmuseum (Apr 14–29); catalog. *Elf englische Zeichner,* Staatliche Kunsthalle Baden-Baden (May 4–Jun 17); travels to Kunsthalle Bremen; catalog. *Henry Moore to Gilbert and George: Modern British Art from the Tate Gallery,* Palais des Beaux-Arts, Brussels (Sep 28–Nov 17); catalog.

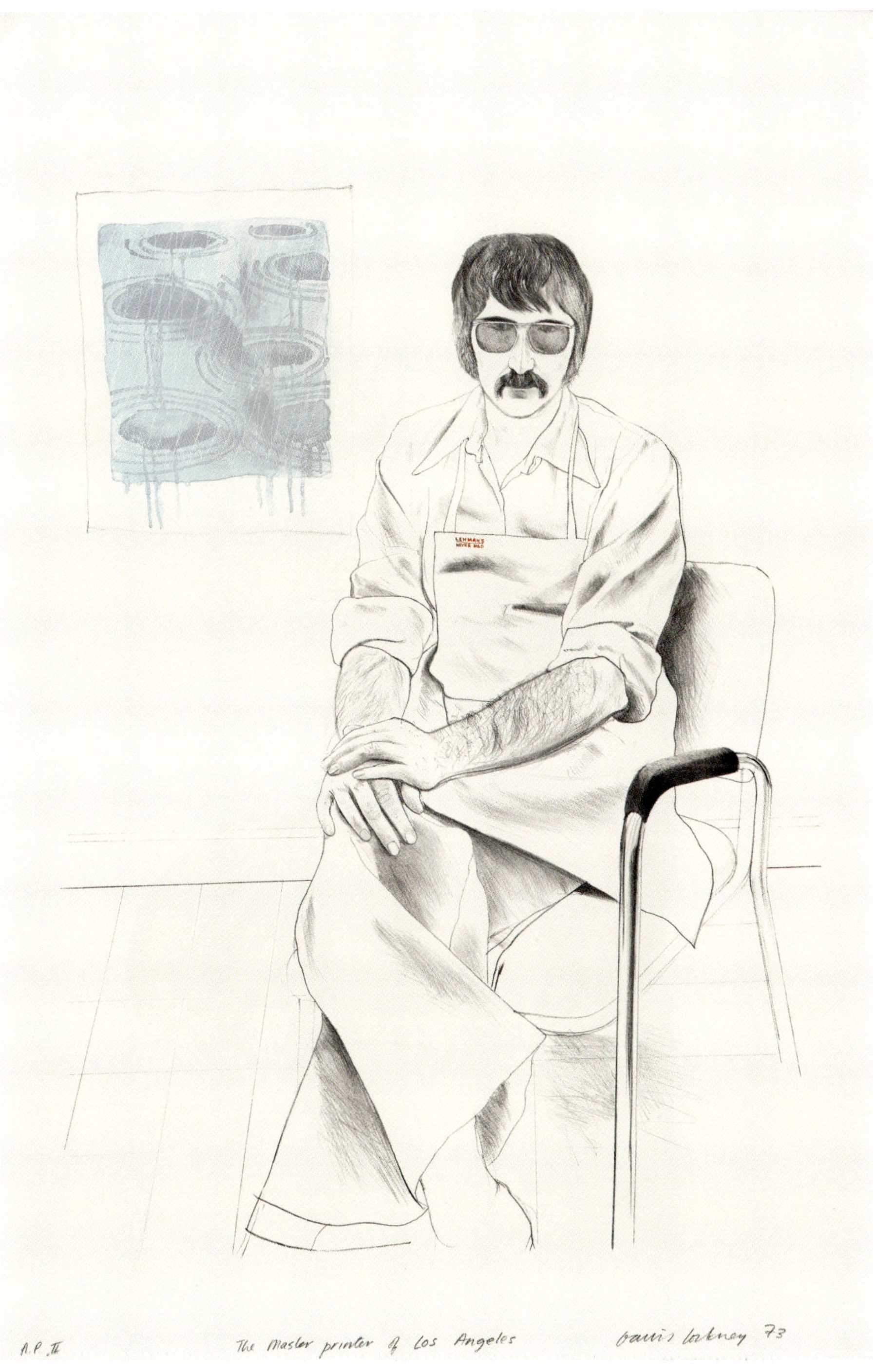
A.P. II
The Master printer of Los Angeles
David Hockney 73

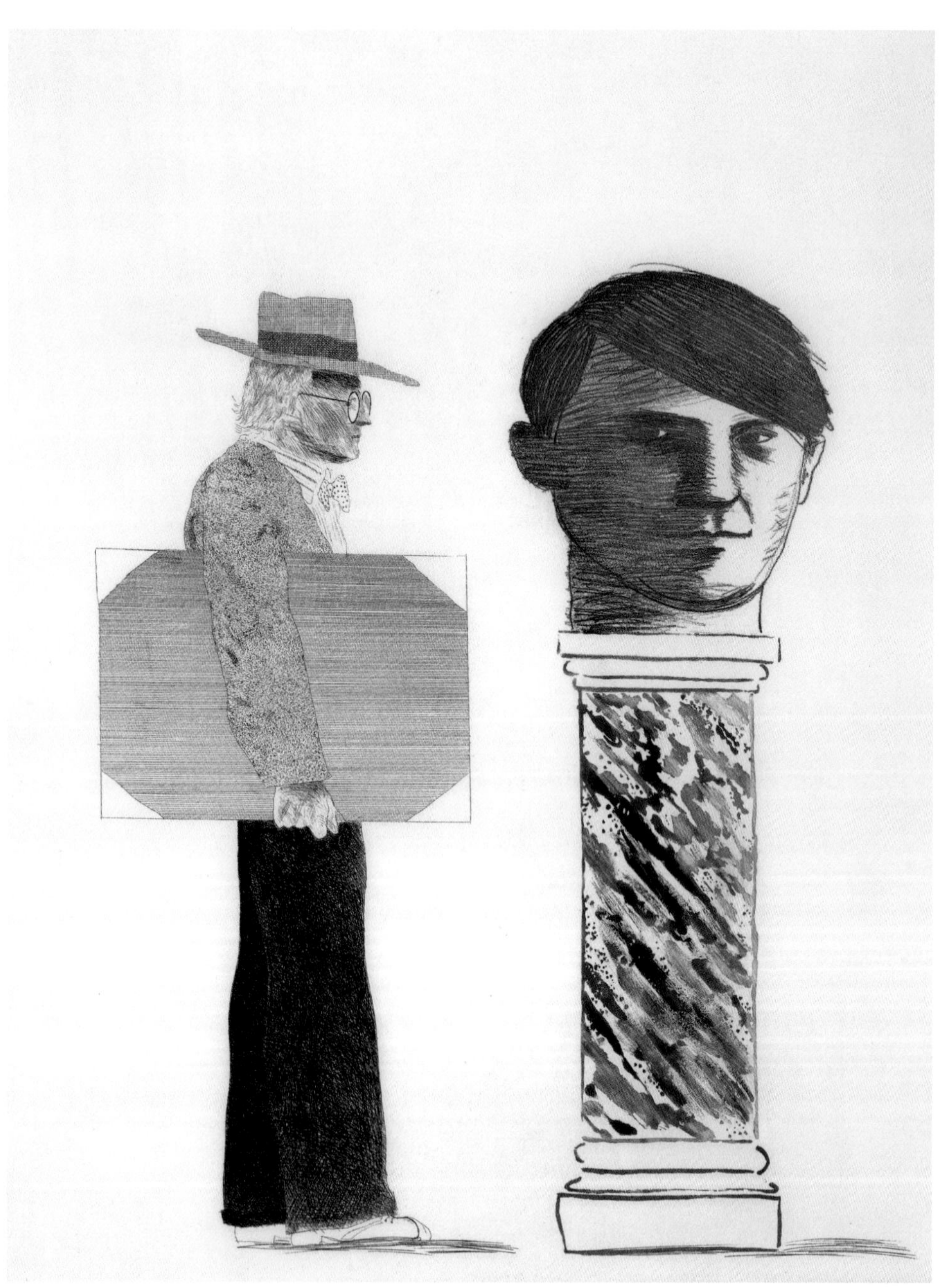

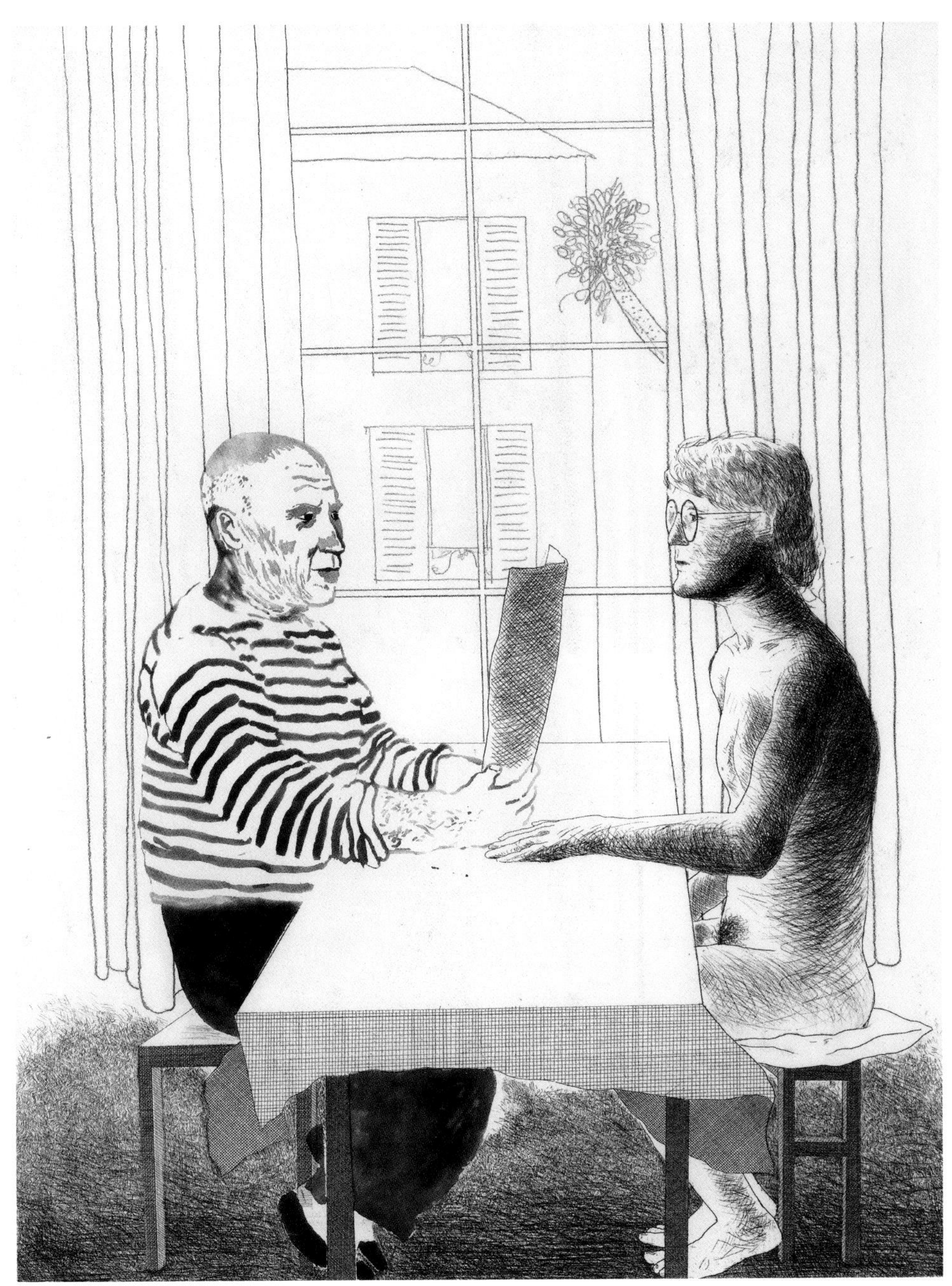

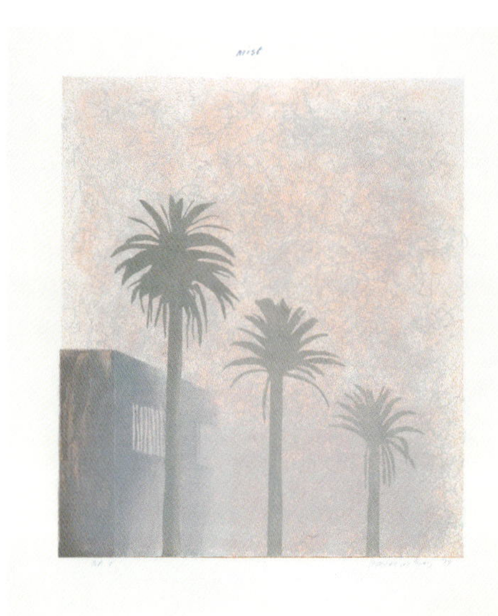

Mist from *The Weather Series,* 1973, lithograph, edition of 98 with 22 proofs, 37 x 32 in. / 94 x 81.3 cm

Rain from *The Weather Series,* 1973, lithograph and screen print, edition of 98 with 25 proofs, 39 x 30 ¹/₂ in. / 99.1 x 77.6 cm

Wind from *The Weather Series,* 1973, lithograph and screen print, edition of 98 with 21 proofs, 40 x 31 in. / 101.6 x 79 cm

Right page: *Sun* from *The Weather Series,* 1973, lithograph and screen print, edition of 98 with 26 proofs, 37 ¹/₂ x 30 ³/₄ in. / 95.5 x 78 cm

Page 130: *The Student: Homage to Picasso,* 1973, etching, edition of 120 with 60 proofs, 29 ³/₄ x 22 ¹/₄ in. / 75.7 x 56.5 cm

Page 131: *Artist and Model,* 1973–1974, etching, edition of 100 with 23 proofs, 22 ¹/₂ x 17 ¹/₄ in. / 57.2 x 48.3 cm

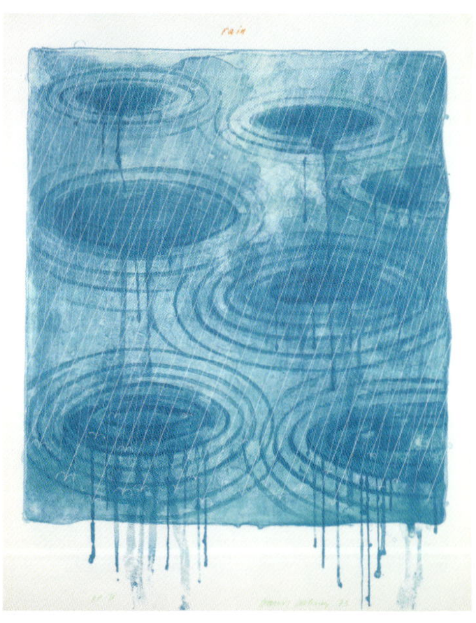

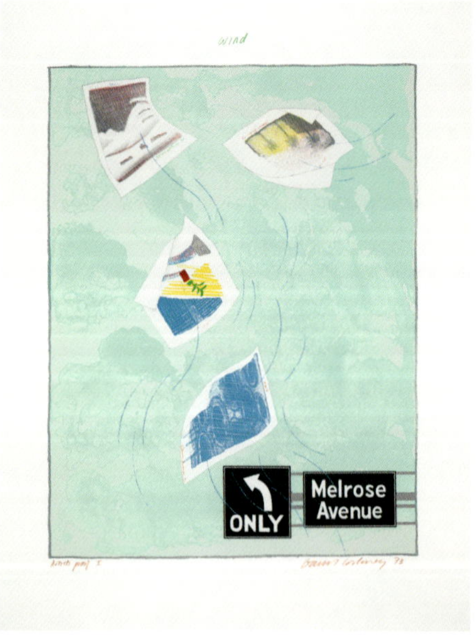

sun

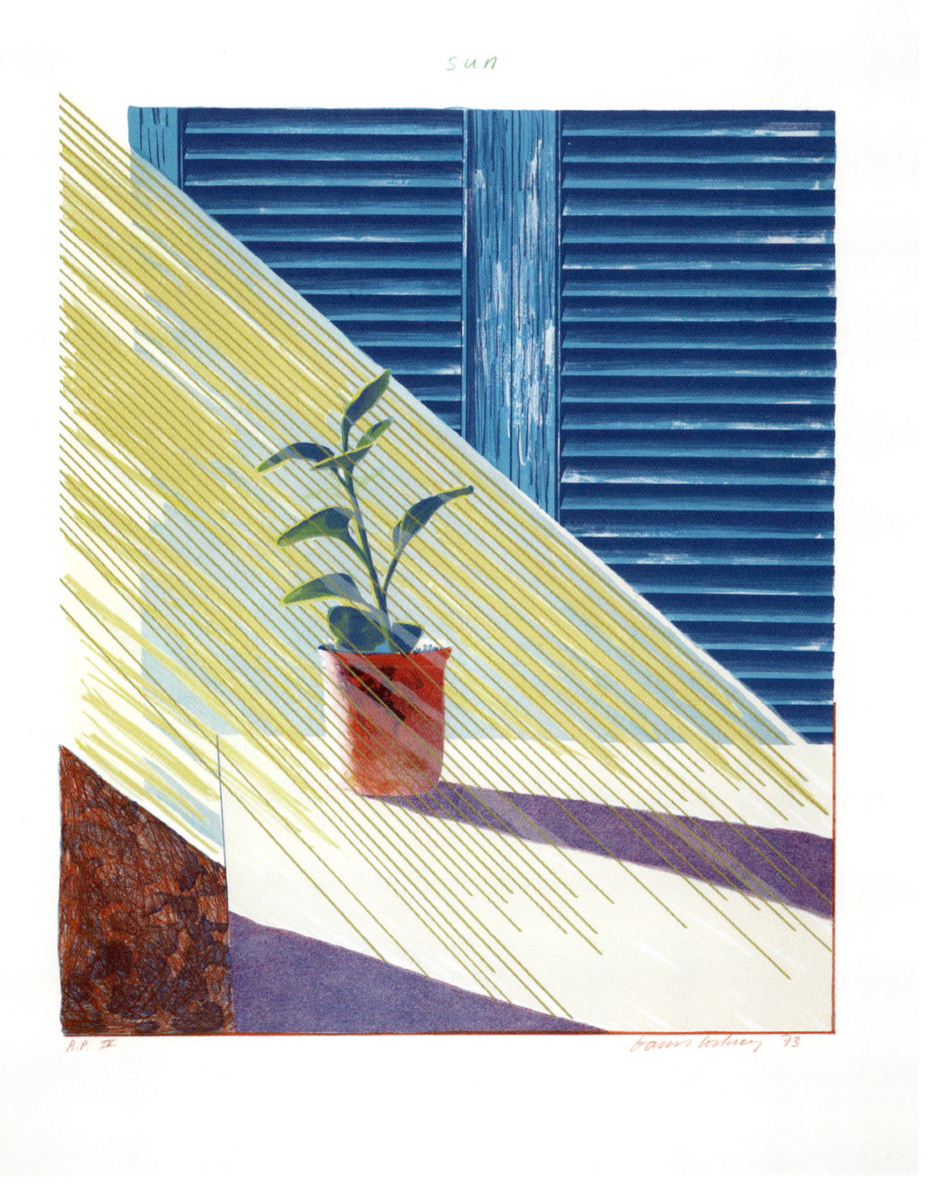

A.P. II
David Hockney 73

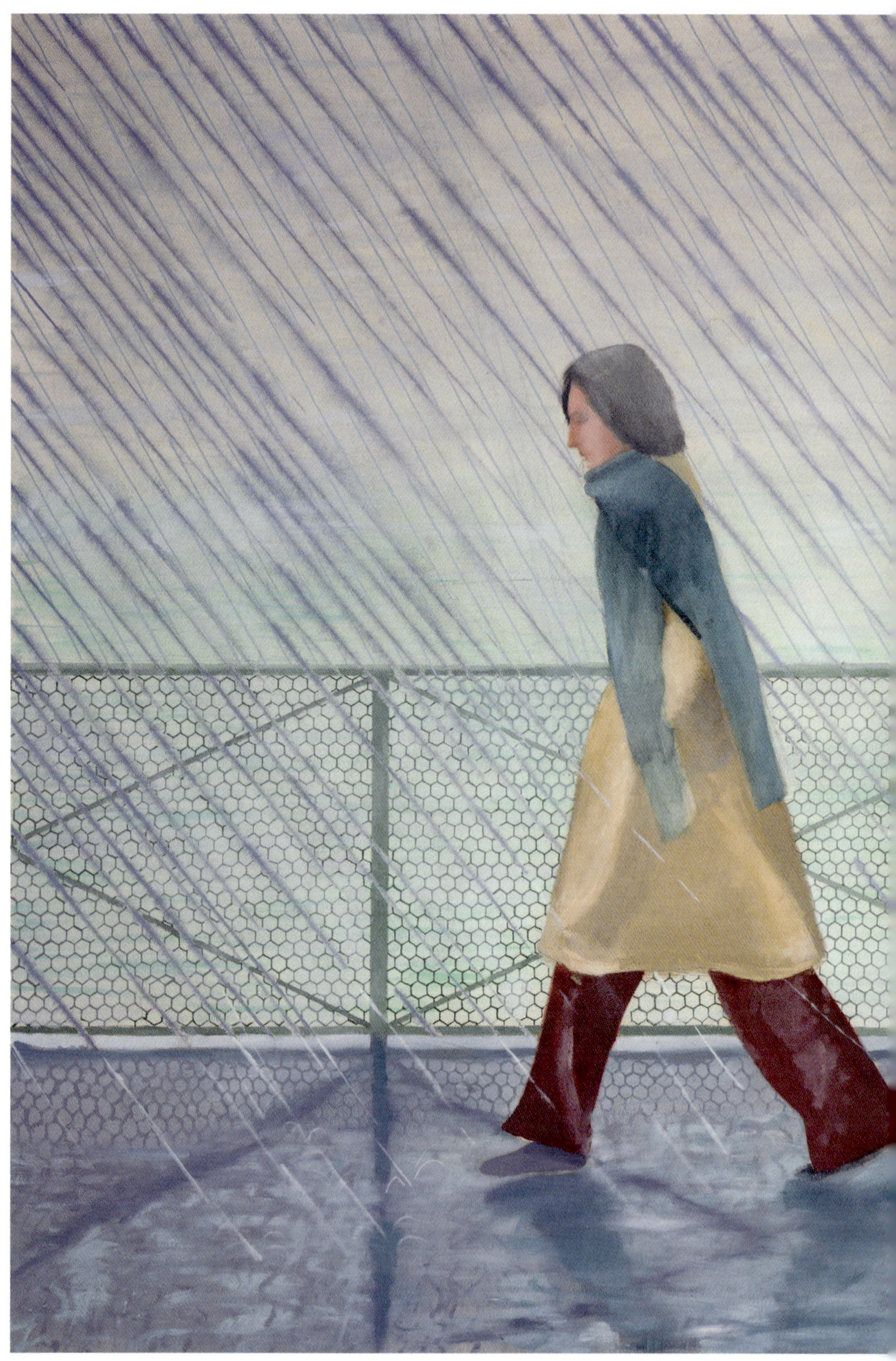

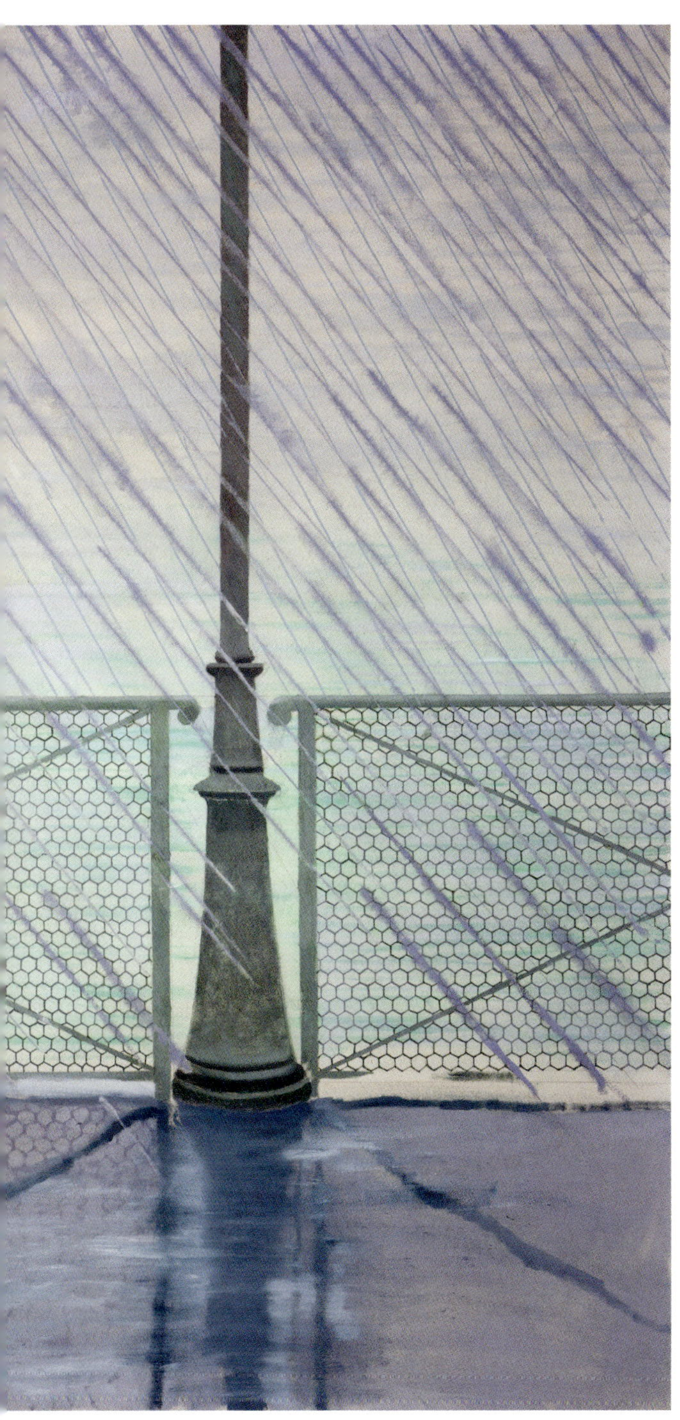

Yves Marie in the Rain, 1973,
oil on canvas, 48 x 60 in. /
121.9 x 152.4 cm

1974

In an interview with Pierre Restany for the catalog to his Paris retrospective at the Musée des Arts Décoratifs in the Louvre, Hockney stresses how much the city has inspired him: "When I left London to come and live and work in Paris, I hadn't the least idea what I was going to paint. I took with me paint, frames, and canvases and set to work. I started a picture based on a drawing done in Italy. I gave it up at the end of six weeks, and went straight on to two new canvases which revealed themselves to be typically Parisian in spirit. It was obvious. I realized as a result that in the paintings and drawings I've done here there is much more of Paris than there is of London in all I've been able to do in London. The reason is simple: it is easier for me to get the necessary detachment in Paris because I don't understand much of the French character or the language. But on the other hand I know how to use my eyes." Asked if he wanted to stay in Paris: "It's much more difficult painting Paris than painting Los Angeles. No-one or hardly anyone has painted Los Angeles whereas Paris has been painted by so many people. By very talented artists, much greater than I am. Also I want to take up the challenge, because it's worth the trouble and I like to make life difficult for myself. If you want to paint anything worthwhile you shouldn't be afraid of stepping up the pressure. That suits me. I'll stay."

He paints a double portrait of Gregory Masurovsky and Shirley Goldfarb (pp. 142/143), two American artists living in Paris: "I was struck by the small studios they've lived in for twenty years, two tiny little rooms…Their relationship is a weird subject: he can't go out of the building without her seeing, but she can…To look at Shirley and Gregory in the studio, I had to remove the wall, as it were. That's why the painting's done as it is. The only way to get the side view of the studio is to take down the wall." While this portrait is still executed in acrylic, his preferred medium for a decade, Hockney returns to oil in two large paintings of windows in the Louvre. The motif for *Contre-Jour in the French Style – Against the Day dans le Style-Français* (p. 139) he finds in an exhibition of French drawings at the Pavillon de Flore: "The first time I went I saw this window with the blind pulled down and the formal garden beyond. And I thought, oh, it's marvelous, marvelous! This is a picture in itself. And then I thought, it's a wonderful subject, and it's very French…perhaps I'll use a more conscious French style: pointillism. It was a way of getting into oil painting again."

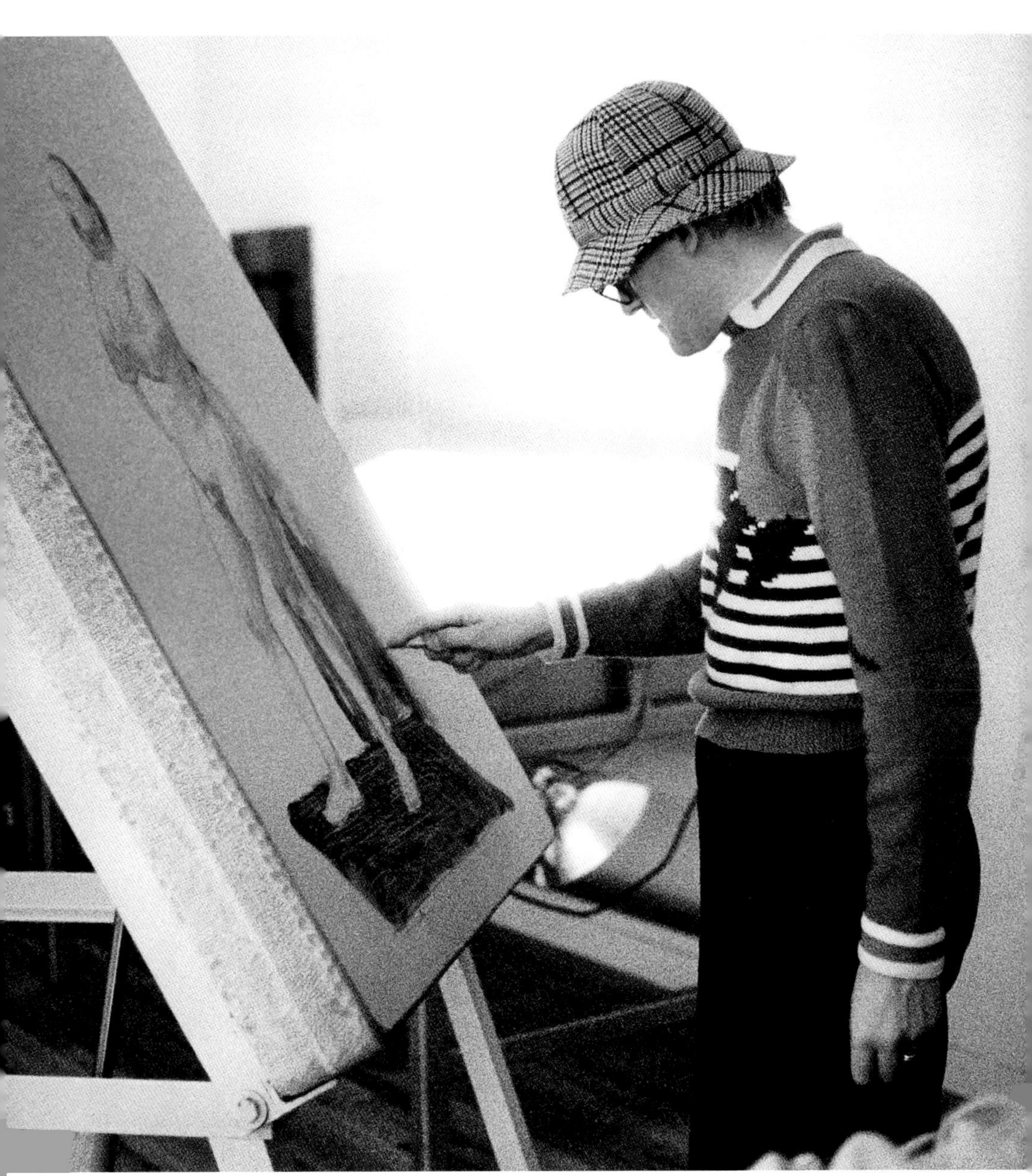

Jack Hazan's film on Hockney, *A Bigger Splash*, is finally released and the artist sees it in London. He is shocked: "I had no idea what this film would be like…We thought it was going to be a 25-minute blurred film with bad sound, that it would be on the Academy Cinema with a Polish version of Shakespeare. We never expected it to be two and a half hours of weeping music." After a showing at the Cannes film festival, David Robinson reports back in the *Times*: "Feature length, it defies classification except that in the broadest terms it is a film portrait of a painter, David Hockney. The film was made over a period of three years, with Hazan and his partner standing by as observers, waiting to snatch on film brief moments when the painter was willing to be filmed and piecing together from the resulting fragments the essence of a personality. The film achieves much more: the images become in a mysterious way an extension of Hockney's own vision. The colours and compositions are those of the paintings. Here is the world of the painter, his friends, his models, and the quiet rooms in which time seems arrested." Robinson also reflects on how uncomfortably close to its subject it gets: "The film centres on the creation of the series of swimming pool paintings and the coincident break-up of the relationship with Peter Schlesinger, the favourite model of four years. Hockney's carefully composed public face protects a very private person; but the significance of the emotional event is exposed in the concern of his friends in his restlessness. Above all, in a sequence where he sketches the boy and the act becomes an assertion of love incomparably more intense than a subsequent scene of physical love-making. This degree of intimacy could be risky, if it were not composed into a portrait so intensely appreciative of the man as artist, the artist as man, and the style of both."

After viewing the film, Hockney hardly can bear the thought that it will be shown again in front of audiences all over the world. "Then I thought, the photography was stunning; but I was still worked up about it. I didn't know what to do. The guy's spent four years making it, a lot of his own money, you can't do anything about it. I realized I couldn't say, 'You can't show the film,' no matter what I thought. It was a problem." In the end they find a similarity between their approaches: "I'm painting this picture of Gregory and Shirley and it's nearly finished," Hockney recounts. "Jack looks at it, quite fascinated, and says, 'You see, David, that's what you do all the time; look at what you're doing to them.' And

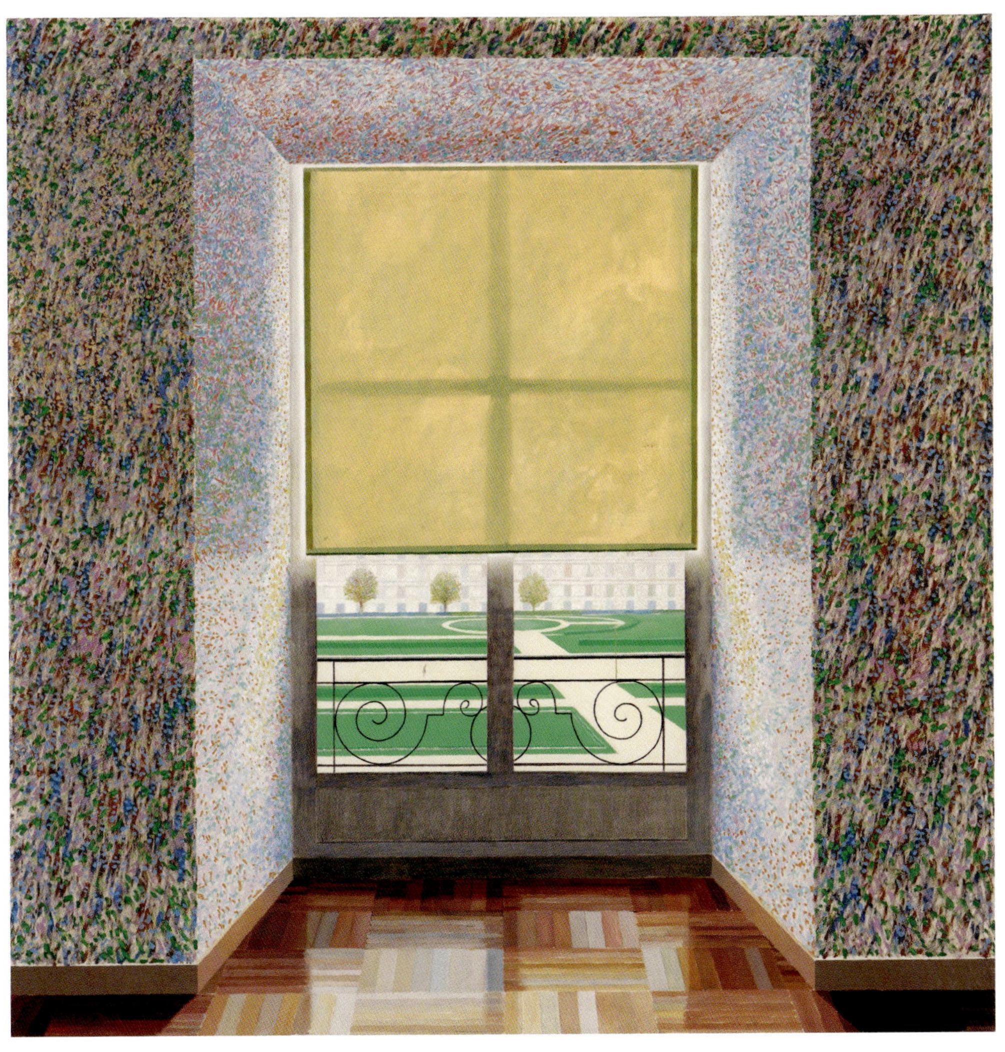

Contre-Jour in the French Style – Against the Day dans le Style-Français, 1974, oil on canvas, 72 x 72 in. / 182.9 x 182.9 cm

Page 137: David Hockney drawing Henry Geldzahler on lithographic stone (print never editioned), Tyler Workshop, Bedford Village, NY, 1974. Photo: Kenneth Tyler

I said, 'I know, I see your point; if Shirley and Gregory say, We don't like that picture, I'm not going to destroy it.'"

After its screening at Cannes, the film is shown in Paris and becomes a success among cineasts. Part of the success is the opening of the retrospective *David Hockney: Tableaux et dessins* at the Musée des Arts décoratifs, where the audience can see the originals of the pictures painted in the film.

In autumn, Hockney receives an invitation to design the stage for Igor Stravinsky's opera *The Rake's Progress* at Glyndebourne Festival Opera under the direction of John Cox. He accepts, and to make the first designs travels to Chateau Marmont in Hollywood (where Stravinsky himself had stayed) along with his assistant Mo McDermott. "Mo advised me straight away to make models, because, he said, if you only make a drawing, somebody else then translates it into the space. The moment he said that I thought, I don't want anybody else to do that, I want to do that myself. So I thought, I will make scale models. I wanted pictorialism, I wanted to bring my own attitudes to sets."

Hockney begins a relationship with Gregory Evans, an American fashion student also enjoying life in Paris, and together they travel to Italy.

Solo: *Tableaux et dessins*, Musée des Arts décoratifs, Paris (Oct 11–Dec 9); catalog with a text by Stephen Spender and an interview by Pierre Restany. *David Hockney*, Kinsman Morrison Gallery, London (Jan–Feb). *Print Retrospective*, D.M. Gallery, London (Mar 7–30). *A Loan Exhibition of Recent Drawings*, Garage Art Limited, London (Jul 3–27). *Drawings*, Dayton's Gallery 12, Minneapolis (Oct 15–Nov 14); catalog. *A Collector's Christmas*, Knoedler Contemporary Prints, New York (Nov 30–Dec 24). *Drawings, Etchings and Lithographs*, La Medusa Grafica, Rome (Dec). *David Hockney*, Michael Walls, New York (Dec).

Film: *A Bigger Splash*, GB, 106 min., dir. by Jack Hazan, written by Jack Hazan and David Mingay, starring David Hockney, Peter Schlesinger, Celia Birtwell, Henry Geldzahler, Mo McDermott, John Kasmin, Ossie Clark, and many others.

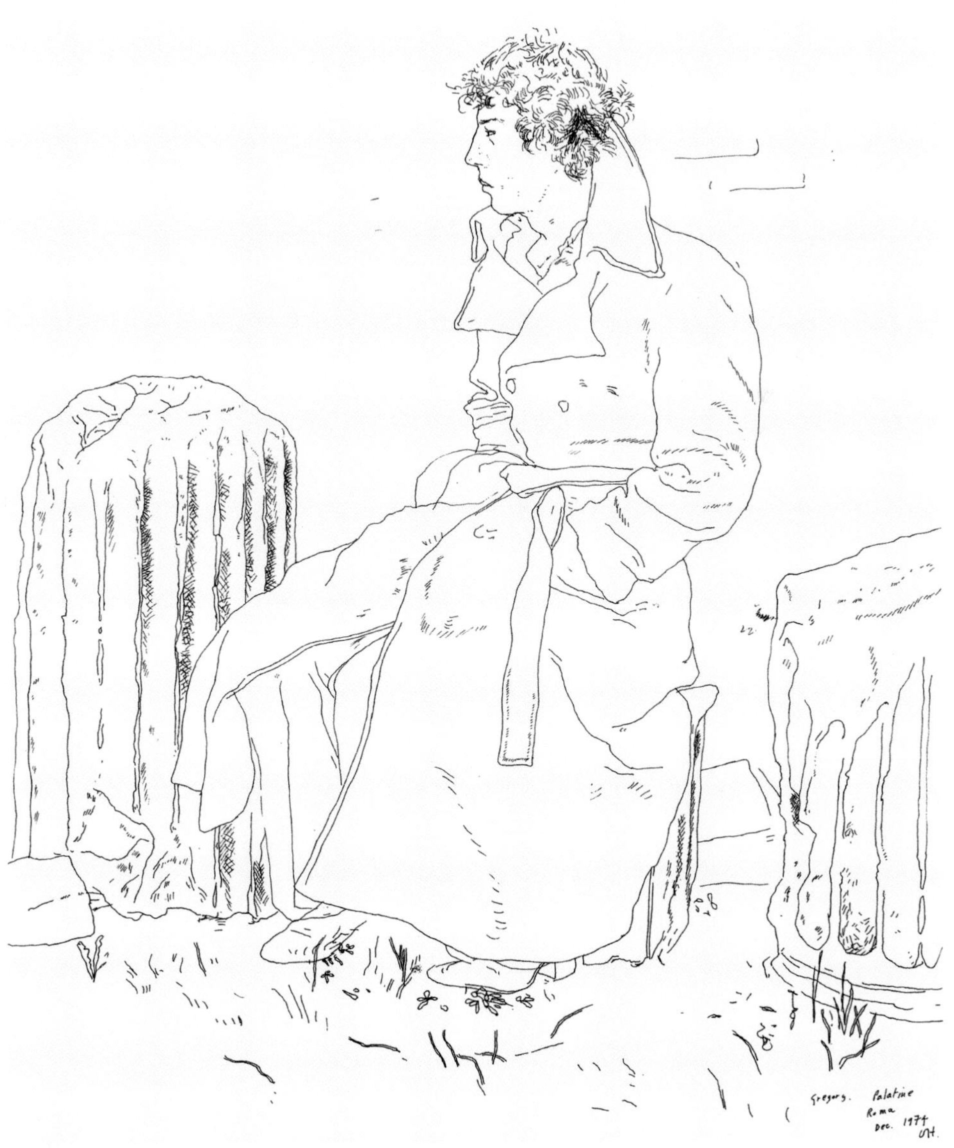

Gregory, Palatine, Roma. Dec. 1974,
ink on paper, 17 x 14 in. / 43.2 x 35.6 cm

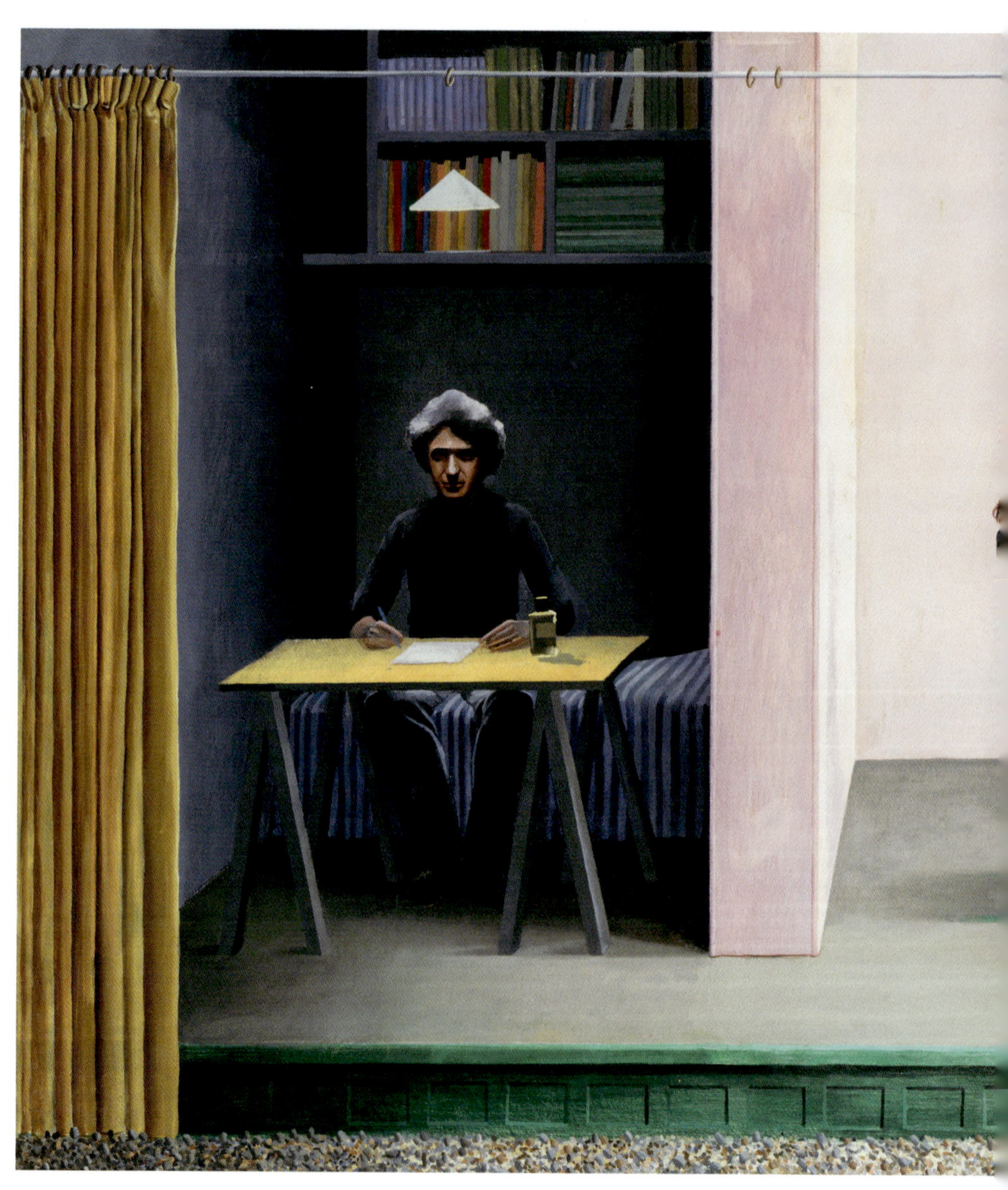

Shirley Goldfarb and Gregory Masurovsky,
1974, oil on canvas, 45 x 84 in. /
114.3 x 213.4 cm

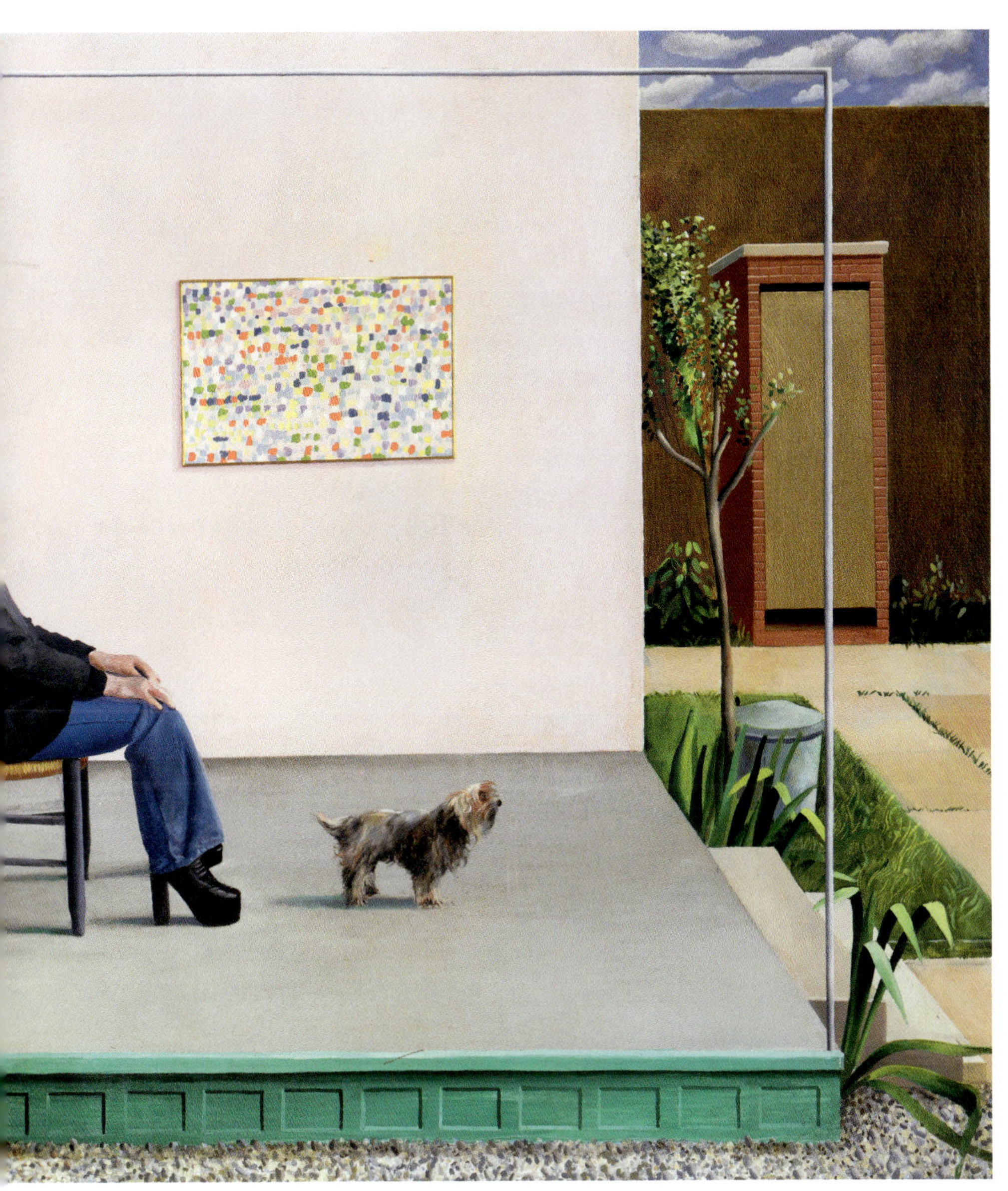

1975

Hockney continues drawing his friends and in an exhibition at Galerie Claude Bernard in Paris in March shows studies of Gregory Evans from their trip to Italy as well as intimate portraits of Celia Birtwell, Yves-Marie Hervé, Henry Geldzahler, and his parents. Meanwhile the Glyndebourne Festival Opera builds Hockney's stage designs for *The Rake's Progress* (pp. 150–151). This requires special attention since the decorations depend on large cross-hatchings in homage to Hogarth's original print cycle: "I had even gone down to Glyndebourne to decide what scale the crosshatching should be for the theater. If it was too small you wouldn't see it, if too big it would be a dominating pattern." The opera premieres in June and is an immediate audience success. Reviews are divided, though (while in the long run this production would prove a classic to be revived again 35 years after its premiere). In the *Times,* William Mann describes the production as "dominated by the new settings of David Hockney who has gone back to Hogarth's engravings, analyzed their technical features, then stirred those around in the cauldron of his imagination until a new synthesis emerged…The technique of cross-hatching results in striped wigs, trees which might almost be human legs wearing tight check trousers, and an entrancing picture-gallery morning room for Tom in London…The effect is more Hockney than Hogarth, particularly in the brothel scene where Mother Goose presides, a monstrous praying mantis upon a huge bed, over her staff and customers who crawl into tiny toy cupboards for enjoyment; and in Bedlam (a visual counterpart to the brothel), where the inmates in their boxes look rather like battery fowls. Hockney's approach, even while stealing prime attention, is well suited to the icy artificiality and mannered wit of the Auden-Kallman libretto and the emotional pendulum of Stravinsky's music; and it makes the ideal background for John Cox's barbed, scrupulously characterized and timed production which revels in the absurdities of the action."

Returning to Paris inspired by his work for the stage, Hockney paints *Invented Man Revealing Still Life* (p. 149) and *Kerby (After Hogarth) Useful Knowledge* (p. 147), a riff on Hogarth's etching for Joshua Kerby's 18th-century treatise on perspective: "I never read Kerby's treatise but I think the frontispiece was just Hogarth's joke…Perhaps he's trying to show you can do all the perspective wrong and the picture'll still look right. He uses reversed perspective; things are smaller at the front and bigger at the back. My painting is a transcription

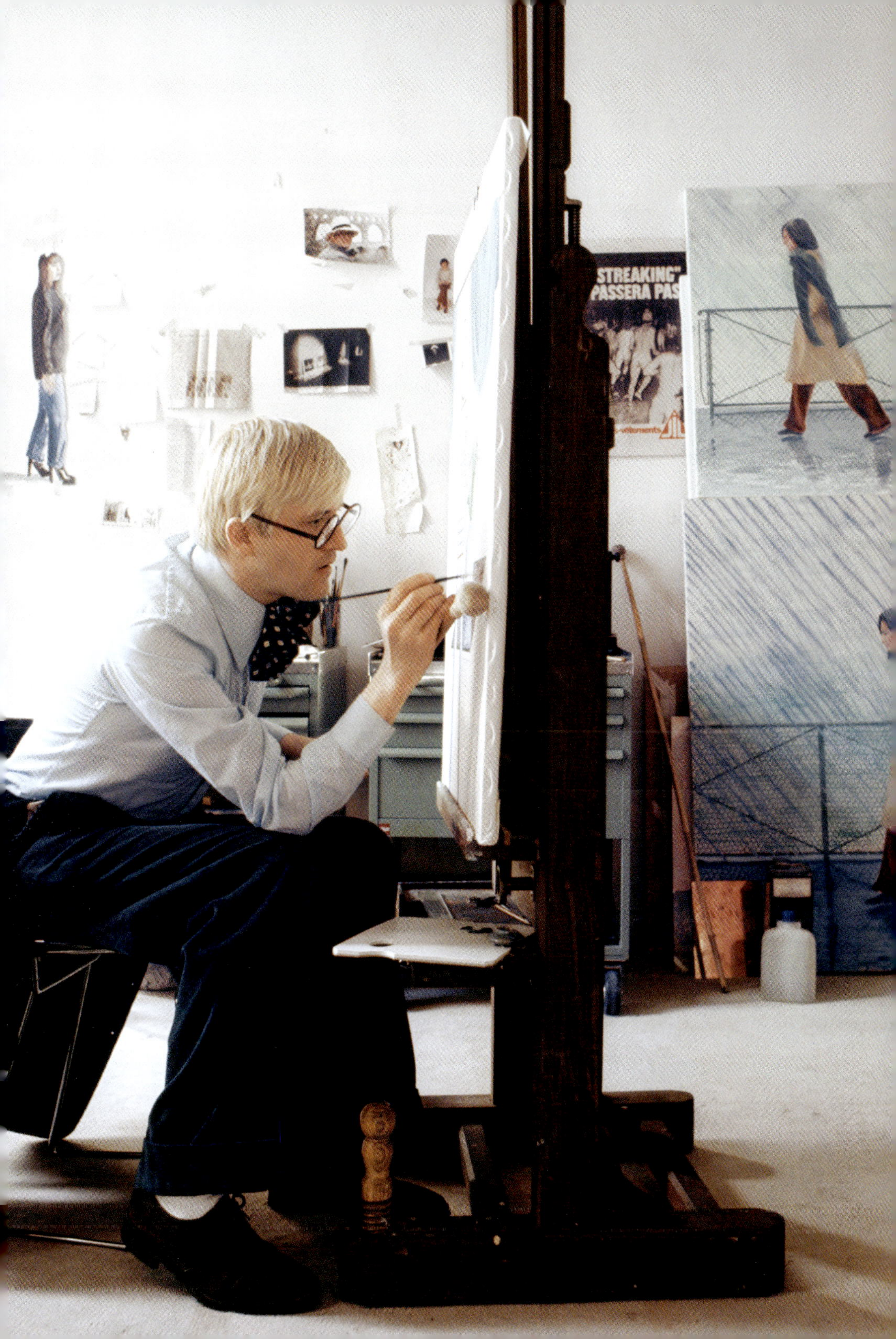
"STREAKING"
PASSERA PAS
vêtements

of his black and white engraving into paint." These paintings mark Hockney's departure from naturalism, and questions of perspective will occupy him for a long time.

In summer he travels to a gay resort on Fire Island close to New York with Henry Geldzahler. Back in Paris, he quickly tires of life there, and in November he packs up his studio and moves to London. Unhappy with his old home in Powis Terrace, he finds new lodgings and studio in Pembroke Gardens in West London. This appears like a happy development: "Not too many people knew I was there. Each time you move back you have a nice period when it's quiet, the phone doesn't ring much, you can get on with work and see only a few friends…I started feeling much better."

Solo: *Early Works*, Alberta College of Art Gallery, Calgary (Jun 6–29). *Designs for The Rake's Progress*, Manchester City Art Gallery, Manchester (Oct 8–26). *Schilderijen, tekeningen en prenten*, Nijmeegs Museum, Nijmegen (Oct 17–Nov 23); catalog with a text by F.J.G. van der Grinten. *David Hockney*, Dorothy Rosenthal Gallery, Chicago (Mar). *Dessins et gravures*, Galerie Claude Bernard, Paris (Apr 15–May 24); catalog. *Drawings and Selected Prints*, Margo Leavin Gallery, Los Angeles (Sep 9–Oct 4).

Group: *Druckgraphik der Gegenwart 1960–1975*, Kupferstichkabinett Berlin (Jun 20–Aug 24); catalog. *European Painting in the Seventies: New Work by Sixteen Artists*, LA County Museum of Art, Los Angeles (Sep 30–Nov 23); travels to Saint Louis and Madison; catalog. *Contemporary British Drawings*, Museu de Arte Moderna, São Paulo (Oct 17–Dec 5); touring exhibition organized by the British Council; travels to Brasilia, Rio de Janeiro, Buenos Aires, Bogota, Mexico City, and Caracas; catalog.

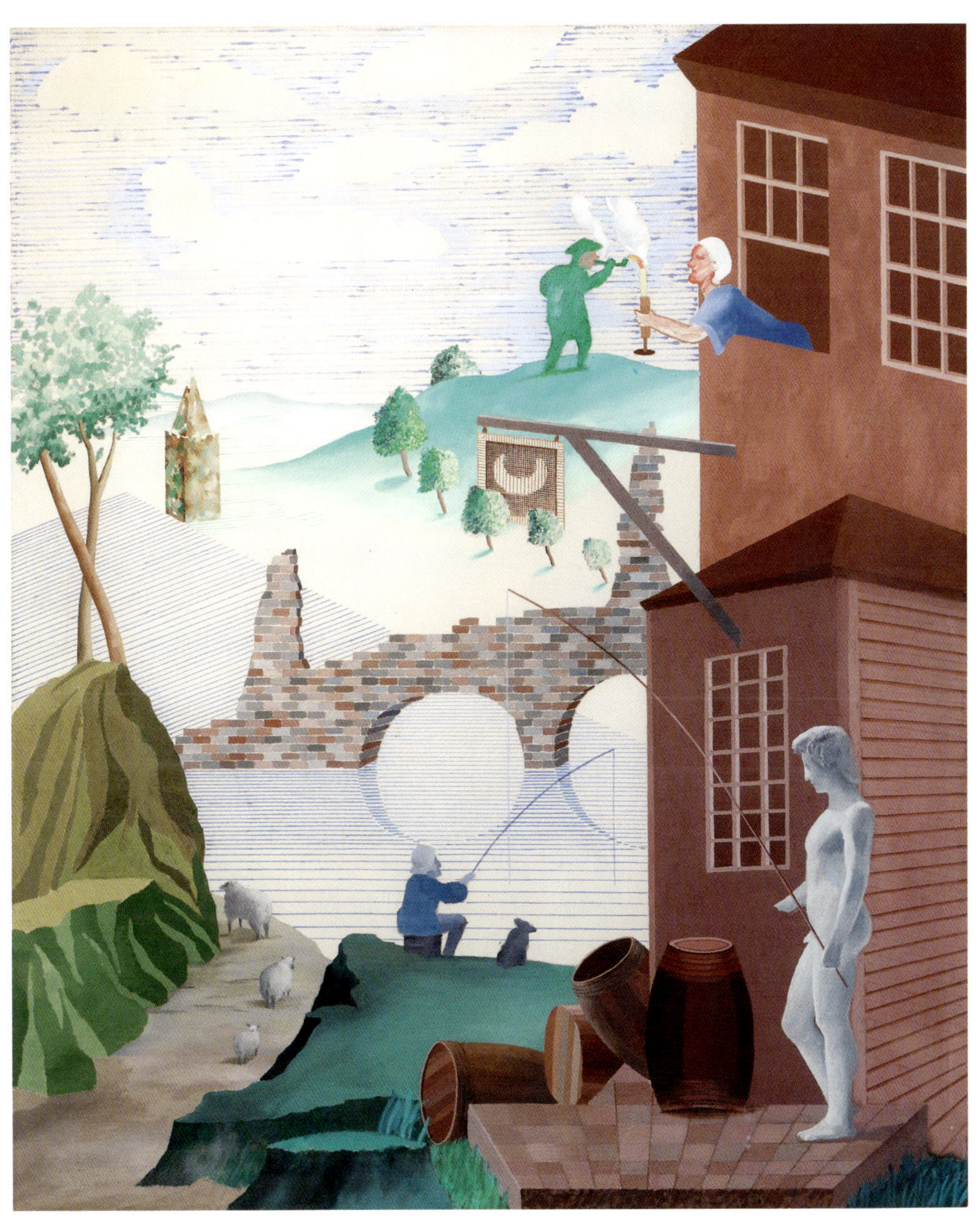

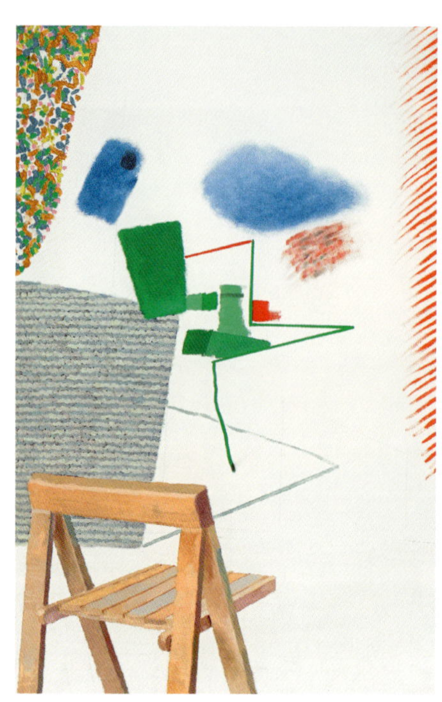

Chair with Photograph, 1975,
oil and pencil on canvas, 36 x 24 in. /
91.4 x 61 cm

Study for "Septentrion," 1975,
pencil and colored pencil on paper,
14 x 17 in. / 35.6 x 43.2 cm

Right page: *Invented Man Revealing
Still Life,* 1975, oil on canvas,
36 x 28 ¹/₂ in. / 91.4 x 72.4 cm

Page 145: David Hockney in
his studio, Paris 1975.
Photo: Dmitri Kasterine

Page 147: *Kerby (After Hogarth)
Useful Knowledge,* 1975, oil on
canvas, 72 x 60 in. / 182.9 x 152.4 cm

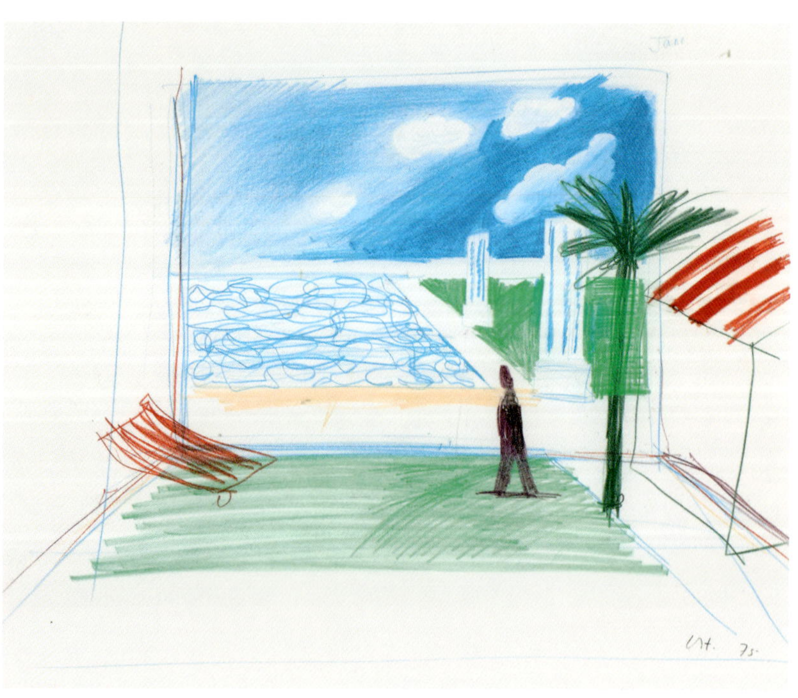

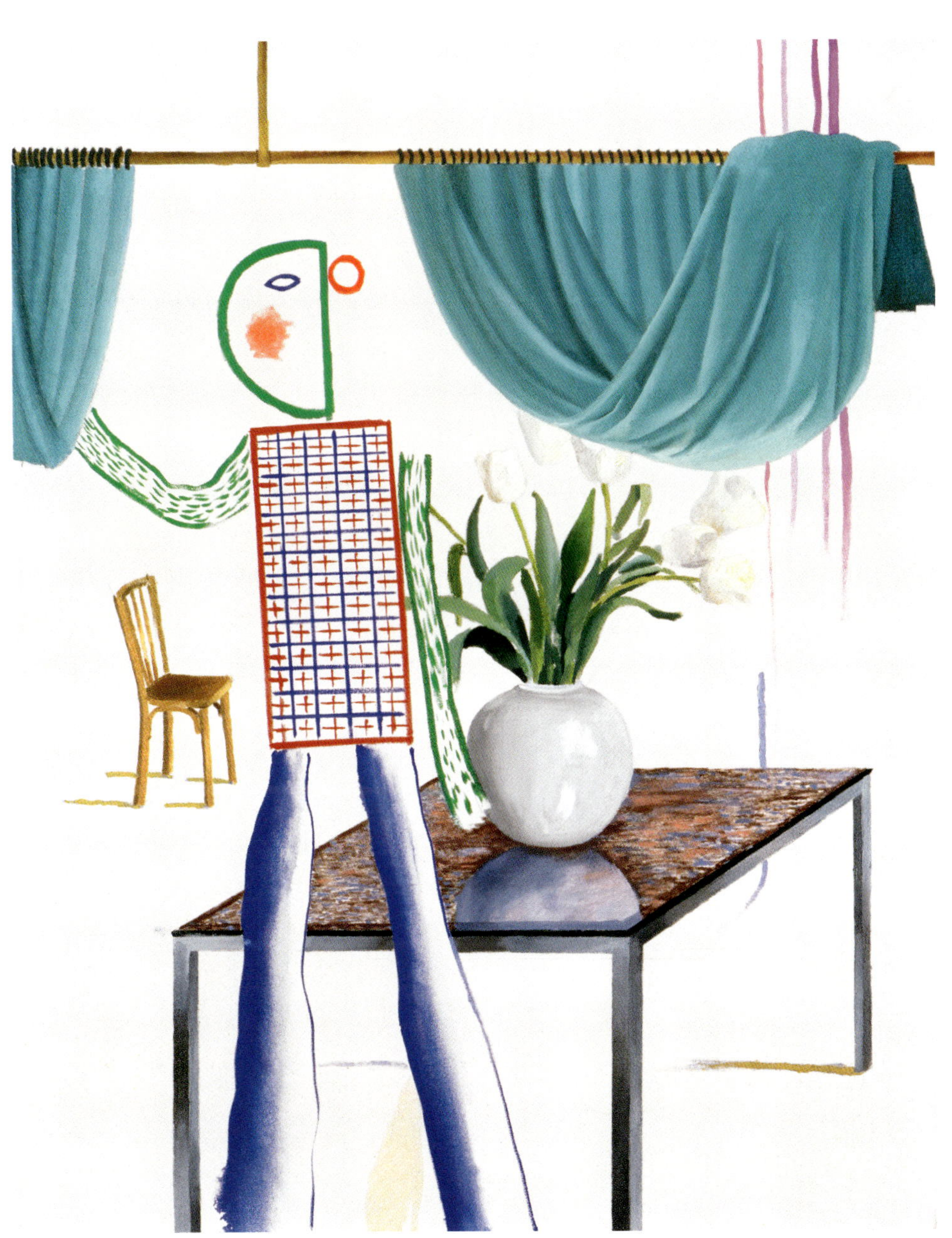

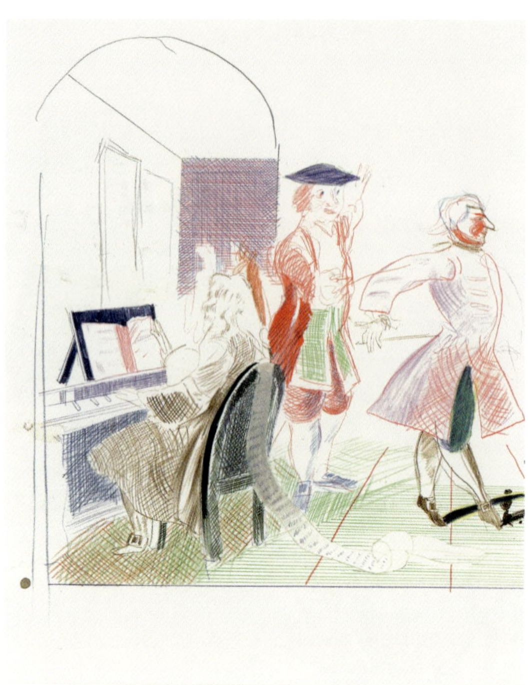

Stage design for Igor Stravinsky's *The Rake's Progress,* 1975

Sketch, crayon on paper, 17 x 14 in. / 43.2 x 35.6 cm

An Assembly, colored ink and collage on paper, 19 ³/₄ x 25 ⁵/₈ in. / 50.2 x 65.1 cm

Right page: *Bedlam,* ink on cardboard, 16 x 21 x 12 in. / 40.6 x 53.3 x 30.5 cm (model)

Street Scene, ink on cardboard, 16 x 21 x 12 in. / 40.6 x 53.3 x 30.5 cm (model)

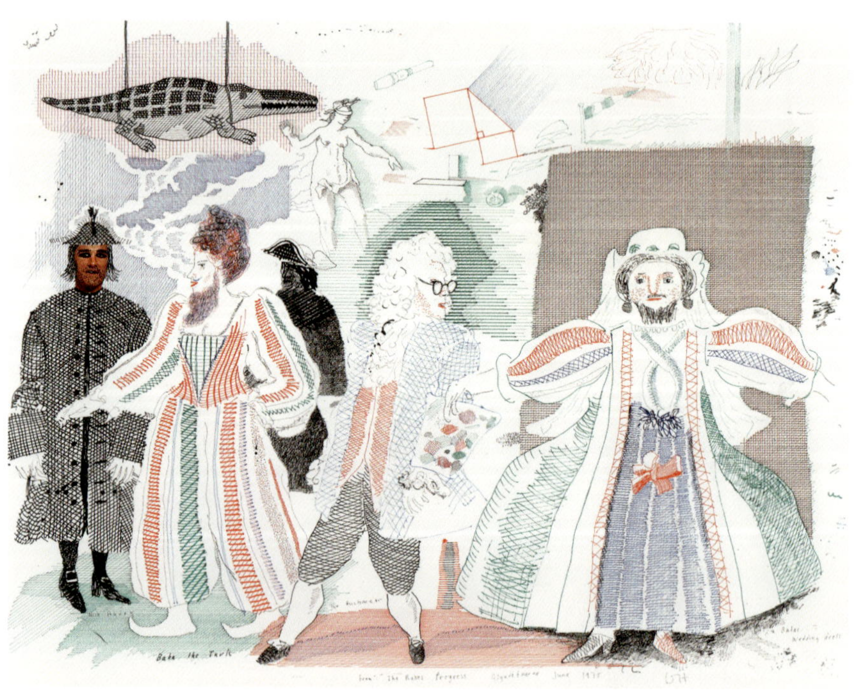

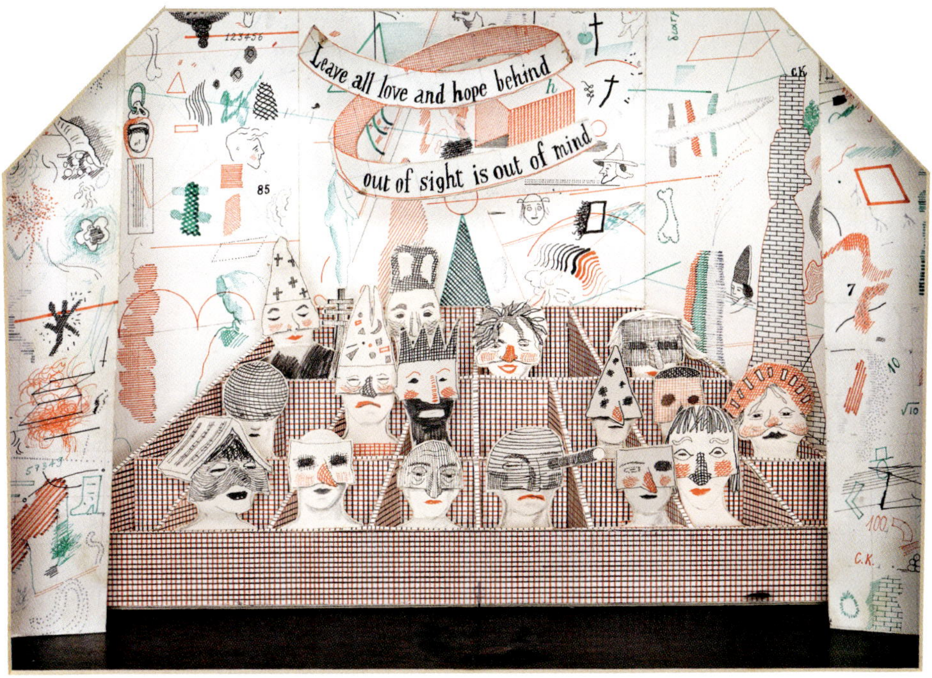

Leave all love and hope behind
out of sight is out of mind

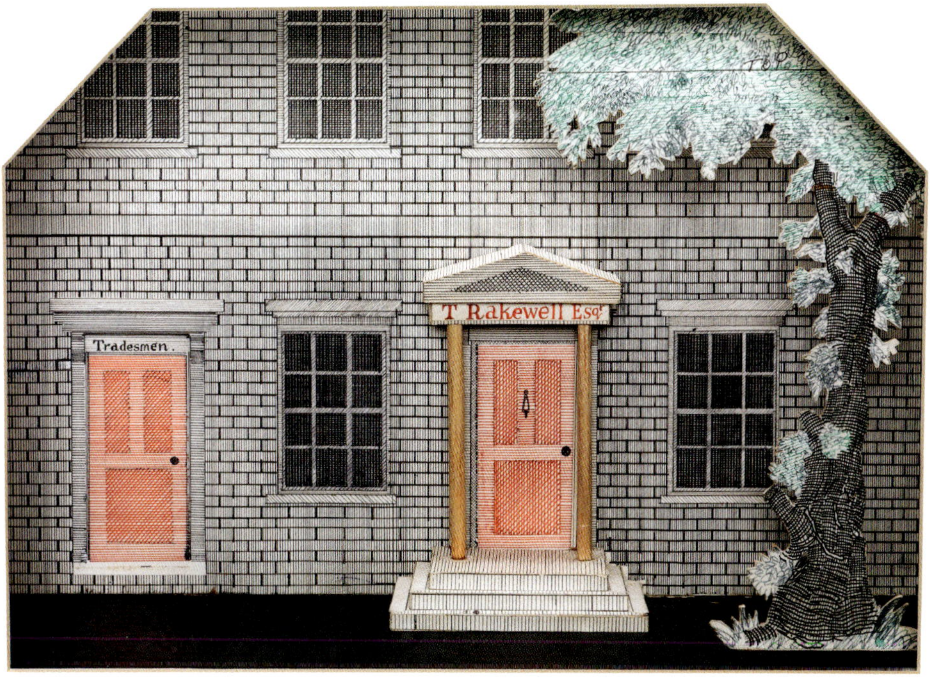

Tradesmen.
T Rakewell Esq

1976

In January, Hockney travels from New York to California with Gregory Evans over two weeks. Arrived in Los Angeles, he makes a series of large portrait lithographs for Gemini (pp. 156–157), including Evans, Nick Wilder, and Mo McDermott, filmmaker Billy Wilder, several studies of Henry Geldzahler, and a revamped double portrait of Christopher Isherwood and Don Bachardy. In the evenings, Hockney enjoys social life, as his new friend Billy Wilder reports: "He is much better-read than I will ever be, and he knows all about movies and the theater. He is a great connoisseur of good music. He tells a good joke and is clever at imitations. Any Hollywood hostess is honored to have him at her party…It's fascinating how a working-class Englishman has become so much part of our community. If you only have one friend and it is Hockney, you are not lost in this world. So try and make it Hockney!"

In March he takes a trip to Australia and New Zealand; in May he goes to visit his parents in England. He cannot finish the painting *My Parents and Myself* (p. 155), which he has started the previous year: "I was never truly satisfied, nor was I satisfied with it as a portrait of them…So I had to struggle on. Now I might have abandoned it had it not been my parents." Again he spends the summer on Fire Island, where at the suggestion of Geldzahler he reads the poem "The Man with the Blue Guitar" by Wallace Stevens: "When I first read it, I wasn't quite sure what it was about, like all poems like that, but I loved the rhythms in it and some of the imagery, just the choice of words is marvelous. Then, when I read it out loud, I loved it even more, because I got the music that it has." He makes first studies for illustrations to the poem in ink on paper.

The autobiography *David Hockney by David Hockney: My Early Years* is published. It has been edited by Nick Stangos from 25 taped hours of the artist talking about his life and thoughts on art. The first edition sells out fast and the book has to be reprinted; yet similar to his experiences with *A Bigger Splash,* Hockney does not enjoy the public attention. "The book has been an enormous success here," he writes to Geldzahler, "and overpraised almost everywhere. It's put me off going to parties—the last one I went to a lady told me she had three copies given for Christmas. I laughed but I can't face talking about it to another person."

While Hockney does not see photography as a fully equal part of his artistic process, but rather as a useful tool to help with the painting, Sonnabend Gallery exhibit a portfolio of *Twenty Photographic Pictures* (pp. 158–159) at the close of

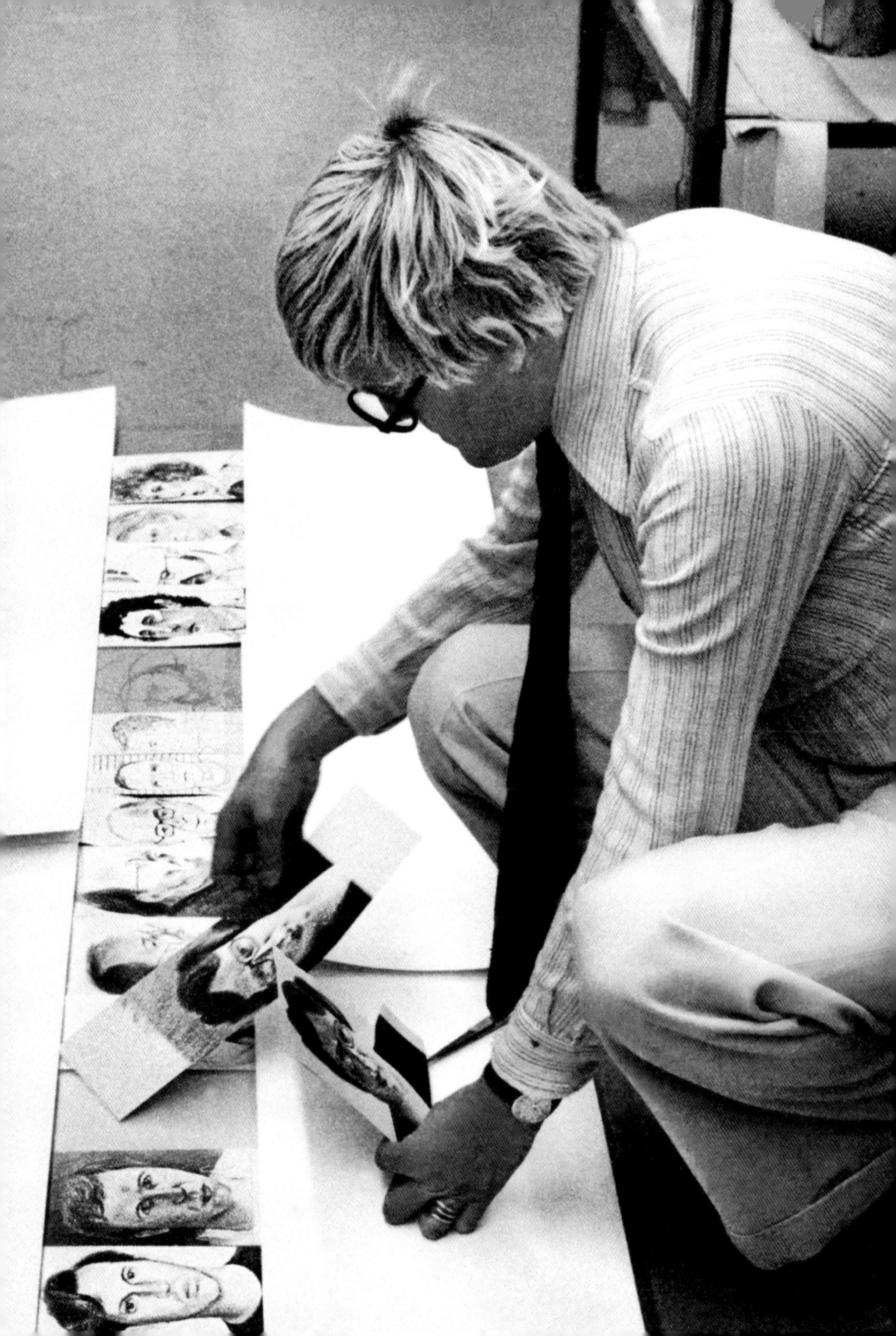

the year. Grace Glueck in the *New York Times*: "Over the years, the 38-year-old former star of Pop art has managed 'obsessively' to fill 55 big albums with his work, all in color, and it's clear that the same Pinteresque hand that wields the brush has snapped the shutter. There is a shimmering Hollywood swimming pool, a bather's long shadow on the bottom ('It's that blue shadow I like,' says Mr. Hockney). There's a nude in the shower, flesh gleaming ('I like the way the light hits that back, like a Bonnard,' says Mr. Hockney). There's a friend seated next to a potted palm in Paris's Luxembourg Gardens ('Only Hockney,' says the artist Robert Rauschenberg, 'could make Paris look like Southern California.')"

Solo: *David Hockney*, Louisiana Museum for Moderne Kunst, Humlebæk (Feb 7–Mar 7). *David Hockney*, Sonja Henie og Niels Onstad Kunstsenter, Høvikodden (Mar–Apr); organized by the Arts Council of Great Britain, travels to Gøteborgs Kunstmuseum, Goteborg; catalog. *David Hockney*, Festival Gallery, Bath (May 28–Jun 19). *Drawings and Paintings 1960–1965*, Waddington Galleries, London (Nov 2–27); catalog. *Obra Gràfica 1961–1974*, Galeria Eude, Barcelona (Mar); catalog. *Works with the Eye*, Nicholas Wilder Gallery, Los Angeles (May 11–29). *Drawings and Prints*, Davis and Long, New York (Jun 7–25). *Paintings, Drawings and Prints*, Lain Art Gallery, Newcastle upon Tyne (Jun 15–Jul 12); catalog. *David Hockney*, Sonnabend Gallery, New York (Oct). *Color Photographs*, Broxton Gallery, Los Angeles (Nov 13–Dec 11). *Twenty Photographic Pictures*, Sonnabend Gallery, New York (opens Dec 1).

Group: *Drawing Now 1955–1975*, Museum of Modern Art, New York (Jan 21–Mar 9); catalog. *Pop Art in England: Anfänge einer neuen Figuration, 1947–1963*, Kunstverein Hamburg (Feb 7–Mar 21); travels to Munich and New York; catalog. *Peter Blake, Richard Hamilton, David Hockney, R. B. Kitaj, Eduardo Paolozzi*, Museum Boymans-van Beuningen, Rotterdam (May 20–Jul 4); catalog.

Publication: *David Hockney by David Hockney: My Early Years*, ed. by Nikos Stangos, introduction by Henry Geldzahler, London: Thames and Hudson; New York: Harry N. Abrams.

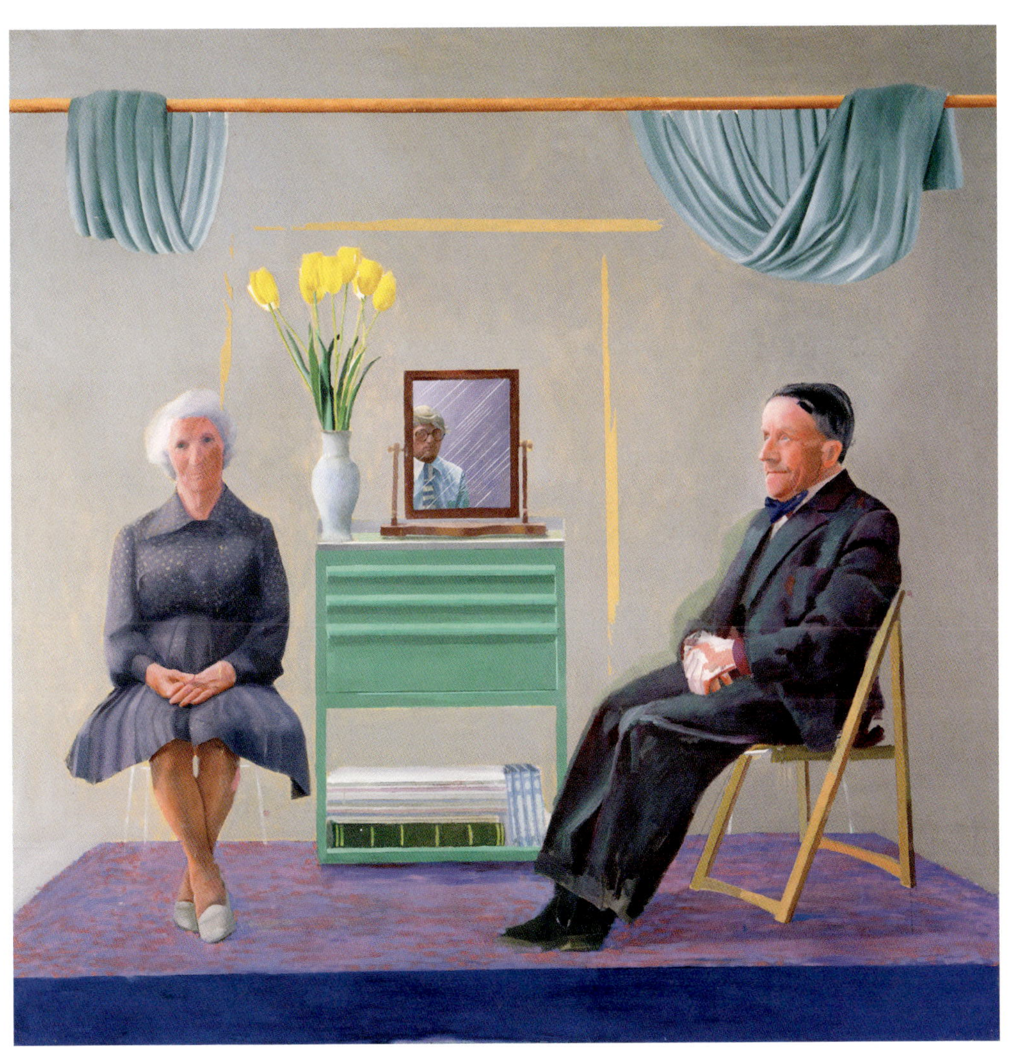

My Parents and Myself, 1976,
oil on canvas with masking tape,
72 x 72 in. / 182.9 x 182.9 cm

Page 153: David Hockney, c. 1976.
Photo: Sidney B. Felsen

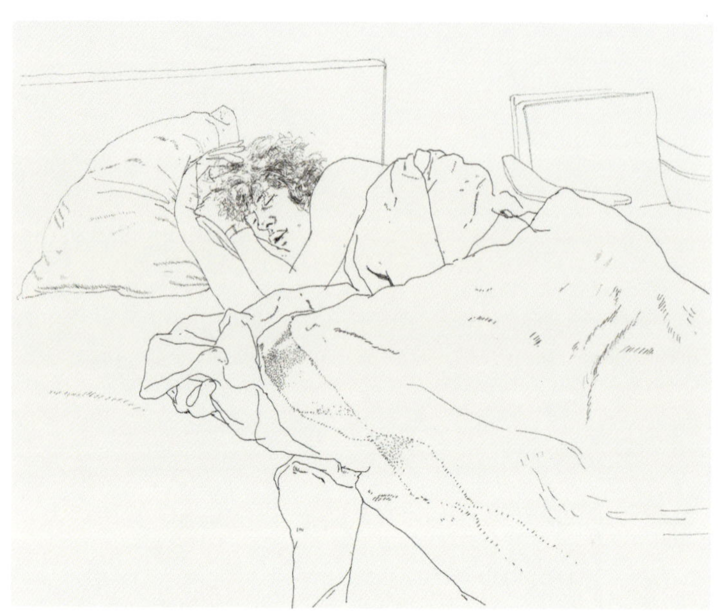

Gregory Asleep, Sunday Inn, Houston, 1976, ink on paper, 14 x 17 in. / 35.6 x 43.2 cm

Nicholas Wilder, 1976, lithograph, edition of 95, 33 x 24 ³/₄ in. / 83.8 x 62.9 cm

Billy Wilder, 1976, lithograph, edition of 43, 38 x 28 in. / 96.5 x 71.1 cm

Right page: *Joe MacDonald,* 1976, lithograph, edition of 99, 41 ³/₄ x 29 ¹/₂ in. / 104.8 x 74.9 cm

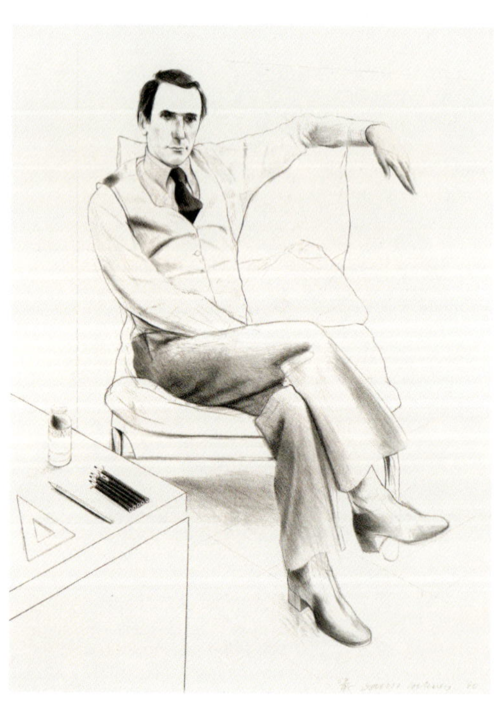

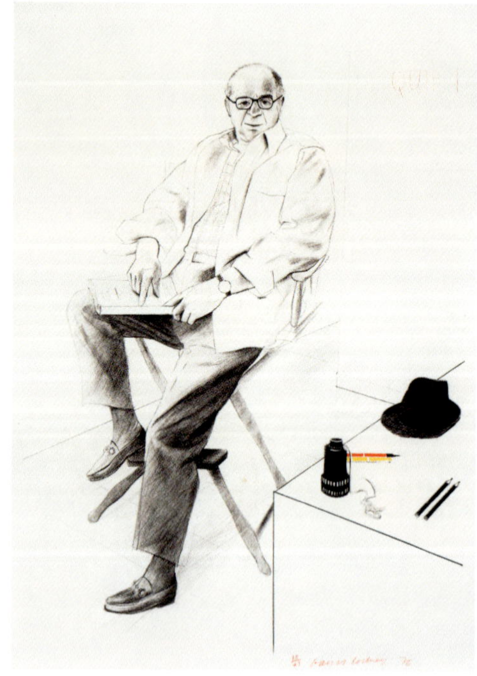

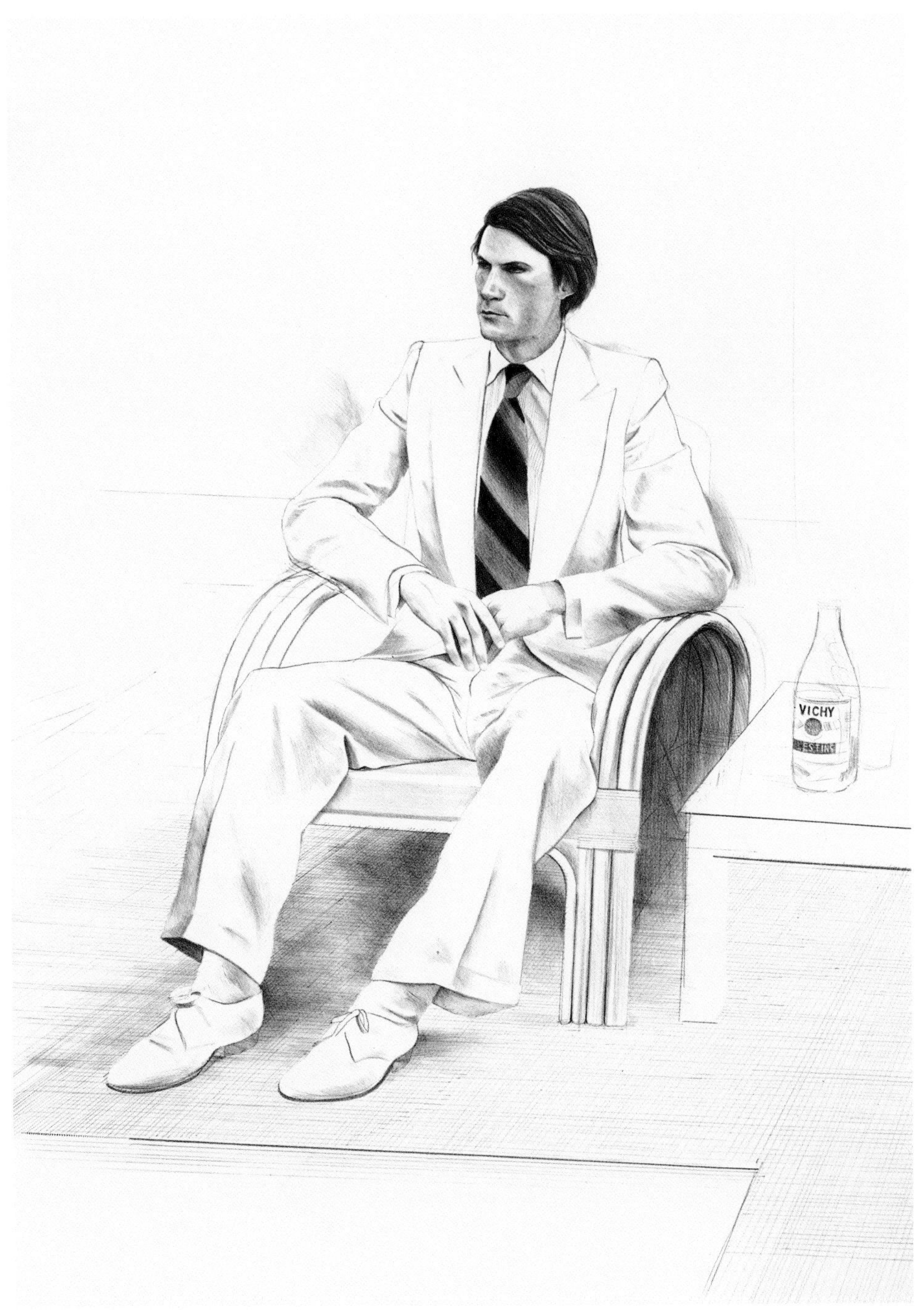

VICHY
CÉLESTINS

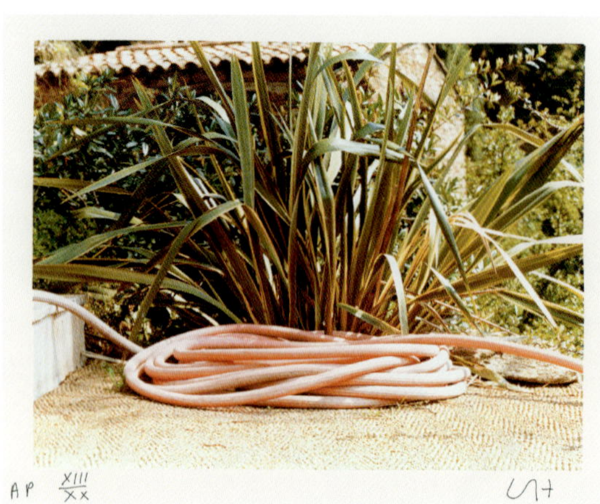

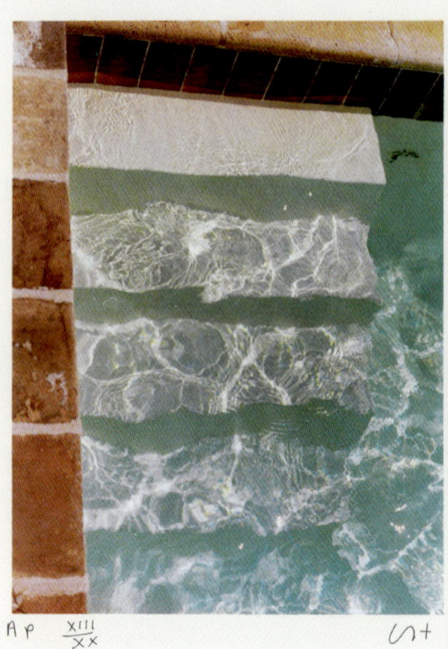

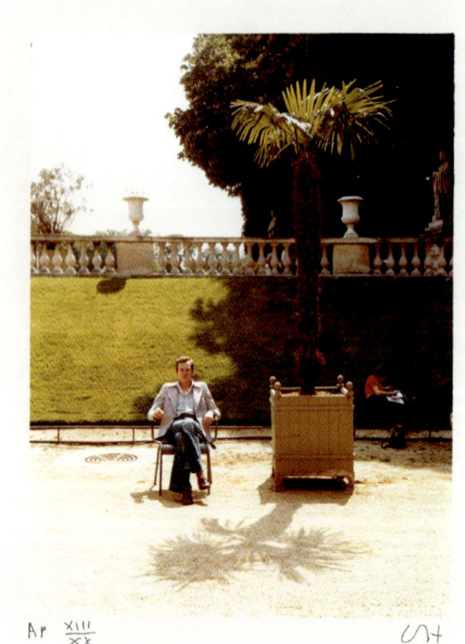

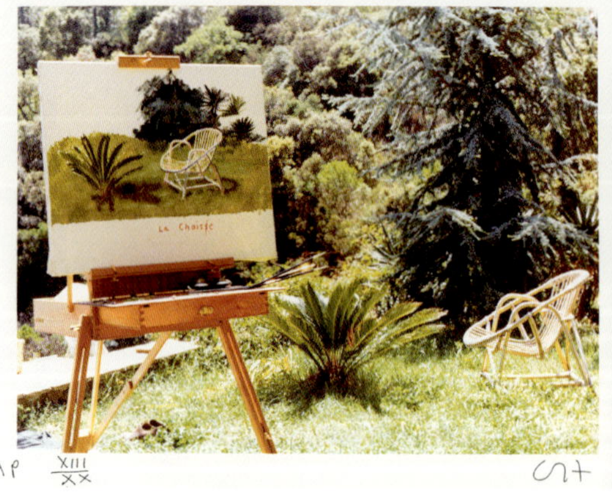

Twenty Photographic Pictures by David Hockney,
series of 20 chromogenic prints, each 8 x 10 ½
or 10 ½ x 8 in. / 20.3 x 26.7 or 26.7 x 20.3 cm,
published by Sonnabend in an edition of 80,
New York 1976

Pink Hose, May 1974
Steps into Water, May 1975
Jean in the Luxembourg Gardens, June 1974
Sur le Motif, May 1974

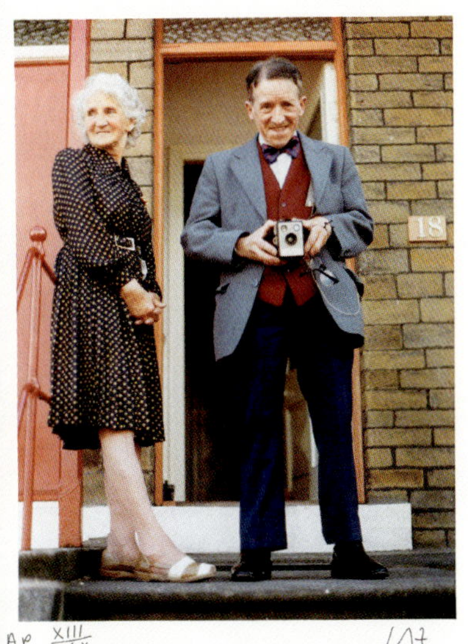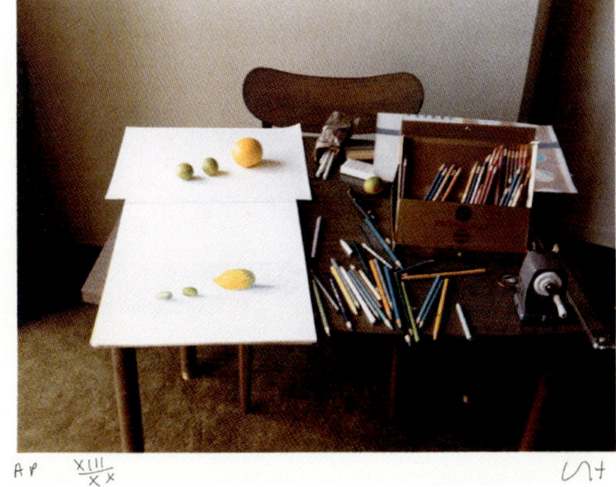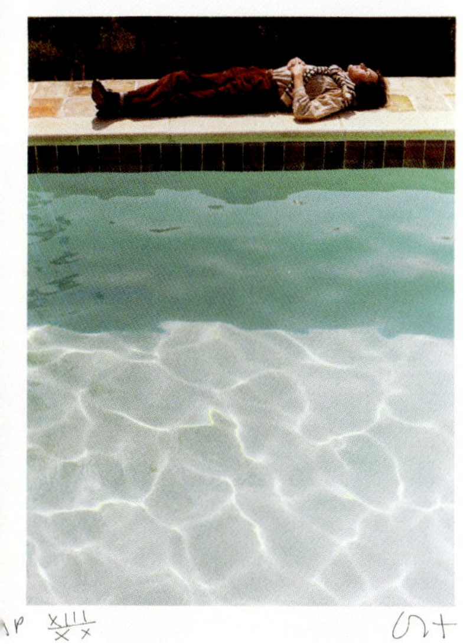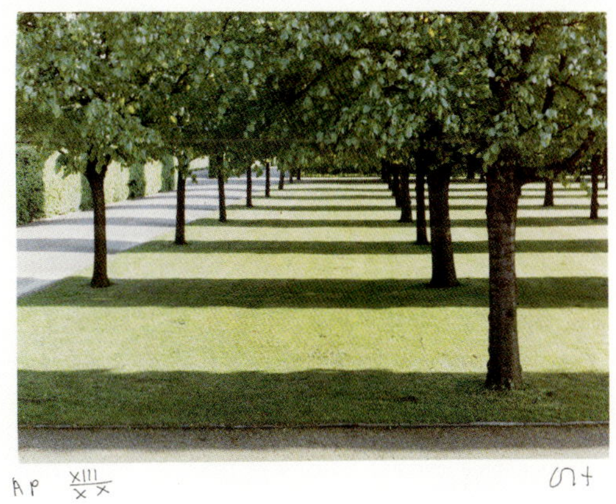

My Parents, Bradford, July 1975
Two Lemons and Four Limes, Santa Monica, 1971
Yves-Marie Asleep, May 1974
Herrenhausen, Hannover, May 1970

1977

The Blue Guitar (subtitled *Etchings by David Hockney, Who Was Inspired by Wallace Stevens, Who Was Inspired by Pablo Picasso*) is published both as a print portfolio and as a book (p. 167). With the help of printer Maurice Payne, Hockney has utilized the color etching method shown to him by Aldo Crommelynck, Picasso's former printer. "The etchings themselves weren't conceived as literal illustrations of the poem," the artist explains, "but as an interpretation of its themes in visual terms. Like the poem, they're about the transformations within art as well as the relation between reality and the imagination, so there are pictures within pictures and different styles of representation." In Pembroke Studios, he paints two more canvases influenced by the topic: *Self Portrait with Blue Guitar* (p. 166) and *Model with Unfinished Self Portrait* (p. 165), the latter of which shows Gregory Evans sleeping in a blue morning robe in front of a canvas of the self-portrait in progress.

The *New Review* runs a double interview with Hockney and R. B. Kitaj as its lead story. Both artists on the cover are naked (apart from a tight undershirt Kitaj wears) and they stress the importance of the human figure in art history and speak out against modernist academicism. "It's perfectly clear that you cannot ignore form in art," Hockney says. "But in the last 50 years form has been made everything and that is as bad as making content everything, when you finish up with banal illustration. In making form everything you finish up with a formalist art that disappears in on itself. I still believe in the old idea that there should be a balance. Without balance you deny some other rather important things and diminish the art by going on toward these uninteresting peripheries. The art is not as big as it could be. And remember this: it is always figures that look at pictures. It's nothing else. There's always a little mirror there. On every canvas there's a little bit of mirror somewhere. You don't get 'Red and Blue Number Three' looking at 'Blue and Brown Number Four.'"

Hockney travels to India with John Kasmin. In summer, as Pembroke Studios is too small to combine daily work and an active social life, he moves back to Powis Terrace, converting the top floor of the previous house into a studio. He is not quite satisfied with the results, it feels like working up a tower far removed from the world. Nevertheless he paints *Looking at Pictures on a Screen* (p. 165) there, a portrait of Henry Geldzahler standing and gazing at reproductions of paintings from the National Gallery, and finally *My Parents* (p. 163),

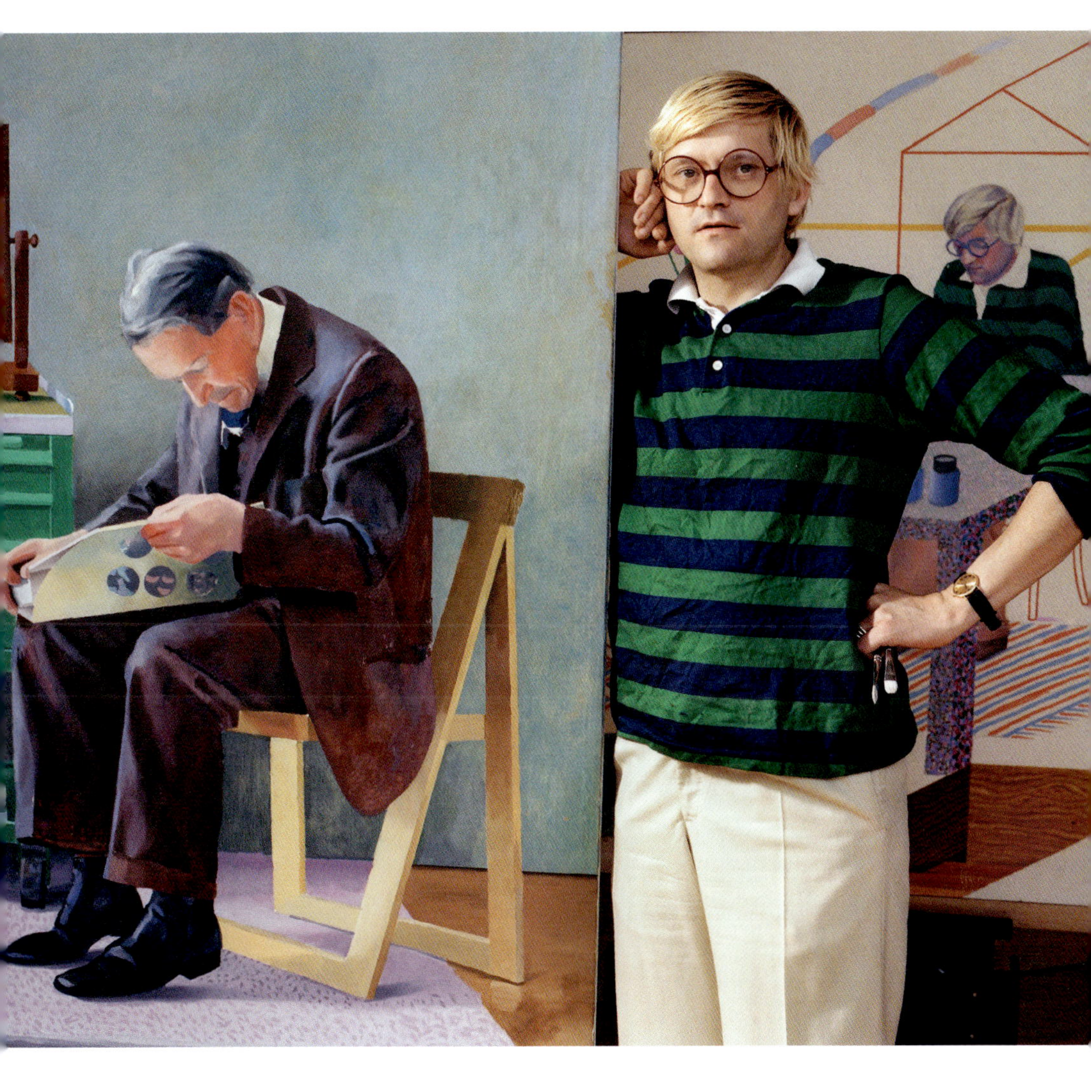

David Hockney, London 1977.
Photo: Born Schwartz

a new attempt at a portrait of his parents this time without his own image included. The latter painting is shown at the *Hayward Annual* along with the *Blue Guitar* etchings. William Feaver in the *Observer*: "At first sight, this is an uneasy composition, the figures being stiff and curiously lurid at the joints, the whole richly varnished. But as it settles on the eye, the subtleties of handling and feeling begin to emerge. Mannered though this painting may be, it is neither jokey nor sub-Ingres, but devoted and altogether fine." Other reviews are more negative, and a debate around the virtues of figurative or more self-consciously modernist art ensues. In an *Art Monthly* interview Hockney explains why for him there is no avant-garde today: "Cubism appeared to most people to be a distortion of reality; it wasn't, but that's how it appeared. People get passionate about that, especially about distortions of the human figure. They wonder why. They know the human figure, and that its foot isn't twice as big as its head. But people couldn't care less about [Carl Andre's] bricks, or Bob Law's paintings. There is no passion for or against them, that's the truth. People think a guy's got a ballpoint pen, and he tries to get £5,000 for the picture, and, well, if somebody's fool enough to pay it, what can you do? But to try and equate that with the struggles of modernism 60 years ago is almost a cheap insult."

In October, Hockney shows his new paintings and the *Blue Guitar* etchings at André Emmerich Gallery in New York. Again, reviews are mixed, and the question of figurative against modernist art is taken up. Hilton Kramer in the *New York Times*: "Inevitably, his new exhibition is something of an event. But what kind of event is it? The new pictures—mostly portraits and self-portraits—are as clever as anything Mr. Hockney has ever done, and there are things in the painting that are, if anything, even finer than what he has attempted in the past. The sheer technical virtuosity that has gone into certain passages of *Looking at Pictures on a Screen* and *Model with Unfinished Self Portrait* is certainly impressive, and will win him many new admirers. His gift for a certain mode of pictorial theatricality—for setting a scene and effectively placing the actors and the props within it—is also very appealing. The people who come to see these pictures obviously take a great delight in them…What we find in this painting—and this, I think, is finally the basis of its appeal—is a kind of 19th-century salon art refurbished from the stockroom of modernism. This, of course, is no small accomplishment in itself, but it ought to be recognized for what it is

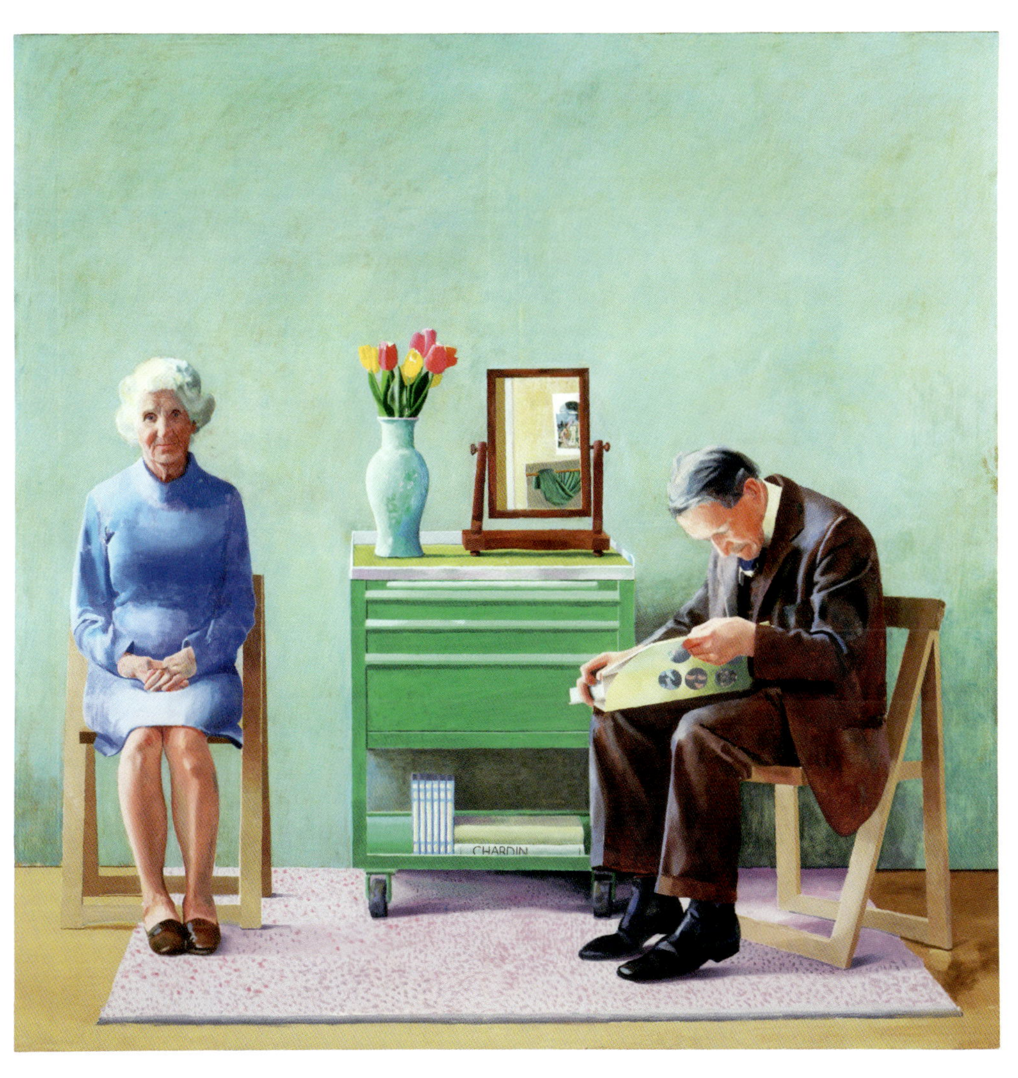

My Parents, 1977, oil on canvas,
72 x 72 in. / 182.9 x 182.9 cm

and not mistaken for something it is not. Mr. Hockney's art, like the success it enjoys, marks the triumphant return of what might be called bourgeois art, only in his case it is bourgeois art compounded out of the very materials that once challenged and offended bourgeois taste. This is indeed the true comedy of it, if we have the wit to see it."

Hockney stays in New York to begin work on designs for Mozart's opera *The Magic Flute*, to be produced by John Cox during the 1978 season at Glyndebourne. He creates more than 30 drops that can be taken up and down to form the background for the stage. This project will occupy him for almost a year, a time during which he produces no other paintings.

Solo: *Zeichnungen und Druckgraphik*, Staatliche Graphische Sammlung, Munich (Feb 24–Apr 17); catalog with a text by Christian Geelhaar. *Drawings and Prints*, Wolverhampton Art Gallery, Wolverhampton (Oct 1–29). *The Blue Guitar*, Gallery One, State University, San Jose (Oct 26–Nov 18). *Paintings and Drawings, 1961–1975*, Galerie Neuendorf, Hamburg (Apr 21–May 20). *David Hockney*, Getler/Pall Gallery, New York (May 17–Jun 25). *David Hockney*, Galerie Bleue, Stockholm (Oct–Nov). *New Paintings, Drawings and Graphics*, André Emmerich Gallery, New York (Oct 29–Nov 16); catalog.

Group: *Kunst um 1970: Die Sammlung Ludwig Aachen*, Künstlerhaus Wien, Vienna (Mar 8–Jun 12); catalog. *Documenta 6*, Kassel (Jun 24–Oct 2); catalog. *Hayward Annual*, Hayward Gallery, London (Jul 20–Sep 4); catalog. *Englische Kunst der Gegenwart*, Künstlerhaus Bregenz (Jul 23–Oct 30); catalog. *Artists' Sets and Costumes*, Philadelphia College of Art, Philadelphia (Oct 31–Dec 17); travels to Bronxville; catalog.

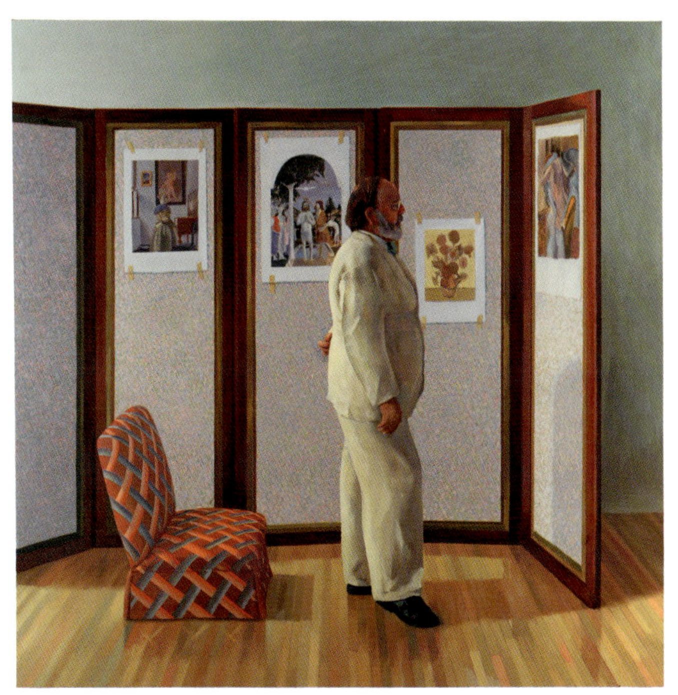

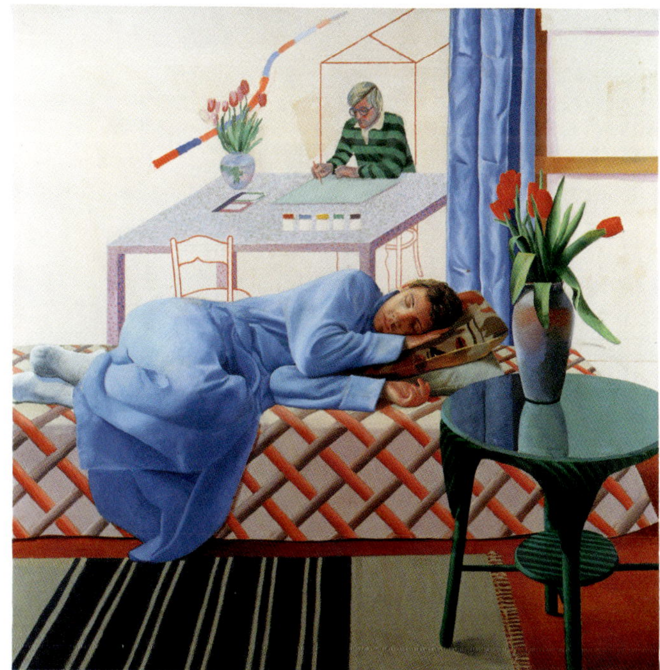

Looking at Pictures on a Screen,
1977, oil on canvas, 74 x 74 in. /
188 x 188 cm

*Model with Unfinished Self
Portrait,* 1977, oil on canvas,
60 x 60 in. / 152.4 x 152.4 cm

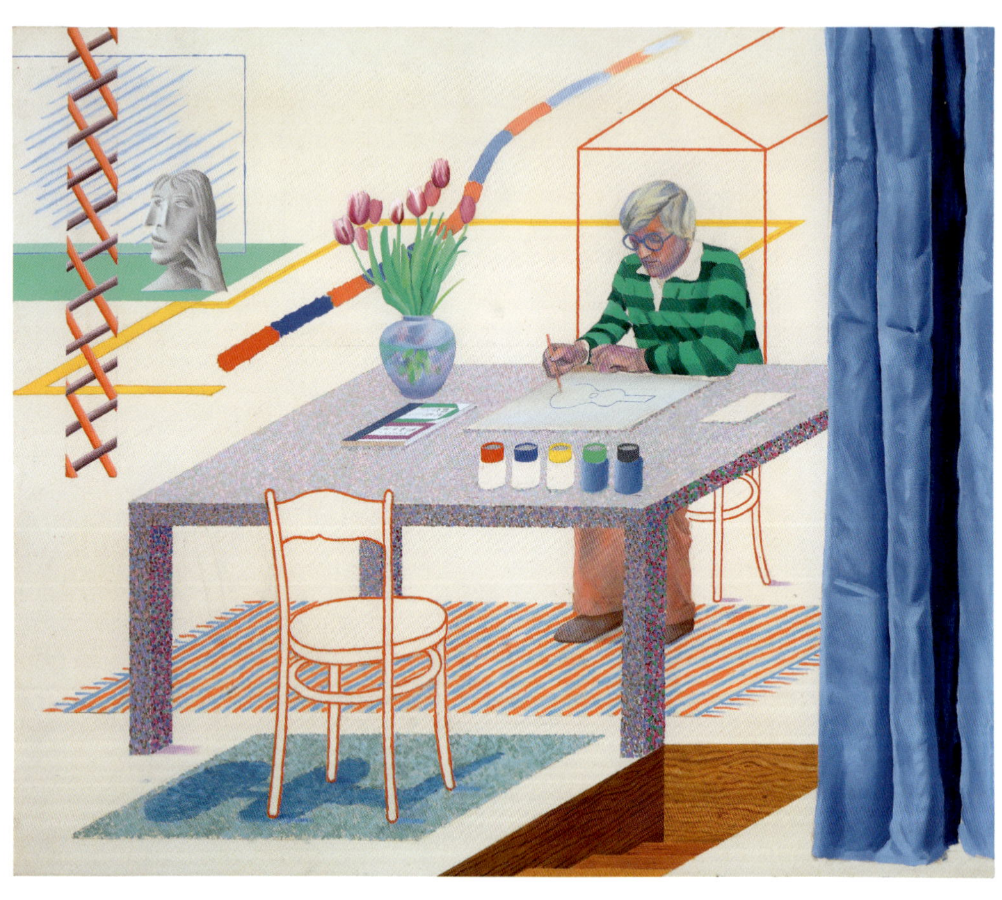

Self Portrait with Blue Guitar, 1977, oil on canvas, 60 x 72 in. / 152.4 x 182.9 cm

Right page: *The Blue Guitar,* 1976–1977, series of 20 etchings, edition of 200, each 20 1/2 x 18 or 18 x 20 1/2 in. / 52.1 x 45.7 or 45.7 x 52.1 cm

The Old Guitarist; Discord Merely Magnifies; It Picks Its Way; Franco-American Mail; A Moving Still Life; Serenade

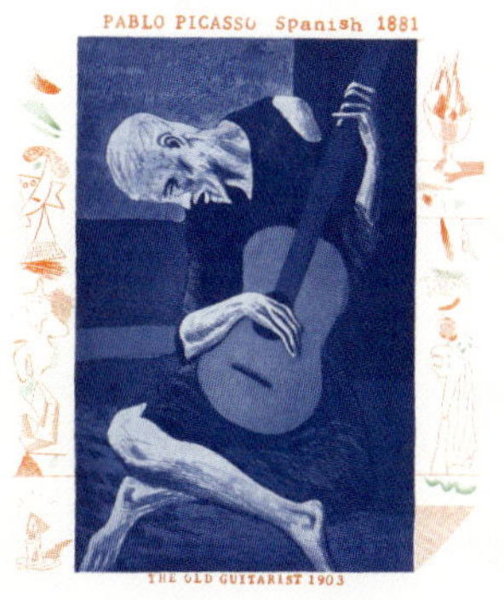

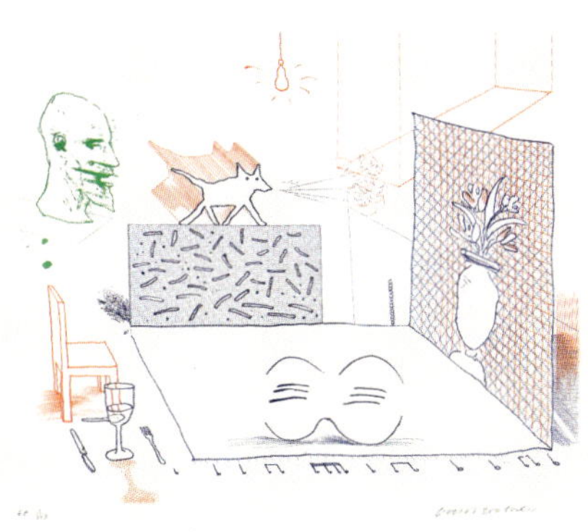

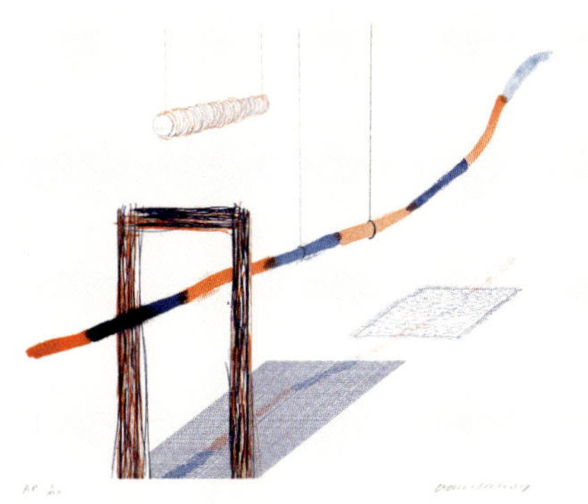

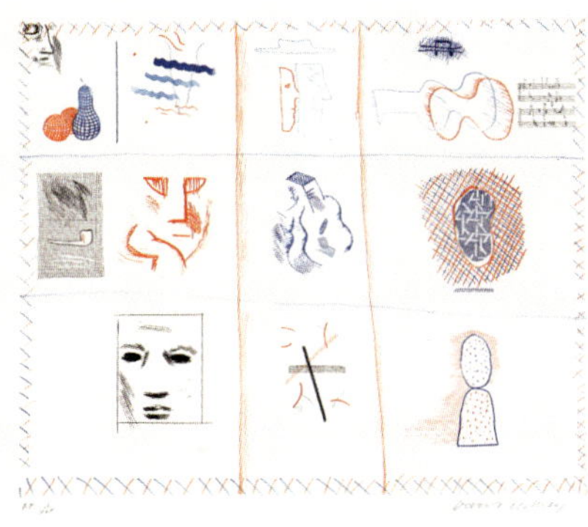

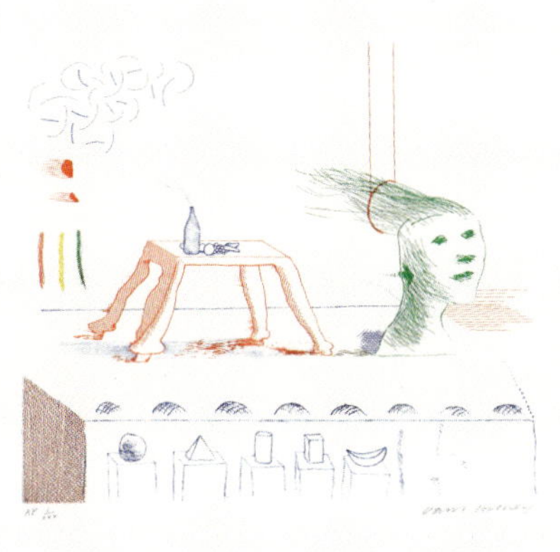

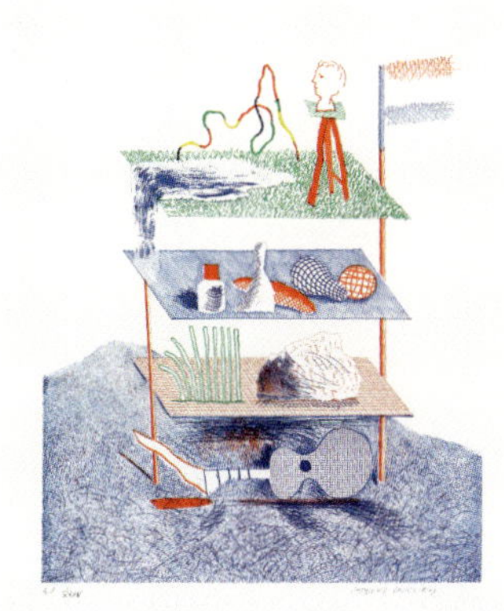

1978

Hockney finishes his designs for John Cox's production of *The Magic Flute* (p. 171). Gillian Widdicombe reports in the *Observer*: "Cox gave Hockney no specific instructions, nor any visual suggestions, for designing *The Flute,* though he did describe in some depth what he believed the opera to be about, and they both thought that the priestly chorus should not look as though it had escaped from a Mormon Tabernacle. Hockney listened to *The Flute* about eight times on the gramophone, then designed the first scene first and worked methodically through to the end… 'I wanted to do it plain, with flats moving in and out, as they did in Mozart's time. I decided, specially in the first bit, that the music was crisp and clear, with a lot of colour and fun. It was only in the nineteenth century that *The Flute* was thought to be so ponderous. I thought I'd begin like an Italian painting, with everything in focus. So I painted the rocky landscape for the opening scene without any tricks of perspective, and took the dragon from the Uccello in the National Gallery."

In spring, Hockney travels to Egypt on a package tour with Peter Schlesinger and fashion model Joe MacDonald, visiting the original places that inspired his settings for *The Magic Flute*. They return for the premiere at the Glyndebourne Festival Opera in May, which proves an overwhelming success. Desmond Shawe-Taylor in the *Sunday Times*: "There is a hint of toy theatre in the succession of 36 drops constructed from Hockney's charming maquettes, with their clean, pure lines and bold, resonant colours that match the solemn or playful, but always crystal clear, Mozartian score. They work beautifully in the theatre."

In August Hockney leaves Powis Terrace to resettle in Los Angeles. On the way, he stops with printer Ken Tyler, who now has his own printshop in Bedford Village near New York. They experiment with a new process: first making colored paper pulp, then pressing the different colors into a mould that is built according to the artist's composition. They produce a series of 29 *Paper Pools* (p. 172): "We were making unique objects, not prints, and it was thrilling work. We worked long hours, but we liked it. Ken is incredibly energetic and inventive. In using this paper pulp technique, you had to be bold. It is the exact opposite of an etching needle. An etching needle has a fine point, you put it on this lovely wax surface and you are drawing with a line. Here line meant nothing. It couldn't be line; it had to be mass, it had to be color."

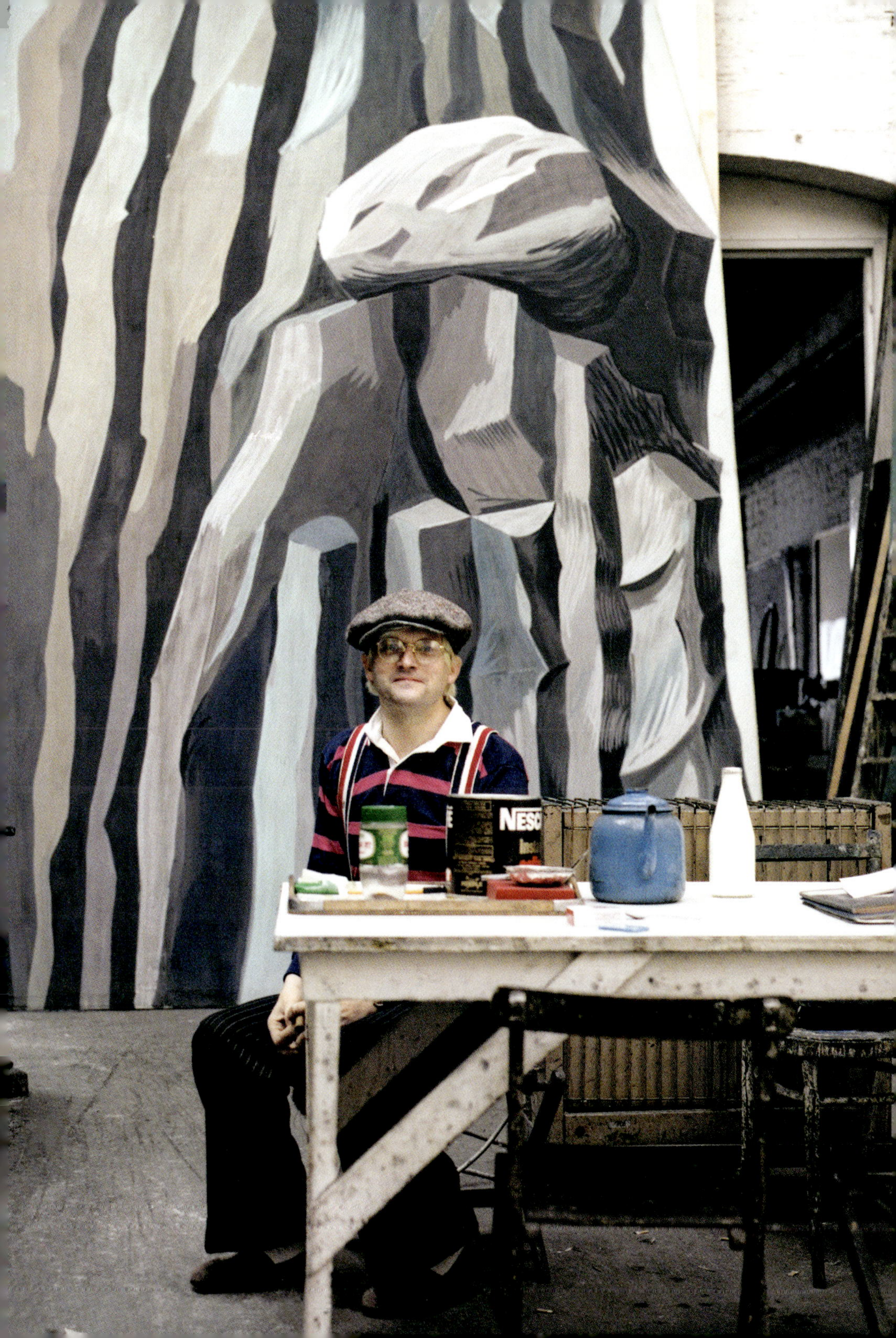

Spending much more time than planned with this body of work, Hockney reaches Los Angeles only in October and gets a new studio on Santa Monica Boulevard. He begins *Canyon Painting* (p. 172) to test a new type of acrylic paint, and then the 20-foot-wide *Santa Monica Blvd.* (pp. 174/175), which portrays figures and facades seen straight from street level: "The Santa Monica Boulevard painting I had blocked in quite quickly, and then I kept struggling with it and altering it. I realized finally that I had probably painted about ten pictures on that canvas and I had kept taking them out. The picture had a horizontal format but the eye didn't move enough across it and the painting was too static." In these paintings, Hockney is looking for a stronger dynamic in his work, but also for a new way of painting Los Angeles after his long absence.

Solo: *Zeichnungen und Druckgraphik 1959–1977,* Albertina, Vienna (Jan–Feb); travels to Tiroler Landesmuseum, Innsbruck; Kulturhaus der Stadt Graz; and Künstlerhaus Salzburg; catalog with a text by Peter Weiermair. *Travels with Pen, Pencil and Ink,* Portland Center for the Visual Arts, Portland (Apr 3–May 14); organized by the International Exhibitions Foundation, Washington, D.C., travels to Yale Center for British Art, New Haven; Minneapolis Institute of the Arts, Minneapolis; Hirshhorn Museum and Sculpture Garden, Washington, D.C.; Art Gallery of Ontario, Toronto; Toledo Museum of Art, Toledo; Fine Arts Museum of San Francisco; Denver Art Museum, Denver; Grey Art Gallery and Study Center, New York (through 1979), and others; catalog with a text by Edmund Pillsbury, London: Petersburg Press. *A Rake's Progress,* Sudley Art Gallery, Liverpool (Apr 1–30). *Drawings, Prints and Photographs,* Nishimura Gallery, Tokyo (Sep 18–Oct 7). *David Hockney,* Century Galleries, Henley-on-Thames (Nov). *Drawings and Prints 1961–1977,* L.A. Louver, Venice, CA (Nov 28–Dec 31).

Group: *20th Century Portraits,* National Portrait Gallery, London (Jun 9–Sep 17); catalog. *Late Twentieth Century Art, Sydney and Frances Lewis Foundation,* Anderson Gallery, Virginia Commonwealth University, Richmond (Dec 5, 1978–Jan 8, 1979); travels to Institute of Contemporary Art, Philadelphia, and many others (through 1983); catalog.

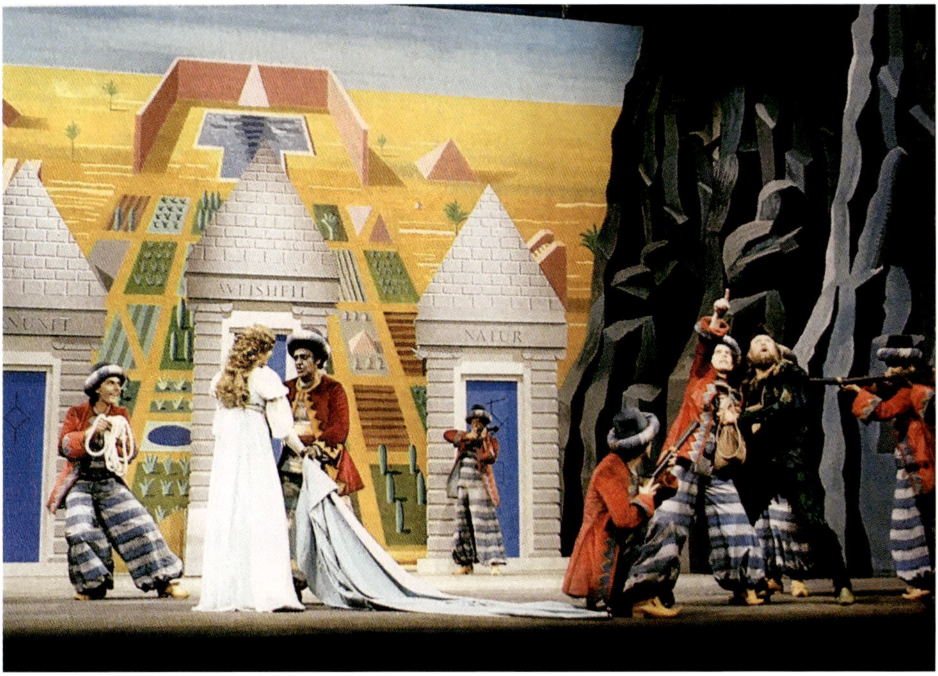

VERNUNFT
WEISHEIT
NATUR

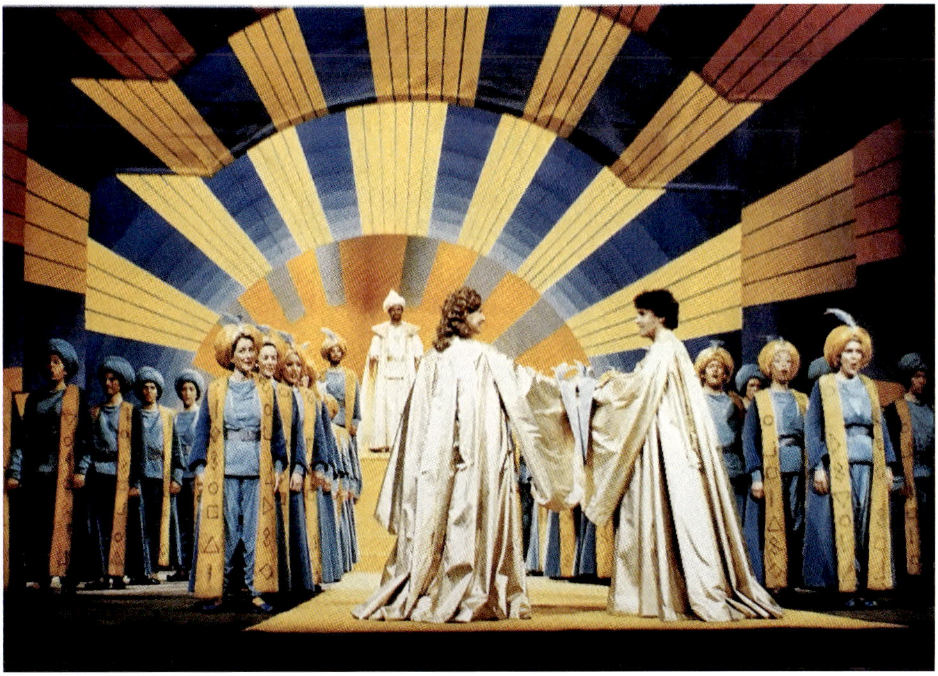

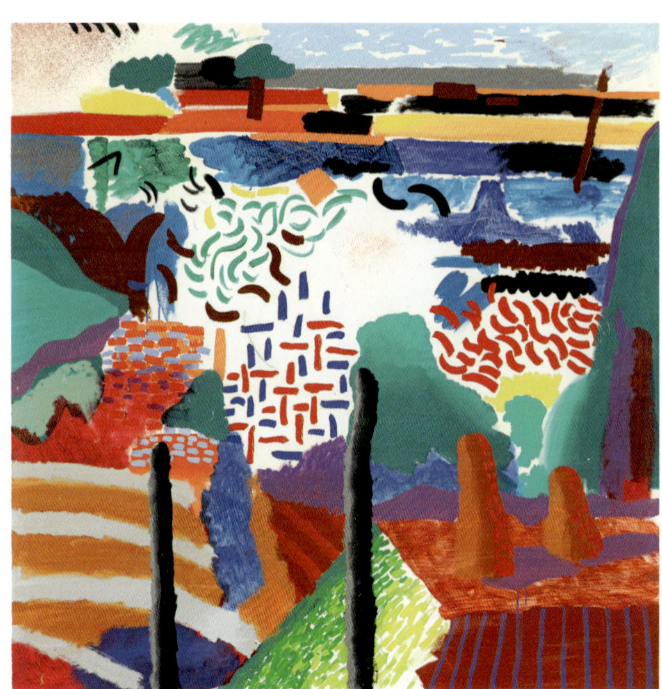

Canyon Painting, 1978,
acrylic on canvas, 60 x 60 in. /
152.4 x 152.4 cm

*Swimmer Underwater (Paper
Pool 16),* 1978, colored and
pressed paper pulp,72 x 85 ½ in. /
182.9 x 217.2 cm

Right page: *Stephen Hawking.
Cambridge, March 11th 1978,*
ink on paper, 17 x 14 in. /
43.2 x 35.6 cm

Page 169: David Hockney in
front of an element of *The Magic
Flute's* rocky landscape set from
Act I, 1978. Photo: Maurice Payne

Page 171: Production of
The Magic Flute, as performed
at Glyndebourne Festival Opera,
Glyndebourne 1978

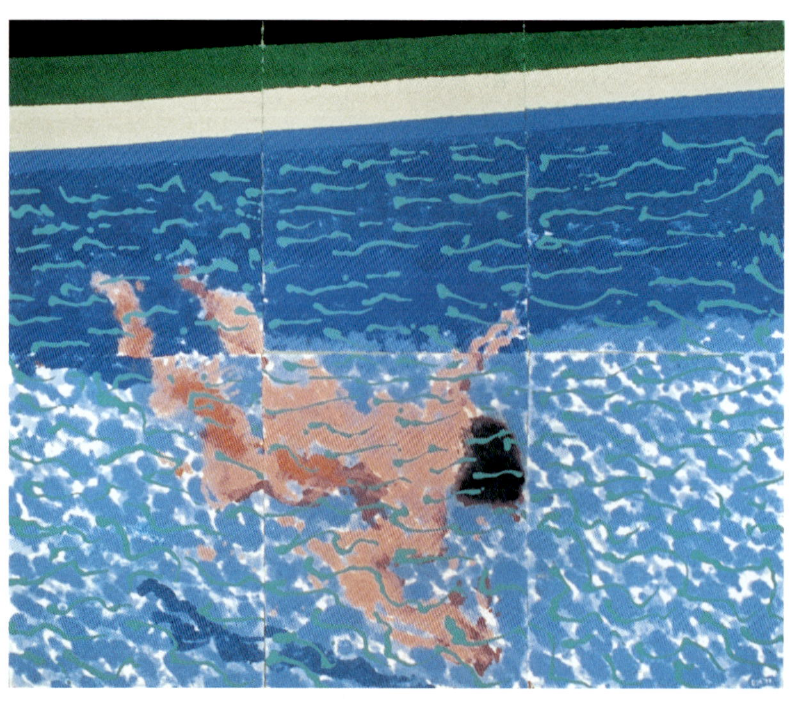

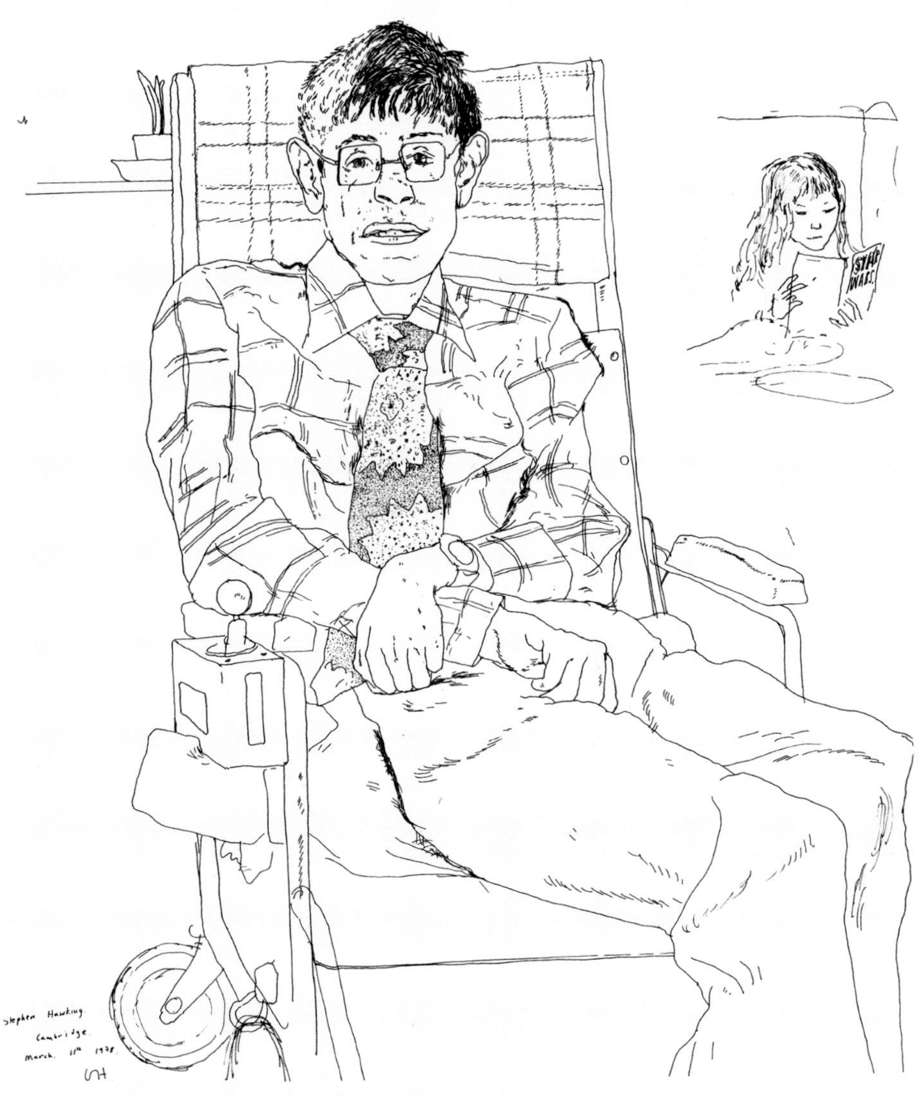
Stephen Hawking.
Cambridge.
March. 11th 1978.
STAR WARS

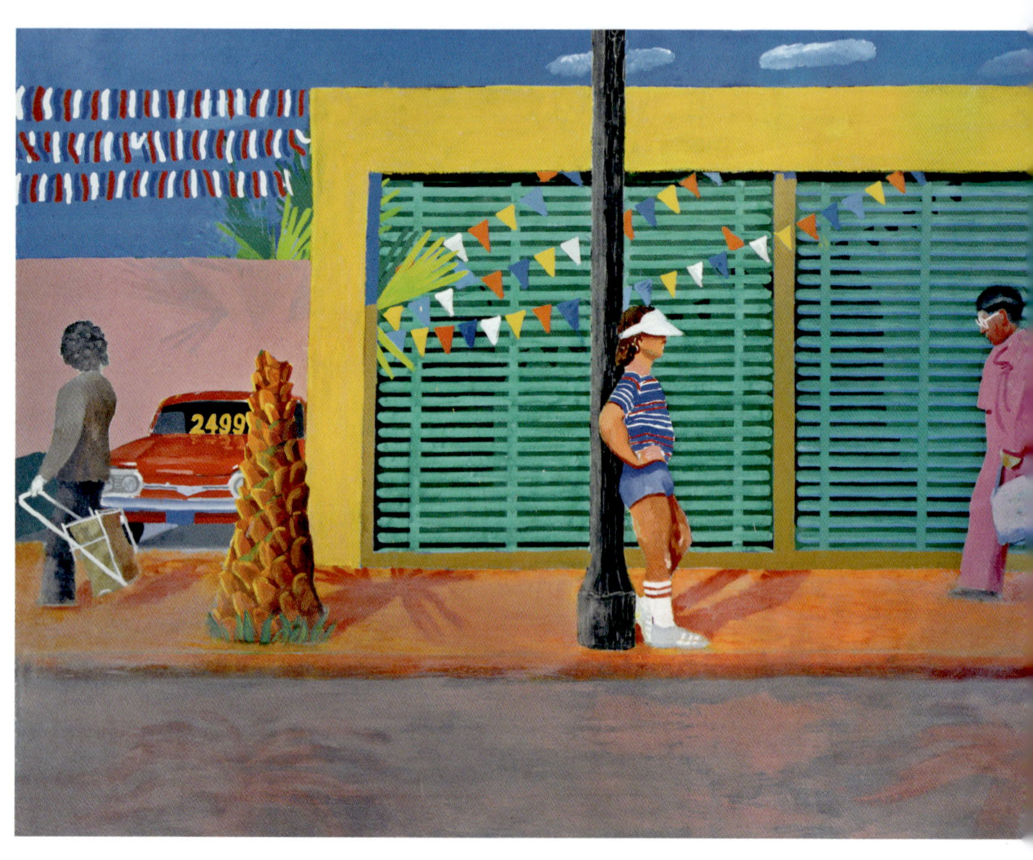

Santa Monica Blvd., 1978–1980,
acrylic on canvas, 86 x 240 in. /
218.4 x 609.6 cm

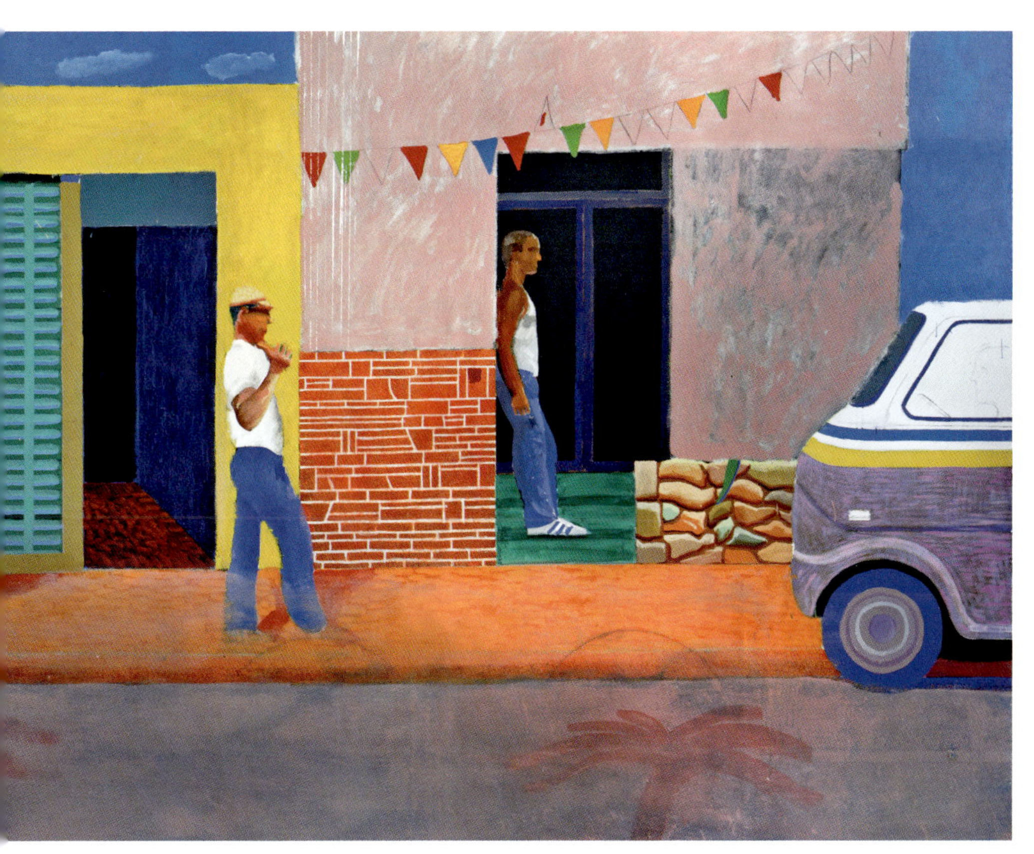

1979

Hockney's father Kenneth dies in February. The artist returns to Bradford to support his mother and attend the funeral.

The *Paper Pools* are exhibited at the closing exhibition of Warehouse Gallery in London's Covent Garden. William Feaver in the *Observer*: "The gallery has never looked more jubilant. Blue waters lap on all sides, spread over multiple sheets of what is, in effect, folio blotting paper…Hockney's images are life-size and hoarding-scale. And he has brought off some scintillating watery effects: shoals of green commas, coalescing blues, ribboning shadows under the diving boards, a freestyle swimmer dissolved into pink underwater blobules."

Also in the *Observer,* Hockney launches an attack on the acquisition politics of the Tate and its director, Norman Reid. Hockney posits that the Tate's collection of British contemporary art should be inclusive, they must "act as a museum of record and try to cover the ground more fully. That is their duty and their job. And it seems to me that it is a job which in recent years they have been doing rather badly…To give just a few examples. In the past 15 years they have not purchased a single work by L. S. Lowry, not one by Patrick Procktor, not one by Euan Uglow, not one by Allen Jones, not one by David Oxtoby." They have also rejected Hockney's offer of a *Paper Pool* at a greatly reduced price, which goes to Bradford City Art Gallery instead. Hockney finds that abstract painters are much more generously represented: "We know that art can be full of joy, and my criticism of the Tate's present attitude is that it is so narrow, so biased in favor of joyless and soulless and theoretical art. In taking this narrow view, they are also being extremely arrogant. It is a view they are trying to impose on the public." Norman Reid answers with his own article a week later, saying that he buys the best art he can. The public weighs in on the letters page, mostly taking Hockney's side.

Back in Los Angeles, Hockney frequents the Gemini workshop to work on several lithographs of Celia Birtwell and Ann Upton (p. 180). He also produces a series of quickly painted portraits in acrylic, using a bold palette, including a portrait of the drag performer Divine (p. 179). He moves into a new house in the Hollywood Hills with Gregory Evans.

Hockney is invited by British director John Dexter to design a triple bill for the Metropolitan Opera in New York, to be premiered in early 1981: the short operas *Les Mamelles de Tirésias* by Francis Poulenc and *L'Enfant et les sortilèges* by

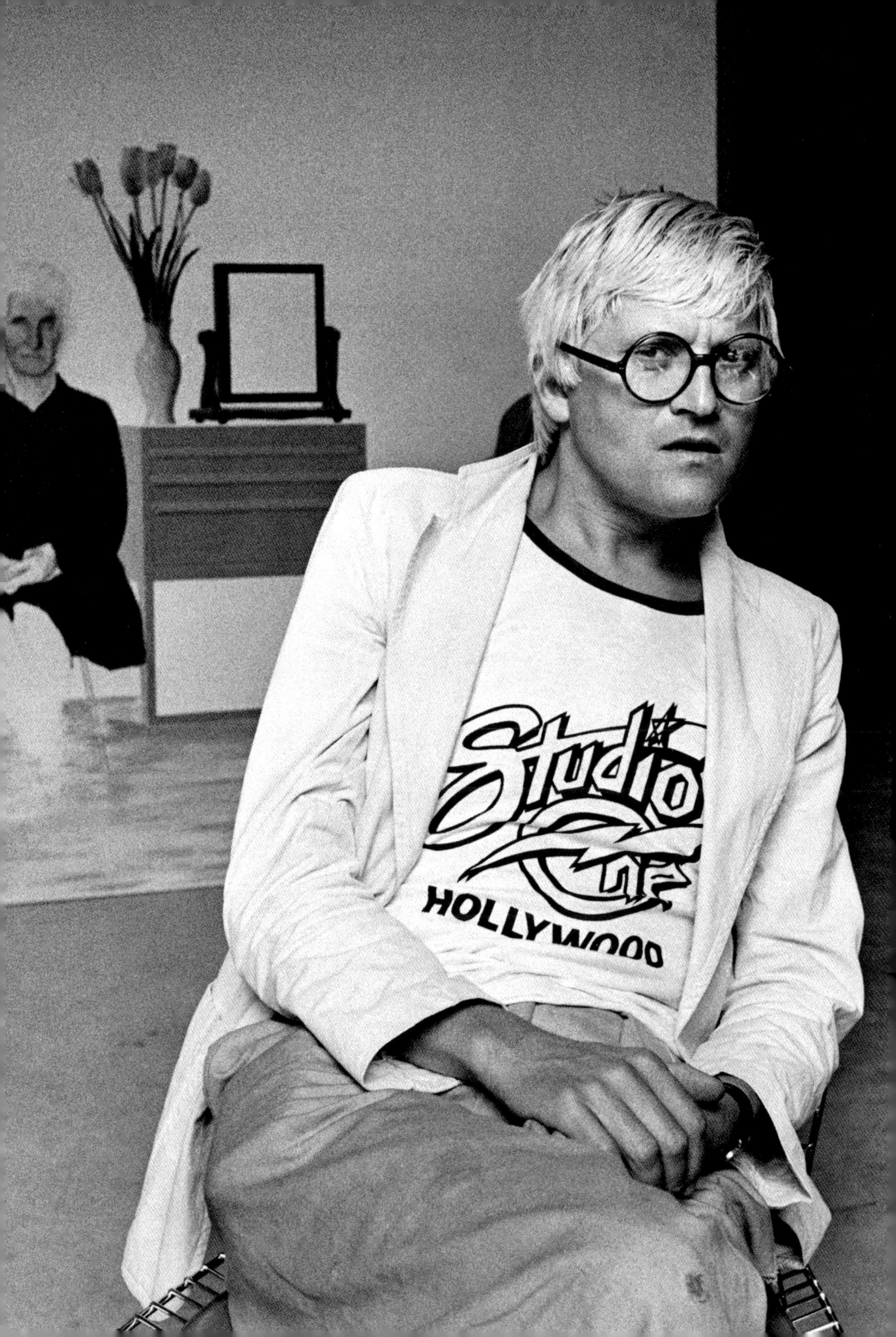

Maurice Ravel as well as Eric Satie's ballet *Parade,* which had once been designed by Picasso. He accepts the invitation and gets to work (pp. 182–183): "The first drawings I made for the triple bill, and I made a lot of them, I called *French Marks* (p. 181) because, listening to that French music by Satie, Poulenc, and Ravel, I thought the one thing the French were marvelous at, the great French painters, was making beautiful marks: Picasso can't make a bad mark, Dufy makes beautiful marks, Matisse makes beautiful marks. So I did a number of drawings using brushes, letting my arm flow free, exploring ways of bringing together French painting and music."

Solo: *Prints, 1954–1977,* Midland Group Gallery, Nottingham (Jan 20–Feb 24); touring exhibition organized by Scottish Arts Council and Petersburg Press; catalog with a text by Andrew Brighton. *The Blue Guitar,* Museum of Modern Art, New York (Apr 10–Jul 10). *Prints and Drawings,* Octagon Gallery, Belfast (May 16–Jun 8). *Paper Pools,* André Emmerich Gallery, New York (Jan 6–27); Warehouse Gallery, London (Feb 6–28). *David Hockney,* Knoedler Gallery, London (Feb). *David Hockney,* André Emmerich Gallery, New York (Mar). *David Hockney,* Gimpel-Hannover and André Emmerich Galleries, Zürich (Sep 1–Oct 13).

Group: *Images of the Self,* Hampshire College Gallery, Amherst (Feb 19–Mar 14). *Narrative Paintings: Figurative Art of Two Generations,* Arnolfini Gallery, Bristol (Sep 1–Oct 20); travels to London, Stoke-on-Trent, and Edinburgh; catalog. *British Art Show,* Mappin Art Gallery, Sheffield (Dec 1, 1979–Jan 27, 1980); organized by the Arts Council of Great Britain, travels to Laing Art Gallery and Hatton Gallery, Newcastle upon Tyne; Arnolfini Gallery, Bristol; and others; catalog. *Four Painters: Derek Boshier, Bridget Riley, David Hockney, Patrick Caulfield,* Scottish National Gallery of Modern Art, Inverleith House, Edinburgh (Dec 1979–Feb 1980).

Publication: *Pictures by David Hockney,* ed. by Nikos Stangos, introduction by David Hockney, London: Thames and Hudson; New York: Harry N. Abrams.

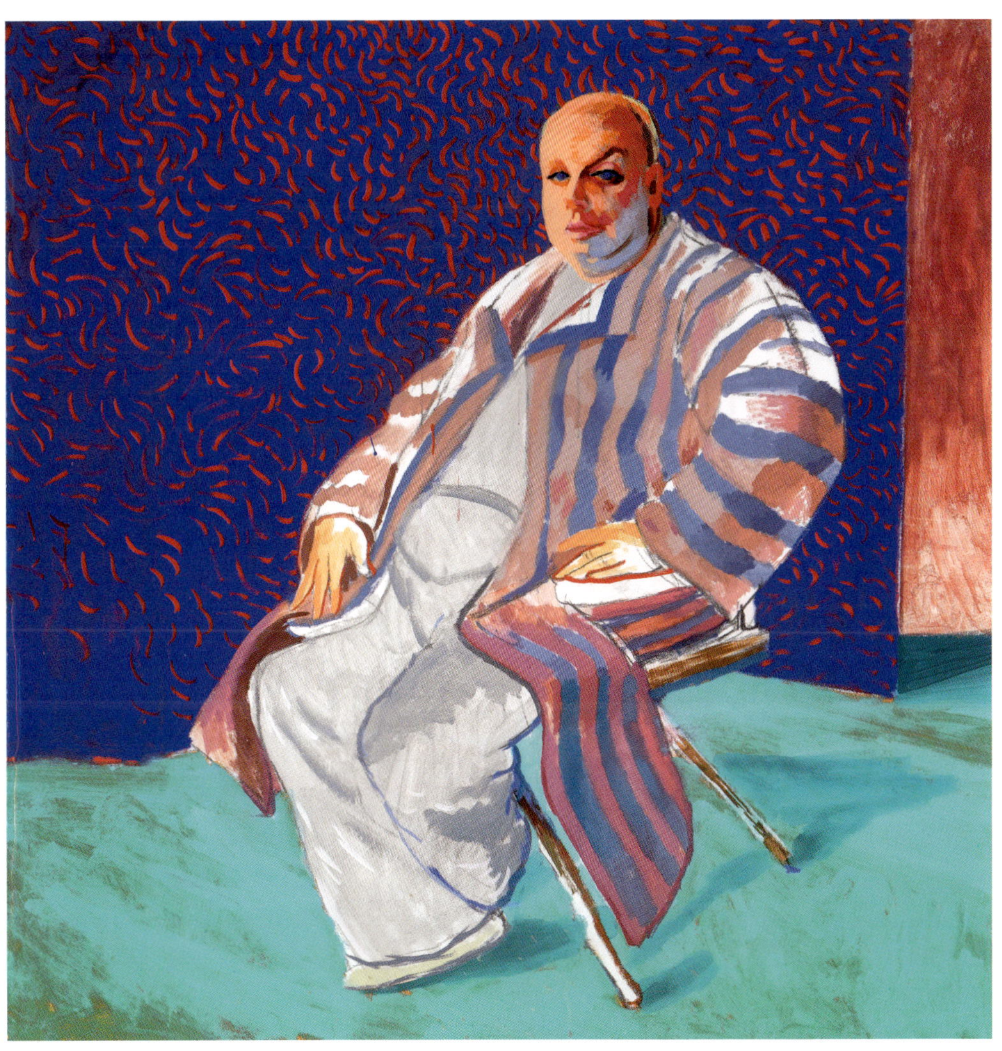

Divine, 1979, acrylic on canvas, 60 x 60 in. / 152.4 x 152.4 cm

Page 177: David Hockney, St. Germain, Paris 1979. Photo: Derek Hudson

Page 180: *A Lot More of Ann Combing Her Hair,* 1979, lithograph, edition of 67, 49 x 36 in. / 124.5 x 91.4 cm

Page 181: *French Marks I,* 1979, gouache on paper, 14 x 17 in. / 35.6 x 43.2 cm

French Marks III, 1979, gouache on paper, 14 x 17 in. / 35.6 x 43.2 cm

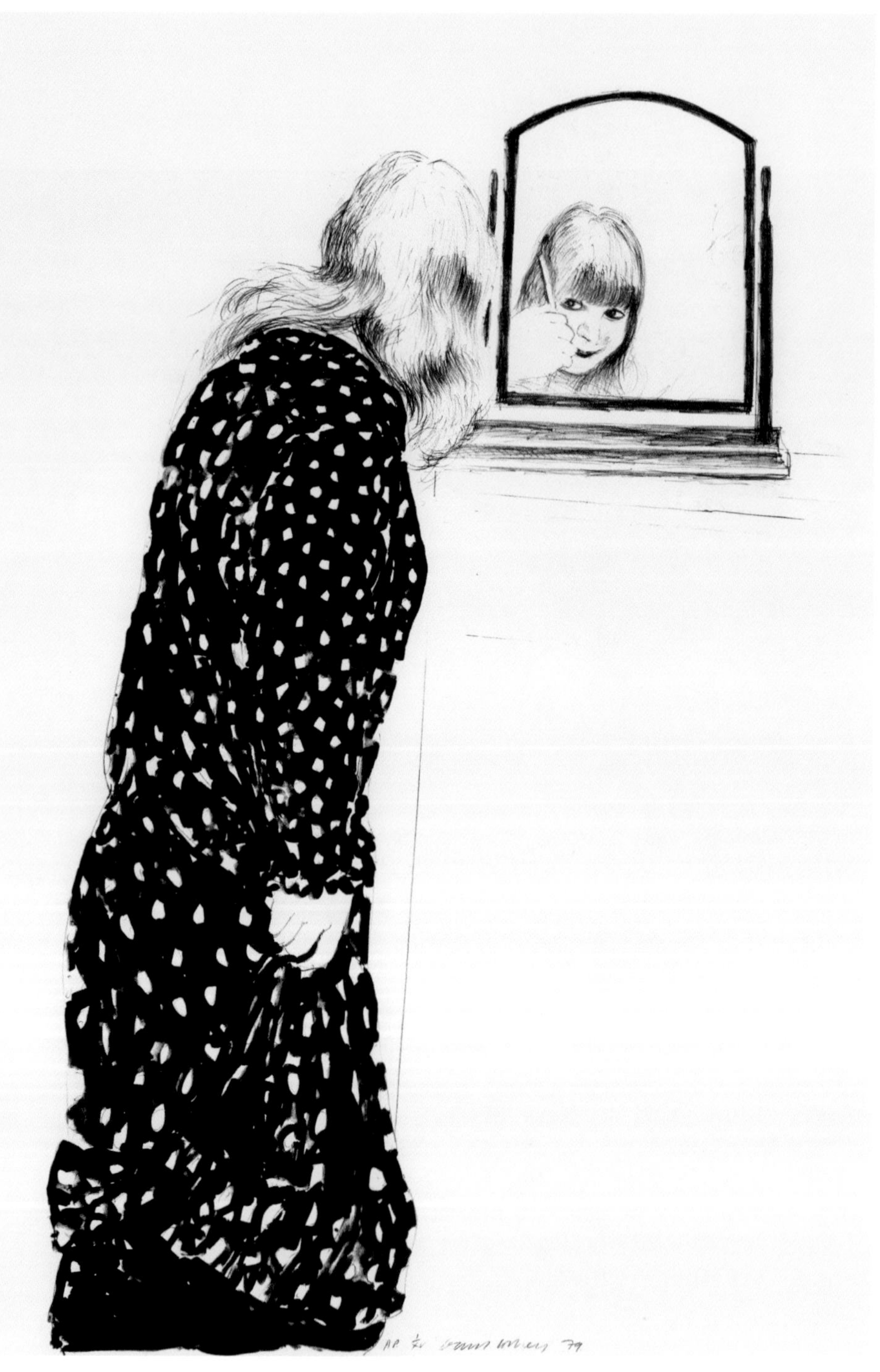

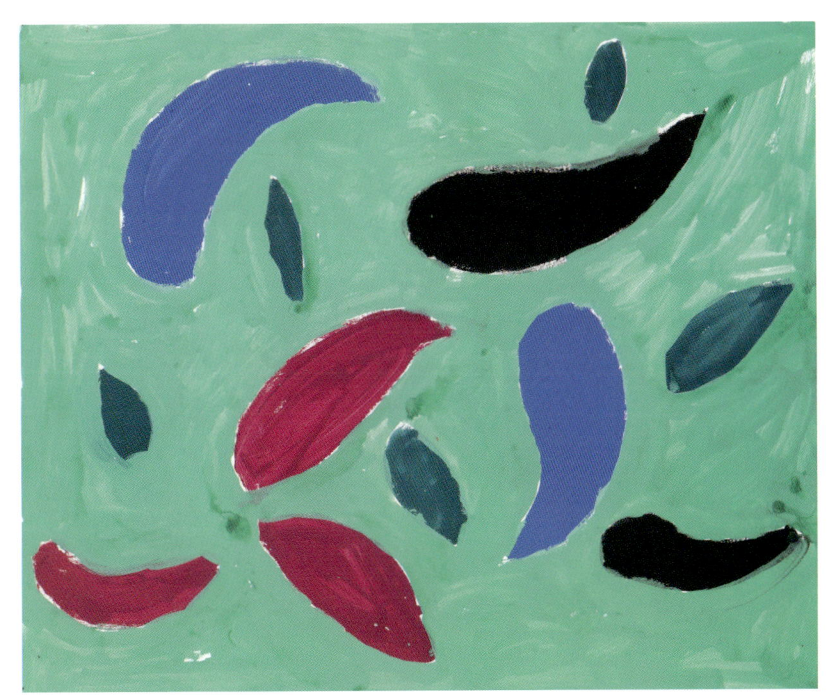

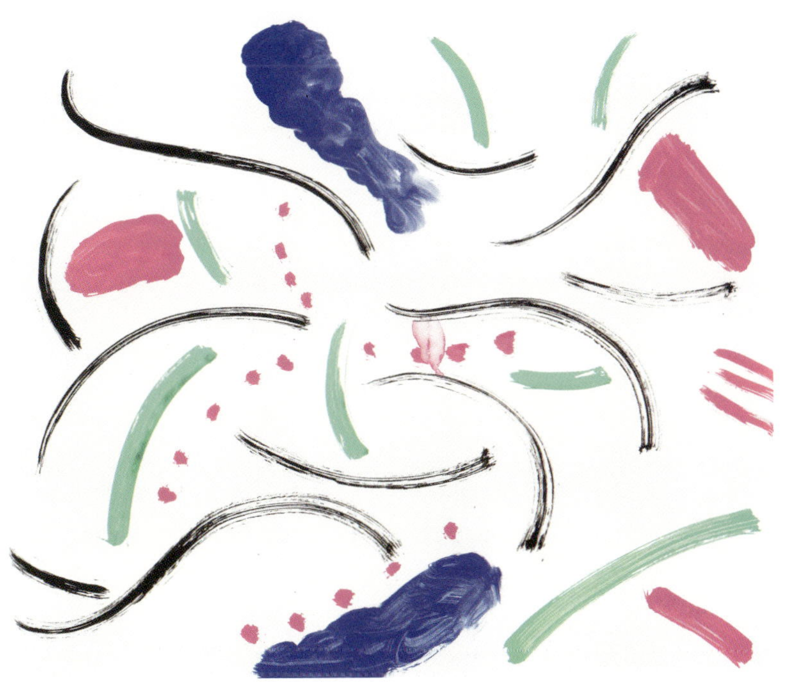

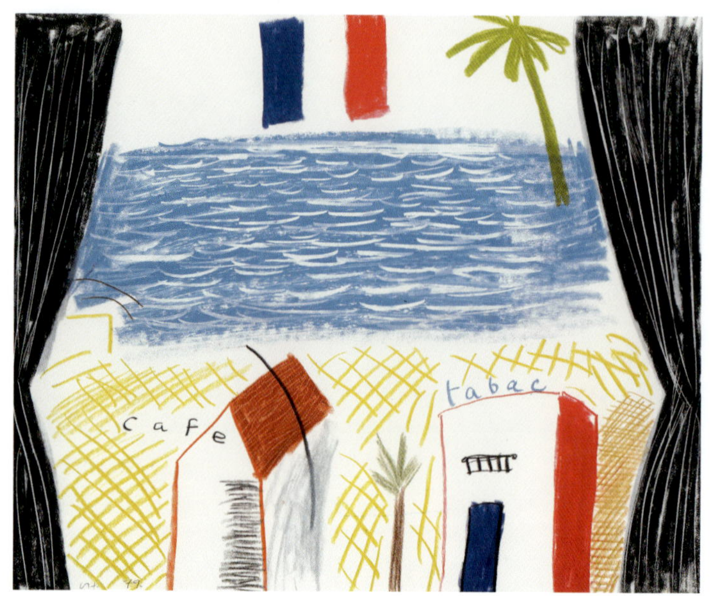

Tabac, Cafe, Curtain and French Flag, 1979, crayon on paper, 14 x 17 in. / 35.6 x 43.2 cm

French Marks with Interior and Trees from *Les Mamelles de Tirésias*, 1979, crayon on paper, 19 x 24 in. / 48.3 x 61 cm

Right page: *Painted Floor with Garden and French Marks* from *L'Enfant et les sortilèges*, 1979, gouache on paper, 19 x 24 in. / 48.3 x 61 cm

Study for Stage with French Flag and Figure from *Parade Triple Bill*, 1979, crayon and gouache on paper, 19 x 24 in. / 48.3 x 61 cm

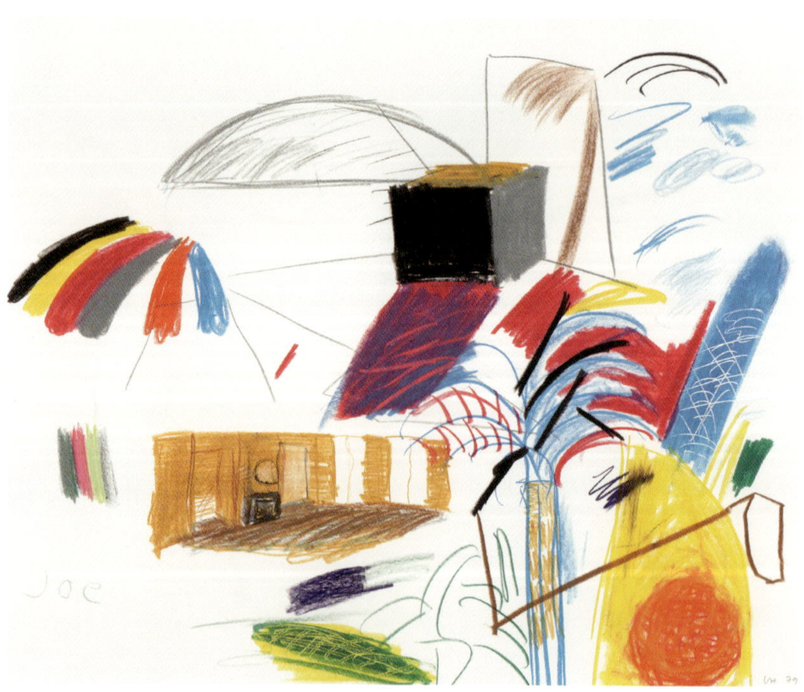

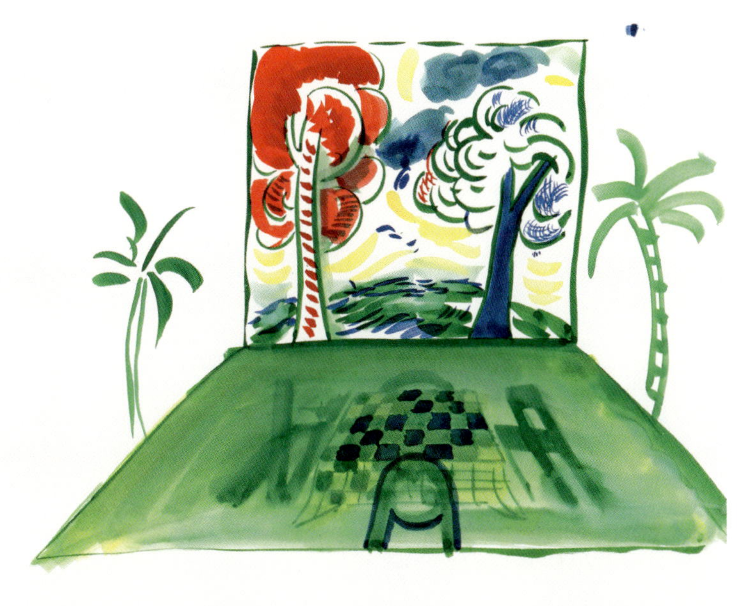

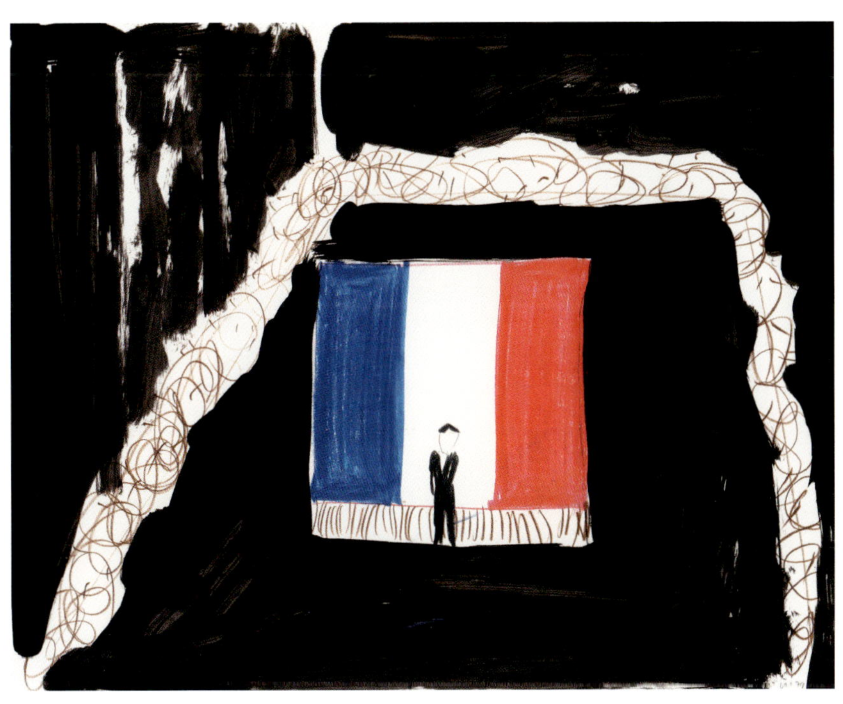

1980

Hockney continues work with director John Dexter on the *Parade Triple Bill* at the Metropolitan Opera (p. 191). Their ideas for the ballet *Parade* do not meet the interest of star dancer Rudolf Nureyev, who is to provide the choreography, and in the end Nureyev has to back out of the production. Dexter's idea is to link all three works visually. They make good progress on *L'Enfant et les sortilèges* (which translates as *The Child and the Spells*): "I decided to start by looking in toyshops," Hockney says. "On a hunch, I bought a set of children's letter blocks, some little dolls and a plastic clockwork squirrel. I put the building blocks on the model stage to spell Ravel…John looked at it and his eyes lit up when he saw the blocks, he said, 'Can we spell Maurice with them?…Of course we can use this; they've all got six sides and we can flick them over and represent with different sides of the blocks things like furniture etc.' That afternoon we blocked the whole thing out. I crudely painted the sides of the blocks, making a fireplace, furniture, books, and so on, to show how they could be transformed." The blocks form a first stage device to connect the pieces, and Hockney goes on painting the drop curtains as sceneries.

In June, Hockney sees the big Picasso retrospective at the Museum of Modern Art. In a letter to R. B. Kitaj he writes: "It's like the National Gallery all painted by one man…No artist ever left such incredible evidence of his experience before; it's like Rembrandt, Piero, Van Gogh and Degas all in one…You really *must* see it." Inspired by the experience, Hockney returns to London to make paintings on themes of music and dance (p. 190) that relate to his work for the stage. He works unusually quickly, and soon has finished 16 canvases.

At the end of August, Hockney travels back to Los Angeles. He hears that the musicians at the Metropolitan Opera in New York are on strike, and it appears doubtful if the triple bill will actually be produced. He works on two paintings that mark a new departure, inspired by his daily trips up and down the Hollywood Hills: "The moment you live up here, you get a different view of Los Angeles. First of all these wiggly lines seem to enter your life, and they entered the paintings. I began *Nichols Canyon* (p. 187). I took a large canvas and drew a wiggly line down the middle which is what the roads seemed to be. I was living up the hills and painting in my studio down the hills, so I was traveling back and forth every day, often two, three, four times a day. I actually *felt* those wiggly lines." The concept was further elaborated in the large canvas *Mulholland Drive: The*

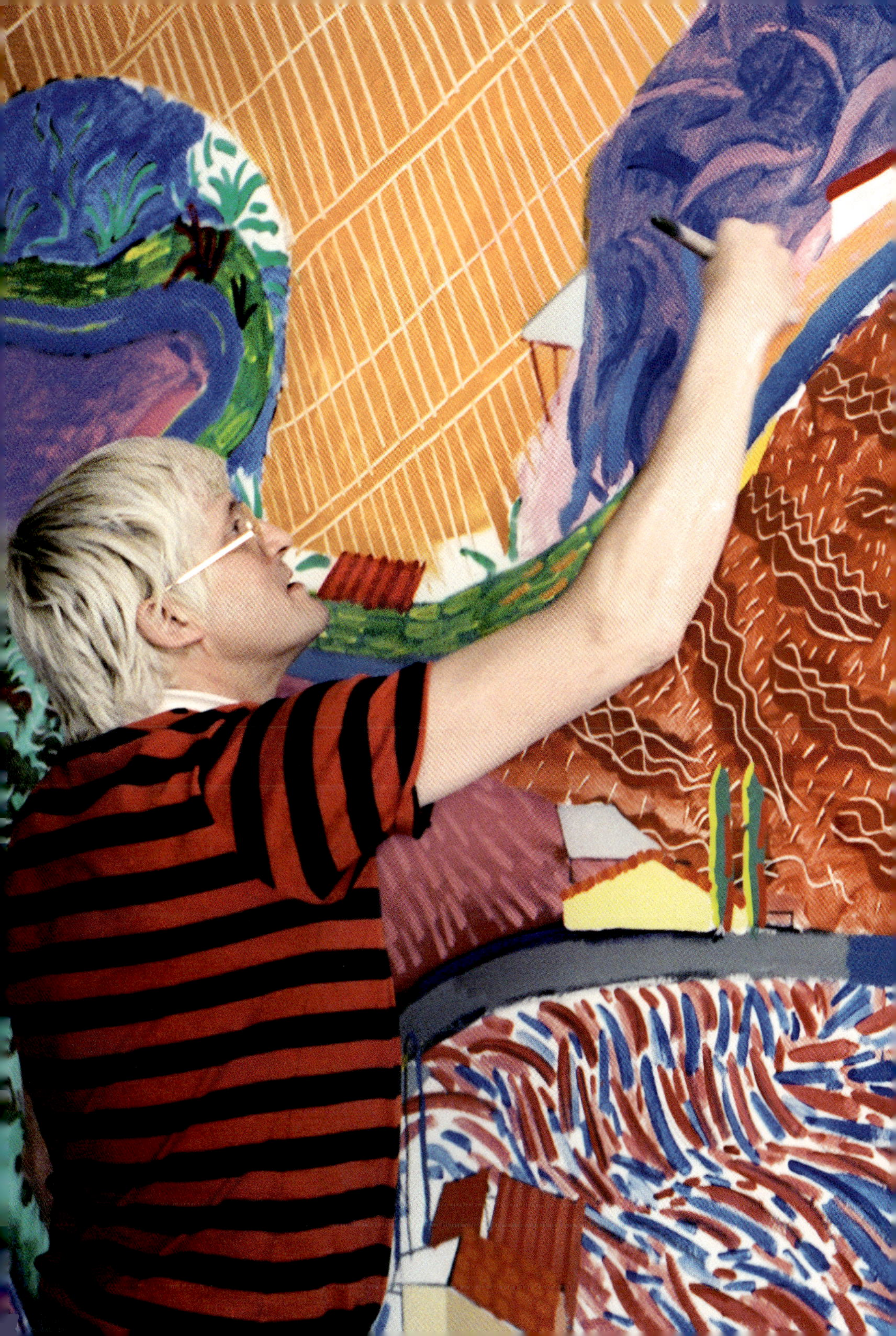

Road to the Studio (pp. 188/189), in which all landmarks and undulation of the drive are painted from memory: "You drive around the painting, or your eye does, and the speed it goes at is about the speed of the car going along the road. That's the way you experience it." This leads Hockney to a free exploration of space in his paintings: "It was all about movement and shifting views. What I was learning was amazing to me. I realized more and more what you could do, how you could chop up space, how you could play inside the space, that only by playing could you make it come alive, and that it only became real when it came to life."

Solo: *Travels with Pen, Pencil and Ink*, Tate Gallery, London (Jul 2–Aug 25); catalog. *Drawings, Theatre Designs, Paintings and Prints*, Graves Art Gallery, Sheffield (Sep 19–Oct 26). *David Hockney*, Laguna Art Museum, Laguna Beach. *David Hockney*, Getler/Pall Gallery, New York (Mar 4–Apr 5). *Drawings*, André Emmerich Gallery, New York (Apr 3–26). *Lithographs 1978–1980*, Tyler Graphics, New York (Jun); catalog. *Prints*, Holsworthy Gallery (Jul 23–Aug 9), catalog. *David Hockney*, Jordan Gallery, London (Aug). *Modern Graphics*, Arum Art Center, Arundel (Aug 23–Sep 27). *Drawings and Prints*, Deweer Art Gallery, Otegem (Sep 20–Oct 28). *David Hockney*, André Emmerich Gallery, New York (Oct 4–22). *David Hockney*, Knoedler/Kasmin Gallery, London (opens Oct 7).

Group: *Contemporary Printed Art: A View of Two Decades*, Museum of Modern Art, New York (Feb 14–Apr 1). *Collaborations*, Northwestern University, Evanston (Sep 28–Oct 26).

Publication: *David Hockney: Paper Pools*, ed. by Nikos Stangos, London: Thames and Hudson; New York: Harry N. Abrams.

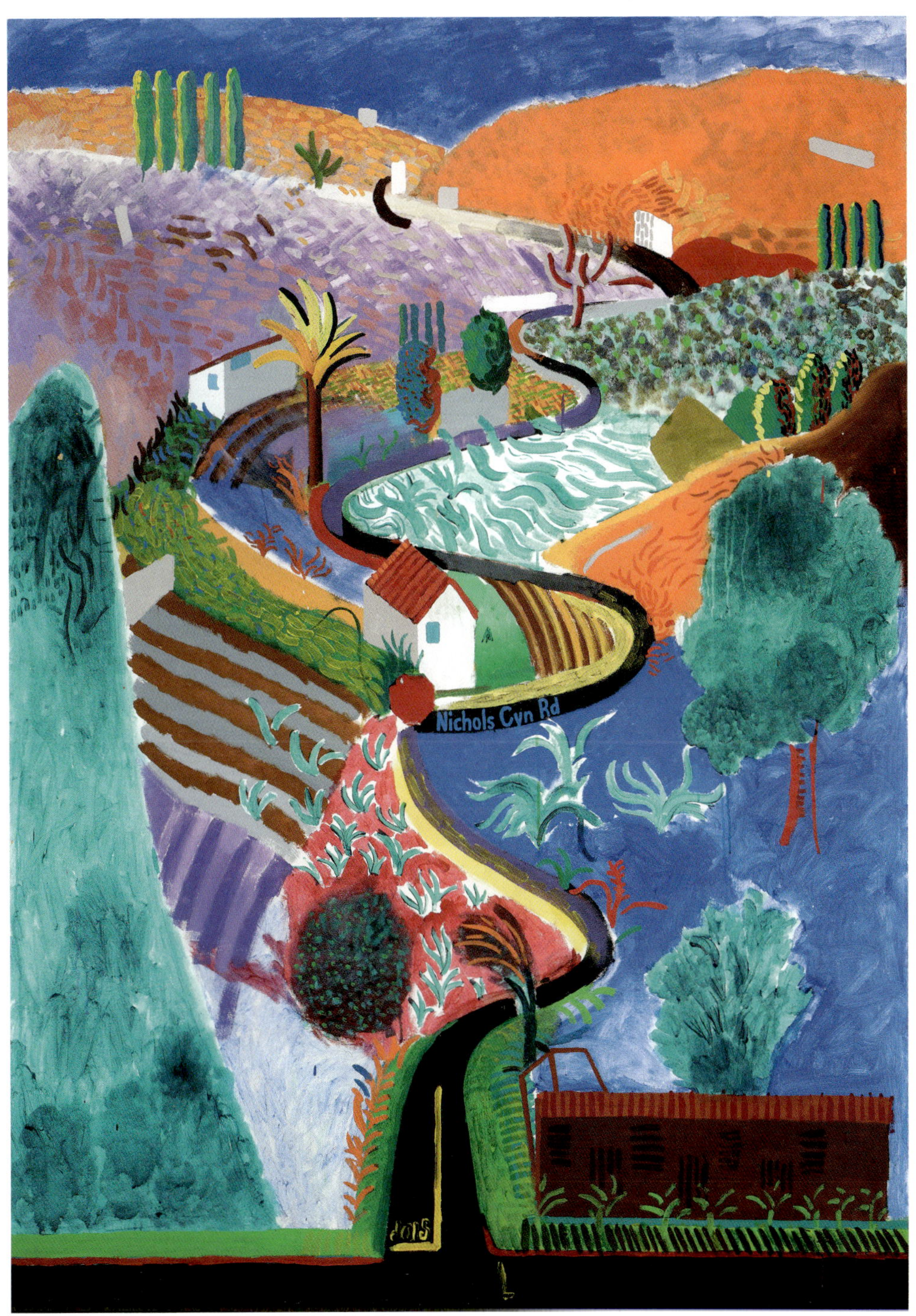
Nichols Cyn Rd

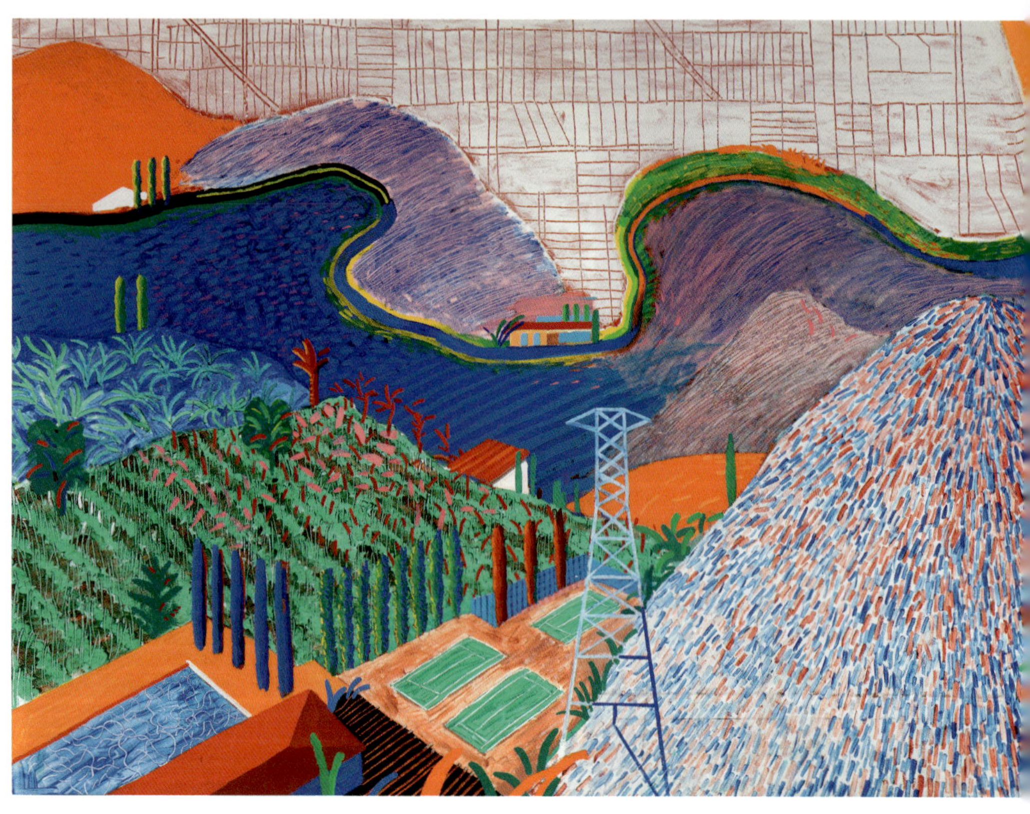

Mulholland Drive: The Road to the Studio, 1980, acrylic on canvas, 86 x 243 in. / 218.4 x 617.2 cm

Page 185: David Hockney in his studio painting *Mulholland Drive: The Road to the Studio,* Los Angeles 1980. Photo: Sidney B. Felsen

Page 187: *Nichols Canyon,* 1980, acrylic on canvas, 84 x 60 in. / 213.4 x 152.4 cm

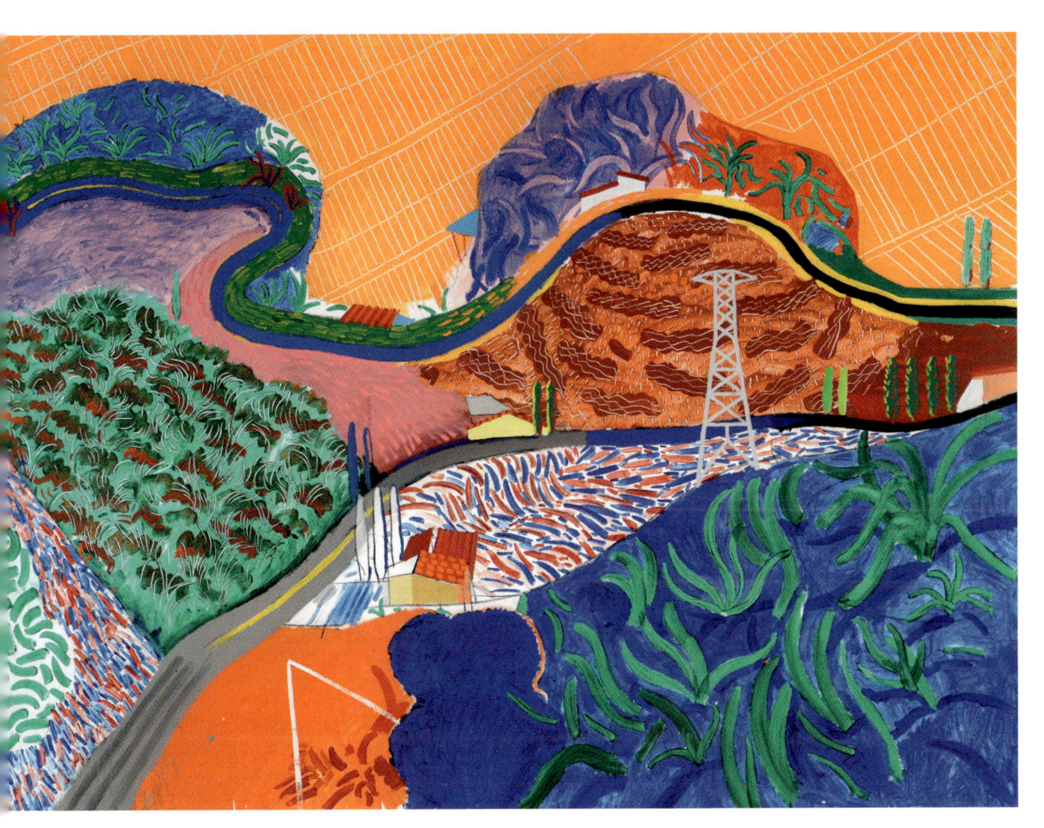

Page 190: *Harlequin,* 1980, oil on canvas, 48 x 36 in. / 121.9 x 91.4 cm

Page 191: Production of *Les Mamelles des Tirésias,* as performed at Metropolitan Opera House, New York 1981

Production of *L'Enfant et les sortilèges,* as performed at Metropolitan Opera House, New York 1981

Harlequin.

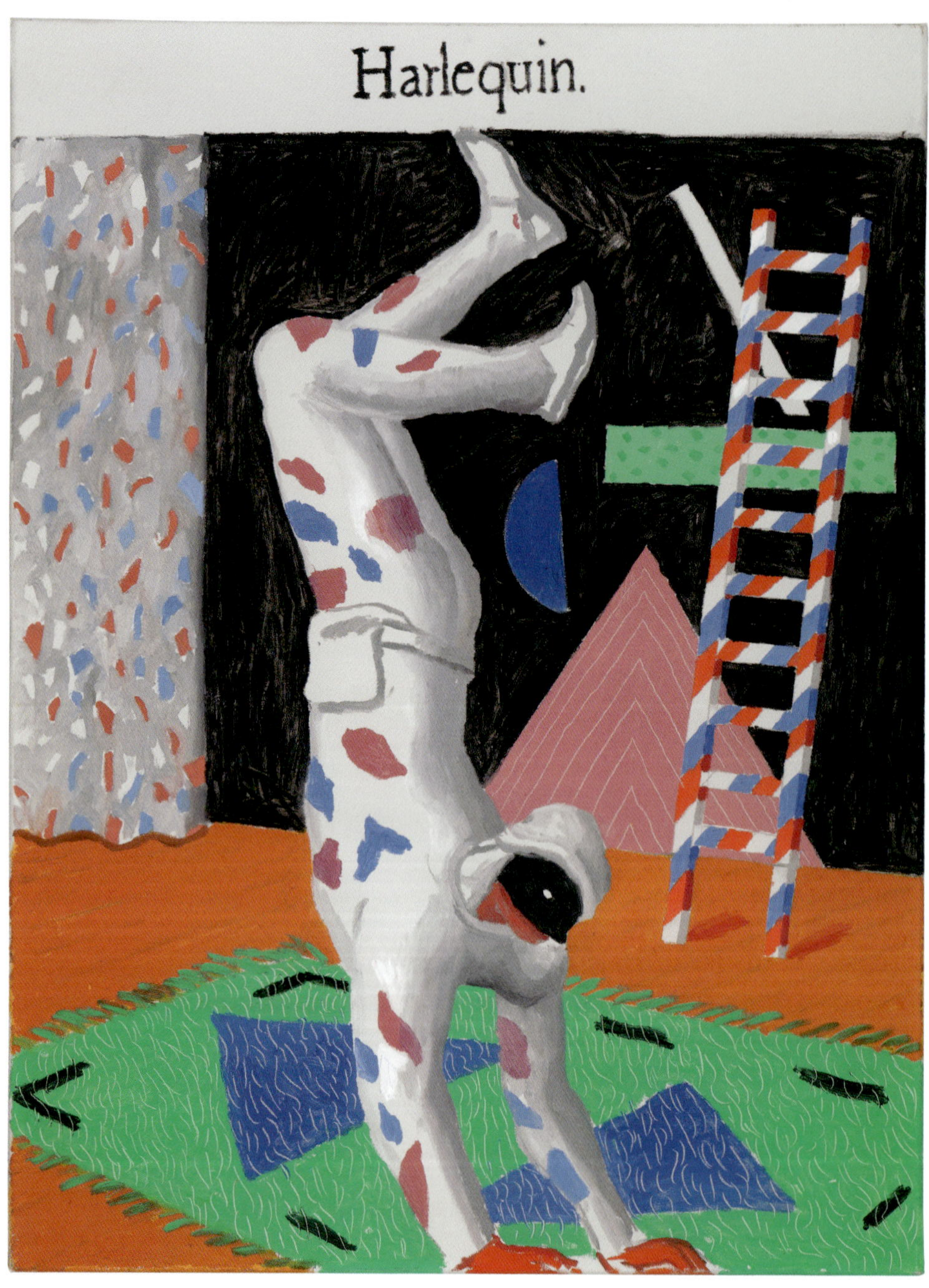

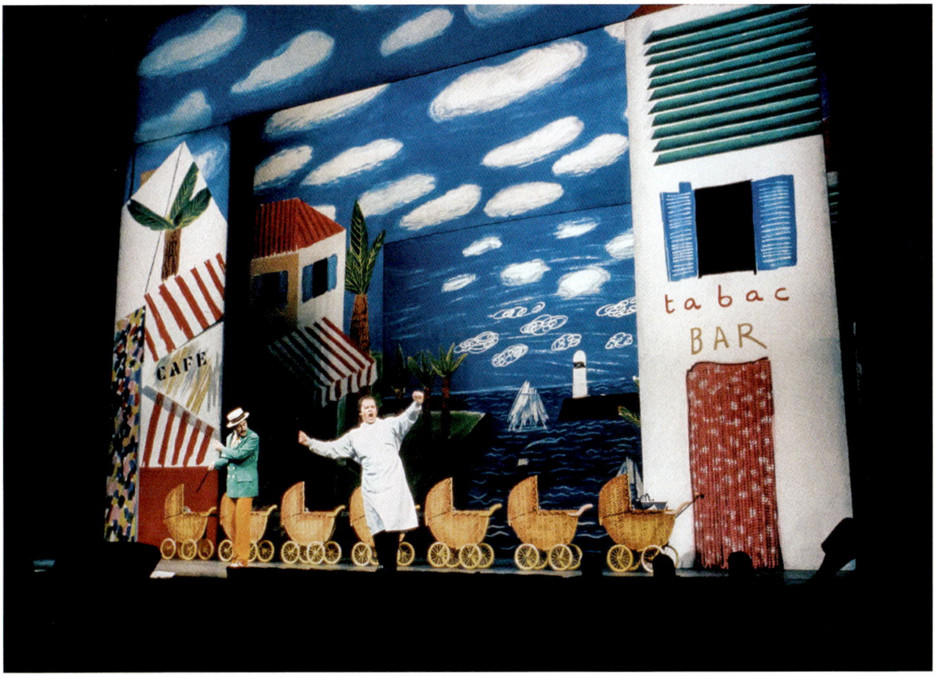

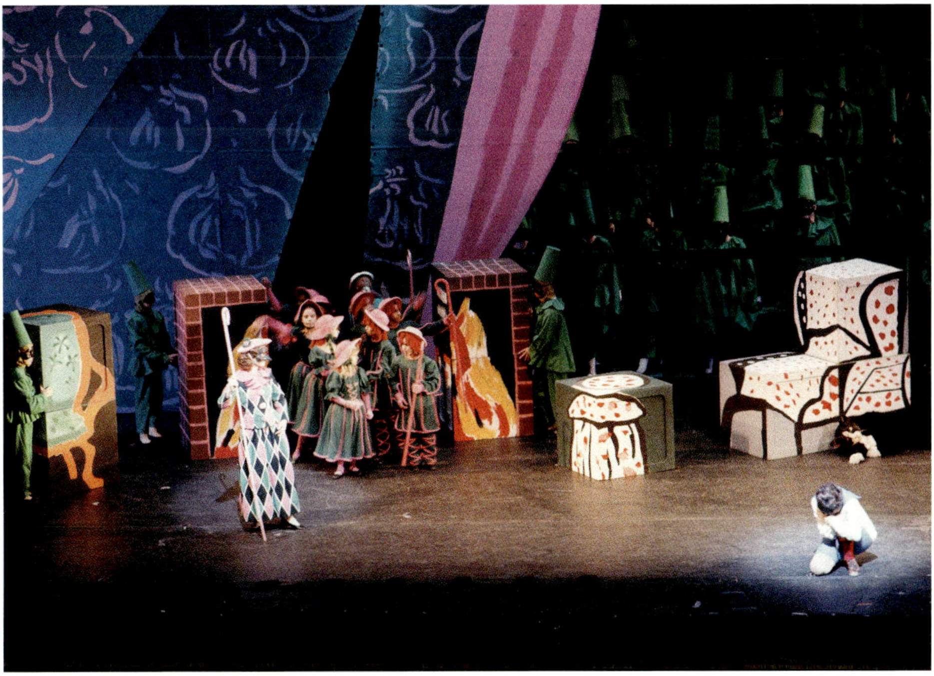

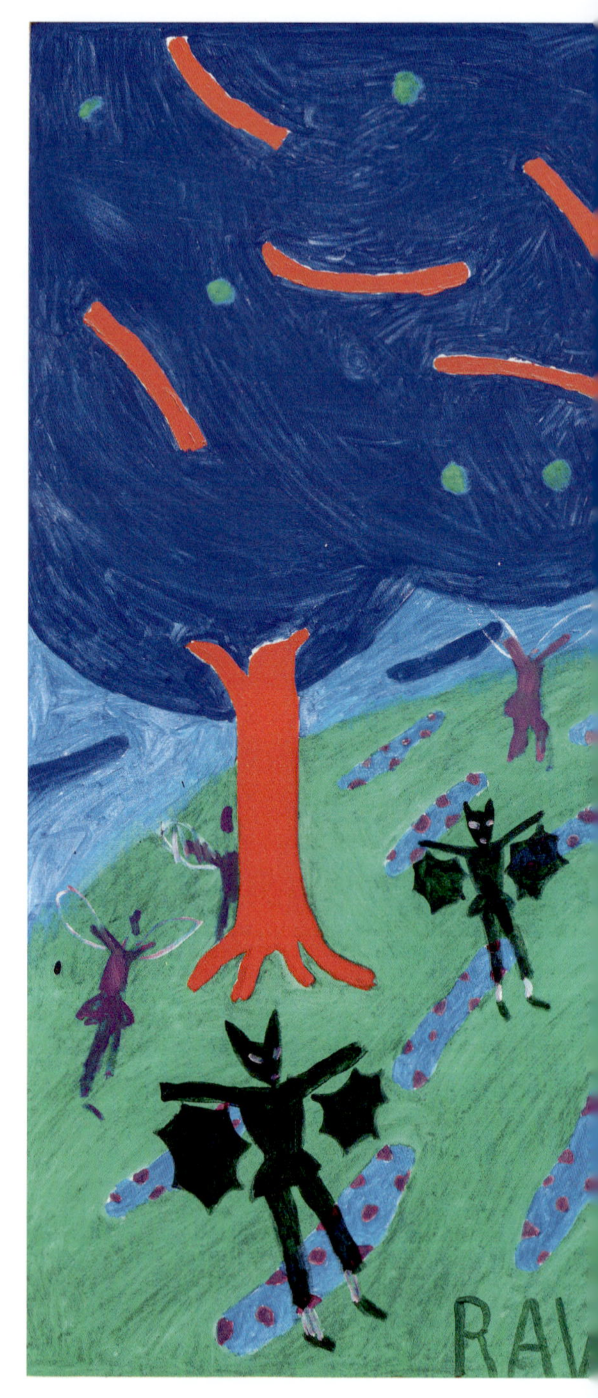

Ravel's Garden with Night Glow,
1980, oil on canvas, 60 x 72 in. /
152.4 x 182.9 cm

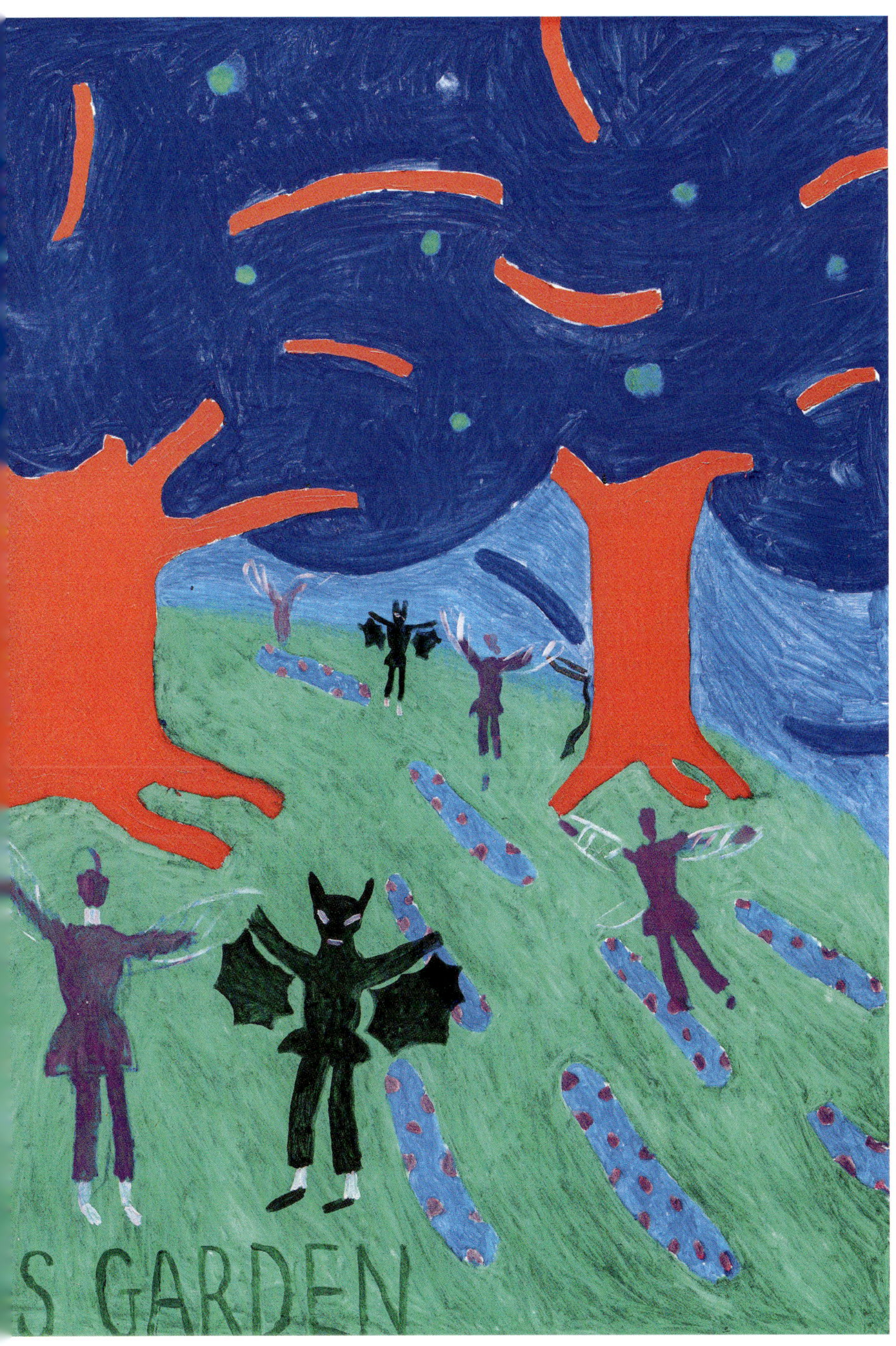
S GARDEN

1981

At the Metropolitan Opera in New York, the musicians' strike is ended, and production of the French triple bill *Parade* can finally go ahead. The program is premiered in February to rave reviews. Donal Henahan in the *New York Times*: "Before we lose ourselves in the forests of detailed explanation and praise, let the medals of honor be passed out right now to those who most deserve them: John Dexter, who directed with unending inventiveness; David Hockney, whose dazzling poster-art sets and witty costumes provided not only color, but also dramatic continuity to the whole night, and Manuel Rosenthal, the 76-year-old French conductor who made his Met debut by reminding us what authority and style can do to shape and vitalize an operatic score…One fluorescent thread, certainly, was the decor of Mr. Hockney, the British painter, who cannily designed the sets so that even Ravel's fragile fairy tale was not swallowed up in this yawning house."

After the premiere, Hockney immediately starts work on a next commission for the Metropolitan Opera, a triple bill of Igor Stravinsky's *Le Sacre du Printemps, Le Rossignol,* and *Oedipus Rex,* to be staged in December (pp. 197, 199). John Dexter later tells the *New York Times* how he got his man: "So I walked up to David one day, while we were in the middle of work on *Parade,* and said, 'How do you fancy three Stravinskys? There's only one rule established: it's all about circles and masks.' Actually, I think if we hadn't been at that kind of fever pitch with *Parade,* David wouldn't have been nudged into doing Stravinsky quite as easily as he was. That and the composer. The idea was to go from the maximum movement of *Sacre*—the maximum, most primitive—to the most sophisticated kind of theater of the lot, which I think the Greek theater was. But the idea was also for the pieces to create an ensemble."

In May Hockney travels to China with Gregory Evans and poet Stephen Spender to produce a book, *China Diary* (pp. 201–203). Chaperoned by the two guides Miss Li and Mr. Lin, they are taken around the sites with great speed: "There was hardly a time when you had half an hour to sit around; so I realized I had to devise a method of drawing quickly or from memory. I started drawing from memory more and more." Hockney closely observes the local artists painting; his most memorable meeting is with an eight-year-old prodigy. The boy is reticent at first, tired of his skills being displayed to tourists, but when Hockney demonstrates his crayons, the mood changes: "The moment I began

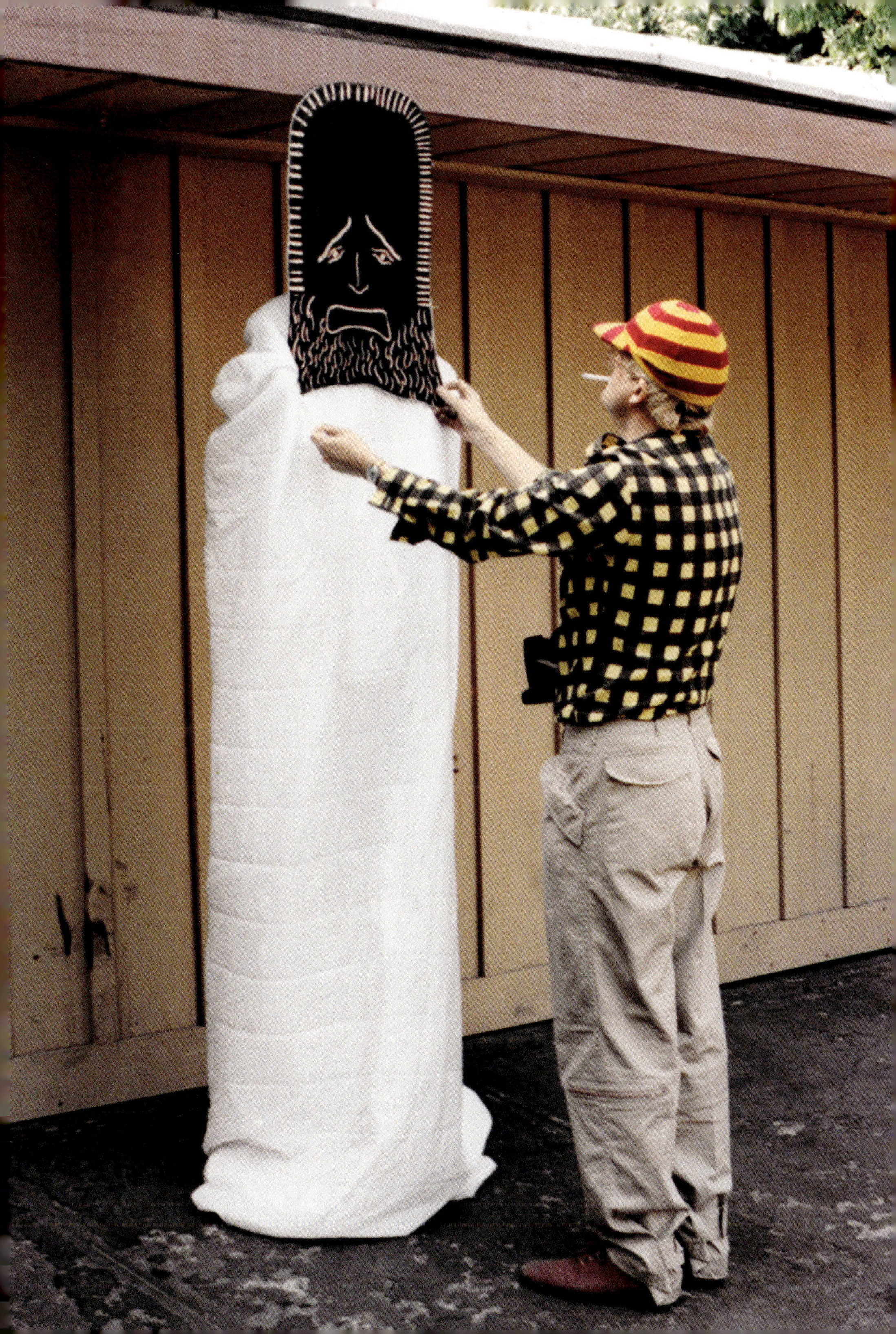

drawing, he grabbed my hand…Then he drew pictures for us, cats, done in the Chinese manner with brushes, which were stunning. Watching him do them was something: the way they were placed on the paper. Everything about them was terrific; he was like a little Picasso, I thought; he was marvelous. When we were leaving, he walked down to the car and he wouldn't let go of my hand. It was very touching. I felt we had communicated without the interpreter…The boy's work made me realize all the beautiful things one could do with the brush, what the brush does; it was his work that made me look at Chinese things with new eyes."

In July, Hockney stages an exhibition at the National Gallery in London for their series *The Artist's Eye*. He develops his display from the 1977 painting *Looking at Pictures on a Screen* (p. 165), portraying Henry Geldzahler looking at four reproductions of work by Vermeer, Piero della Francesca, Van Gogh, and Degas. To that he adds both the original masterpieces and their original reproductions, allowing viewers to compare impressions. Hockney's text in the catalog (p. 200) argues in favor of the value of reproductions: "You can take the cheap photographic copy home. You can pin it up next to your bed. You can have a look at it at night. You can wake up and have a look at it in the morning. And it's giving off pleasure in strange ways that go on and on." For him, the value of these reproductions is related to the photographic medium, which is not merely the mechanical process: "Now I think the best use for photography, the *best* use for it, is photographing other pictures. It is the only time it can be true to its medium, in the sense that it's real. This is the only way that you can take a photograph that could be described as having a strong illusion of reality. Because on the flat surface of the photograph is simply reproduced another flat surface—a painting."

December sees the premiere of the Stravinsky bill at the Metropolitan Opera; reviews mostly compare it with the earlier *Parade* triple bill. Anna Kisselgoff in the *New York Times*: "Five of the six works seen in these two seasons were first presented by Serge Diaghilev's Ballets Russes and both programs refer back to original productions that were highly experimental in their time. It is perhaps a commentary upon our own time that the Met cannot come up with their equivalent in new work. So it is, in fact, presenting the dead avant-garde. Yet these particular works are hardly all classics and if they no longer shock, most look very much alive on their own terms. The Stravinsky evening is superior to the *Parade*

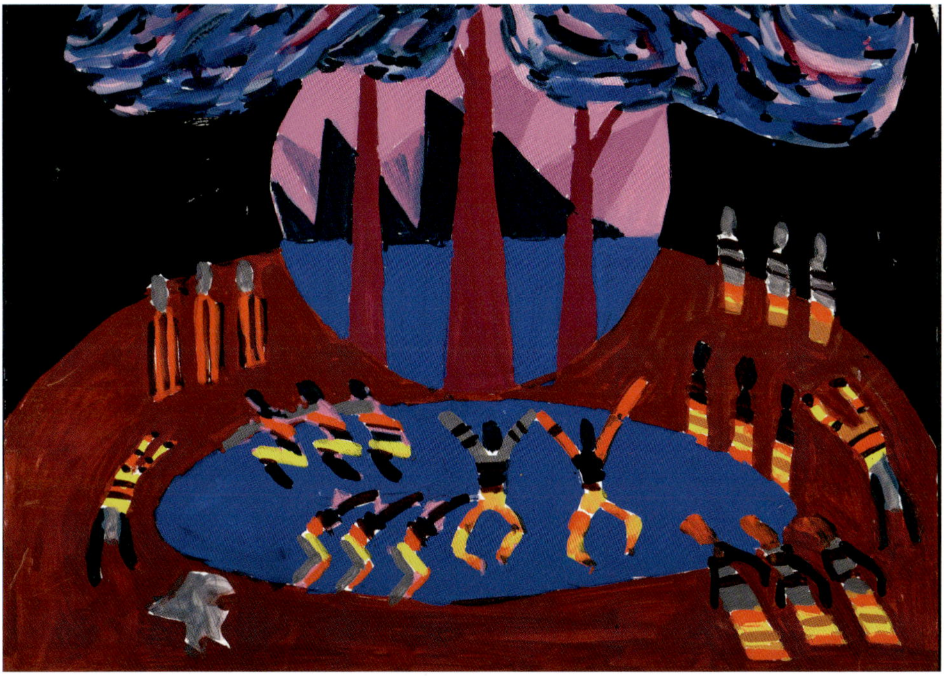

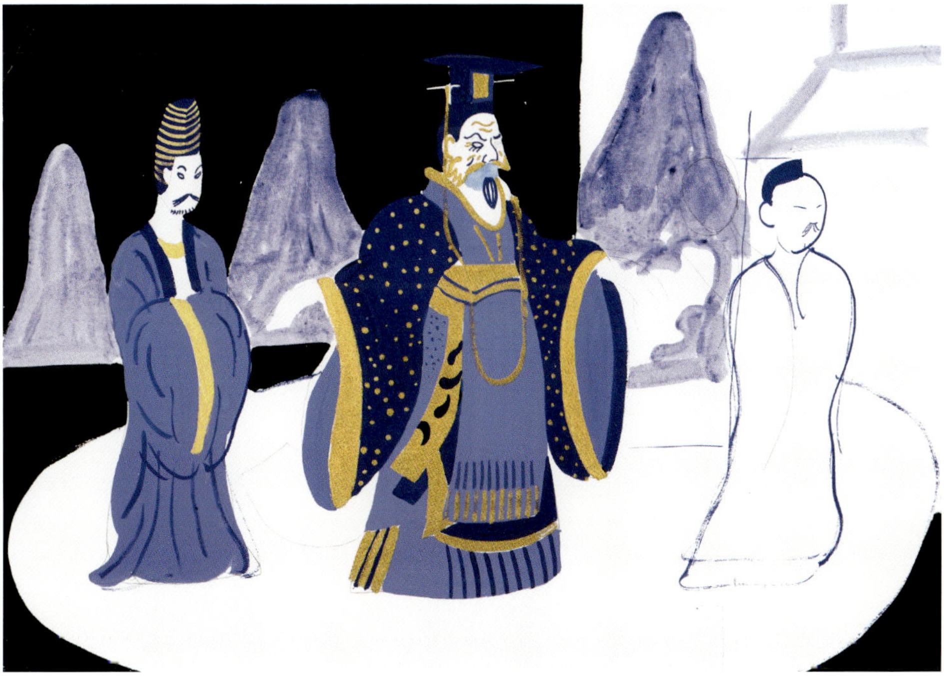

bill in its unity of conception and esthetic logic. Last season, Mr. Dexter and Mr. Hockney forced an artificial connection among the three pieces by linking them with new commedia dell'arte figures extraneous to them as independent works. An anti-war theme, tied to the period in which the works were presumably conceived, was equally arbitrary. In *Stravinsky,* Mr. Dexter and Mr. Hockney are more subtle, or at least more abstract. The links are decorative, seen in the symbolism of real or painted masks on faces and backcloths, and the repetition of the circular motif as a ritual sign."

Having spent the second half of the year in New York and Los Angeles, Hockney visits Bradford and London for Christmas, as he does in most years. It is cold and gray, and he paints his *Hollywood Hills House* (pp. 204/205) from memory, adding a picture of Stan Laurel and Oliver Hardy that his father had once painted, a real postcard of a Renaissance painting, and in the foreground models for the opera stage.

Solo: *Stage Designs for "The Rake's Progress" and "The Magic Flute,"* Ashmolean Museum, Oxford (May 18–Jun 28). *The Artist's Eye: David Hockney. Looking at Pictures on a Screen,* National Gallery, London (Jul 1–Aug 31); catalog *Looking at Pictures in a Book* with a text by David Hockney. *David Hockney,* Castelli Graphics, New York (Mar 14–Apr 4). *Paintings and Drawings for "Parade,"* André Emmerich Gallery, New York (Mar 26–Apr 18); travels to Riverside Studios, London (May 5–June 7). *Celia and Flowers: 1965–1980,* Knoedler Gallery, London (opens May 27). *David Hockney,* Galerie Claude Bernard, Paris (Jun 12–Aug 1). *Blue Guitar,* Meta Galleria, Florence (Jun). *Parade von Eric Satie,* Galerie Herbert Meyer-Ellinger, Frankfurt am Main (Sep 23–Nov 21). *Opere grafiche,* Galleria del Cavallino, San Marco (Sep). *Zeichnungen und Grafik,* Galerie Kammer, Hamburg (Oct–Nov).

Group: *A New Spirit in Painting,* Royal Academy of Arts, London (Jan 15–Mar 18); catalog. *Westkunst,* Museen der Stadt Köln (May 30–Aug 16); catalog. *Art in Los Angeles,* LA County Museum of Art, Los Angeles (Nov 20, 1981–Jan 31, 1982); catalog. *Instant Fotografie,* Stedelijk Museum, Amsterdam (Dec 4, 1981–Jan 17, 1982); catalog.

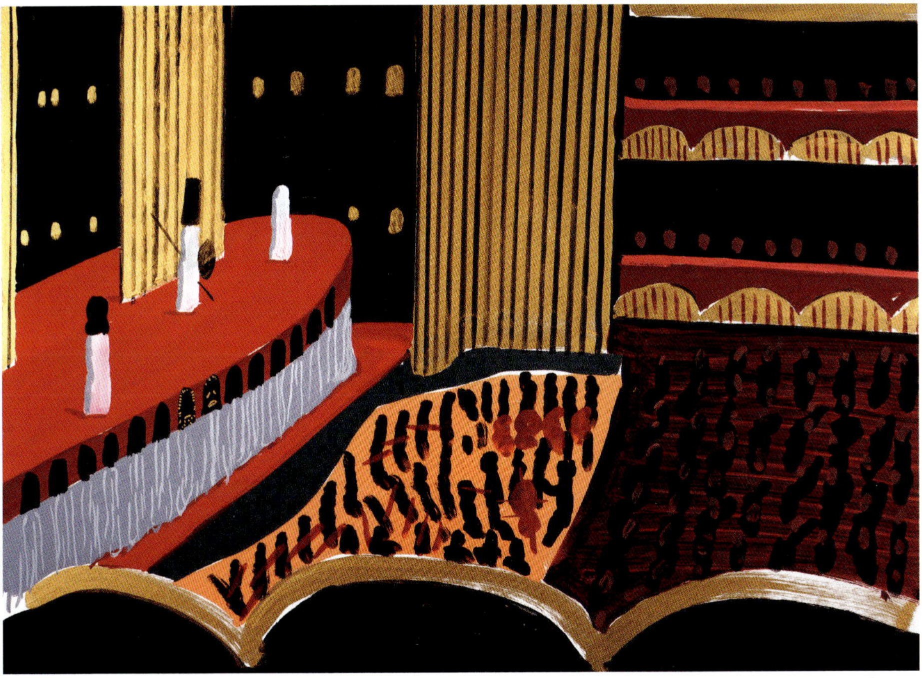

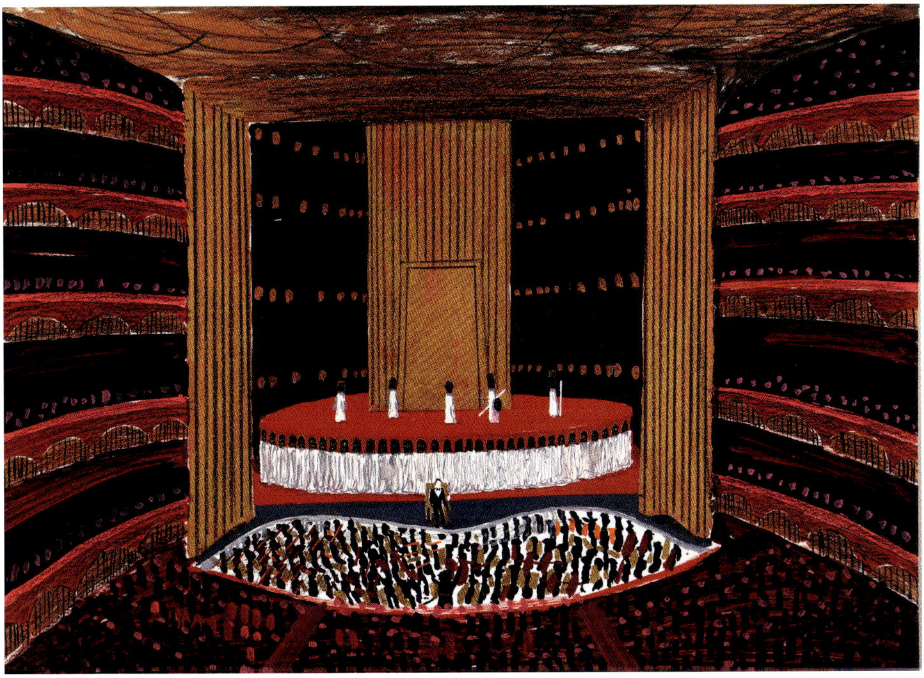

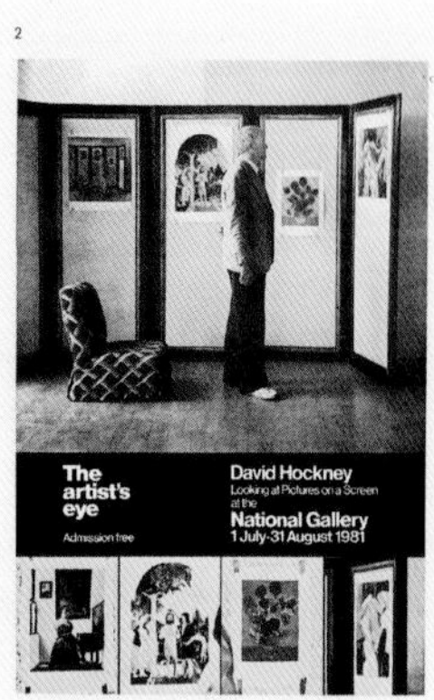

Poster of *The Artist's Eye* exhibition, 1981

**The
artist's
eye**

David Hockney
Looking at Pictures in a Book
at the
NATIONAL GALLERY

1 July – 31 August 1981

So I decided, Well, these pictures were all from the National Gallery; why not put in this picture of mine which has all the others painted in them, smaller? And then here were the real ones, the real objects that were the source of the pleasure. So we put them up in the room with the screen, with the reproductions, and with my painting.

Then I thought, What would that signify? What would you get from it? And then I thought, Well, one thing that can come across quite clearly is if a painting is really wonderful, even in a reproduced form, even a *cheap* reproduced form, it can still give off a lot of its magic. You can't quite define what it is—magic is a good term, it seems to me. And I've even noticed this magic sometimes in postcards of paintings.

I was once in Albi at the Toulouse-Lautrec Museum where they have a small painting by Vuillard, of Lautrec. And they have a very beautiful postcard. I think the postcard is stunning. I saw it and I thought, My God, the postcard is even giving off real vibrations like the painting, of the sheer delight. I thought the painting was delightful, it was unbelievably simple and fresh. Vuillard must have just looked and watched Lautrec, probably almost out of the corner of his eye, and sketched it in very quickly, this feeling of looking at Monsieur Lautrec at work. And it had all the freshness and delight that his mind must have had as he looked up and saw Lautrec—wearing yellow trousers and a red shirt.

I purchased all the stock of these postcards and sent them to friends. And I must admit that most of the friends told me later that the morning they got the postcard and looked at it how thrilling it was—even a postcard, the very object they were holding. And I thought Well it's true, this, you can get the magic to come, even off reproductions.

Panchromatic photograph of coloured postcard.
Edouard Vuillard: *Portrait of Toulouse-Lautrec* (Albi, Musée Toulouse-Lautrec)

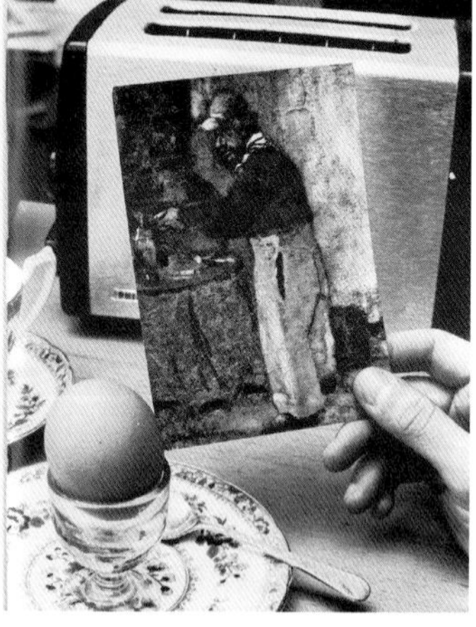

paper or book. They show you pictures that are extremely unrealistic, in the sense that you never saw anything like that if you were at the sporting event. You've never seen anybody suspended in air. You have never seen the ball stood still. And in photographs they *seem* still. Because it's got very little time in it. The sports photograph is a fraction of a second and that's what you see. But that is not what you felt. You felt the time moving on, in the sporting event. The photograph has great difficulty in depicting time. And if we go back to the Piero—I suggested, in this painting, this bird was still, but another part was not. Well, of course, painting, imaginative painting, can do this. And in this sense it is much closer to true experience. It tells of the experience more vividly.

About sixty years ago most educated people could draw in quite a skilful way. Which meant they could tell other people about certain experiences in a certain way. Their visual delights could be expressed. And today people don't draw very much. They use the camera. My point is they're not truly, perhaps, expressing what it was they were looking at—what it was about it that delighted them—and how that delight forced them to make something of it, to share the experience, to make it vivid to somebody else. If the few skills that are needed in drawing are not treated seriously by everybody, eventually it will die. And then all that will be left is the photographic ideal which we believe too highly of.

So here's my short plea for an art of depiction to be kept up. And that means, when I say, 'keeping it up,' I mean there are certain things in an art of depiction that can be taught to anybody, and especially, one would think, any educated person.

Because slowly what would happen, of course, is that primitive art would develop again and the skills slowly

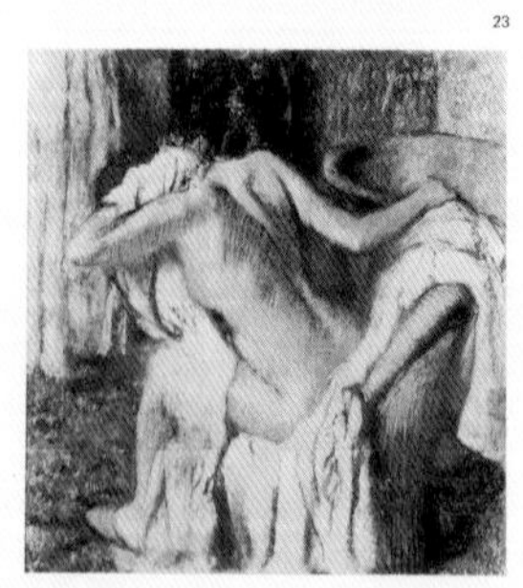

Edgar Degas: *After the Bath* (National Gallery)

Essay by David Hockney in
Looking at Pictures in a Book,
London: National Gallery, 1981

Right page: *Tian An Men Square with Monument to the People's Heroes and the Mao Tse-Tung Memorial Hall, China,* 1981, watercolor on paper, 14 x 17 in. / 35.6 x 43.2 cm

Mountains and Trees, Kweilin, 1981, watercolor on paper, 14 x 17 in. / 35.6 x 43.2 cm

Page 195: David Hockney working on a mask for Igor Stravinsky's *Oedipus Rex* in the driveway of his residence, Los Angeles 1981. Photo: Sidney B. Felsen

Page 197: Stage design for Igor Stravinsky's *Le Sacre du Printemps,* 1981; *Dancers I,* gouache on paper, 22 ¹/₂ x 30 in. / 57.2 x 76.2 cm

Stage design for Igor Stravinsky's *Le Rossignol,* 1981; *Emperor and Courtiers,* gouache on paper, 22 ¹/₂ x 30 in. / 57.2 x 76.2 cm

Page 199: Stage design for Igor Stravinsky's *Oedipus Rex,* 1981; *Raised Stage with Orchestra,* gouache and tempera on paper, 29 x 40 in. / 73.7 x 101.6 cm

Oedipus Raised Stage with Central Column, Narrator and Auditorium, gouache on illustration board, 29 x 40 in. / 73.7 x 101.6 cm

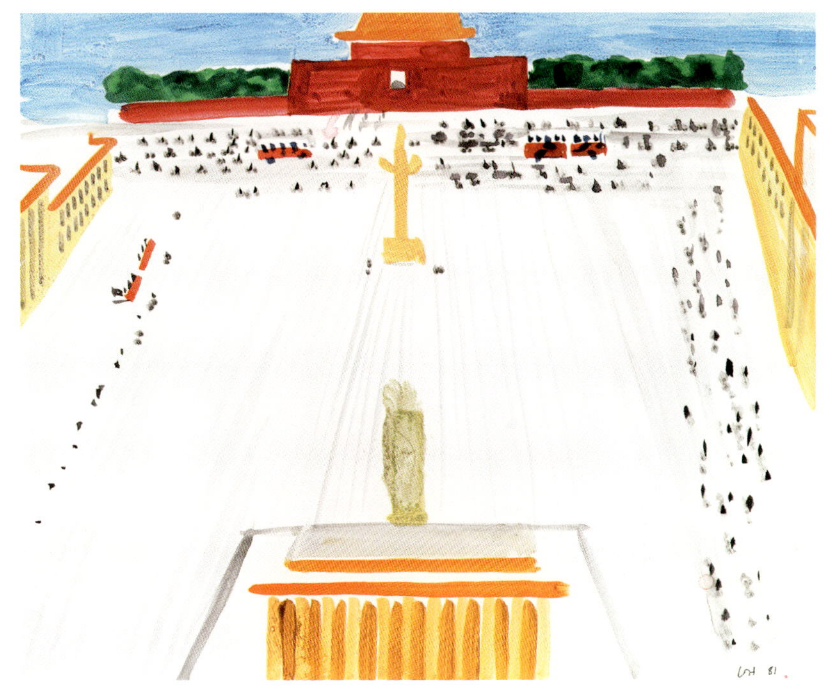

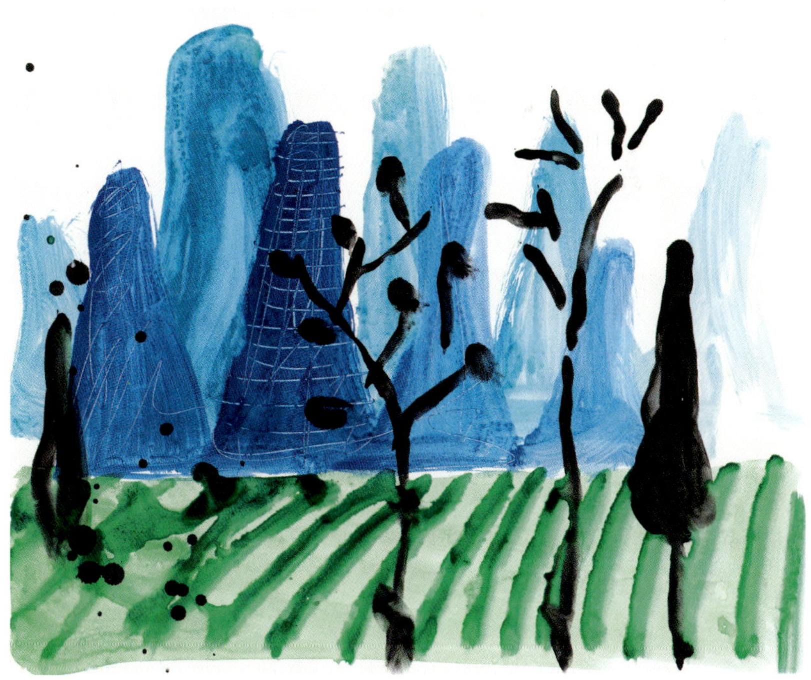

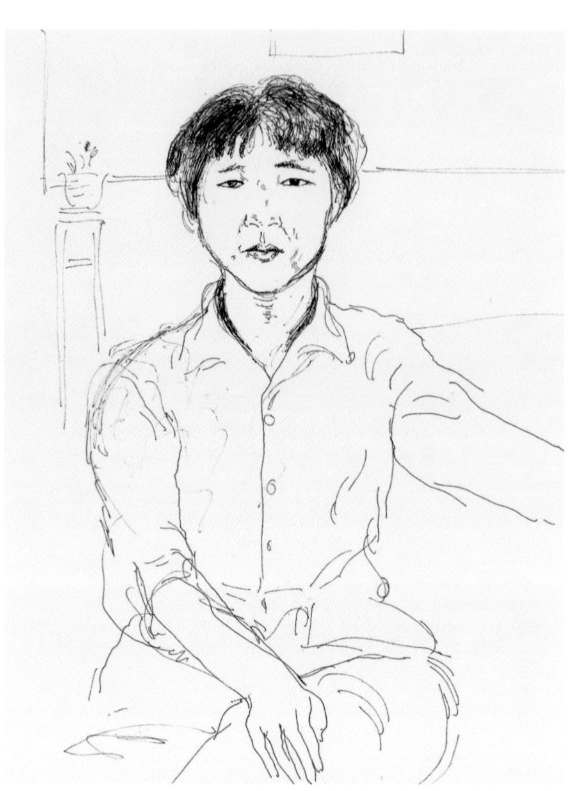

Guide in Sian, China, 1981, ink on paper, 17 x 14 in. / 43.2 x 35.6 cm

Mr. Lin and Child, 1981, ink on paper, 14 x 17 in. / 35.6 x 43.2 cm

Mr. Lin Standing, China, 1981, ink on paper, 27 x 12 in. / 68.6 x 30.5 cm

Right page: *Tian An Men Square, Peking (with Buses and Bicycles), China,* 1981, watercolor on paper, 14 x 17 in. / 35.6 x 43.2 cm

Peking View, China, 1981, watercolor on paper, 14 x 17 in. / 35.6 x 43.2 cm

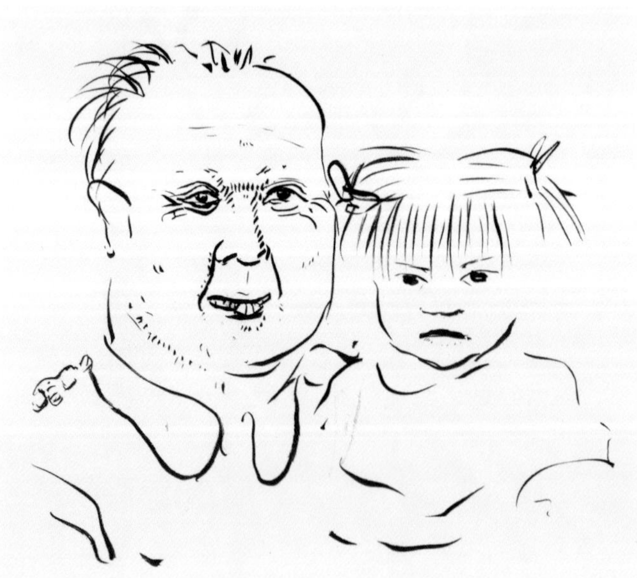

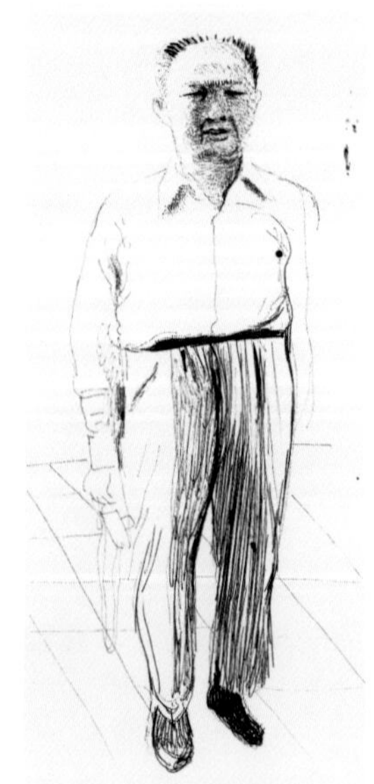

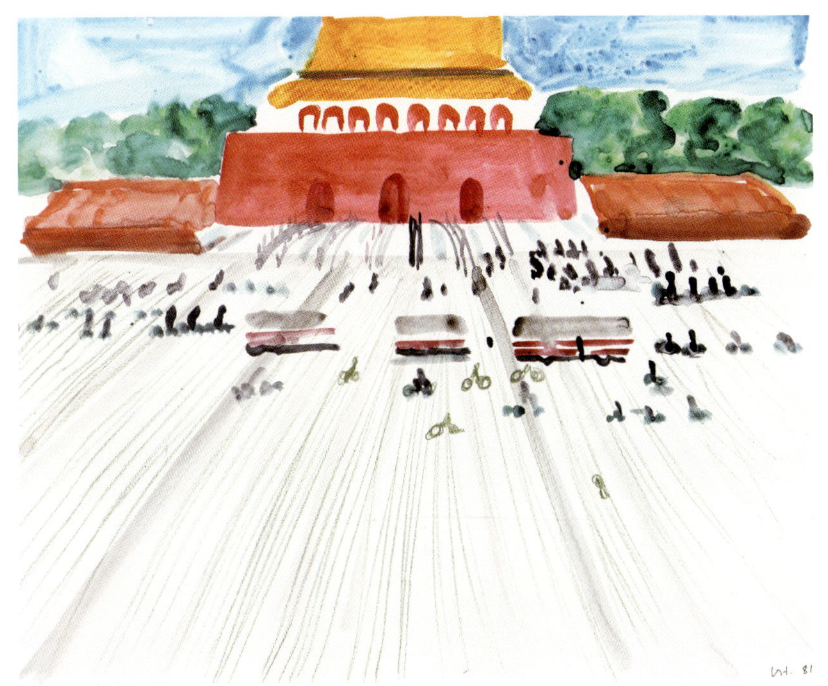

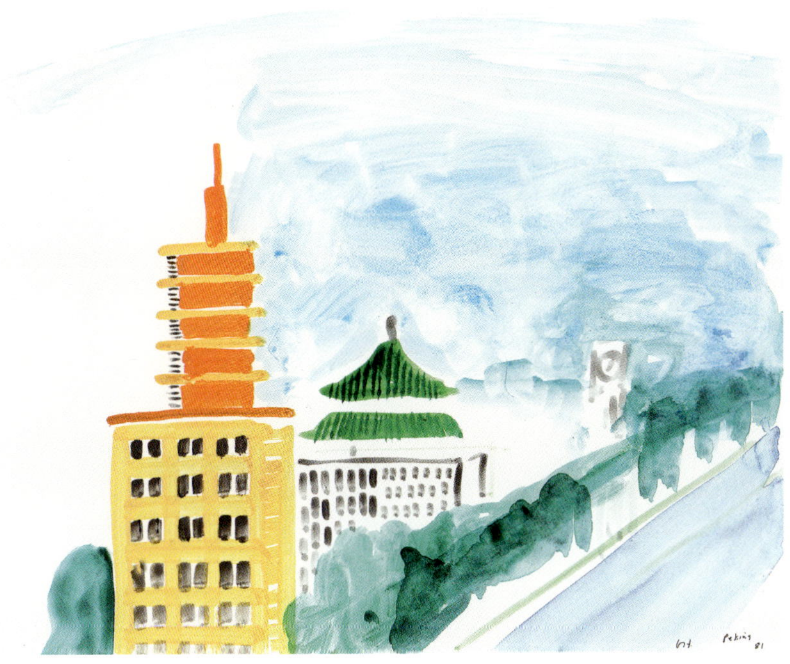

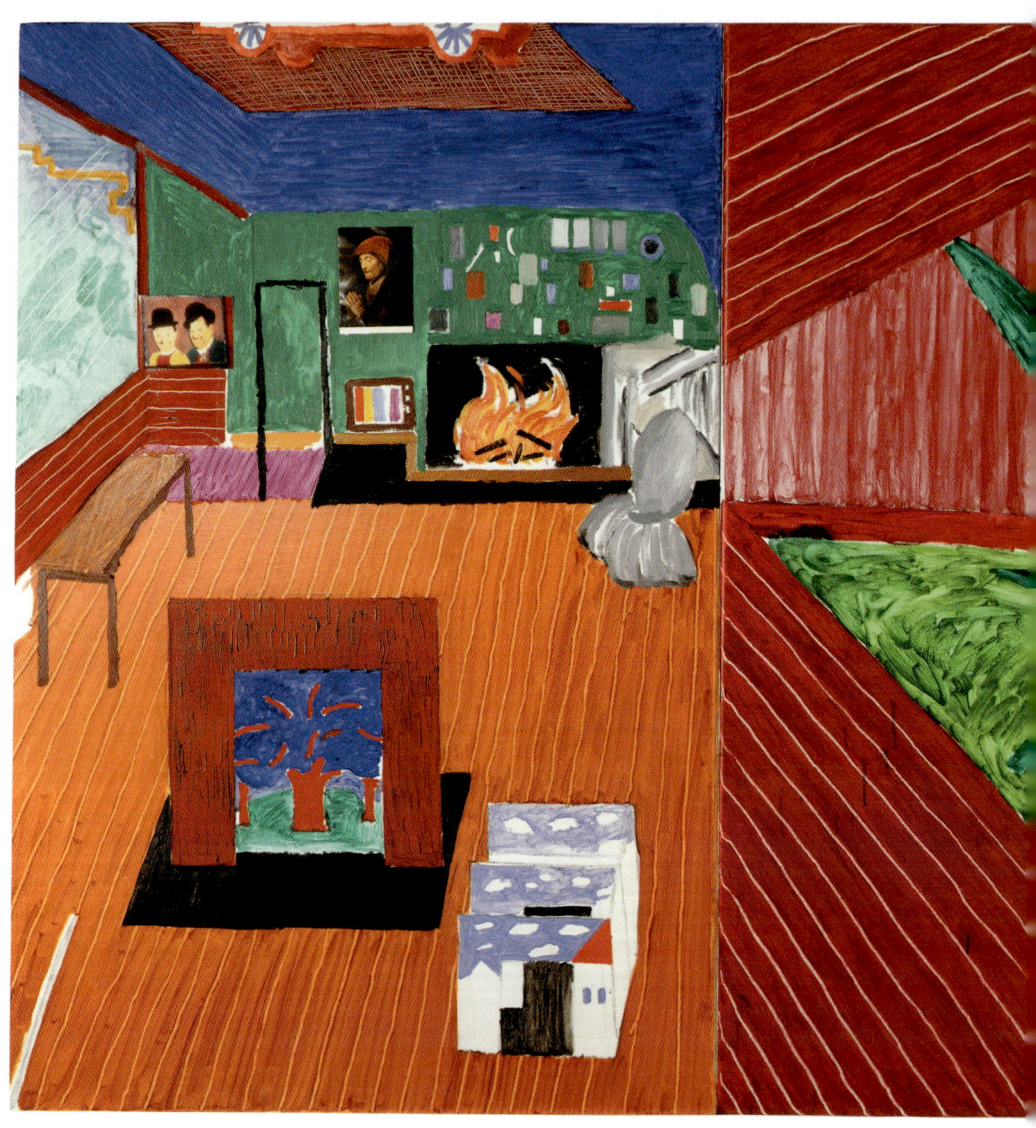

Hollywood Hills House, 1981–1982, oil,
charcoal, and collage on 3 canvases,
60 x 120 in. / 152.4 x 304.8 cm

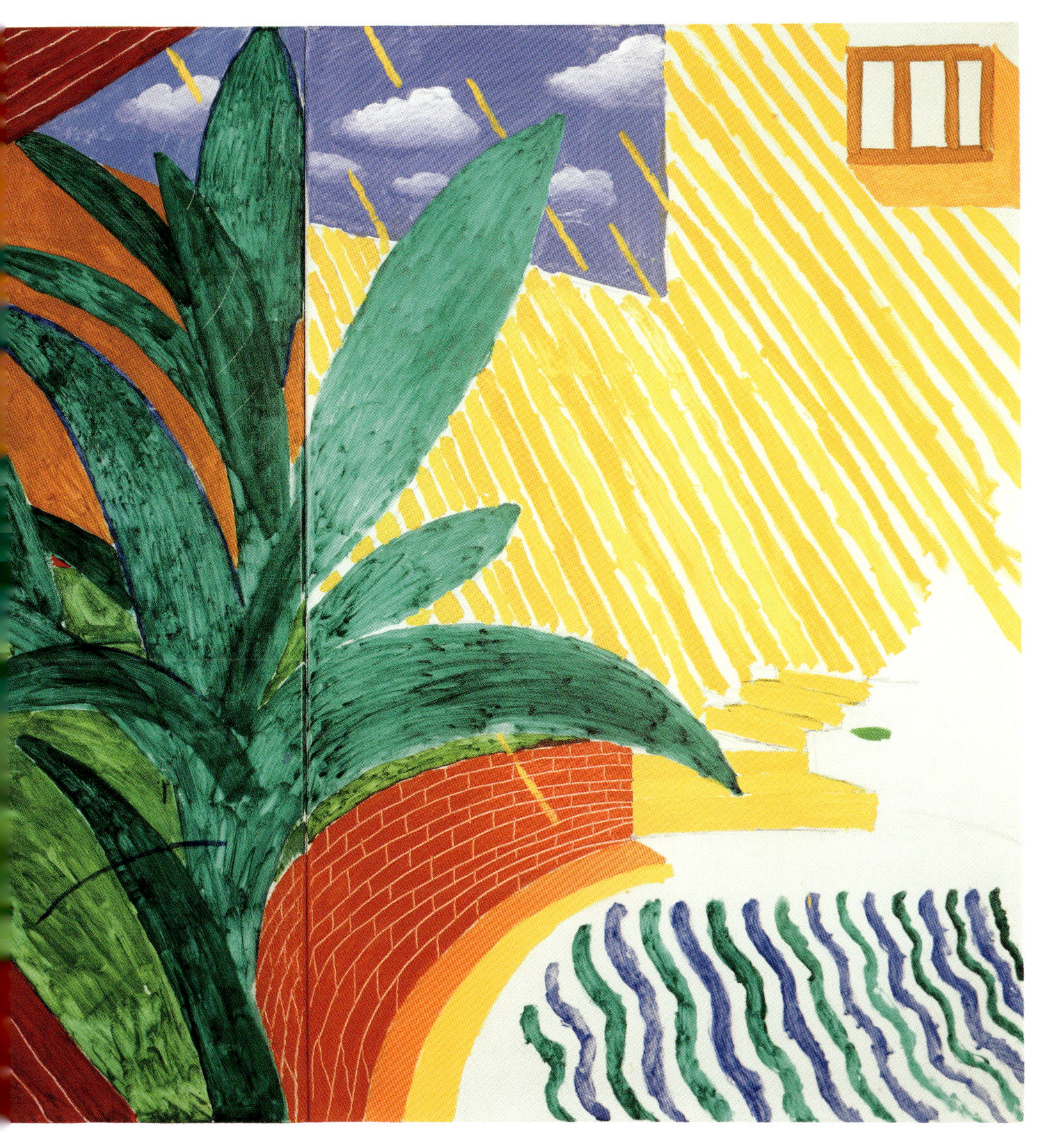

1982

Hockney buys the house in Hollywood Hills and has it painted in vibrant colors. He starts on a series of large-format gouaches, when he receives a visit from Alain Sayag, curator of the Centre Pompidou in Paris, who has talked the artist into doing a photography show and now browses thousands of photos to make a selection. Hockney is still unconvinced by the possibilities of the medium: "All you can do with most ordinary photographs is stare at them—they stare back, blankly—and presently your concentration begins to fade. They stare you down. I mean, photography is all right if you don't mind looking at the world from the point of view of a paralyzed cyclops—*for a split second*. But that's not what it's like to live in the world."

They use a Polaroid camera to document Sayag's choices and Hockney starts experimenting with the medium. He has made composite photographs since the early 1970s as studies for paintings; now he photographs the house and garden and puts the Polaroids together in grids that combine multiple views into one picture (pp. 209–210): "It worked so well that I couldn't believe what was happening when I looked at it. I saw all these different spaces, and I thought: 'My God! I've never seen anything like this in photography.' Then I was at the camera night and day. I bought a thousand dollars of Polaroid film straight away! Within a week I'd done very complex things. I quickly discovered that I didn't have to match things up at all. In fact, I couldn't possibly match them, and it wasn't necessary. The joiners were much closer to the way we actually look at things, closer to the truth of the experience."

Soon he has completed 150 joiners, some of which are shown at André Emmerich Gallery in June. Andy Grundberg in the *New York Times*: "By photographing at different angles and distances, Hockney forces a number of perspectival disparities to appear. The surface of his swimming pool reads as flat against the gallery wall while its surroundings zoom off into the distance... Faces present themselves simultaneously in profile and staring straight ahead. Hockney has long admired Picasso; this is as close as he has yet come to paying homage by style."

Hockney also adds joiners to his photography exhibition at Centre Pompidou in July. He sums up his changed feelings in his essay for the show's catalog: "It's as if the medium was fixed in this one view of the world; photographers seem to be excessively concerned with subject matter, and they may not necessarily relate

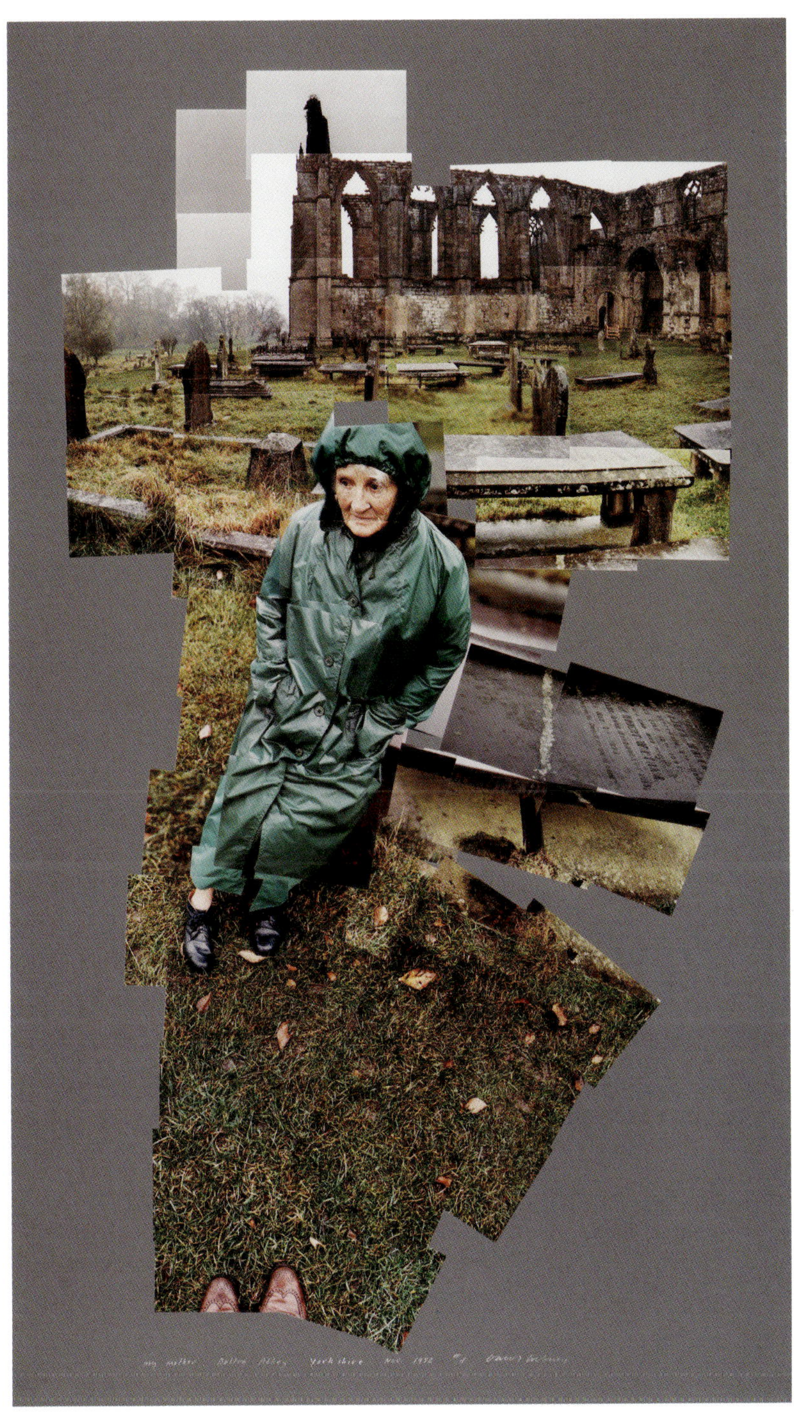
my mother, Bolton Abbey, Yorkshire, Nov. 1982 #1   David Hockney

to form the way a painter does. I believe that only an artist's approach will extend photography as a medium…The Cubists were deeply involved in depicting reality more accurately than had been previously done, and I think they did in fact succeed. It seems strange that photography was not influenced by Cubism."

Hockney switches from Polaroids to a Pentax camera to avoid having white borders around each shot. He creates joiners on travels though the American West, including the Grand Canyon (pp. 212/213), and to Yorkshire with his mother (p. 207). As the work becomes more complex and cannot be immediately executed since the artist has to wait for the films to be developed, he starts making notes and diagrams for their assembly.

Solo: *David Hockney photographe,* Musée national d'art moderne, Centre Georges Pompidou, Paris (Jul 7–Sep 12); catalog with texts by Alain Sayag and David Hockney; English edition: *Photographs,* London: Petersburg Press. *Sources and Experiments,* Sewall Art Gallery, Rice University, Houston (Sep 7–Oct 15); catalog with a text by Esther de Vécsey. *Hockney and Poetry,* Michael Parkin Fine Art, London (May 12–Jun 12); catalog with texts by Michael Parkin and Mark Glazebrook. *Drawing with a Camera,* André Emmerich Gallery, New York (Jun 3–25). *Composite Polaroids,* Knoedler Gallery, London (Jun 29–Jul 31). *Drawings and Photographs of China,* Knoedler Gallery, London (Nov 2–Dec 4). *Incisioni, litografie, manifesti, libri,* La Libreria Giulia, Rome (opens Dec 3). André Emmerich Gallery, New York (Dec).

Group: *1960–1980: Attitudes / Concepts / Images,* Stedelijk Museum, Amsterdam (Apr 9–Jul 11); catalog. *Carnegie International,* Carnegie Institute, Pittsburgh (Oct 23, 1982–Jan 2, 1983); catalog. *Painter as Photographer,* John Hansard Art Gallery, Southampton (Nov–Dec); touring exhibition organized by the Arts Council of Great Britain. *Paper as Image,* Sunderland Arts Centre (Nov–Dec), touring exhibition organized by the Arts Council of Great Britain.

Publication: Stephen Spender and David Hockney, *China Diary,* London: Thames and Hudson; New York: Harry N. Abrams.

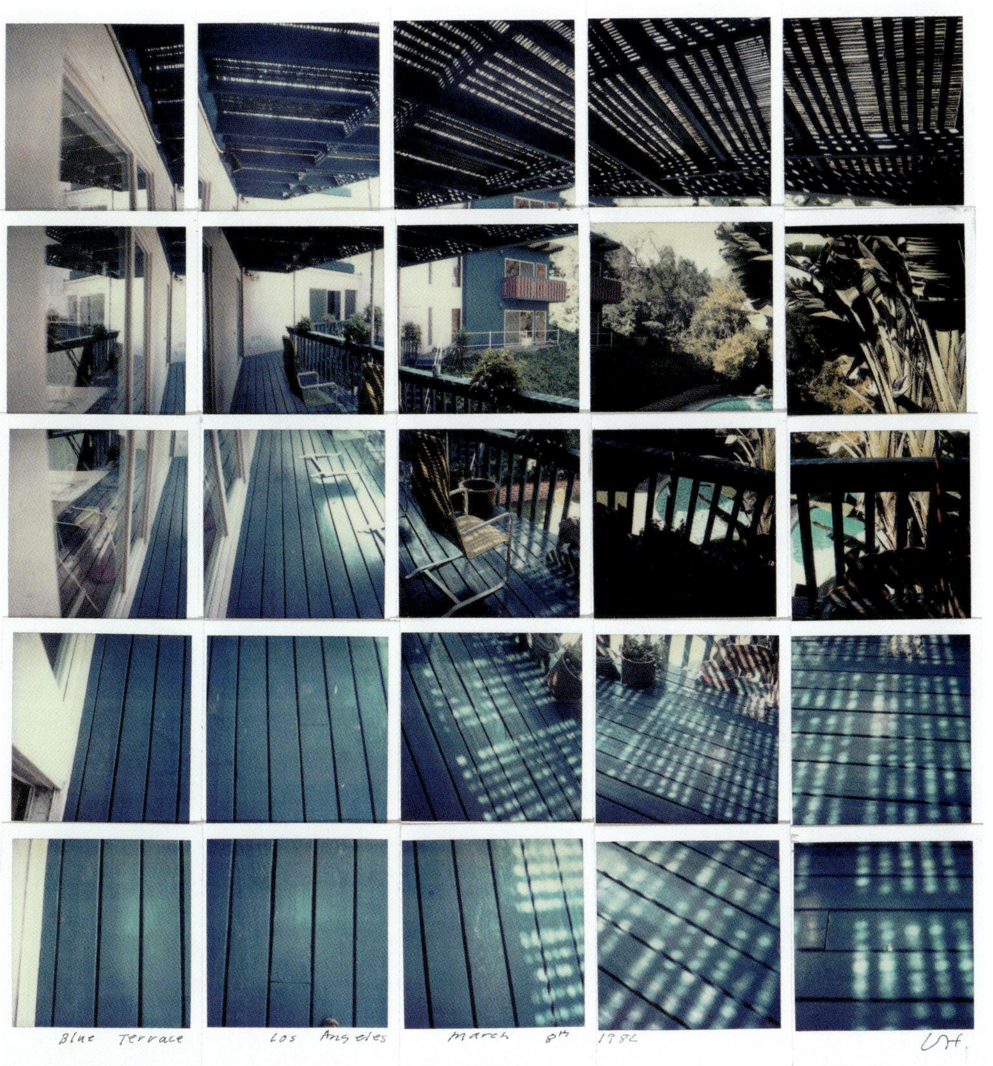

Blue Terrace Los Angeles March 8th
1982, composite Polaroid,
17 ¹/₂ x 17 ¹/₂ in. / 44.5 x 44.5 cm

Page 207: *My Mother, Bolton
Abbey, Yorkshire, Nov. 1982,*
photographic collage, edition of 20,
44 ¹/₄ x 24 ¹/₄ in. / 122.5 x 61.5 cm

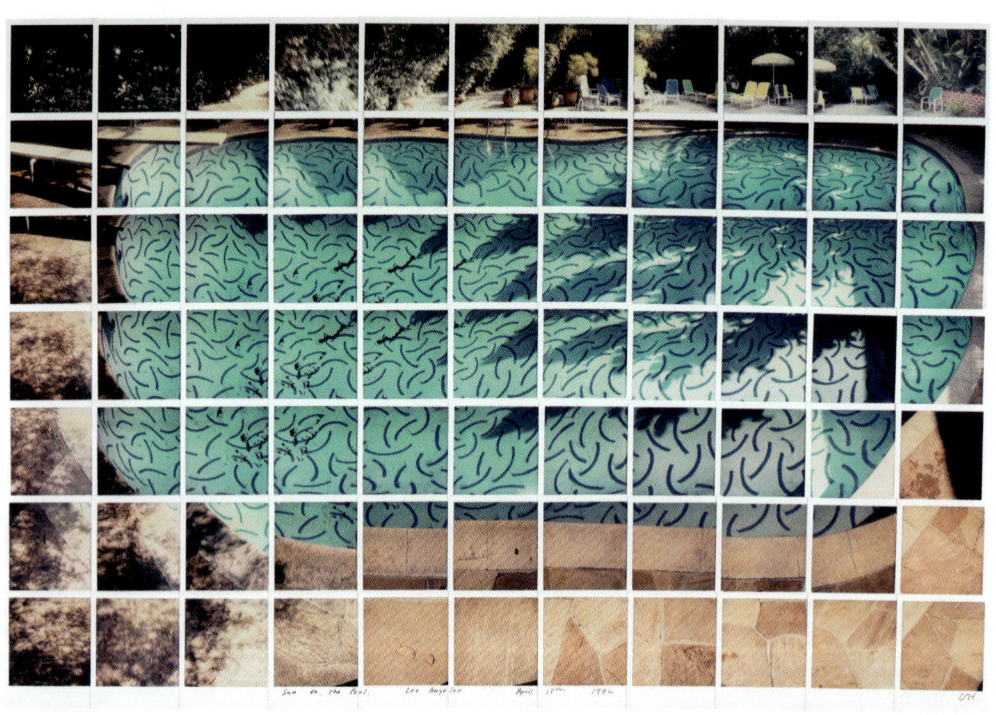

Sun on the Pool Los Angeles April 13th 1982, composite Polaroid, 24 ³/₄ x 36 ¹/₄ in. / 63 x 92.1 cm

Right page: *Henry Cleaning His Glasses Los Angeles March 20th 1982,* composite Polaroid, 42 x 20 in. / 106.7 x 50.8 cm

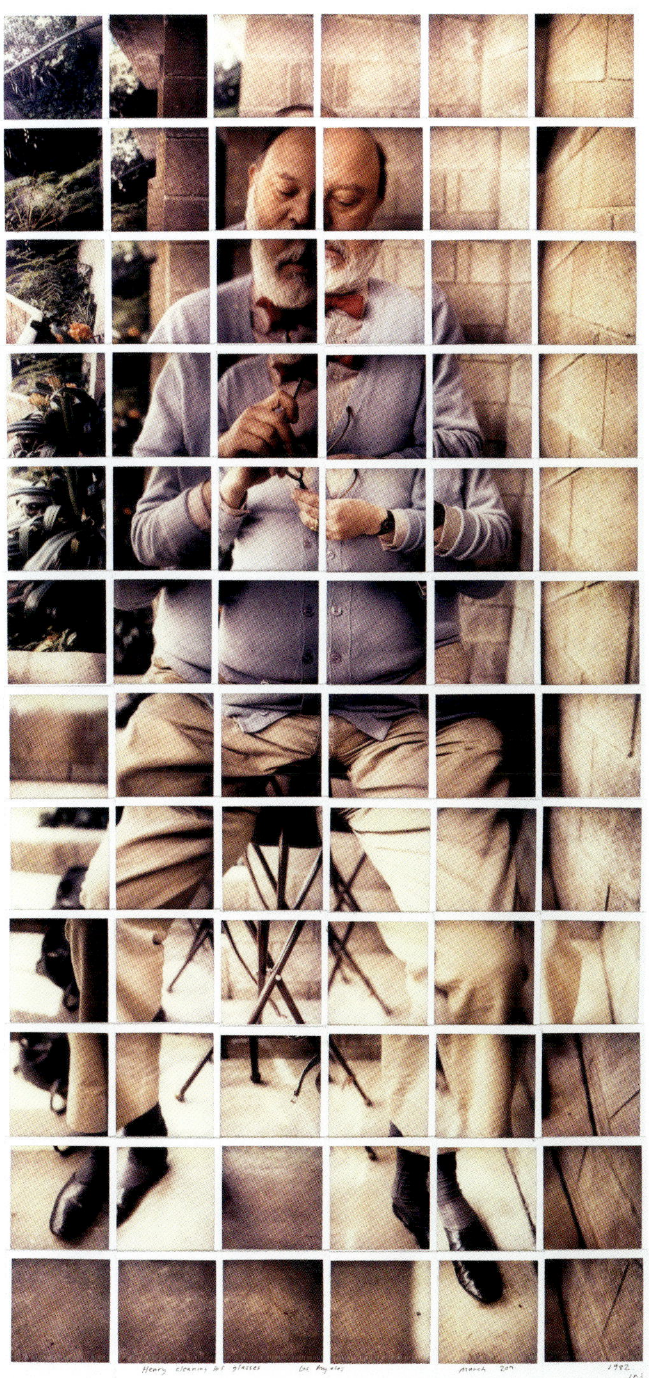

Henry cleaning his glasses   Los Angeles   March 20th   1982.

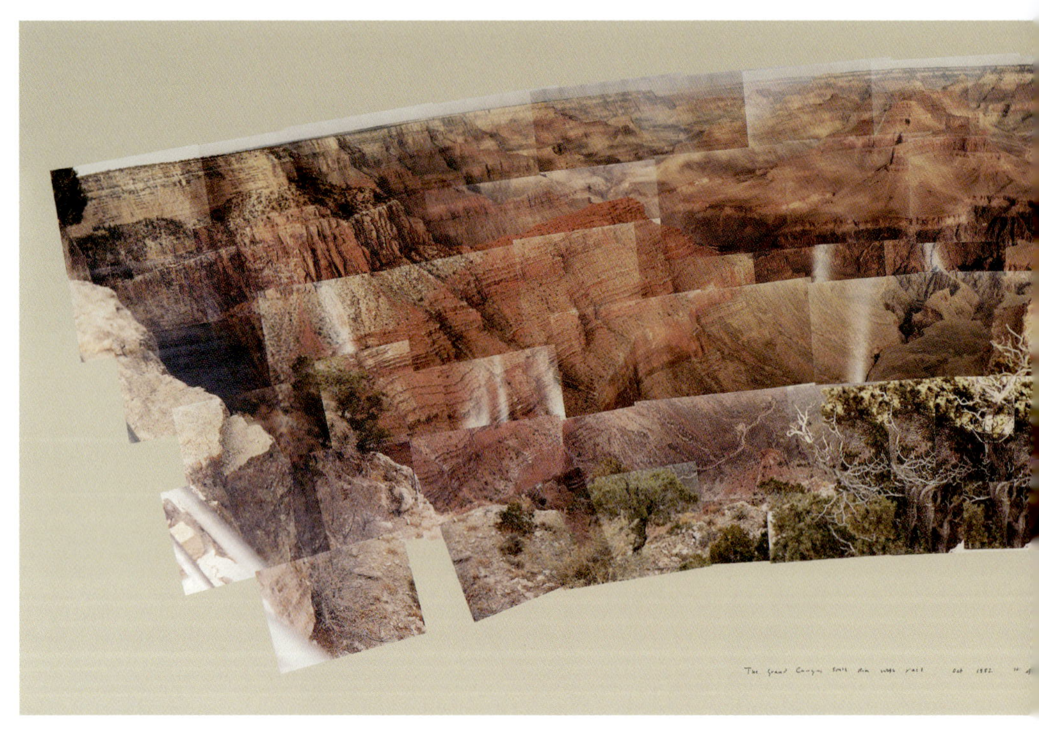

*The Grand Canyon South Rim
with Rail, Oct. 1982*, photographic
collage, edition of 10, 42 x 136 in. /
106.7 x 345.4 cm

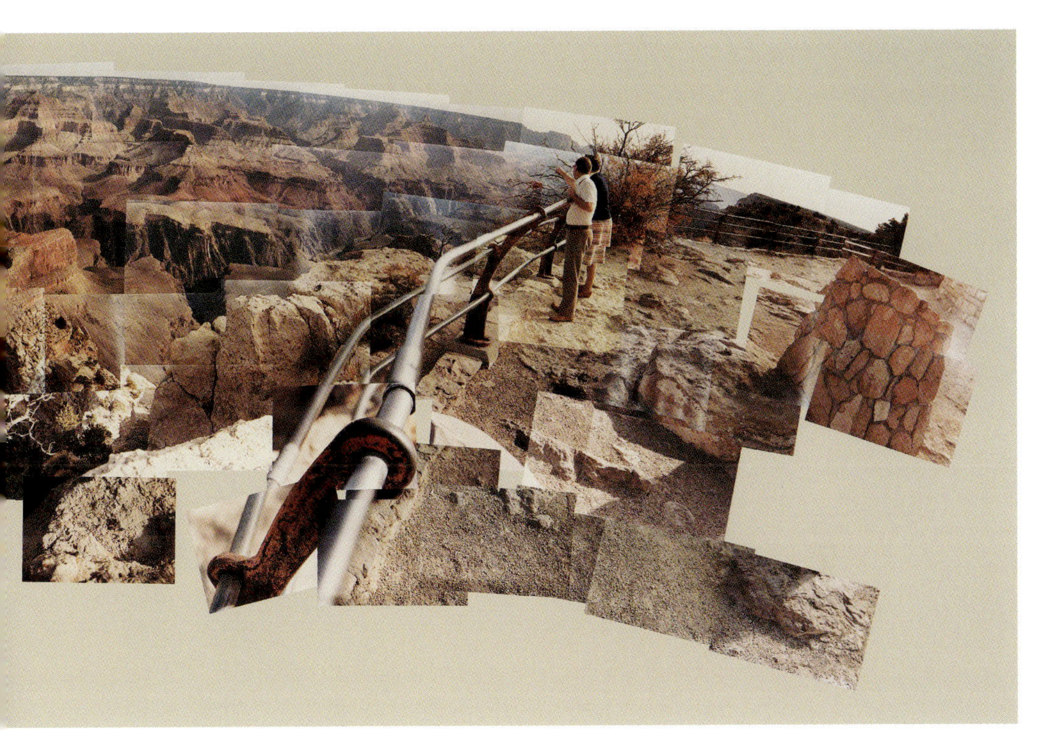

1983 On New Year's Day, Hockney creates a complex photocollage of his mother and friends playing Scrabble (p. 221): "I joined in too, though I couldn't concentrate much on the game because I was taking pictures. It was while I was doing this piece that I saw that I was using narrative for the first time, using a new dimension of time."

In February he goes to Japan for a congress on works on paper. He makes photographs for a number of joiners (p. 221), developing the film back in England: "What really excited me was when I pieced together the Zen Garden in Kyoto…it was then and really only then that I began to realize that one of the areas I was really examining was perspective, that this was what you could alter in photography."

Continuing his explorations of perspective, Hockney studies Chinese scroll paintings at the Metropolitan Museum in New York and the British Museum in London and he reads George Rowley's *Principles of Chinese Painting* from 1959. Rowley writes: "A scroll painting must be experienced in time like music or literature. Our attention is carried on laterally from right to left, being restricted at any one moment to a short passage which can be conveniently perused…In the European tradition, the interest in measurable space destroyed the 'continuous method' of temporal sequence used in the Middle Ages and led to the fifteenth century invention of the fixed space of scientific perspective. When the Chinese were faced with the same problem of spatial depth in the T'ang period, they reworked the early principles of time and suggested a space through which one might wander and space which implied more space beyond the picture frame. We restricted space to a single vista as though seen through an open door; they suggested the unlimited space of nature as though they had stepped through that open door and had known the sudden breathtaking experience of space extending in every direction and infinitely into the sky." The implications for Hockney are immense: "It was an attack on perspective—it was all about the spectator's being in the picture, not outside it—an attack on the window idea, that Renaissance notion of the painting's being as if slotted into a wall, which I'd always felt implied the wall and hence separation from the world. The Chinese landscape artists, with their scrolls, had found a way to transcend that difficulty. In my own photocollages, some of the ones I'd done on my trip to Japan earlier that year, I'd been pushing the notion of the observer's head swiveling about in a world

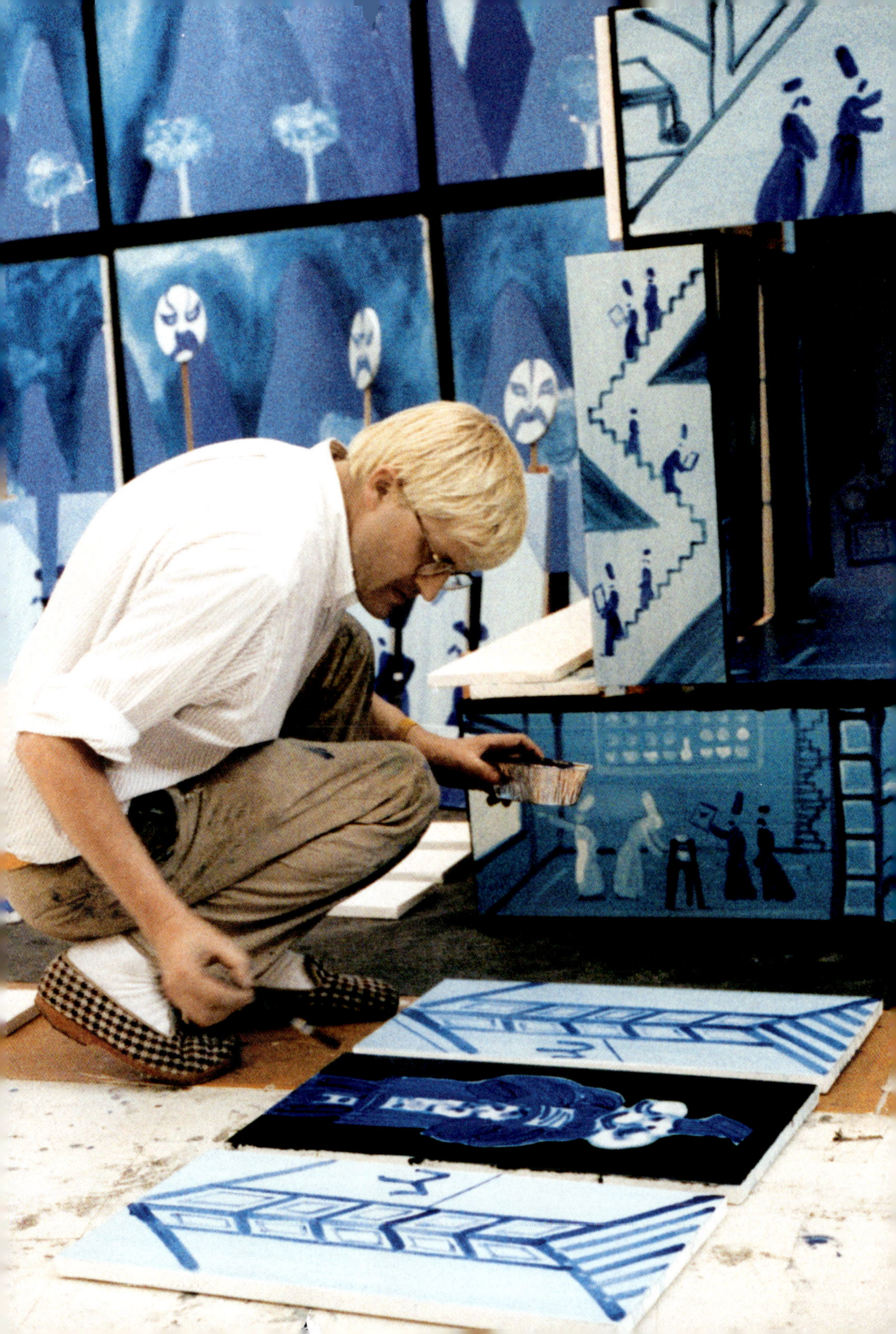

which was moving in time, but I'd really only just begun to try and deal with how to portray movement of the observer's whole body across space. And that's precisely what these Chinese landscape artists had mastered, according to Rowley."

Martin Friedman, director of the Walker Art Center in Minneapolis, invites Hockney to organize an exhibition of his stage designs (p. 217). The artist agrees, but since he does not find it interesting to simply show his sketches and models, he starts building almost life-size models of one or two scenes for each production. The work turns out much more complicated than expected and six weeks before the opening he moves to Minneapolis to work in situ. Friedman observes: "Oddly enough, the more he worked on the re-creation, the more free-form it became. The set for *Le Rossignol* is close to total abstraction. It no longer looks exactly like the performed version; it now consists of a series, a big series of paintings, in which the elements appear almost montage-fashion—and it's much, much more interesting." The exhibition proves a large success and over the next two years travels to Mexico City, Ontario, Chicago, San Francisco, and London, where it is reviewed by John Russell Taylor as "brilliant and unflagging inventiveness to be sure, but also every evidence of the blood, sweat, and tears which must have gone into the creation of these apparently effortless delights."

For six weeks during the preparation of the exhibition, Hockney draws a self-portrait almost every day (p. 219). It is a stocktaking, of his age (he has become quite hard of hearing, and his current relationship with the much younger Ian Falconer proves difficult because of their disagreements about social habits), and of his self-image: "They were drawn mostly early in the morning. I noticed if you did this they were always different: not only did you have different expressions, you also had totally different moods and feelings, and that affects your mind. I realized that your mood is reflected in the way you draw the lines and marks. You also try to pick up the mood of the sitter, so in a portrait of someone else there are two moods. In a self-portrait it is the same mood...The self-portraits do reflect the fact that even I was beginning to panic a little bit about the massive amount of work I had taken on."

In November, Hockney delivers a lecture "On Photography" at the Victoria and Albert Museum in London, in which he describes human perception as "many points of focus and many moments." He argues against the photographic way of seeing where "the foreground abruptly ends at a point some distance from

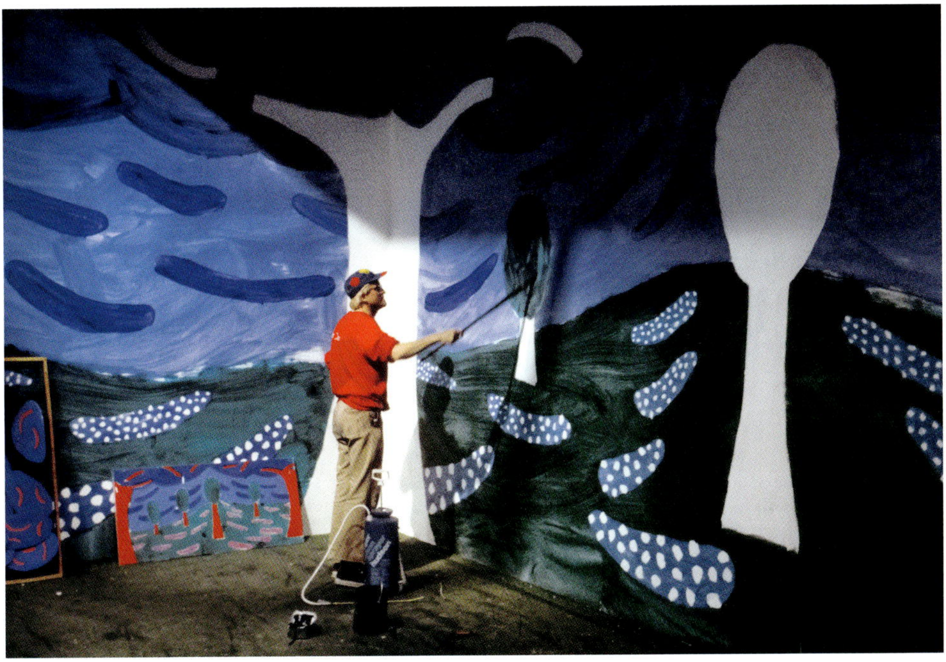

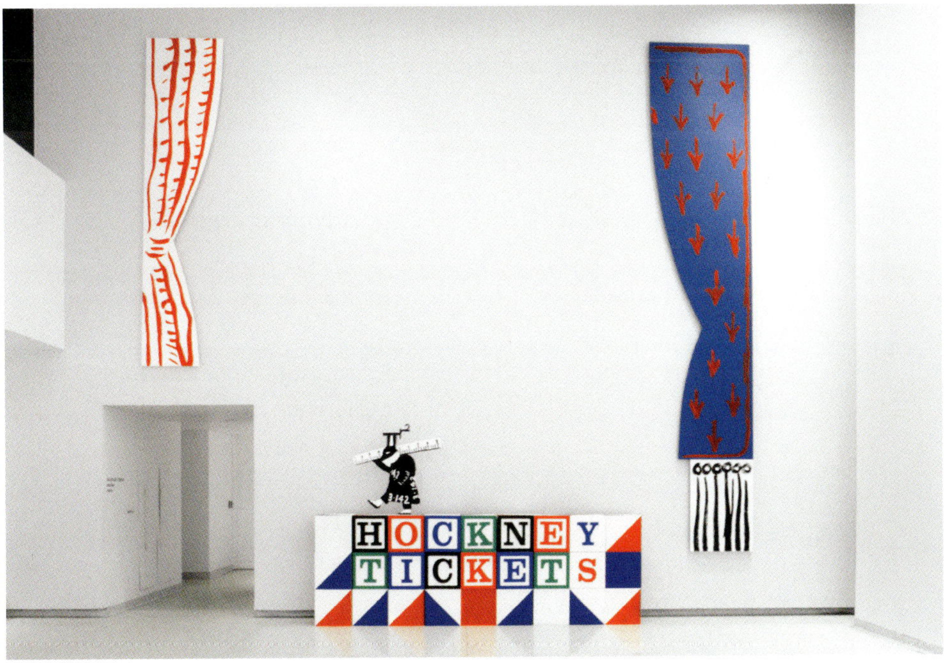

HOCKNEY
TICKETS

you and you know you are not there, you are not connected with what is seen, even though it's seen from one point representing the viewer. There is actually a void between where you would be standing to see it this way, and the bottom of the picture. You might think, what does it matter about the ground since we do not look at it. On the contrary, we scan the ground before us at all times with great care; we would not move forward if we could not see it... The problem with a window on the world is that there must be a wall around the window, and this wall is cutting us off from what is seen." He goes on to describe how he tried to step out through that window with his photocomposites, incorporating elements of cubism and adding the important layer of time, especially in his photos from earlier in the year: "I made pictures of a walk in a Zen garden where I attempted to show the experience of walking, so that one might see the entire experience, in time. It means that you must look with your memory. Then it led me to believe that we're always looking with our memory... I came to the conclusion that there is no such thing as objective vision. There can never be, because even the memory of the first instant of looking is then part of the perception, and it adds up and it adds up. It brought me closer to the way we actually experience the activity of seeing, and it actually led me back to drawing and painting, with a whole new sense of the possibilities to be found there."

Solo: *David Hockney,* Frankfurter Kunstverein, Frankfurt am Main (Mar 15–Apr 24); catalog with a text by Peter Weiermair. *Photographs by David Hockney,* Hayward Gallery, London (Nov 9, 1983–Feb 5, 1984); touring exhibition organized by the British Arts Council, London; catalog with a text by Mark Haworth-Booth. *Hockney Paints the Stage,* Walker Art Center, Minneapolis (Nov 20, 1983–Jan 22, 1984); travels to Museo Rufino Tamayo, Mexico City; Art Gallery of Ontario, Toronto; Museum of Contemporary Art, Chicago; Fort Worth Art Museum, Fort Worth; San Francisco Museum of Modern Art, San Francisco; and Hayward Gallery, London (through 1985); catalog with texts by Martin Friedman, John Cox, John Dexter, David Hockney, and Stephen Spender, New York: Abbeville Press; London: Thames and Hudson. *Drawings for the Theatre,* Nishimura Gallery, Tokyo (Feb–Mar). *New Work with a Camera,* André Emmerich Gallery, New York (May 7–Jun 3); L.A. Louver, Venice, CA (May 14–Jun 25); and Richard Gray Gallery, Chicago (May 14–Jun 30). *David Hockney,* Knoedler/ Emmerich Gallery, Zurich (Jun–Jul). *Kasmin's Hockneys: 45 Drawings,* Knoedler/Kasmin Gallery, London (Jul 5–Aug); catalog. *David Hockney,* Bjorn Bengtsson, Varberg (Sep–Oct). *New Work with a Camera,* Nishimura Gallery (Oct 3–29) and Nagase Photo Salon (Oct 3–15), Tokyo; catalog. *David Hockney in America,* William Beadleston, Inc. Fine Art, New York (Nov 8–Dec 10); catalog with a text by Christopher Finch.

Publication: David Hockney, *On Photography: A Lecture at the Victoria and Albert Museum,* New York: André Emmerich Gallery.

Film: *David Hockney: Joiner Photographs,* USA, 50 min., dir. by Don Featherstone.

Honor: Honorary Degree at the University of Bradford.

Self Portrait with Check Jacket, 1983, charcoal on paper, 30 x 22 ¹/₂ in. / 76 x 57.2 cm

Self Portrait Looking over Glasses, 1983, charcoal on paper, 30 x 22 ¹/₂ in. / 76.2 x 57.2 cm

Self Portrait without Shirt, 1983, charcoal on paper, 30 x 22 ¹/₂ in. / 76.2 x 57.2 cm

Page 215: David Hockney working on sets for the exhibition *Hockney Paints the Stage* in his studio, Los Angeles 1983. Photo: Sidney B. Felsen

Page 217: David Hockney installing *Hockney Paints the Stage,* Walker Art Center, Minneapolis 1983

Hockney Paints the Stage, exhibition view, Walker Art Center, Minneapolis 1983

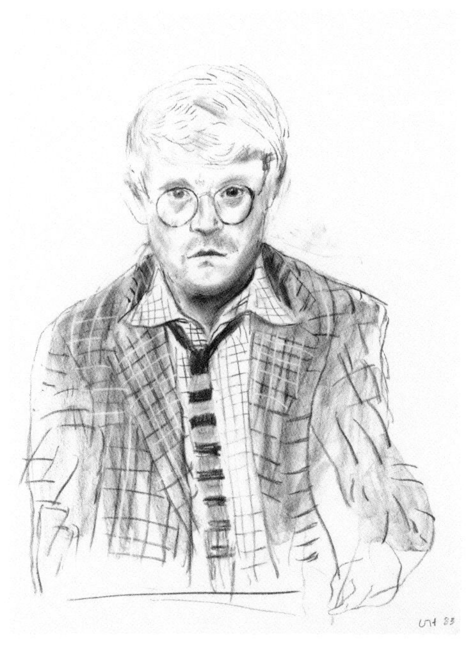

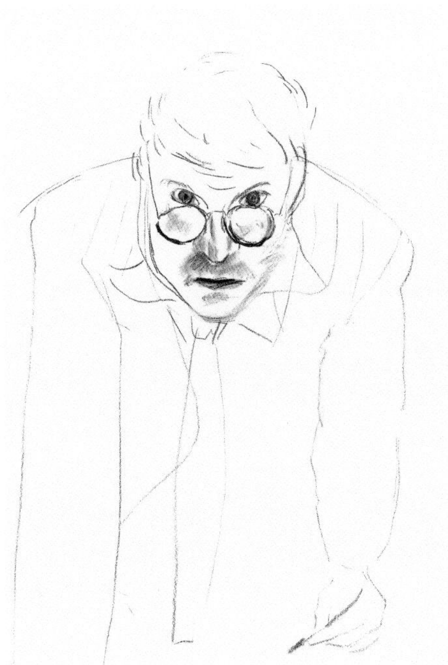

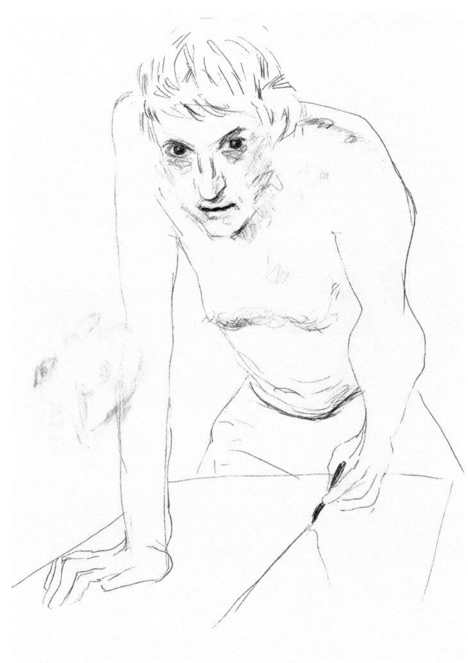

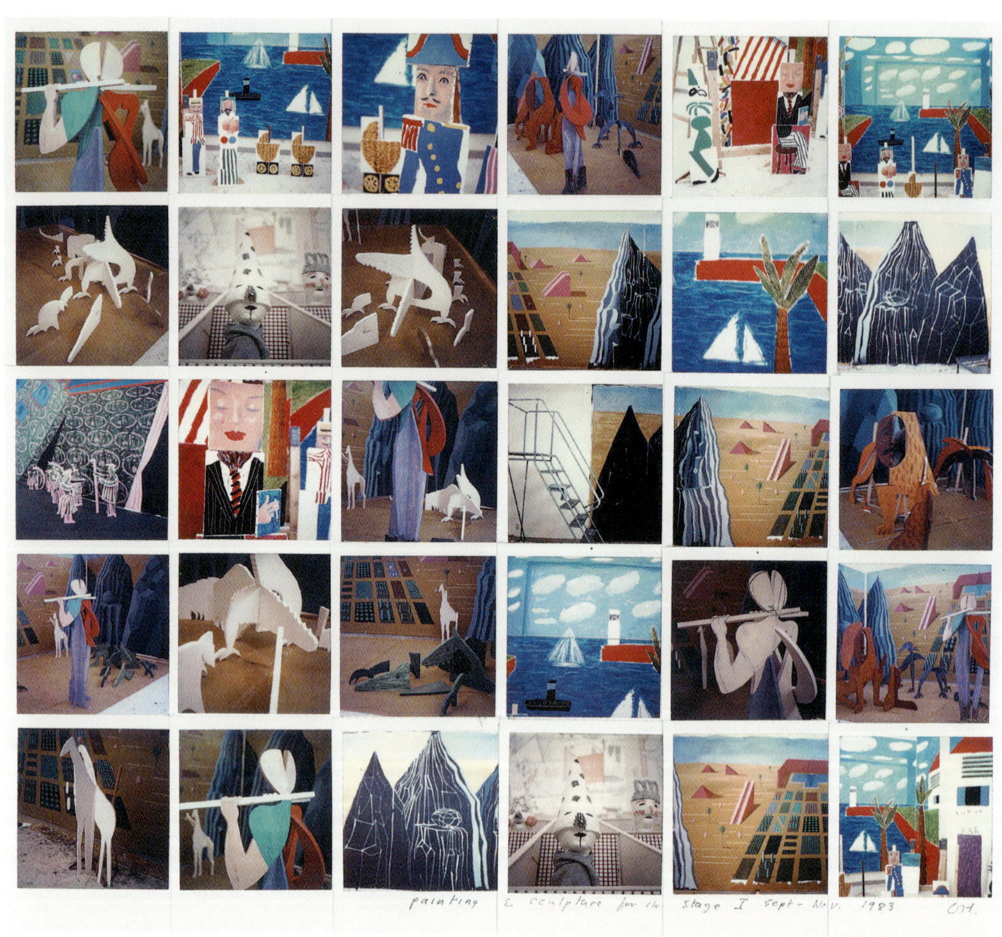

Painting and Sculpture for the Stage I, Sept–Nov 1983, composite Polaroid, 18 x 20 in. / 45.7 x 50.8 cm

Right page: *Walking in the Zen Garden at the Ryoanji Temple, Kyoto, Feb. 1983*, photographic collage, edition of 20, 40 x 62 ¹/₂ in. / 101.5 x 158.8 cm

The Scrabble Game, Jan 1st 1983, photographic collage, edition of 20, 39 x 58 in. / 99.1 x 147.3 cm

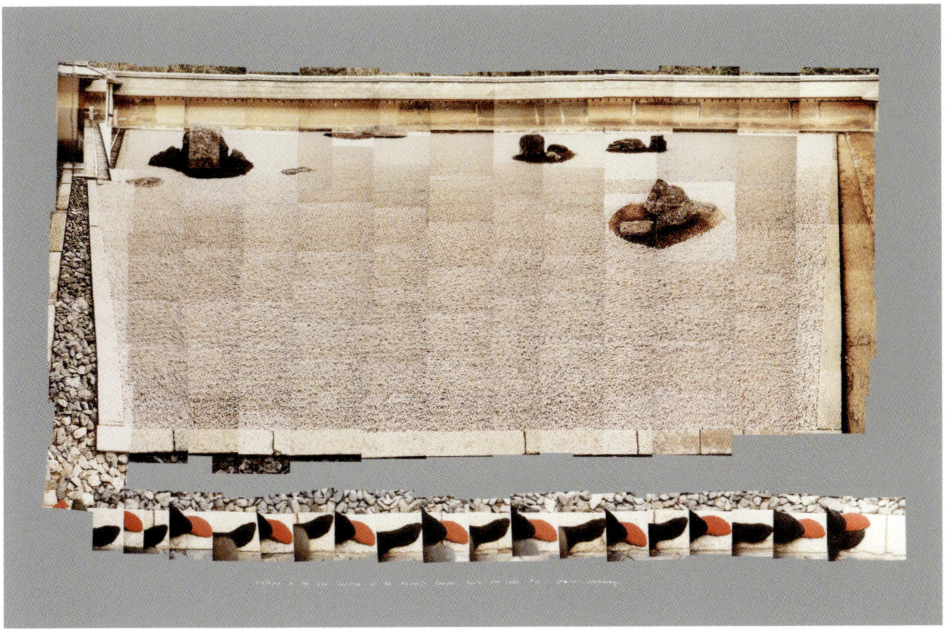

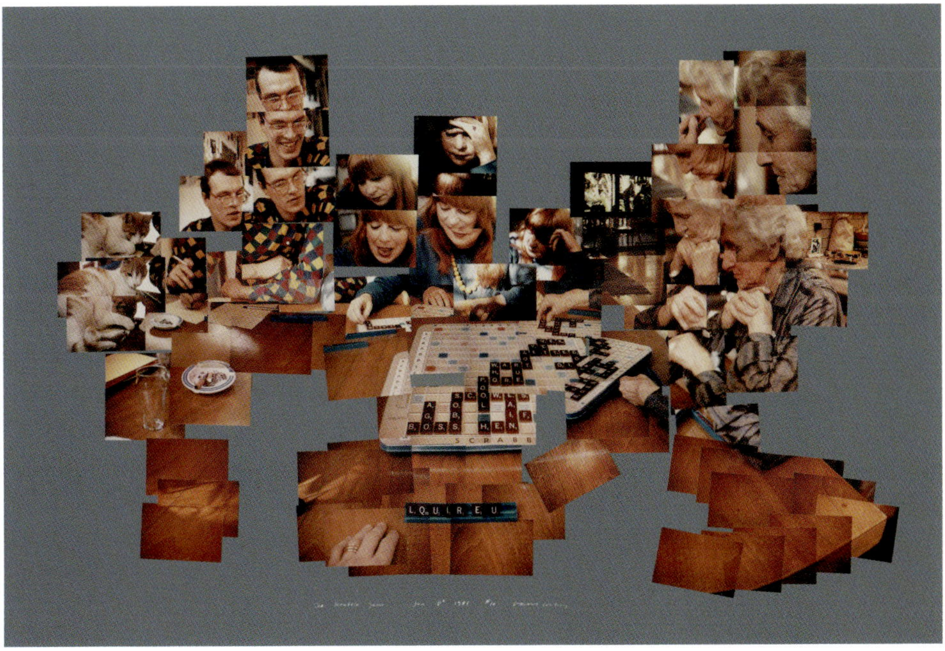

1984

After mainly working on photographs and stage design for almost four years, Hockney paints again, portraying friends such as Celia Birtwell or Christopher Isherwood in a style that moves very close to the subject, resulting in surprising shapes (pp. 225, 229): "Have you ever noticed," the artist asks Lawrence Weschler, "how when you look at things close up, you sometimes shut one eye—that is, you make yourself like a camera? Otherwise, things start to swim... The Cubists, you know, didn't shut their eyes. People complained about Picasso—how he distorted the human face. I don't think there are any distortions at all. For instance, those marvelous portraits of his lover Marie-Therese Walter which he made during the thirties—he must have spent hours with her in bed, very close, looking at her face. A face looked at like that *does* look different from one seen at five or six feet. Strange things begin to happen to the eyes, the cheeks, the nose—wonderful inversions and repetitions. Certain 'distortions' appear, but they can't be distortions, because they're reality. Those paintings are about that kind of intimate seeing."

Influenced by the narrative approach of Chinese scrolls, Hockney paints *A Visit with Christopher and Don, Santa Monica Canyon* (pp. 226/227): "I was trying to create a painting where the viewer's eye could be made to move in certain ways, stop in certain places, move on, and in so doing reconstruct the space across time for itself... The problem was how to prevent the eye from stopping, from getting stuck. For instance, that's why both Don and Christopher are rendered transparently. When you look at Christopher, you see him, but when you move along to the bedroom and you're looking at the bed, he dissolves in a sense into patterns of green and blue and red paint."

Hockney travels to Mexico City with Gregory Evans and David Graves for the opening of *Hockney Paints the Stage.* Their car breaks down in the village of Acatlán and they move into the Hotel Romano Angeles. Hockney loves the central courtyard of the hotel with its gallery and palms and stays for a week, sketching while the others wait (pp. 230/231). Back in LA, printer Ken Tyler shows him a new method of lithography on transparent sheets of Mylar, through which the different colors can be registered more easily. Hockney takes Tyler and Evans to the hotel again to try out the technique. Tyler remembers: "The garden that David loved so much in the courtyard was all fakery, like something that a poor Latino family might have created in Los Angeles in their backyard, but he

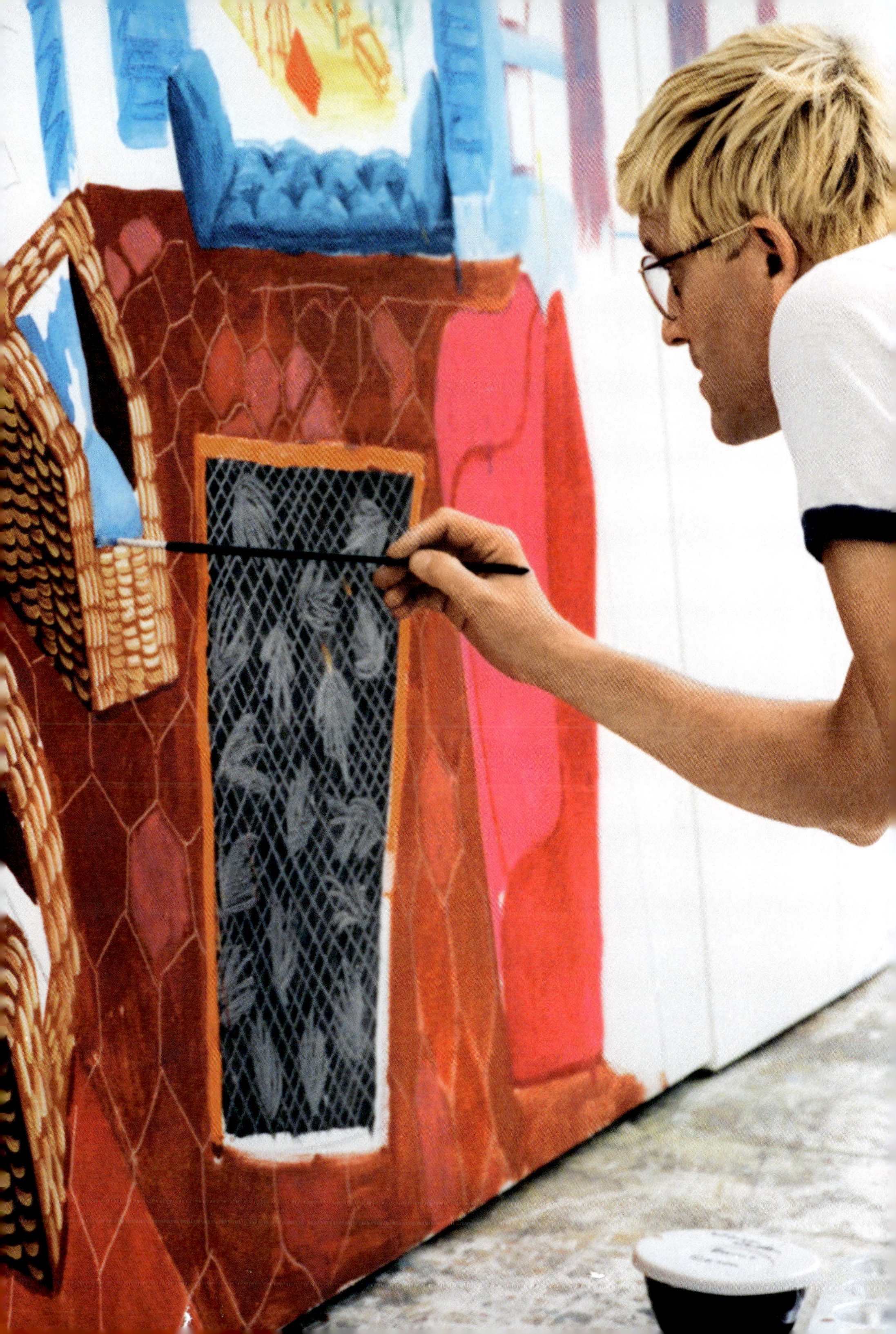

thought it was wonderful and it turned him on. So with his magical mind he created this luscious thing…"

In October, Hockney opens an exhibition of recent paintings, gouaches, drawings, and photocollages at André Emmerich Gallery in New York. The photocollage *Nude, 17th June 1984* (p. 229) is inspired by the famous calendar shot of a naked Marilyn Monroe seen from above, here embodied by actress Theresa Russell for the Nicolas Roeg film *Insignificance*. Her body is both fragmented and its parts multiplied through countless viewpoints: "Only erotic photographs inspire you immediately to look for more than 30 seconds," Hockney says, "and my pin-up requires you to look very slowly, you are forced to move over every inch of her body, which makes it more interesting, more erotic."

Solo: *Photo-Composites*, Milwaukee Art Museum, Wisconsin (May 31–Sep 20). *Hockney's Progress*, Abbot Hall Art Gallery, Kendal (Jun 30–Sep 2). *Ausgewählte Druckgrafik*, Knoedler Gallery, Zürich (Apr 14–May 5). *Print Retrospective*, Thordén Wetterling Galleries, Stockholm (Apr 28–Jun 6); travels to Thordén Wetterling Galleries, Gothenburg (Sep 8–Oct 10). *Prints*, Mira Godard Gallery, Toronto (Jun). *New Work*, Richard Gray Gallery, Chicago (Sep). *David Hockney*, Associated American Artists Gallery, New York (Sep–Oct). *Salon Exhibition, 15 Years*, Marianne Deson Gallery, Chicago (Sep 14–Oct 16). *New Work: Paintings, Gouaches, Drawings, Photo Collages*, André Emmerich Gallery, New York (Oct 13– Nov 3); catalog. *Photographic Collages*, Carpenter + Hochman Gallery, Dallas (opens Dec 13).

Group: *The Folding Image: Screens by Western Artists of the Nineteenth and Twentieth Centuries*, National Gallery of Art, Washington, D.C. (Mar 4–Sep 3); travels to Yale University Art Gallery, New Haven; catalog. *Drawings, 1974–1984*, Hirshhorn Museum and Sculpture Garden, Washington, D.C. (Mar 15–May 13); catalog. *The Figure in Contemporary Art*, Maier Museum of Art at Randolph College, Lynchburg (Mar 18–Apr 15). *Olympian Gestures*, LA County Museum of Art, Los Angeles (Jun 7– Oct 7). *Reading Drawings: A Selection from the Victoria and Albert Museum, London*, The Drawing Center, New York (Jun–Jul).

Publication: *David Hockney: Cameraworks*, with a text by Lawrence Weschler, London: Thames and Hudson; New York: Alfred A. Knopf.

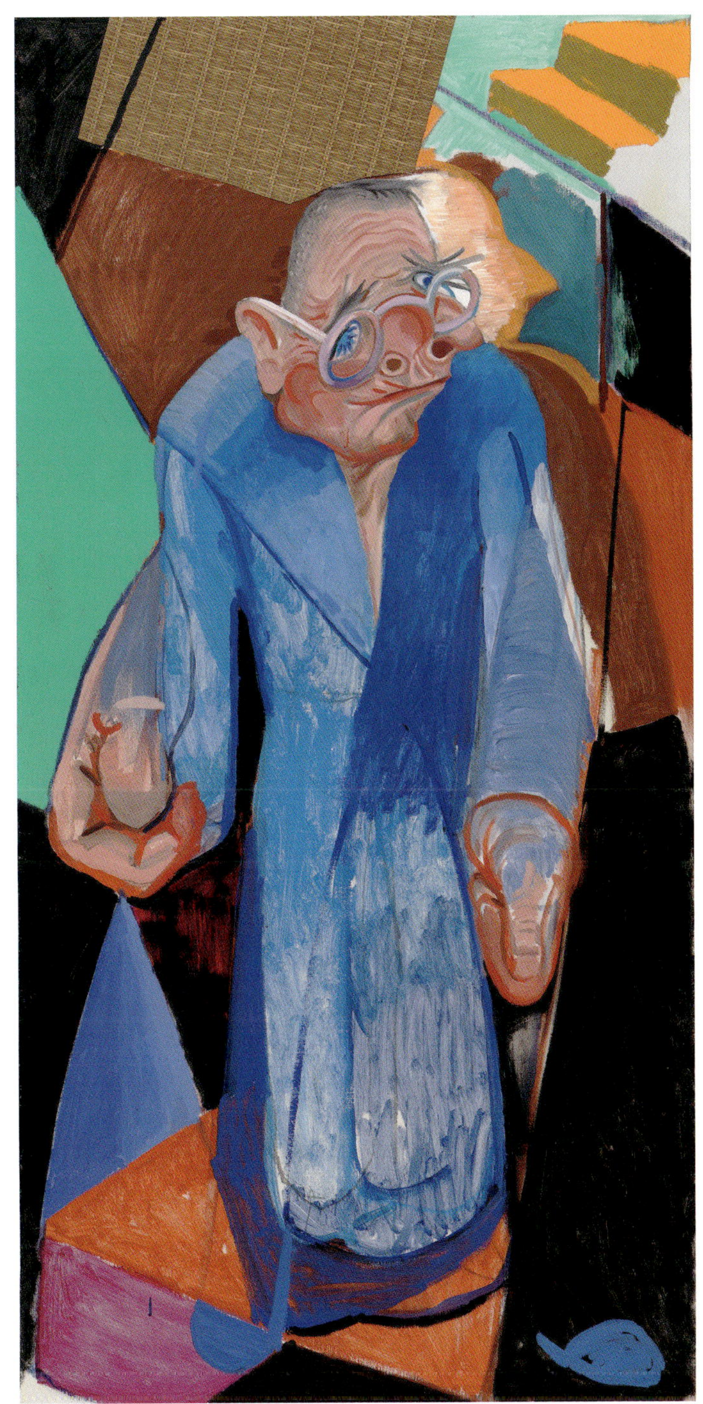

Christopher Isherwood, 1984,
oil and contact paper on canvas,
72 x 36 in. / 182.9 x 91.4 cm

Page 223: David Hockney in
his studio, Los Angeles 1984.
Photo: Sidney B. Felsen

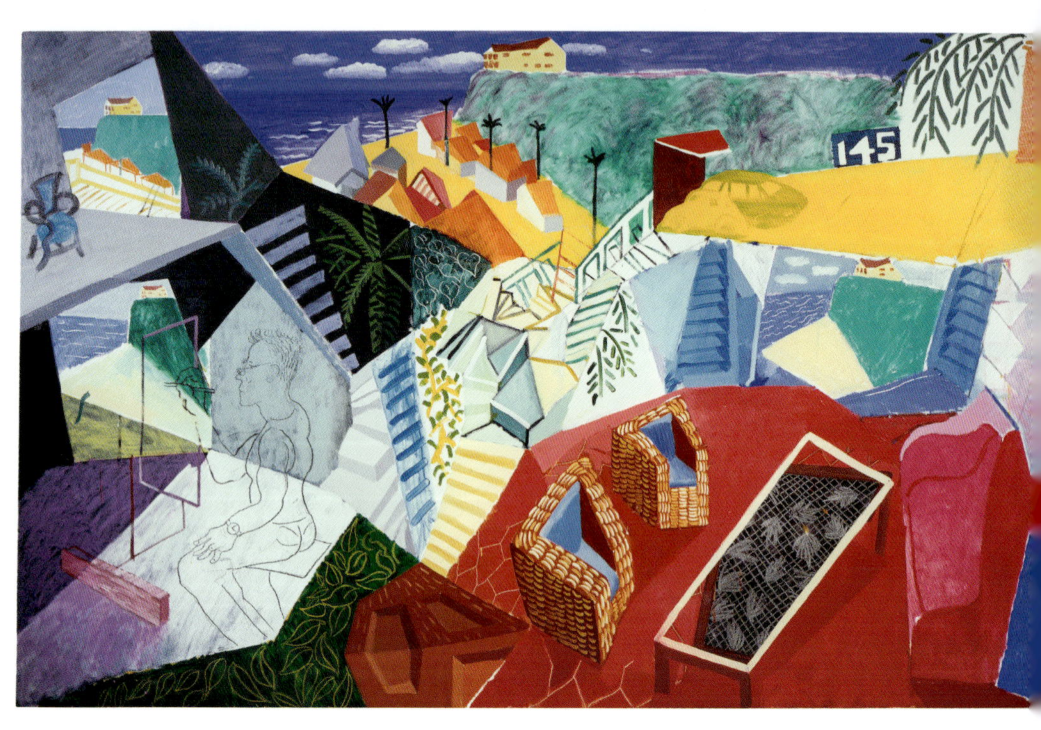

*A Visit with Christopher and Don,
Santa Monica Canyon,* 1984,
oil on 2 canvases, 72 x 240 in. /
182.9 x 609.6 cm

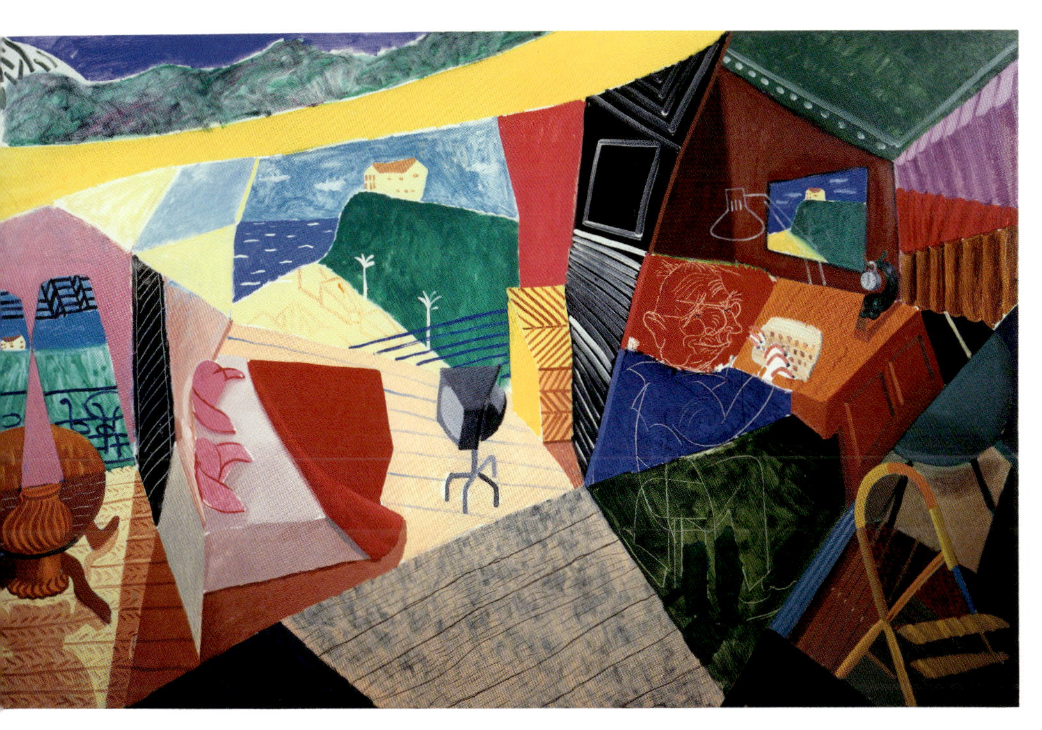

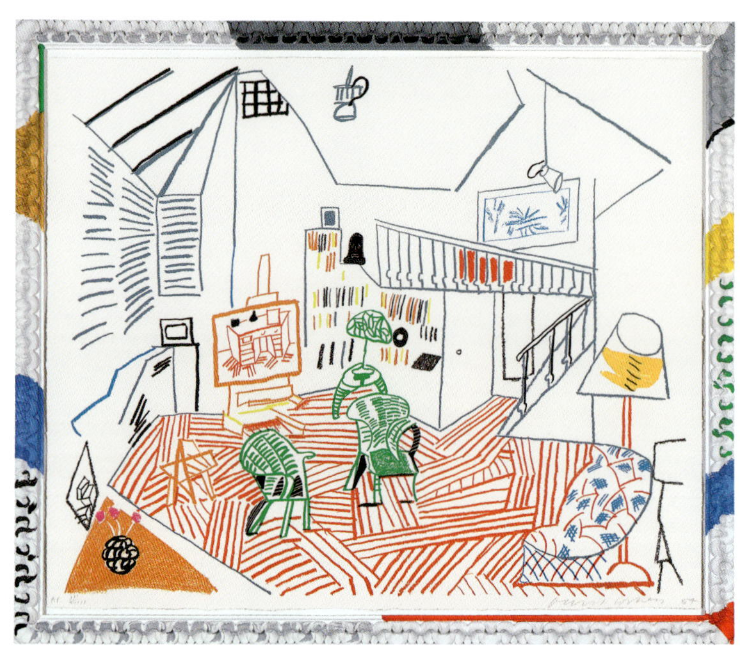

Pembroke Studio Interior,
1984, lithograph, hand-painted frame, edition of 70,
46 x 55 in. / 116.8 x 139.7 cm framed

A Visit with Mo and Lisa,
Echo Park, Los Angeles,
1984, gouache, crayon, and pencil on 2 sheets of paper,
60 x 202 in. / 152.4 x 513.1 cm

Right page: *Nude, 17th June 1984,* photographic collage,
edition 1 of 20, 71 1/4 x 48 in. /
181 x 122 cm

An Image of Celia, State I,
1984–1986, lithograph,
edition of 10 with
8 proofs, 49 1/2 x 39 in. /
125.8 x 99.1 cm

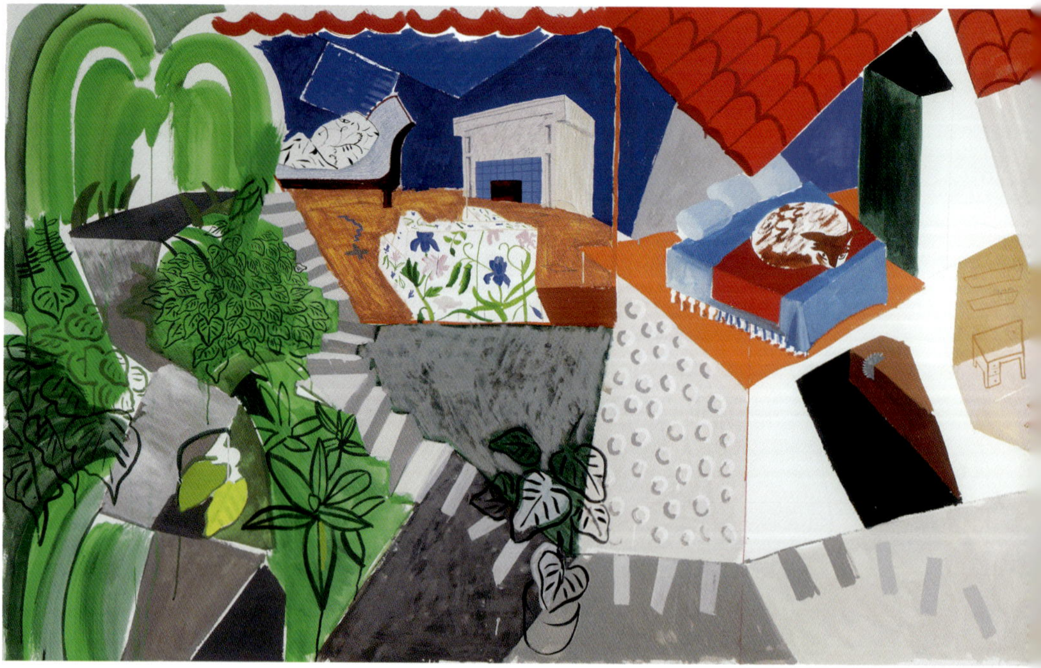

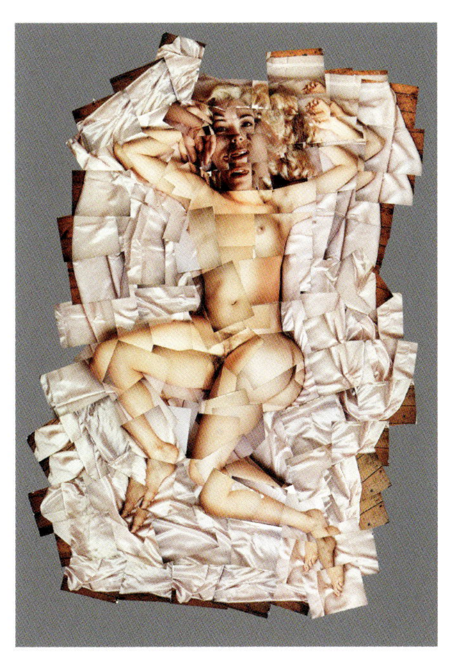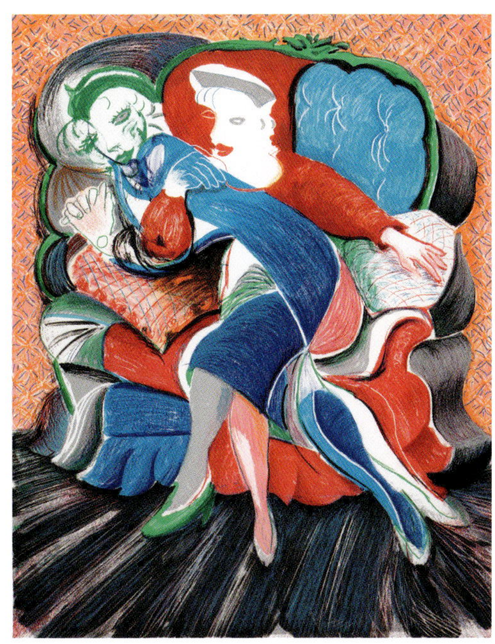

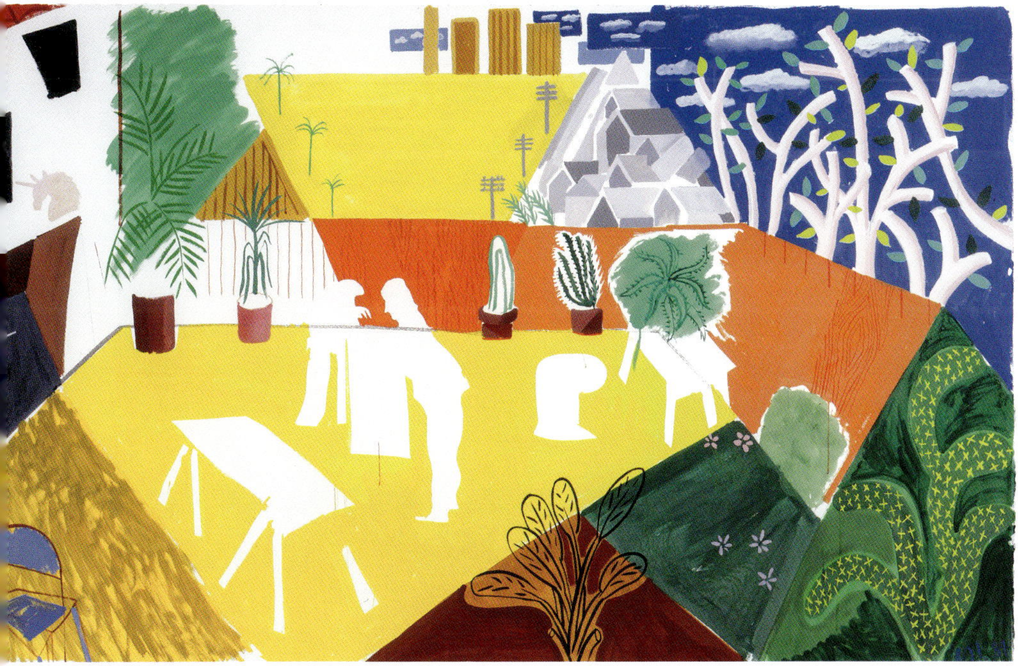

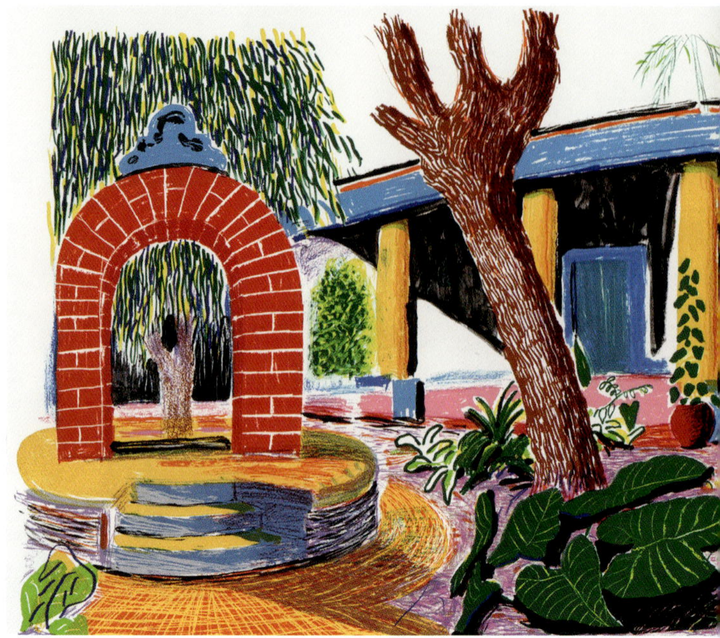

Hotel Acatlan: Second Day, 1984,
lithograph on 2 sheets of paper,
edition of 98, 28 $^3/_4$ x 76 in. /
73 x 193 cm

Hotel Romano Angeles, Acatlan,
1984, oil on 2 canvases,
36 x 120 in. / 91.4 x 304.8 cm

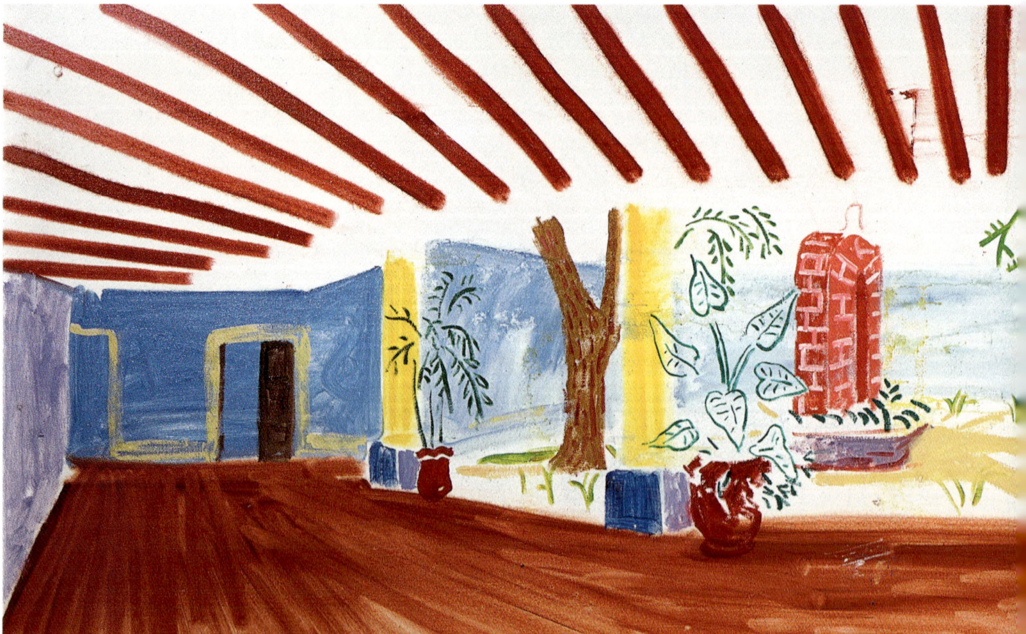

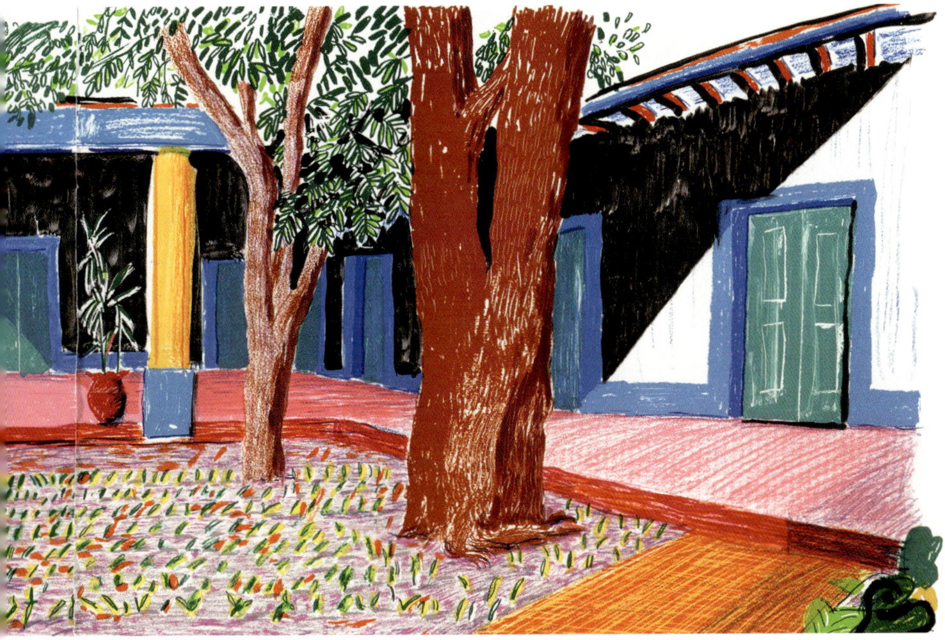

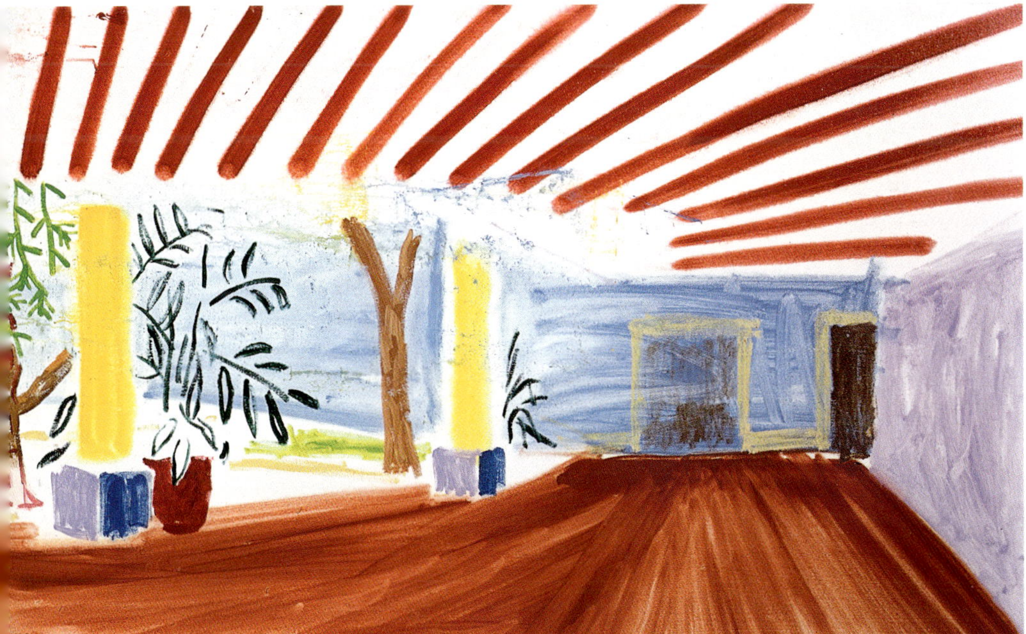

1985

After his visits to the Hotel Romano Angeles, Hockney creates a big painting from the sketches he has made, *A Walk around the Hotel Courtyard, Acatlán* (pp. 242/243). In April he writes to R. B. Kitaj: "I am now doing a painting of a courtyard of a Mexican hotel. I loved the space of it when I first discovered it, and went back to stay for five days. It has so many different perspectives that you are forced to move your eye constantly over the surface of the canvas. It is a totally impossible view from one point, yet there is a clarity and order about the picture. The effect of the space is extremely strong, yet it is not an illusion you want to walk in to—because you are already in the picture and walking round—every viewer so far feels this." The painting is shown later in the year in the exhibition *Wider Perspectives Are Needed Now* at Knoedler Gallery in London and L.A. Louver in Los Angeles.

For some time, Hockney has grown increasingly hard of hearing. After testing a new hearing aid, he writes to Kitaj: "Music is more alive again and sound seems spatial, and made me think that over the last years to compensate for my muffled ears I developed a strong visual space sense. I say this because I'm very aware I seem to see in another way that has to do with noticing movement of the eye (time) and perception of space. A blind man develops his hearing to define his space; could not a deaf person develop his sight…Anyway there's no doubt that either from the theater or somewhere else I became more aware of space and time. All the photography is to do with it, and all the subsequent paintings, and something is happening in the paintings that seems like a new kind of pictorial space to me."

Over three months, Hockney creates a 41-page pictorial essay for the December issue of French *Vogue* (pp. 237–241). It serves as an introduction to Hockney's thoughts on perspective, illustrated by examples from his recent work: "The idea of the moving spectator is of course old, and only comes under attack with the introduction of one-point perspective in the Renaissance. This could have been due to the problems of depicting the crucifixion. When Giotto depicts the crucifixion he does it in the medieval way, an action through time from one picture to the next, Christ carrying the cross up the hill etc. Yet the actual execution contains no action (your head is not chopped off—an arrow does not pierce your heart). With the invention of one point perspective time stops and space is fixed, giving objects in space a fixed position and a feeling of weight and volume…The invention must have led to the camera obscura and

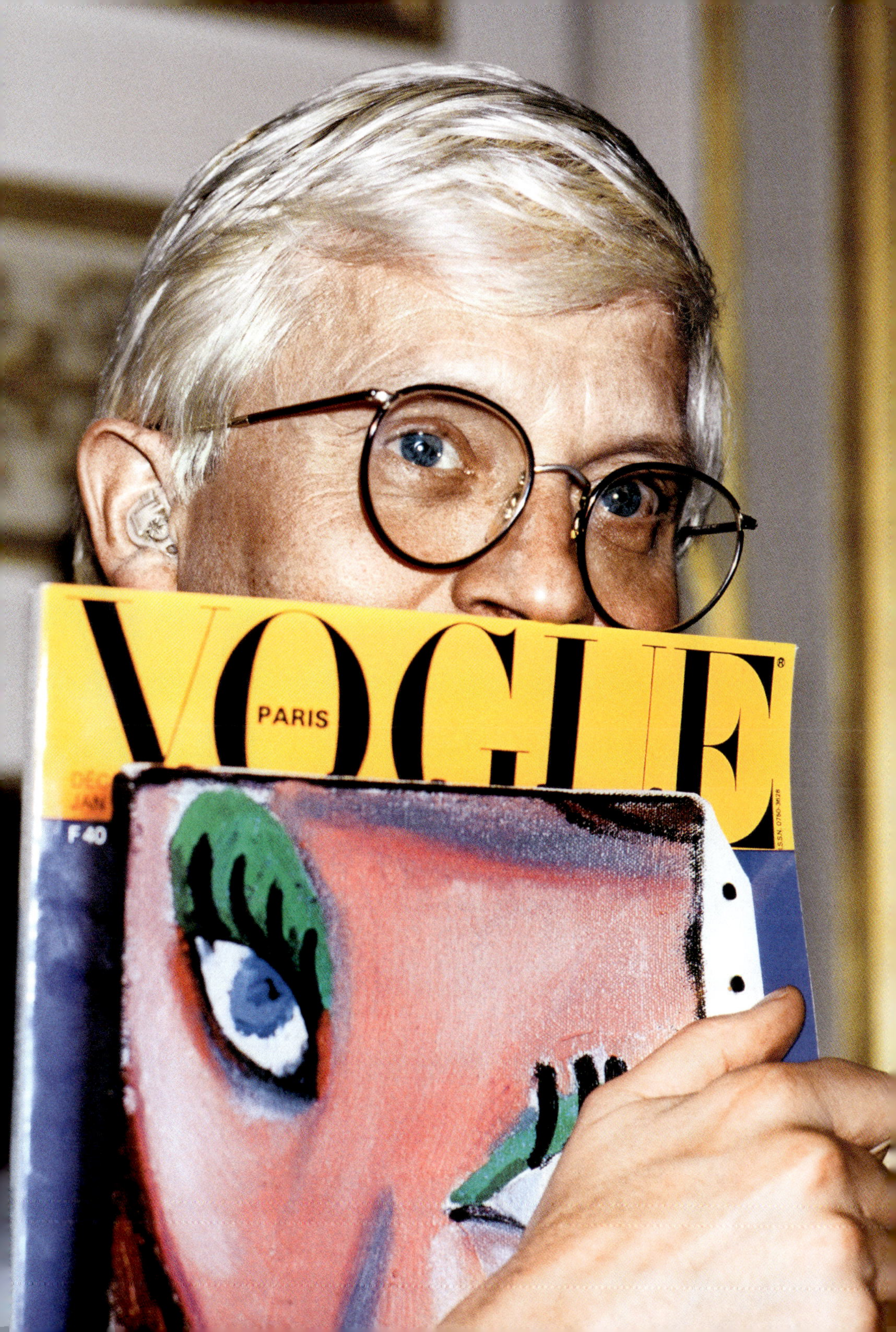

VOGUE
PARIS
DÉC
JAN
F 40
I.S.S.N. 0750-3628

hence the camera of today, always seeing the world in the same way. It makes a static world, and seems to take away our bodies, for to make perspective work we have to stand still, close one eye and look at the world through a hole. Now let us begin a journey to a more complex perspective that puts us in this world. What happens if we reverse perspective?" This reverse perspective can be seen in paintings and photocollages of chairs and a paint trolley (p. 236) that carries a copy of *Vogue* in the bottom compartment. Hockney's most complex photocollage to date, *Place Furstenberg, Paris* (p. 236), along with the painting *A Walk around the Hotel Courtyard, Acatlán,* show how far he has come subverting perspectival conventions.

Solo: *David Hockney,* College Art Gallery, New Paltz (Oct); travels to State University of New York, Albany; and College of Santa Fe. David Hockney, Lloyd Shin, Wilmette (Jan). *New Color Lithographs,* Tyler Graphics Ltd., Bedford Village (May). *Prints from the 1960s and 70s,* Eugenia Cucalón Gallery, New York (May 24–Jun 28). *Portraits,* Barbara Krakow Gallery, Boston (Jun 15–Jul 27). *Wider Perspectives Are Needed Now,* Knoedler Gallery, London (opens Jul 25). *Drawings, Prints and Photocollages,* Greg Kucera Gallery, Seattle (Jul–Aug). *Eight New Lithographs,* Richard Gray Gallery, Chicago (Aug). *David Hockney,* Jane Corkin Gallery, Toronto (Sep 14–Oct 8). *Paintings of the Early 1960s,* André Emmerich Gallery, New York (Sep 19–Oct 19); catalog with a text by Nicholas Wilder. *New Work,* André Emmerich Gallery, New York (Dec 5, 1985–Jan 4, 1986). *Images et pensées pour le Magazine Vogue Paris,* Galerie Claude Bernard, Paris (Dec 10, 1985–Jan 15, 1986). *Wider Perspectives Are Needed Now,* L.A. Louver, Venice, CA (Dec 17, 1985–Jan 18, 1986).

Group: *From Manet to Hockney: Modern Artists' Illustrated Books,* Victoria and Albert Museum, London (Mar 20–May 19); catalog. *A Second Talent: Painters and Sculptors Who Are Also Photographers,* The Aldrich Contemporary Art Museum, Ridgefield, CT (Sep 22–Dec 15); catalog. *The Painter's Music / The Musician's Art,* collaboration with the chamber ensemble "An die Musik," Helen Frankenthaler, David Hockney, Robert Motherwell, and Kenneth Noland, Solomon R. Guggenheim Museum, New York (Nov 17).

Publication: David Hockney, *Martha's Vineyard and Other Places: My Third Sketchbook from the Summer of 1982,* New York: Harry N. Abrams.

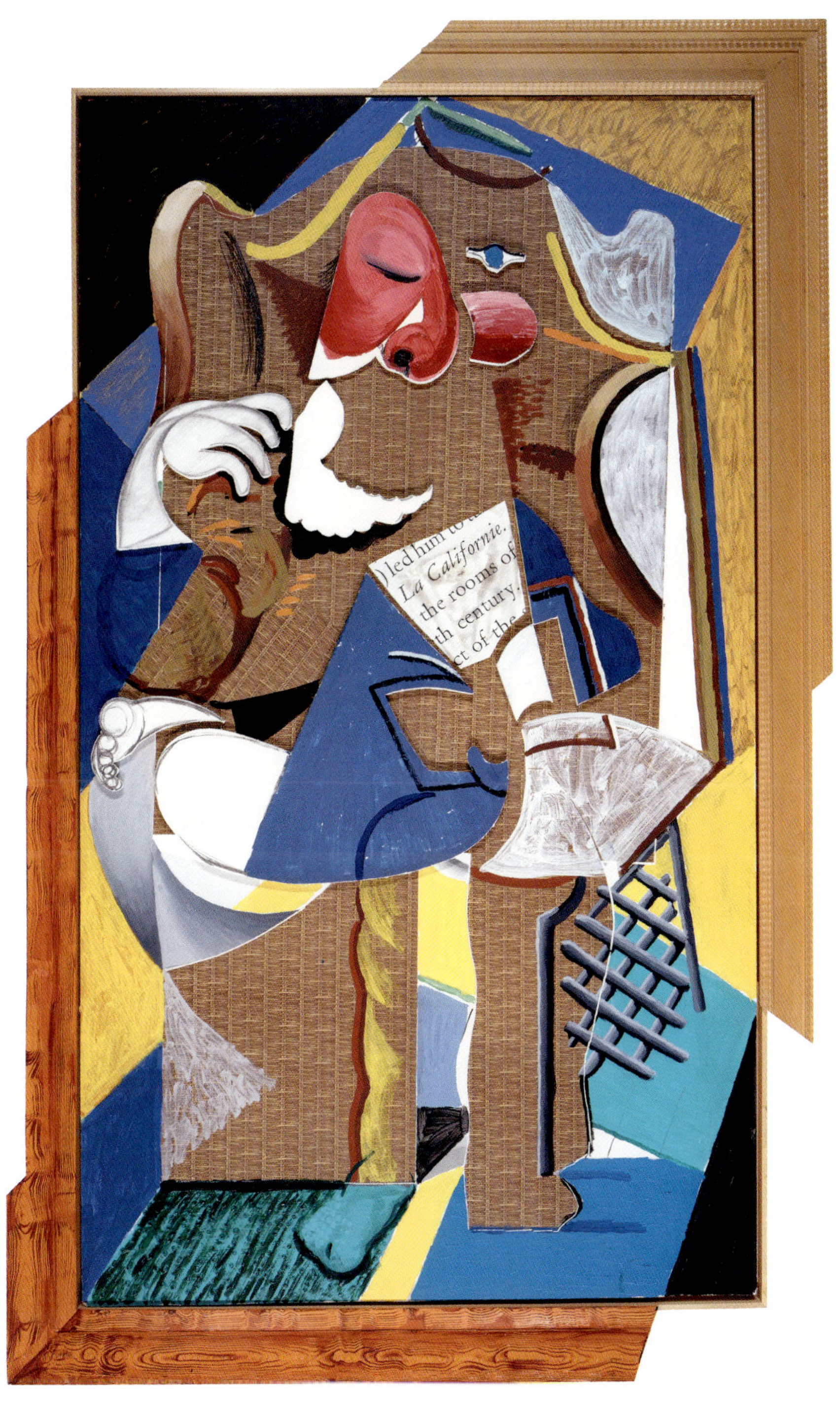
led him to
La Californie,
the rooms of
th century,
ct of the

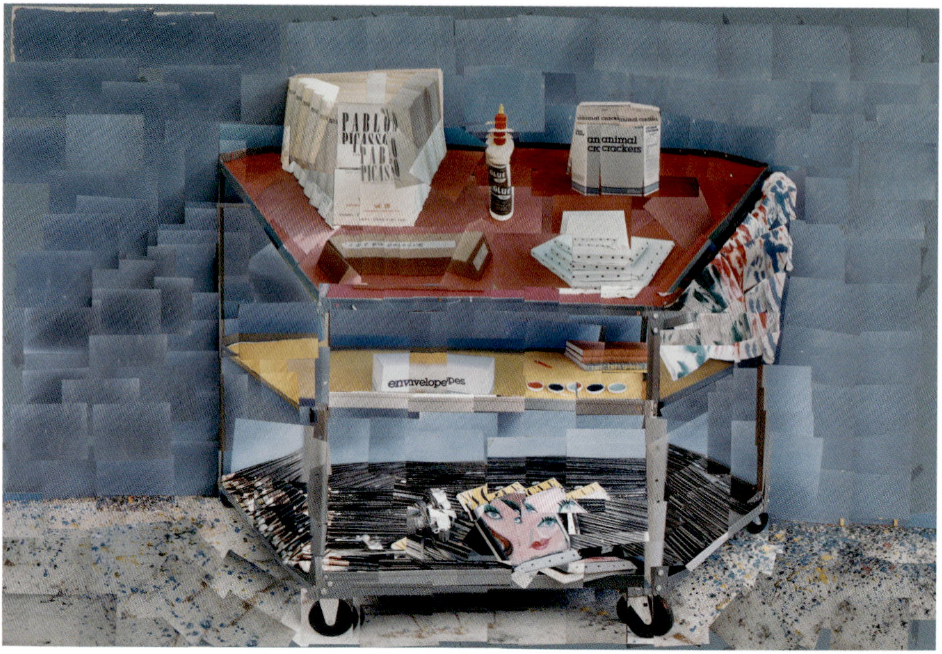

PABLO
PICASSO
PABLO
PICASSO
an animal crackers
envelopes

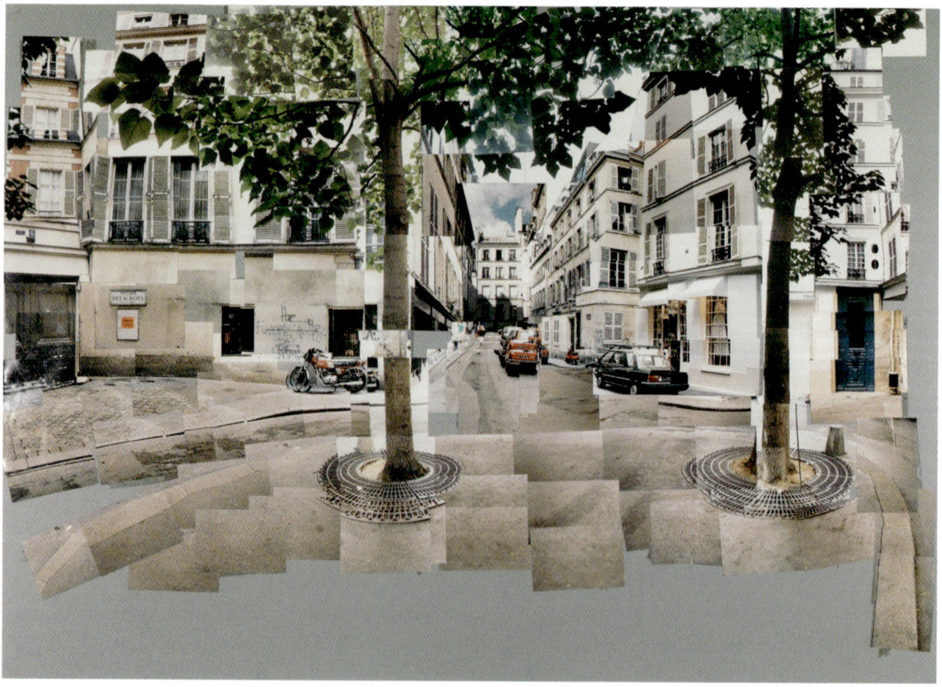

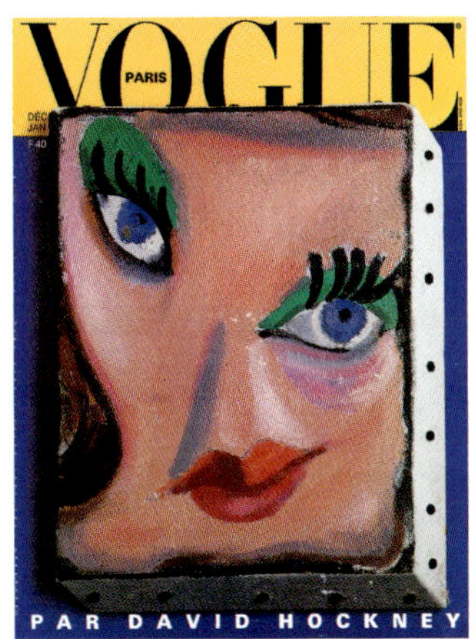

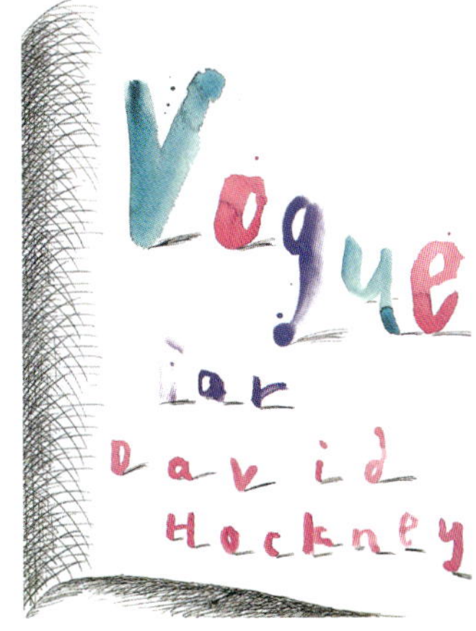

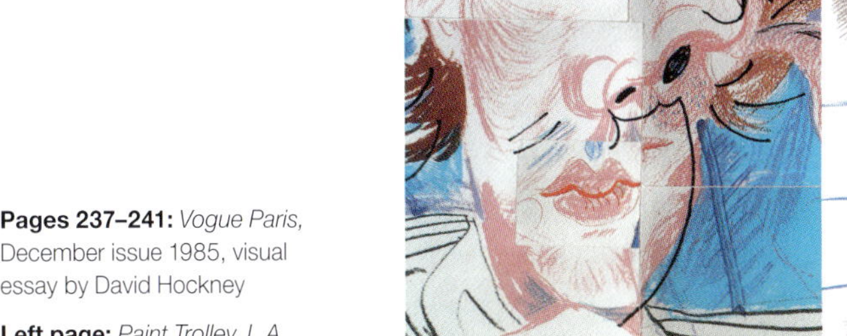

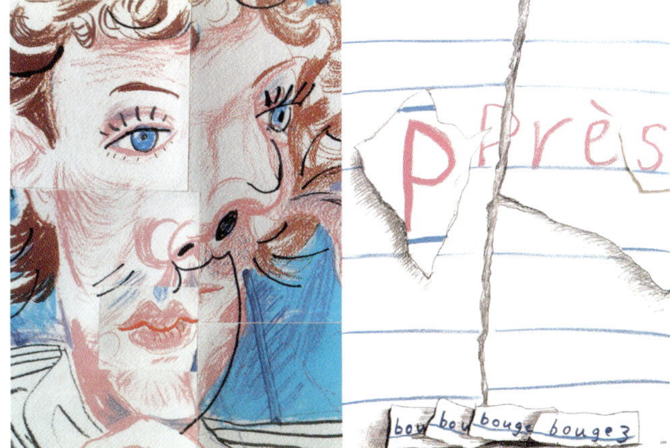

Pages 237–241: *Vogue Paris*, December issue 1985, visual essay by David Hockney

Left page: *Paint Trolley, L.A. 1985,* photographic collage, edition of 2, 40 x 60 in. / 101.5 x 152.4 cm

Place Furstenberg, Paris, August 7, 8, 9, 1985, photographic collage, edition of 2, 43 ¹⁄₂ x 61 ¹⁄₂ in. / 110.5 x 156.2 cm

Page 233: David Hockney at the *Vogue* launch evening, Paris 1985. Photo: Frederic Reglain

Page 235: *Henry Reading,* 1985, collage, acrylic, contact paper, and charcoal on gatorboard in artist's frame, 82 x 48 in. / 208.3 x 121.9 cm

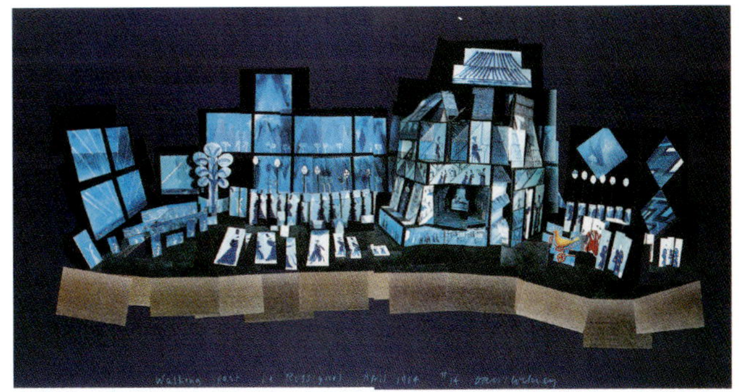

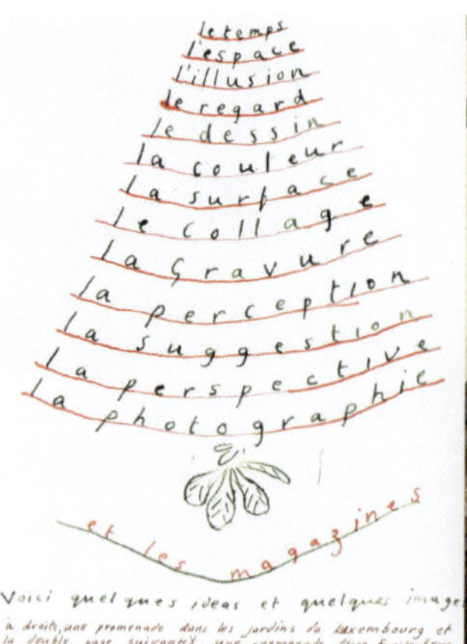

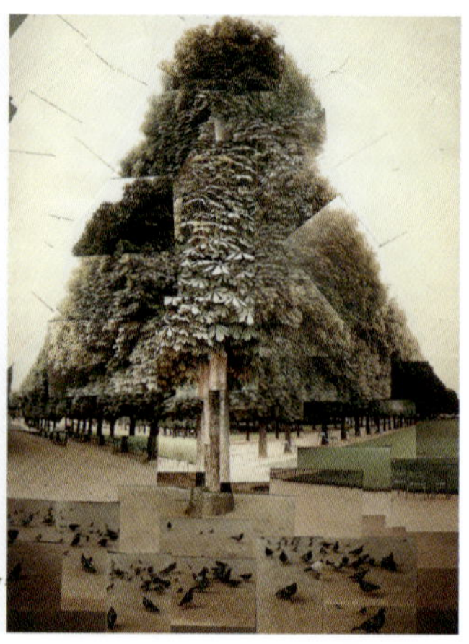

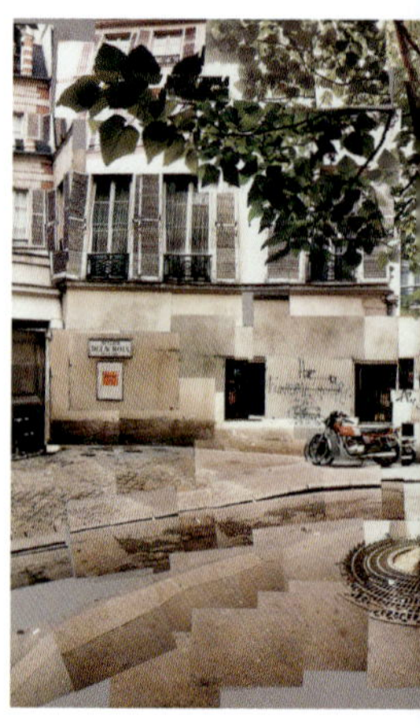

Voici quelques idées et quelques images
à droite, une promenade dans les jardins du Luxembourg et
la double page suivante, une promenade Place Furstenberg

Commençons un voyage dans
un pays où la perspective est
plus complexe et qui nous place
dans ce monde-là.

Qu'est-ce-qui se passe si
nous inversions la perspective?

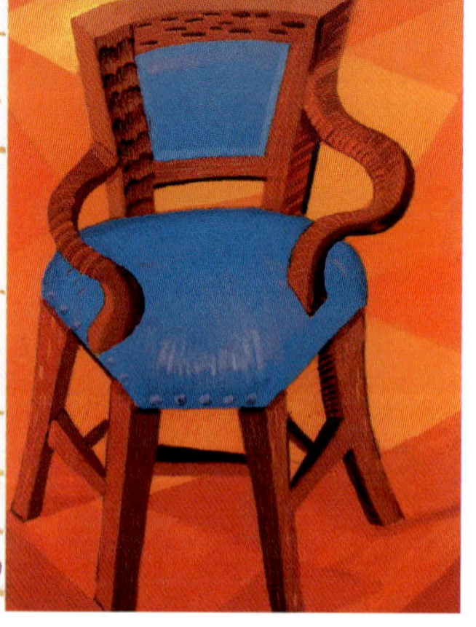

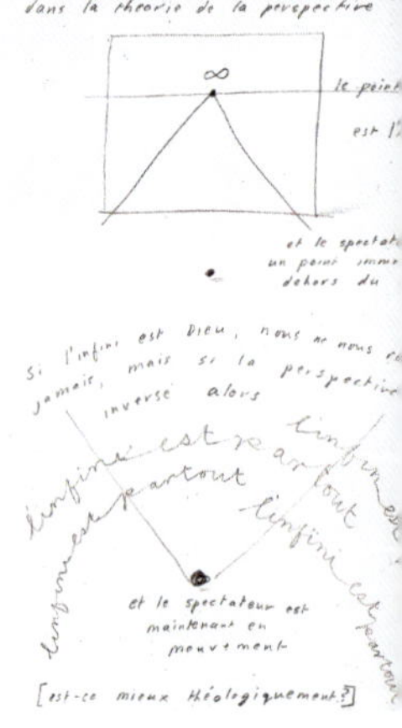

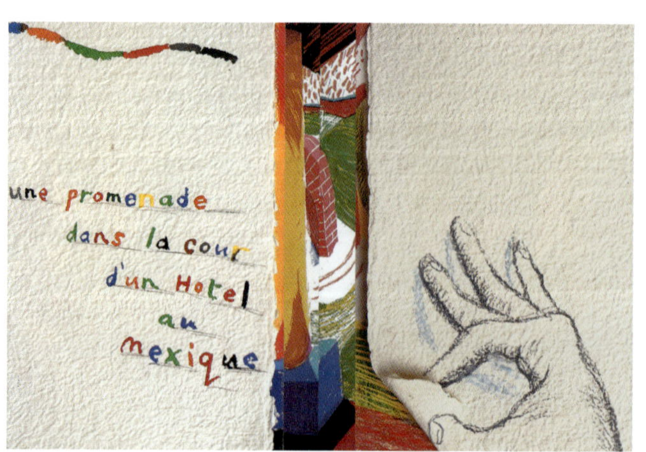

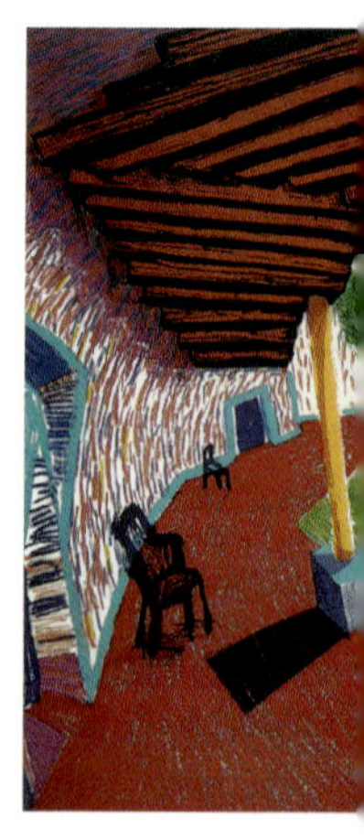

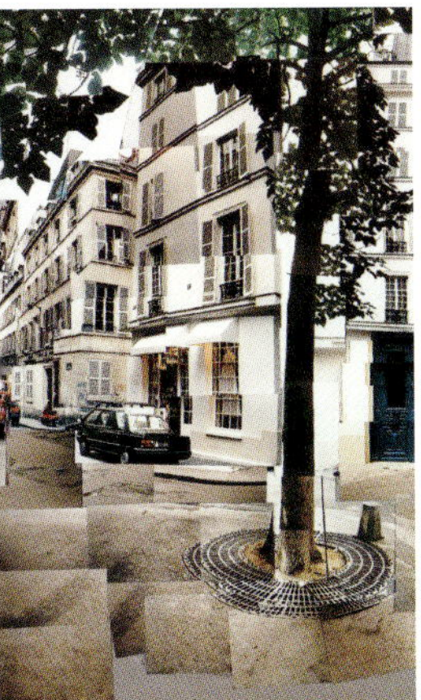

La leçon de perspective

C'est, bien sûr, une vieille idée que de considérer le spectateur en mouvement. Elle fut détruite par l'invention de la perspective, l'unique point de fuite, l'artifice pictural de la Renaissance. Cela fut peut-être dû aux difficultés de peindre la crucifixion.

Lorsque Giotto peint la crucifixion, il le fait d'une manière médiévale : c'est-à-dire une suite d'événements traversants le temps, d'un tableau à l'autre, le Christ portant la croix jusqu'en haut du mont.

Mais cette exécution n'est pas une action, (votre tête n'est pas coupée, aucune flèche ne transperce votre cœur.)

Le temps s'arrête, et l'espace devient fixe lorsqu'on utilise le procédé de la perspective, donnant ainsi une impression de poids et de volume aux objets dans l'espace. La souffrance du Christ est rendue plus appréciable par la perspective et gagne en expression, mais le problème est toujours ; "qu'est-ce-que cela peut bien nous faire ?"

Nous ne sommes ni près ni attachés visuellement parce que nous voyons. (en revanche, on peut l'être émotivement.)

Cette invention précéda celle de la chambre obscure, et par la suite l'appareil de photo tel que nous le connaissons aujourd'hui, voyant le monde de la même façon. C'est donc un monde statique, un monde qui supprime notre matérialité. Pour que cette perspective puisse fonctionner, nous sommes obligés de ne pas bouger, de fermer un œil pour regarder ce monde avec l'autre, à travers un petit trou. (et voilà l'angoisse du photographe aujourd'hui.)

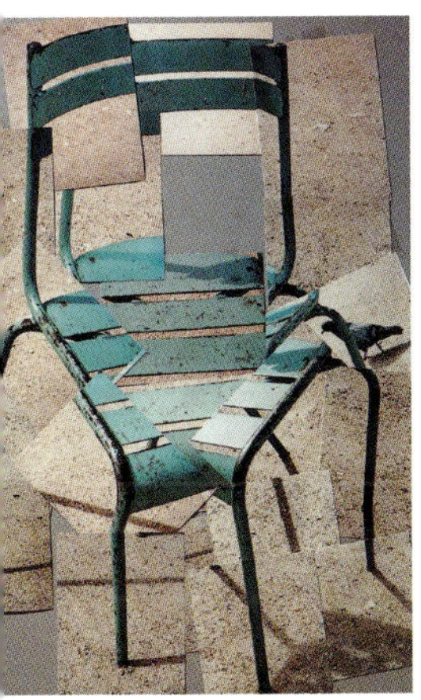

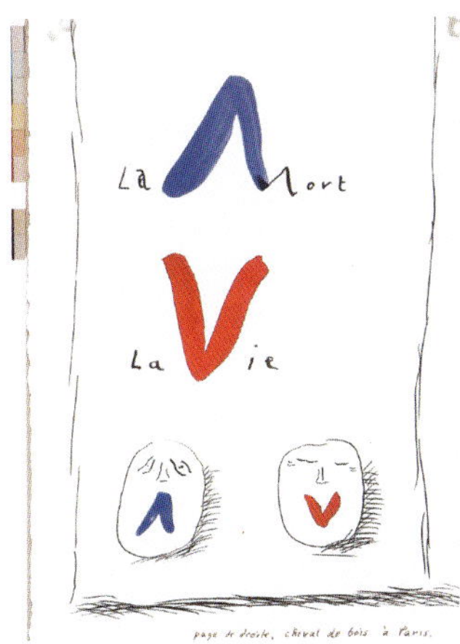

page de droite, cheval de bois à Paris.

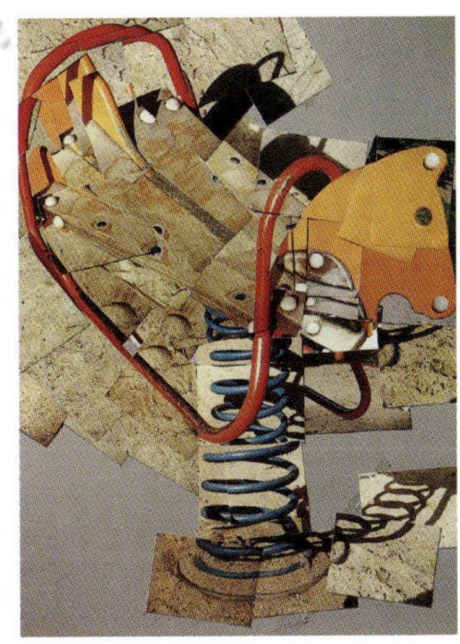

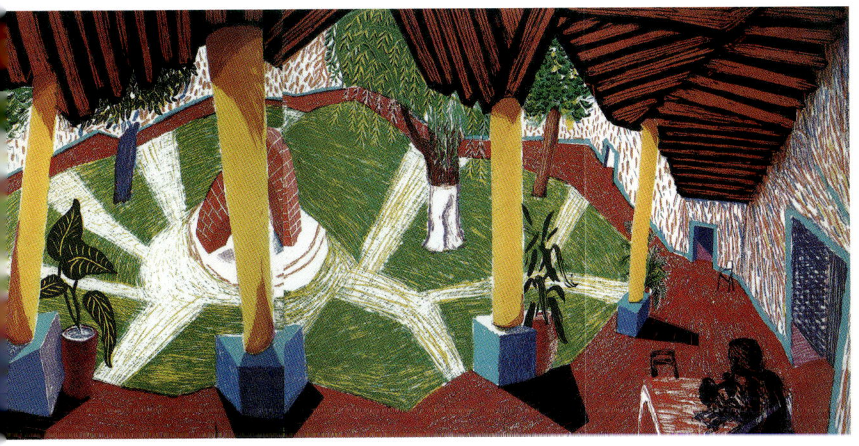

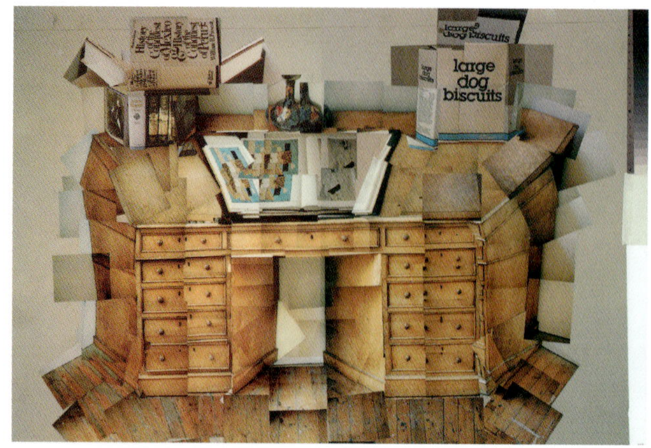

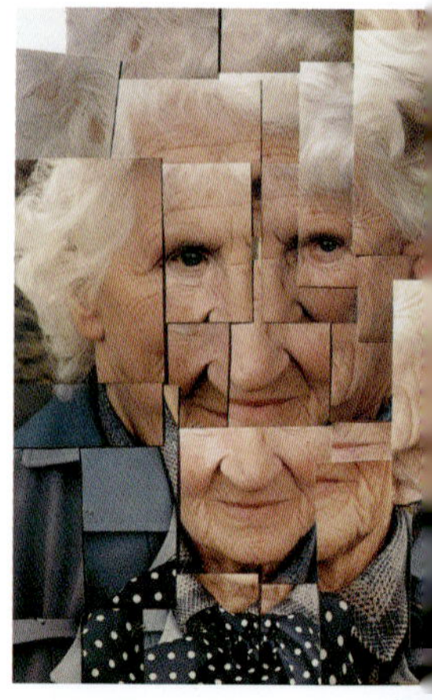

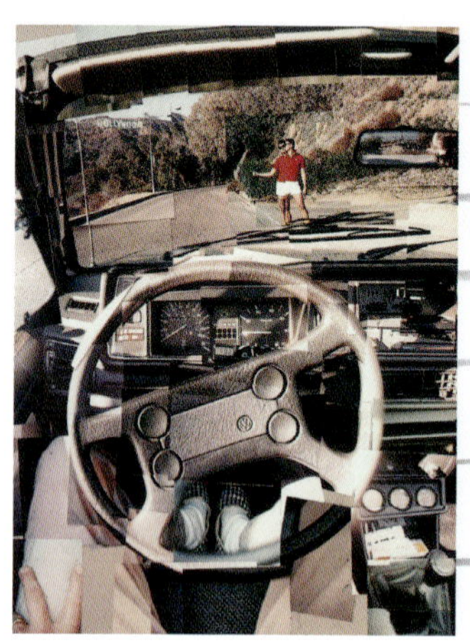

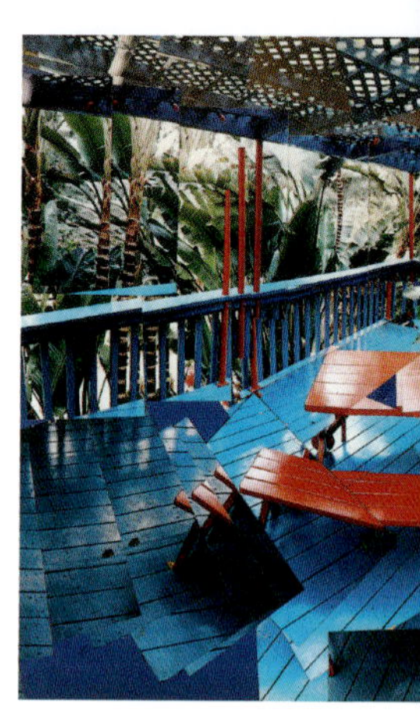

Voici à gauche une scène typiquement Hollywoodienne

et sur les pages précédentes, Mo McDermott + Lisa

Lombardi dans leur maison d'Echo Park à Los Angeles.

les doubles pages suivantes sont à propos des

différentes heures de la journée à Los Angeles.

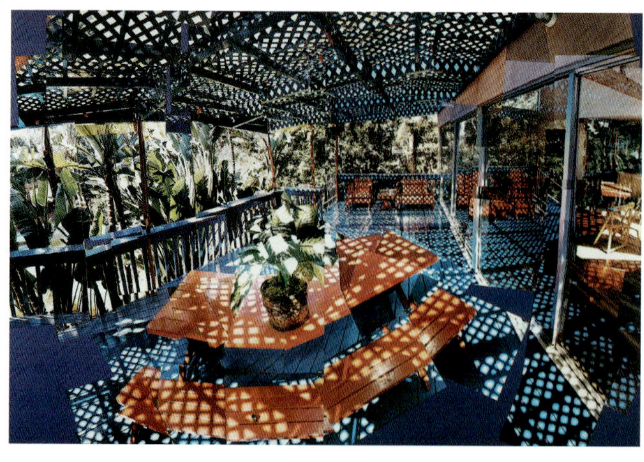

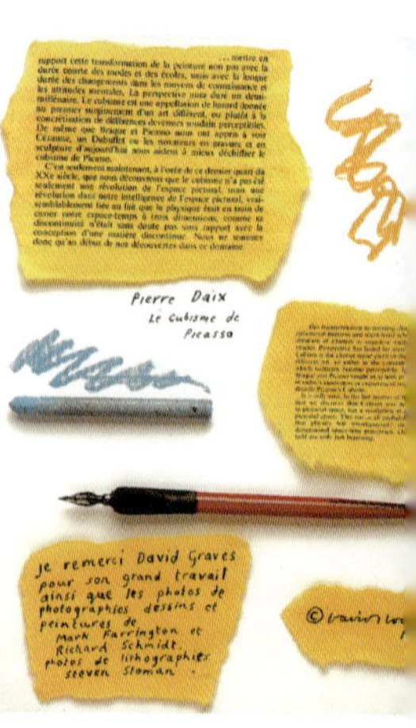

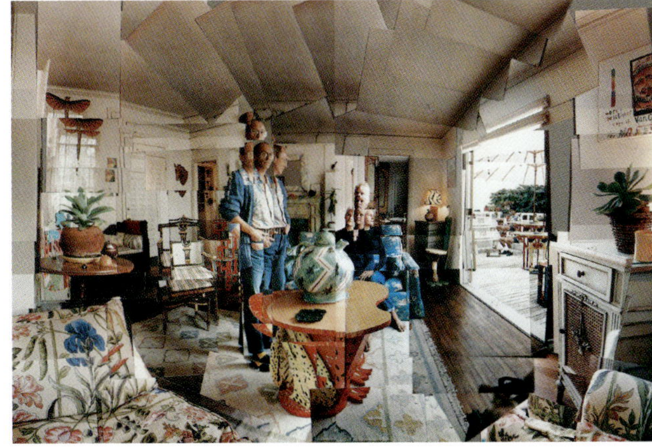

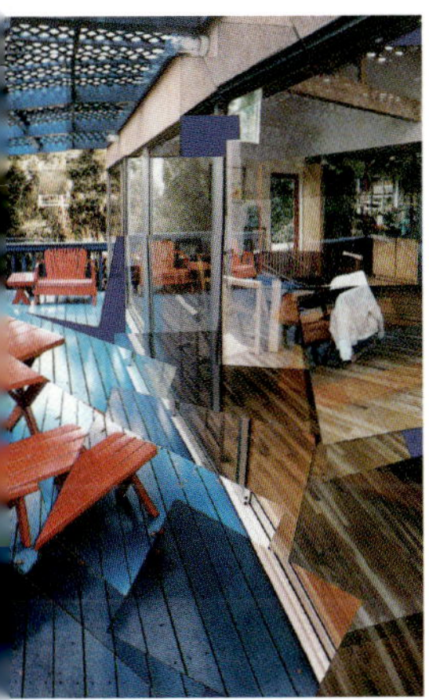

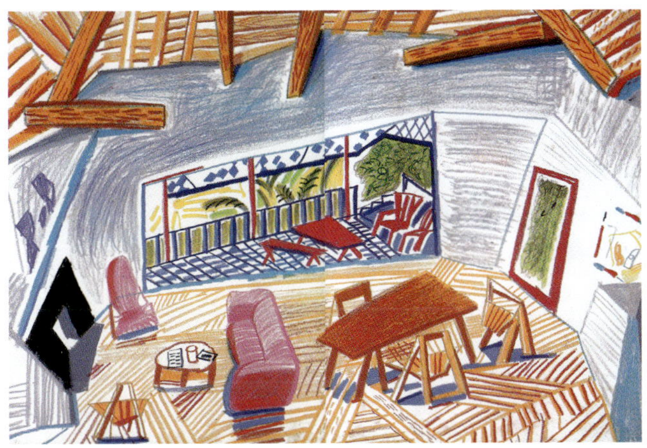

BY DAVID HOCKNEY

he Chinese landscape painting is a walk through a landscape, the spectator is involved and surrounded and partici-
nates. The static viewpoint is avoided.

is collage depicts a reconstruction of a theatre presentation of Stravinsky's opera "Le Rossignol", based on Hans
Andersen's story. My construction told the whole story and was meant to reveal itself as the spectator walked
nd could look round the corners. No single photograph would be able to show this experience, as I made this
myself, constructing the picture by walking past the piece. It is the movements of the spectator that gives it another
on. Movement is life. Lack of movement, death.

ere are more pictures and thoughts on Time; Space; Illusion; Seeing; Drawing; Colour; Surface; Collage;
; Perception; Suggestion; Perspective; Photography; and Magazines.

he perspective lesson. The idea of the moving spectator (the spectator now has life) is of course old, and only
nder attack with the introduction of one point perspective in the Renaissance. This could have been due to the
a of depicting the crucifixion.

hen Giotto depicts the crucifixion he does it in the medieval way, an action through time from one picture to the
rist carrying the cross up the hill etc. Yet the actual crucifixion contains no action (your head is not chopped off—
does not pierce your heart).

ith the invention of one point perspective time stops and space is fixed, giving objects in space a fixed position
king of weight and volume. For the depiction of Christ's suffering this would be an expressive gain, but this
is, what does it do to us?

e are not close or connected visually (emotionally, of course, we can be) with what is seen. The invention must
te the camera obscura and hence the camera of today, always seeing the world in the same way. It makes a static
d seems to take away our bodies, for to make perspective work we have to stand still, close one eye and look at the
rough a hole. (The photographer's problem today).

ow let us begin a journey to a more complex perspective that puts us in this world.

hat happens if we reverse perspective?

ith the moving spectator there are now changes in some of our concepts of distance (distance from where ?), so
uld be felt closer and more connected to us, in fact psychological distance has now more meaning.

hapes of things are now not what we thought they were, the representation on a flat surface is now a different
an (all representations are now seen as abstractions—which they always were).

ven images of man are not as we thought, and the world is made more enchanting.

he idea of the fixed image suggests we are separate from others and objects. Images must change to grasp
is.

the previous pages Mo McDermott and Lisa Lombardi in the house in Echo Park, Los Angeles.
re is a small Hollywood scene and the next pages are about different times of day in Los Angeles.

paix sur Terre.

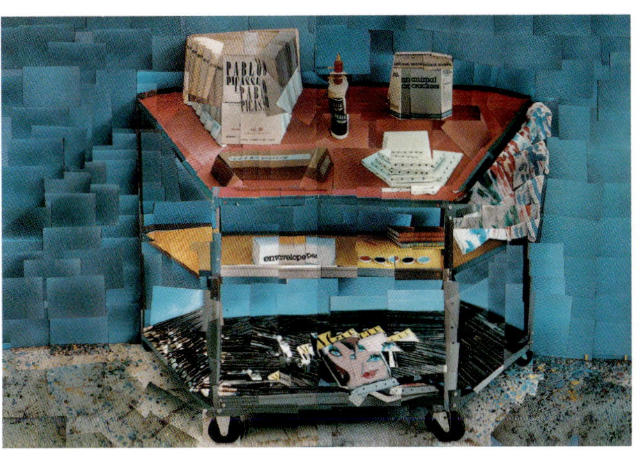

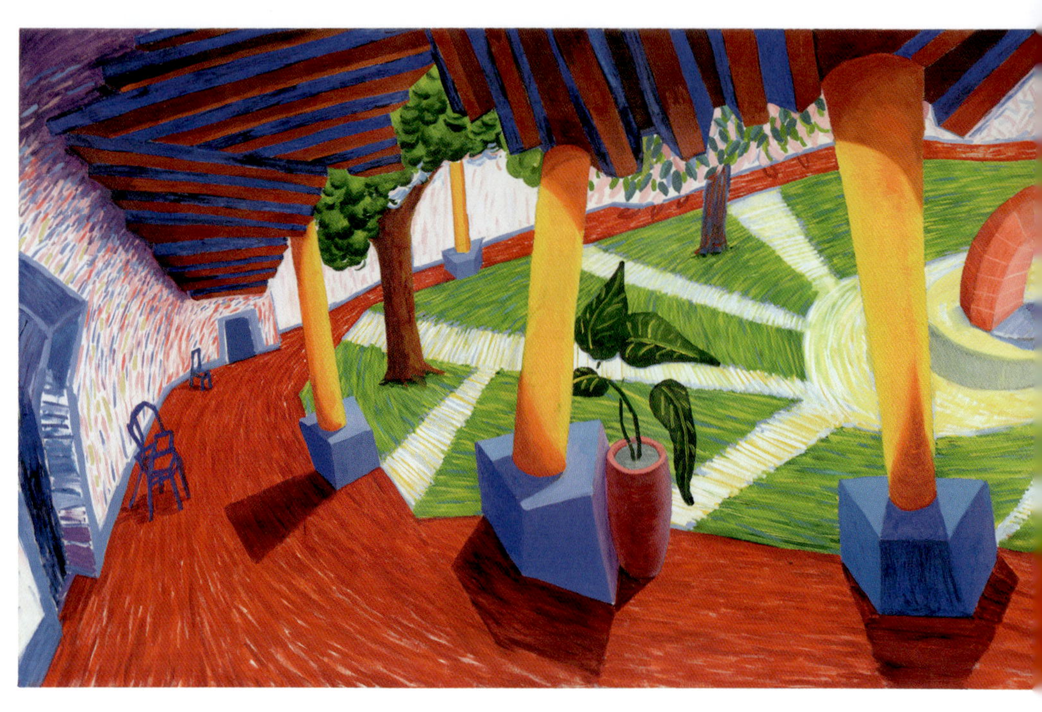

*A Walk around the Hotel Courtyard,
Acatlán*, 1985, oil on 2 canvases,
72 x 240 in. / 182.9 x 609.6 cm

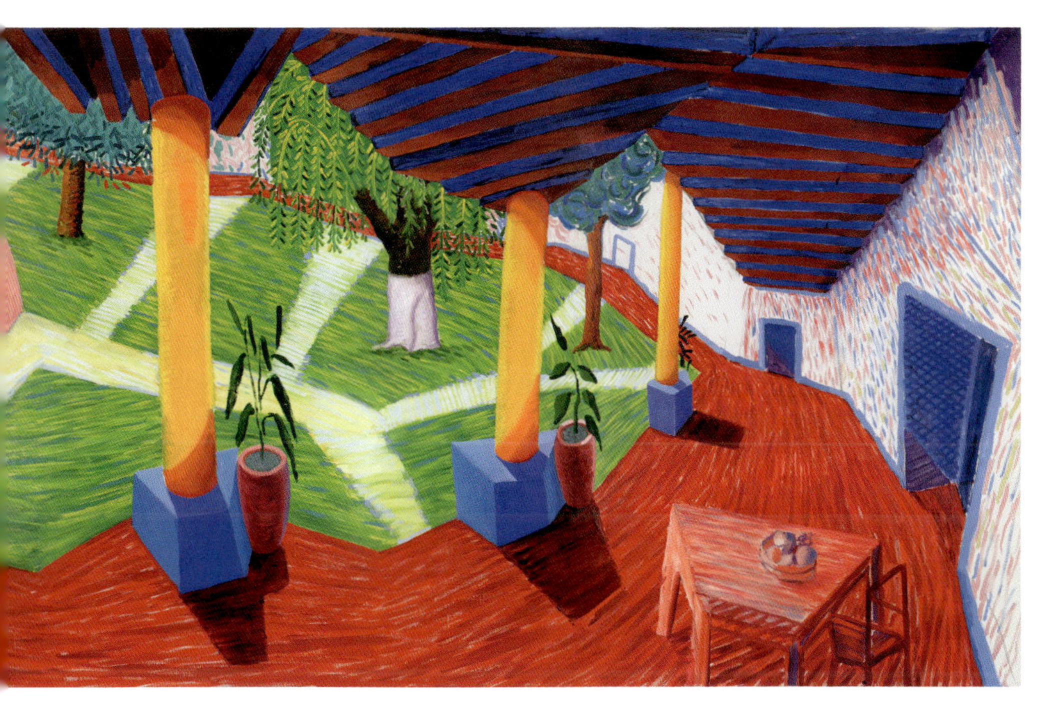

1986

Inspired by his work in different printmaking techniques, Hockney starts experimenting with an office-quality photocopying machine. By switching the cartridges and putting each sheet repeatedly through the machine, he finds he can layer colors similarly to the lithography process. He can reduce or enlarge the image, collage parts together and copy them again, and so create works on paper without the help of an assistant. He calls them homemade prints. In a conversation with Lawrence Weschler, he describes the advantages: "Over the years, I've made a lot of prints working in several different master printshops. It's an exciting process, but I've always been bothered by the lack of spontaneity: how it takes hours and hours, working alongside several master craftsmen, to generate an image. How you're continually having to interrupt the process of creation from one moment to the next for technical reasons. But with these copying machines, I can work by myself—indeed you virtually have to work by yourself; there's nothing for anyone else to do—and I can work with great speed and responsiveness. In fact, this is the closest I've ever come in printing to what it's like to paint." The method also allows him to integrate different materials for pictorial effect, such as the photocopy of a city map in *Mulholland Drive, June 1986* (p. 249), or of his own shirt in *Self Portrait, July 1986* (p. 248).

On invitation of producer Michael Deakin, Hockney takes part in the BBC series *Painting with Light* (p. 247), trying out the Quantel Paintbox, a computer program for creating graphics. The image is painted with an electronic pen on a touchboard and transmitted to a television screen. While the technique proves very limited, it offers new possibilities all its own. "I'm painting with light on glass," Hockney comments. "The only equivalent where you would get colors like this is stained glass itself where you can get a richness of color that even paint can't give. It has almost a neon glow."

With David Graves and his new assistant Charlie Scheips, Hockney travels to the Mojave Desert to make photographs. On the way he discovers a crossing, where over a week he photographs his last, most complex, and most painterly photocollage, *Pearblossom Hwy., 11–18th April 1986* (pp. 250/251)—"a panoramic assault on Renaissance one-point perspective," as the artist calls it. The occasion is a commission by *Vanity Fair* to illustrate a story by Gregor von Rezzori, but in the end the work is not published due to the ambitiousness of the project.

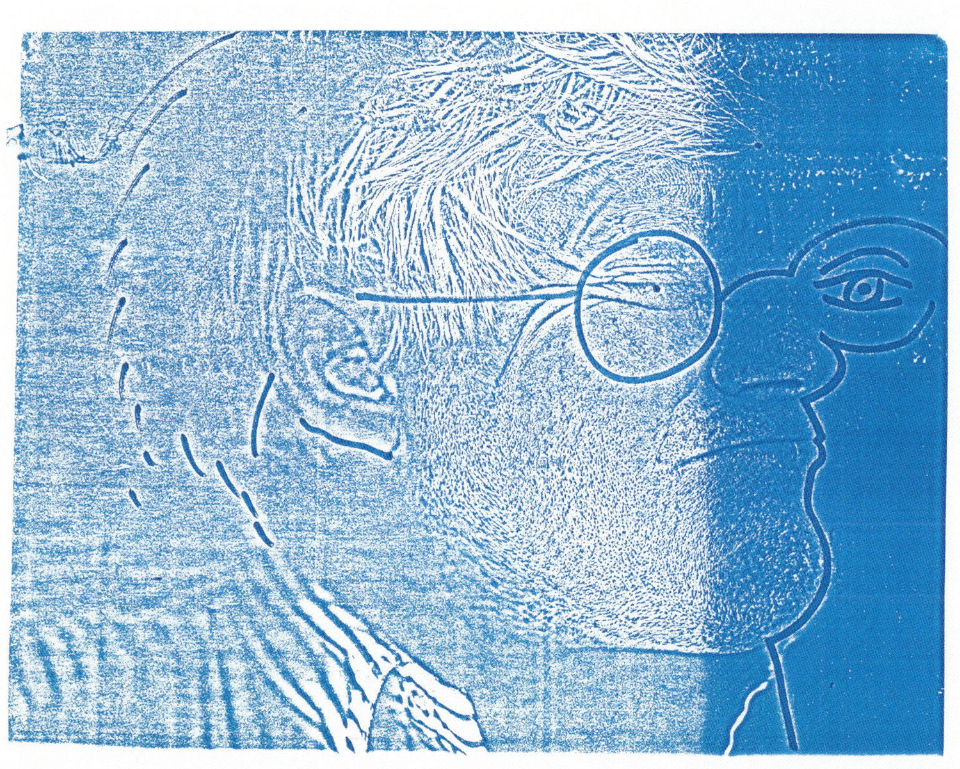

Self Portrait, 1986, homemade print,
8 ½ x 11 in. / 21.6 x 27.9 cm

Page 247: David Hockney tries out
the Quantel Paintbox in the BBC
series *Painting with Light,* 1986

It is first shown in September at the International Center of Photography in New York. Andy Grundberg in the *New York Times*: "The most complex and awesome piece in the show is also one of the newest: *Pearblossom Hwy.*, made last April. Essentially a picture of the intersection of two roads in the Southwest, with mountains in the background and trash in the foreground, the $6^{1}/_{2}$-by-10-foot image consists of hundreds of individual exposures—more than a hundred in the sky alone. The perspective is as flat as a smashed soda can, and the sun-drenched colors force us to see the whole before we decipher its parts. The subject is to some extent a metaphor for Hockney's photocollages, for they are about the intersection of painting issues with photographic ones, and the intersection of art with everyday life."

Solo: *David Hockney,* Berkeley Art Museum, Berkeley (Feb 7–Mar 21). *Moving Focus Prints from Tyler Graphics Ltd.,* Tate Gallery, London (Mar 26–May 11); catalog. *Photographs by David Hockney,* Museum of Arts, Boca Raton (Apr 12–May 15); organized by the International Exhibitions Foundation, Washington, D.C., travels to Aspen, Davenport, Lawrence, Madison, Santa Barbara, and others (through 1989); catalog with texts by Mark Haworth-Booth and David Hockney. *David Hockney's Photocollages: A Wider Perspective,* International Center of Photography, New York (Sep 14–Nov 9), travels to Tel Aviv and Cambridge, MA (through 1987). *Photocollages,* Tynte Gallery, Adelaide (Mar 1–23); catalog. *Prints from Tyler Graphics 1984–1986,* Thordén Wetterling Galleries, Gothenburg (Mar 3–Apr 6). *Gouaches and Photocollages,* Gallery One, Toronto (Apr 26–May 14). *Still Lives and Landscapes,* Knoedler Gallery, London (Aug–Sep). *David Hockney,* Galerie Kaj Forsblom, Helsinki (Aug 6–Sep). *Homemade Prints,* André Emmerich Gallery, New York (Dec 6, 1986–Jan 3, 1987); Knoedler Gallery, London (opens Dec 9); L.A. Louver, Venice, CA (Dec 6, 1986–Jan 17, 1987); and Nishimura Gallery, Tokyo (Dec 1986–Jan 1987); catalog.

Group: *Forty Years of Modern Art,* Tate Gallery, London (Feb 19–Mar 27); catalog. *Musique et art au XXème siècle,* Palais des Beaux-Arts, Brussels (Feb 22–Apr 6). *Der Maler und das Theater im 20. Jahrhundert,* Schirn Kunsthalle, Frankfurt am Main (Mar 1–May 19); catalog. *Interaction: Art-Music-Art,* Camden Arts Center, London (Nov 12–Dec 21).

Film: *Painting with Light: David Hockney,* GB, 45 min., dir. by David Goldsmith.

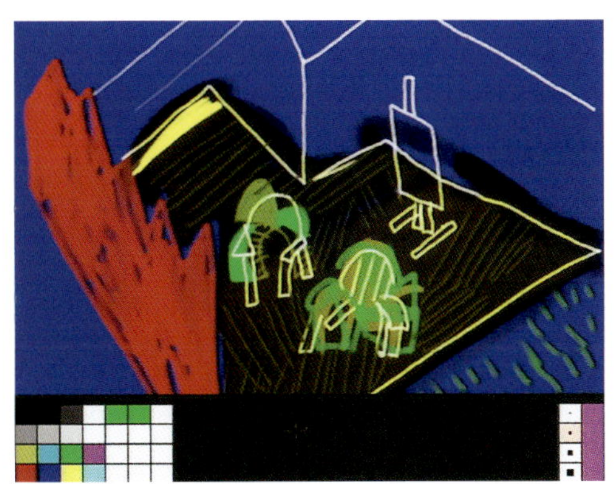
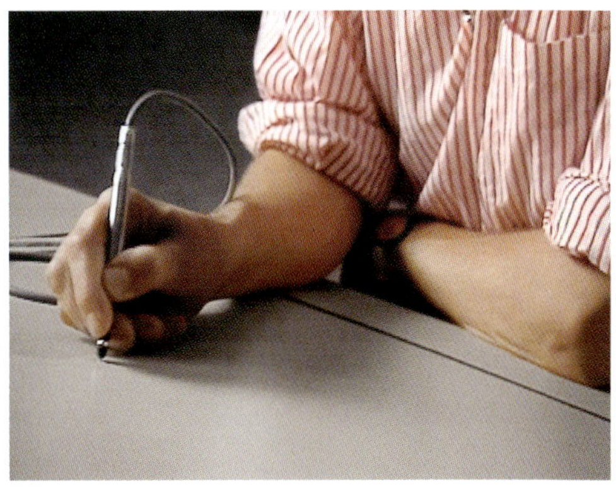
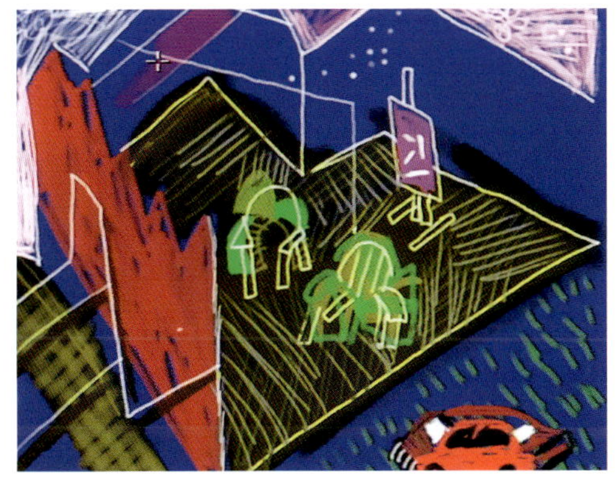
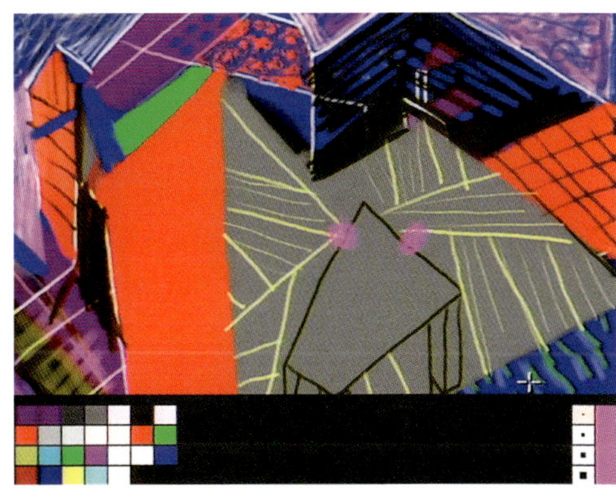
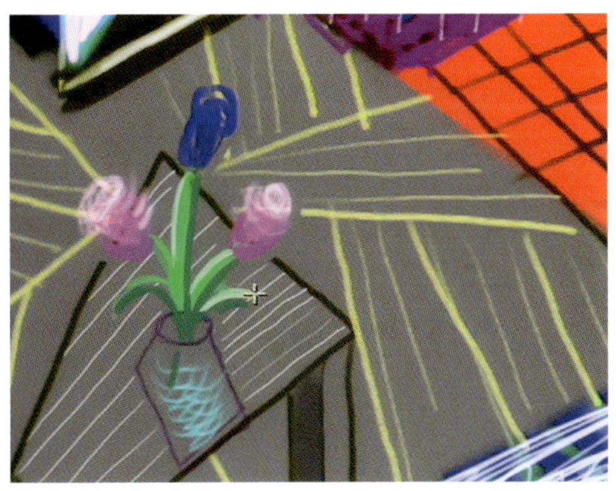
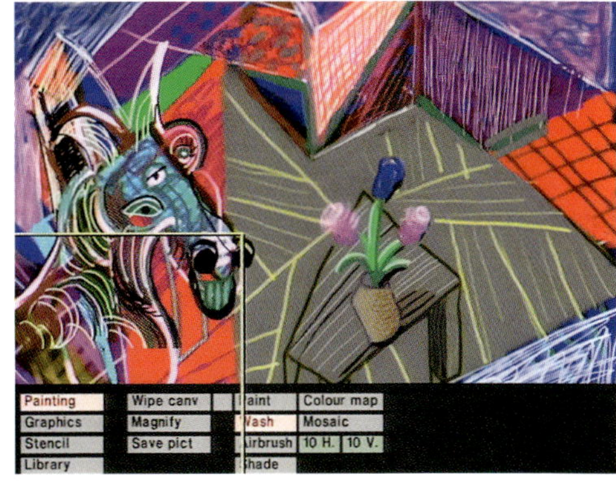

Painting
Graphics
Stencil
Library
Wipe canv
Magnify
Save pict
Paint
Wash
Airbrush
Shade
Colour map
Mosaic
10 H.
10 V.

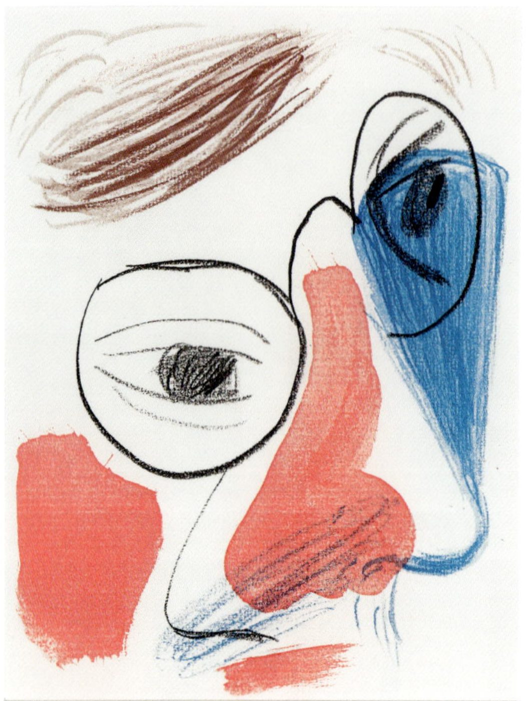

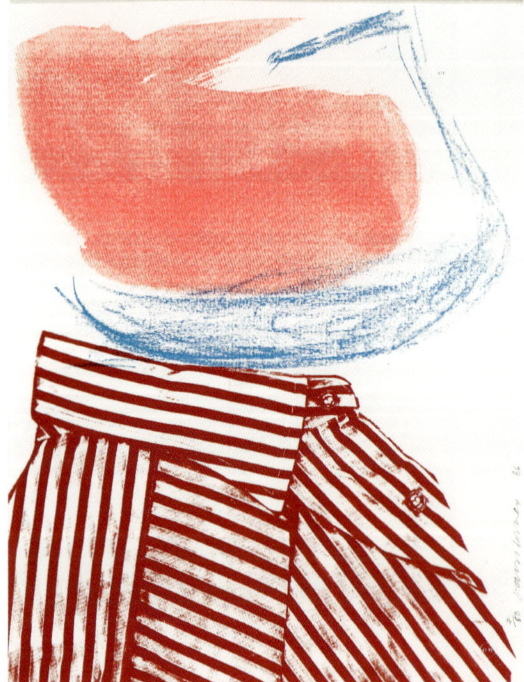

Self Portrait, July 1986, homemade
print on 2 sheets of paper, edition
of 60, 22 x 8 ¹/₂ in. / 56 x 21.5 cm

Right page: *Black Plant on Table,
April 1986*, homemade print on
6 sheets of paper, edition of 30,
22 x 25 ¹/₂ in. / 55.9 x 64.8 cm

Mulholland Drive, June 1986,
homemade print, edition of 50,
11 x 17 in. / 27.9 x 43.2 cm

Pages 250/251: *Pearblossom
Hwy., 11–18th April 1986 (Second
Version),* photographic collage,
71 ¹/₂ x 107 in. / 181.6 x 271.8 cm

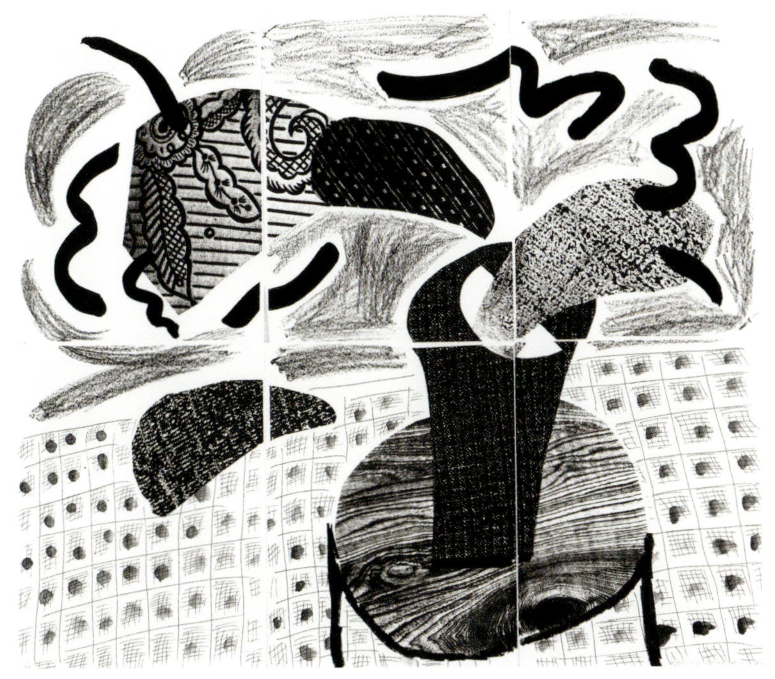

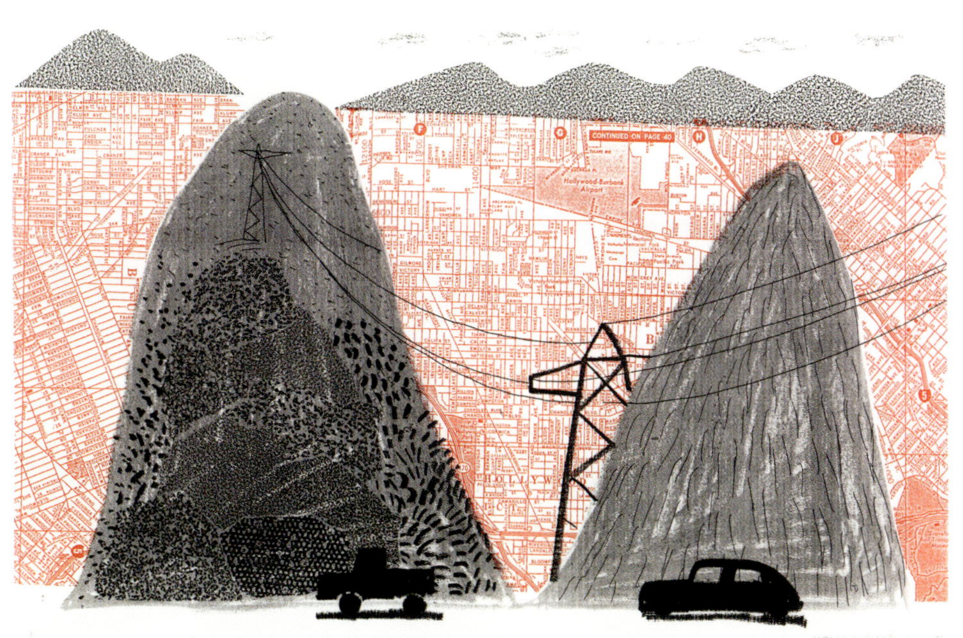

CONTINUED ON PAGE 40
Hollywood-Burbank
Airport
HOLLYW
F   G   H   J

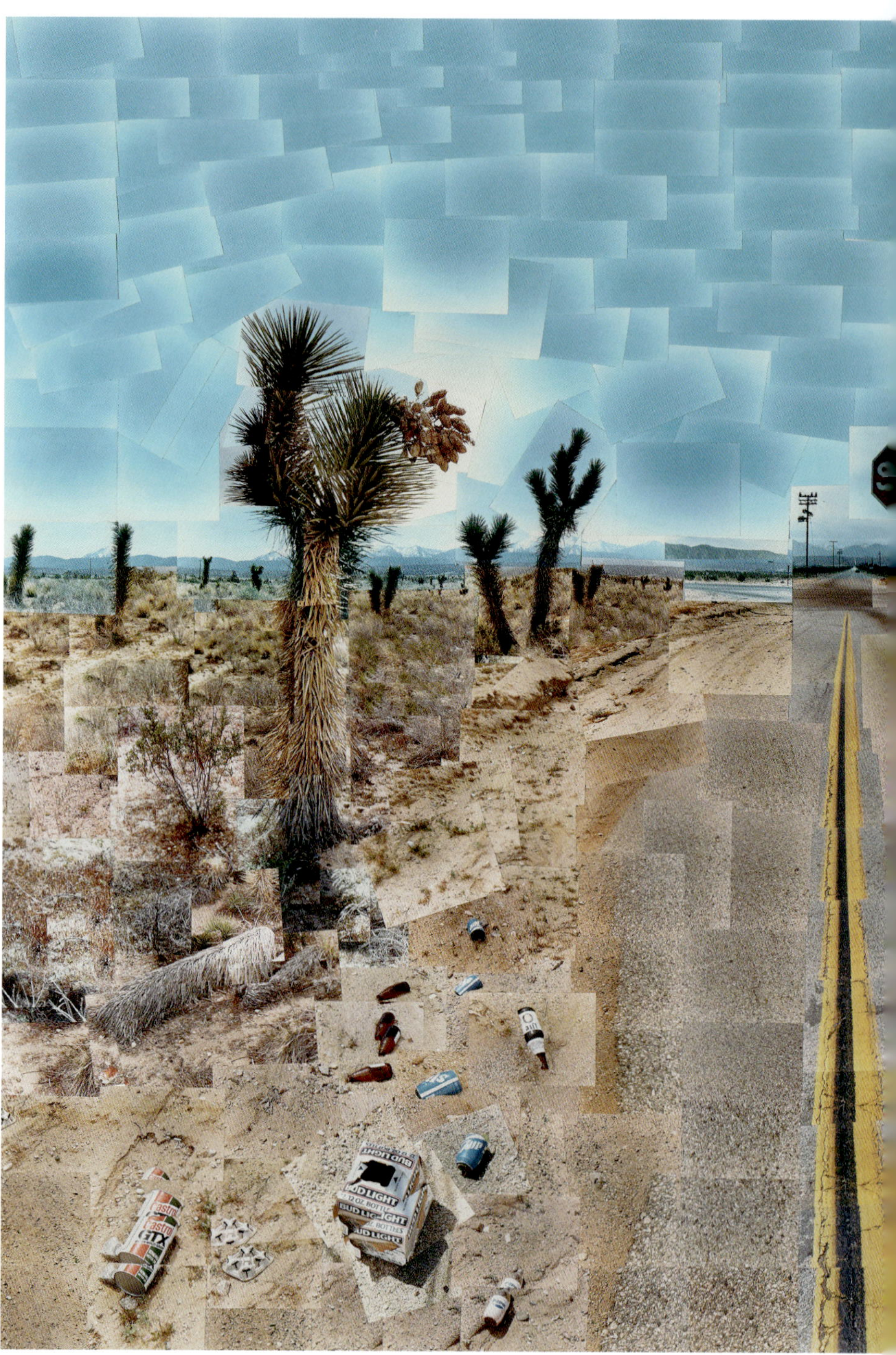

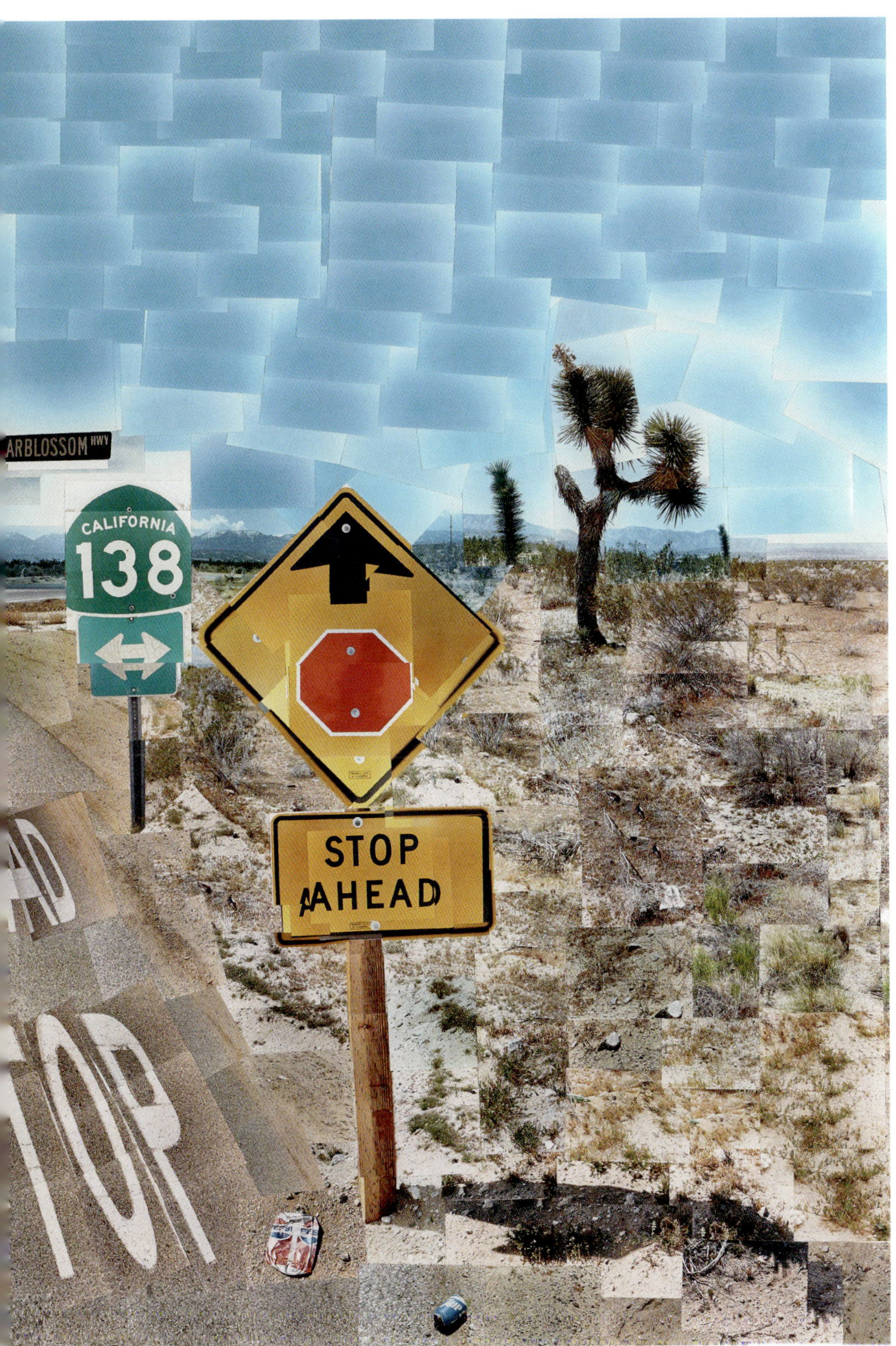
ARBLOSSOM HWY
CALIFORNIA
138
STOP
AHEAD

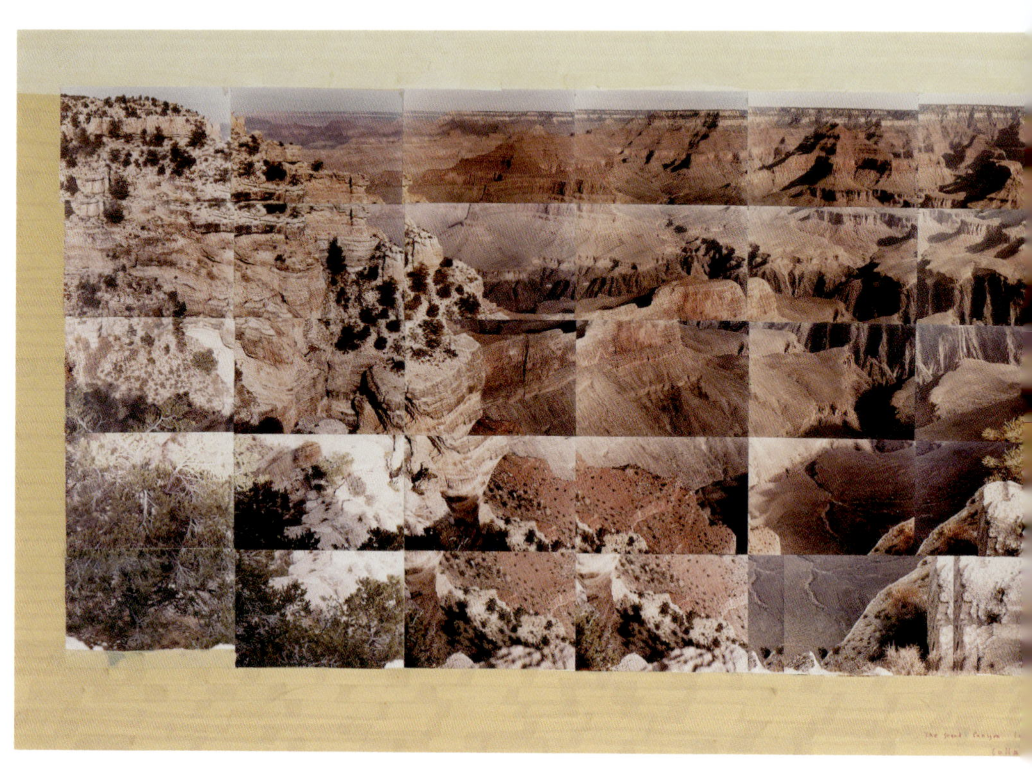

*The Grand Canyon Looking North II,
September 1982, Collage #2, Made
May 1986,* photographic collage,
44 ½ x 127 in. / 113 x 322.6 cm

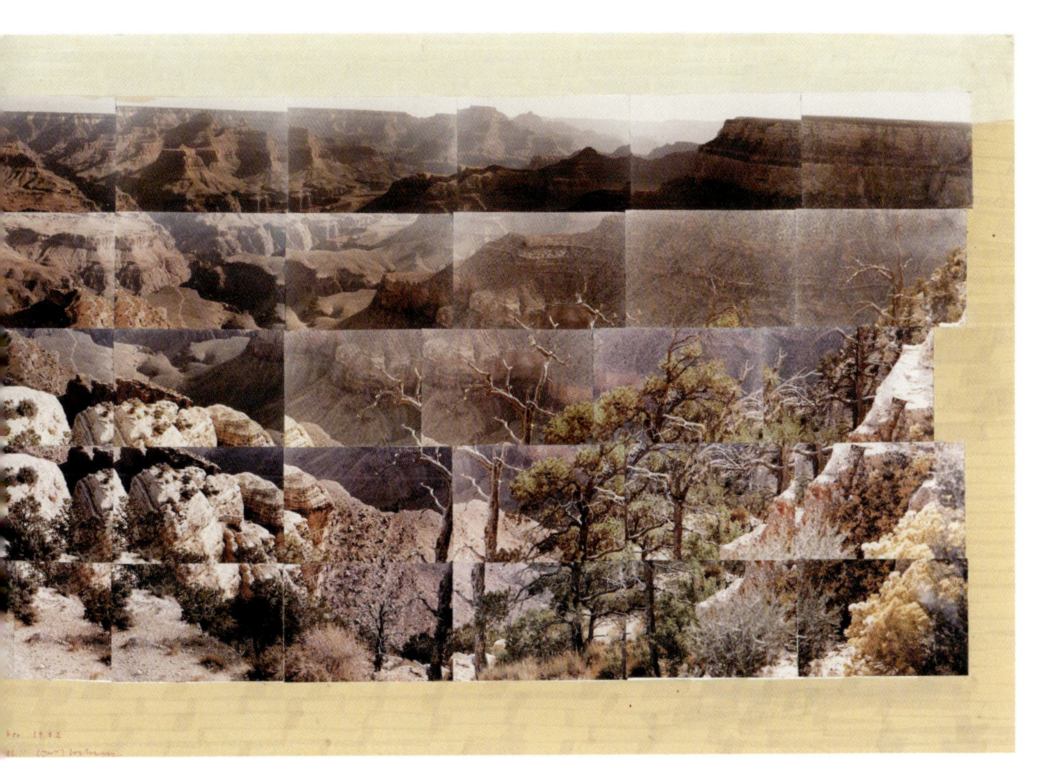

1987

Hockney acquires a color laser photocopier and uses it to both make reproductions of his paintings and new works by selecting and manipulating details from previous drawings. He also creates four-color prints for newspapers, which can directly be printed with the rest of the paper and still be an original work. "It's not every day that you can buy a David Hockney masterpiece for 18p," proudly proclaims the *Telegraph and Argus,* which on February 24 comes with a Hockney spread entitled *Bradford Bounce* (pp. 260/261). Near Bradford, his friend Jonathan Silver buys the old Salts Mill in Saltaire and renovates it to open a Hockney gallery, with works from his own collection and some on loan from the artist and his family.

Hockney now owns a dachshund, Stanley, who makes first appearances in smaller works, and soon after a second dog. These are briefly mentioned when Waldemar Januszczak from the *Guardian* visits him in Los Angeles for an article titled "Hockney at 50": "From my experiences of a long warm afternoon in the Hockney household, the whole world comes to see him. The phone never stops ringing. An assortment of males, young and old, secretaries, workmen, assistants, biographers, hangers-on, visitors from abroad, people doing books, people who make the tea, people who look after Hockney's two noisy little dogs, gardeners, college friends from Bradford, and me, all of us buzz around the lopsided house clinging to a hillside like drones around a hive…How far has he reached in his philosophical experiments with photography and perspective? Far enough, he sighs, looking like an old alchemist who has just boiled his last toad. There will be no more photography. No more theatre. No more collaborations. He feels, he says, ready now to begin painting—at last."

All through the year, Hockney works on the stage design for Richard Wagner's *Tristan und Isolde* at the Los Angeles Music Center Opera, which opens in early December (pp. 257–259). The production is directed by Jonathan Miller, and there is less cooperation than in Hockney's previous stage projects. Yet the artist delivers some of his most stunningly painterly backdrops, as described by John Russell in the *New York Times*: "When the action moved in Act III to Tristan's castle in Brittany, Hockney set the scene in a huge bare fortified space, granitic in its every detail…When this tableau was revealed, something happened that is in general much reprobated. The house burst into applause, thereby drowning out one of Wagner's most heartfelt inspirations. Thereafter, Hockney made the

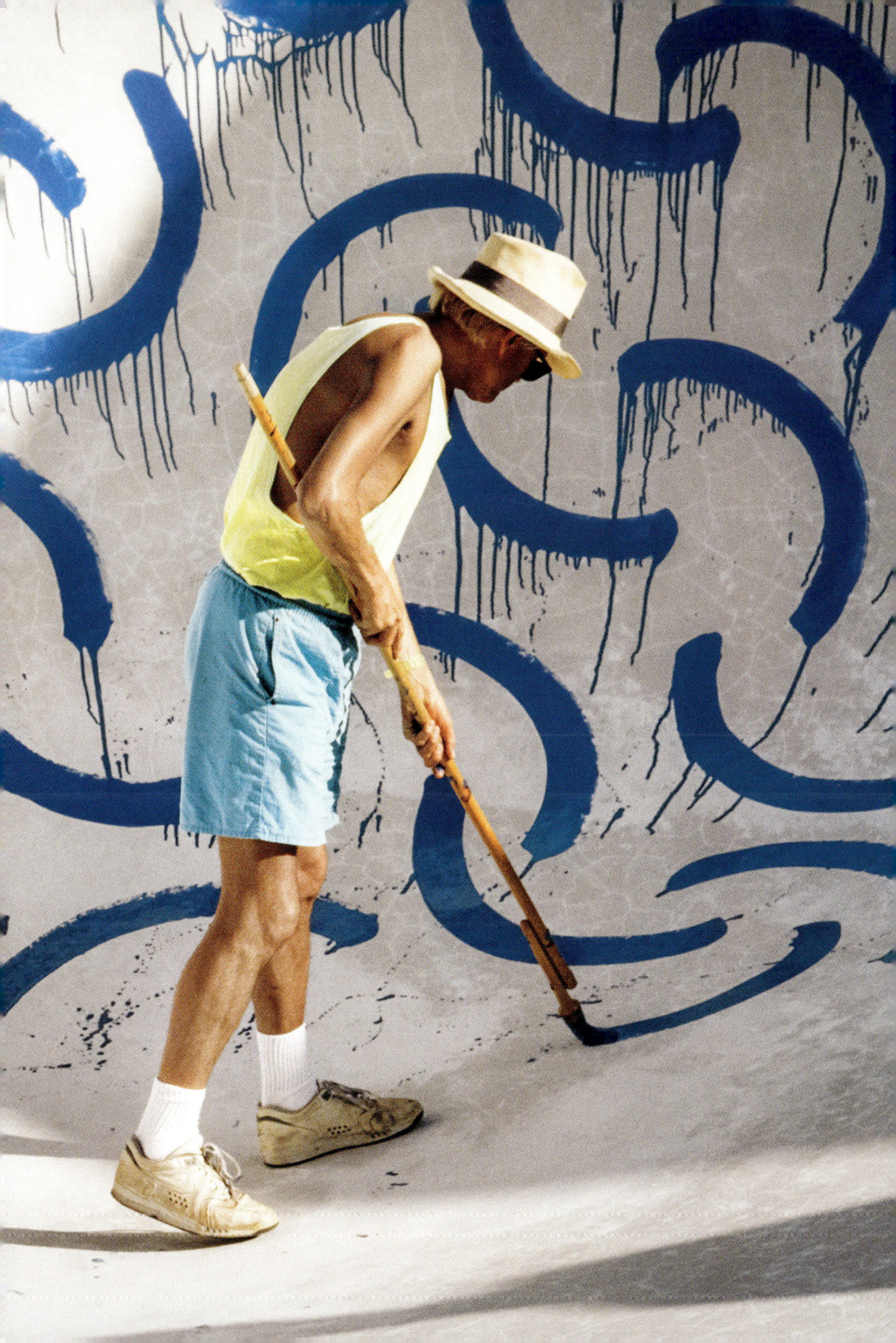

bright day come and go, conjured up shifts of light and color that defied time and set it at naught, and brought us back to a dry boneyard of the heart that only Tristan's wild fancies could irrigate. Isolde's arrival could not have been better prepared. And at the very end, when Wagner leaves the orchestra to sum up the long evening on its own, Hockney rose to the notorious challenge and whisked us in a matter of seconds to a world in which all life was extinguished and all light doused, and from there to a transfigured universe in which time past, time present and time to come were somehow in equilibrium. It was as awesome a moment as we shall ever see on a stage."

Solo: *Faces 1966–1984,* Laband Art Gallery, Loyola Marymount University, Los Angeles (Jan 30–Mar 14); catalog with a text by Marco Livingstone. *David Hockney,* National Museum of Photography, Film and Television, Bradford (Mar). *A Rake's Progress and Other Etchings,* Fitzwilliam Museum, Cambridge (Jul 14–Oct 4). *Photocollages and Polaroids,* New Mexico State University Art Gallery, Las Cruces (Nov–Dec). *Moving Focus: Graphics, Drawings, Photocollages,* Erika Meyerovich Gallery, San Francisco (Jan 22–Mar 22). *Master Prints 1963–1986,* Galerie Herbert Meyer-Ellinger, Frankfurt am Main (Apr 28–Jun 27).

Group: *British Art in the Twentieth Century: The Modern Movement,* Royal Academy of Arts, London (Jan–Apr); catalog. *Contemporary Southern Californian Art,* Taipei Fine Arts Museum, Taipei (Apr 4–Jun 14); catalog. *Photography and Art: Interactions since 1946,* LA County Museum of Art, Los Angeles (Jun 4–Aug 30); travels to Fort Lauderdale, Queens, and Des Moines (through 1988); catalog. *The Artist's Mother: Portraits and Homages,* Heckscher Museum, Huntington (Nov 14, 1987–Jan 3, 1988); travels to Washington, D.C.; catalog. *Contemporary American Stage Design,* Milwaukee Art Museum, Milwaukee (Sep 3–Nov 1); catalog. *The World Is Round: Contemporary Panoramas,* Delaware Art Museum, Wilmington (Nov 20, 1987–Jan 10, 1988); travels to Southampton, Nashua, Albany, New Paltz, and Yonkers (through 1989); catalog.

Publications: Marco Livingstone, *David Hockney,* London: Thames and Hudson. Eric Shanes, *Hockney Posters,* London: Pavilion Books.

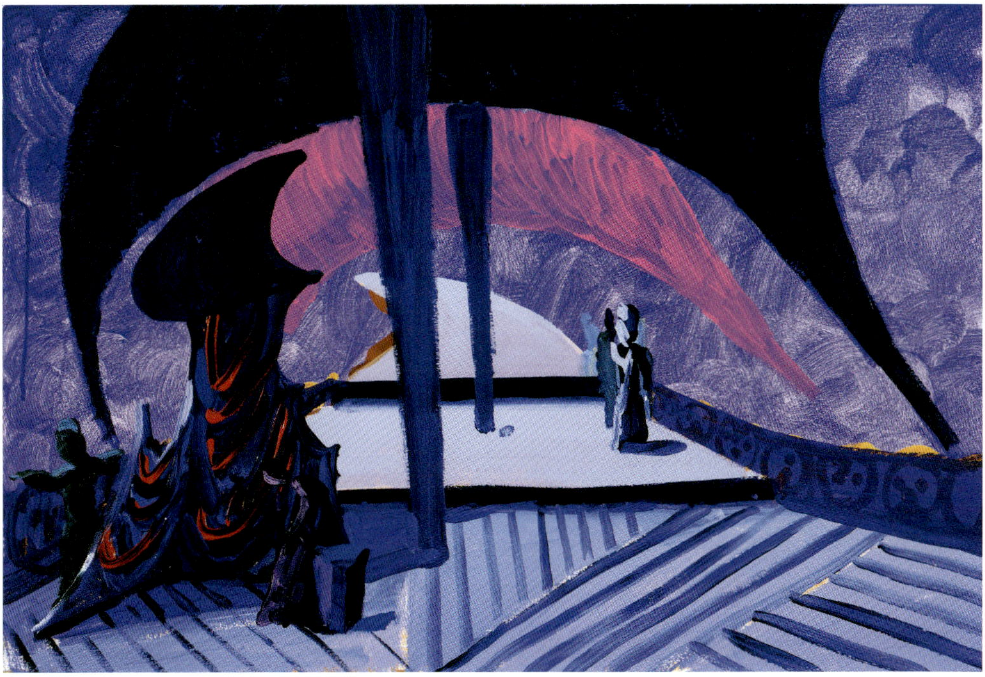

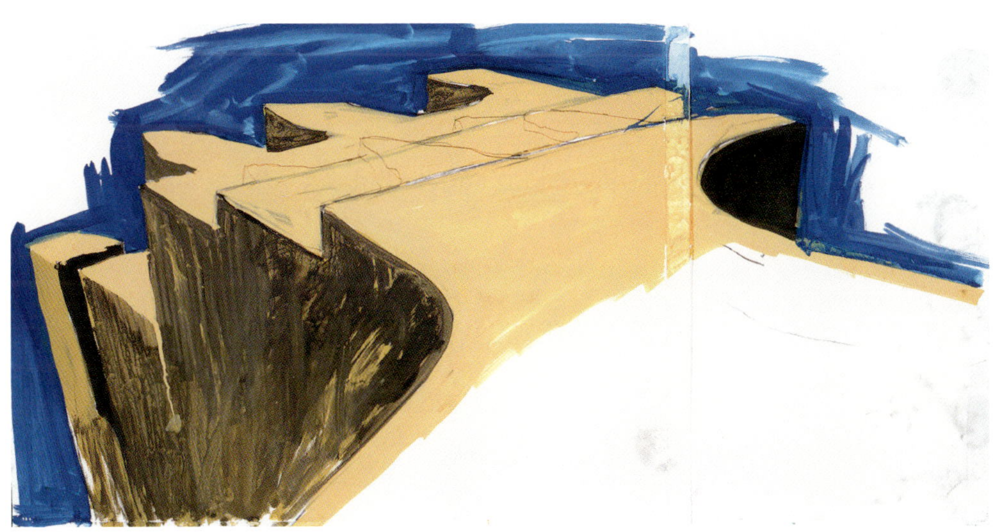

Tristan on the Ship, acrylic on canvas, 24 x 36 in. / 61 x 91.4 cm

Act III, Cliff Sketch, pencil and gouache on paper, 22 $^1/_4$ x 44 $^1/_4$ in. / 56.5 x 112.4 cm

Page 255: David Hockney painting a swimming pool, Los Angeles 1987. Photo: Jim McHugh

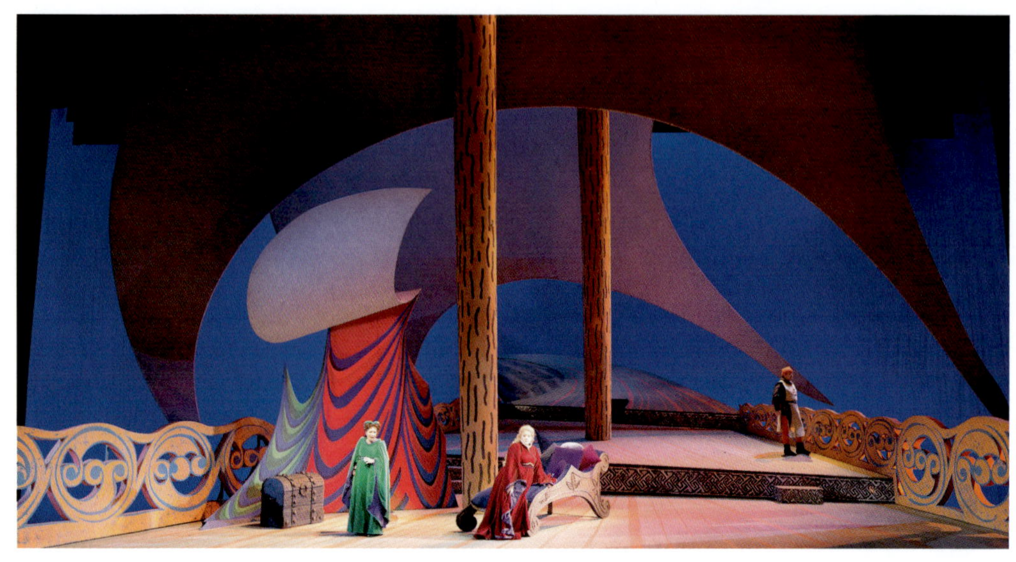

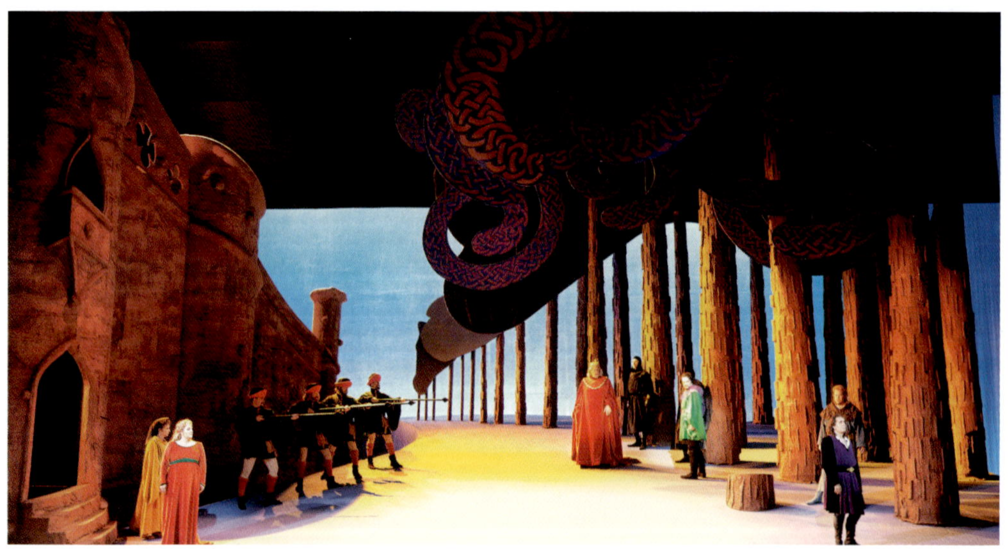

Production of *Tristan und Isolde*,
as performed at Los Angeles Music
Center Opera, Los Angeles 1987

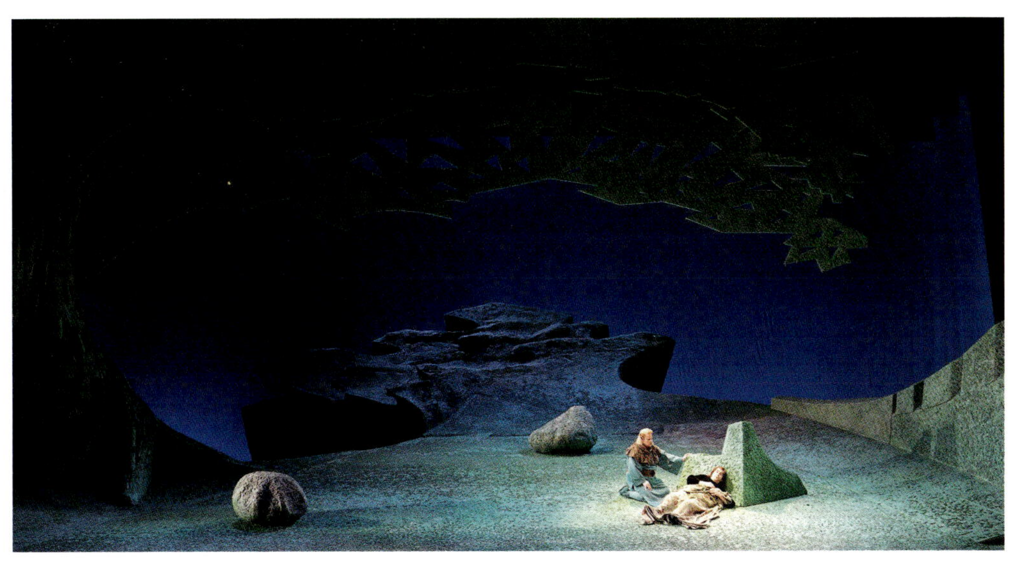

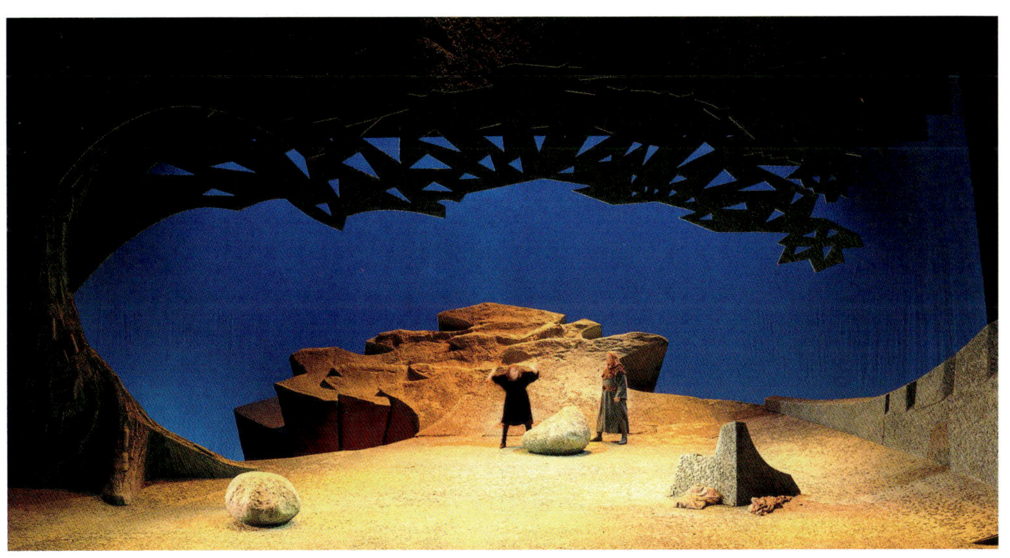

Pages 260/261: *Bradford Bounce, Feb. 1987,* color xerox on 2 panels, 15 x 22 in. / 38 x 55.9 cm

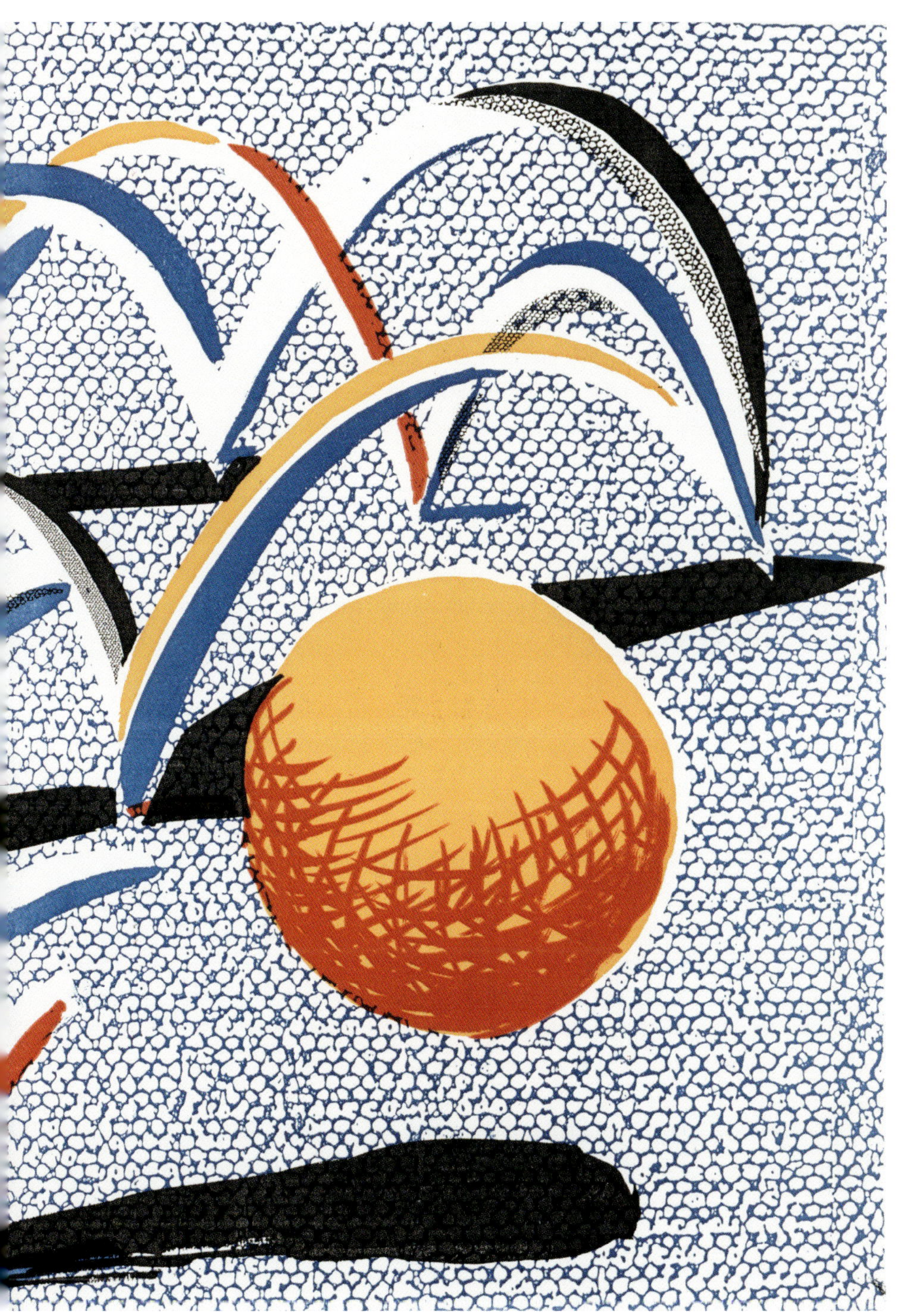

1988

On February 4, *David Hockney: A Retrospective,* organized by Maurice Tuchman and Stephanie Barron, opens at the Los Angeles County Museum of Art (pp. 270/271). It is his first retrospective since 1970, and he selects the works and plans the layout himself. In one room he even recreates his Hollywood studio with actual models for opera stage designs and a number of homemade prints on the wall. His friend Henry Geldzahler begins his essay in the accompanying catalog with the words: "Basic to David Hockney's art from the first has been the need to communicate directly with the viewer. Hockney is not at all involved in the creation of beauty as an end in itself. It is exactly this didactic urgency, this need to be heard plainly and to be understood clearly, which is the basis of his phenomenal popularity." And indeed, the exhibition proves to be the most popular contemporary art exhibition at the museum ever. It then travels to the Metropolitan Museum of Art in New York. John Russell in the *New York Times*: "At both ends of the show, the visitor can place Mr. Hockney as a man with deep local and familial roots (one of his brothers has been Mayor of Bradford, by the way). He also emerges as a very gifted though not always docile student, a painter and printmaker who has done enviably well not only for himself but also for those who have handled his work, and a man of restless and almost universal curiosity who has never been content to do the same thing over and over again." He closes his review with the remark that the images on show are "the work of a thoughtful and generous spirit who wants us to see better and—who knows?—perhaps to behave better as a result. Given the scale of the show, every visitor will find things in it that he doesn't like. But it is the work of an artist who digs deep within himself without ever appearing to do so."

At the end of the year, the exhibition travels to the Tate Gallery in London. When Hockney hears that the Thatcher government is considering new anti-homosexual laws, he threatens to pull back crucial paintings from the exhibition, which would then have to be canceled. In the end, the show can take place as scheduled, and Hockney adds some of his latest paintings. Julian Spalding in *Burlington Magazine*: "The last room in the exhibition contains some of Hockney's most recent work. It has been hung by himself, with pictures placed all over the walls, creating the effect of a visually encompassing dance. It is difficult to assess the achievement of each canvas, though Hockney does seem to be aiming at a new vividness of portrayal that is both startling and sweet. However,

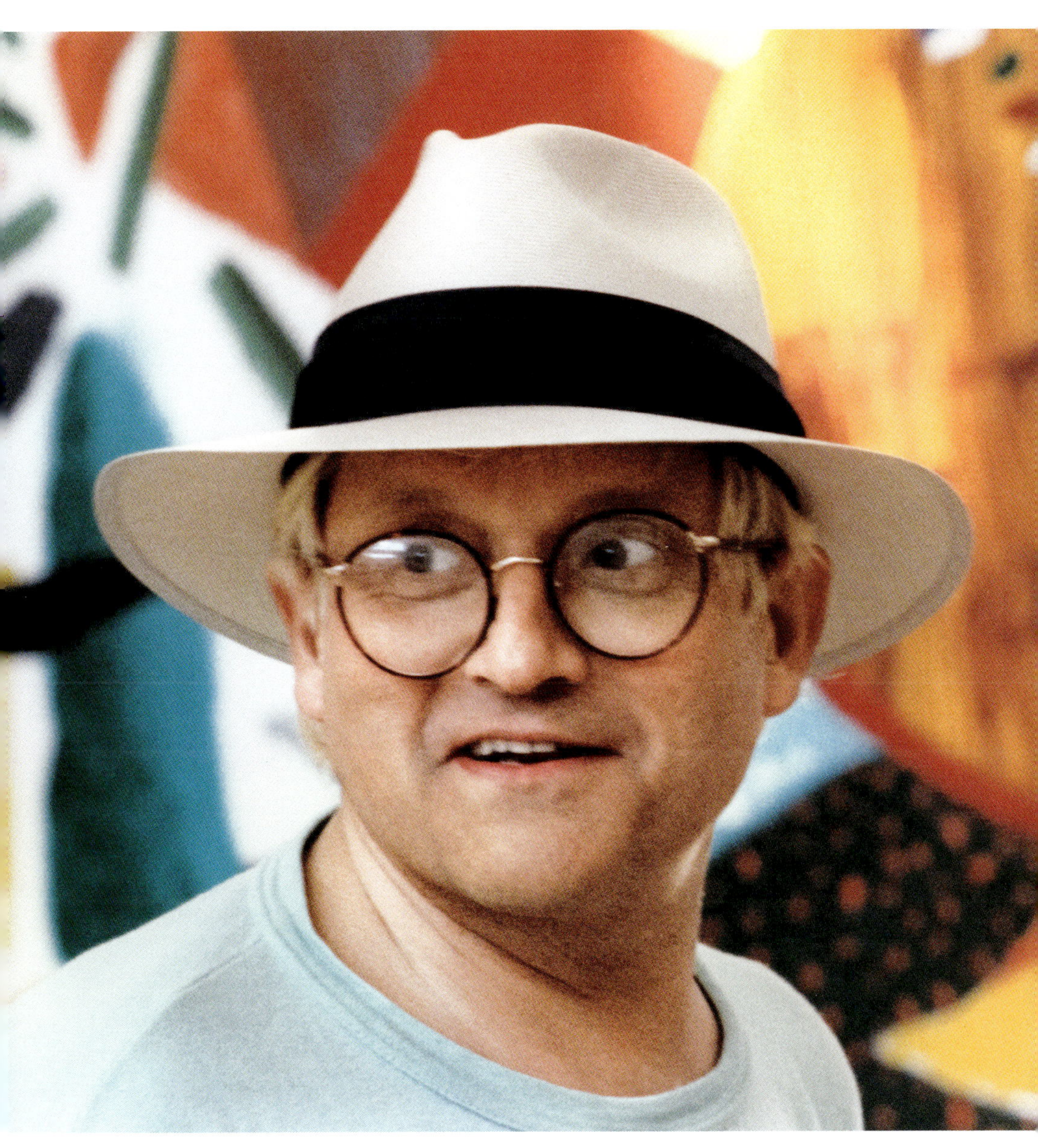

David Hockney in his studio,
Los Angeles 1988. Photo:
Sidney B. Felsen

Page 265: *Van Gogh Chair*, 1988,
acrylic on canvas, 48 x 36 in. /
121.9 x 91.4 cm

individual qualities are not, in a show like this, what ultimately counts. The overall effect is what is important. Had the organizers been more sympathetic to Hockney's true lines of interest, which were neither restricted to painting nor to a rigid chronology, then the whole exhibition could easily have been as uplifting as the disjointed but inspired last room."

The small portraits of friends and family described here are the first fruits of Hockney's return to painting in this year. He also produces three portraits of chairs inspired by van Gogh's paintings (p. 265), after he has been invited by the Fondation Vincent van Gogh in Arles to contribute to the centenary of the Dutch artist's arrival in that city. Hockney paints van Gogh's chair in reverse perspective.

In his new Malibu beach home, Hockney also starts a series of paintings of the sea (pp. 267, 269): "The beach house was owned by an old lady who had lived here for decades—an amateur painter actually. She'd built a small studio on the hill at the back of the house with an electric lift to get her into it. I enjoy using that lift too and so do the dogs!…When you live this close to the sea, when it literally comes up and splashes the windows, it is not the horizon line which dominates, but the close movement of the water itself. It's like fire and smoke, endlessly changing, endlessly fascinating…"

Extending his work on the photocopier, Hockney begins using a fax machine and sends pictures around the world from what he calls *The Hollywood Sea Picture Supply Co. Est. 1988* (p. 268): "Many of them were made up from paintings of the sea, stretched on one machine, reduced in another way, crammed in, pasted up, made into a collage and then into a fax. I began sending them out to various people who immediately responded by asking me how I got such clear pictures from a fax machine…There's no such thing as a bad printing machine. To make half-tones, for instance, you don't use washes for something to look like a wash, you use opaque gray; the machine read the opaque gray and made the dots it-self…I played with the faxes for about six months. Next to the fax machine I had a new black and white laser copier with which I now began to do all kinds of things, not just reduce: I could use it to bend images, play with variations or put one image inside another." The images become more and more complicated and need to be printed out on several sheets and assembled correctly: "As people became aware of what I was doing, they would call and ask me to send the latest

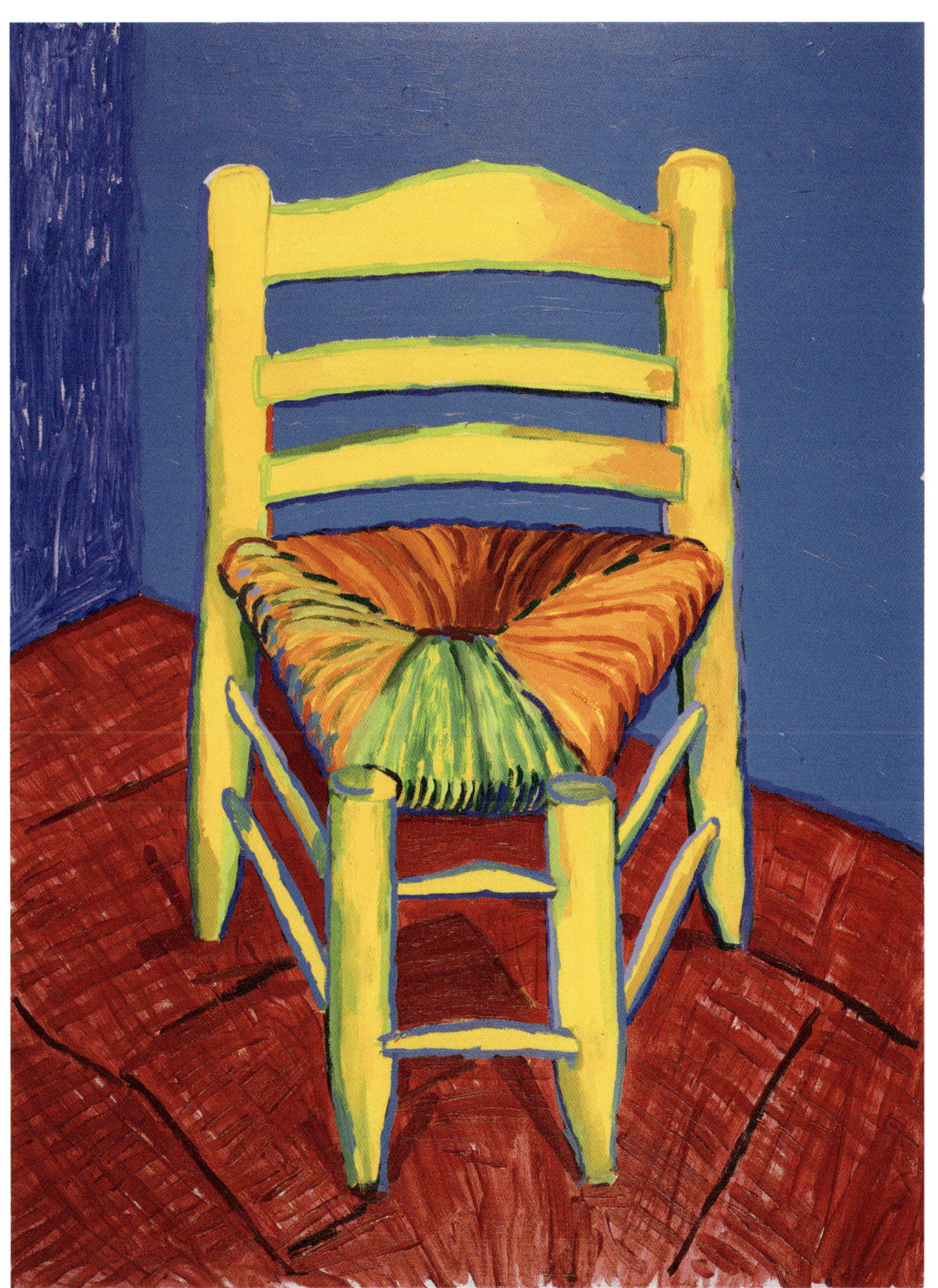

fax. First I would send a detailed plan of how the pages should be pasted together, followed by the work itself. My phone bills became enormous! Then I realized that people have different kinds of fax machines at the other end—old ones and new ones. The old ones were incredibly slow sometimes. Once I send one to an old machine, they rarely get another!"

Solo: *A Retrospective,* LA County Museum of Art, Los Angeles (Feb 4–Apr 24); travels to Metropolitan Museum of Art, New York (Jun 18–Aug 14) and Tate Gallery, London (Oct 26, 1988–Jan 3, 1989); catalog ed. by Maurice Tuchman and Stephanie Barron, texts by Henry Geldzahler, Anne Hoy, R.B. Kitaj, Christopher Knight, Gert Schiff, Kenneth E. Silver, and Lawrence Weschler, New York: Harry N. Abrams. *Portrait Drawings, a 20 Year Survey,* André Emmerich Gallery, New York (Jun 2–Jul 29). *Selected Prints,* Douglas Drake Gallery, New York (Jun 9–Jul 23). *Prints,* Pace Prints, New York (Jun 23–Aug 1). *Weather Series,* Pence Gallery, Santa Monica (Sep 10–Oct 15). *David Hockney,* Seibu, Tokyo (Oct 13–25). *A Private View,* Editions Graphiques, London (Oct 26–Nov 12); catalog. *Etchings and Lithographs, 1961–1986,* Waddington Graphics, London (Oct 26–Nov 19); catalog. *Some New Paintings,* Knoedler Gallery, London (opens Oct 27); catalog. *Etchings / Aquatints,* Fieldborne Galleries, London (Nov 1–Dec 16). *Photocollagen, Cameraworks,* Dany Keller Galerie, Munich (Nov 29, 1988– Jan 21, 1989). *David Hockney's Images of His Model Celia, 1973–1986,* Carl Schlosberg Fine Arts, Los Angeles (opens Dec 4).

Publications: *Hockney on Photography: Conversations with Paul Joyce,* London: Jonathan Cape. Peter Webb, *A Portrait of David Hockney,* London: Chatto and Windus; New York: E.P. Dutton.

Film: *A Day on the Grand Canal with the Emperor of China,* USA, 46 min., dir. by Philip Haas, written by and starring David Hockney.

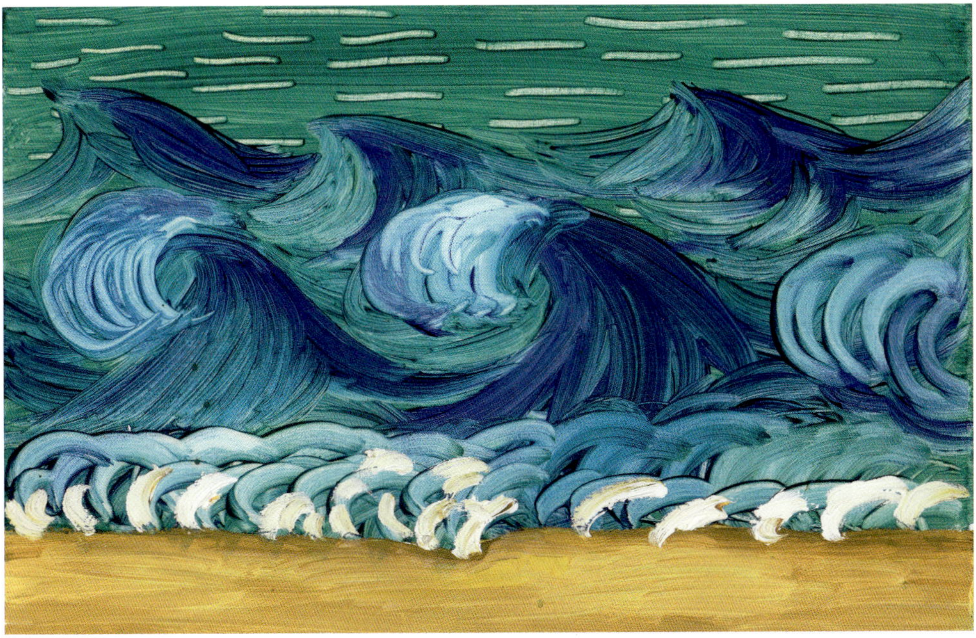

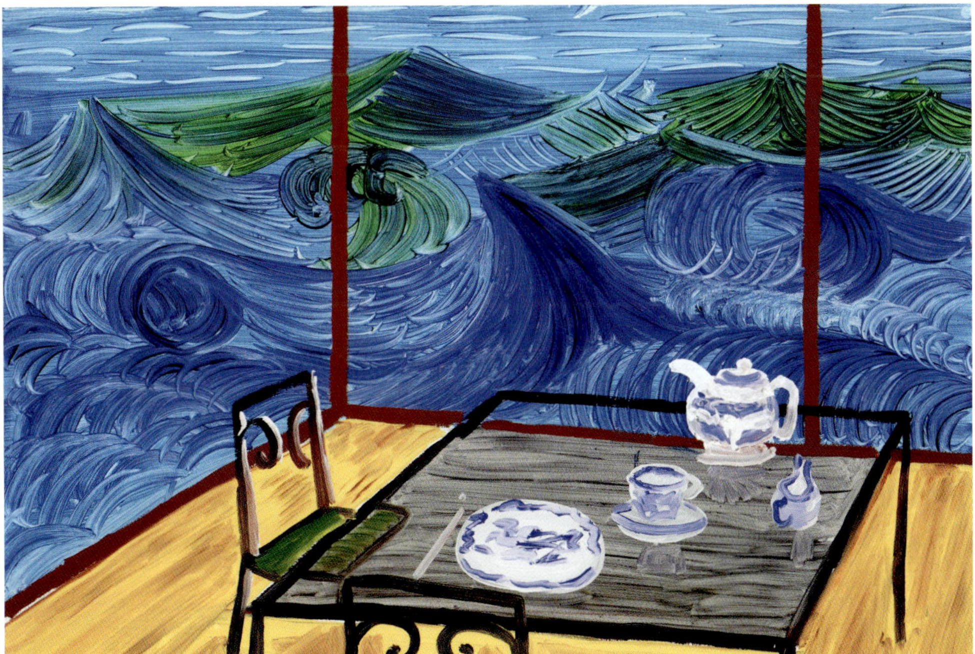

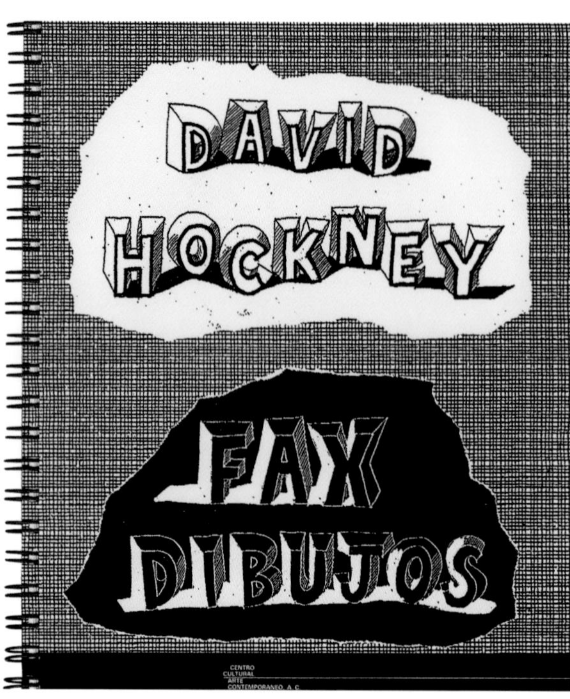

Faxes sent in 1989 as published in *David Hockney: Fax Dibujos,* Centro Cultural Arte Contemporaneo, Mexico City 1990; Catalog cover; *Yet Another Picture from The Hollywood Sea Picture Supply Co.,* fax drawing, 1989, 8 ¹/₂ x 17 in. / 21.6 x 43.2 cm

Right page: *Livingroom at Malibu with View,* 1988, oil on canvas, 24 x 36 in. / 61 x 91.4 cm

Beach House with Waves I, 1988, oil on canvas, 24 x 36 in. / 61 x 91.4 cm

Page 267: *Blue Waves with Gold Sand,* 1989, oil on canvas, 10 ¹/₂ x 16 ¹/₂ in. / 26.5 x 42 cm

Breakfast at Malibu, Wednesday, 1989, oil on canvas, 24 x 36 in. / 61 x 91.4 cm

Pages 270–271: *David Hockney: A Retrospective,* exhibition views, LA County Museum of Art, Los Angeles 1988

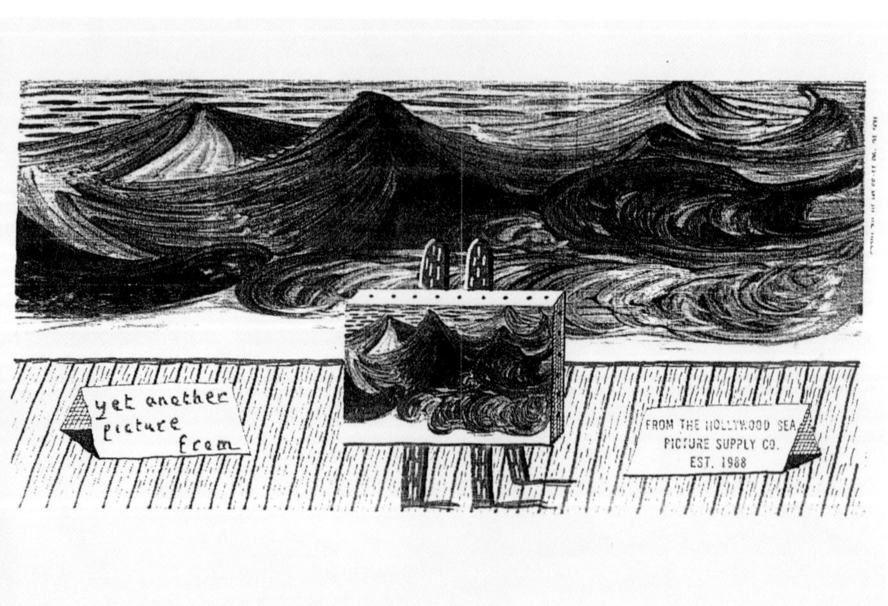

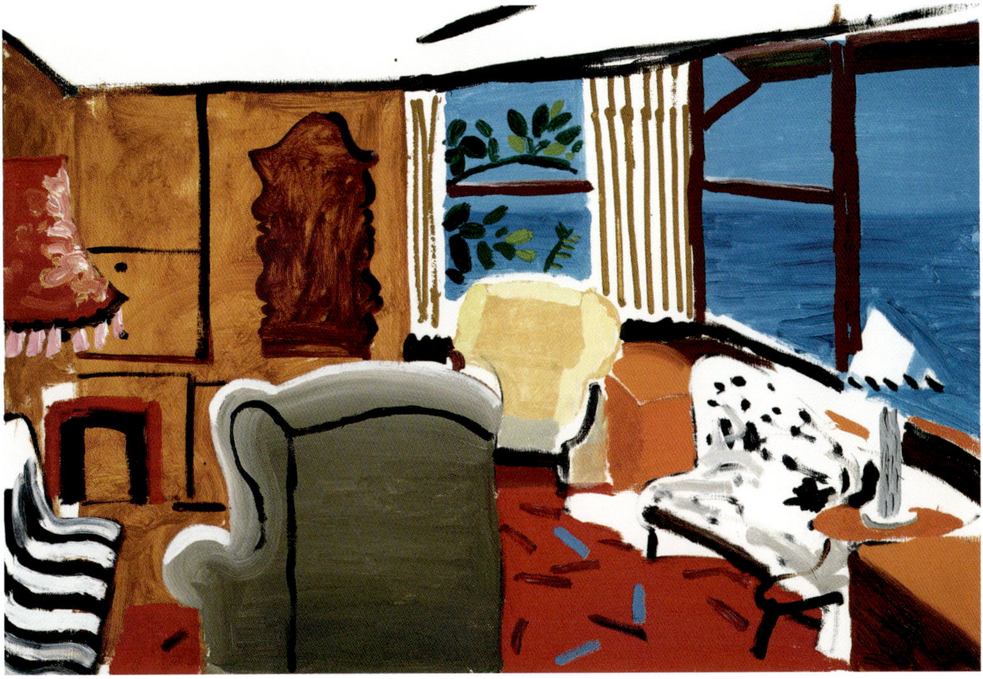

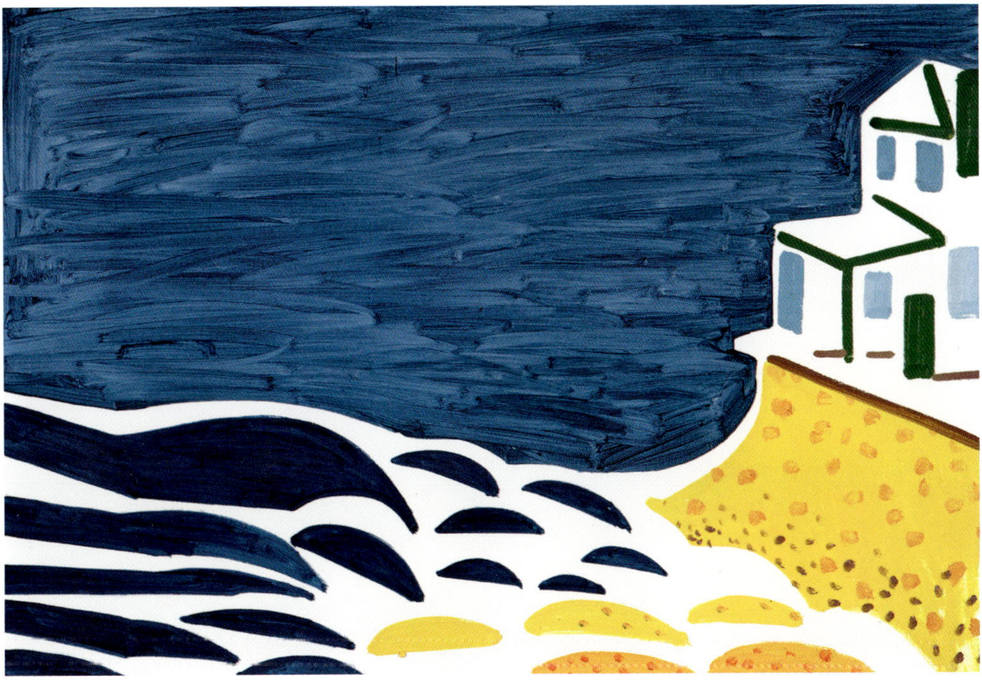

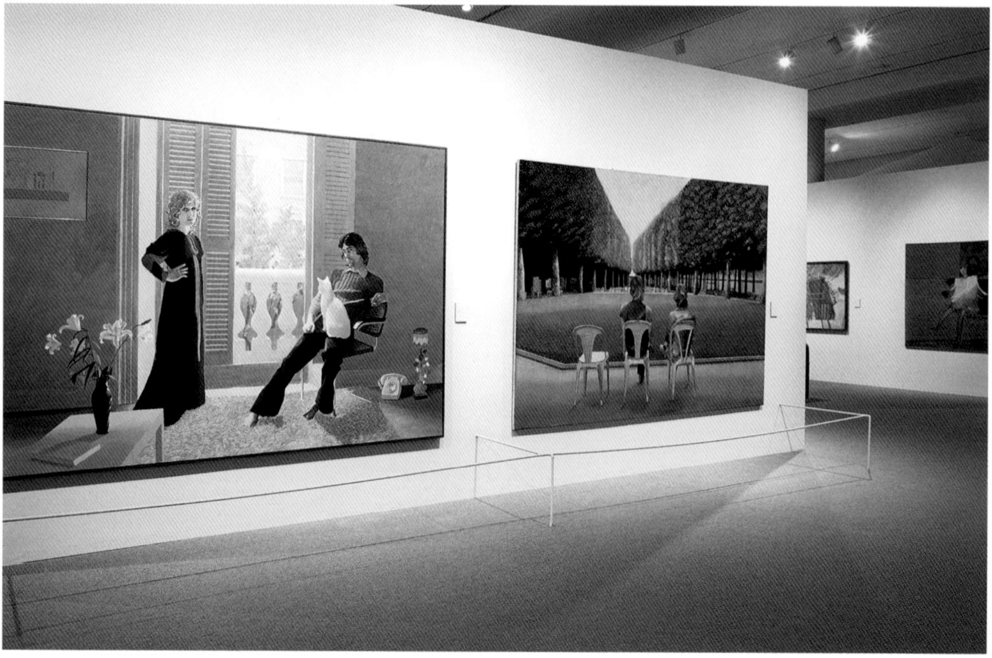

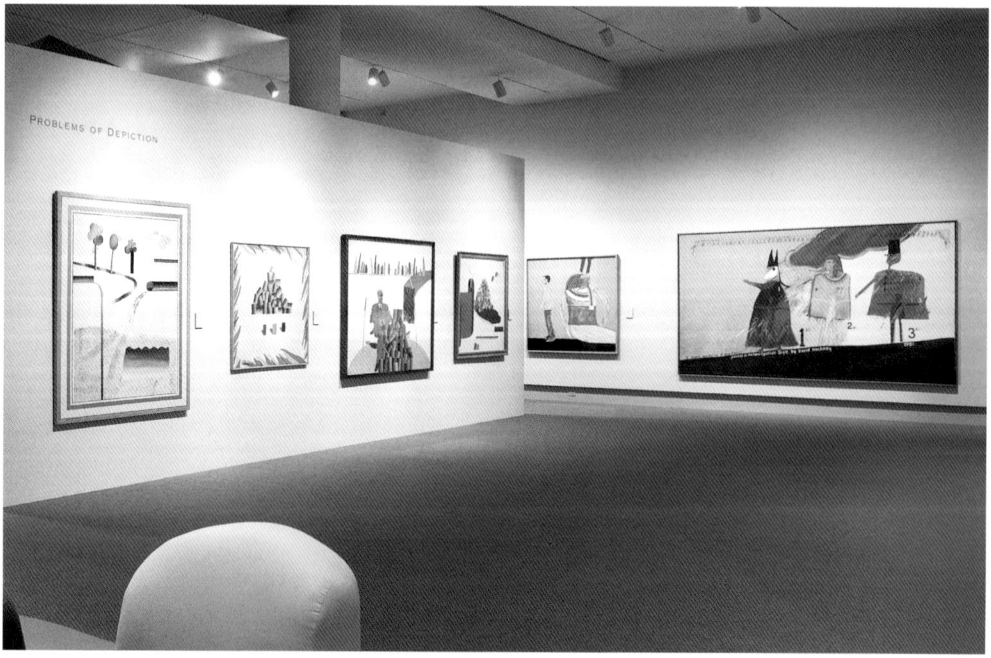

PROBLEMS OF DEPICTION

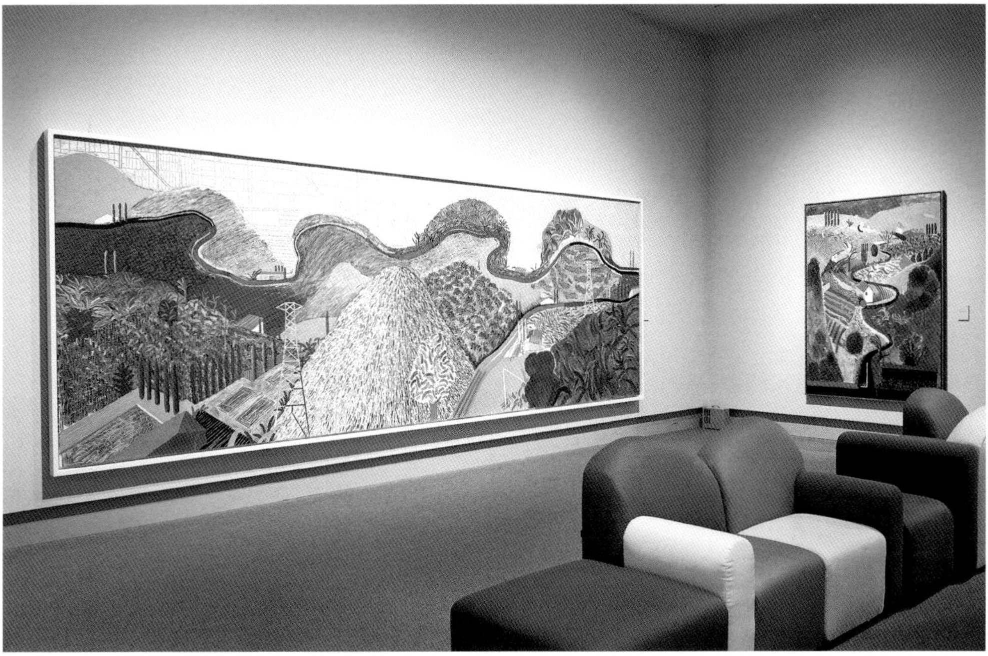

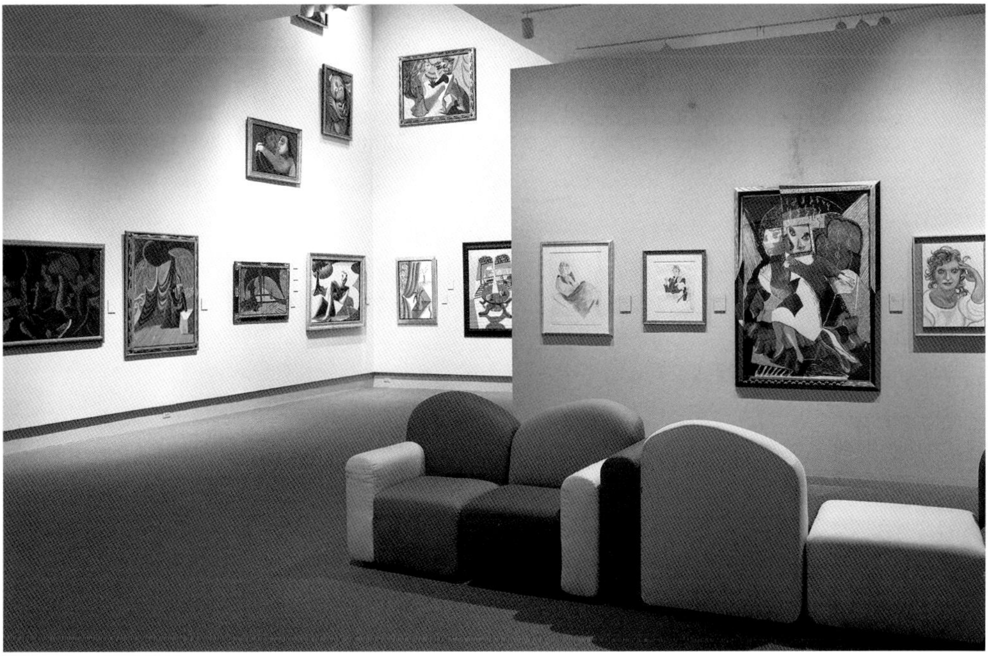

1989

Hockney continues creating small-format paintings: portraits of visitors at his Malibu house, sea pictures, and a series of pretty plant paintings that he gives to friends suffering from AIDS. The artist also continues his fax work, including an alphabet (pp. 275–277) that he later sends out to writers asking them for a poem, a story, or any kind of reply, among them Stephen Spender, Julian Barnes, William Golding, Seamus Heaney, Kazuo Ishiguro, Doris Lessing, Arthur Miller, Iris Murdoch, Joyce Carol Oates, Susan Sontag, John Updike, and Gore Vidal. The book will be published in 1991.

The artist is invited to take part in the São Paulo Biennial taking place in October. The original idea is to show paintings, but since willing lenders prove difficult to find so shortly after his touring retrospective, Hockney suggests a big fax exhibition: "So we got a map of the room in São Paulo and made an exact model of it so that we could make some faxes specifically to fit the wall." Because the phone lines in Brazil do not prove up to the task, in the end they have to cheat and fax the sheets from one room to the next in Los Angeles, pack them in suitcases, and have an assistant carry them to São Paulo. As planned, the exhibition takes place without the artist being present, which disappoints some in the audience. "But many people saw the philosophical side, the interesting side, the use of printing to make original works. I assume that even though people think my work is very popular, it often takes them time to see what I am really doing, to see what it is I am exploring, that it is not just a wild thing, but something that grows out of something else, and will grow into something else again."

In November, Hockney's friend Jonathan Silver organizes a live event during which Hockney faxes a 144-sheet composite image, *Tennis* (pp. 278/279), to Salts Mill in Saltaire near Bradford. Martin Wainwright in the *Guardian*: "David Hockney's latest work of art arrived in his home city of Bradford last night in a welter of spray-on glue and sheets of fax paper, and to the sound of Wagner's 'Ride of the Valkyries.' Sheet by acid-sprayed, conservation-guaranteed sheet, 144 pieces of a huge jigsaw of tubes and angles beeped and fluttered from four laser facsimile machines in Sir Titus Salt's former alpaca mill, while 5,000 miles away at his home in California, Mr Hockney—already master of computer, photocopy, and snipped-photograph art—was feeding the composite picture into his own fax… Bent over the light-flashing, peeping fax machines, the mill and gallery's owner, Jonathan Silver, checked detailed assembly instructions previously

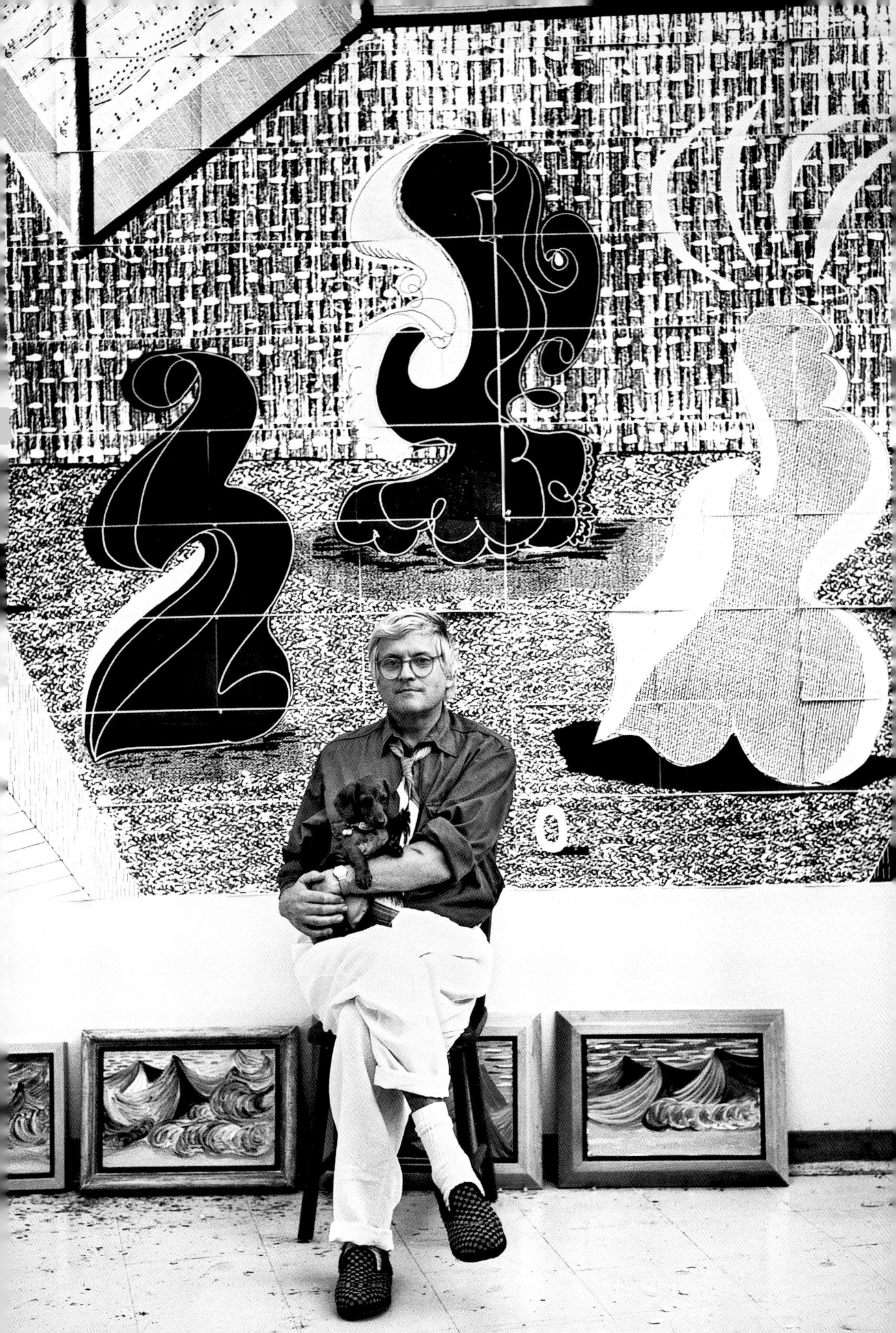

faxed by the artist. One of Bradford's less orthodox businessmen—with ponytail and Geldof stubble—he flicked pellets with Hockney at Bradford grammar and sold the young artist's paintings through the chain of clothes shops he established in the North after taking his A levels. Hockney has repaid the debt with numerous studies of Silver, one in varieties of lurid green, another suggesting the gallery owner is about to explode from high blood pressure. Both looked on among the gallery's 100 Hockneys, ranging from a teenage pencil sketch of the Yorkshire Wolds to oils done last Christmas."

Solo: *David Hockney at the Royal College of Art,* Gardner Centre, University of Sussex, Brighton (Mar 5–May 27); catalog. *Homemade Prints,* Cleveland Center for Contemporary Art (Mar 31–May 26). *David Hockney,* Odakyu Grand Gallery, Shinjuku (Apr 26–May 22); travels to Gunma, Funabashi, and Osaka; catalog. *David Hockney,* Modern Museum of Art, Santa Ana (Sep 3–Nov 5). *Photographs of China,* Nishimura Gallery, Tokyo (Jan 23–Feb 10); catalog. *New Paintings,* André Emmerich Gallery, New York (Mar 30–Apr 22); catalog. *Graphics and Photocollages 1965–1988,* Art Gallery Artium, Tokyo (Apr 12–May 14). *Neue Bilder,* Galerie Hans Neuendorf, Frankfurt am Main (May 17–Jun 30); catalog with an interview by Anders Stephenson. *Fotografias,* Galeria 57, Madrid (opens Jun 20). *A Selection of Prints,* Richard Green Gallery, Los Angeles (Jun 24–Jul 22). *Flower, Chair, Interior,* Nishimura Gallery, Tokyo (Oct 23–Nov 25); catalog. *Some New Pictures,* L.A. Louver, Venice, CA (Dec 6, 1989–Jan 6, 1990); travels to The Contemporary Museum, Honolulu; catalog with a text by Peter Goulds. *Illustrations for Six Fairy Tales from the Brothers Grimm,* Björn Olsson Gallery, Stockholm (Dec 9, 1989–Jan 20, 1990); catalog.

Group: *Fantasies, Fables and Fabrications: Photo-Works from the 1980s,* Delaware Art Museum, Wilmington (May 12–Jul 2); travels to Amherst, New Hampshire, and Kansas City (through 1990); catalog. *Summer Exhibition,* Royal Academy of Arts, London (Jun 10–Aug 20). *XX Bienal de São Paulo* (Oct 14–Dec 10); catalog.

Award: Praemium Imperiale for Painting, Japanese Art Association, Tokyo.

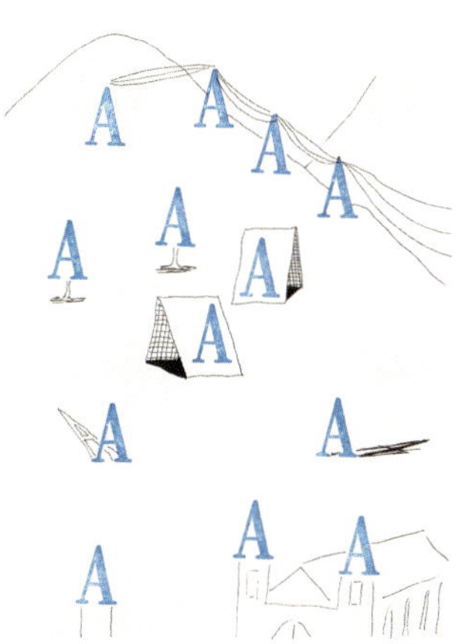 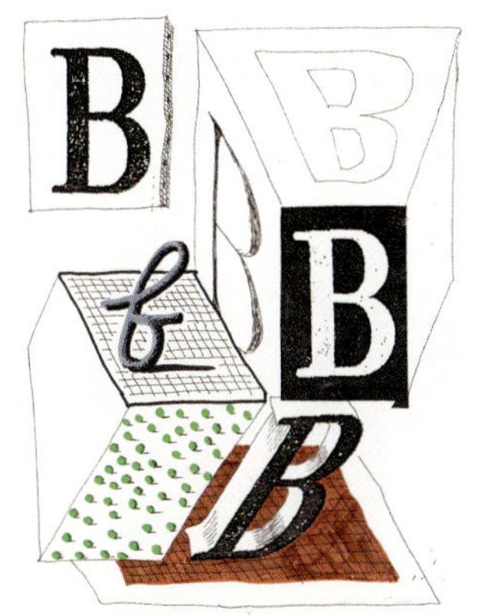 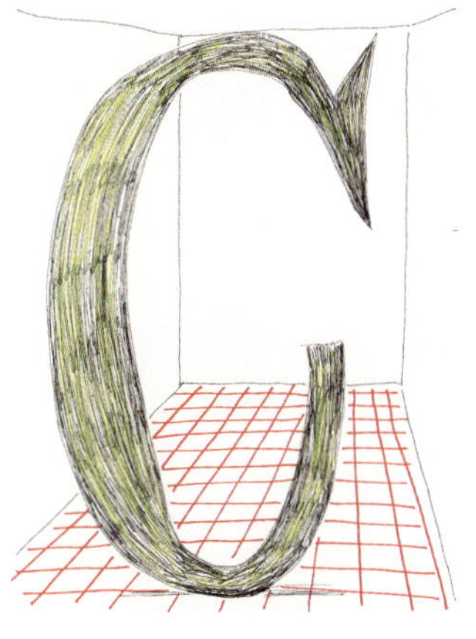

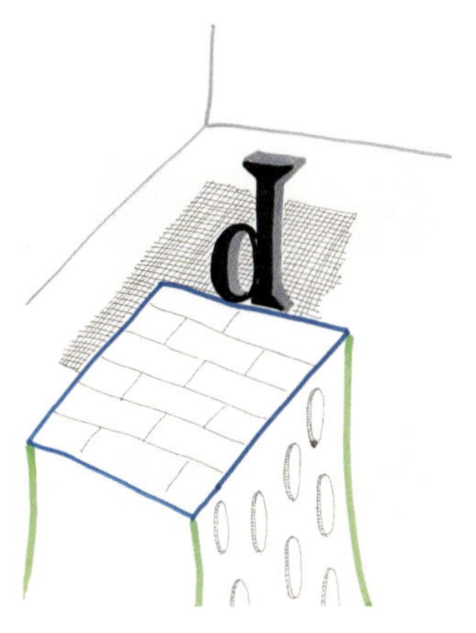 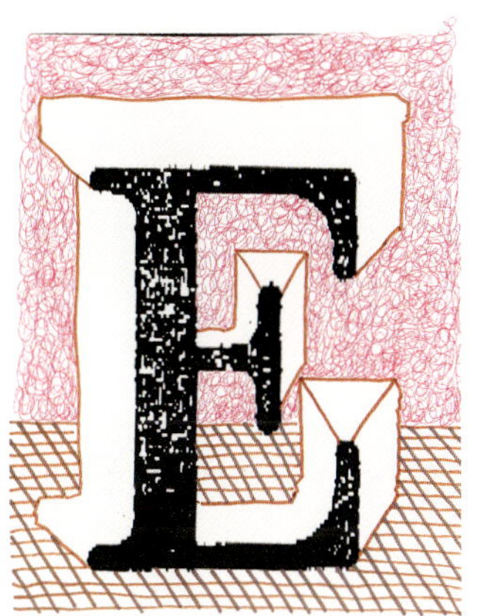 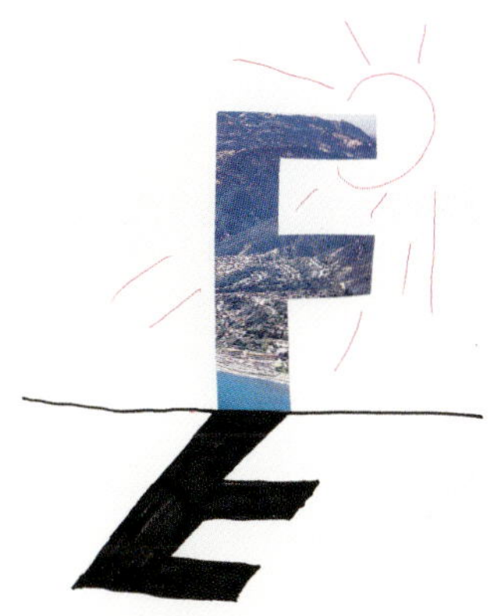

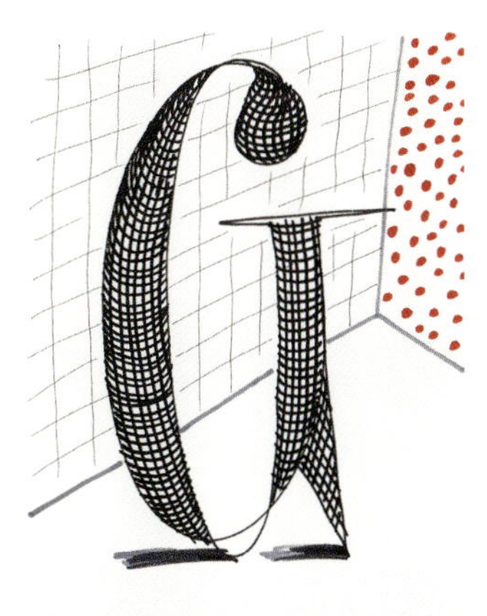 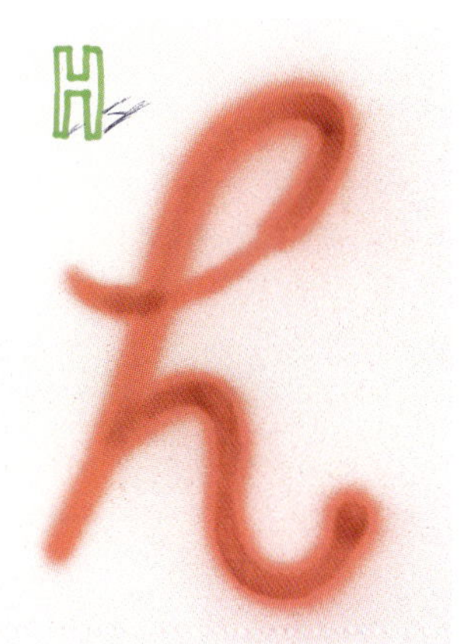 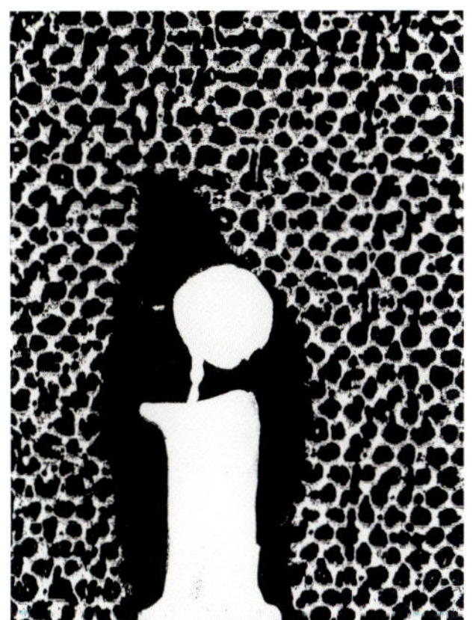

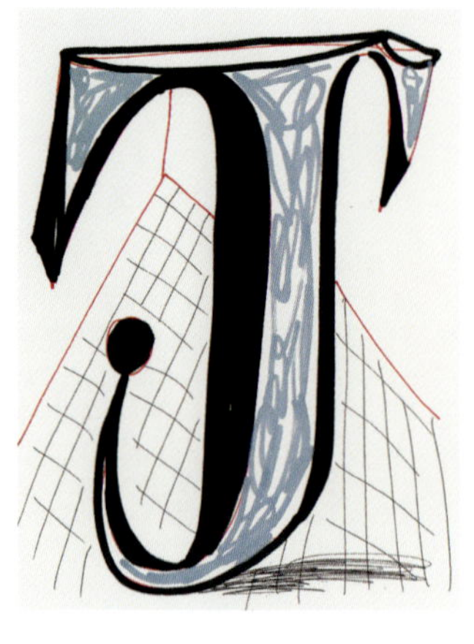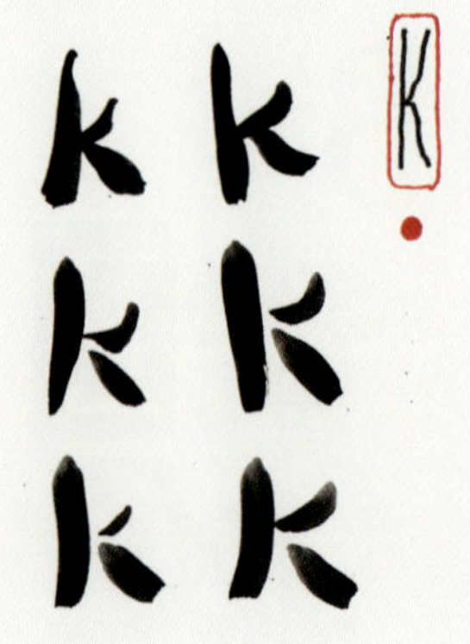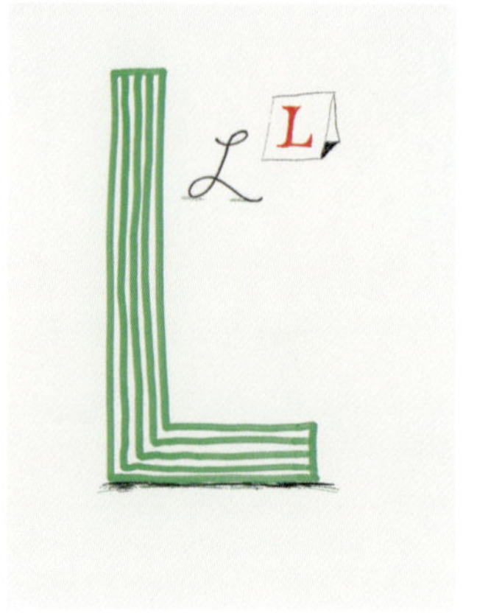

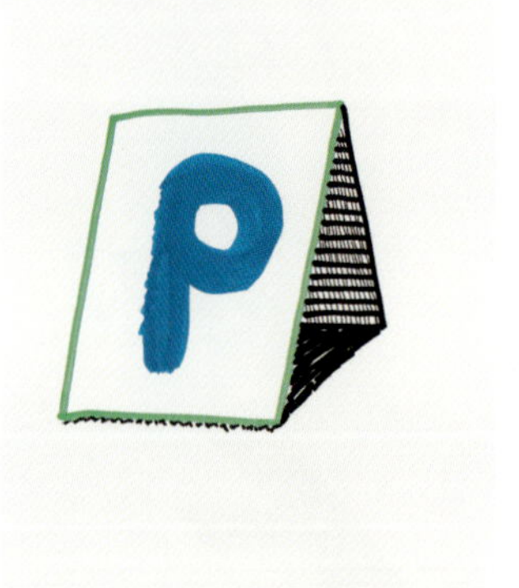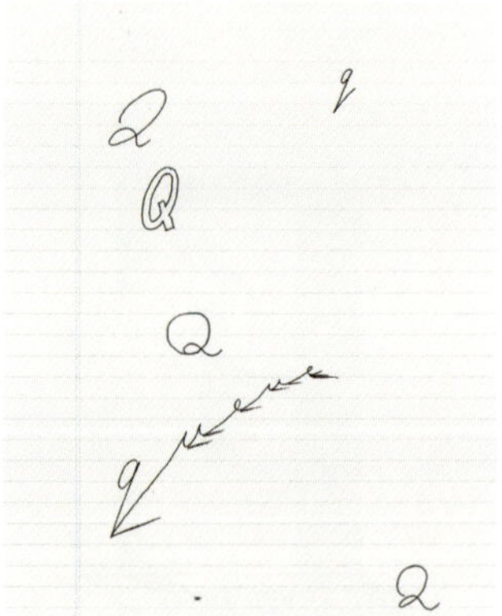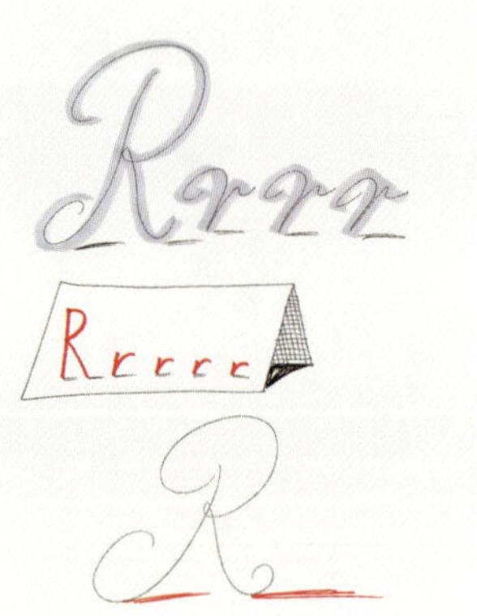

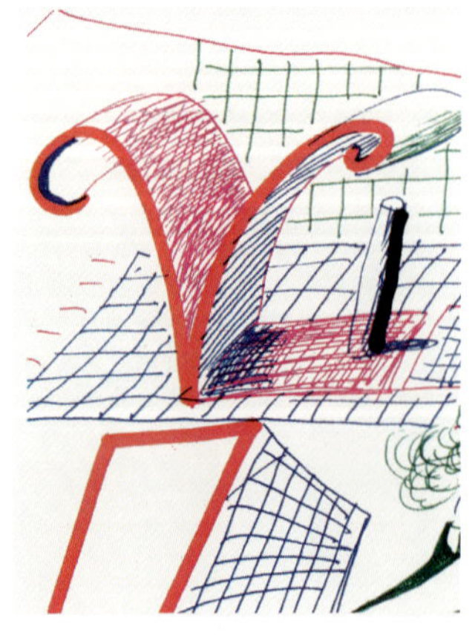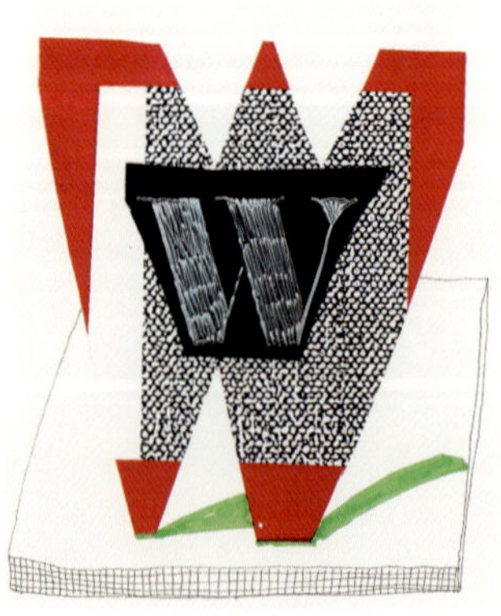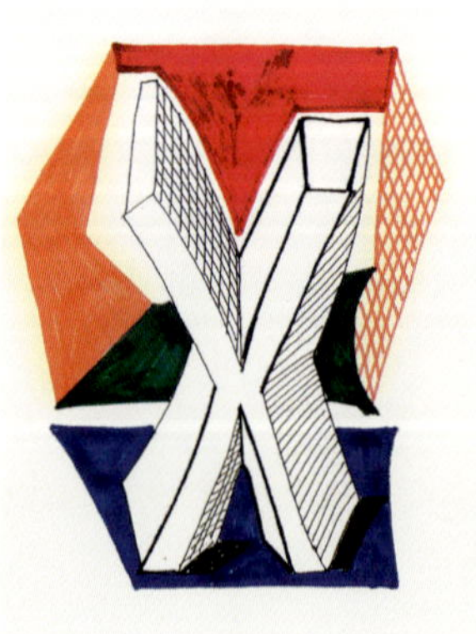

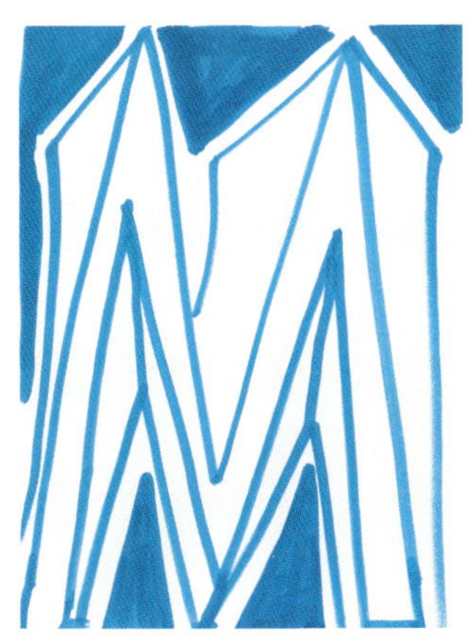

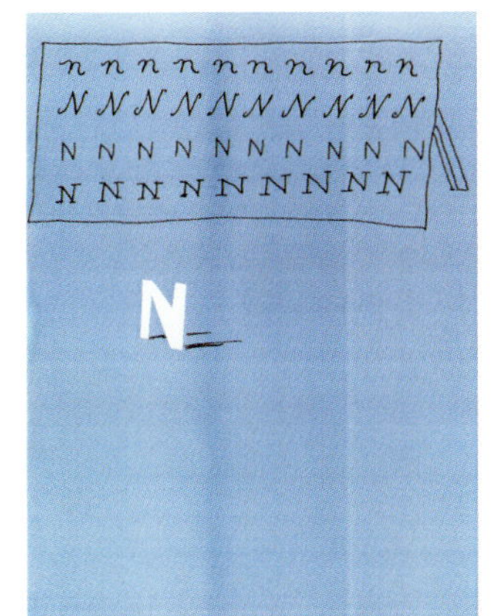

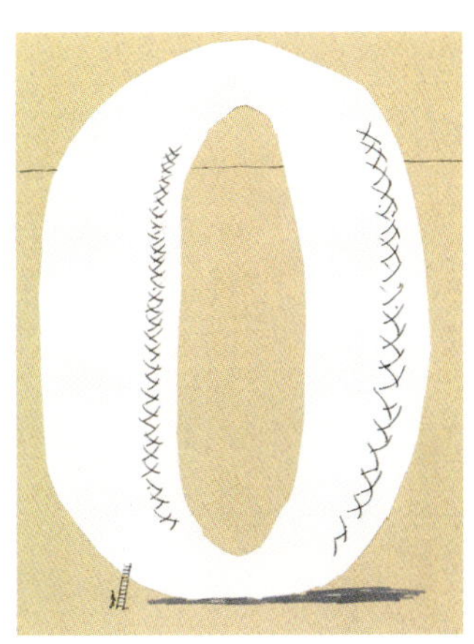

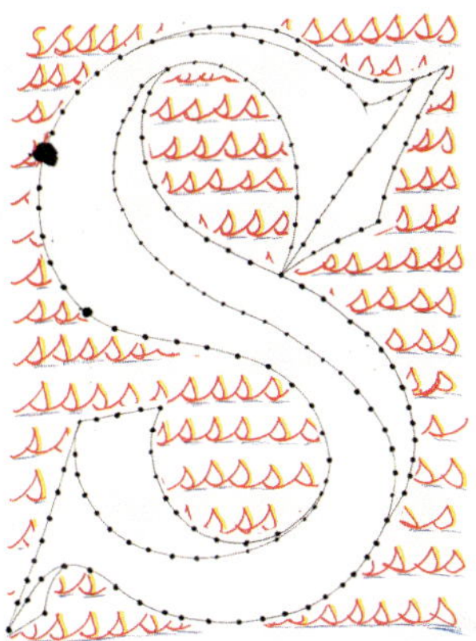

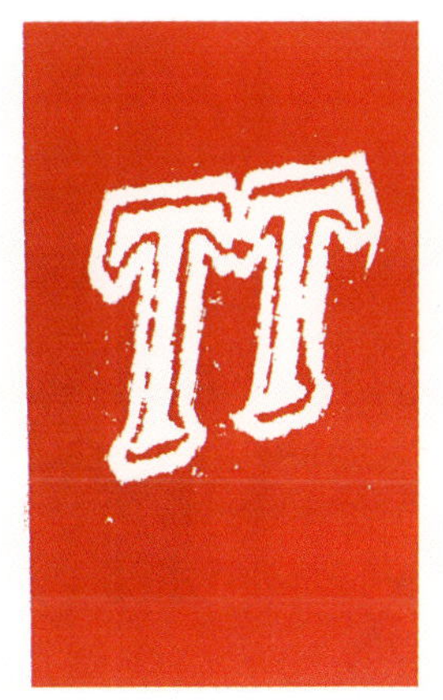

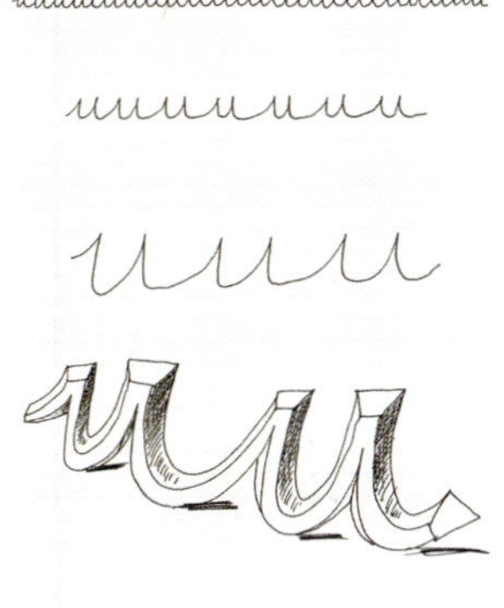

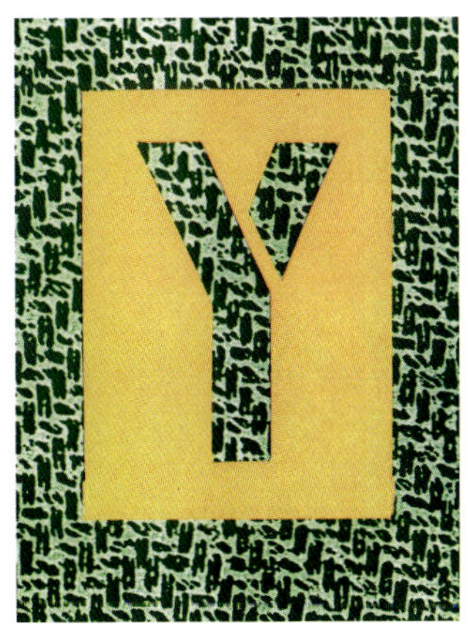

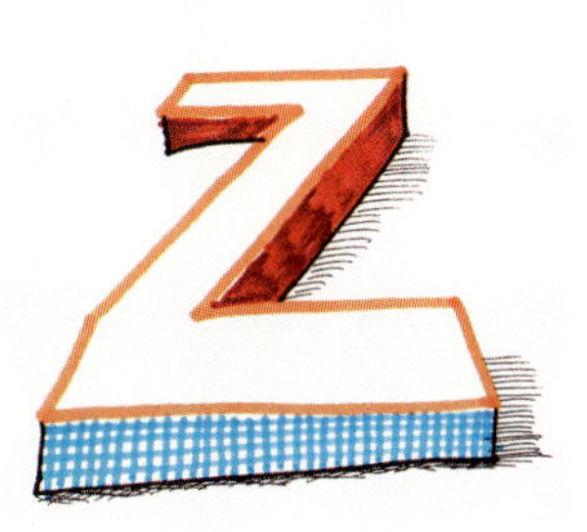

Pages 275–277: *The Alphabet Book,* 1989, 26 works, various markers, ball pen, India ink, crayon, spray paint, collage, laser copy, xerox, and rubber stamp on paper, each 11 x 8 ½ in. / 27.9 x 21.6 cm

Page 273: David Hockney in his studio, Los Angeles 1989. Photo: Herb Ritts

Pages 278/279: *Tennis,* 1989, faxed drawing on 144 sheets of paper, 102 x 168 in. / 259.1 x 426.7 cm

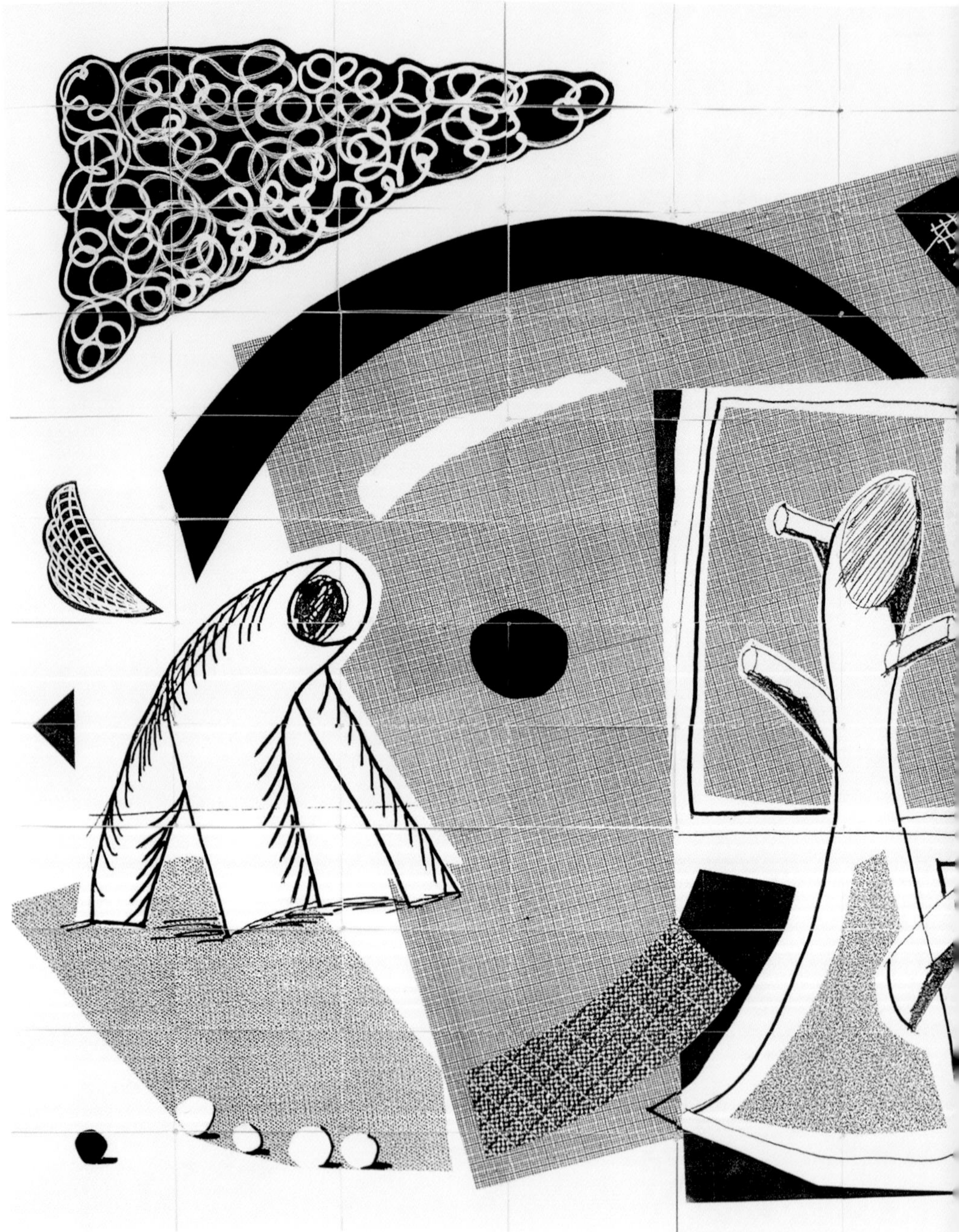

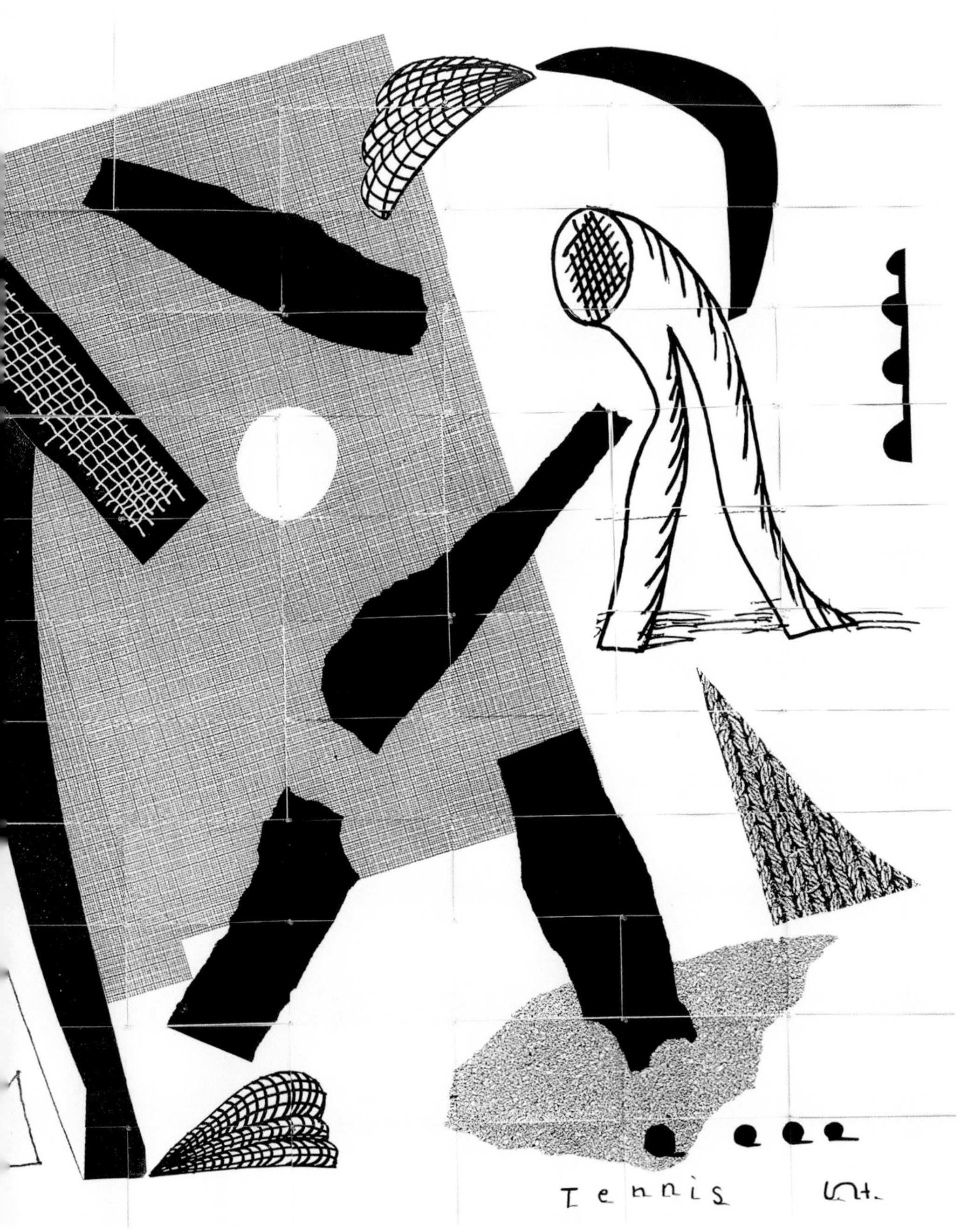

Tennis

1990

Hockney creates a "Wagner drive," a one-and-a-half-hour car trip between the Pacific Coast Highway and the Santa Monica Mountains soundtracked by musical excerpts, to which selected guests are invited. Lawrence Weschler tells of "Hockney pacing the car just right so that Wagner's transitions seamlessly matched the road's own curves and croppings, and the constrictions and the dilations of the endlessly changing view. Mainly orchestral passages from *Parsifal,* as you looped in and among the canyons and then finally back up the main spine of the mountains for the return toward the shore. And if Hockney had managed to time things just right—and usually he had—the music itself would now be reaching its most thrilling climax yet (Siegfried's funeral), exactly one hour and twenty minutes into the drive, just as the car rounded a final bend, suddenly divulging a stupendous sudden view of one last valley at the very moment the sun was sinking behind the far darkened slope." The same scenery also serves as the subject for a series of landscape paintings, most notably *Pacific Coast Highway and Santa Monica* (pp. 288/289).

Hockney attends a conference on new computer technology with his assistant Richard Schmidt. Using the Oasis program for Apple Macintosh, he creates his first drawing on a computer, which he prints out on his laser color printer. He also buys a still-video camera which records analog images directly on floppy disc: "I bought the camera, used it, and at first thought the result was a bit fuzzy, that there was something not that good about it, until I explored it more and understood the way it recorded color…I realized color was coming out in a different way, no film was being used, the camera was seeing and putting digits onto a disc. I then put the disc into a little machine tied to the printer and you could print the photographs practically any size. If you printed four on a page, they were more sharply focused and the color seemed rather rich and rather unphotographic." Hockney produces the series *40 Snaps of My House* (p. 283) and sends them to friends as a little book. His next series is of *112 L.A. Visitors* (pp. 284–285), whom he stands in front of a painting and photographs in five composite images, which are printed in life-size. Barbara Isenberg visits from the *Los Angeles Times*: "Watch him in the studio with his new camera. He's photographing everyone who comes by—the framer, his hair stylist, a museum curator, this reporter—and taking those photographs from camera to video monitor to print in just minutes…Already Hockney's using it to design exhibitions, even to

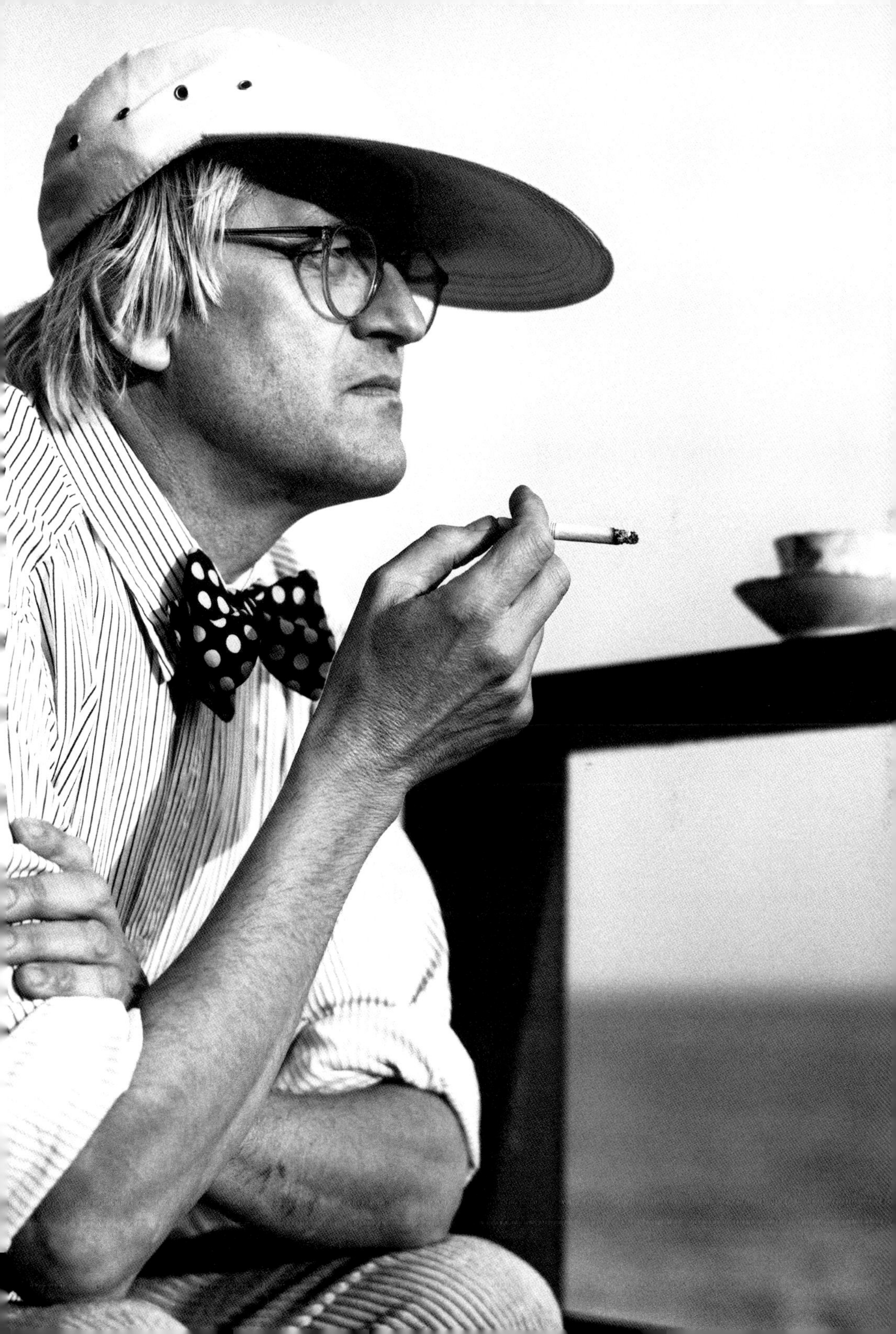

work out immediate problems in his paintings. There's a laser print up on the wall above a painting of the Santa Monica Mountains, and, he says, he'll sometimes photograph half a painting, print out an image from the copier, draw on it in color, then redraw it on canvas."

In September, Hockney begins work on the stage set for Giacomo Puccini's *Turandot* (pp. 286–287) in collaboration with Ian Falconer, who also designs the costumes. The premiere at the Lyric Opera of Chicago will be in January 1992, and together with assistant Richard Schmidt they construct a big model of the stage and use Handycams to record the designs under different lighting conditions. They work day and night until in November Hockney suffers a mild heart attack and remains hospitalized for a week.

Solo: *Fax Prints,* Walker Art Center, Minneapolis (Apr 1–29). *Dibujos en fax de David Hockney,* Centro Cultural Arte Contemporaneo, Mexico City (Oct 1990–Jan 1991); catalog. *Prints from the Sixties and Seventies,* Lorence-Monk Gallery, New York (Feb 3–24). *Cameraworks,* Miriam Shiell Fine Art, Toronto (Apr 2–28). *Early Drawings,* Paul Kasmin Gallery, New York (Jun 19–Jul 28). *Prints and Photographs,* Douglas Drake Gallery, New York (Nov 30, 1990–Jan 19, 1991). *Things Recent,* André Emmerich Gallery, New York (Dec 5, 1990–Jan 5, 1991); catalog *Things Recent and a Catalogue with New Kinds of Reproduction.*

Group: *Glasgow's Great British Art Exhibition,* Glasgow Museum, Glasgow (Mar 27–May 9); catalog. *The Assembled Photograph,* Wright State University, Dayton (Apr 1–May 13). *Friends of the Royal Academy,* Royal Academy of Arts, London (summer).

Publications: David Hockney, *Picasso,* New York: Hanuman. *David Hockney (Shinchosha's Super Artists),* Tokyo: Shinchosha.

Honor: Commitment to Life IV Award, AIDS Project Los Angeles.

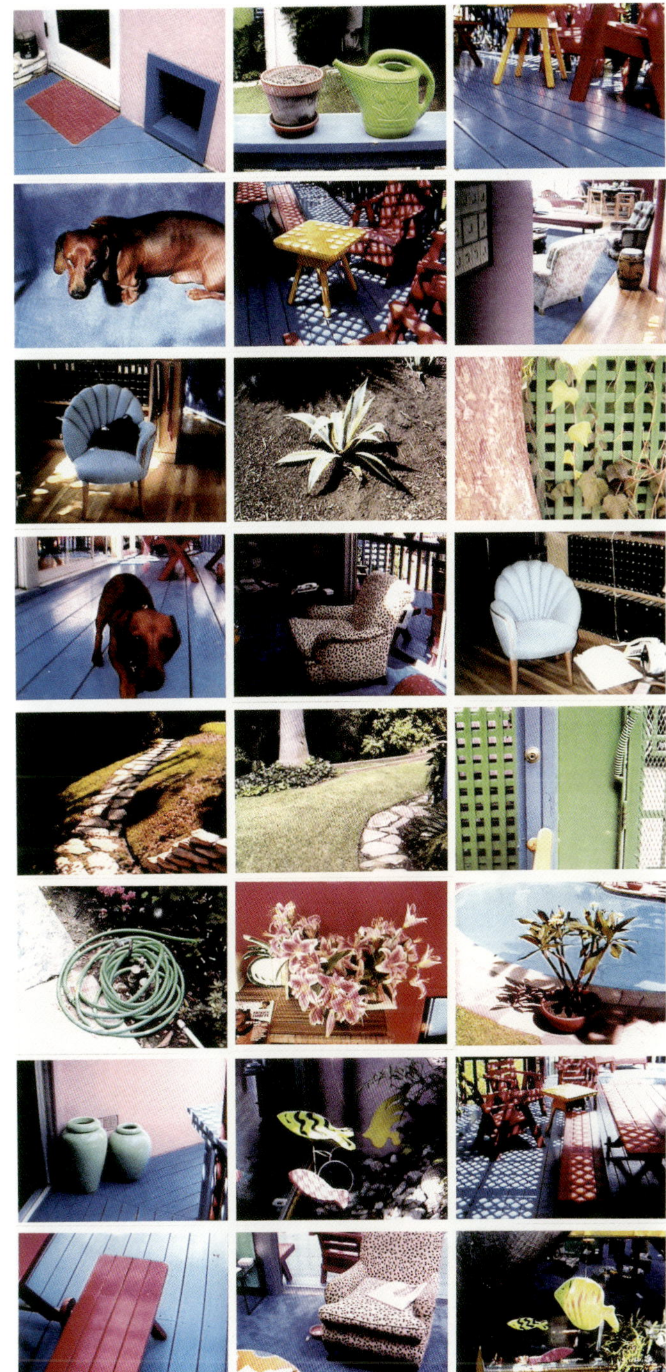

40 Snaps of My House, August 1990 (detail), color laser prints, 90 x 48 in. / 228.6 x 121.9 cm overall

Page 281: David Hockney, Los Angeles 1990. Photo: Greg Gorman

Pages 284–285: *112 L.A. Visitors 1990–1991* (details), color laser-printed still video portraits, each sheet 22 ¹/₂ x 30 in. / 57.2 x 76.2 cm

Pages 286–287: Stage designs for *Turandot,* 1990, scale models; left page: Act I; Act II, Scene I; right page: Act II, Scene II; Act III, Scene II

Pages 288/289: *Pacific Coast Highway and Santa Monica,* 1990, oil on canvas, 78 x 120 in. / 198 x 304.8 cm

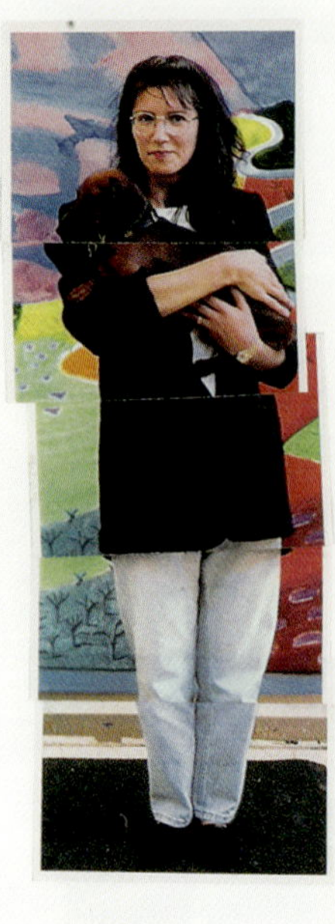
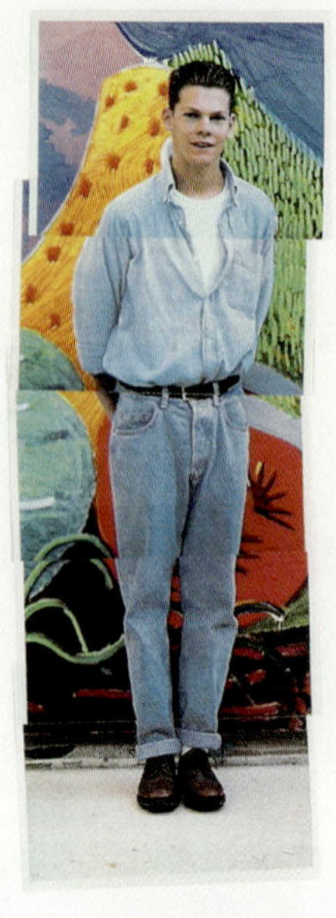
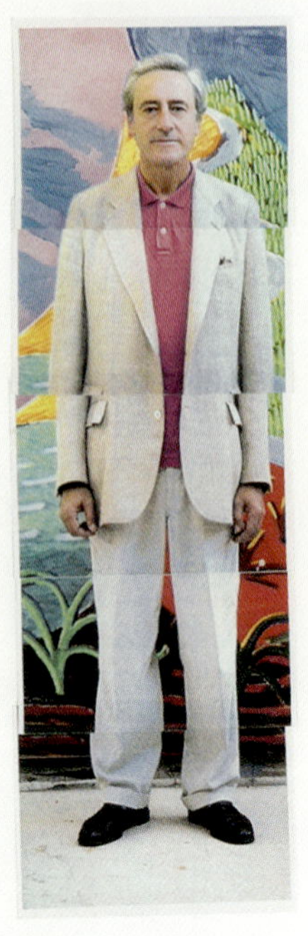
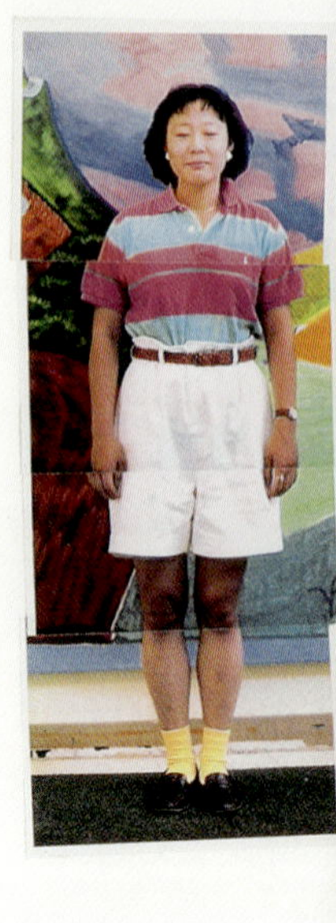
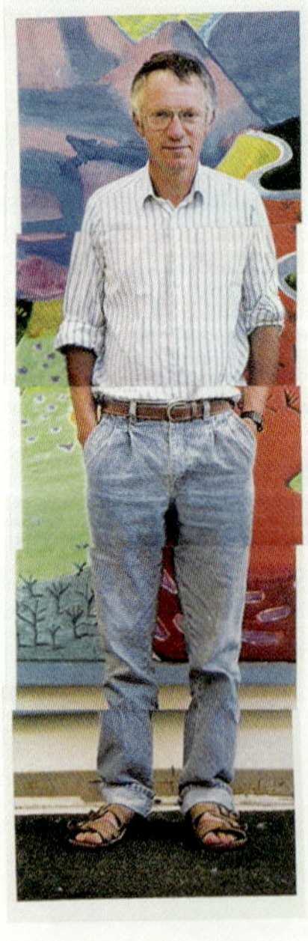
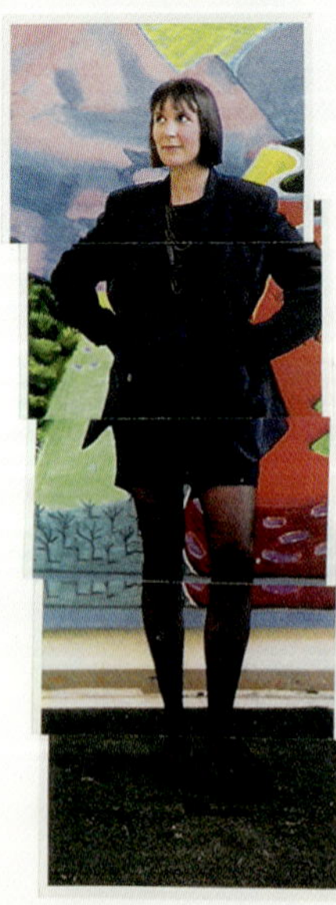
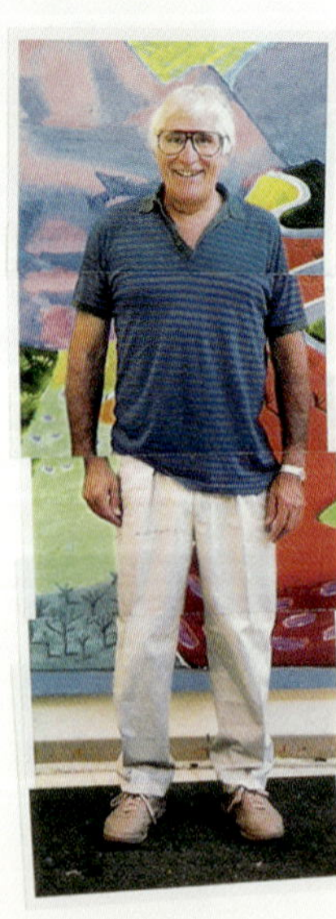
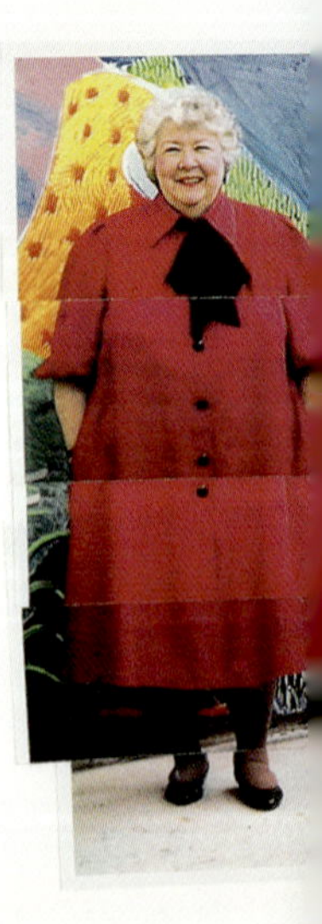

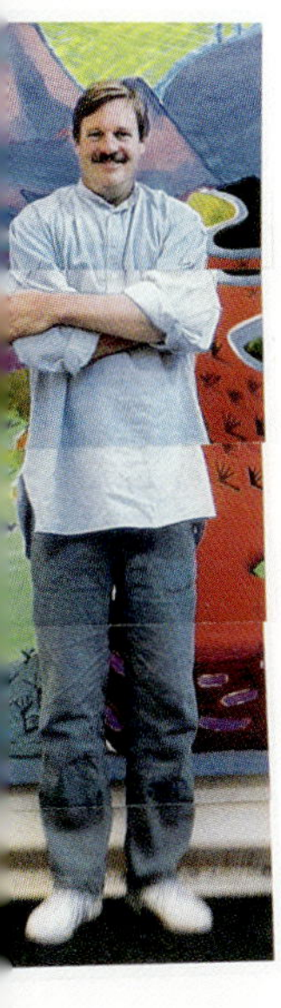
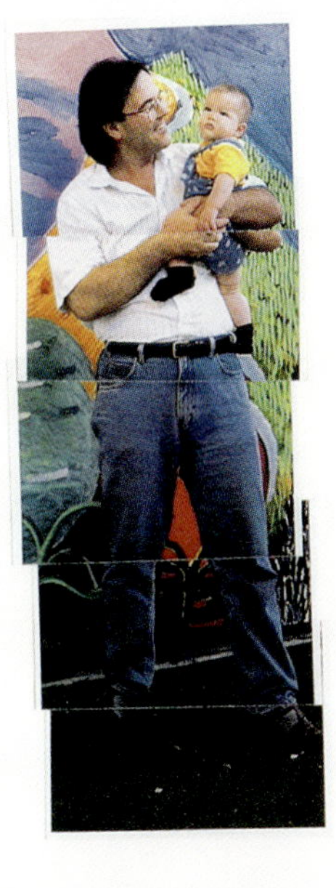
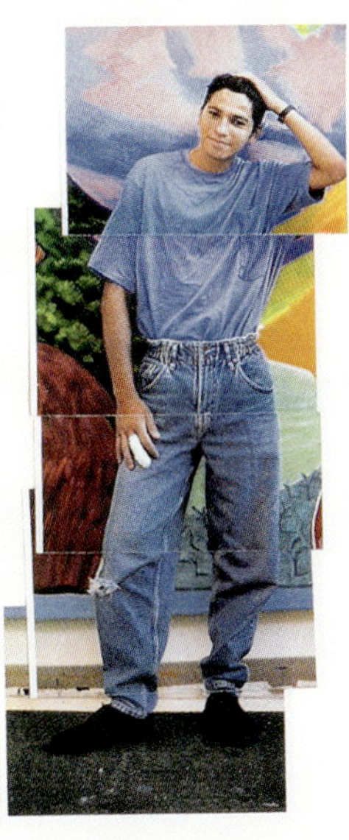
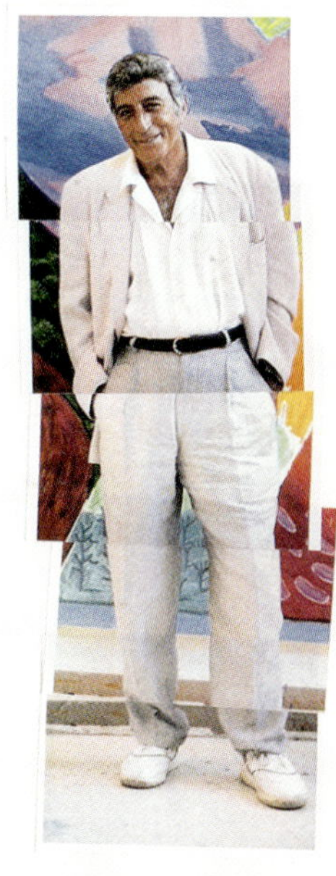
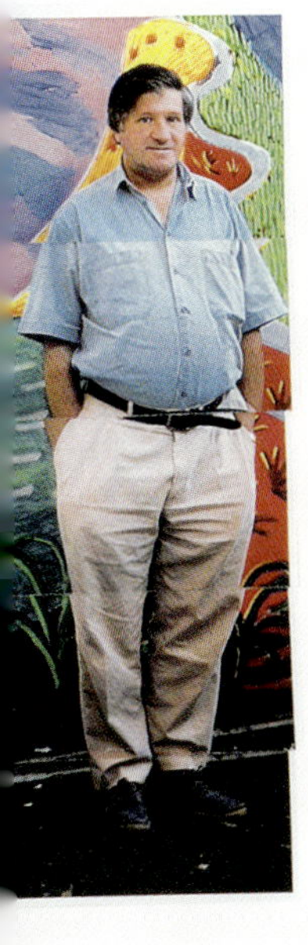
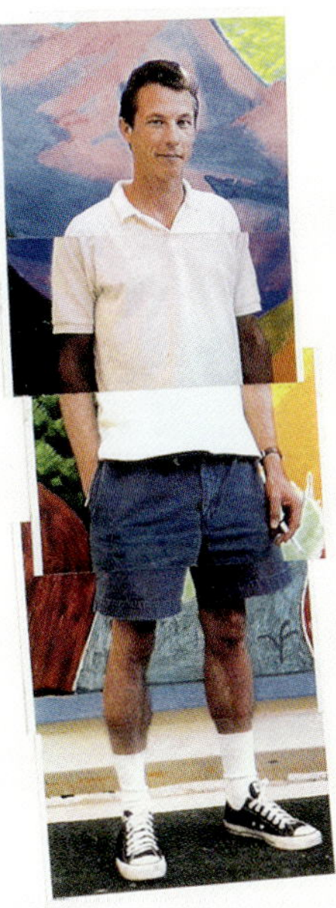
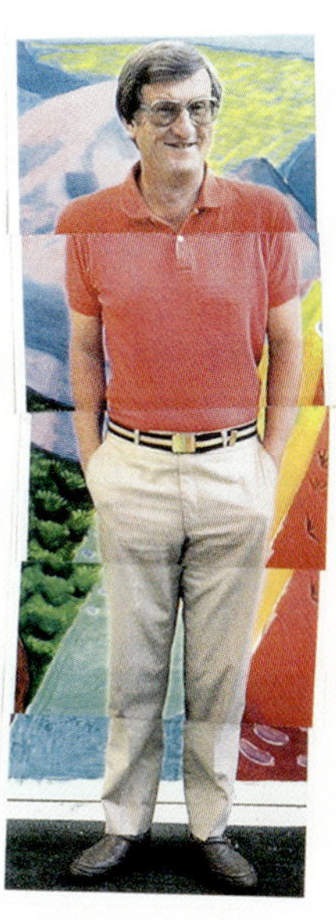
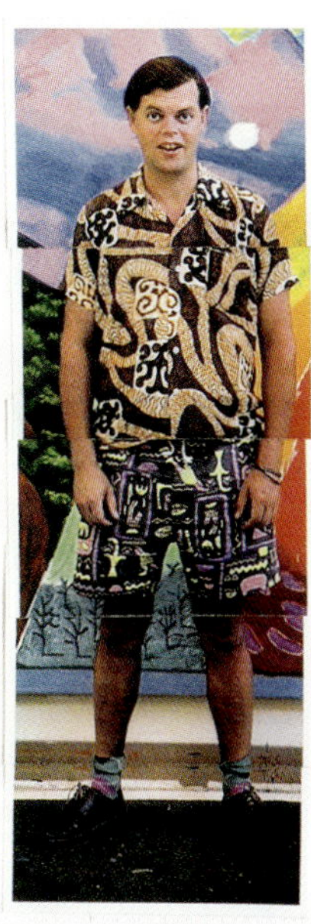

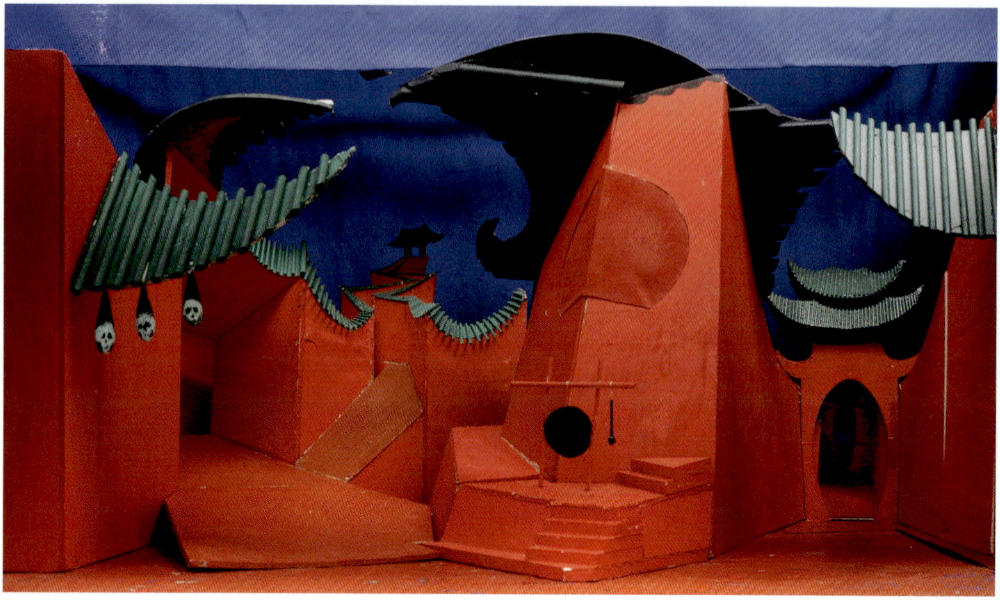

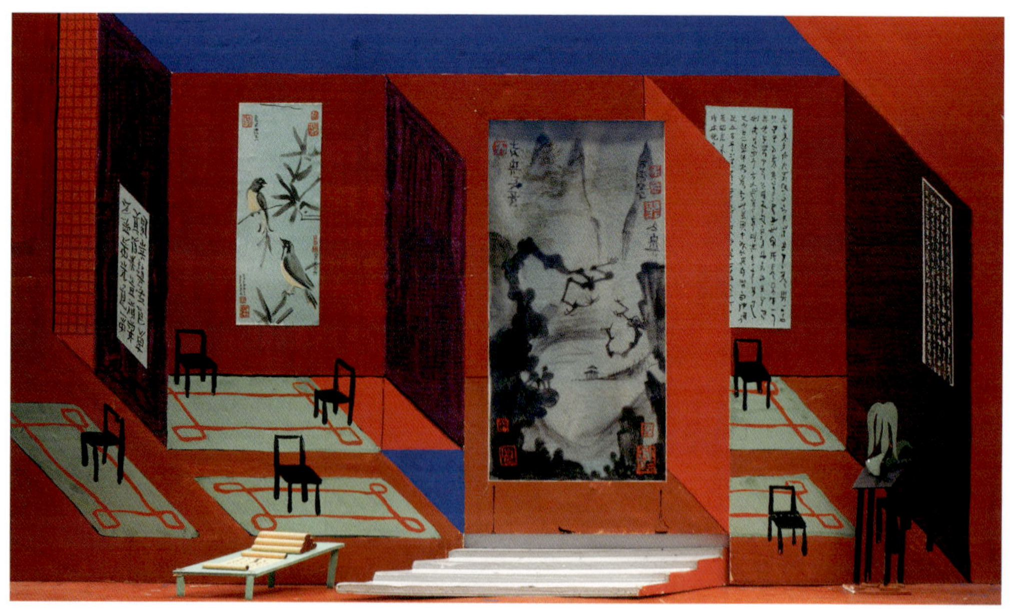

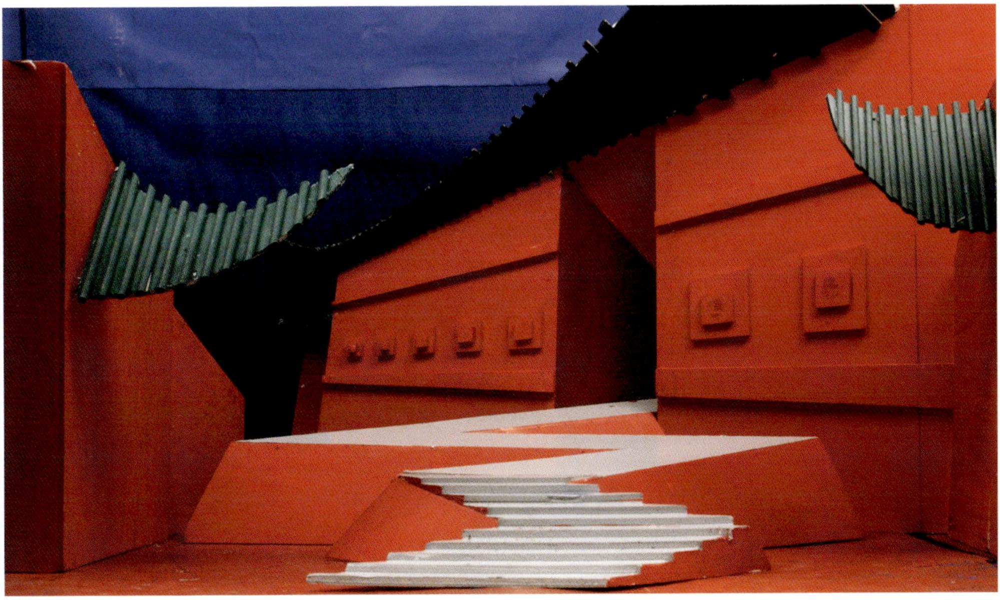

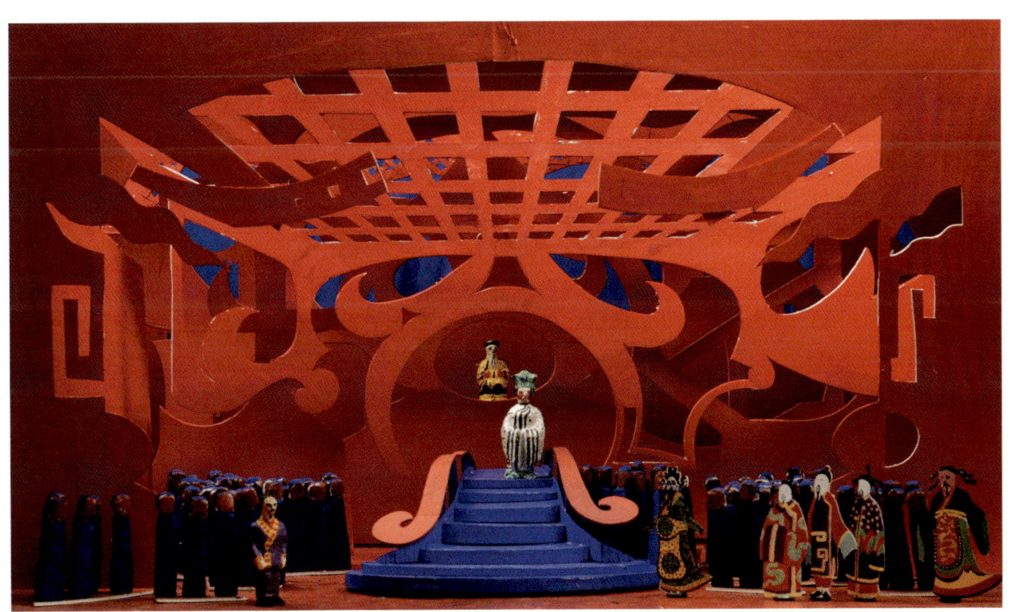

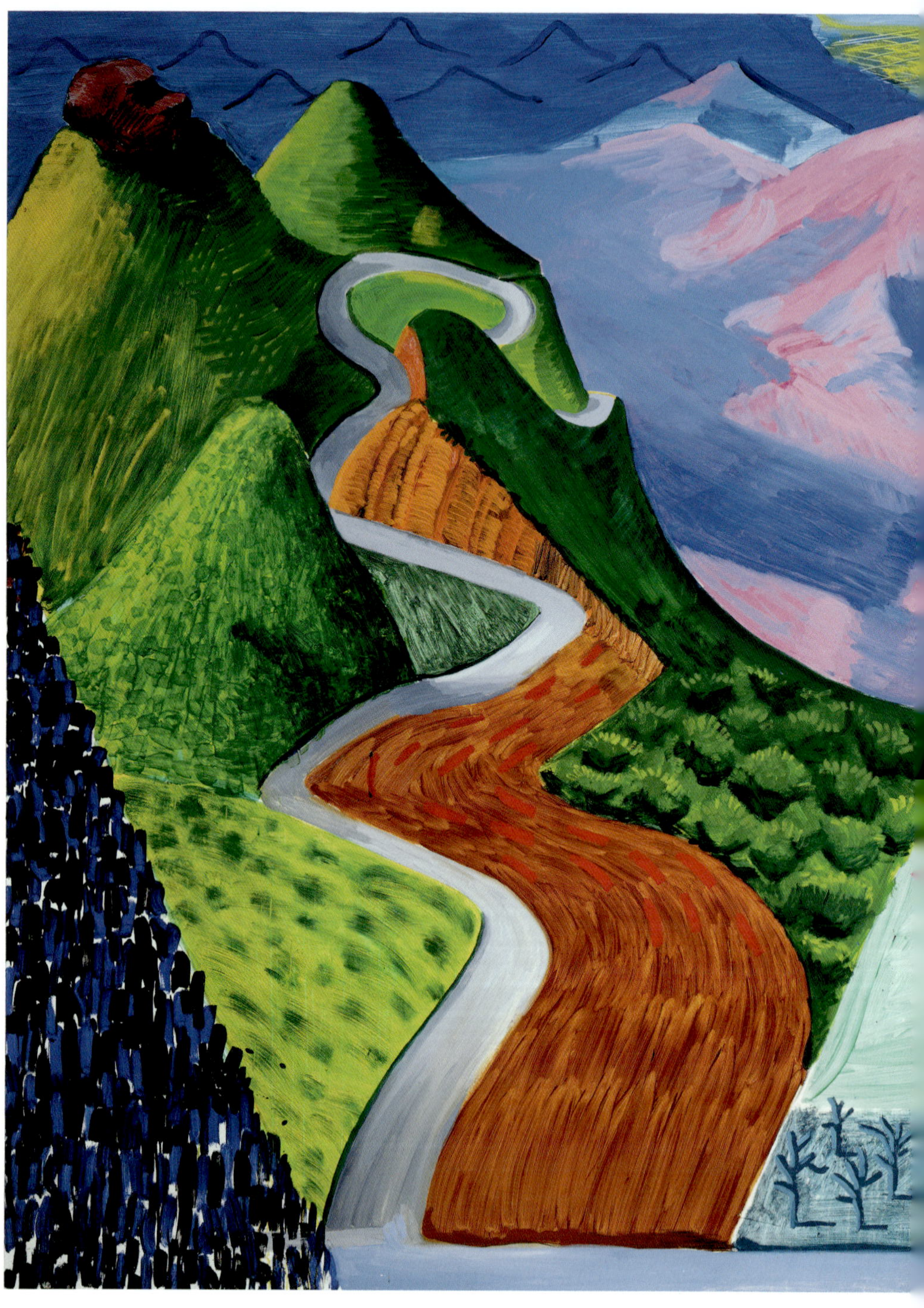

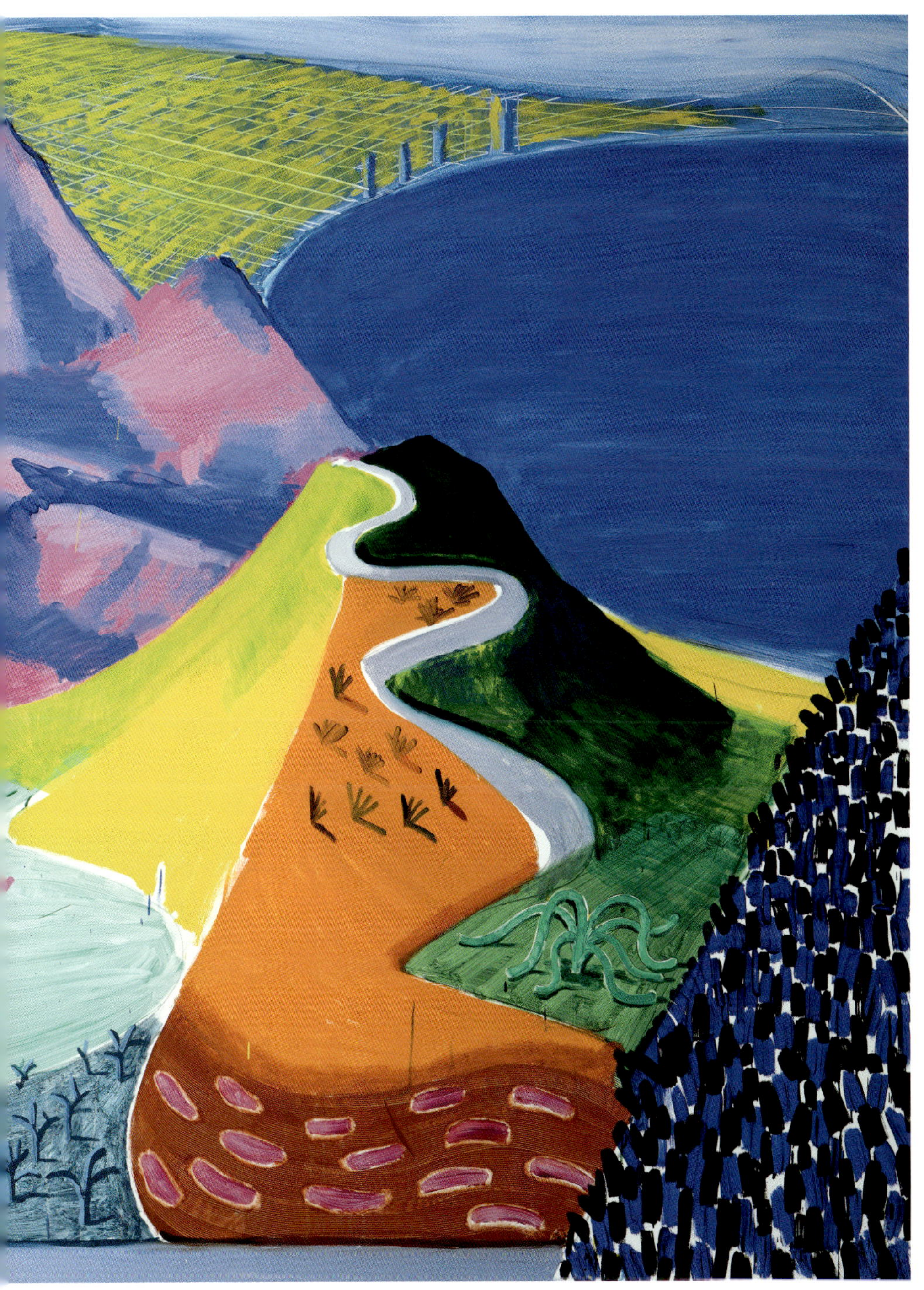

1991

While he does not give up smoking, Hockney leads a somewhat healthier life after his heart attack, training on walking machines and eating better food. His work rate remains undiminished. While he is still creating the stage design for *Turandot* with Ian Falconer, Geordie Greig visits him for the *Sunday Times*: "Locked away in his studio, he refuses all calls (except from his 90-year-old mother in Bradford). Hockney says he does little else but work: painting, faxing, photographing, photocopying, drawing—in fact experimenting with anything in the name of art. 'I'm having fun. If any artist tells you he's not having fun in his studio, there is something wrong with him. He has to, even if his work is pessimistic. Art has to have some hope because it believes it can get a message across,' he preaches, upbeat and talkative, bouncing around his studio in sneakers, white jeans, and a turquoise t-shirt. He revels in his new opera designs. There are no drawings, just a 15 foot theatre with figures and set all modeled in minute detail. 'It will be three hours of absolute magic. I will make the eye hear more and the ear see more. I love the music and delight in finding forms to fit it,' he said... His delight in his work is irrepressible as he dashes next door to switch on a giant TV set to show a video of *Turandot* filmed from his model theatre. 'It's all more fun than a train set,' he grinned."

In June, Hockney's electronic photographs from the previous year are exhibited at the National Museum of Photography, Film and Television in Bradford. Eamonn McCabe in the *Guardian* on this part of his oeuvre: "Hockney's playful pictures are great fun; they will not replace the chemical process if only because the technology cannot yet produce a decent print. He implied he didn't particularly care whether or not they were art. 'They're reasonably easily made and I regard a lot of my work as research anyway. We live in an age where the artist is forgotten. He is a researcher. I see myself that way.' Everything in Hockney's life is an exploration and exploring is, for him, the major role of the artist."

In July, Hockney goes to Chicago to oversee production at the Lyric Opera. He travels with John Fitzherbert, Richard Schmidt, and Bing McGilvray in a camper van; they work at the opera house especially on the lighting for a week, and on the way back make a detour through Monument Valley and to the Grand Canyon. Back in Los Angeles, Hockney immediately begins painting again. The new pictures show landscape motifs inspired by what he has seen, but also seemingly abstract forms, that together explore natural and pictorial spaces. Paintings

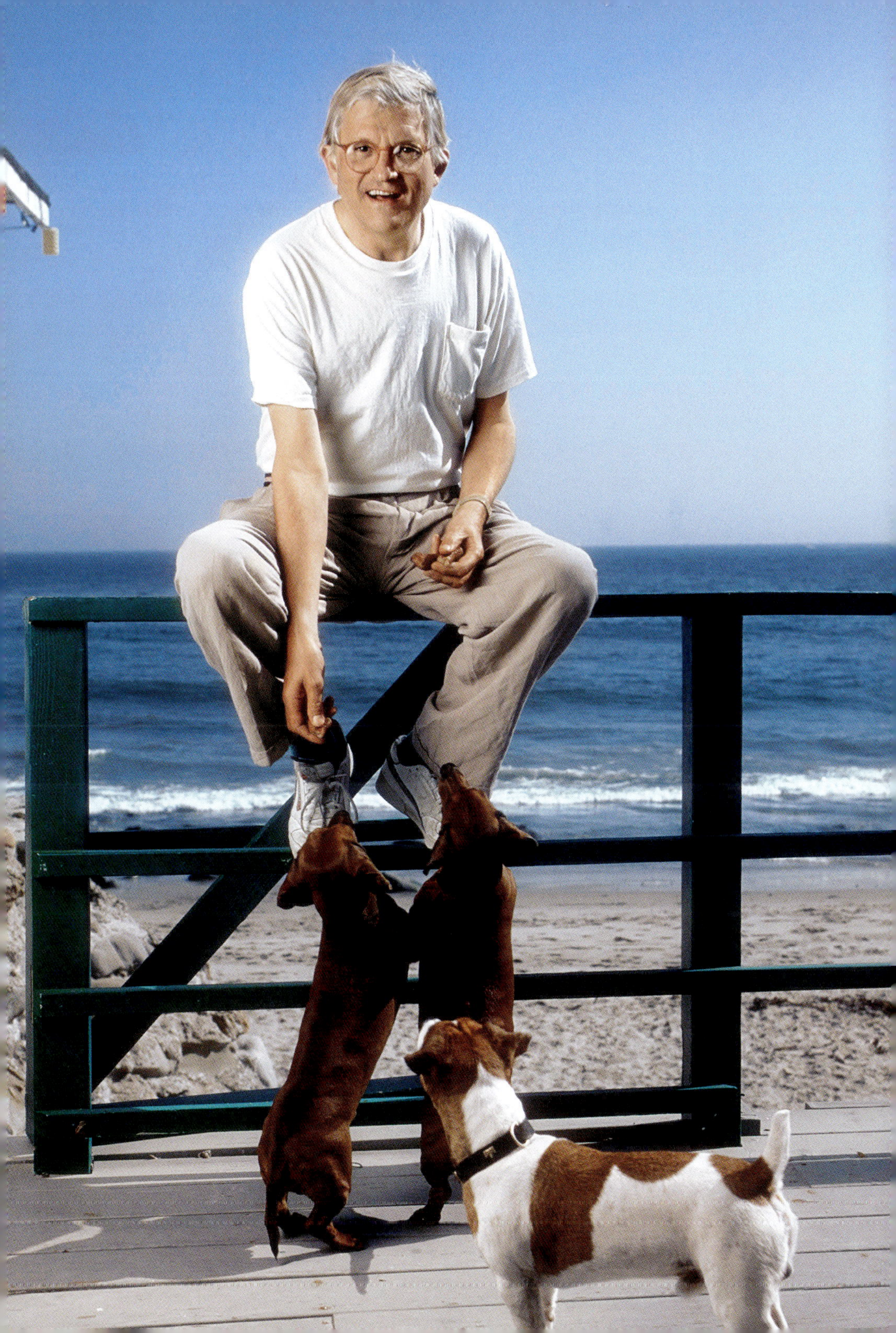

such as *What about the Caves* (pp. 294/295) in turn inspire Hockney's work on his next opera production, Richard Strauss's *Die Frau ohne Schatten* for the Royal Opera House at Covent Garden in London, due to open next November: "The first thing I made for *Die Frau,* on a small model, was an abstract representation of a river, like a snake. I put little dots on it which were actually derived from the textures that were appearing in these paintings. *Turandot* is mostly architectural interiors; even the garden, which is nearest to nature, is a Chinese garden, stylized, formal, not raw nature. In *Die Frau,* on the other hand, we are dealing with nature in the wild…and I knew these paintings were going to influence its design."

Solo: *David Hockney's New Electronic Snaps,* National Museum of Photography, Film and Television, Bradford (May 29–Sep 29); catalog with a text by Colin Ford. *Doll Boy,* Hamburger Kunsthalle, Hamburg (Nov 6, 1991–Jan 12, 1992); catalog ed. by Uwe M. Schneede, text by Ulrich Luckhardt. *Cavafy Etchings,* The British Museum, London. *Graphic Inventions: A Selection of Works on Paper by David Hockney in the 1960s,* Knoedler Gallery, London (opens Apr 9); catalog.

Group: *Setting the Stage: Contemporary Artists Design for the Performing Arts,* Columbus Museum of Art, Columbus (Feb 24–Apr 21); catalog. *Pop Prints 1959–1982,* Tate Gallery, London (Mar 6–Jun 23). *Individual Realities in the California Art Scene,* Sezon Museum of Art, Tokyo (May 11–Jun 10); travels to Amagasaki; catalog. *Seven Master Printmakers,* Museum of Modern Art, New York (May 16–Aug 13); catalog. *Pop Art,* Royal Academy of Arts, London (Sep 13–Dec 15), travels to Museum Ludwig, Cologne; Centro de Arte Reina Sofía, Madrid; and Montreal Museum of Fine Arts, Montreal (through 1993); catalog. *Memoire de la Liberté,* Musée national d'art moderne, Centre Georges Pompidou, Paris (Oct 1–Nov 30); catalog.

Publication: *Hockney's Alphabet,* ed. by Stephen Spender, texts by Douglas Adams, Anthony Burgess, T.S. Eliot, William Golding, Seamus Haney, Erica Jong, Doris Lessing, Norman Mailer, Arthur Miller, Iris Murdoch, Joyce Carol Oates, Susan Sontag, John Updike, Gore Vidal, and others, London: Faber and Faber.

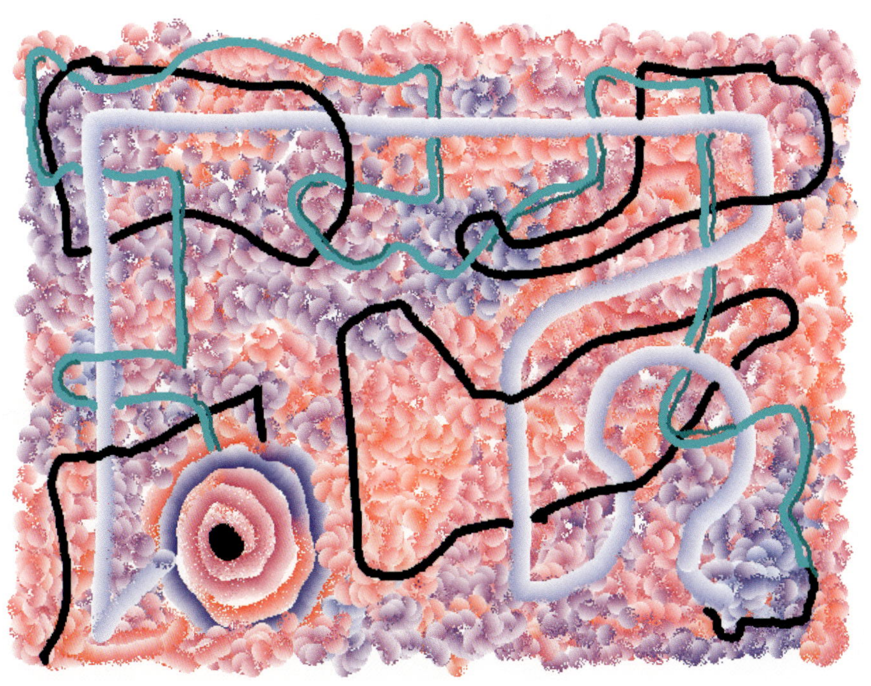

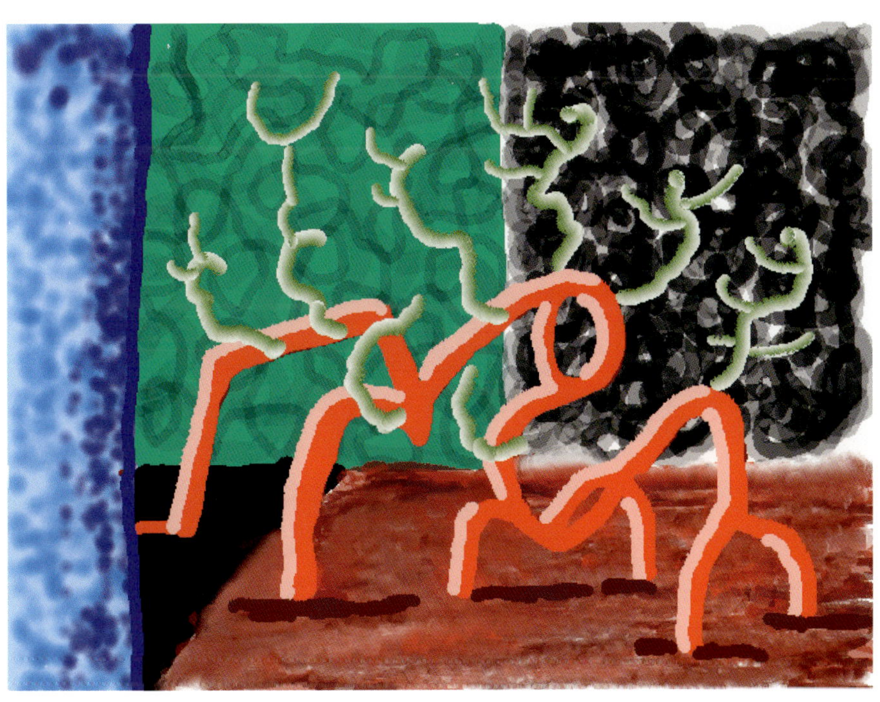

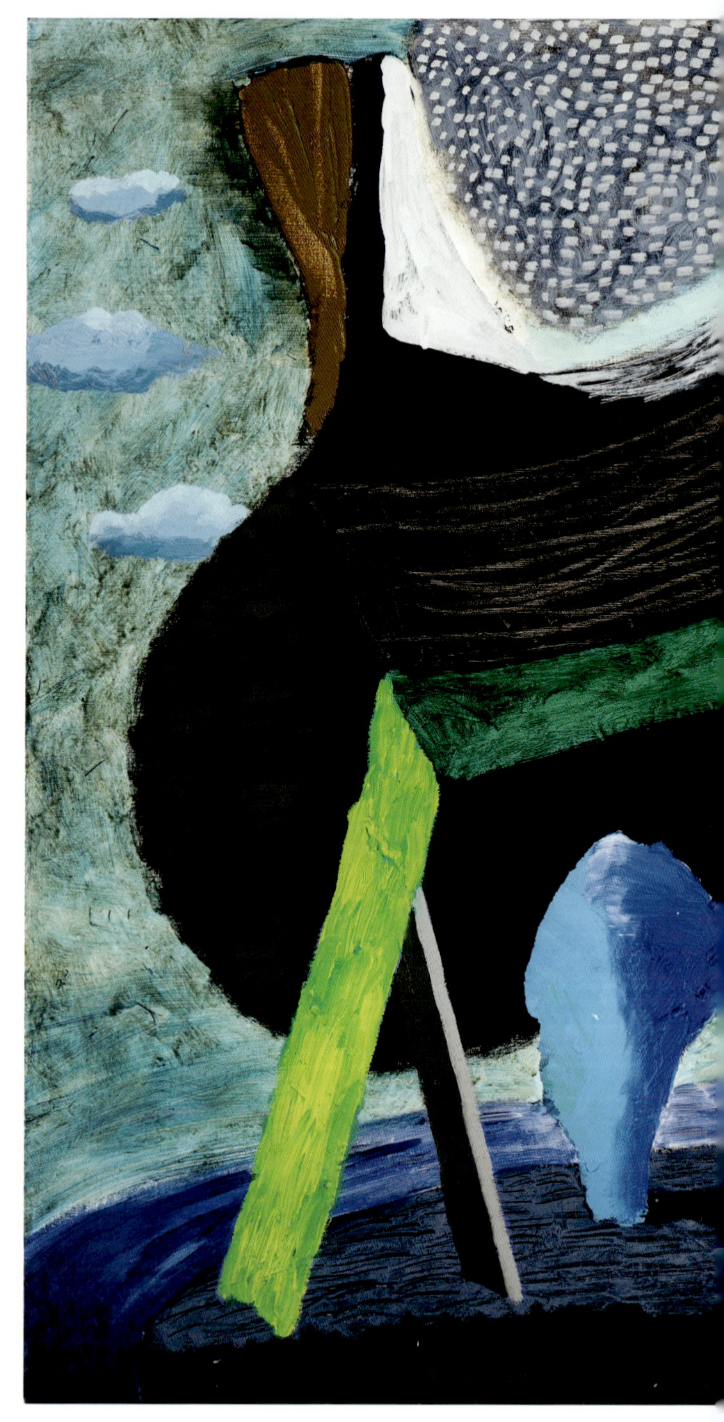

What about the Caves, 1991,
oil on canvas, 36 x 48 in. /
91.4 x 121.9 cm

Page 291: David Hockney
with his dogs on the terrace of
his beach house, Malibu 1991.
Photo: Paul Harris

Page 293: *Monday Morning
Flowers,* 1991, computer drawing

Sunday 1, Walking Plant, 1991,
computer drawing

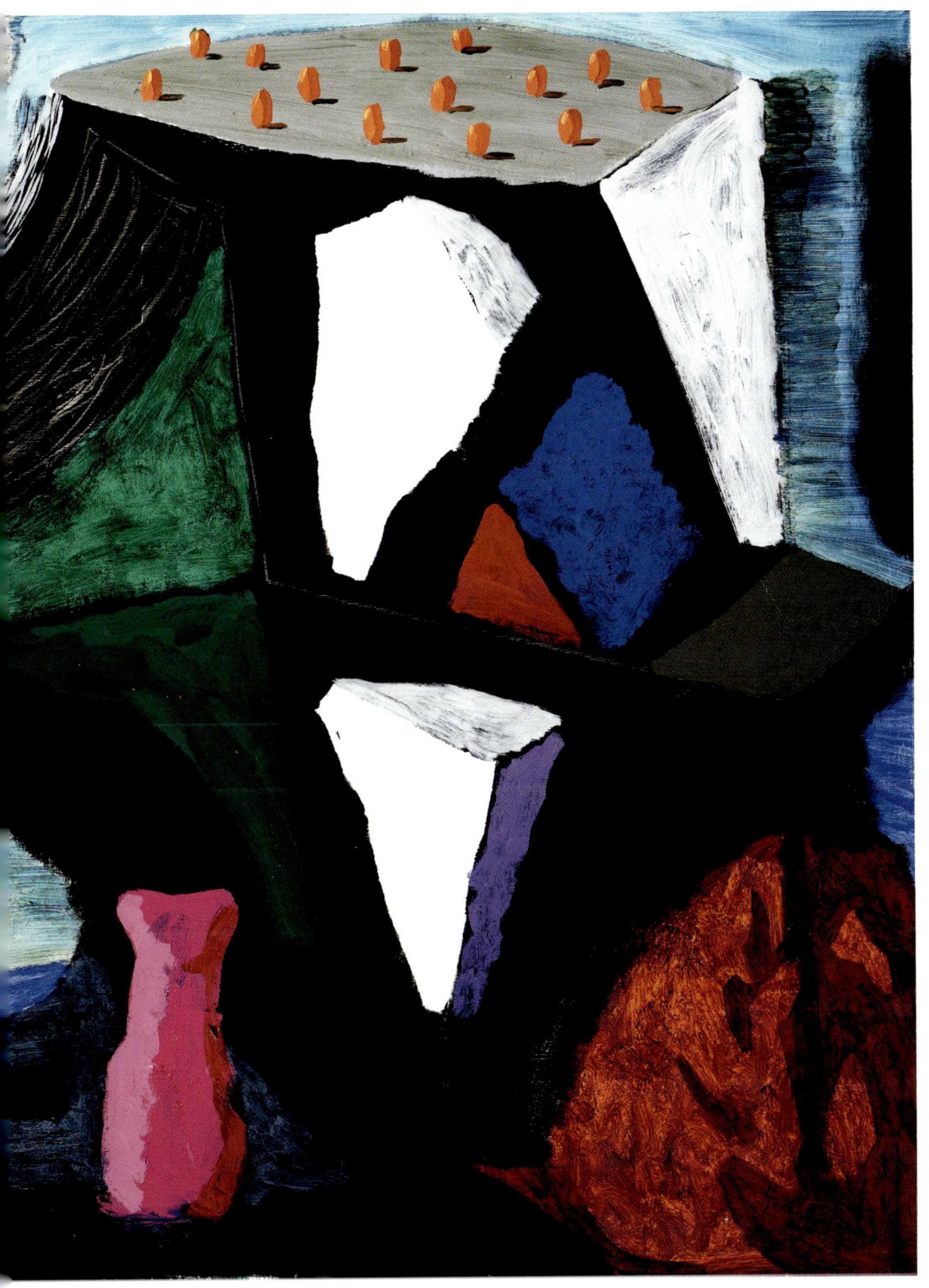

1992 In January, the new *Turandot* production has its premiere at the Lyric Opera of Chicago. According to John von Rhein's review in the *Chicago Tribune,* it is "a show from which you emerge literally humming the scenery. The company's first presentation of Puccini's swan song in 22 years arrived Saturday night at the Civic Opera House all decked out in David Hockney's fantastical sets and collaborator Ian Falconer's lavish costumes, looking like the million bucks it probably cost the Lyric and San Francisco, who are sharing the production. Consistently inventive, realized with high-tech precision, this 'designer opera' evokes the chill barbarity of Puccini's fairy-tale China in a virtuosic burst of bold colors, stylized shapes, witty perspectives, and liquid lighting. This *Turandot* may not qualify as Hockney's most successful designs for the operatic stage—for my taste, his French triple-bill at the Met still holds that honor—but it may well be his most eye-filling."

Hockney paints a series of *Very New Paintings* (pp. 299–301), investigations in space and color influenced by his opera set designs, taking up the continuing struggle between abstraction and representation: "Someone said that the *Very New Paintings* are abstract narratives. Certainly a great deal of thought and feeling have gone into them. For example, here at the beach I am between two great forces, the mountains and the sea. The mountains were made by a great force of nature, a thrusting force, which calmed in time, leaving them here, grand and peaceful. While below the other thrust continues, the endless movement of the sea. These forces are present, I believe, in the paintings. They are also quite sexual…Perhaps these paintings seem a jumble to the viewer at first. They take time to unfold. They're a bit mind-boggling, but they are meant to be. The viewer can roam freely within them, finding his or her own space. That's why there are no figures in them. You construct your own space mentally."

Expectations for the production of *Die Frau ohne Schatten* (pp. 302/303) at London's Royal Opera, directed by Hockney's old collaborator John Cox, are high. Anthony Peatty visits the team for the *Independent*: "I asked David Hockney about *Frau*'s ending which, even in the best productions, can seem to go on rather, as the Voices of the Unborn Children resound from offstage and the life force, fruitfulness and the shadow are celebrated onstage. Would they cut any of it at Covent Garden? 'Oh no,' he explained, in the same terms he once used when justifying the length of the love duet in *Tristan,* 'it takes that

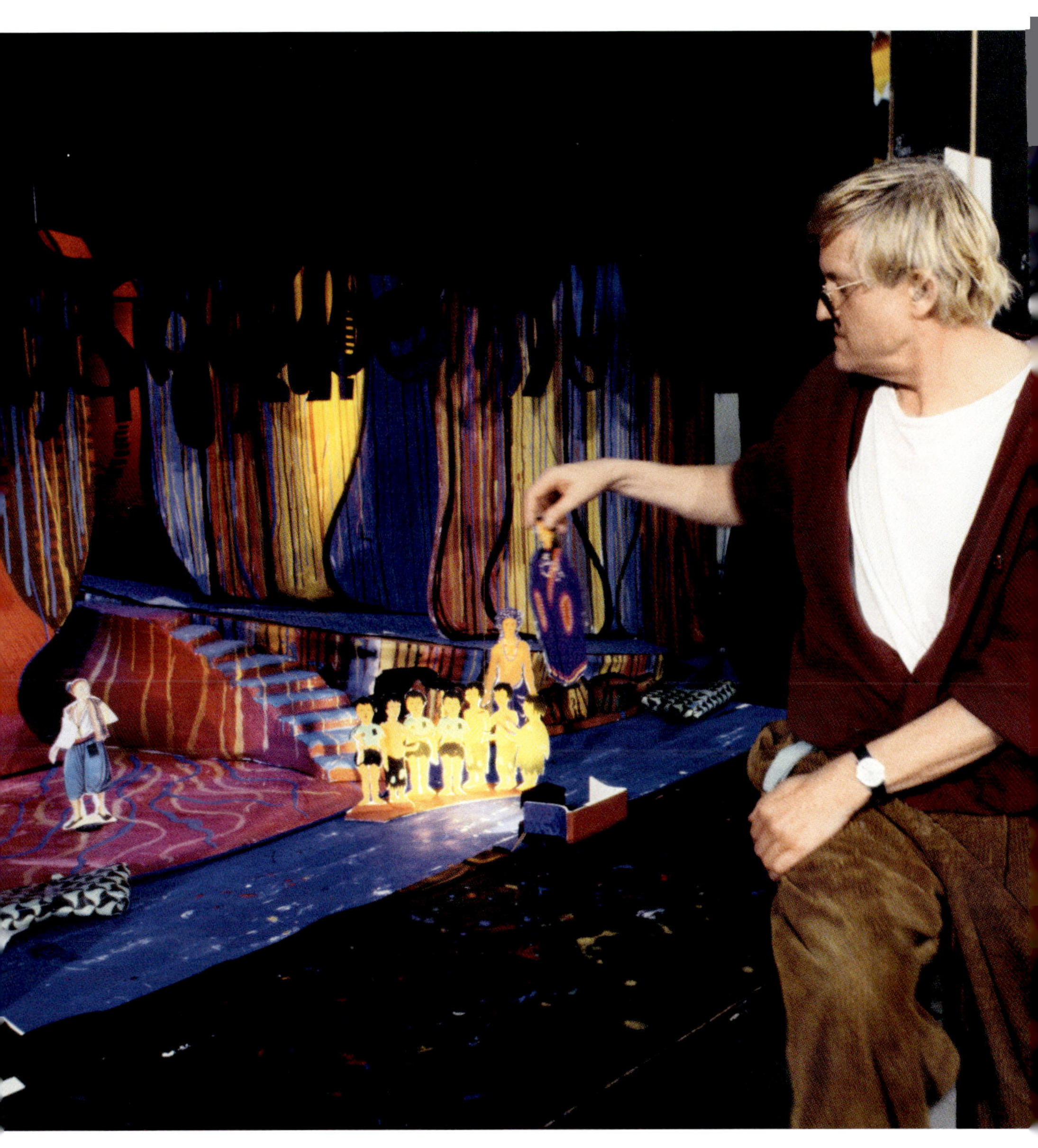

David Hockney with his model for the
opera *Die Frau ohne Schatten*, 1992.
Photo: Jim McHugh

long to reach ecstasy.' John Cox answered the same question with a grin, 'We need all that music for the designs.' Perhaps they mean the same thing." The production lacks time for rehearsals and the necessary technical fine-tuning, though. Hockney remembers: "Even by the dress rehearsal not everything was lit right...on each of the subsequent five nights, adjustments were made. The last performance was without doubt the best, the only one when all the cues were correct with the music. The singers, too, were at their best because it was being broadcast. I sat there and I don't think there was anybody in the theatre who enjoyed it more than I did. And then it was gone, disappeared..." *Die Frau ohne Schatten* will remain Hockney's last stage design for an opera.

Solo: *Seven Paintings,* Tate Gallery, London (Feb 18–Jul 26). *David Hockney,* Palais des Beaux-Arts, Brussels (Jun 12–July 26); travels to Fundación Juan March, Madrid (Sep 18–Dec 20) and Palau de la Virreina, Barcelona (Jan–Feb 1993); catalog. *Hockney's Opera,* Bunkamura Museum of Art, Tokyo (Jun 13–Jul 12); travels to Sapporo, Nagoya, Kobe, Hiroshima, and Ibaraki; catalog with texts by Stephen Spender, Hideo Takahashi, Kazuo Yamawaki, and Shin'ichiro Osaki. *Grafiek,* Museum Boymans-van Beuningen, Rotterdam (Jul 26–Oct 4); catalog with a text by Manfred Sellink. *Recent Pictures,* Richard Gray Gallery, Chicago (Jan 11–Feb 11); catalog. *New Pictures and Still Video Portraits,* Nishimura Gallery, Tokyo (Jun 12–Jul 11); catalog.

Group: *Ready Steady Go: Paintings of the Sixties from the Arts Council Collection,* Royal Festival Hall, London (Jan 21–Feb 23); travels to Bath; catalog. *Collaborations: Recent Work from Tyler Graphics,* Aldrich Museum of Contemporary Art, Ridgefield (Jan 26–May 3). *Chaos to Order,* Art Museum of Southeast Texas, Beaumont (Mar 28–Jun 14). *This Sporting Life, 1878–1991,* High Museum of Art, Atlanta (May 16–Sep 13); travels to Houston, Santa Clara, Wilmington, and New York (through 1993); catalog. *New Acquisitions / New Work / New Directions,* LA County Museum of Art, Los Angeles (Jun 18–Jul 26). *Singular and Plural: Recent Accessions, Drawing and Prints 1945–1991,* Museum of Fine Arts, Houston (Jul 12–Aug 23).

Honor: Honorary Doctorate, Royal College of Art, London.

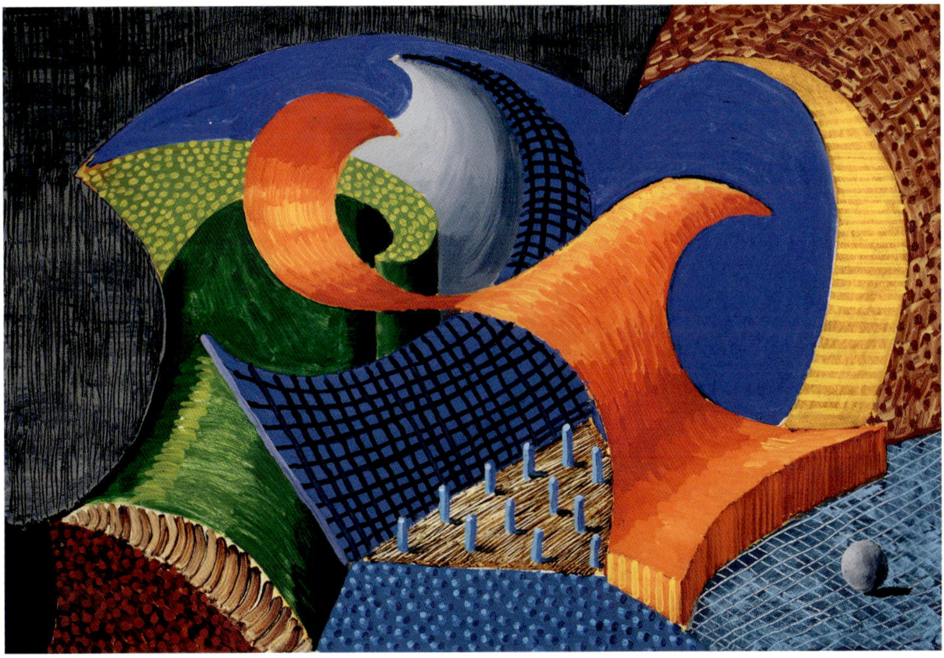

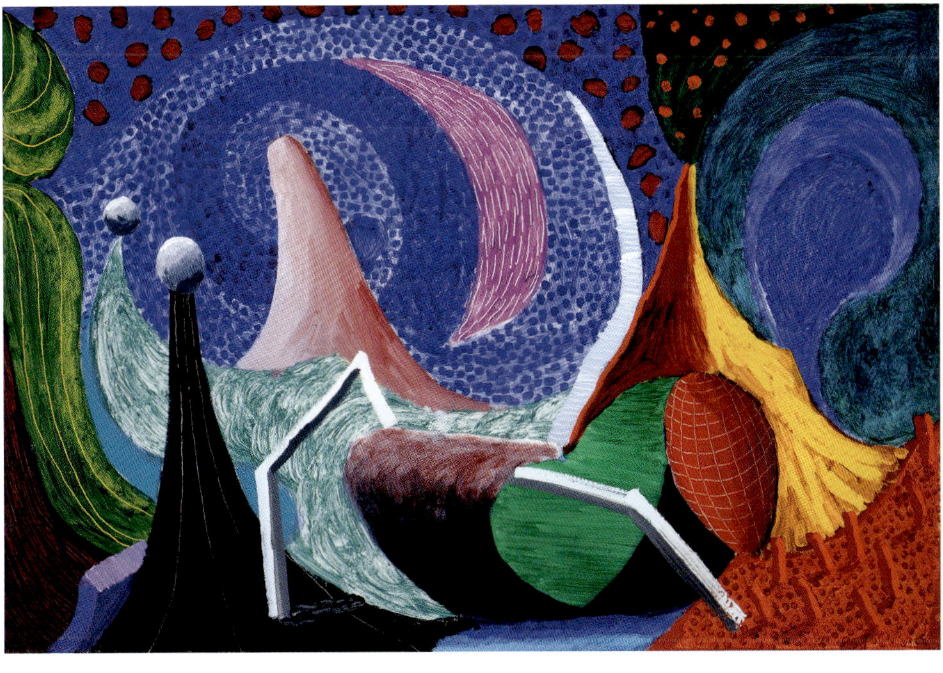

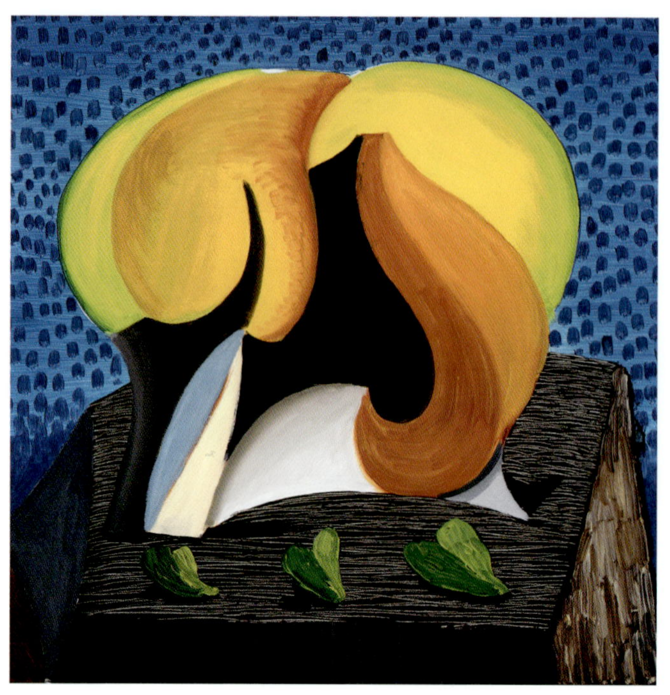

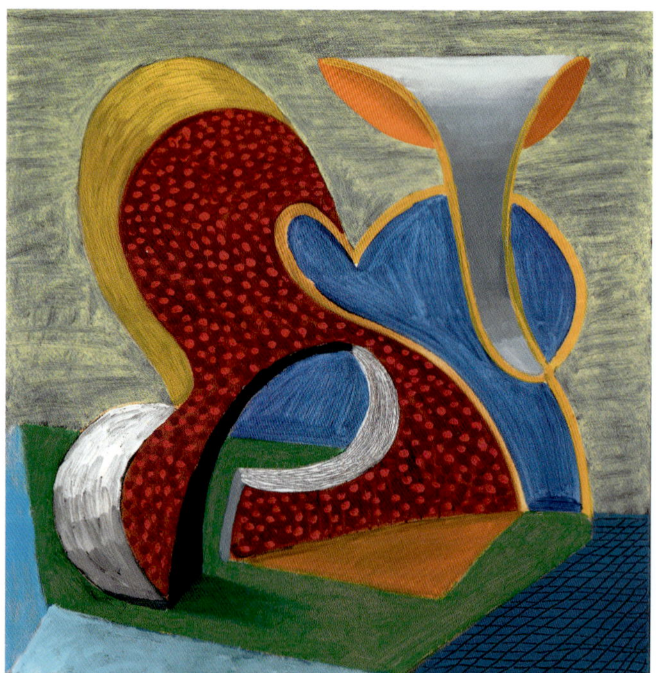

The First V.N. Painting, 1992, oil on canvas, 24 x 24 in. / 61 x 61 cm

The Fourth V.N. Painting, 1992, oil on canvas, 24 x 24 in. / 61 x 61 cm

Right page: The Seventh V.N. Painting, 1992, oil on canvas, 36 x 48 in. / 91.4 x 121.9 cm

The Sixth V.N. Painting, 1992, oil on canvas, 36 x 48 in. / 91.4 x 121.9 cm

Page 299: The Eleventh V.N. Painting, 1992, oil on canvas, 24 x 36 in. / 61 x 91.4 cm

The Twenty Fourth V.N. Painting, 1992, oil on canvas, 24 x 36 in. / 61 x 91.4 cm

Pages 302–303: Production of Die Frau ohne Schatten, as performed at the Royal Opera House, London 1992

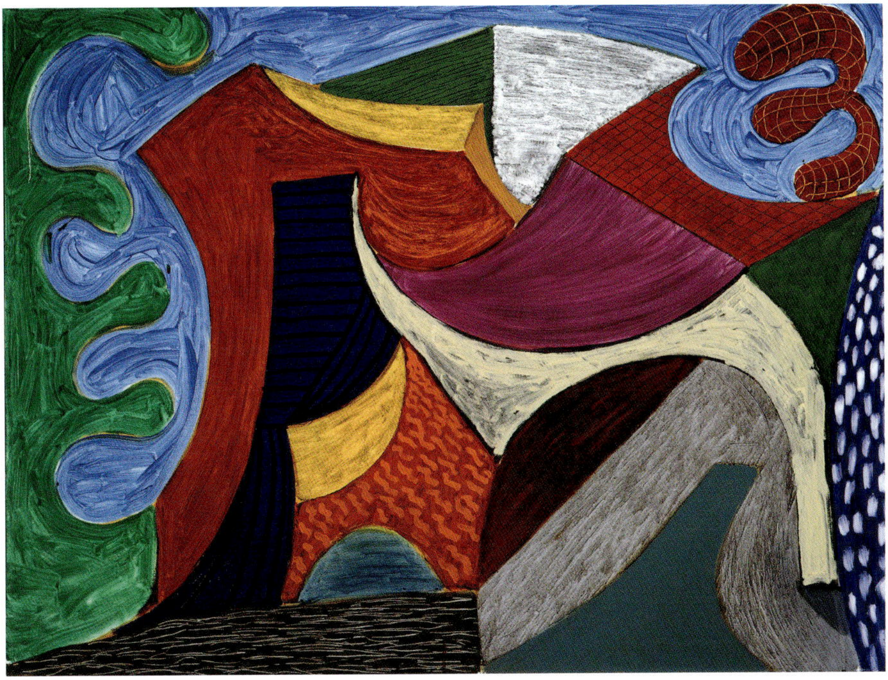

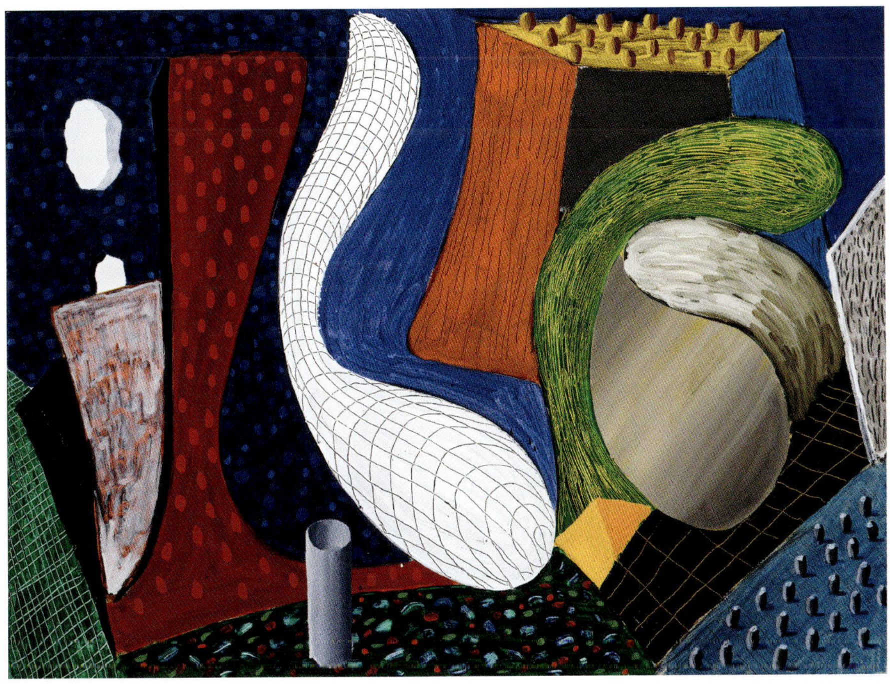

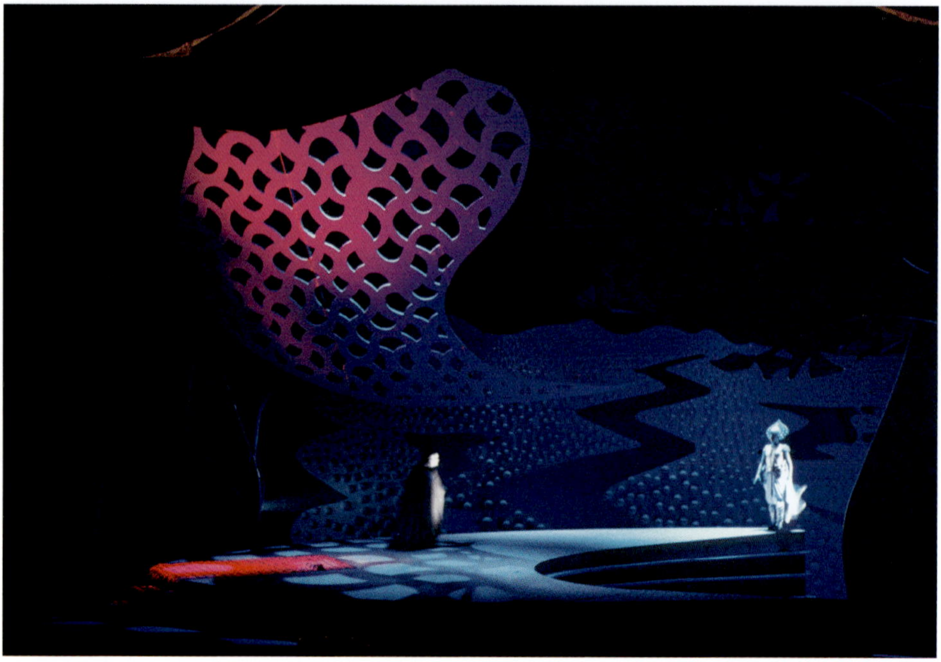

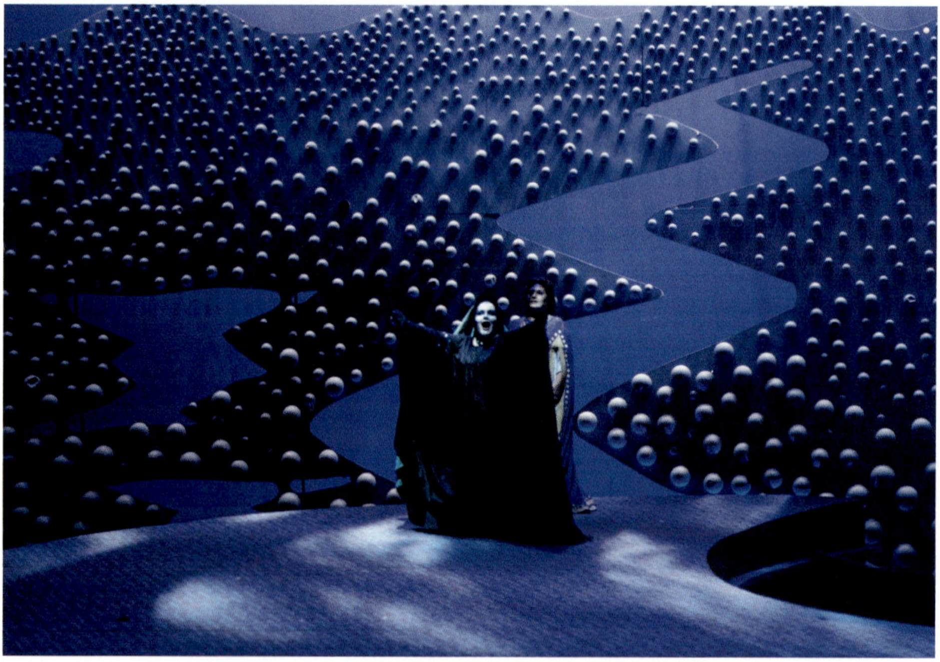

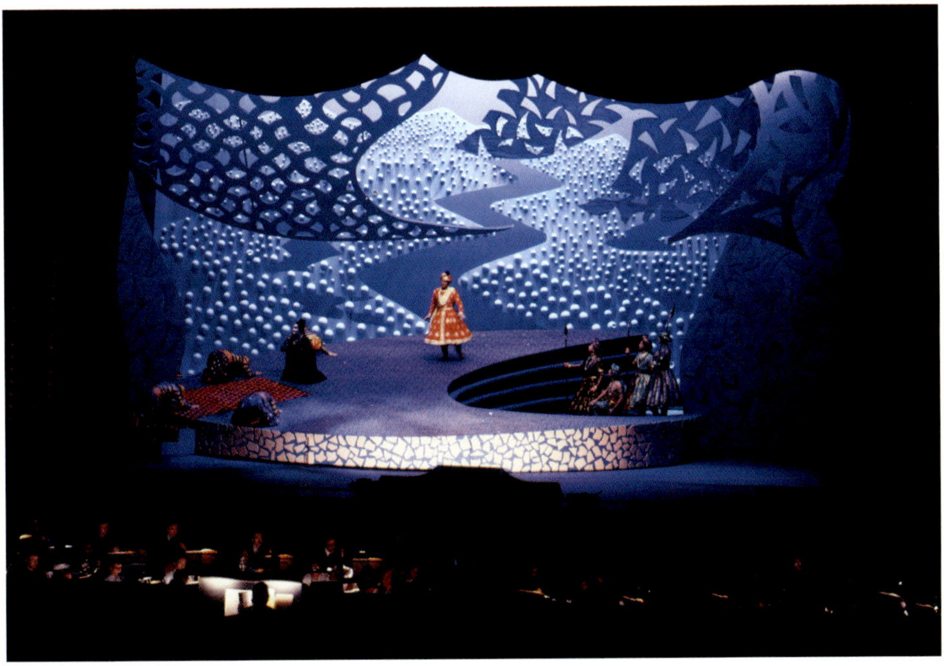

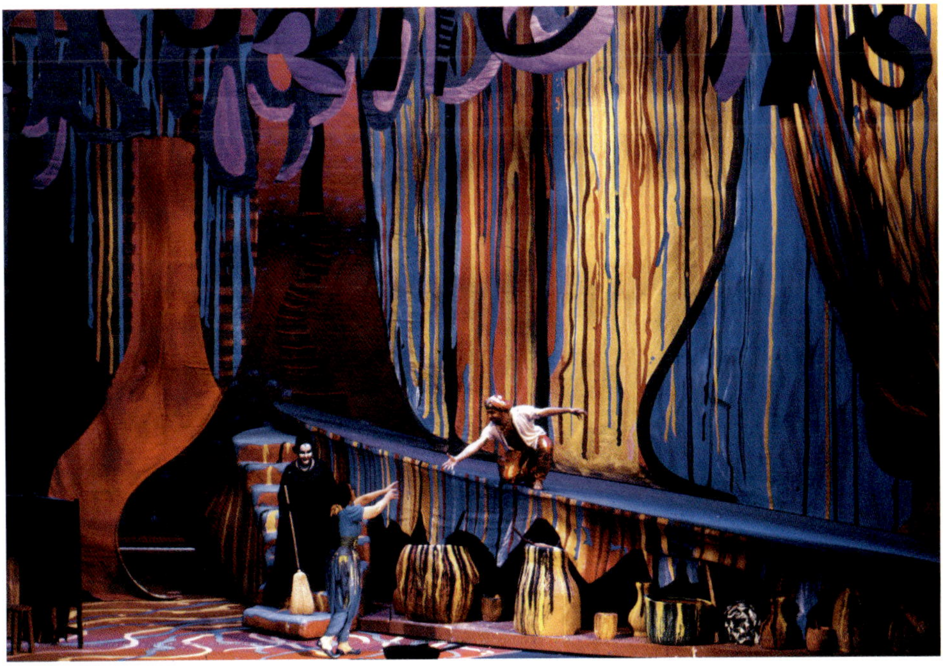

1993

Hockney shows the complete series of *Very New Paintings* at André Emmerich Gallery in New York in January. Roberta Smith in the *New York Times* has mixed feelings: "In some ways, these are among the best paintings Mr. Hockney has produced in a while, although it's all relative. As with much of his work, they are once removed, more like paintings of paintings than the real thing… They are cute, smart, and in a certain way irresistible, the way bonbons are; but like bonbons, they lack essential nutrition." During summer the paintings are shown in Glasgow at William Hardie Gallery. Richard Cork in the *Times* takes away a more positive impression: "These works are determined to remain unpredictable, perpetually on the move; and their habit of jumping from one kind of handling to the next matches their way of looking at the world… This is an uneven show, notably lacking the cool, seductive placidity which made his Californian paintings so beguiling a quarter of a century ago. At their best, though, the restless images end up affirming the delights of motion, vitality, and unquenchable visual curiosity with great exuberance. Now in his late fifties, Hockney gives no sign here of dozing on his reputation and resorting to popular formulae. His appetite for experiment remains keen, and he would rather struggle towards the unknown than remain content with polishing facile, well-worn solutions."

The series marks Hockney's return to the public eye as a painter, and interest is further enhanced by the publication of the second part of his autobiography, titled *That's the Way I See It*. A number of home stories appear in publications on both sides of the Atlantic. They show the artist enthusiastic about his art, but living a more secluded life, partly due to his deafness, partly sombered by the fact that many of his friends have died of AIDS. Trip Gabriel in the *New York Times* sees a dark edge to the new paintings and asks whether a decade of AIDS has made his work more gloomy: "Mr. Hockney answered elliptically, by telling the story of his visit to the big Matisse retrospective that ended on Tuesday at the Museum of Modern Art in New York: 'I spent about five hours in there. It was one of the highest and deepest pleasures I've had. But I remember there was a painting of a little still life, just a pot of flowers and a bust on a table, and it's painted in 1942. You look at the date and you think, in Europe they were just ripping themselves apart. It's ghastly.' He paused to gather his thoughts. 'I'm glad he painted it. I'm very glad somebody sat down and did something like that.'"

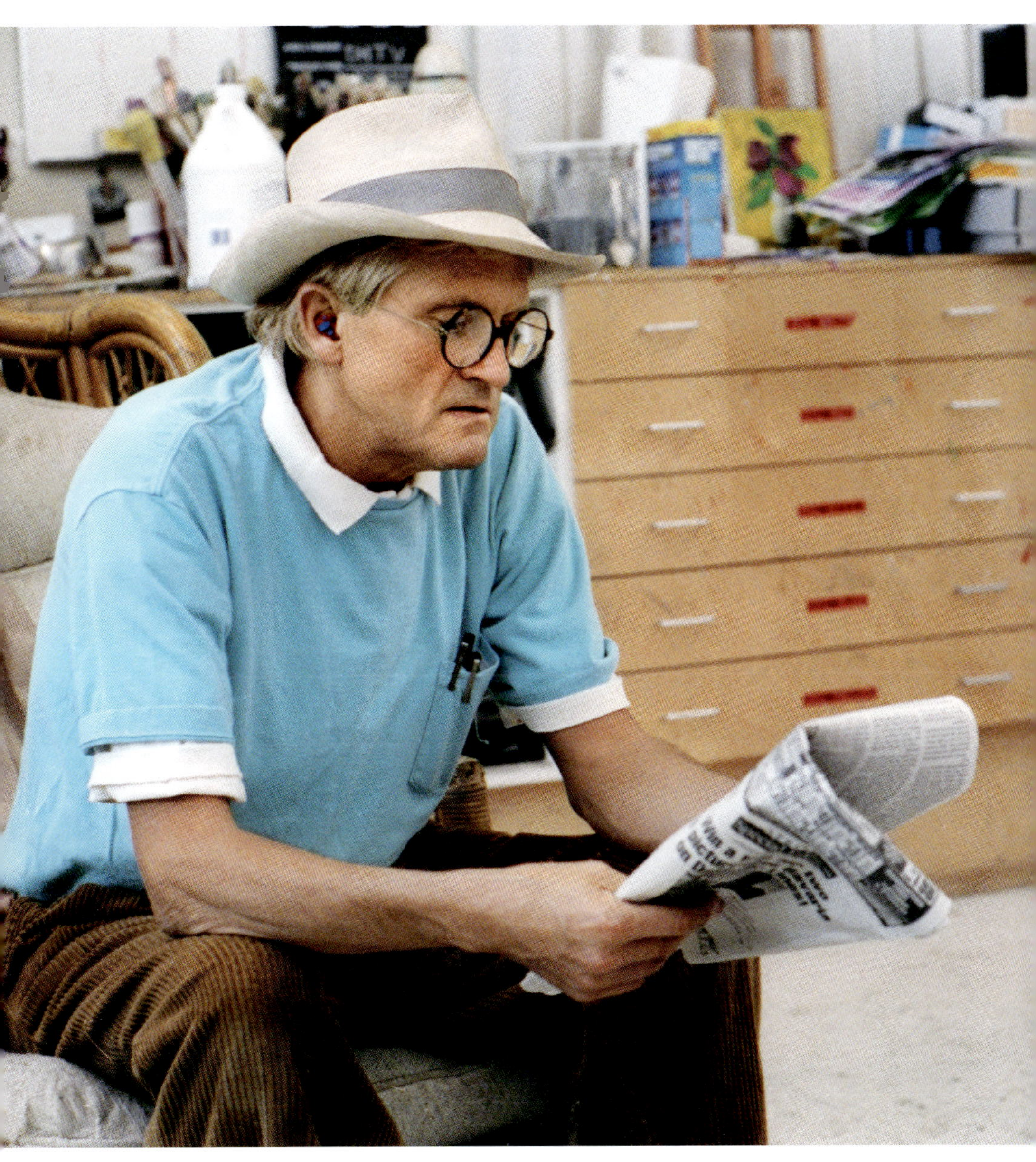

David Hockney in his studio, Los Angeles
1993. Photo: Sidney B. Felsen

In Salts Mill in Saltaire, Hockney's friend Jonathan Silver exhibits the *Very New Paintings* together with an exclusive set of large laser-printed photographs of the Yorkshire landscape (p. 308). Over the year, Hockney begins several new series: small portrait paintings and drawings from life of his dachshund dogs Stanley and Boodgie (p. 307); *Painted Environments* that present a three-dimensional assemblage of a painted canvas on its easel, surrounded in the room with painted elements, photographed and then laser-printed (pp. 310/311); and large-scale crayon drawings of his seated friends and family, executed with particular attention to their hands (p. 309).

Solo: *Paintings and Prints from 1960,* Tate Liverpool (Apr 7, 1993–Feb 13, 1994); catalog with a text by Penelope Curtis. *Illustrations from Six Fairy Tales from the Brothers Grimm, 1969,* Royal Festival Hall, London (Apr 12–May 9); organized by South Bank Centre, London; travels to Southampton, Yeovil, Aberystwyth, Salisbury, and many others (through 2010); catalog with a text by Peter Webb. *25 Years of Printmaking,* Gantry Arts Centre, Southampton (May 15–Jun 13); organized by Edinburgh Printmakers Workshop & Gallery and Berkeley Square Gallery, London; travels to Yeovil, Aberystwyth, Salisbury, Accrington, and others (through 1995). *Some Very New Paintings,* André Emmerich Gallery, New York (Jan 7–Feb 13); travels to William Hardie Gallery Glasgow (Jun 28–Aug 27) and 1853 Gallery, Saltaire (Sep 1–Nov 30); catalog. *Works on Paper,* Athena Fine Arts, New York (Jan 14–Feb 20). *Now: David Hockney,* Lung Men Gallery, Taipei (Dec 11, 1993–Jan 9, 1994).

Group: *Photoplay: Works from the Chase Manhattan Collection,* Center for the Fine Arts, Miami (Jan 9–Mar 1); travels to Monterrey, Caracas, São Paulo, Buenos Aires, and Santiago (through 1994); catalog. *Sixties Art Scene in London, 1957–1969,* Barbican Art Gallery, London (Mar 11–Jun 13); catalog. *Summer Exhibition,* Royal Academy of Arts, London (Jun 15–Aug 15); catalog. *The Portrait Now,* National Portrait Gallery, London (Nov 19, 1993–Feb 6, 1994); catalog.

Publication: David Hockney, *That's the Way I See It,* ed. by Nikos Stangos, London: Thames and Hudson; San Francisco: Chronicle Books.

Stanley, 1993, crayon on paper,
22 ¹/₂ x 30 ¹/₄ in. / 57.2 x 76.8 cm

Stanley, 1993, crayon on paper,
30 ¹/₄ x 22 ¹/₂ in. / 76.8 x 57.2 cm

Boodgie, 1993, crayon on paper,
30 ¹/₄ x 22 ¹/₂ in. / 76.8 x 57.2 cm

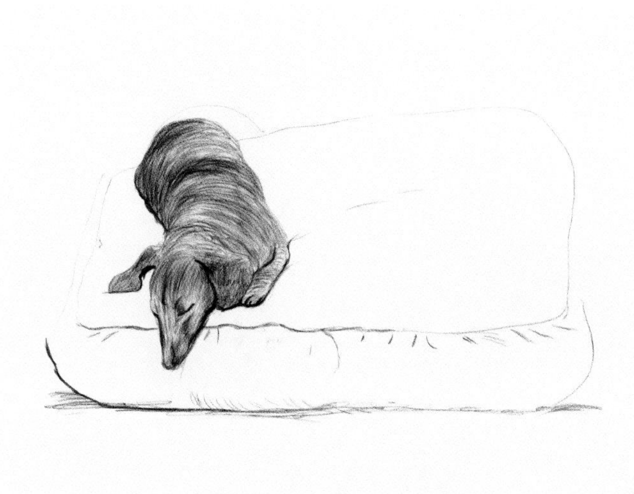

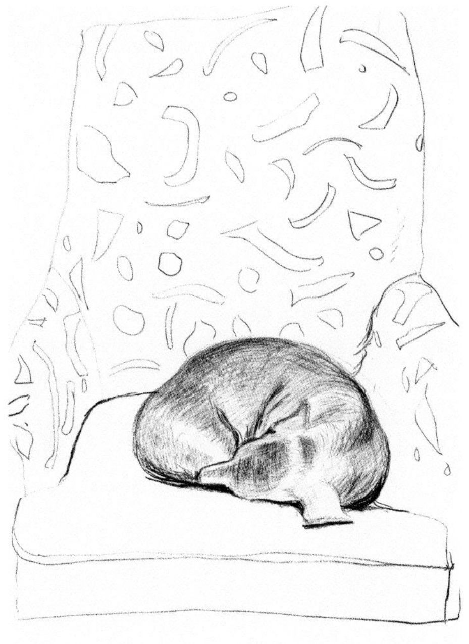

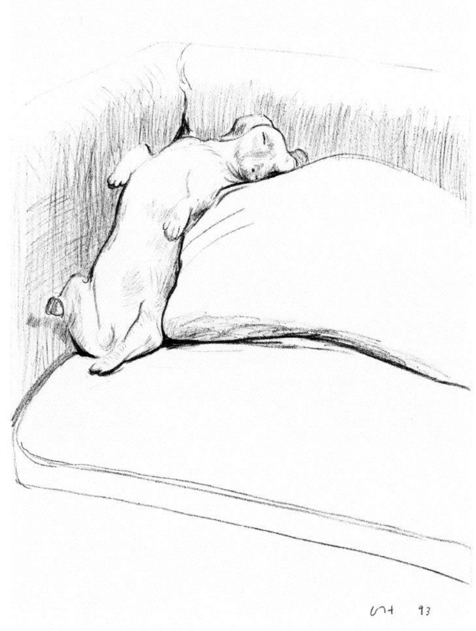

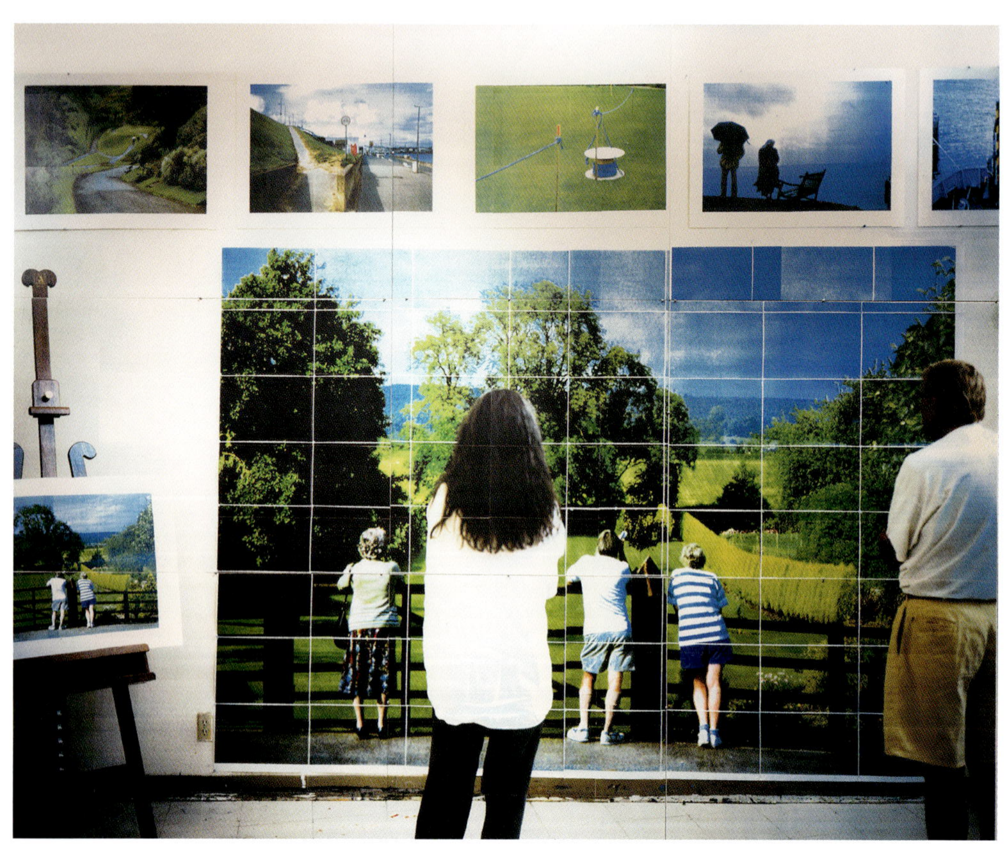

David Hockney and Karen Kuhlman Looking at Photographs of Yorkshire, 1993, 9 color laser-printed photographs, 120 ¹/₄ x 151 ¹/₂ in. / 305.4 x 384.8 cm overall

Right page: *Mum, Dec 29th 1993,* crayon on paper, 30 ¹/₄ x 22 ¹/₂ in. / 76.8 x 57.2 cm

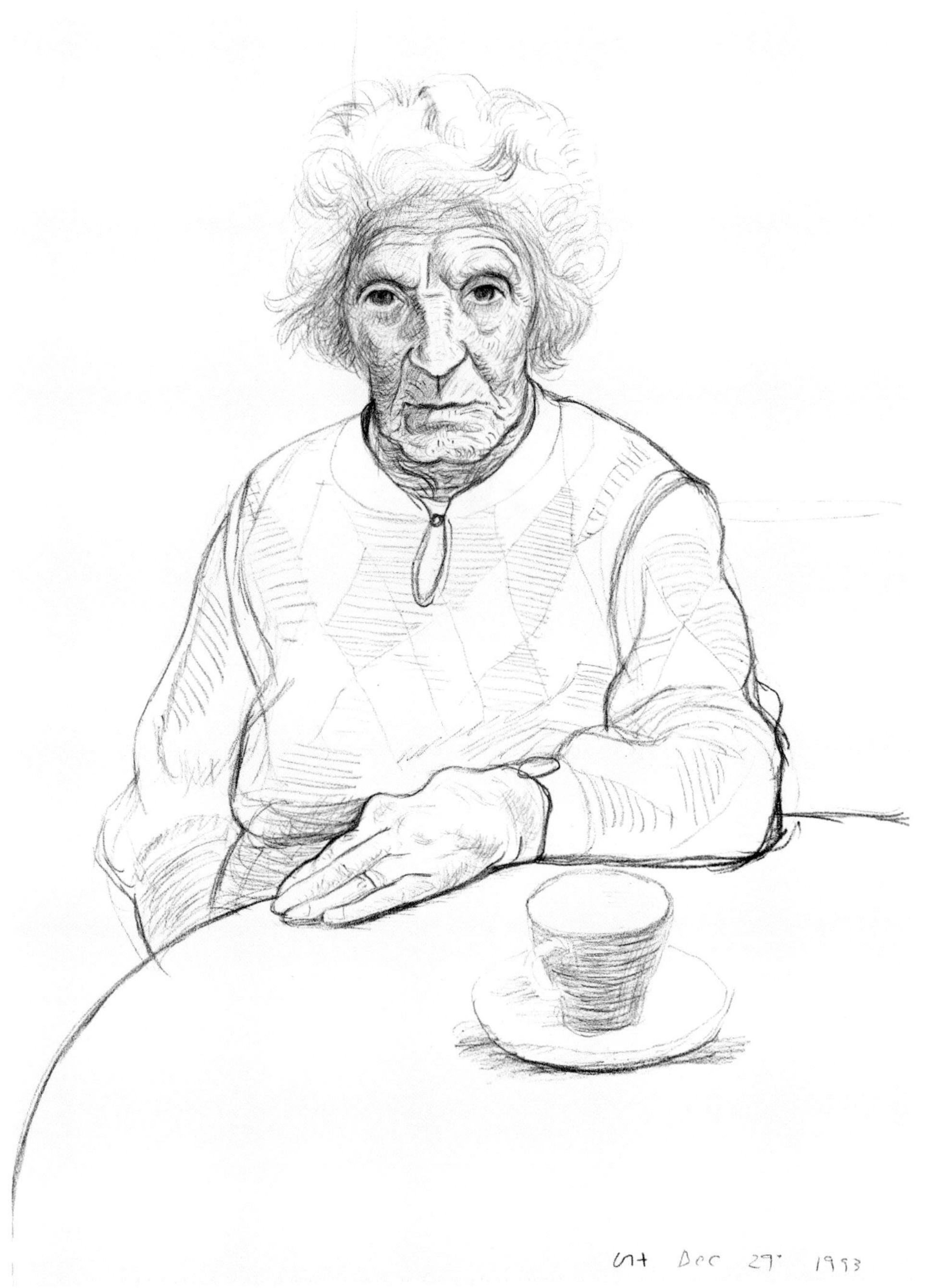

un Dec 29ᵗ 1993

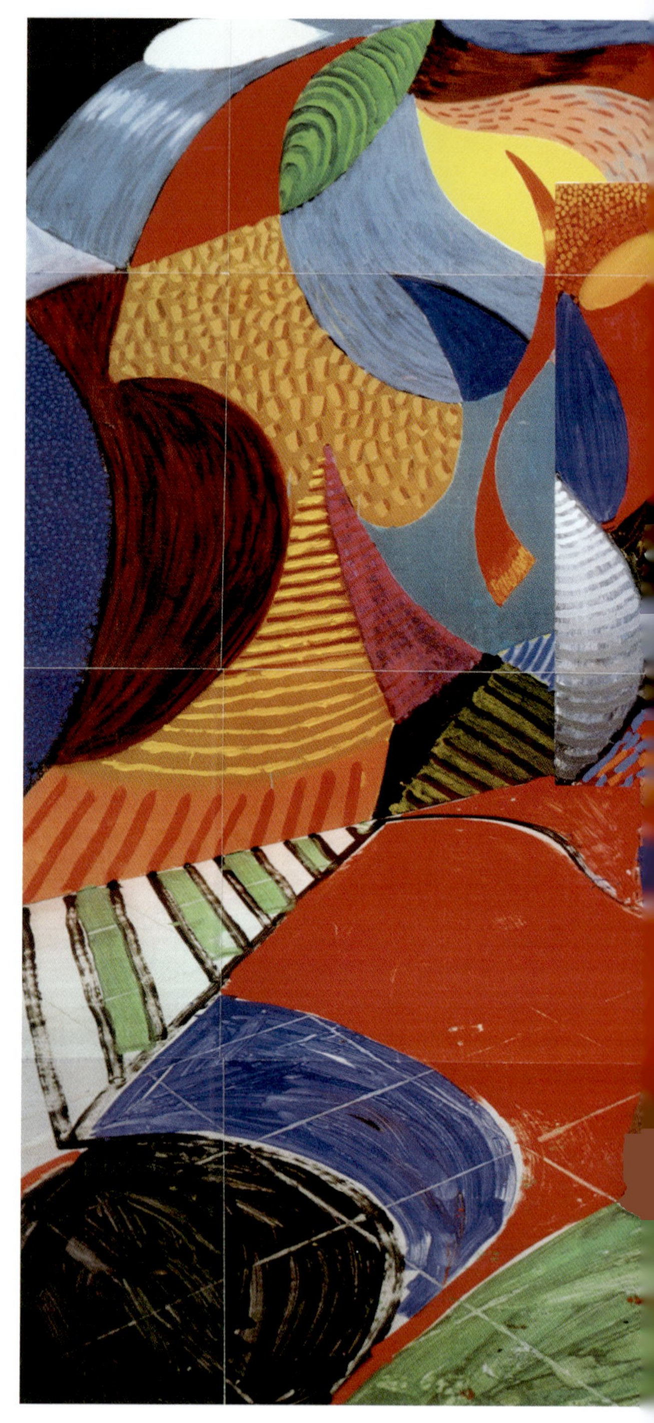

Painted Environment I, 1993, 16 color
laser-printed photographs mounted
on archival board, edition of 25,
36 $^{1}/_{4}$ x 44 $^{1}/_{4}$ in. / 92.1 x 112.4 cm

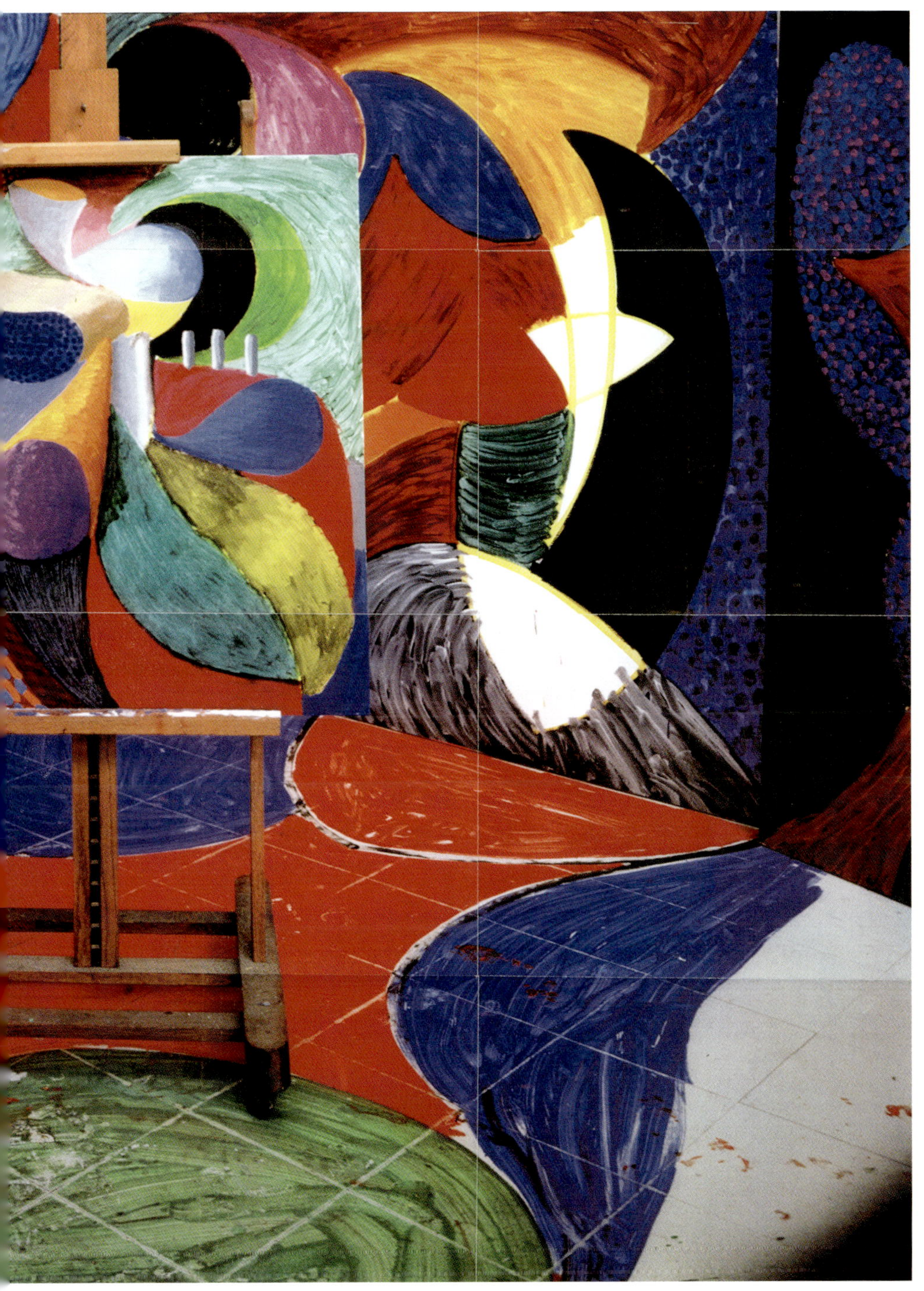

1994

Hockney continues with his large-format drawings of family members and friends, and more than 70 are on show in an exhibition in his friend Jonathan Silver's 1853 Gallery at Salts Mill near Bradford, *New Drawings,* subtitled *Some Drawings of Family, Friends and Best Friends* (pp. 315–317). The best friends are Hockney's two dachshunds, Stanley and Boodgie: "They had to be drawn rather quickly," he explains to the *Independent,* "and I had to make sure paper was all over the house and studio as to move away and get it meant the dogs moved as they always follow me." His human sitters have to bring a little more patience, as Silver, himself a frequent model, describes in his notes for the exhibition: "Being drawn by David is intense, exhausting, and very rewarding. He does not let you sit necessarily in a comfy position, asking you to position your eyes at an angle, or to turn your head to the side. To watch David drawing is equally exhausting—he seems to be in his own world of examination transcendentally in a passage of his own time and space—gazing at you with a penetration right into the centre of your soul. His face twists and turns, his eyes dart about and screw up, his whole body is acutely heightened in a dynamo of intense scrutiny. His lips move up and down like the sea, and often his tongue is out! Emerging from one of these sessions, usually about two hours, you feel as if there has been a union between artist and model—that union being transferred by crayon onto paper. The bigger the effort made in the union between the two of us, the stronger the picture. At the end I feel exhausted, simultaneously liberated." For the catalog to the exhibition, Hockney films details of the drawings with a video camera, treating the still images and printing them out on his laser printer as a way of reproduction.

In August, Hockney's close friend Henry Geldzahler dies from cancer, and the artist visits him during the last days. The sense of loss is great and shared with many; Geldzahler was an inspirational influence throughout the American art world, as his obituary in the *New York Times* describes: "An omnipresent figure on the social scene, he was a close friend of many artists, and his rotund, bearded figure made him a favorite subject of their work. Mr. Geldzahler was nearly as well known for a celebrated portrait of him and his friend Christopher Scott painted in 1969 by David Hockney as for any of his accomplishments; the painting, now owned by David Geffen, changed hands in late 1992 for $1.1 million. But Mr. Geldzahler was also painted by Larry Rivers, Alice Neel, and Frank

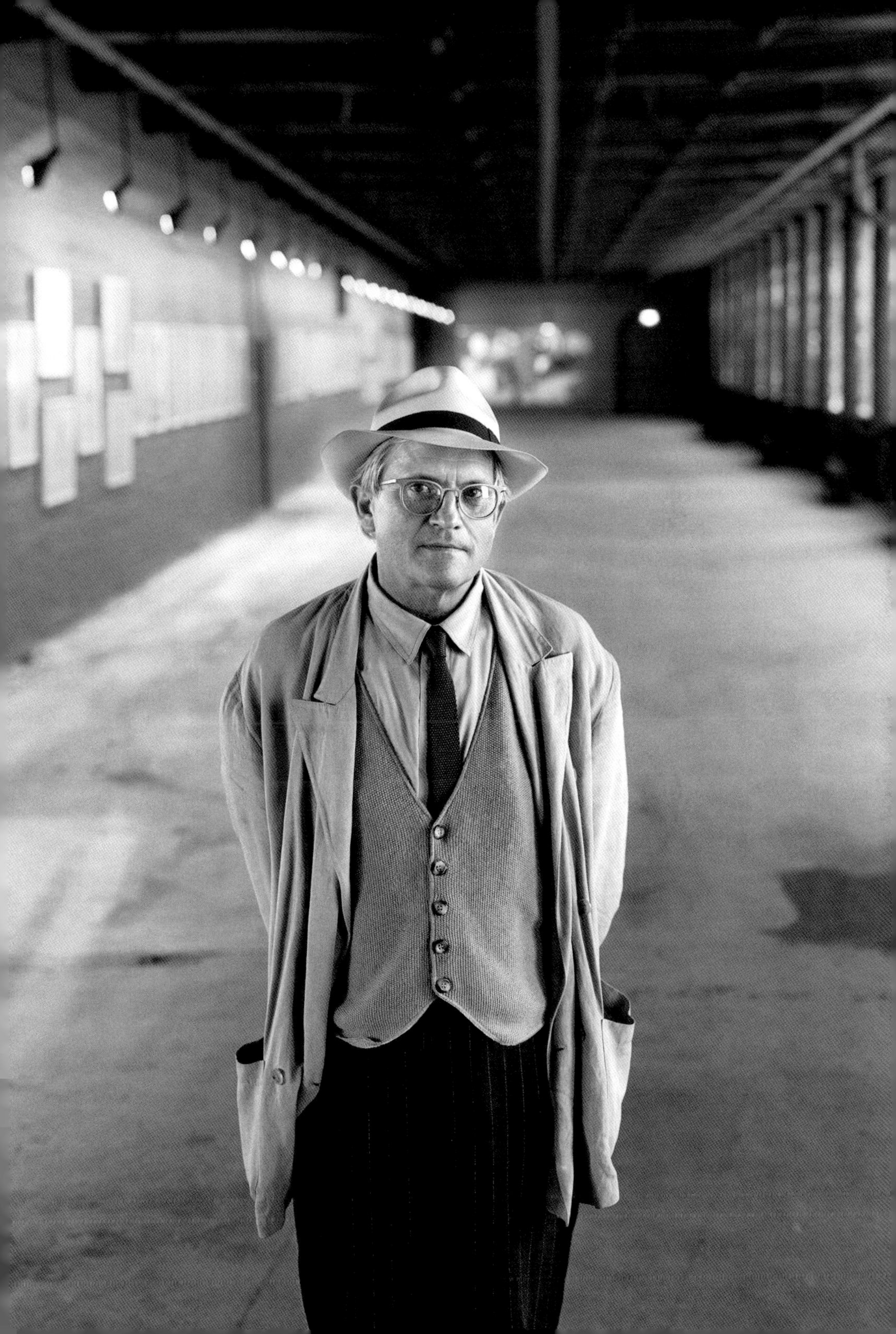

Stella, among others; he was also depicted in sculptures by Marisol and George Segal and featured as the centerpiece of 'happenings' staged by Claes Oldenburg. Andy Warhol, who once said, 'Henry gave me all of my ideas,' made a film consisting only of Mr. Geldzahler smoking a cigar for 90 minutes."

Hockney designs the settings for *Operalia 94,* Placido Domingo's opera competition for young talent, broadcast live from Mexico City in September: "I thought nobody is using colour well on TV," he tells Michael Church from the *Sunday Telegraph,* "and I think I've found a way of making it look wonderful, even though it's live. I've done so much videoing of paintings recently. I think it's worth going a stage further."

Solo: *Hockney in California,* Takashimaya Art Gallery, Tokyo (Apr 21–May 10); travels to Marugame Genichiro-Inokuma Museum of Contemporary Art, Kagawa (May 15–Jun 19); Koriyama City Museum of Art, Fukushima (Jun 25–Jul 24); and Chiba Sogo Museum of Art, Chiba (Jul 29–Aug 23); catalog. *25 Years of Printmaking,* Joy Tash Gallery, Scottsdale (Jan 20–Feb 29). *New Prints,* Richard Gray Gallery, Chicago (Jan 22–Feb 26). *Some New Paintings, Drawings, Prints and Gouaches 1989–1994,* L.A. Louver, Venice, CA (Mar 19–Apr 23). *David Hockney's Pools,* André Emmerich Gallery, New York (Apr 21–May 27). *New Drawings,* 1853 Gallery, Saltaire (Jun 28–Aug 19); catalog. *Some Even Newer Paintings (Being Gouache on Paper),* André Emmerich Gallery, New York (Sep 9–Oct 15). *Some More New Prints,* Gemini G.E.L., Los Angeles (opens Oct 24); catalog. *New Works,* Nishimura Gallery, Tokyo (Nov 8–Dec 10); catalog.

Group: *Out of Print: British Printmaking 1946–1976,* Musée du dessin et de l'estampe originale, Gravelines, (Jun 12–Sep 30); touring exhibition organized by the British Council, London, travels worldwide (through 2001); catalog. *Painting and Sculpture: Recent Acquisitions,* Museum of Modern Art, New York (Jun 16–Sep 11). *Hogarth and Hockney: The Rake's Progress,* The Art Institute of Chicago (Sep 10, 1994–Feb 5, 1995).

Publications: Paul Melia and Ulrich Luckhardt, *David Hockney,* Munich: Prestel. Kenneth E. Silver, *David Hockney,* New York: Rizzoli. *Off the Wall: Hockney Posters,* ed. by Brian Baggott, London: Pavilion Books.

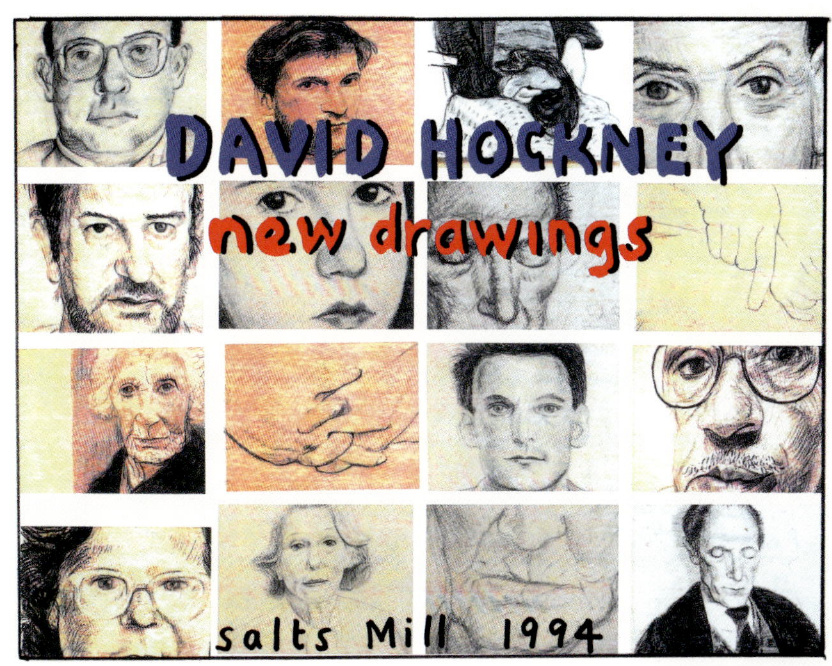

DAVID HOCKNEY
new drawings
salts Mill 1994

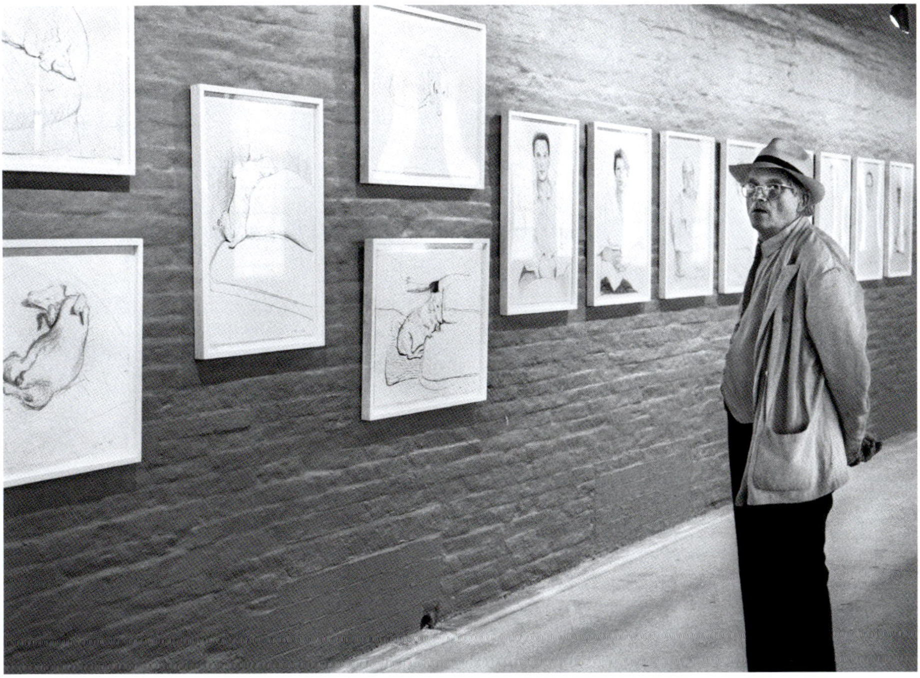

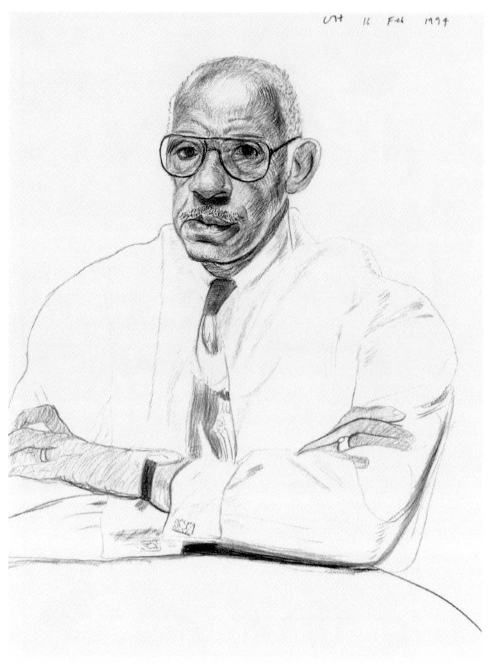

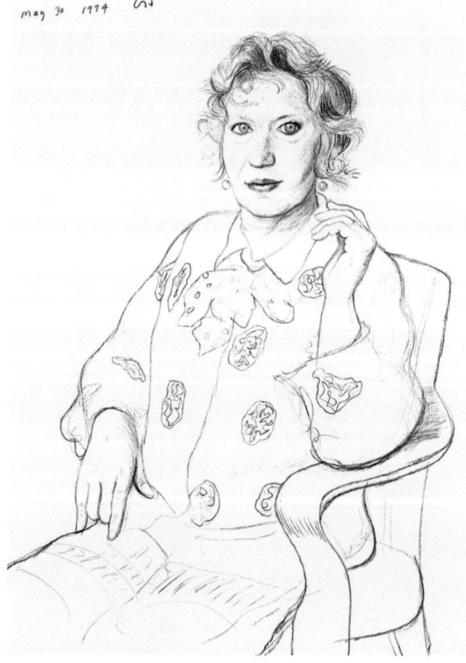

Dr. Leon Banks, 16 Feb 1994,
crayon on paper, 30 ¹/₄ x 22 ¹/₂ in. /
76.8 x 57.2 cm

Celia Birtwell, May 30 1994,
crayon on paper, 30 ¹/₄ x 22 ¹/₂ in. /
76.8 x 57.2 cm

Right page: *Mum, 10 March 1994,*
crayon on paper, 30 ¹/₄ x 22 ¹/₂ in. /
76.8 x 57.2 cm

Betty Freeman, Feb 1 1994,
crayon on paper, 30 ¹/₄ x 22 ¹/₂ in. /
76.8 x 57.2 cm

Dr. Wilbur Schwartz, 15 Feb 1994,
crayon on paper, 30 ¹/₄ x 22 ¹/₂ in. /
76.8 x 57.2 cm

Jonathon Brown, Jan 2nd 1994,
crayon on paper, 30 ¹/₄ x 22 ¹/₂ in. /
76.8 x 57.2 cm

Pages 313 and 315 bottom:
David Hockney at his exhibition
New Drawings, 1853 Gallery, Salts
Mill, Saltaire 1994. Photos: Craig
Easton

Page 315 top: *1853 Gallery Catalogue Cover,* 1994, color laser copy
of still movie video images with
gouache and Sharpie felt marker,
8 ¹/₂ x 11 in. / 21.6 x 27.9 cm

Page 318: *Gouache Drawing,* 1994,
gouache and Uni-paint marker on
paper, 22 ¹/₂ x 30 ¹/₄ in. /
57.2 x 76.8 cm

Gouache Drawing, 1994, gouache
and Uni-paint marker on paper,
22 ¹/₂ x 30 ¹/₄ in. / 57.2 x 76.8 cm

Page 319: *P.O.T.,* 1994, gouache
on 4 sheets of paper, 4 panels,
44 ¹/₂ x 60 ¹/₂ in. / 113 x 153.8 cm

P.E.T., 1994, gouache on 4 sheets
of paper, 4 panels, 44 ¹/₂ x 60 ¹/₂ in. /
113 x 153.8 cm

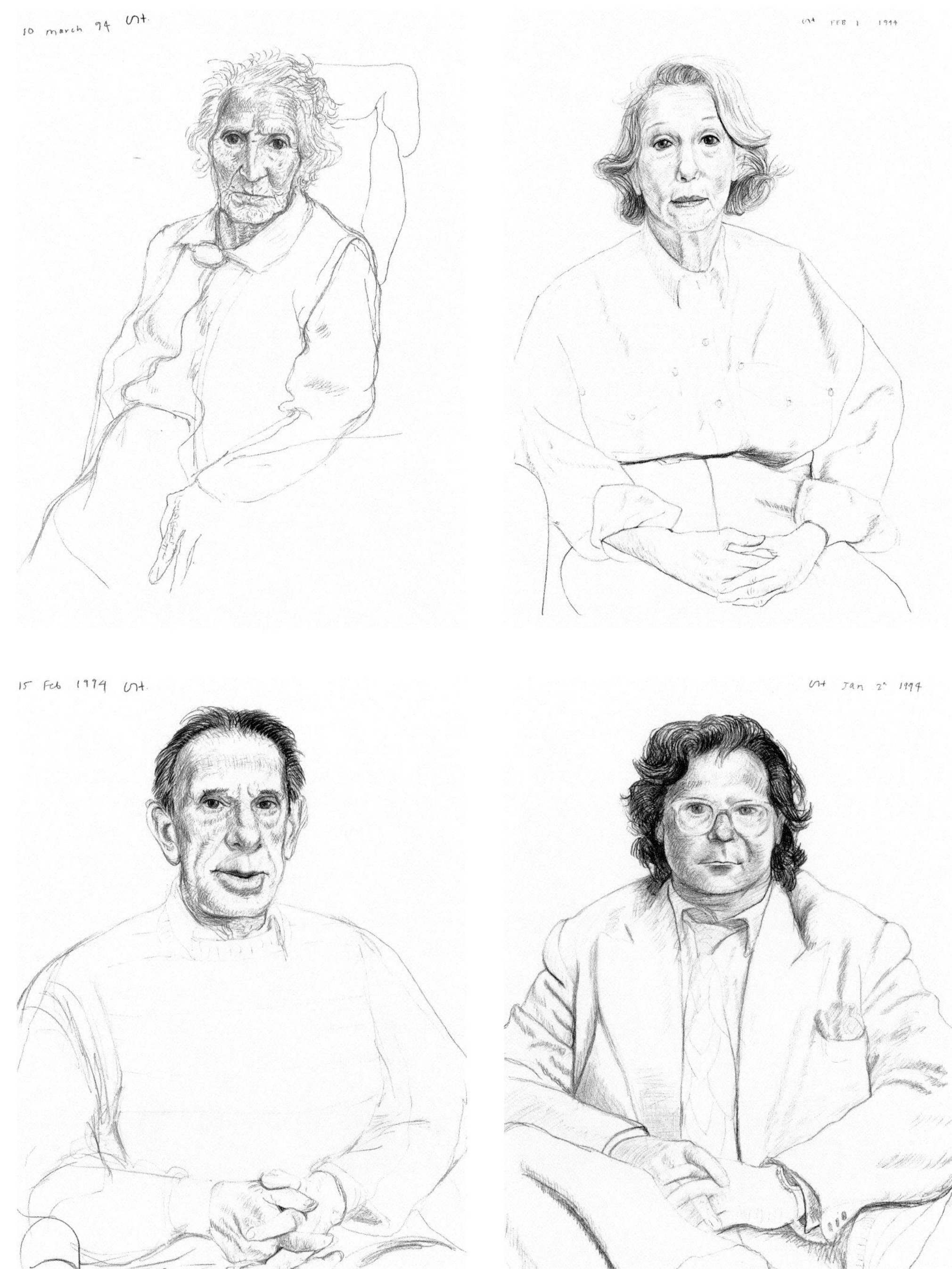

10 march 94 DH.
DH. FEB 1 1994
15 Feb 1994 DH.
DH Jan 2ⁿ 1994

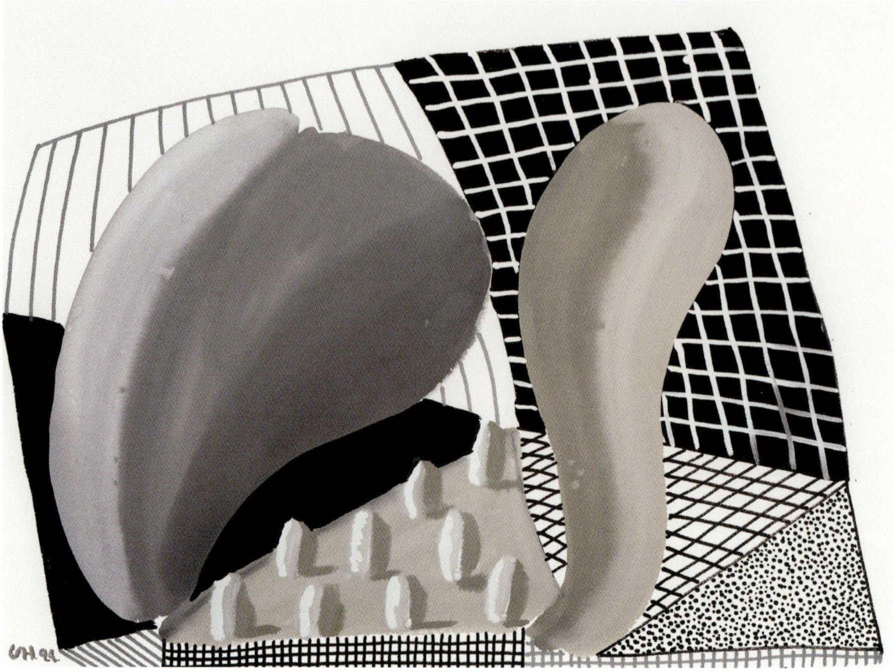

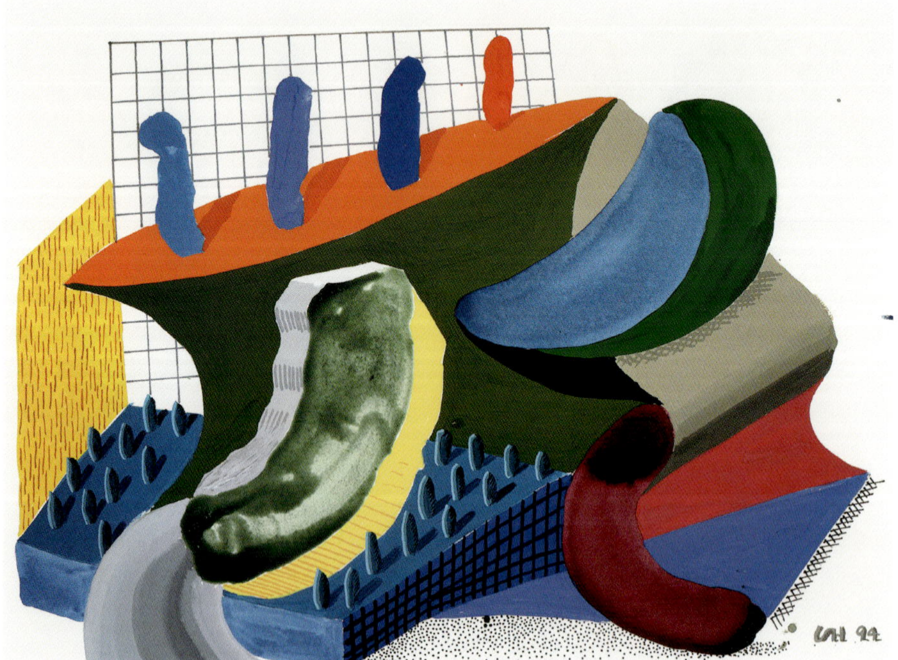

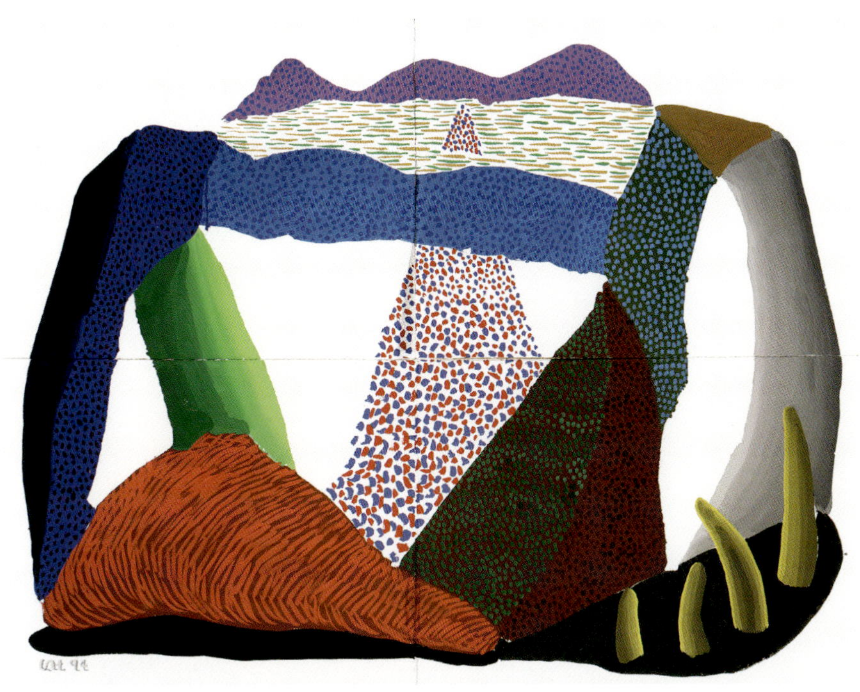

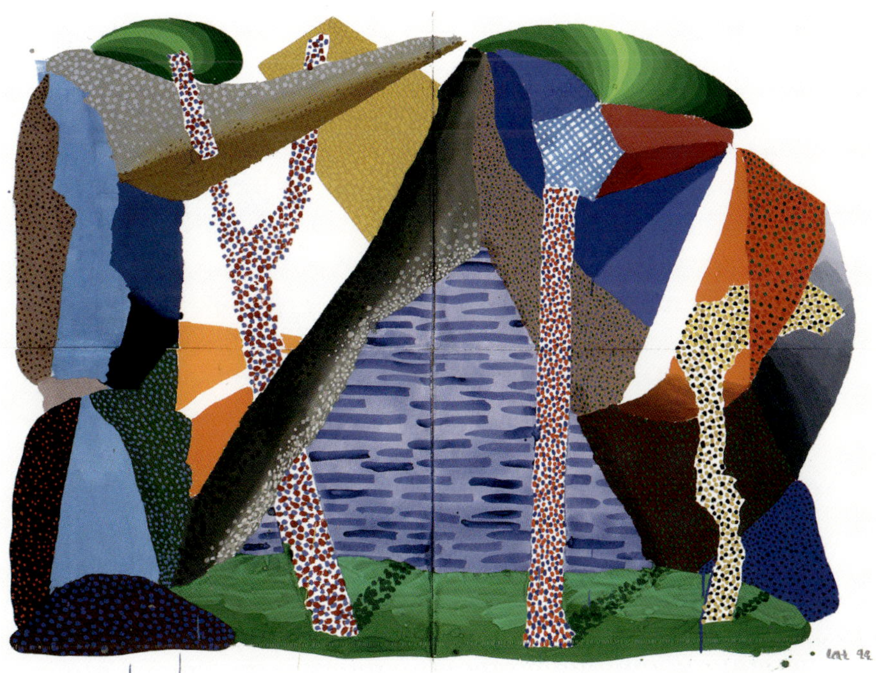

1995 Hockney is now painting several series at once. There are small canvases of simple still lifes that feature fruit or flowers, an exercise getting him back into figurative painting. There are pictures of his two dachshunds, Stanley and Boodgie, now painted in oil on canvas (pp. 328/329): "Beyond the dogs themselves, the true subject of these pictures is affection. For the first time I wanted to paint in what you might call a 'perceptive' way, putting on canvas what I saw. It was not so much their movements, but their deep natural nature. Somehow I really feel that their wisdom is perhaps greater than ours. Of course, the dogs don't know, aren't interested in what I am actually doing. Dogs can't be. And sometimes they pee on the canvases." Also, from his custom of photographing paintings in progress in the studio and making new graphic works out of the photos, Hockney develops a series of works called *Painting as Performance* (pp. 325–327)—taking up the idea of his *Painted Environments* of 1993 and putting them under changing lights. The artist explains the key work in the series: "*Snail's Space* changed quite a bit. The original painting is on two canvases measuring 84 by 240 inches, but I decided to continue the painting on the floor immediately in front of it, so we constructed a three-dimensional extension using real cubes, cones, and cylinders. Then I decided to experiment with computer-controlled lighting, the type they use at pop concerts, to physically change the appearance of colors within the painting. It demands a dark room to start with; we then arranged a computer program of subtle light changes lasting around eight minutes. I called it *Painting as Performance,* meaning if you put a sequence of lights on it, it is passing through time, which in turn means a performance. From when it begins to when it stops, it is theater and painting combined."

An exhibition in April at the L.A. Louver Gallery presents selections from all three work groups together with a good helping of drawings. Due to the technical demands *Snail's Space* is shown without the effects (that will only be realized in the following year), but William Wilson in his review for the *Los Angeles Times* still singles it out: "*Snail's Space* is a superbly realized painting for painting's sake, like a symphony that constantly reinvents its own harmonics. Measuring 7 by 20 feet, it is nearly the size of Picasso's 1937 *Guernica*, echoing that masterpiece's horizontal format. If Picasso was up to anything in that great painting, it was to prove that Cubism was capable of saying something about real life in a big

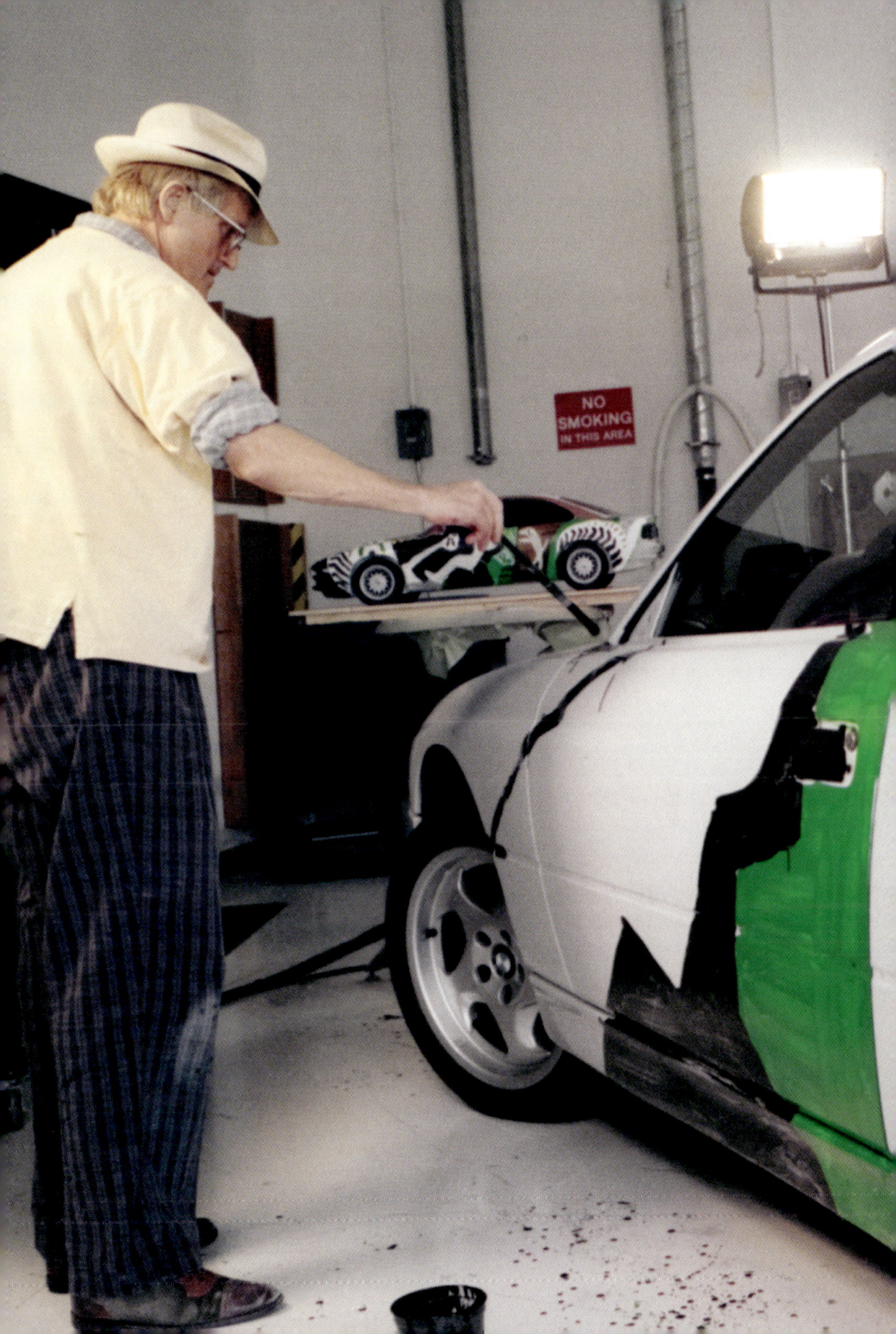

NO
SMOKING
IN THIS AREA

way. It's hard to avoid a hunch that Hockney, here, wants to demonstrate that Cubism still has something to say about real life. *Snail's Space* looks like an inner landscape, the artist's visualization of the path of life. If that's the case, then life, according to Hockney, is a tortured way full of curves that turn back on themselves, meaningless except in the beauty of its own absurdity. It takes great courage to admit to such a vision. But it can't be easy to live with." Also in April, Hockney finishes his work painting the BMW Art Car (p. 321), a project where the car manufacturer gives a model to a famous artist for a redesign. Hockney's painting opens up the frame of the car, showing elements of the engine on the hood, of a driver in the door, but also the green of the landscape one is crossing distributed all over the vehicle.

The Hamburger Kunsthalle presents a large retrospective of Hockney's drawings in August. It proves immensely popular for a contemporary drawings show with more than 40,000 visitors. Eduard Beaucamp in *Frankfurter Allgemeine Zeitung*: "The drawings are like diaries: they put us in the presence of Hockney's friends, of artists and writers, of his parents and collectors; they speak of love affairs, of travels to Egypt and Eastern Asia. Most of all they speak of life in California, where Hockney, fleeing Europe, found what his great forebears searched in Italy, what Matisse and Bonnard were looking for at the Côte d'Azur: the light, which rendered objects in full clearness, brightness of color, plasticity, a spacious landscape, and also a luxurious social meeting place. These are the ingredients of an art that enjoys itself as well as the world. This art cultivates an exuberant mixture of traditional, partly purposefully academic, and modernist forms that had lost their meaning and can now be filled with saucy new content, brimming with private topics and messages. Absolutist demands of the previous orthodoxy are answered with a proliferation of mixed forms, a play with the possibilities of looking at and making art, a separation of different artistic positions, and a strict denial of universal claims to validity." The exhibition then travels to the Royal Academy in London (and later to the Los Angeles County Museum of Art). William Feaver reviews the London leg of the show in the *Observer*: "Gaping studio interiors and panoramic abstractions are Hockney's current alternative to portraiture. They suggest a Land of Faraway, a refuge from life's unhappy aspects. Insouciant dachshunds may doze but the rest of Hockney's circle, subjected to his scrutiny, look understandably anxious. Hung in a group

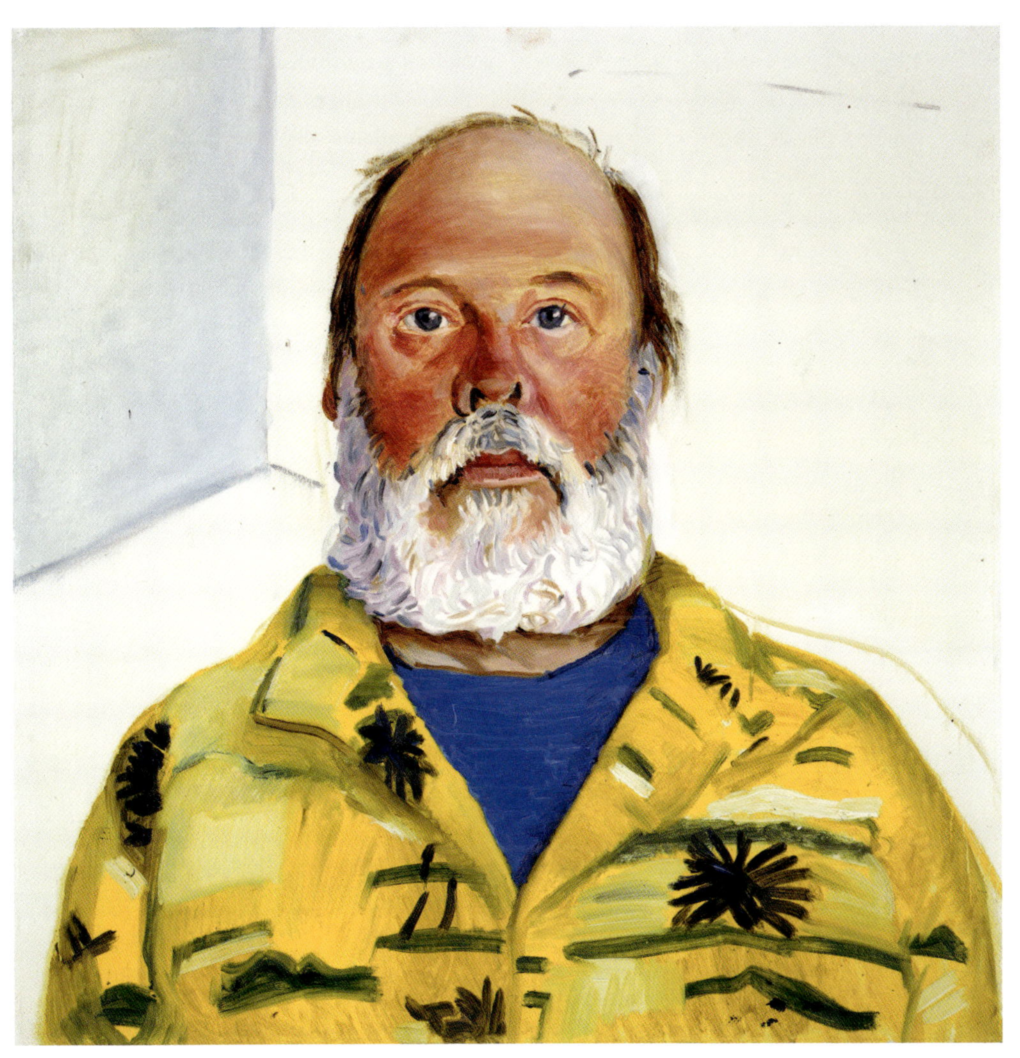

Henry, 1988, oil on canvas,
24 x 24 in. / 61 x 61 cm

Page 321: David Hockney painting the
BMW Art Car at Designworks, Newbury
Park 1995. Photo: Sidney B. Felsen

on one wall, some are dully drawn, some are cubistically squished candidates for the funny farm. But for most there is an undertone of apprehension. Hockney has no use for pathos; he's too canny for that…Drawing is good practice. It's the surest way of looking, the best way of paying attention, as direct a way as any of being poetic. Watching over his mother, now in her nineties, Hockney draws her. At the deathbed of Henry Geldzahler, one of his oldest friends, he draws. Such drawings aren't necessarily any the better for being valedictory, but they are timely, unadorned, and that's enough."

In autumn, Hockney visits a Monet retrospective at the Art Institute of Chicago, which hugely inspires him: "You don't need an art critic to tell you Monet was a great artist. You can see it yourself; you absolutely can. I came out of that exhibition and it made me look everywhere, everywhere intensely. That little shadow on Michigan Avenue, the light hitting the leaf. I thought: 'My god, now I've seen that. He's made me see it.' Most people don't see things like that. They can't get pleasure like that, can they? Monet gives it to you though, for he was a generous spirit, and you can then take pleasure in looking at things freshly…"

Solo: *Mr. and Mrs. Clark and Percy,* Brighton Museum and Art Gallery, Brighton (Mar 28–May 14); travels to Birmingham Museum and Art Gallery, Birmingham (May 20–Jul 2) and Manchester City Art Galleries, Manchester (Jul 8–Sep 3); catalog. *Zeichnungen 1954–1994 / A Drawing Retrospective,* Hamburger Kunsthalle, Hamburg (Aug 22–Oct 22); travels to Royal Academy of Arts, London (Nov 7, 1995–Jan 28, 1996) and LA County Museum of Art, Los Angeles (Feb 15, 1995–Apr 28, 1996); catalog with texts by Ulrich Luckhardt and Paul Melia. *David Hockney,* Alan Cristea Gallery, London (Jan 11–Feb 11). *Some Large New Paintings and Twenty-Five Dogs Upstairs,* L.A. Louver, Venice, CA (Apr 7–May 6); catalog. *David Hockney,* Nishimura Gallery, Tokyo (Apr 24–May 20). *David Hockney,* 1853 Gallery, Saltaire (Jun 26–Oct 1). *David Hockney,* Gemini G.E.L. at Joni Moisant Weyl, New York (Sep 14–Oct 31).

Group: *Art Works: The PaineWebber Collection of Contemporary Masters,* Museum of Fine Arts, Houston (Jun 2–Sep 24); travels to Detroit, Boston, Minneapolis, San Diego, and Miami (through 1997); catalog. *46th International Art Exhibition La Biennale di Venezia,* Venice (Jun 11–Oct 15); catalog. *Unser Jahrhundert: Menschenbilder, Bilderwelten,* Museum Ludwig, Cologne (Jul 9–Oct 8); catalog. *Pierrot: Melancholie und Maske,* Haus der Kunst, Munich (Sep 15–Dec 3); catalog.

Publications: Peter Clothier, *Modern Masters: David Hockney,* New York: Abbeville Press. Paul Melia (ed.), *David Hockney: Critical Introductions to Art,* with texts by Nannette Aldred, Andrew Causey, Simon Faulkner, William Hardie, and Alan Woods, Manchester: Manchester University Press.

Honor: Honorary Doctorate, University of Oxford.

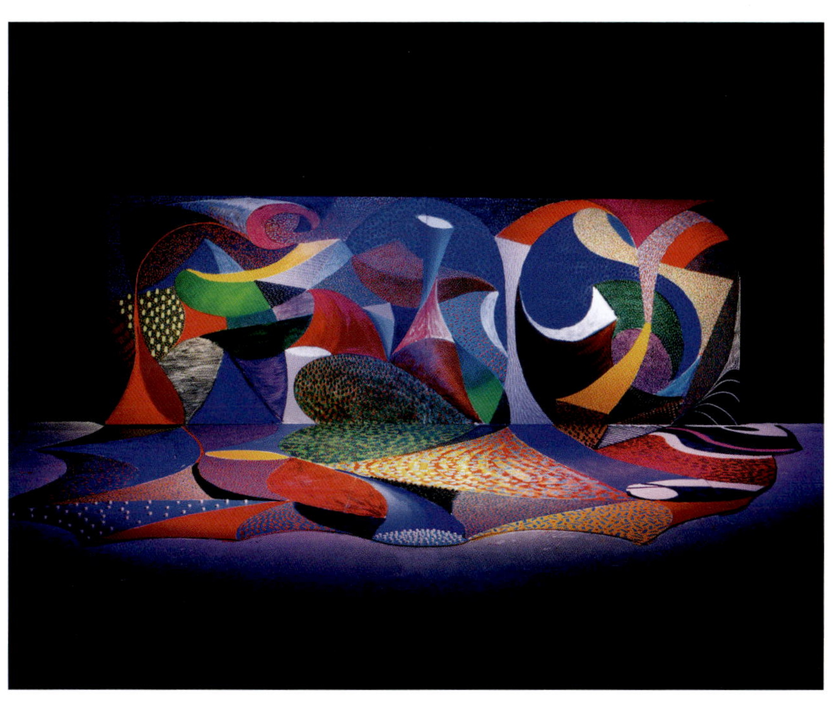

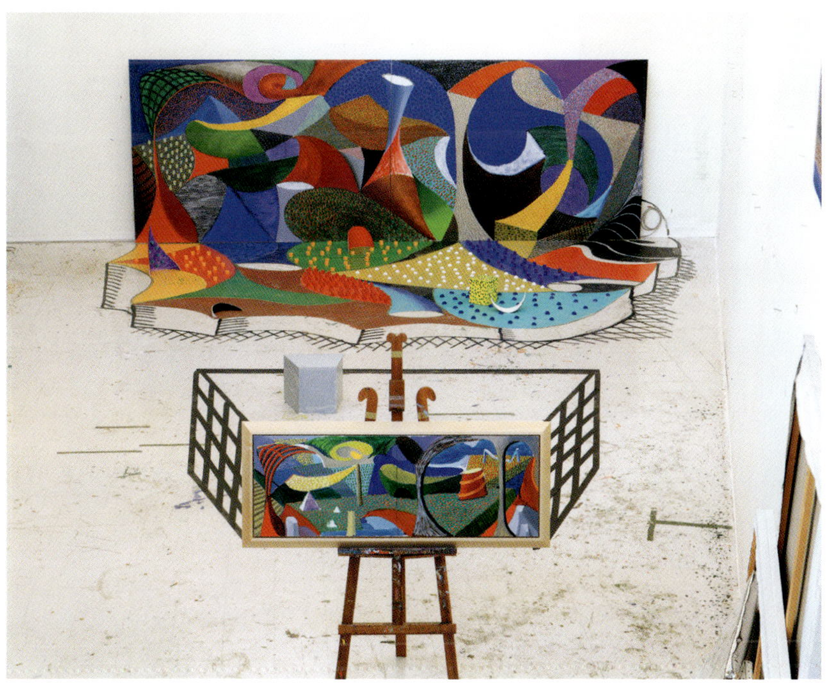

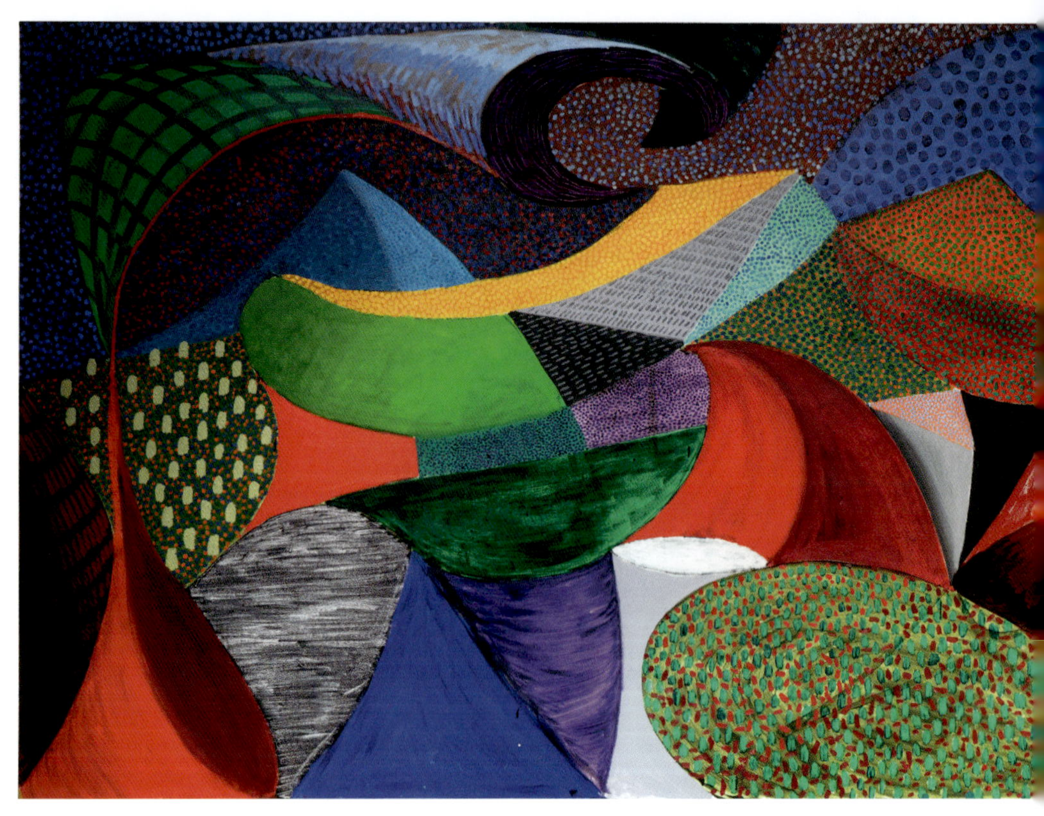

Snail's Space with Vari-Lites, "Painting as Performance," 1995–1996, oil on 2 canvases, acrylic on canvas-covered masonite, wood dowels, 84 ¼ x 264 x 135 in. / 214 x 670.6 x 343 cm, permanent installation, Smithsonian American Art Museum, Washington, DC

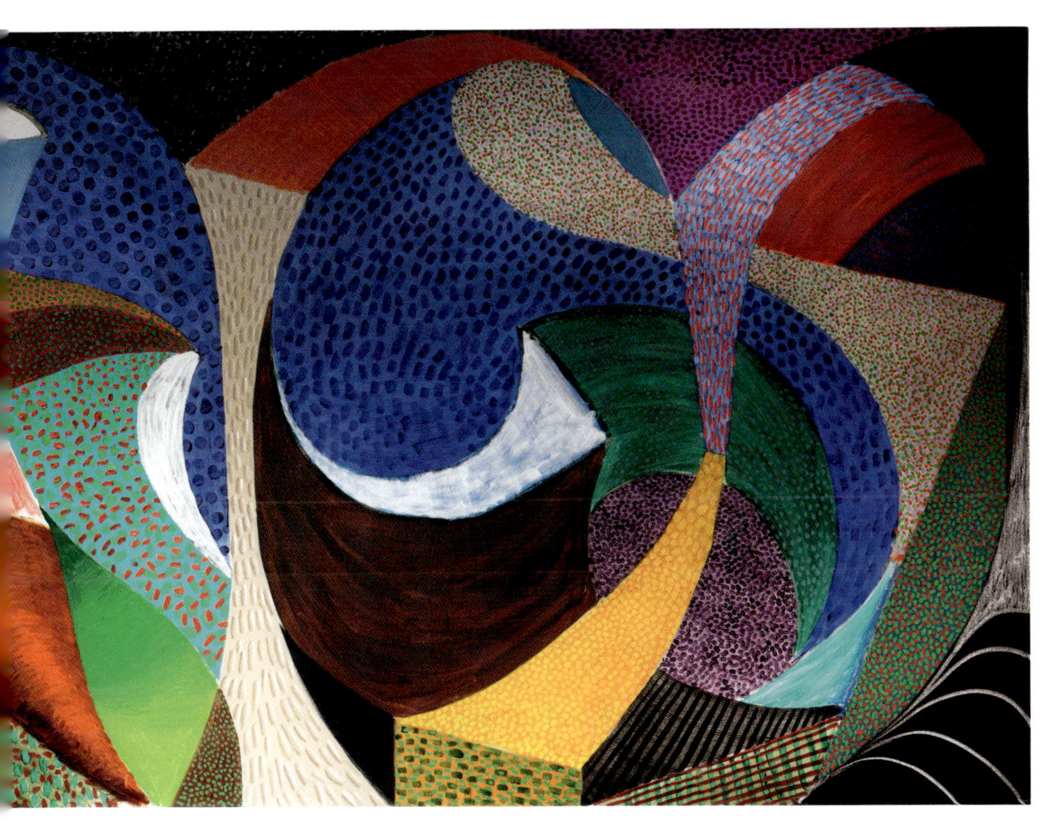

Page 325: *Snail's Space,* 1995, oil on 2 canvases, 84 x 240 in. / 213.4 x 609.6 cm

The studio, Los Angeles, March 29, 1995

Pages 328/329: David Hockney in his studio, Los Angeles, March 1995

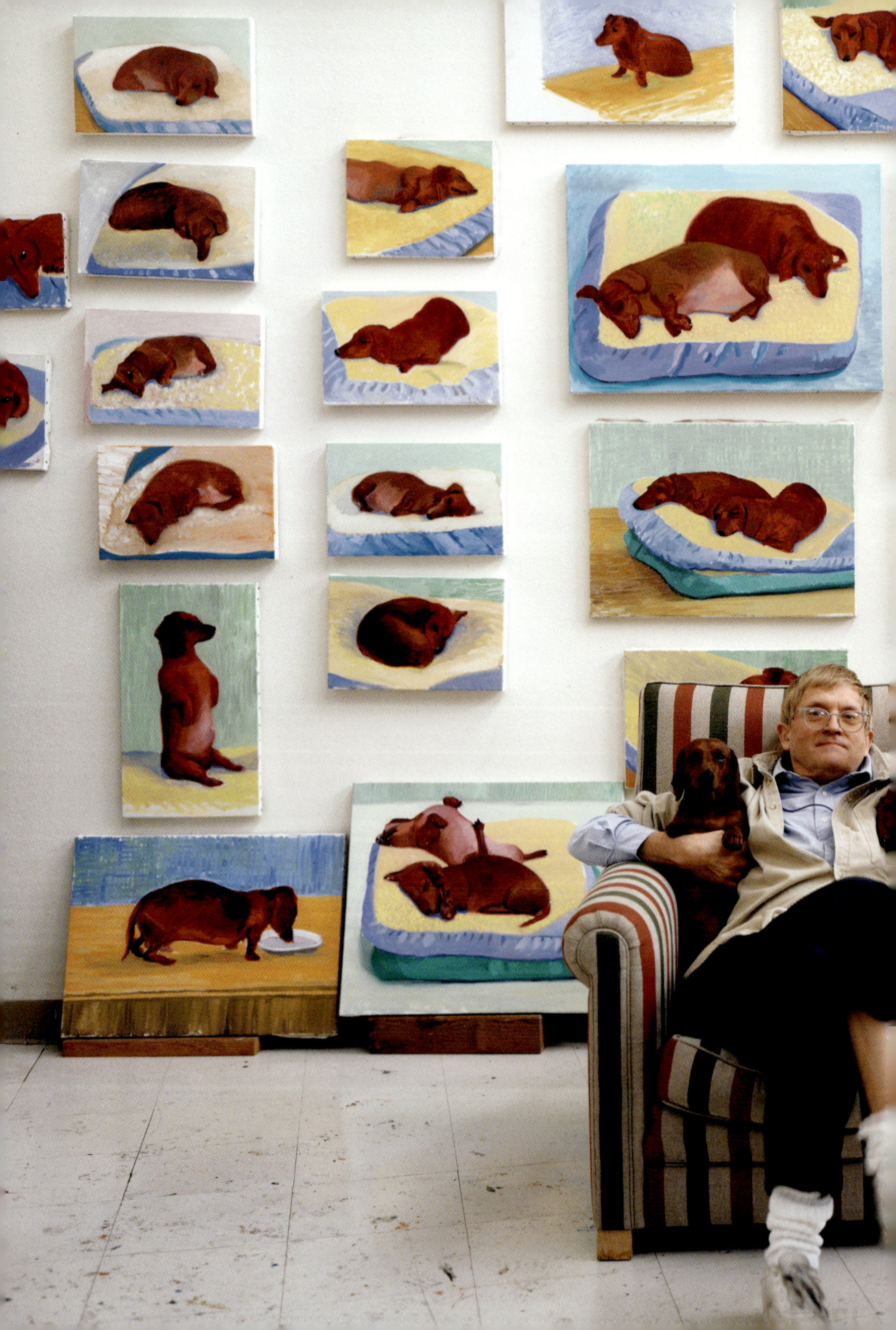

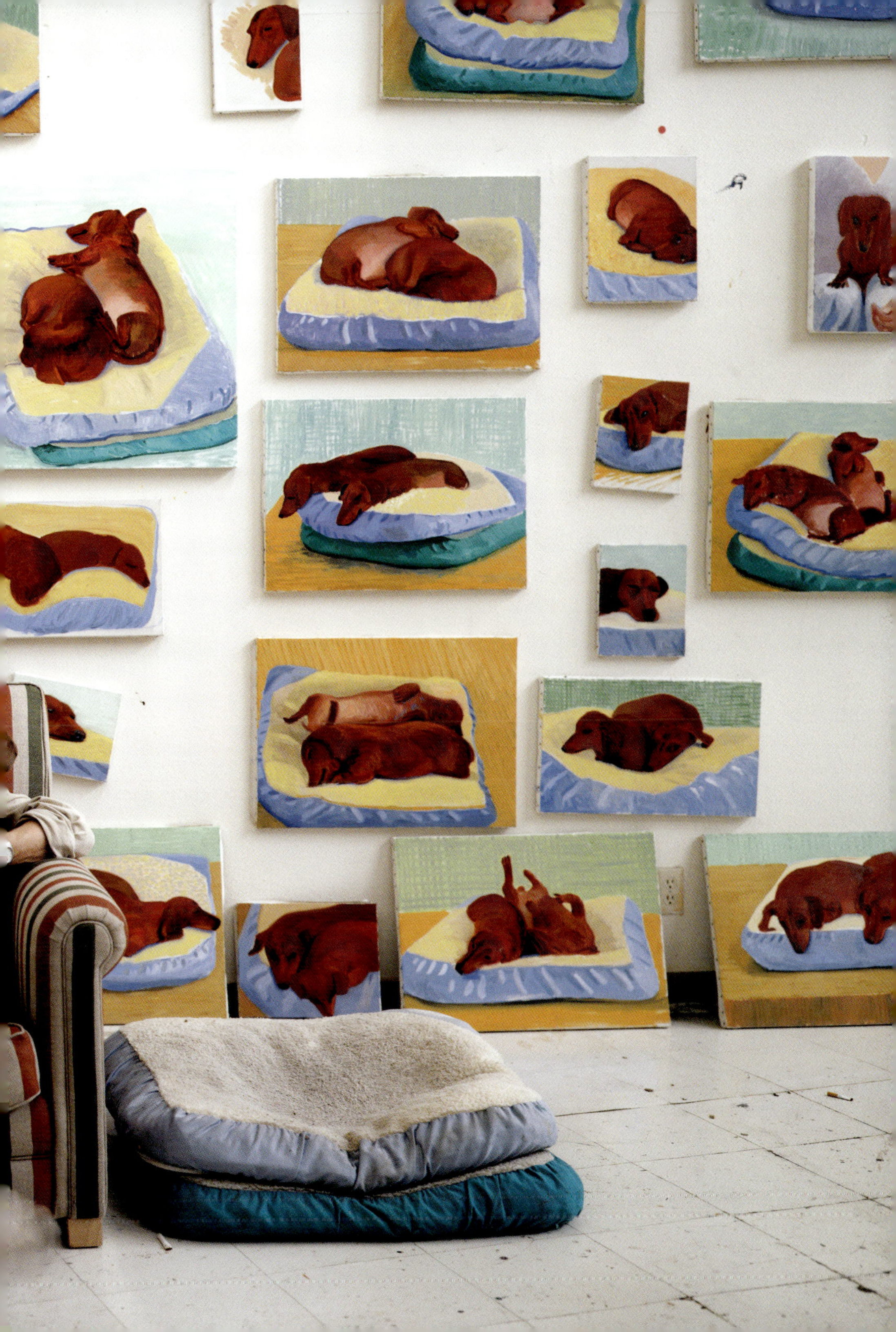

1996

While visiting Holland in spring, Hockney sees a Vermeer retrospective at the Mauritshuis in The Hague and draws huge inspiration from the Dutch painter's work, which he applies to a series of still lifes (pp. 334–337): "What so impressed me about the Vermeers was the condition and the vibrancy of the color. Every other picture in that museum looked dull in comparison. How can these paintings glow like this! He put the paint on so carefully, in transparent layers so you get those vibrant blues. Stunning…I've learned a lot about transparent glazes in oil painting over the years; I've made it my business to. Seeing how Vermeer handled the paint, and beyond that how he controlled the light on to his subjects, sent me back into the studio with tremendous energy. In fact, I decided the best place to paint the flower studies was the far end of the studio, at the top of the stairs, just outside the loo. It might seem a bit peculiar, but that was where the north light came down in just the correct way, at a certain time of day…It's terrific when I really get painting: squeezing the paint out and using it so it doesn't even have time to get a skin on it; working in the evenings where I'll set something up; and then continuing on it first thing in the morning. And as soon as I get going, I develop. I'm never short of what to do. Just give me enough time and I'll work it out."

The portraits of this time (pp. 331, 333) look markedly somber, reflecting not just the sitter, but mostly the artist's mood—Hockney has separated from John Fitzherbert, while his mother is recovering from an operation, Jonathan Silver is suffering from cancer, and many friends have died, the latest being Ossie Clark, murdered by a former lover. "Those portraits were painful to me," he later tells Lawrence Weschler, including his self-portraits: "When I looked at myself, I just saw pain in my face. Some people said, 'It didn't even look like you.' And I thought, 'Oh, you've no idea what I look like when I'm on my own looking in a mirror. You've no idea what I see.'"

In November, a Hockney retrospective goes on view in Manchester City Art Gallery, titled *You Make the Picture.* Reviews are very mixed, with Andrew Graham-Dixon in the *Independent* stating that "Hockney was a more interesting artist when he thought less about the nature of representation and more about sex," whereas John Russell Taylor in the *Times* sees a more consistent development: "If this has the air of an arbitrary progression, the sense of it becomes apparent as you walk round the show. Even at a glance the pictures give so much

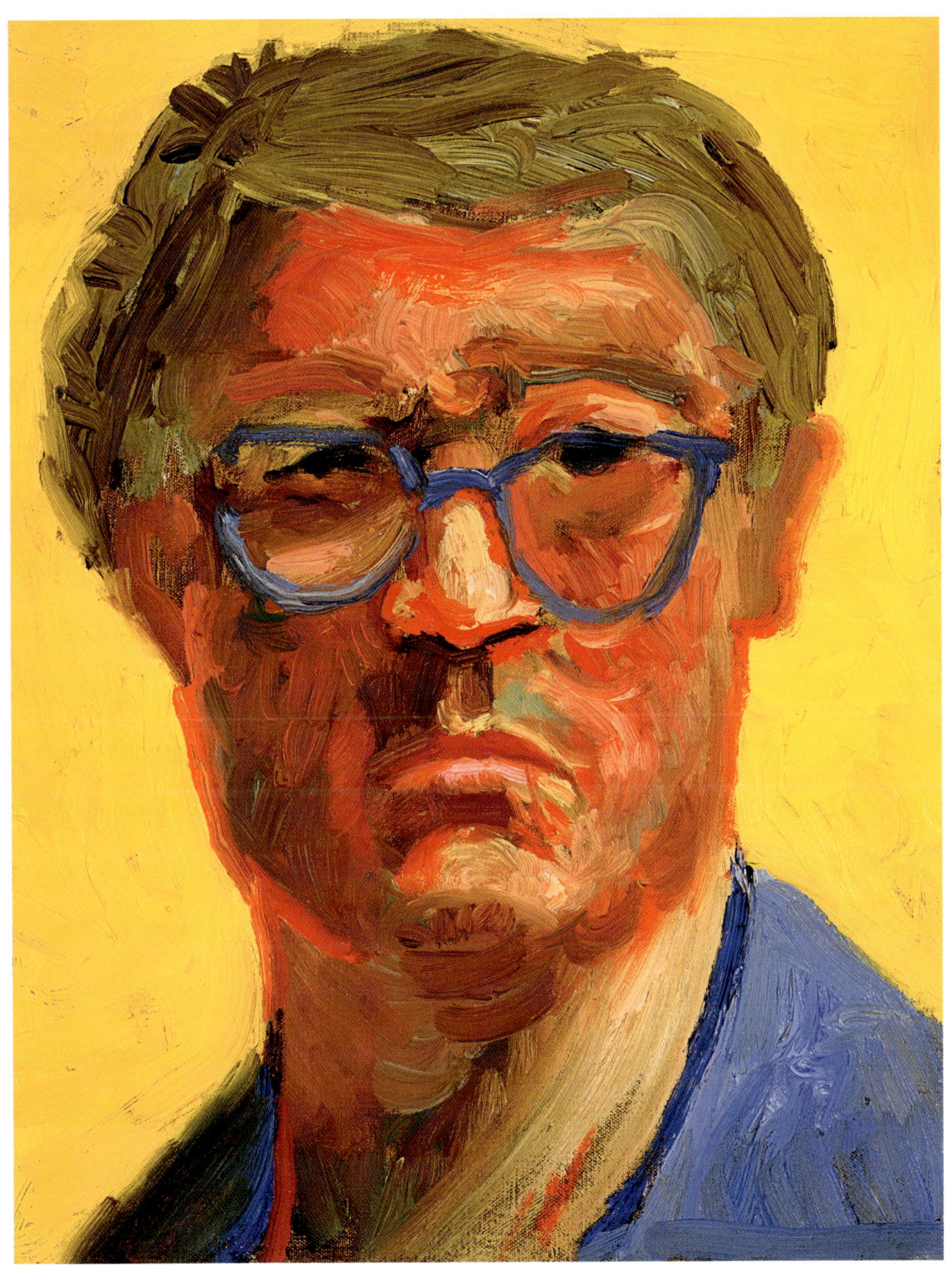

sensuous pleasure that the suspicion immediately arises that there is something in Hockney that gets up the nose of ingrained English puritanism. But if so, the puritans are oddly unobservant, for whatever Hockney's image as a hedonist, his development is deeply thought-out. Everything in this show demonstrates the rigorous logic and consistency in what he does. It starts with the photocollages because it was through them that he came to question the whole Western convention of perspective and pictorial space…Hockney is as much a conceptual artist as any who claim loudly to be so. It is just that he sees before he thinks, and what he thinks is always at the service of what he sees."

Solo: *Paintings and Photographs of Paintings,* Kunsthaus Wien, Vienna (Feb 8–Apr 14). *The Prints of David Hockney,* Center for Contemporary Graphic Art, Tokyo (Apr 20–Jun 2). *A Print Retrospective 1954–1995,* Museum of Contemporary Art, Tokyo (Oct 9–Dec 15); catalog with texts by Takeshi Sakurai and Hideyuki Kido. *You Make the Picture: Paintings and Prints 1982–1995,* Manchester City Art Galleries, Manchester (Nov 15, 1996–Feb 2, 1997); catalog with a text by Paul Melia. *Selected Drawings,* L.A. Louver, Venice, CA (Feb 16–Mar 16). *David Hockney,* Nishimura Gallery, Tokyo (Mar 5–23). *Painting as Performance,* André Emmerich Gallery, New York (May 7–Jun 15). *Paintings and Photographs of Paintings,* Robert Miller Gallery, New York (May 7–Jun 15). *David Hockney,* L.A. Louver, Venice, CA (May 11–Jun 8). *David Hockney,* Alan Cristea Gallery, London (Oct 23–Dec 1). *Important Works,* Galerie Berndt, Cologne (Nov 8, 1996–Feb 1997).

Group: *Thinking Print: Books to Billboards, 1980–1995,* Museum of Modern Art, New York (Jun 19–Sep 10); catalog. *Les Sixties, années utopies,* Musée d'histoire contemporaine, Paris (Oct 25–Dec 29); travels to Brighton Museum, Brighton; catalog. *A Marriage of Styles: British Art in the Fifties and Sixties,* National Gallery of Victoria, Melbourne (Dec 13, 1996–Jan 27, 1997); catalog.

Publications: *David Hockney: 20 Photographs,* Los Angeles: David Hockney Studio. Marco Livingstone, *David Hockney,* London: Thames and Hudson.

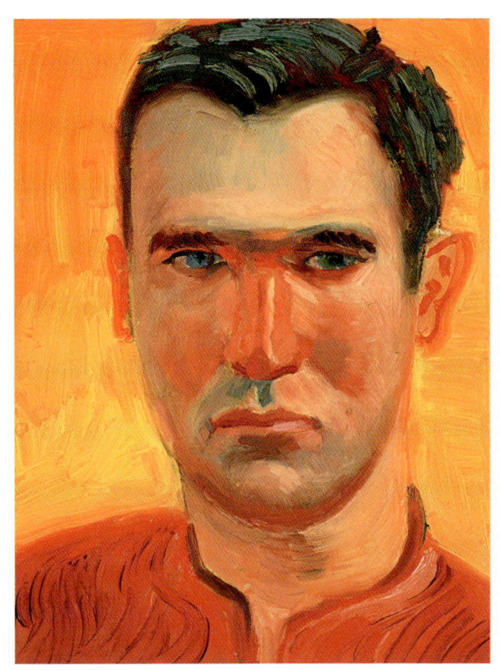

Michael Smith, December 10, 1996, oil on canvas, 13 ³/₄ x 10 ³/₄ in. / 34.9 x 27.3 cm

Maurice Payne, December 10, 1996, oil on canvas, 13 ³/₄ x 10 ³/₄ in. / 34.9 x 27.3 cm

Mum, December 29, 1996 from *Portrait Wall*, 1996–1997, oil on canvas, 13 ³/₄ x 10 ¹/₂ in. / 34.9 x 26.7 cm

Page 331: *Self Portrait, November 1996,* oil on canvas, 13 ³/₄ x 10 ³/₄ in. / 34.9 x 27.3 cm

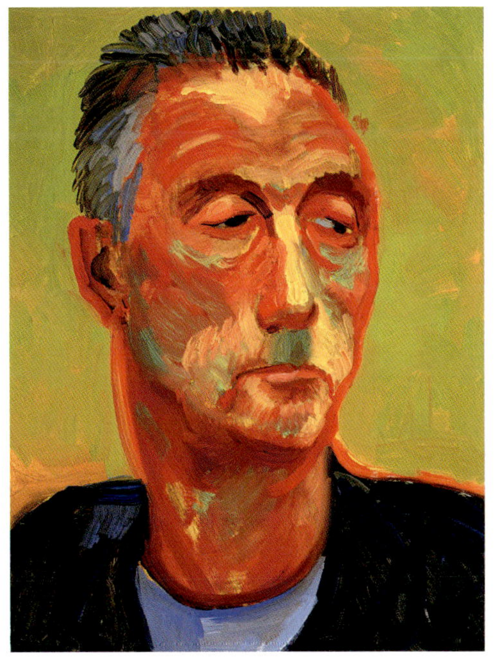

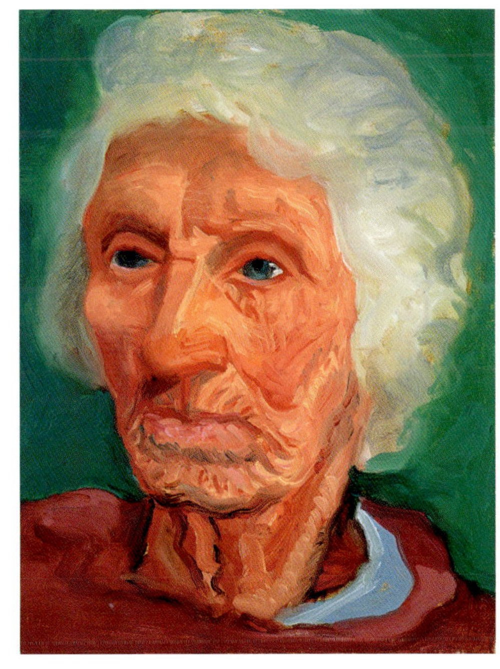

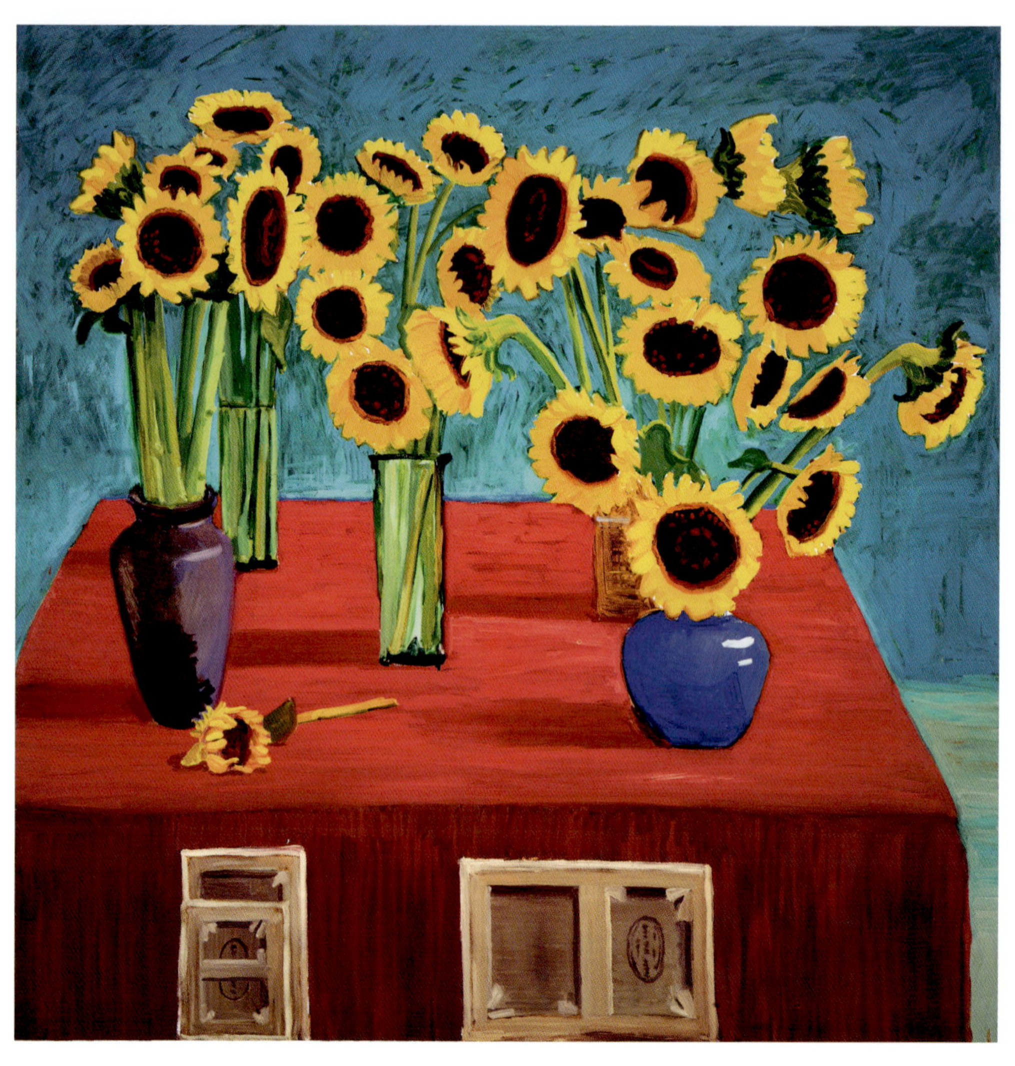

30 Sunflowers, 1996, oil on canvas,
72 x 72 in. / 182.9 x 182.9 cm

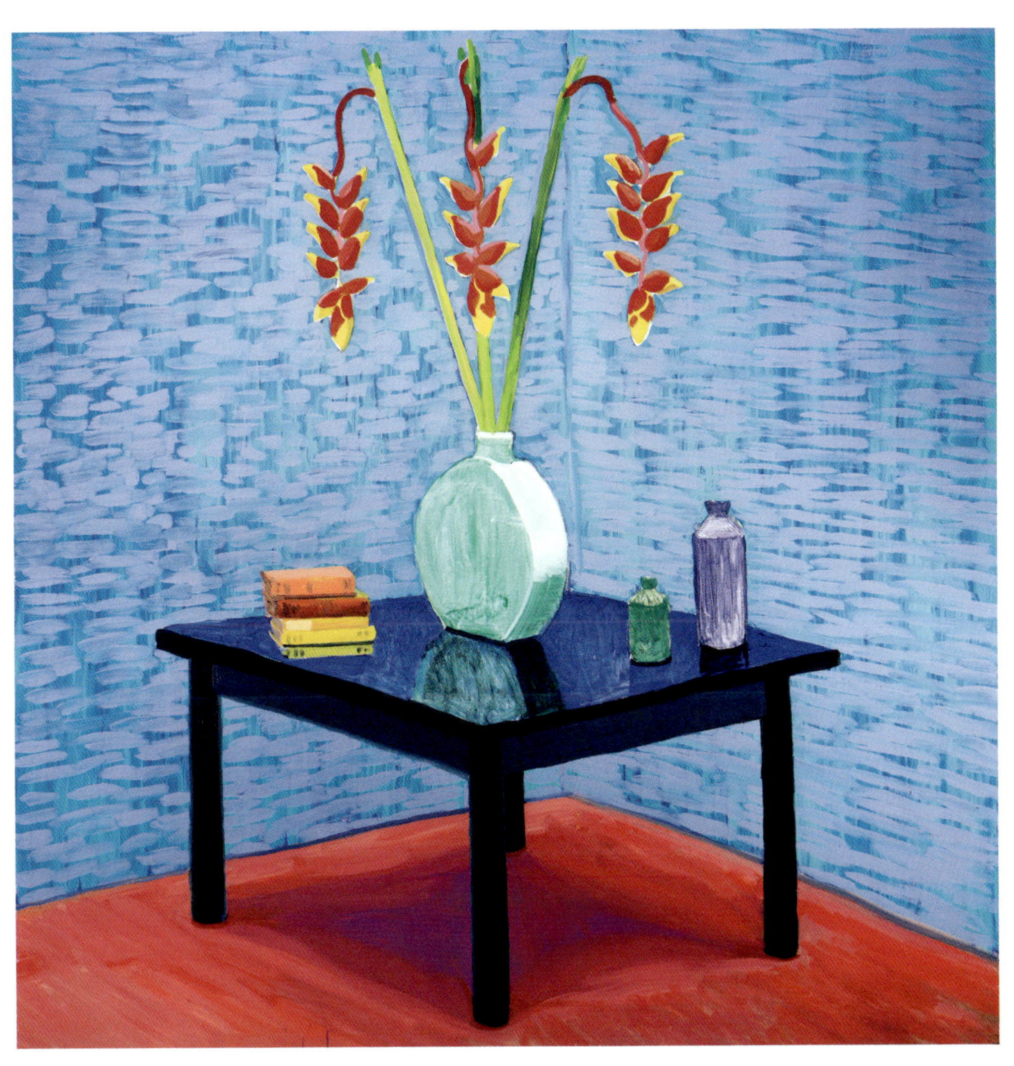

Halaconia in Green Vase, 1996,
oil on canvas, 72 x 72 in. /
182.9 x 182.9 cm

Pages 336/337: *White Lilies and
Orchid* (center) at David Hockney's
studio, Los Angeles 1996

1996 | 335

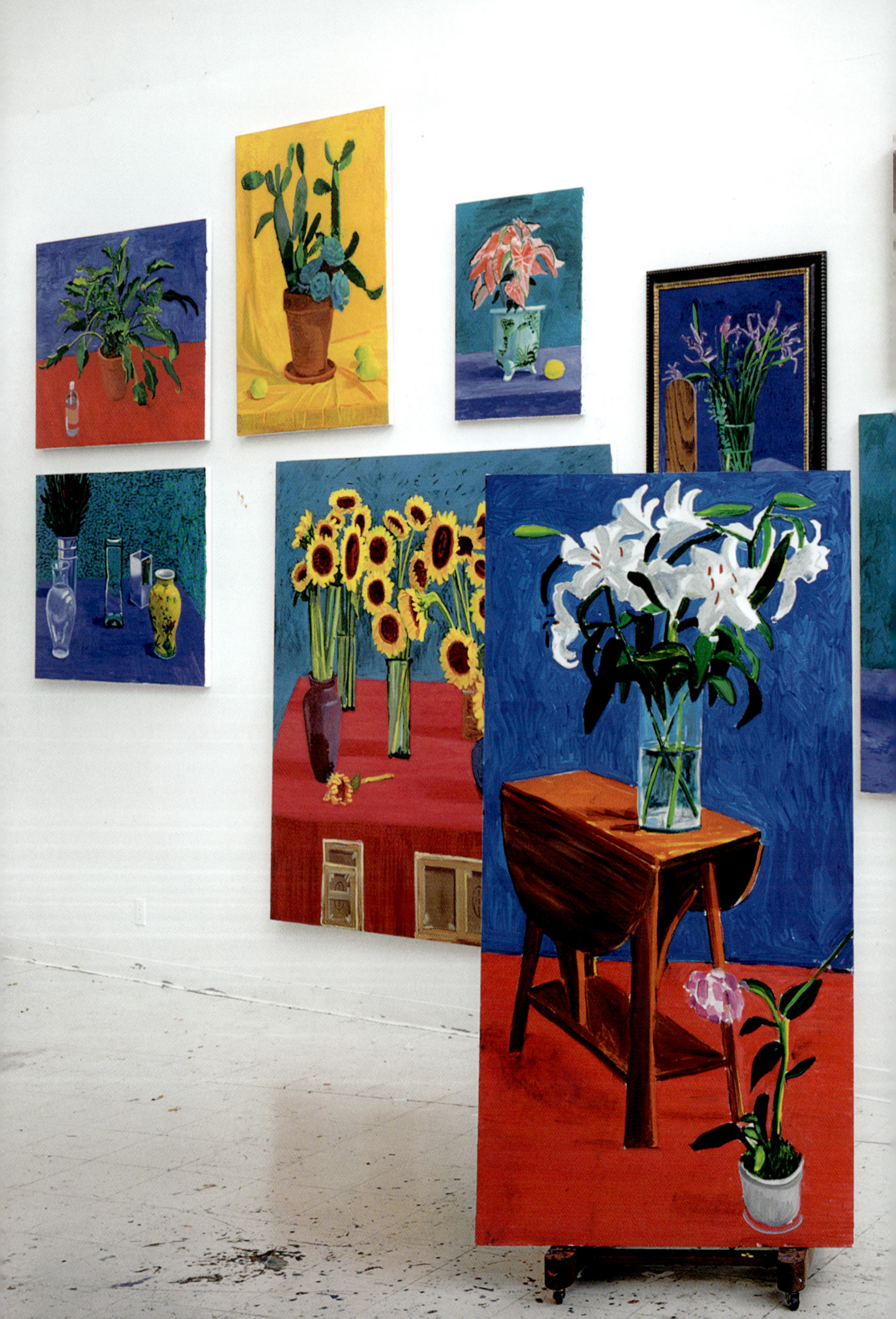

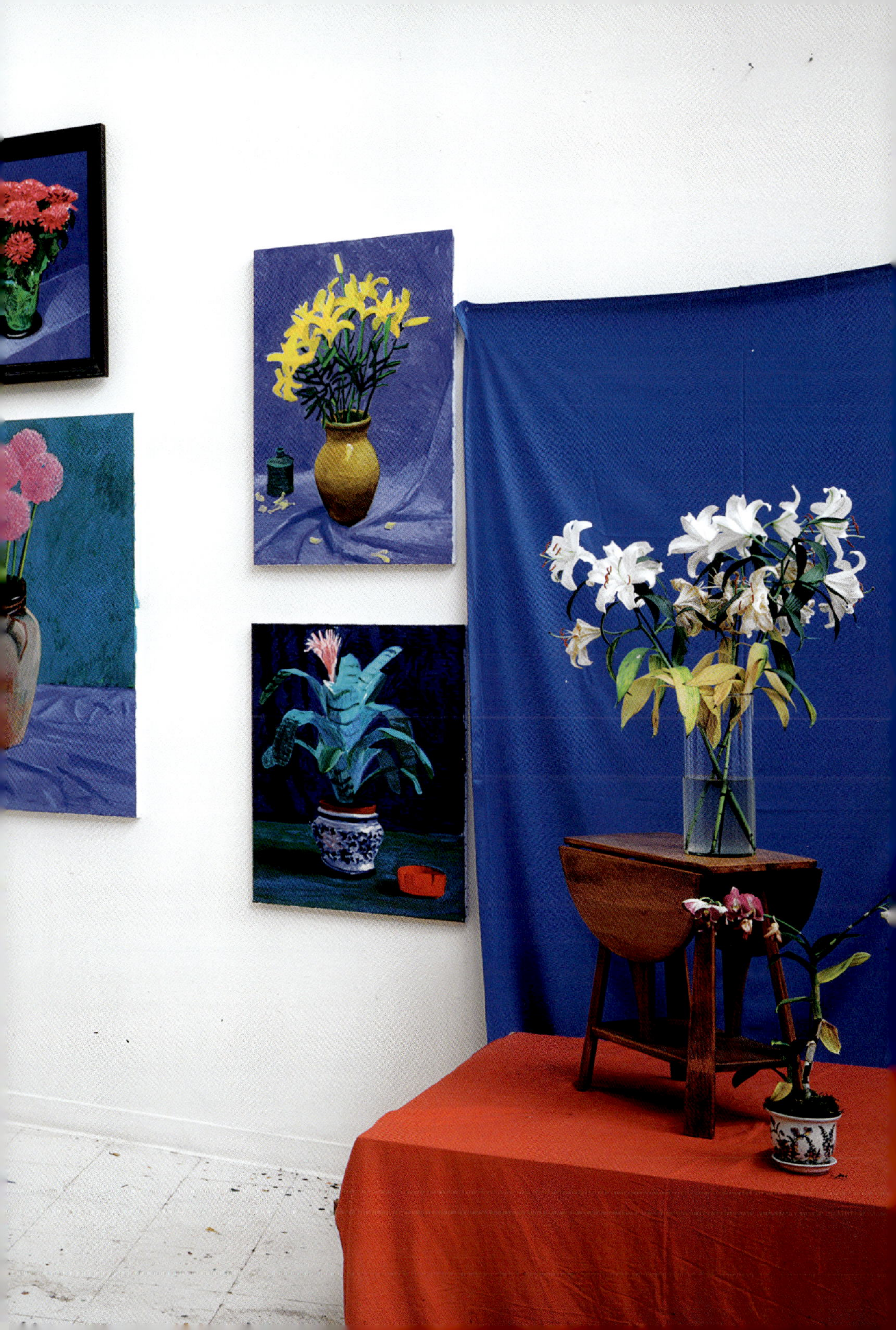

1997

Hockney has a first solo exhibition at his new London gallery, Annely Juda Fine Art. Critics struggle especially with the flower paintings, which in these days of Young British Art appear to them as somewhat conservative. Martin Gayford in the *Telegraph*: "*Flowers, Faces and Spaces* prominently features, as its title suggests, paintings of vases of sunflowers, lilies, and more exotic blooms. That is, one of the least cool, Californian, cheeky, and irreverent subjects imaginable—the staple theme of greetings cards and middle-of-the-road calendars. Has Hockney become hackneyed?... Vases of tulips especially were a common sight in his pictures of the seventies. Indeed, those were much gentler portraits of flowers than this batch; these, the best of them at any rate, have a startling, even unnerving quality that one doesn't normally expect from a flower piece. This comes partly from the colour. Colouristically, if not in other ways, Hockney has grown brighter and brasher as he has grown older. 'People are timid about colour,' he remarked recently. Here, though, his colour combinations are sometimes bold to the point of foolhardiness: sunshine-yellow sunflowers against an electric-turquoise wall and a crimson table, lemon-yellow lemons on an orange cloth beside a cactus with blue flowers. These are colours that zing off the canvas and hit you in the eye. Whether that is a pleasant or an unpleasant experience, however, is a matter of taste."

In June, Hockney drives the roads between Los Angeles and Santa Fe, admiring the landscape of the American West and making one of his regular trips to the Grand Canyon. He celebrates his 60th birthday in Los Angeles, but then moves to Yorkshire for several months, to spend time with his mother and especially his old friend Jonathan Silver, who is dying from cancer. He starts painting the local landscape (pp. 342–343): "In a sense those Yorkshire paintings came out of the ideas of the great spaces of the West, but it did occur to me straightaway that Yorkshire is one place where you have enormous vistas...you can see everything as you drive, from Bridlington to Wetherby, just east of York, down Garrowby Hill and up it again, and I realized here's a subject and here's a way to paint it. Jonathan was urging me all the while to 'paint Yorkshire.' I had never stayed this long in Yorkshire. I was forced to see it afresh." Hockney also paints Salts Mill, the dilapidated building which Silver has transformed into a cultural center bringing new life to the small town (pp. 344/345): "I'd painted Saltaire, for Jonathan; I wanted him to see it as I see it now, and also for him to know

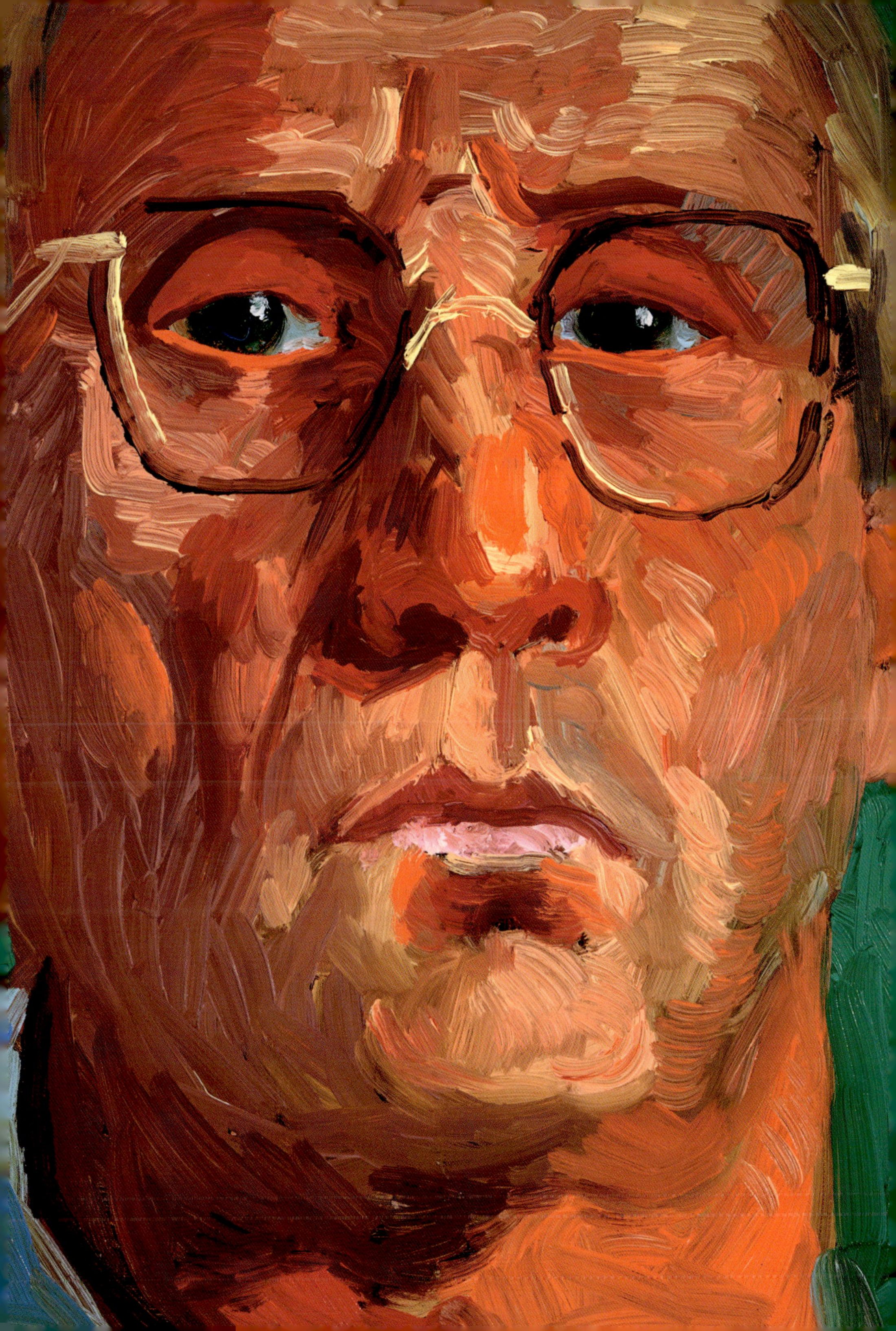

how I'd remembered it as well. Salts Mill is about time and the history of the place, and many places like it. By that I mean, for instance, the rows of houses to the right of the Mill never came down the hill like that. You would actually have to be inside the Mill looking out to achieve that perspective effect. But I grew up in Bradford in small terraces jammed together just like that, and I remember Saltaire as a busy working mill—literally the hub of the whole community."

Hockney finishes the painting a week before Silver's death. On his return to Los Angeles, the artist continues to paint the Yorkshire landscape from memory.

Solo: *Snail's Space with Vari-Lites, "Painting As Performance,"* National Museum of American Art, Washington, D.C. (Jun 6–Sep 14). *Retrospektive Photoworks,* Museum Ludwig, Cologne (Dec 19, 1997–Mar 15, 1998); travels to Kunsthalle Krems, Vienna; Galleria d'arte moderna e contemporanea, Turin; Maison Européenne de la Photographie, Paris; Musée de l'Elysée, Lausanne; National Museum of Wales, Cardiff; Liljevalchs Konsthall, Stockholm; Waino Aaltonen Museum of Art, Turku; and Museum of Contemporary Art, Los Angeles (through 2001); catalog ed. by Reinhold Mißelbeck, texts by Jochen Poetter, Christophe Blaser, Daniel Girardin, and Anke Solbrig, Heidelberg: Edition Braus. *David Hockney,* Nishimura Gallery, Tokyo (Apr 4–May 2). *Flowers, Faces and Spaces,* Annely Juda Fine Art, London (May 1–Jul 19); catalog. *David Hockney,* Galerie Kaess-Weiss, Stuttgart (Oct 11–Nov 4). *David Hockney,* Galerie Maurice at Rosenbaum Fine Art Gallery, Boca Raton (Nov 20–Dec 19).

Group: *Networking: Art by Post and Fax,* Spacex Gallery, Exeter (Feb 15–Mar 23); travels to Worcester, Dunstable, Reading, Glasgow, Wakefield, Belfast, and Bexley (through 1998); catalog. *Sunshine and Noir: Art in L.A. 1960–1997,* Louisiana Museum for Moderne Kunst, Humlebæk (May 16–Sep 7); travels to Wolfsburg, Turin, and Los Angeles (through 1999); catalog. *Summer Exhibition,* Royal Academy of Arts, London (Jun 1–Aug 17). *Hockney to Hodgkin: British Master Prints 1960–1980,* New Orleans Museum of Art; New Orleans (Jul 12–Aug); catalog.

Film: *David Hockney: Pleasures of the Eye,* Germany, 55 min., dir. by Gero von Boehm, narrated by Philip Hurdwood.

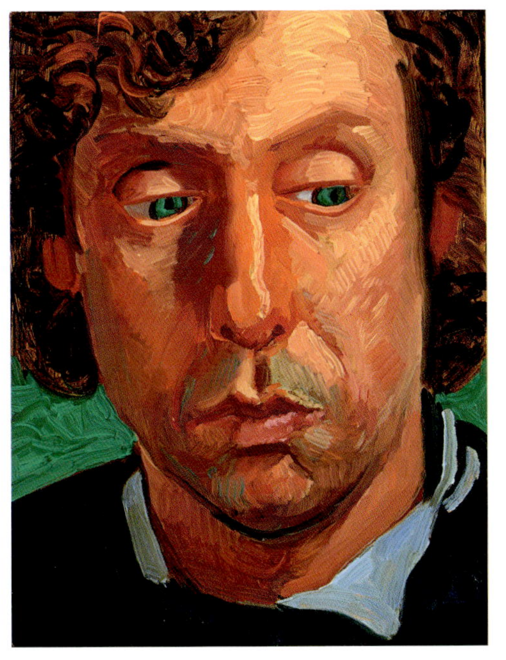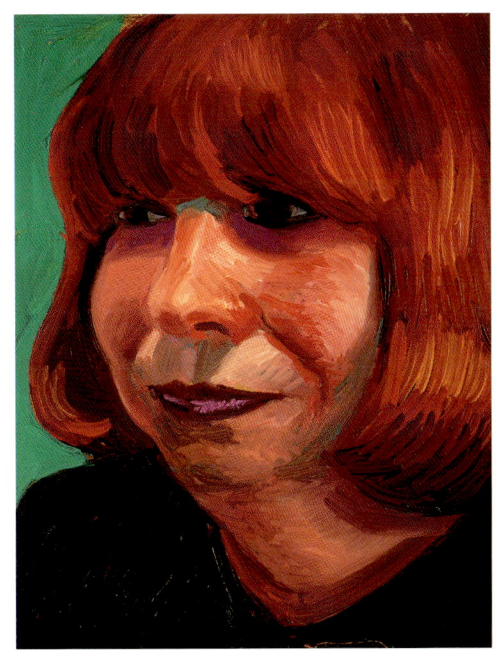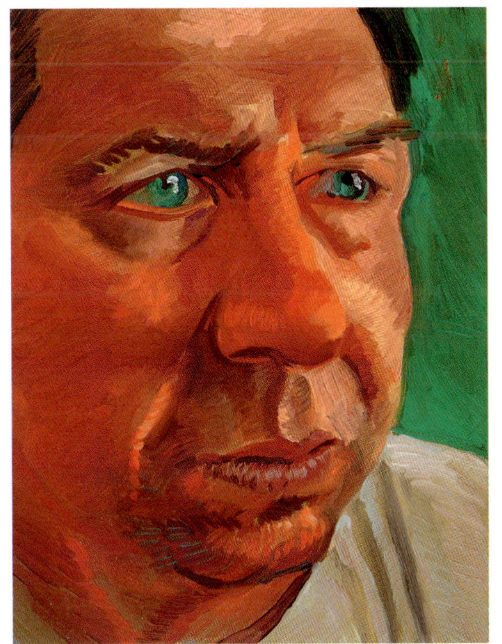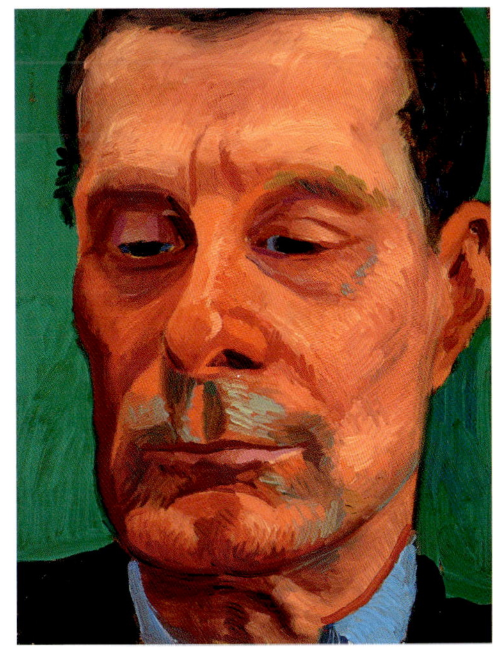

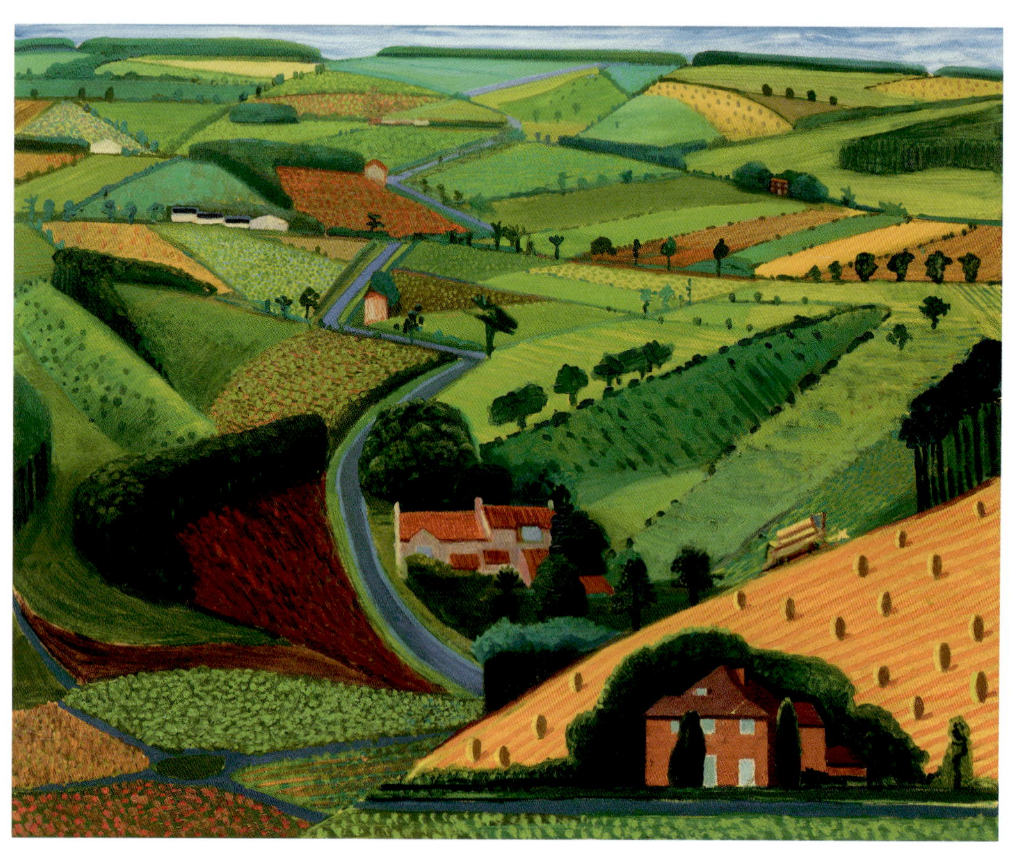

The Road across the Wolds, 1997,
oil on canvas, 48 x 60 in. /
121.9 x 152.4 cm

Right page: *The Road to York through
Sledmere,* 1997, oil on canvas,
48 x 60 in. / 121.9 x 152.4 cm

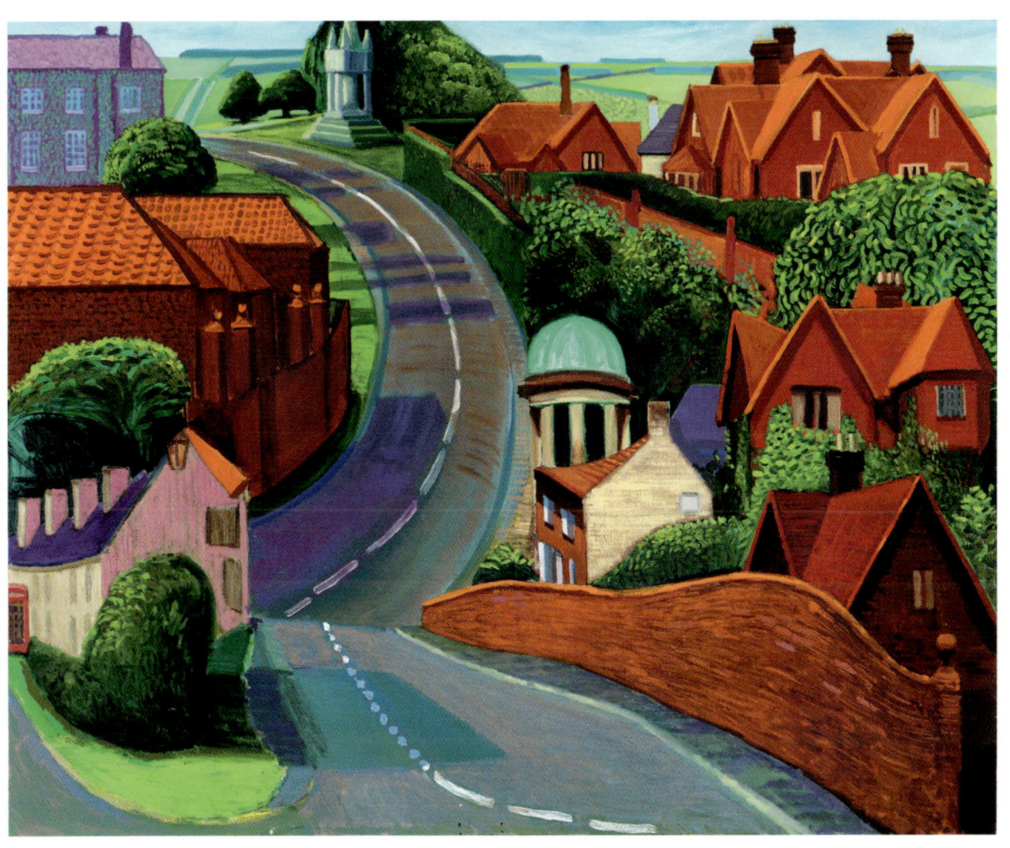

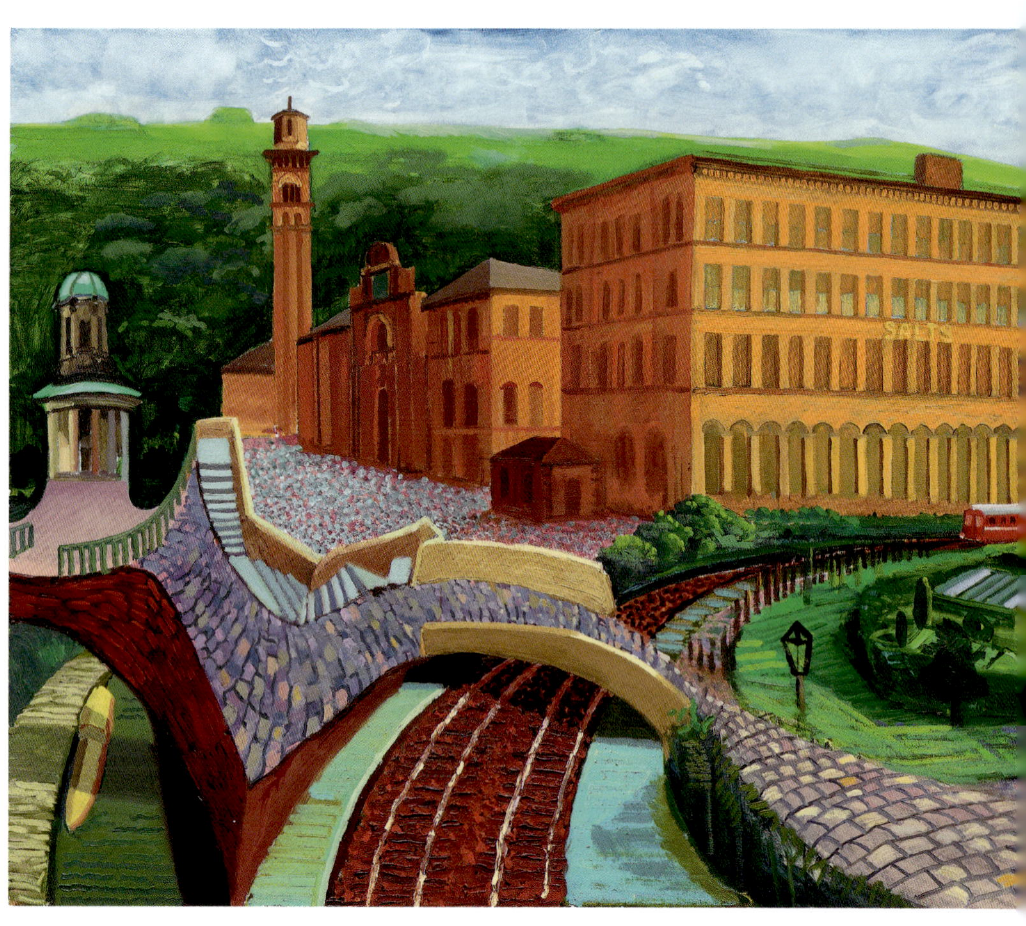

Salts Mill, Saltaire, Yorkshire, 1997,
oil on 2 canvases, 48 x 120 in. /
121.9 x 304.8 cm

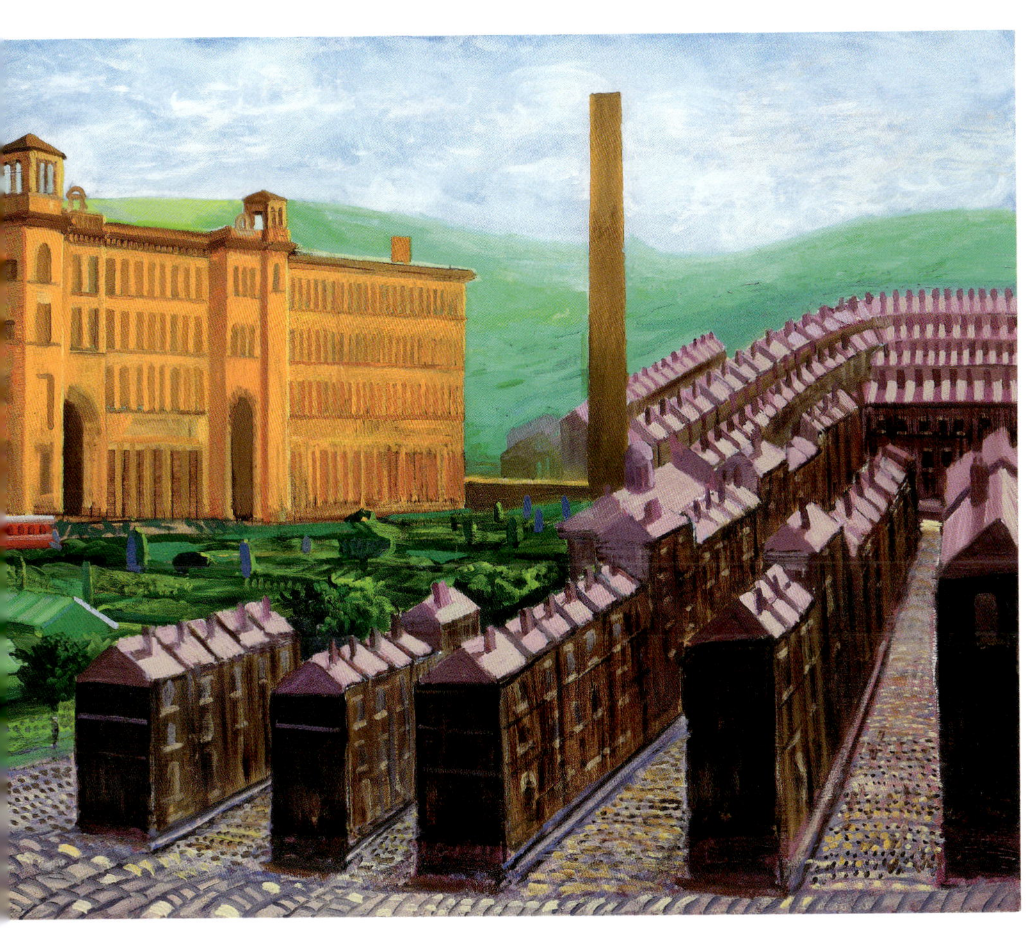

1998

With *Garrowby Hill* (p. 349), painted from memory in Los Angeles, Hockney finishes his series of Yorkshire landscapes. A selection of them are shown at Salts Mill in Saltaire. Alfred Hickling in the *Guardian*: "The problem with memory is that it produces tricks and distortions—things seem bigger, brighter, more condensed than they actually are. Hockney's Yorkshire is splayed across the canvas with all these distortions intact. As scenic views they are hardly accurate, but as images filtered and redrawn they are all the more truthful for it."

Inspired by a retrospective of 19th-century landscape artist Thomas Moran, Hockney paints the Grand Canyon (pp. 352/353), an idea he has been pondering for years. He bases the composition on his photo-composite *Grand Canyon Looking North,* made in 1986 (pp. 252/253), but again works largely from memory: "It was January, not the best time to see the Grand Canyon…so I decided not to go. I didn't want to be influenced by atmospherics. I wanted to paint it how I remembered it, with real color and pigments, strong pure color put on right." The painting is made up of 60 small canvases that add up to the biggest format Hockney has ever used. It is presented at a landscape exhibition at the National Museum in Washington, D.C., and solo shows at L.A. Louver and the Museum of Fine Arts in Boston. William Wilson in the *Los Angeles Times* finds that Hockney "contradicts traditional practice by not dulling hues as they fade into the distance, so backgrounds tend to pop to the surface, flattening the canvas. How can you do that and create an illusion of space? Hockney's never after the illusion. He's after the sensation…*A Bigger Grand Canyon* is pretty awesome. Size and wide-screen format add to the sensation of space but, oddly enough, so does the grid format. It imparts the feeling of looking at something dimensional through something flat like a window."

Hockney publishes an article in *Modern Painters* where he counters the common thesis of the death of painting with his own thesis of the death of television as we know it by hands of the Internet, and the death of the camera as a reliable witness now that photos are routinely manipulated. These ideas mirror his own return from photography to painting: "Both the photograph and reality itself are being called into question. We are losing confidence in the camera's ability to show us what the world looks, and feels, like. All images are artificial in some way…but what the hand, the eye, and the heart can do—and paint—can never be replaced."

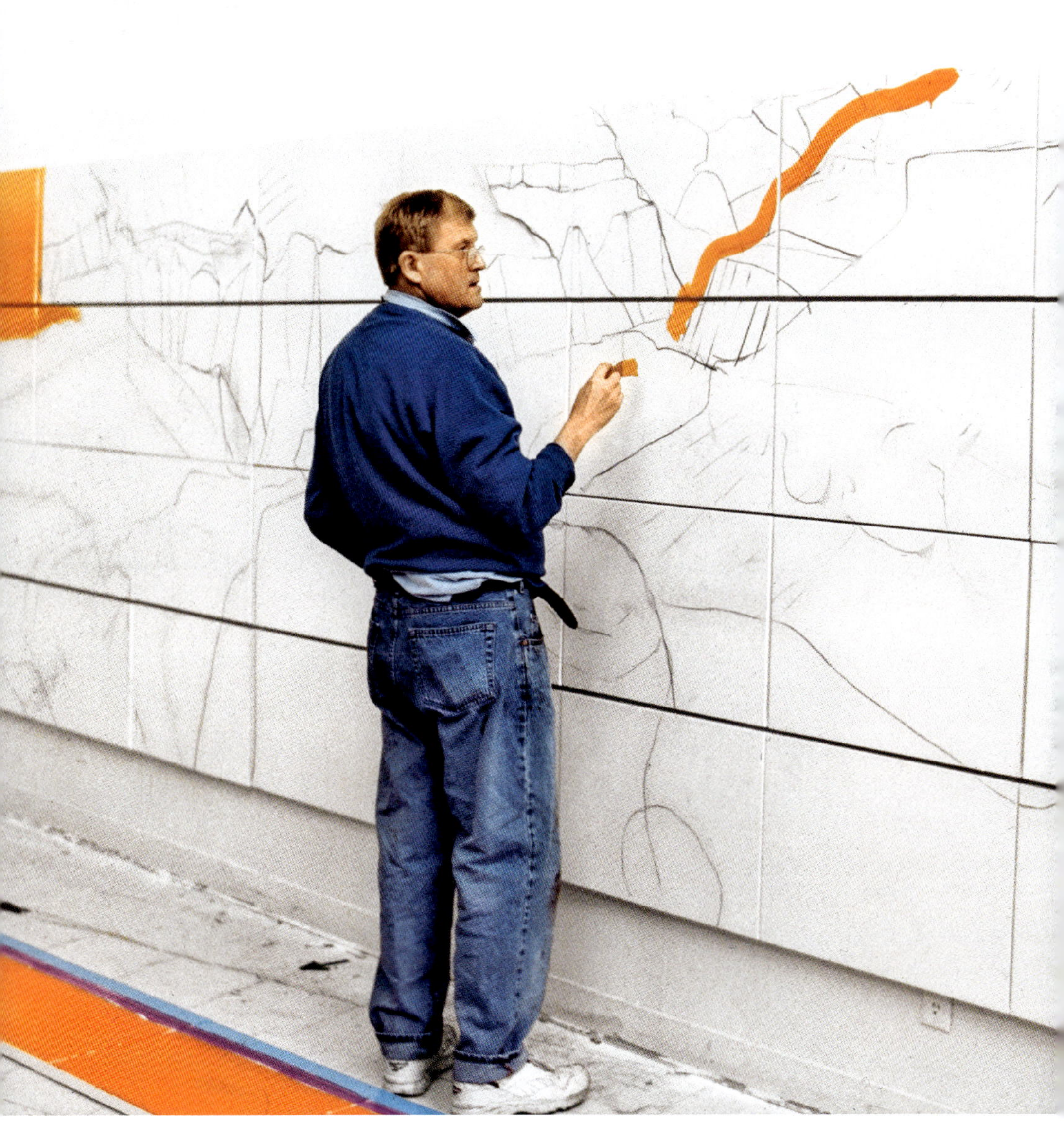

David Hockney in his studio painting
A Bigger Grand Canyon, Los Angeles
1998. Photo: Richard Schmidt

In autumn, Hockney paints *A Closer Grand Canyon* (pp. 350, 351) on 96 panels. This time he actually visits the canyon and for a week every morning goes out to Powell Point on the South Rim, where he sits and draws: "I'd just think about the space…It is about the only place on earth that really makes you look in every direction. You feel small. And the longer you look the more thrilling that becomes." Hockney also creates a series of etchings of people, chairs, and flowers, experimenting with various techniques. He invites his old collaborator Maurice Payne to set up a printing studio in the Hollywood Hills home, and Payne comes up with the strategy of preparing etching plates and leaving them lying about so the artist can start work spontaneously when inspiration hits.

Solo: *New Paintings by David Hockney,* Museum of Fine Arts, Boston (Apr 24–Aug 23); brochure with a text by Barbara Stern Shapiro. *A Bigger Grand Canyon,* National Museum of American Art, Washington, D.C. (Jun 19–Sep 7). *David Hockney,* Galerie Meyer-Ellinger, Frankfurt am Main (Apr 2–May 30). *Looking at Landscape, Being in Landscape,* L.A. Louver, Venice, CA (Sep 15–Oct 24); catalog with an interview by Lawrence Weschler. *Prints 1954–1995,* Peter Gwyther Gallery, London (Oct–Dec).

Group: *Head First: Portraits from the Arts Council Collection,* City Gallery, Leicester (Jan 17–Feb 28); touring exhibition organized by Hayward Gallery for the Arts Council of England, travels to Southampton, Kendal, Newcastle, Bath, Sheffield, and Hull (through 1999); catalog. *Masterpieces of British Art from the Tate Gallery,* Metropolitan Museum, Tokyo (Jan 23–Mar 29); travels to Hyogo Prefectural Museum of Modern Art, Kobe; catalog. *The Power of the Poster,* Victoria and Albert Museum, London (Apr 2–Jul 26); catalog. *Modern British Art,* Tate Liverpool (May 23, 1998–Apr 1, 1999). *In over Our Heads: The Image of Water in Contemporary Art,* San Jose Museum of Art, San Jose (Jun 13–Sep 20). *Photoimage: Printmaking 60s to 90s,* Museum of Fine Art, Boston (Jul 7–Sep 27); travels to Des Moines Art Center, Des Moines; catalog. *Innenleben: Die Kunst des Interieurs,* Städtische Galerie im Städelschen Kunstinstitut, Frankfurt am Main (Sep 25, 1998–Jan 10, 1999); catalog.

Publication: *David Hockney's Dog Days.* London: Thames and Hudson; Boston: Bulfinch Press.

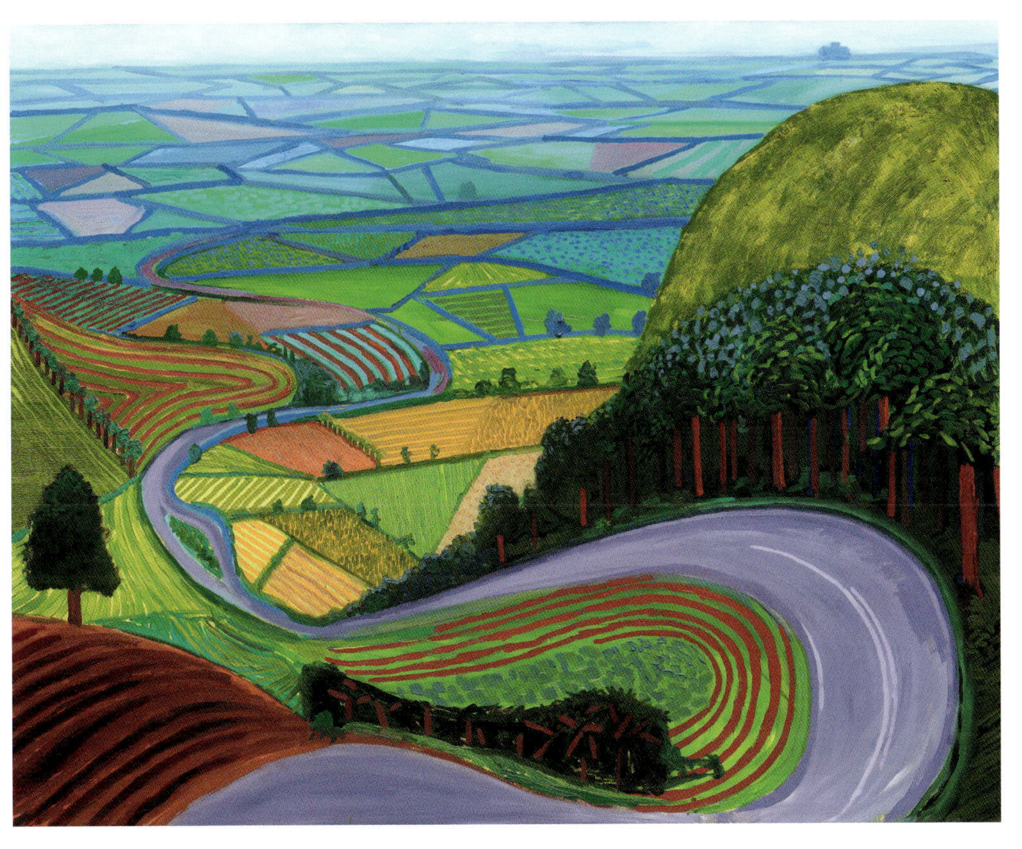

Garrowby Hill, 1998, oil on canvas,
60 x 76 in. / 152.4 x 193 cm

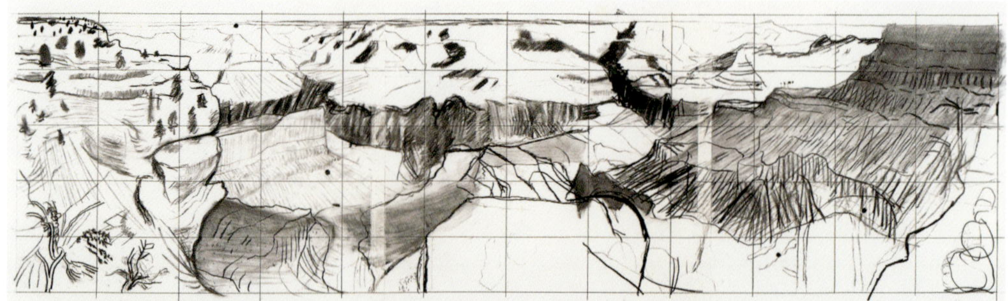

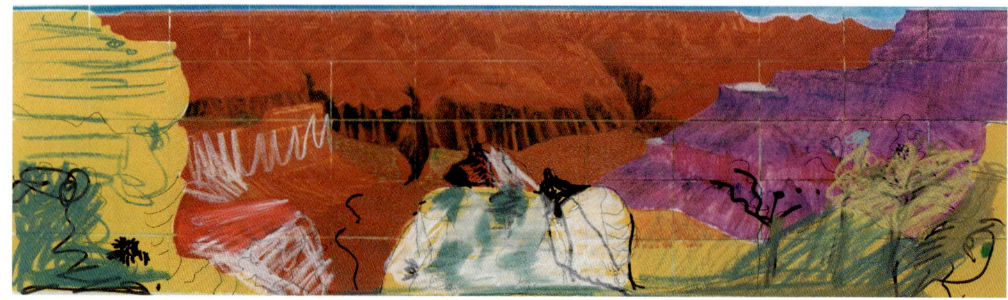

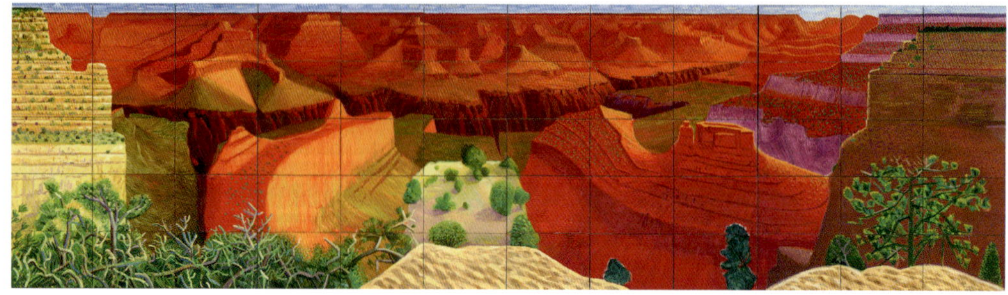

Composition study for *A Bigger Grand Canyon,* 1998, charcoal, pencil, ink, and tape on 3 sheets of paper, 22 ¹/₂ x 78 ³/₈ in. / 57.2 cm x 199.1 cm

Study VIII for *A Bigger Grand Canyon,* 1998, crayon and ink on color laser copy, 11 x 17 in. / 27.9 x 43.2 cm

A Closer Grand Canyon, 1998, oil on 60 canvases, 81 ¹/₂ x 293 in. / 207 x 744.2 cm

Right page: Study I for *A Closer Grand Canyon, Tower of Set,* 1998, oil pastel on paper, 19 ³/₄ x 25 ¹/₂ in. / 50.2 x 64.8 cm

Study II for *A Closer Grand Canyon, Near Pima,* 1998, oil pastel on paper, 19 ³/₄ x 25 ¹/₂ in. / 50.2 x 64.8 cm

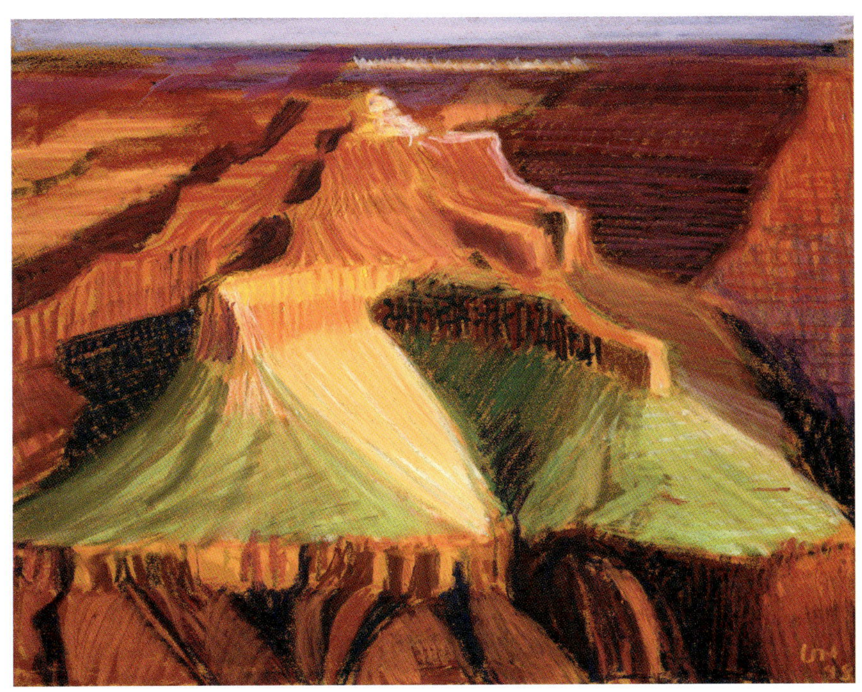

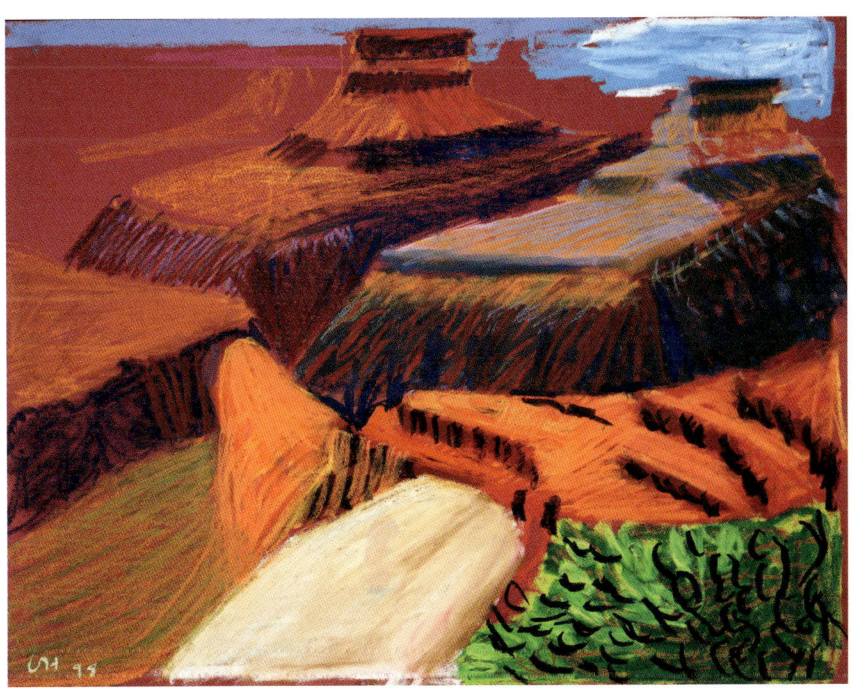

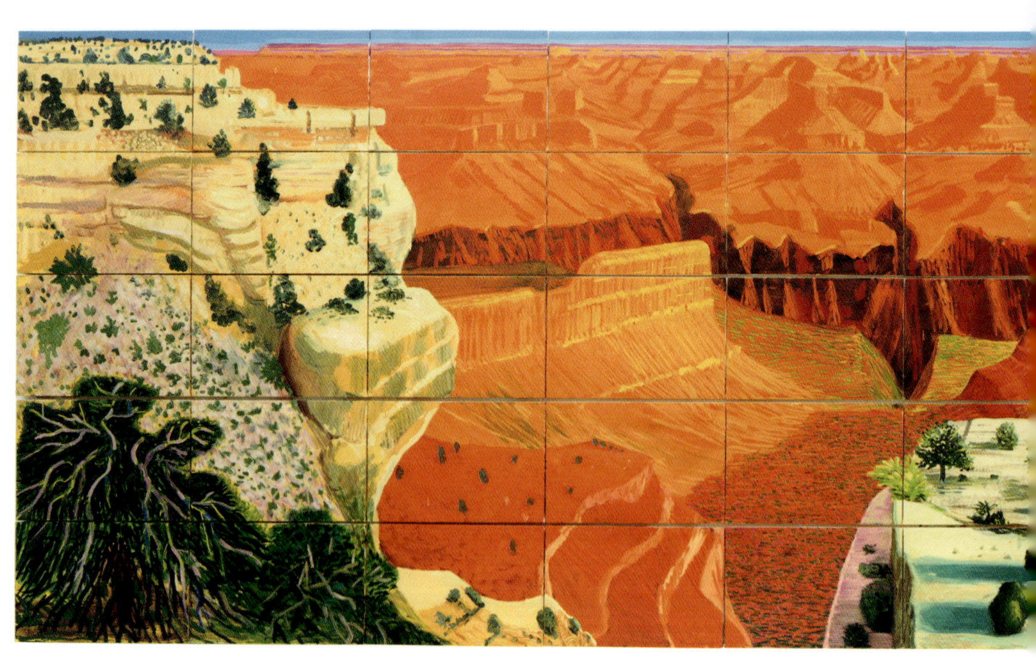

A Bigger Grand Canyon, 1998,
oil on 60 canvases, 81 ½ x 293 in. /
207.1 x 744.2 cm

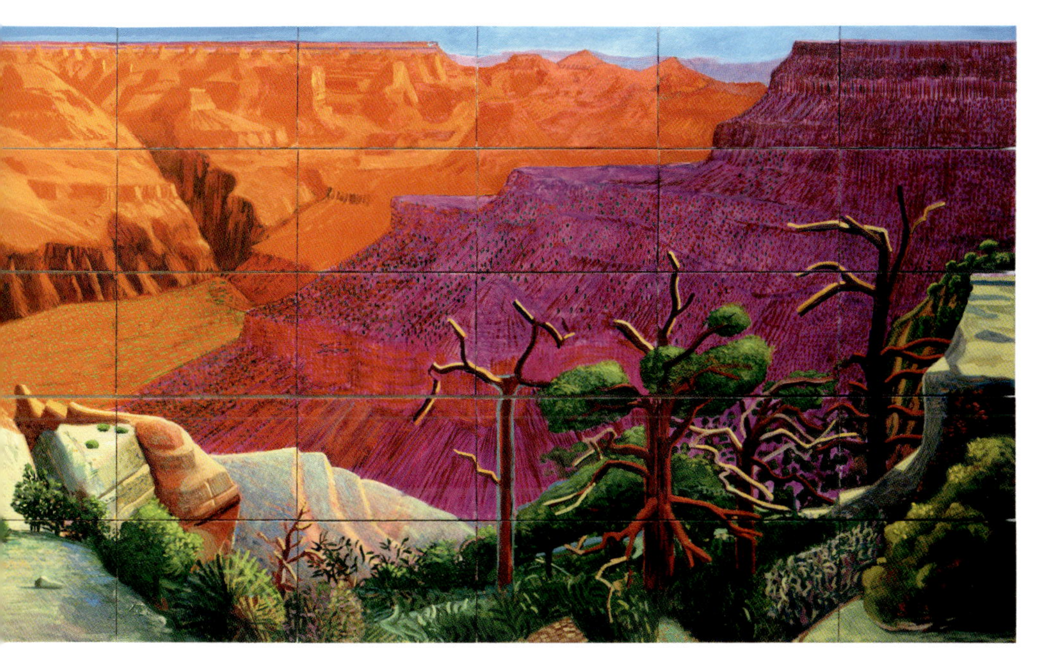

1999

In Paris, Hockney simultaneously shows at the Centre Pompidou, the Musée Picasso, and the Maison Européenne de la Photographie. His Pompidou exhibition, titled *Espace / Paysage,* explores the artist's ideas of space and landscape, juxtaposing key works from different eras. Meanwhile in London, Hockney sees an exhibition of Ingres portraits at the National Gallery, which he visits three times, especially for the drawings. He tells Lawrence Weschler of the discovery he makes: "Those pencil portraits of Ingres's were mind-boggling. For one thing their size—how small they turn out to be when you get to see them in person. The images are seldom more than twelve by eight inches, incredibly detailed and incredibly assured. If you draw at all, you know that's very rare and not at all easy. I bought the catalog, brought it back here to LA, studied it some more, read every word, blew up some of the drawings on the copier over there, and one morning, studying the blowups, I found myself thinking, 'Wait, I've seen that line before. Where have I seen that line?' And suddenly I realized, 'That's Andy Warhol's line'…In Andy's case we know he was using a slide projector…and now look at this, especially the clothes, the fall of the draped cloak, the ruffle around the neck, the gathered sleeve, and then her expression, its palpable freshness: the speed of the line, its boldness, its absolute confidence, no awkwardness, no hesitancy. Of course, Ingres wasn't using a slide projector, but he might well have been using a camera, a refracting instrument of some sort."

Hockney is convinced that Ingres used a camera lucida. He takes up the tool himself and starts a series of portrait drawings (pp. 357–359): "At first I found the camera lucida very difficult to use. It doesn't project a real image of the subject, but an illusion of one in the eye. When you move your head everything moves with it, and the artist must learn to make very quick notations to fix the position of the eyes, nose, and mouth to capture 'a likeness.' It is concentrated work. I persevered and continued to use the method for the rest of the year—learning all the time."

In May, Hockney visits his mother as her health takes a turn for the worse. She dies at the age of 98, surrounded by her children and family.

Hockney begins more detailed research on optical devices known to the Old Masters; he finds that they emerged in the 16th century, that use of lenses, mirrors, or the camera obscura became more widespread in realist art of the 17th

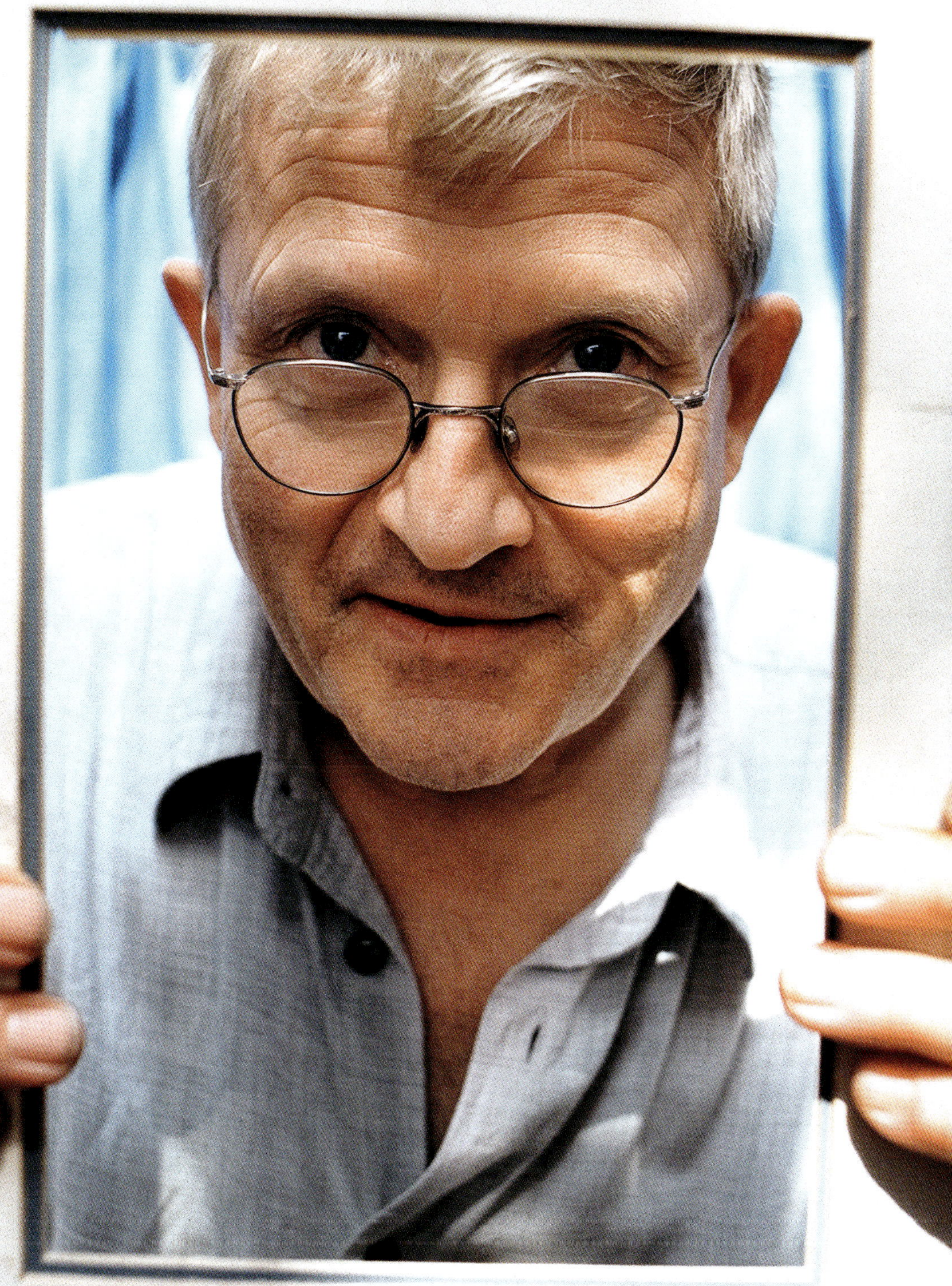

and 18th centuries through painters such as Vermeer, Caravaggio, or Canaletto, and that in the first half of the 19th century the lens-based view became the ruling aesthetic, when: "Suddenly something happens. And that, of course, is the invention of photography—or, to be more precise, the invention of various methods for chemically fixing the sort of lens-cast image that up till then had required the interposition of a human hand." Hockney publishes an article on his discoveries in *RA Magazine,* which provokes a huge reaction. He further develops his theses in dialog with art historians Martin Kemp, David Graves, Gary Tinterow, and many others. In autumn, he takes part in a symposium on "Ingres and Portraiture" at the Metropolitan Museum in New York.

Solo: *Espace / Paysage,* Musée national d'art moderne, Centre Georges Pompidou, Paris (Jan 25–Apr 26); catalog ed. by Didier Ottinger. *Dialogue avec Picasso,* Musée Picasso, Paris (Feb 8–May 3); catalog with texts by Didier Ottinger, Jean Clair, Marc Fumaroli, Simon Faulkner, Pierre Sterckx, and Caroline Hancock. *David Hockney,* National Gallery of Australia, Canberra (Oct 12, 1999–Jan 26, 2000). *David Hockney,* Leslie Sacks Fine Art, Los Angeles (Feb 20–Mar 24). *Space and Line,* Richard Gray Gallery, New York (Apr 29–May 28); travels to Annely Juda Fine Art, London (Jun 30–Sep 11); catalog with a text by Marco Livingstone. *Recent Etchings,* Pace Prints, New York (May 5–Jun 5); catalog. *Recent Etchings,* L.A. Louver, Venice, CA (Jun 29–Aug 28). *David Hockney,* Alan Cristea Gallery, London (Jun 30–Aug 30). *Four Decades of Selected Graphics,* Leslie Sacks Fine Art, Los Angeles (Sep 13–Oct 18). *David Hockney,* Nishimura Gallery, Tokyo (Oct 12–Nov 20). *Dog Wall,* Pace Prints, New York (Nov 23–Dec 30). *David Hockney,* Mira Godard Gallery, Toronto (Nov 27–Dec 18).

Group: *Examining Pictures: Exhibiting Paintings,* Whitechapel Gallery, London (May 6–Jun 26); travels to Chicago and Los Angeles; catalog. *Innovation / Imagination: 50 Years of Polaroid Photography,* Ansel Adams Center, San Francisco (May 11–Jul 18). *Summer Exhibition,* Royal Academy of Arts, London (Jun 1–Aug 15); catalog; Hockney wins the Charles Wollaston Award.

Publication: *Hockney on Art: Conversations with Paul Joyce,* London: Little, Brown.

Film: *David Hockney: In Perspective,* France, 52 min., by Monique Lajournade and Pierre Saint-Jean, dir. by Monique Lajournade.

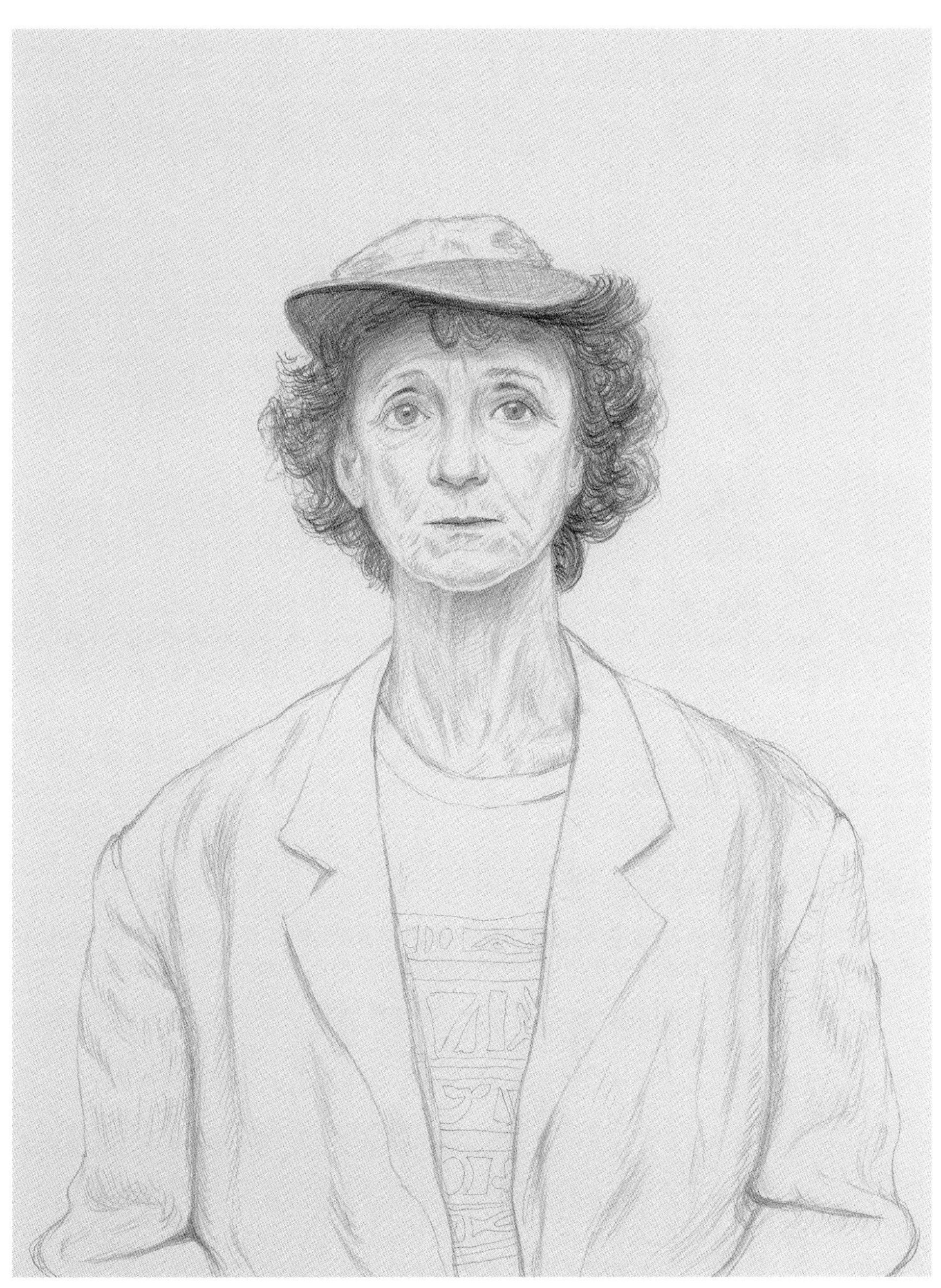

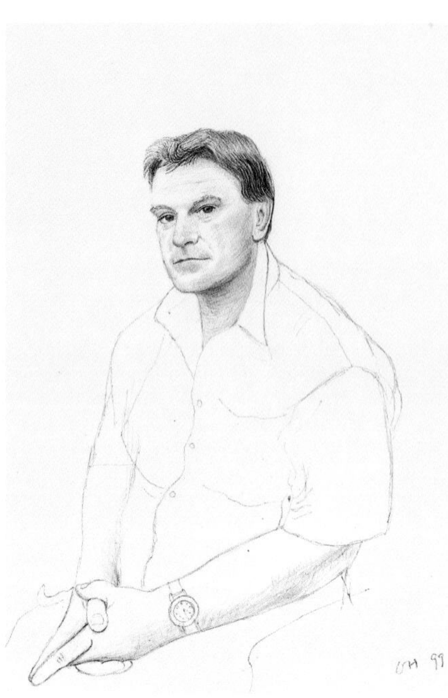

Bing McGilvray, London, 18th June 1999, pencil on paper using a camera lucida, 19 x 15 in. / 48.3 x 38.1 cm

Margaret Hockney, Bridlington, 1st May 1999, pencil on paper using a camera lucida, 10 x 7 in. / 25.4 x 17.8 cm

Ken Wathey and Sophie, Bridlington, 30th April 1999, pencil on paper using a camera lucida, 10 x 7 in. / 25.4 x 17.8 cm

Page 355: David Hockney, 1999. Photo: Eleanor Bentall

Page 357: *Lindy. Marchioness of Dufferin and Ava. London. 17th June 1999,* pencil on paper using a camera lucida, 15 x 16 ⁷/₈ in. / 38 x 42.9 cm

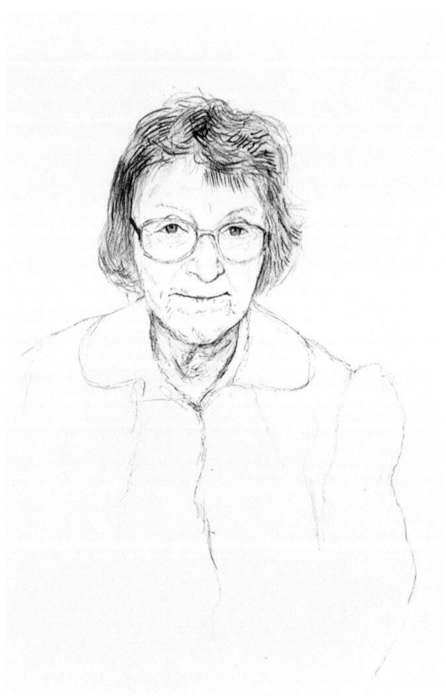

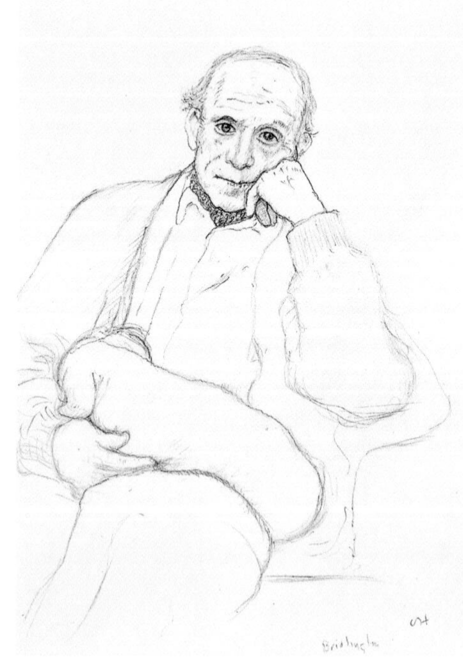

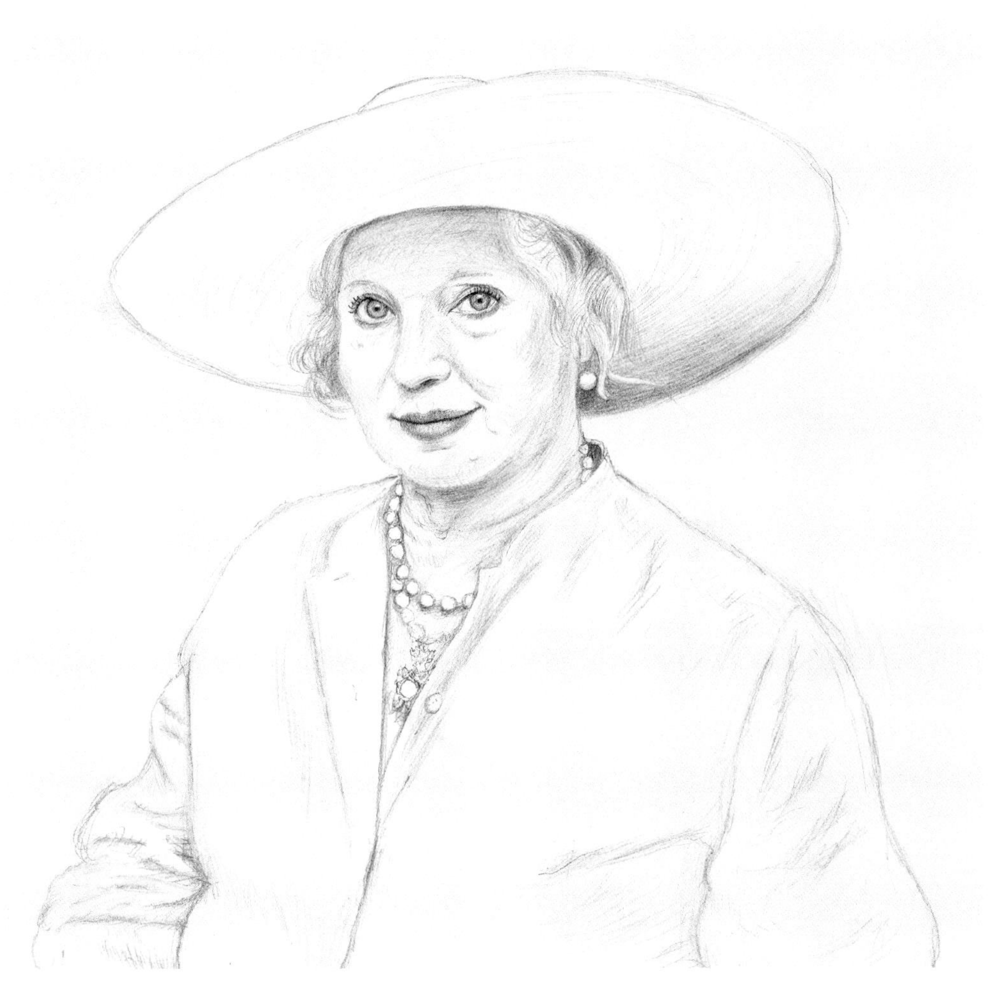

Celia Birtwell. London. 19th June 1999, pencil and white crayon on paper using a camera lucida, 15 x 13 ⅝ in. / 38 x 34.6 cm

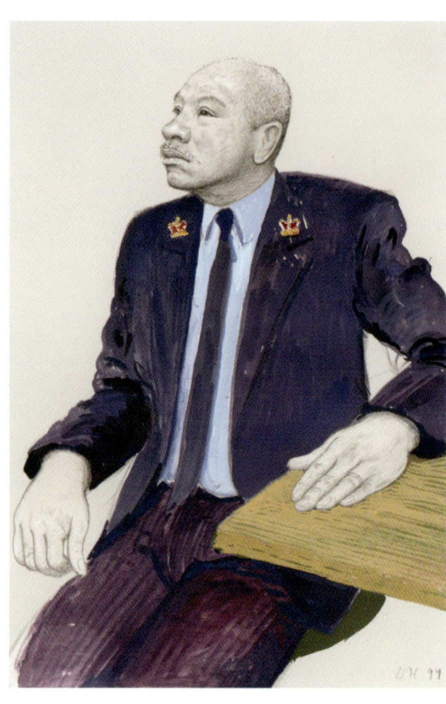

12 Portraits after Ingres in a Uniform Style, 1999, pencil, white crayon, and gouache on paper using a camera lucida, each 22 ⅛ x 15 in. / 56.2 x 38 cm

Vincent Simon, London, 16th December 1999

Jack Kettlewell, London, 13th December 1999

Maria Vasquez, London, 21st December 1999

Right page: *Ken Bradford, London, 20th December 1999*

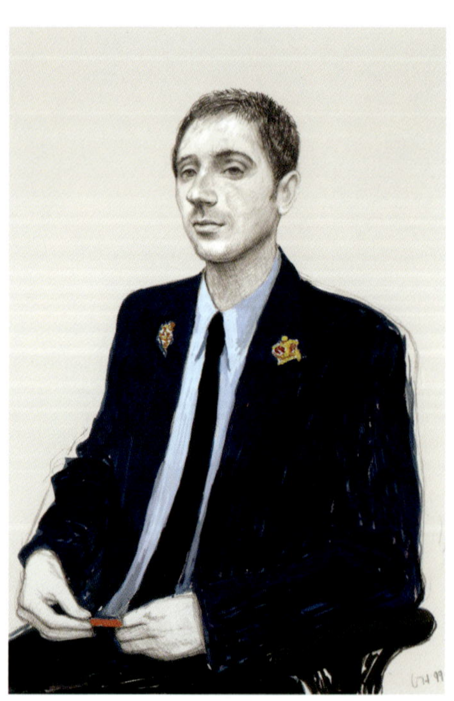

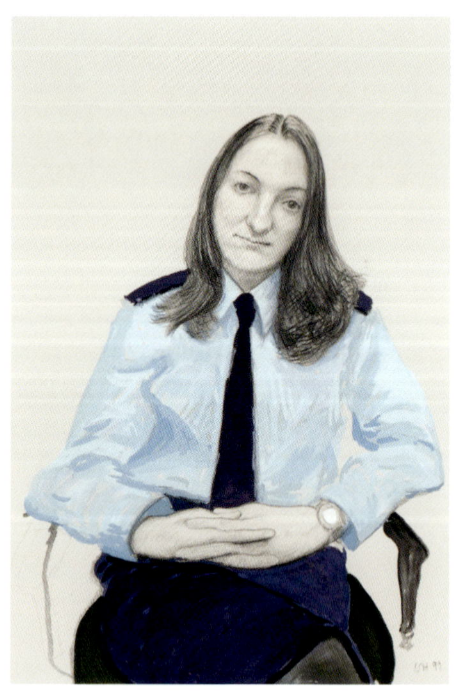

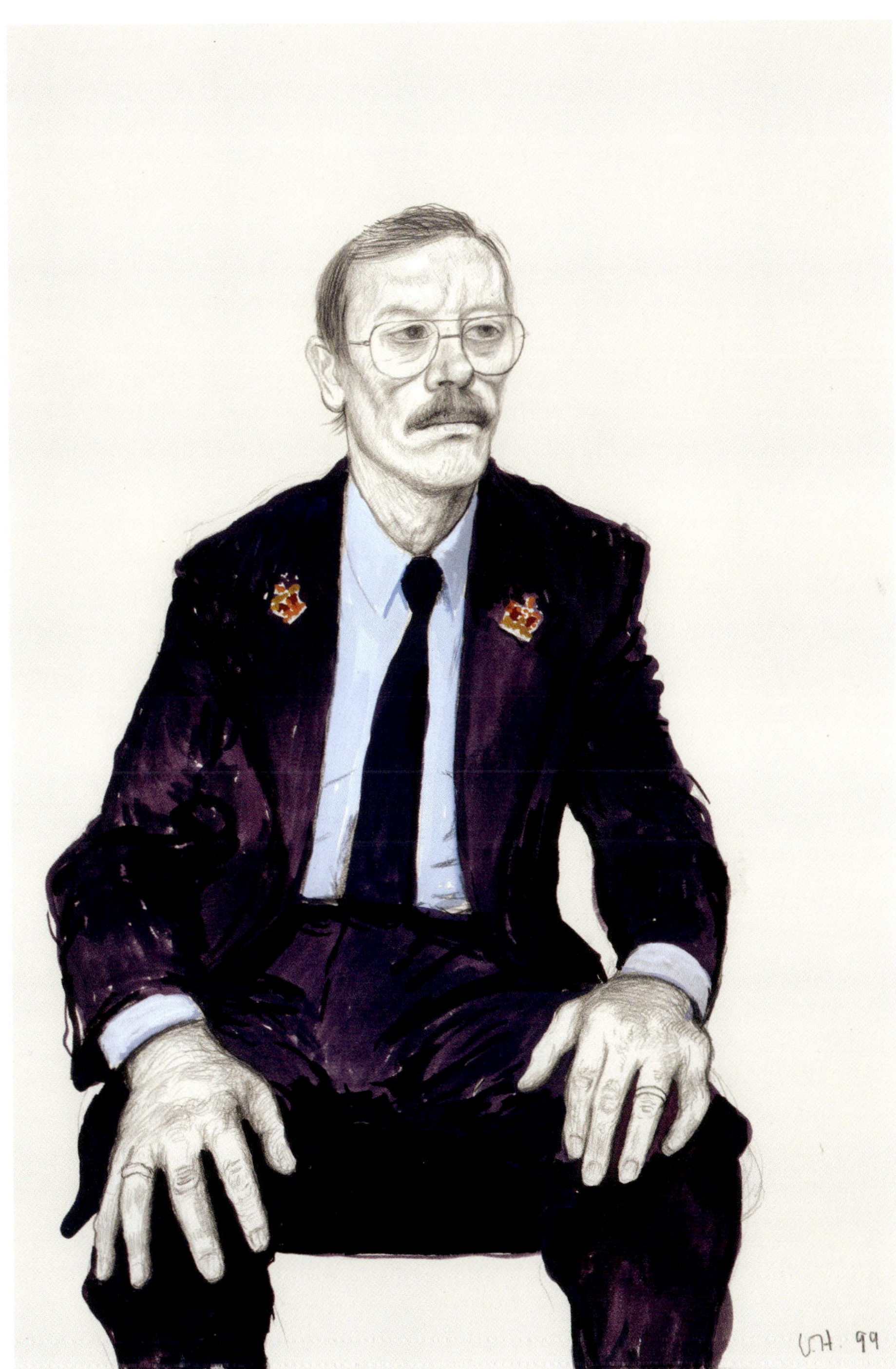

2000 Hockney begins writing a book about the forgotten optical devices of the Old Masters. Practically all evidence for his theory has to be visual, as there are no text sources, possibly because artists have always been secretive about their methods. He makes photocopies of works of Western art through time and chronologically fastens them to a studio wall, soon dubbed *The Great Wall* (pp. 368–371), beginning with a Byzantine mosaic around 1150 and closing with a van Gogh portrait from 1889. Judging from a new, startlingly realistic manner of portraying the human face in Bruges in the early 15th century, Hockney feels the use of lenses must have started with the work of Jan van Eyck or the Master of Flémalle. This appears too early, though. Hockney meets with the experimental physicist Charles Falco, and Lawrence Weschler is present to voice the doubts: "'What about Van Eyck in Bruges? Isn't the problem that there's no good evidence of the existence, let alone widespread dissemination, of such lenses, at that place at that time?' None of us was subsequently able to recall precisely what Falco said in response—but somewhere buried in the subclause of a subclause he noted how, 'Of course, a concave mirror has exactly the same optical properties as a lens'—a throwaway comment that veritably stunned Hockney and Graves. Really?! 'Sure,' Falco continued. 'Try it yourself. In the morning, in the bathroom, take your shaving mirror—you know, the one that magnifies the image of your face—when it's bright outside and still dark on your bathroom's inner wall, aim the lens at the world outside the window so the gathered light bounces off the mirror and onto the darkened wall…and what you'll get is a Technicolor perfect image of the world outside. Upside down, granted.'" With Falco's help, they continue a more scientific approach to their optical research, e.g. finding broken perspective lines and spots of soft focus in a work by Lorenzo Lotto that suggest the use of a lens which had to be adjusted several times.

Public interest is less scientific, as Andrew Marr reports in the *Observer*: "'Did the old masters cheat?' That was the inflammatory cover line above David Hockney's new thinking on how a cascade of the greatest names in Western art—including Caravaggio, Raphael, Frans Hals, Vermeer, Velazquez, and Ingres—used lenses to trace out their pictures. That was how they achieved their near-miraculous use of perspective; that was how they caught transient smiles with such a swagger. Hockney would regard none of this as cheating: 'The lens can't draw a line, only the hand can do that, the artist's hand and eye. This whole insight about

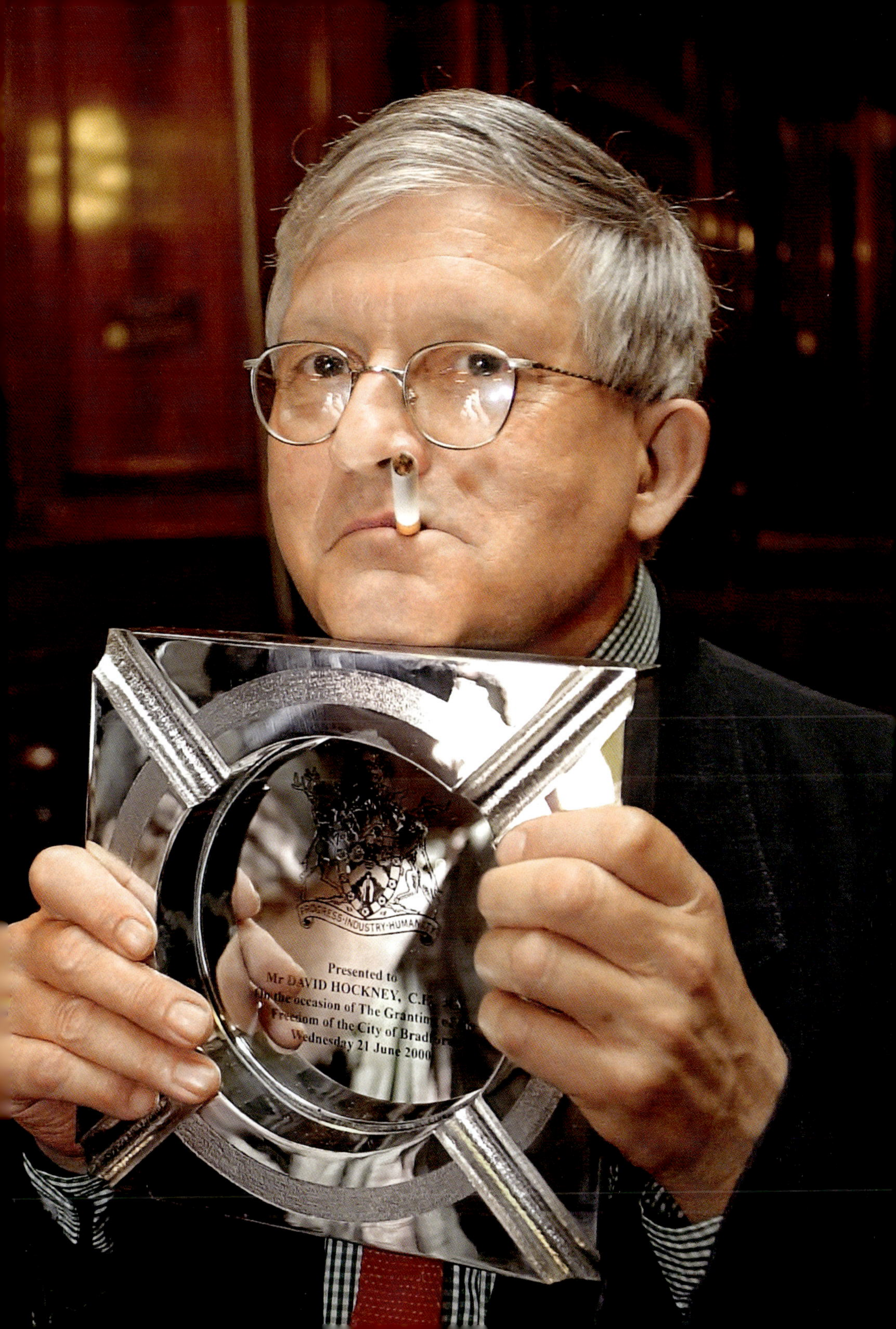
PROGRESS·INDUSTRY·HUMANITY
Presented to
Mr DAVID HOCKNEY, C.H.
On the occasion of The Granting of the
Freedom of the City of Bradford
Wednesday 21 June 2000

optical aids doesn't diminish anything; it merely suggests a different story.' Even so, the audacity and verve of his argument, overturning a long tradition of art connoisseurship with the flick of a pencil, has arrived like a depth-charge in the art world."

Hockney exhibits *12 Portraits after Ingres in a Uniform Style* (pp. 360–361), drawn with the help of the camera lucida, in a group show of modern answers to Old Masters at London's National Gallery. They depict the gallery wardens so that visitors will casually come across his models and be able to judge the verisimilitude of the works for themselves.

While Hockney spends the summer in rainy London, he paints views of his LA garden and the California landscape from memory (pp. 366, 367).

Solo: *Likeness: Recent Portrait Drawings by David Hockney,* Armand Hammer Museum of Art, Los Angeles (Apr 25–Jun 4). *Visions and Revisions,* Pillsbury and Peters Fine Art, Dallas (Jan 8–Feb 26); catalog. *David Hockney,* Leslie Sacks Fine Art, Brentwood (Apr 29–May 27). *David Hockney,* L.A. Louver, Venice, CA (Jul 14–Aug 12). *A Print Retrospective 1961–1999,* Alan Cristea Gallery, London (Sept 12–Oct 14); catalog.

Group: *Modern Art despite Modernism,* Museum of Modern Art, New York (Mar 16–Jul 26); catalog. *How You Look at It: Fotografien des 20. Jahrhunderts,* Sprengel Museum, Hanover (May 14–Jun 8); travels to Städische Galerie am Städelschen Kunstinstitut, Frankfurt am Main (Aug 23–Dec 11); catalog. *Encounters: New Art from Old,* National Gallery, London (Jun 12–Sep 17); catalog. *American Perspectives: Photographs from the Polaroid Collection,* Metropolitan Museum of Photography, Tokyo (Sep 12–Nov 12); catalog. *Painting the Century: 101 Portrait Masterpieces 1900–2000,* National Portrait Gallery, London (Oct 26, 2000–Feb 4, 2001); catalog. *Then and Now,* Bradford Gallery and Cartwright Hall Gallery, Bradford (Nov 25, 2000–Feb 11, 2001).

Honor: Freedom of the City of Bradford Award, University of Bradford.

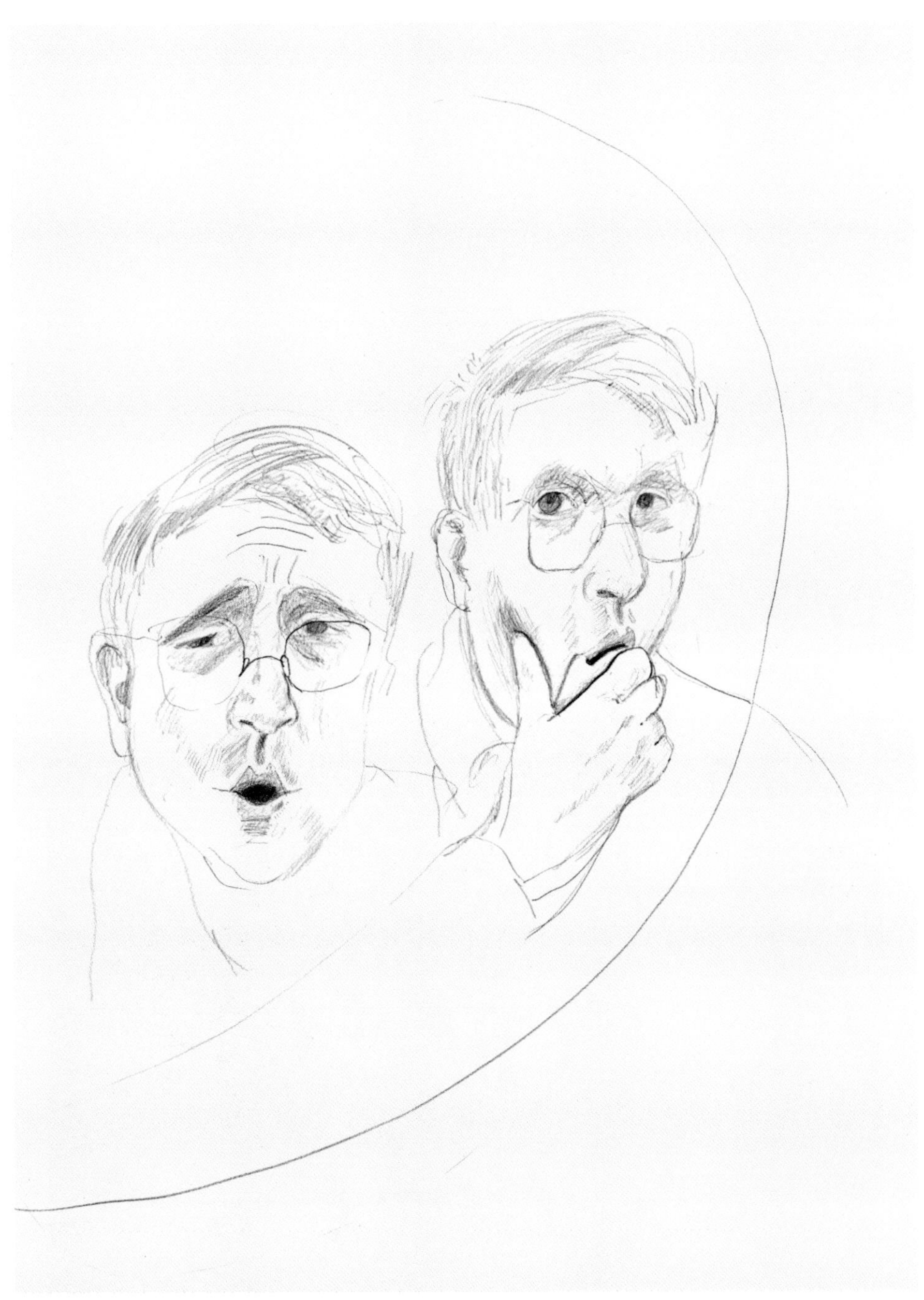

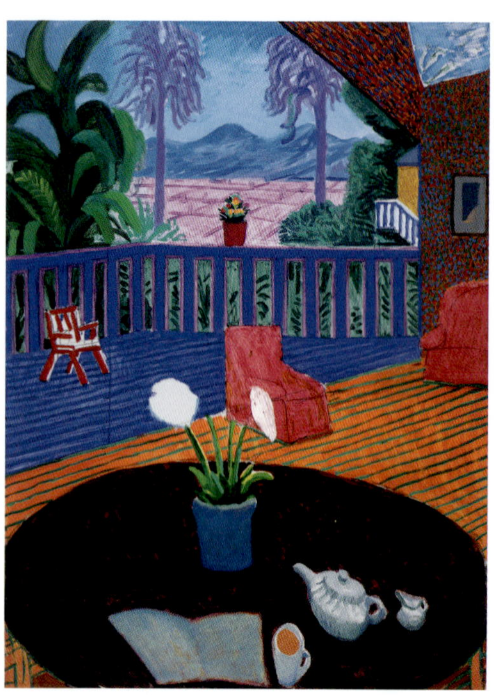

The San Fernando Valley Seen from the Breakfast Table, 2000, oil on canvas, 48 x 36 in. / 121.9 x 91.4 cm

My Garden in L.A., London, July 2000, oil on canvas, 36 x 48 in. / 91.4 x 121.9 cm

Page 363: David Hockney with a silver ashtray received during a ceremony giving him the Honorary Freedom of the City of Bradford, 2000. Photo: Paul Barker

Page 365: *Double Self Portrait, Los Angeles, February 1, 2000,* pencil on paper using a convex mirror, 30 x 22 in. / 76 x 56 cm

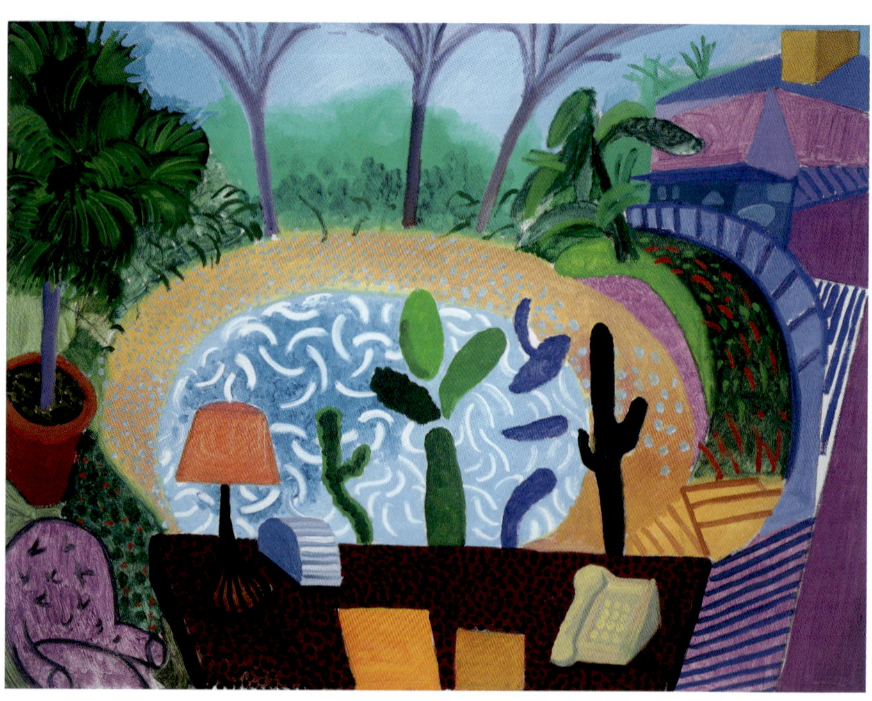

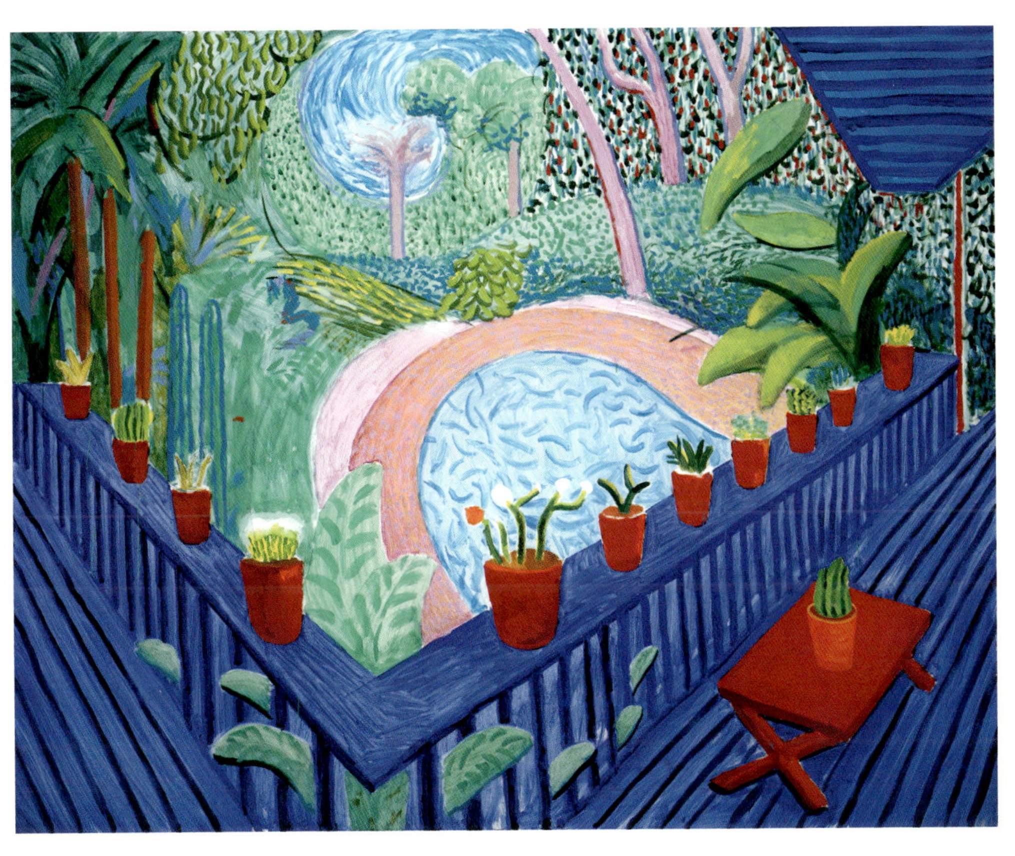

Red Pots in the Garden, 2000,
oil on canvas, 60 x 76 in. /
152.4 x 193 cm

Pages 368–371: Details from
The Great Wall, 2000, color laser
copies on 18 panels, 96 x 864 in. /
243.8 x 2194.6 cm overall

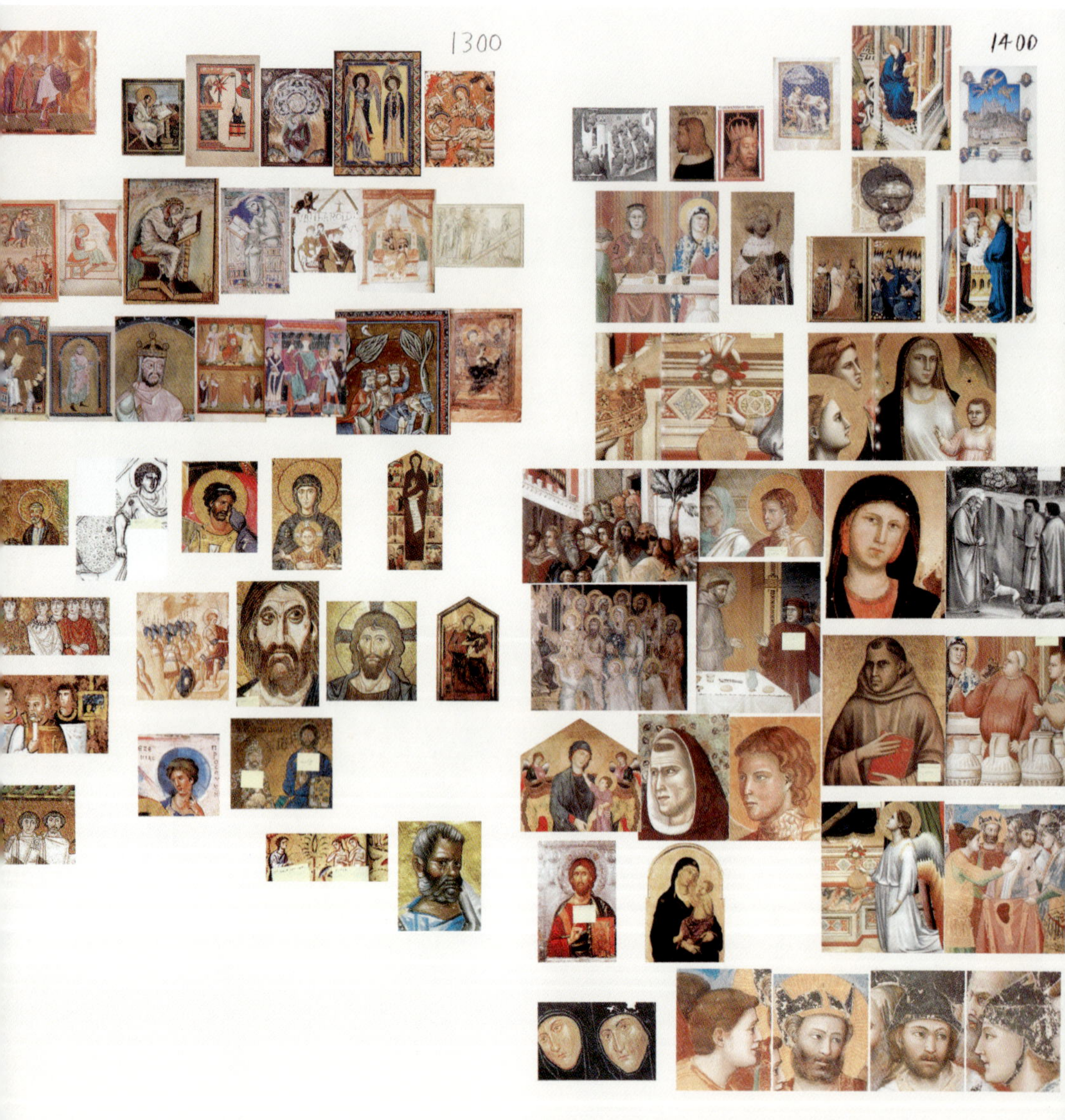

1450

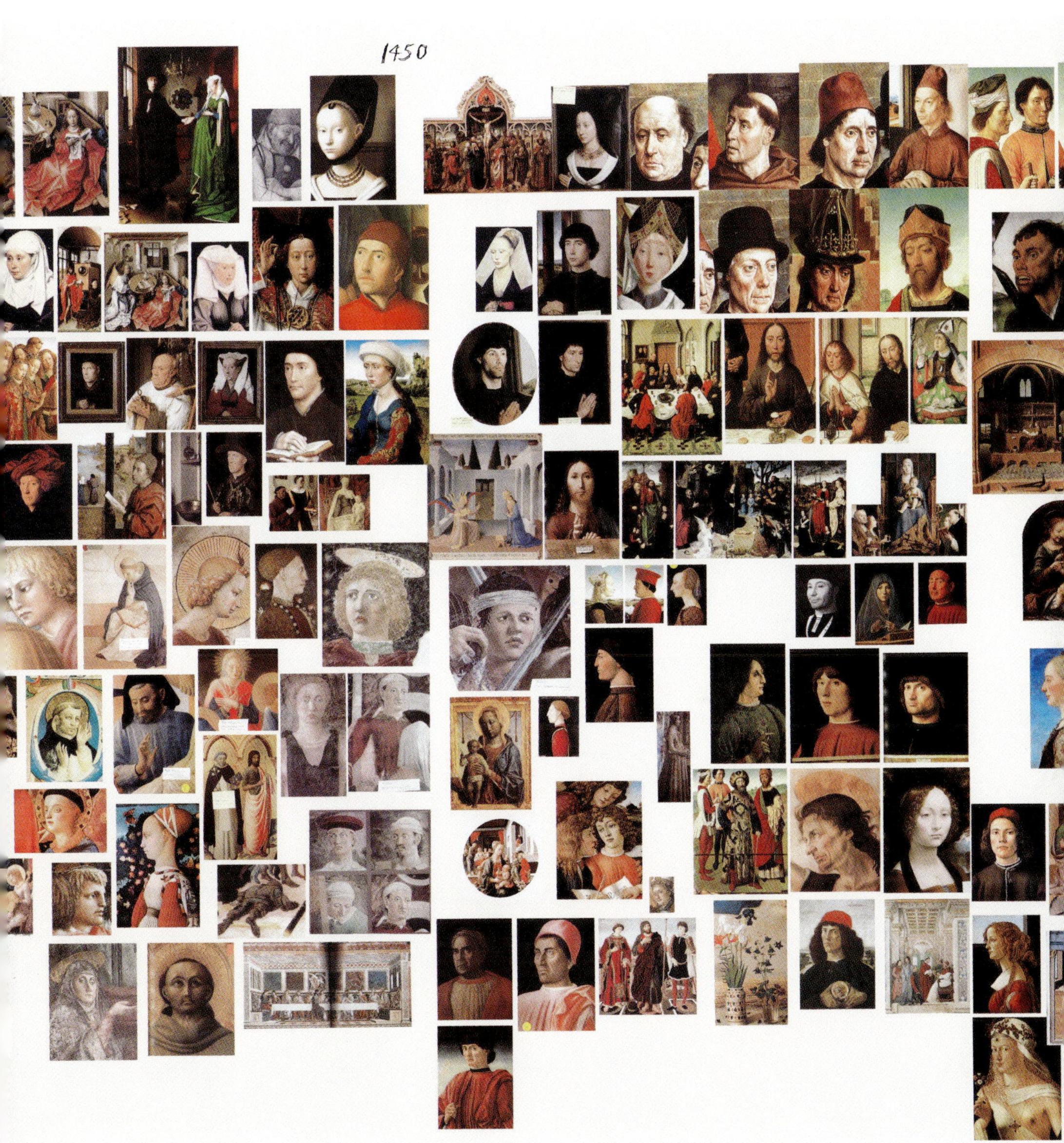

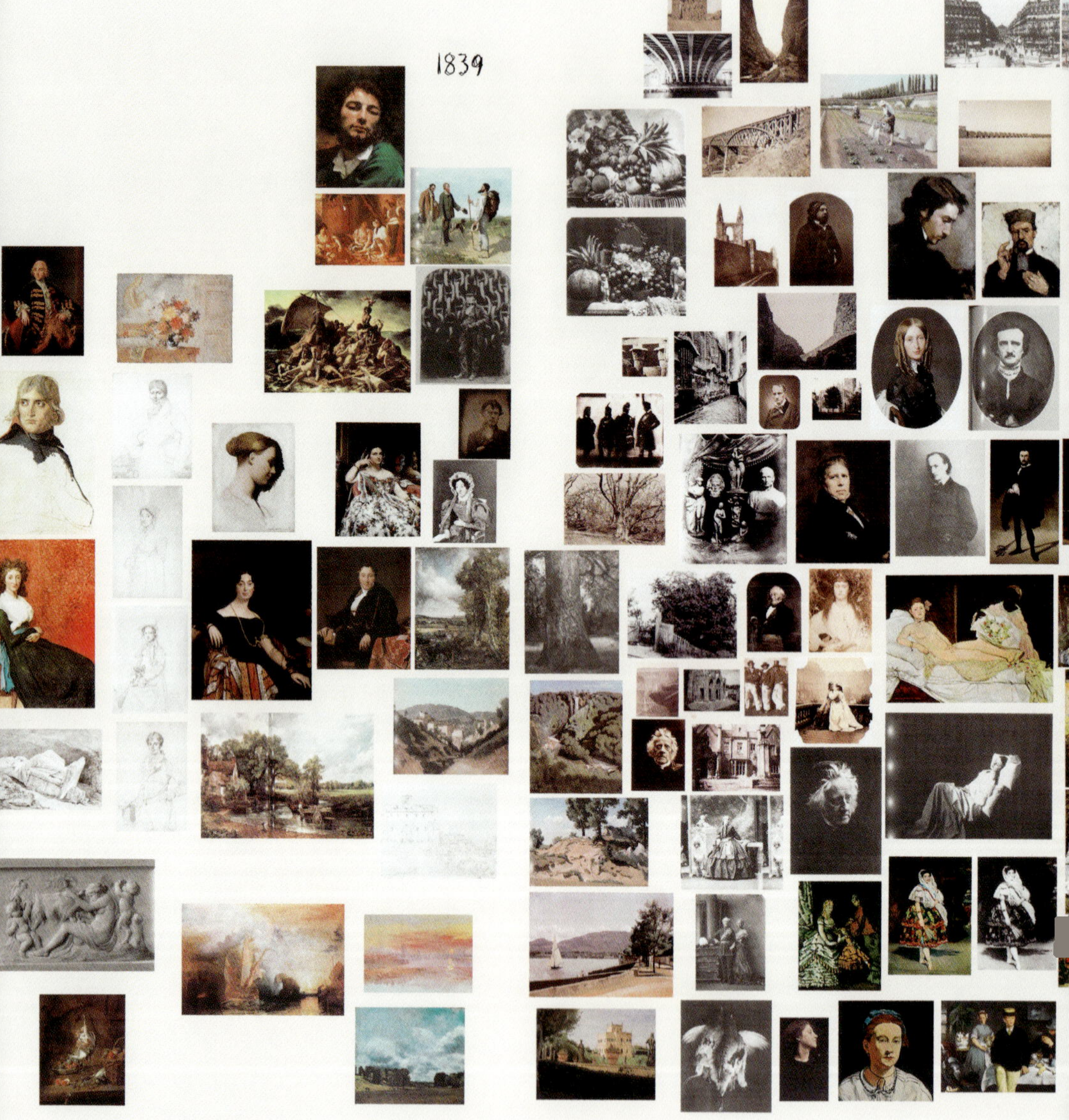
1839

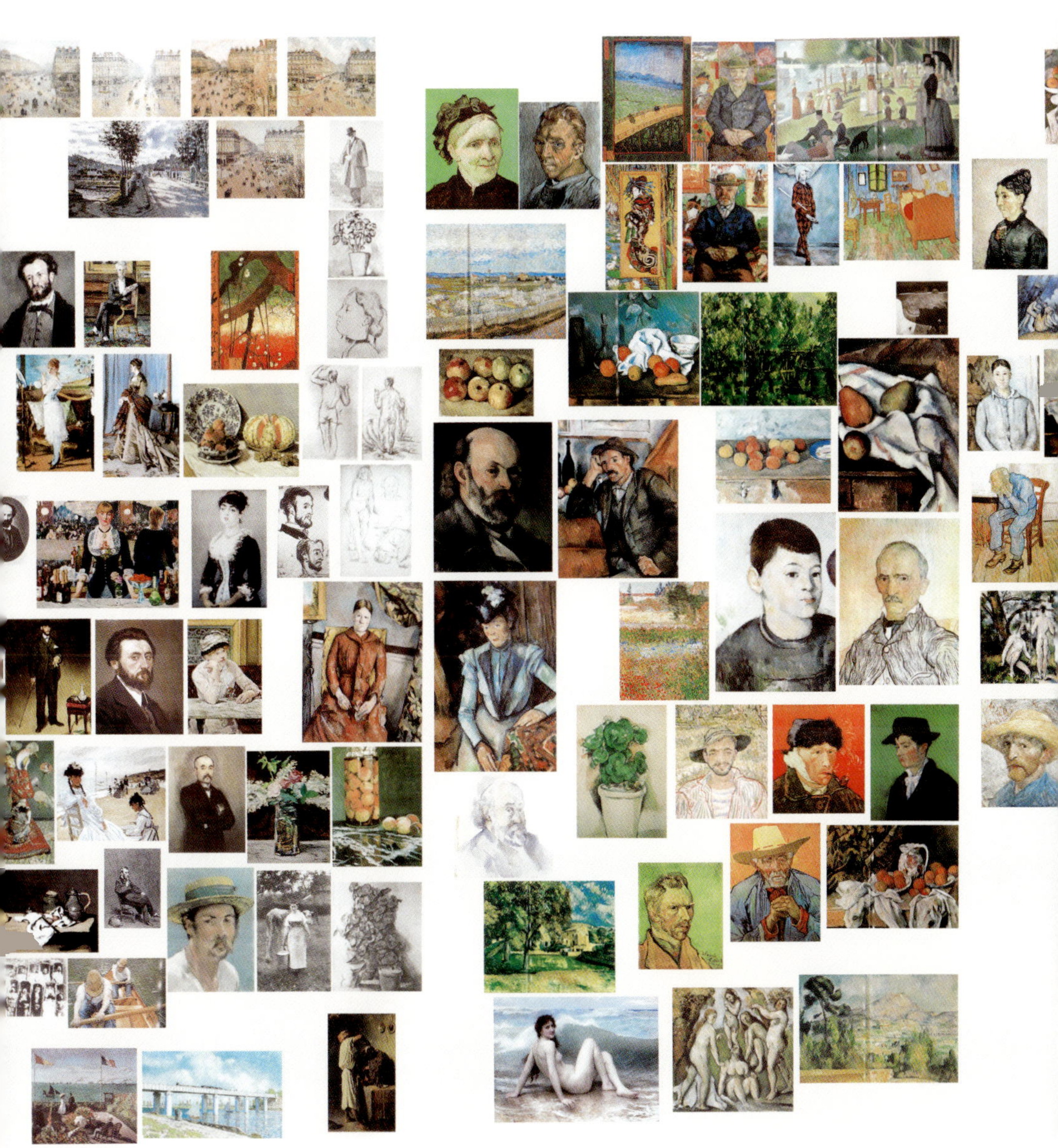

2001   Hockney's book *Secret Knowledge: Rediscovering the Lost Techniques of the Old Masters* is published, illustrating his complete theory on the use of lenses, camera obscuras, and other optical instruments by painters since the 15th century. The book is much discussed, so that the BBC approaches the artist for an accompanying 90-minute TV show. Peter Robb in the *Guardian*: "The delight of Hockney's book is the stimulus it gives us to look afresh at paintings we know well, to think and see for ourselves. His remarks on visual detail are brilliant. I think his larger thesis is essentially right, if not equally pertinent or fruitful in all its parts. New insights sometimes have to fight the tide of a faintly tedious obsession with the minutiae of mechanical technique."

The debate leads to a two-day conference in December organized by Lawrence Weschler for the New York Institute for the Humanities. Speakers include Susan Sontag, who remarks that if great artists had used lenses it would be like finding out that the great lovers of history had used Viagra; Chuck Close, who believes that a painter will use any trick or tool to make a better painting; and scientists who conduct their own experiments extracting images from primitive lenses. Invited prominent art historians remain distant, as Sarah Boxer reports in the *New York Times*: "Svetlana Alpers, a professor emerita at the University of California at Berkeley, suggested that Mr. Hockney, who has often used photographs in his work, secretly wanted to 'kick free of the lens habit.' 'Why not just go for it, David?' she said. 'The old masters did.' Rosalind Krauss, the Meyer Shapiro Professor of Modern Art and Theory at Columbia University, questioned the epiphany that started it all for Mr. Hockney. To say there is no difference between the lines of Ingres and Warhol, she suggested, is wrong. Ingres's drawn line 'swells and narrows.' Warhol's traced line is 'flaccid, inert, and everywhere equally broad,' the essence of technology…And Mr. Hockney said: 'I enjoyed it. I learned some things.' Then he added, 'I will now go back to my studio.'"

Afterward Hockney tells Weschler: "I've been getting bored with the whole controversy…For a short time, but only a very short time, I wondered if there were some way I could adapt optics to my new purposes. But I quickly realized that no, the trouble with optics is the trouble with photography: it's not real enough, it's not true enough to lived experience. The Chinese say that painting draws on three things: the eye, the heart, and the hand. And I longed to return to the hand."

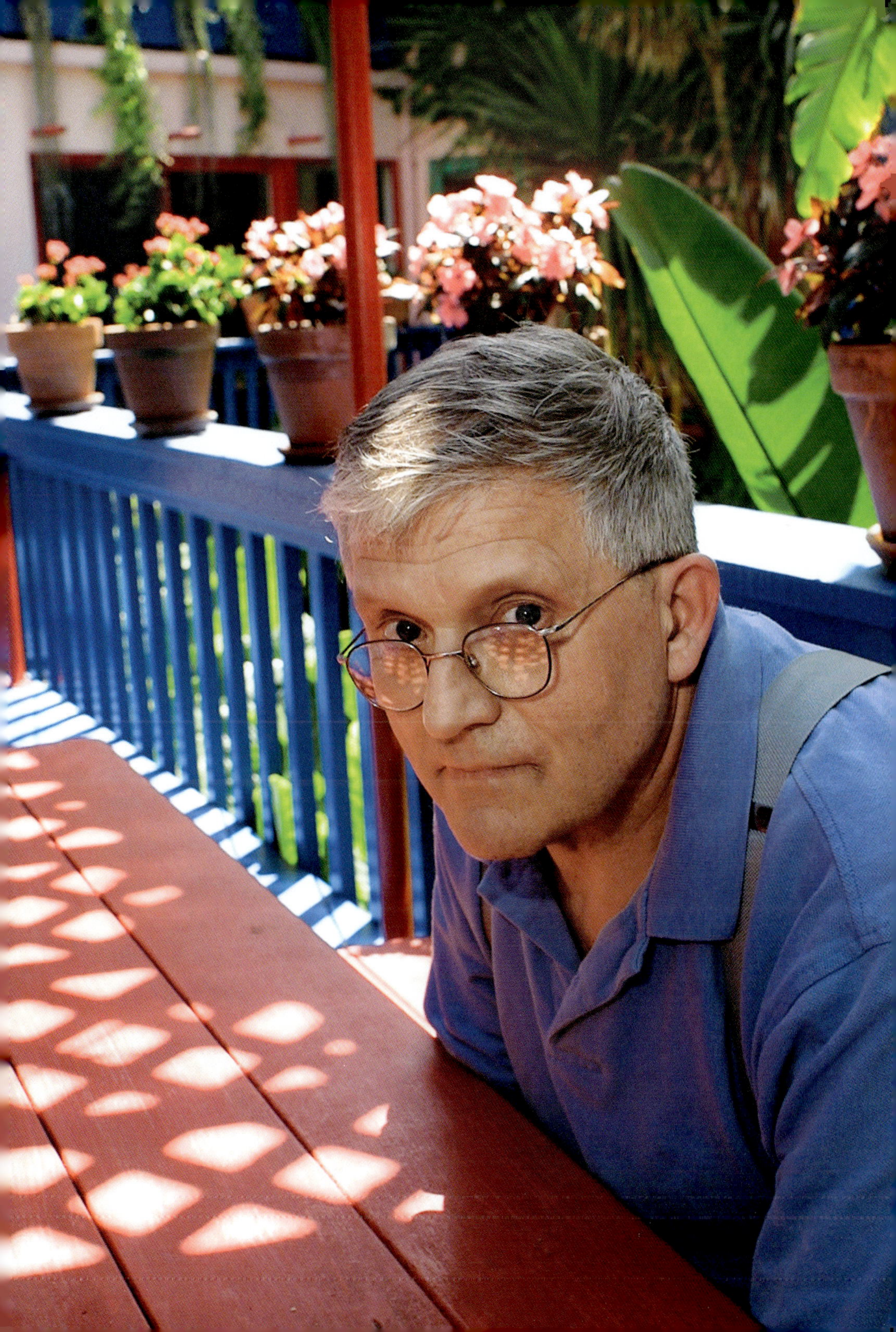

Meanwhile a large Hockney retrospective opens at Bundeskunsthalle Bonn, titled *Exciting Times Are Ahead* (pp. 378–379). Marco Livingstone in *Burlington Magazine*: "The decision to start with the newest work provides a parallel to the reverse perspective employed by Hockney in his recent art, replacing the fixed viewpoint of traditional one-point perspective to give wider vistas reliant on the spectator's own choice of position. The sense of rediscovering even the most familiar of the paintings of the 1960s and 1970s through the lens of Hockney's post-cubist experiments makes for an unusually fresh reassessment of the artist's production over four decades."

Solo: *Exciting Times Are Ahead,* Kunst- und Ausstellungshalle der Bundesrepublik Deutschland, Bonn (Jun 1–Sep 23); catalog with texts by Kay Heymer, Alexandra Kapp, Paul Melia, Didier Ottinger, and Pierre Sterckx; travels as *Maleri 1960–2000* to Louisiana Museum for Moderne Kunst, Humlebæk (Oct 12, 2001–Jan 27, 2002); catalog with a text by Poul Erik Tojner. *David Hockney,* Galerie Kaess-Weiss, Stuttgart (May 5–Jun 10). *Selected Graphics 1964–1998,* Leslie Sacks Fine Art, Los Angeles (Oct 6–Nov 3). *Close and Far,* Galerie Lelong, Paris (Nov 8–Dec 22); catalog with a text by Jean Frémon.

Group: *Pop Art: US/UK Connections, 1956–1966,* Menil Collection, Houston (Jan 26–May 13); catalog. *Les années Pop, 1956–1968,* Musée national d'art moderne, Centre Georges Pompidou, Paris (Mar 7–Jun 18); catalog. *Out of Line: Drawings from the Arts Council Collection,* York City Art Gallery, York (Jun 2–Jul 15); organized by Hayward Gallery, London, travels to Sheffield, Llandudno, Stoke-on-Trent, and Eye; catalog. *Summer Exhibition,* Royal Academy of Arts, London (Jun–Aug); catalog. *Treasures for a Queen: A Millennium Gift to Cincinnati,* Cincinnati Art Museum, Cincinnatti (Jun 17–Sep 2); catalog. *Great British Paintings from American Collections: Holbein to Hockney,* Yale Center for British Art, New Haven (Sep 27–Dec 30); travels to San Marino, CA; catalog. *Szenenwechsel XX,* Museum für Moderne Kunst, Frankfurt am Main (Sep 28, 2001–Mar 3, 2002); catalog. *Vancouver Collects,* Vancouver Art Gallery (Oct 6, 2001–Feb 10, 2002); catalog.

Publication: David Hockney, *Secret Knowledge: Rediscovering the Lost Techniques of the Old Masters,* London: Thames and Hudson; New York: Viking Studio.

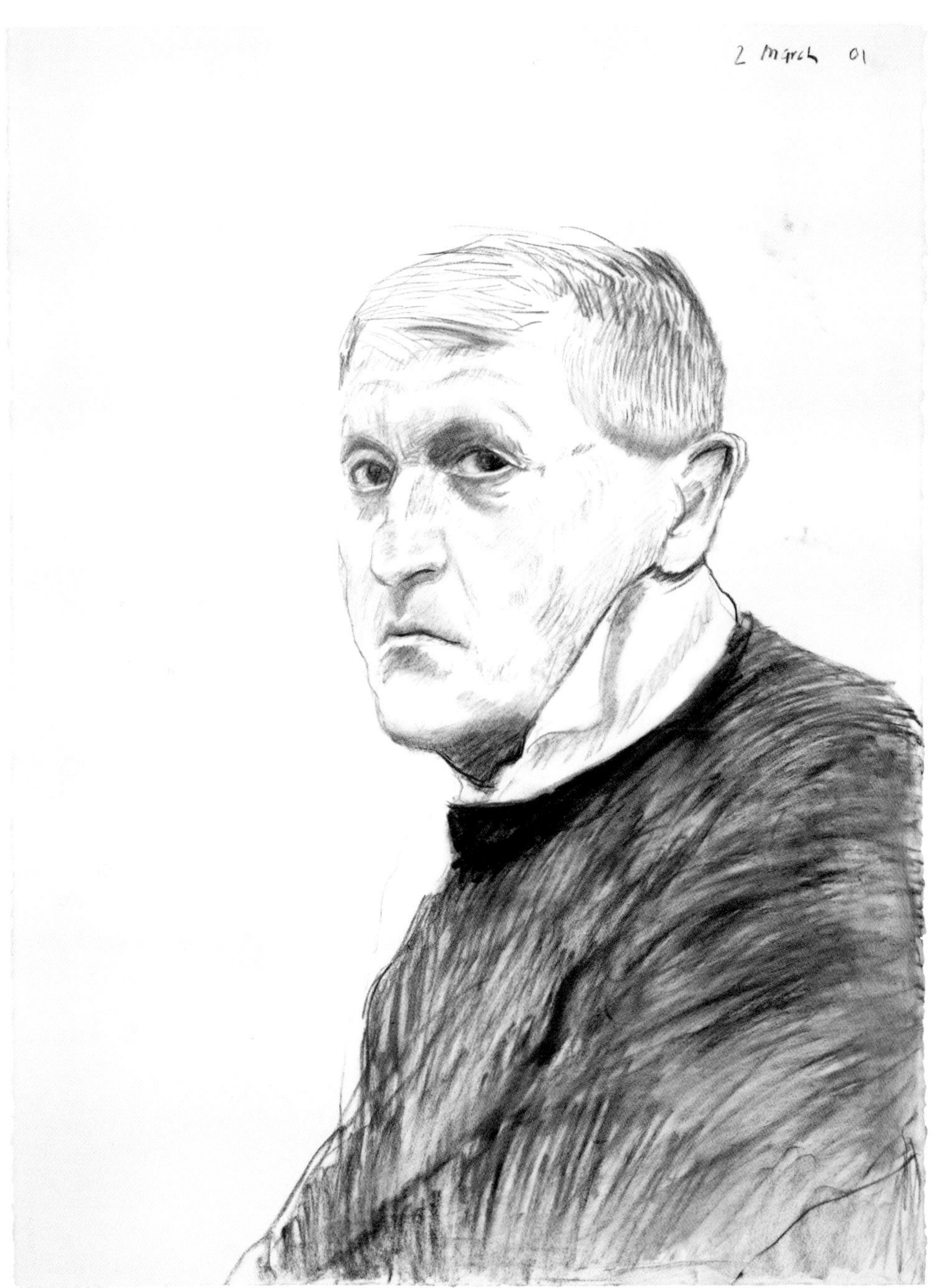

2 March 01

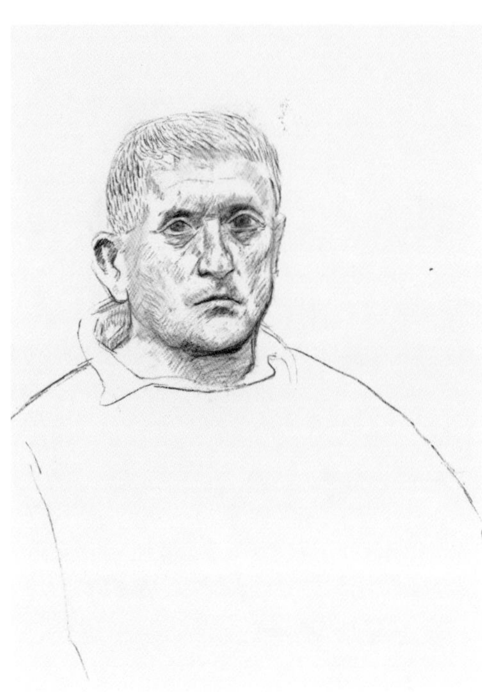

Self Portrait, Weekend of 3/3/01, 2001, charcoal on paper, 30 x 22 ¼ in. / 76.2 x 56.5 cm

Self Portrait, March 4, 2001, charcoal on paper, 30 x 22 ¼ in. / 76.2 x 56.5 cm

Self Portrait, 2001, charcoal on paper, 30 x 22 ¼ in. / 76.2 x 56.5 cm

Right page: *Guest House Garden II,* 2001, oil on canvas, 56 x 76 in. / 142.2 x 193 cm

Guest House Garden, March 7th 2001, charcoal on paper, 22 ¼ x 30 in. / 56.5 x 76.2 cm

Page 373: David Hockney at home, Los Angeles 2001. Photo: Monica Almeida

Page 375: *Self Portrait, 2 March 2001,* charcoal on paper, 30 x 22 ¼ in. / 76 x 56.5 cm

Pages 378–379: *David Hockney: Exciting Times Are Ahead,* exhibition views, Kunst- und Ausstellungshalle der Bundesrepublik Deutschland, Bonn 2001

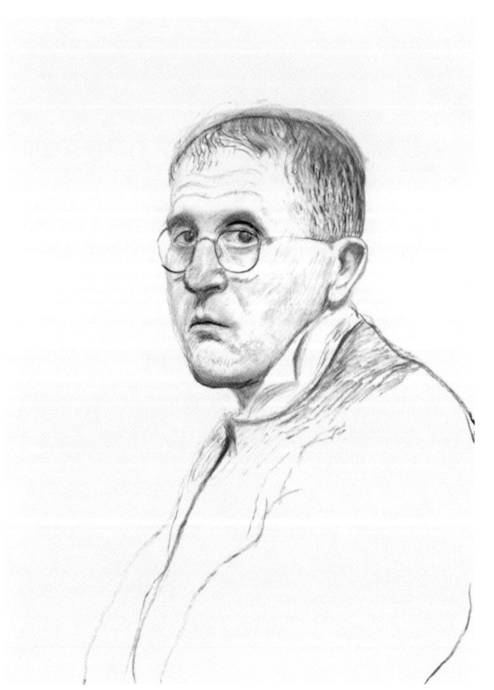

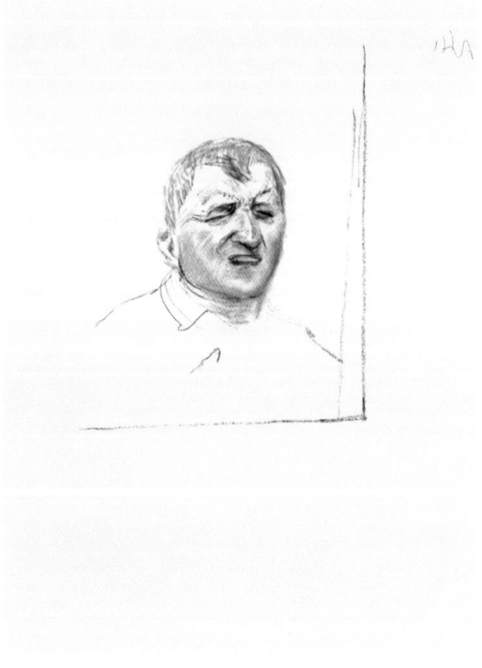

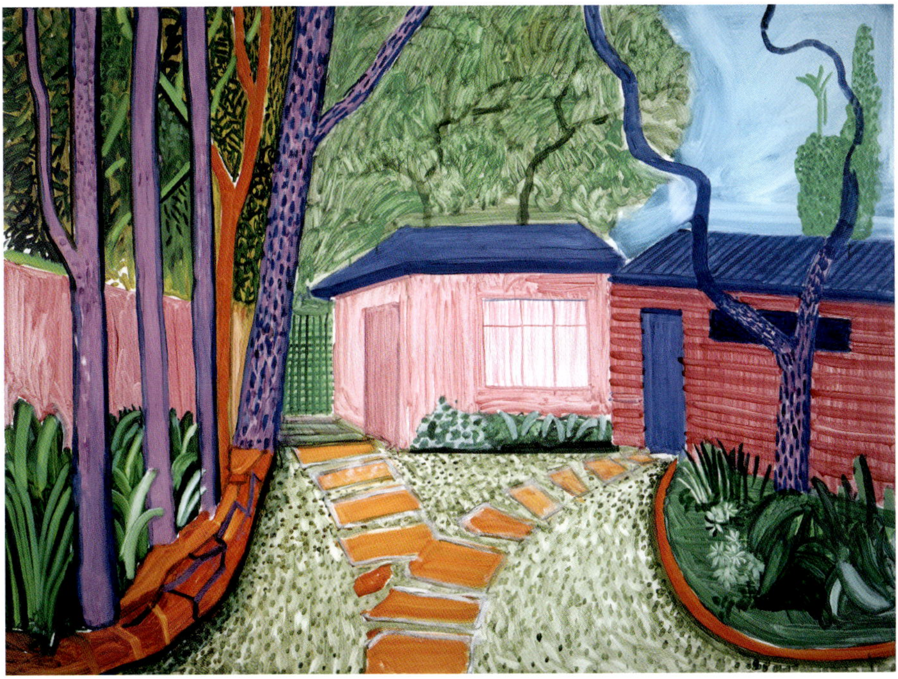

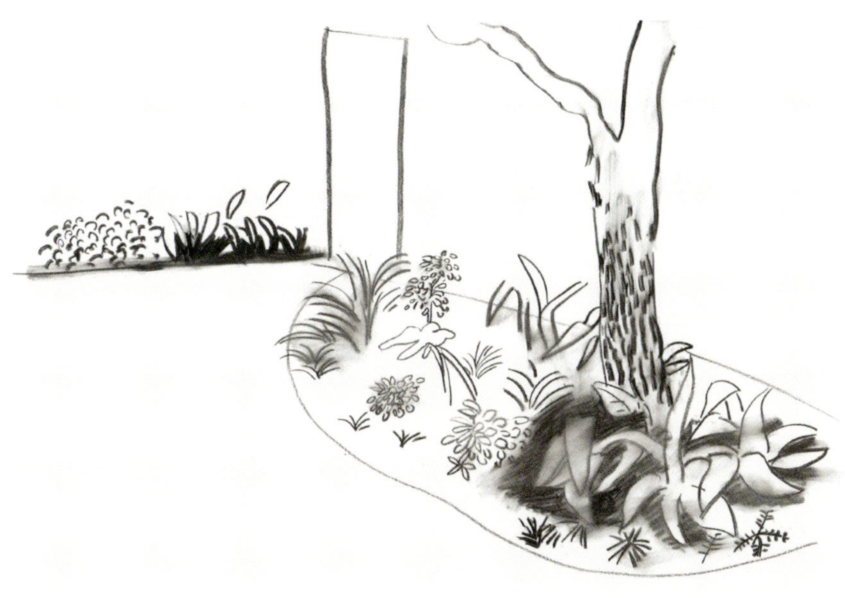

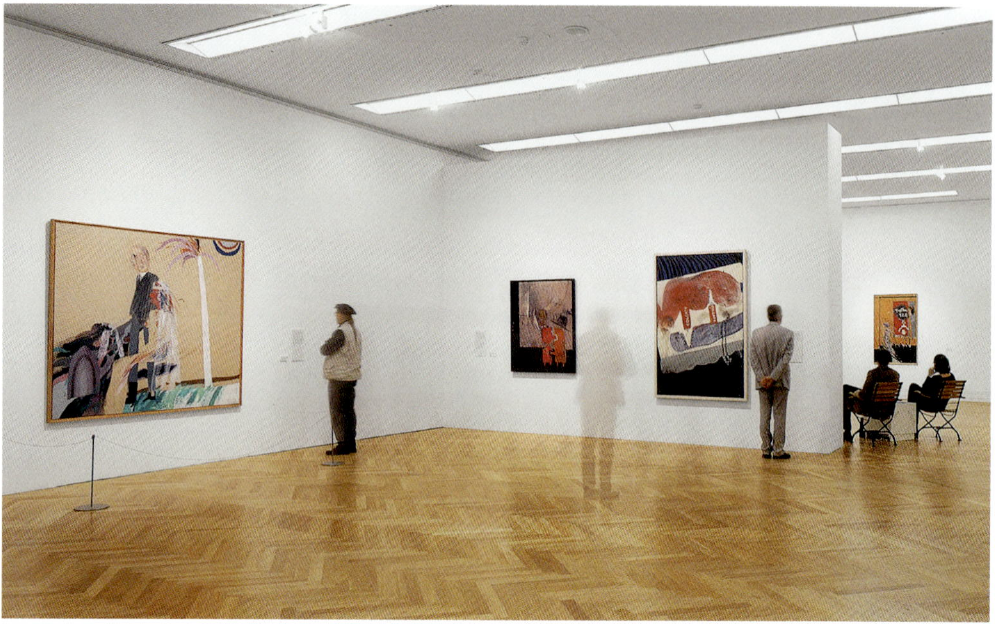

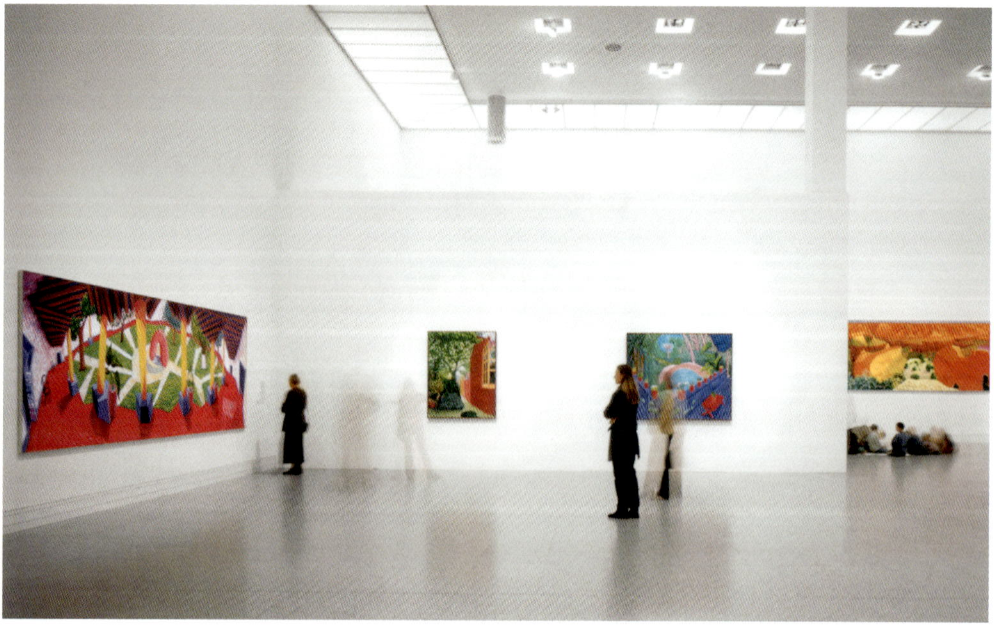

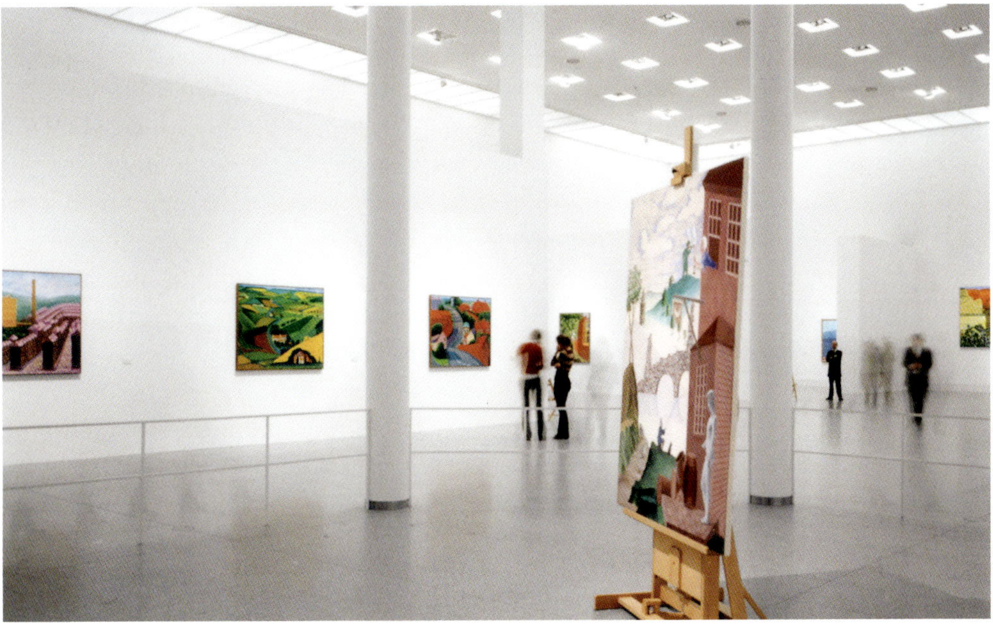

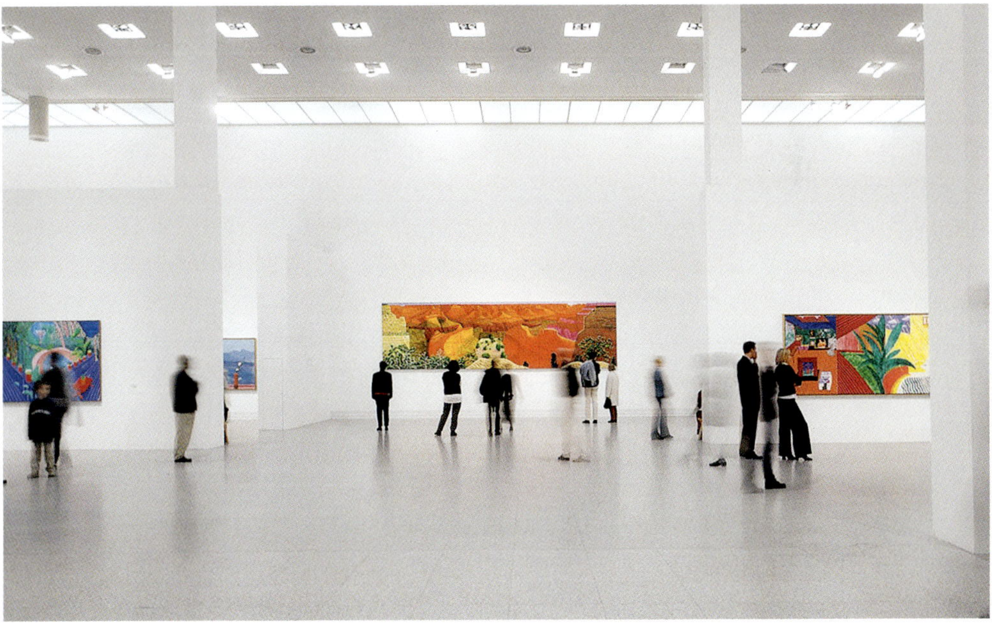

2002

After seeing an exhibition of Chinese painting in New York, Hockney starts trying out watercolors and continues working in this medium when he travels to London. "It's the most direct method of laying in a mark," he says, "flowing from the eye, the heart, down the arm to the hand, through the tip of your instrument, everything flowing very quickly and seamlessly. Oil painting in a sense you have to push. Watercolor just flows… The thing is it does take a while to master the techniques—having to work, say, from light to dark, because unlike with oils, you won't be able subsequently to daub a light color over a dark one. Everything has to be thought out in advance—and I realized it would take time to master all this. I had to ask myself, was I going to be willing to take six months to learn all this? Well I was, and I did, and it took even longer, mastering the medium, innovating new techniques, but by the end I'd broken into this looser, more immediate way." He soon works in large formats on several sheets laid together, painting portraits and double portraits from life, alongside smaller studies and still lifes.

Hockney also has his own portrait painted by Lucian Freud and vice versa (pp. 381, 383, 390/391). The agreement is that each of the artists will sit for the other, though in the end this proves an unequal deal: "I sat for 120 hours for Lucian; he would only sit for three hours for me. He wouldn't co-operate, really. Too restless. The difference between us is, Lucian is shy and I'm a chatterbox, except when I am painting. I don't let people talk when I paint. Well, I don't mind people talking, but I don't answer back because I'm tuned out. Lips moving are very hard to get. Actually Lucian and I talked quite a lot when he was painting me. He let me smoke, too, but only if I didn't tell Kate Moss, who was also sitting for him and who also smokes."

While Hockney spends most of the year in England, he makes several trips abroad hunting for landscape motifs: "To have longer periods of twilight (when color is not bleached but extremely rich) one has to go north. I made a trip to Norway in May, was very taken with the dramatic landscape and returned to go much further north, when in June the sun never sets at all. You can see the landscape at all hours, 24 hours a day. There is no night. I found myself deeply attracted to it, and then went to Iceland twice to tour the island." He returns with many sketches from which he paints a series of multi-sheet watercolors (pp. 384–387).

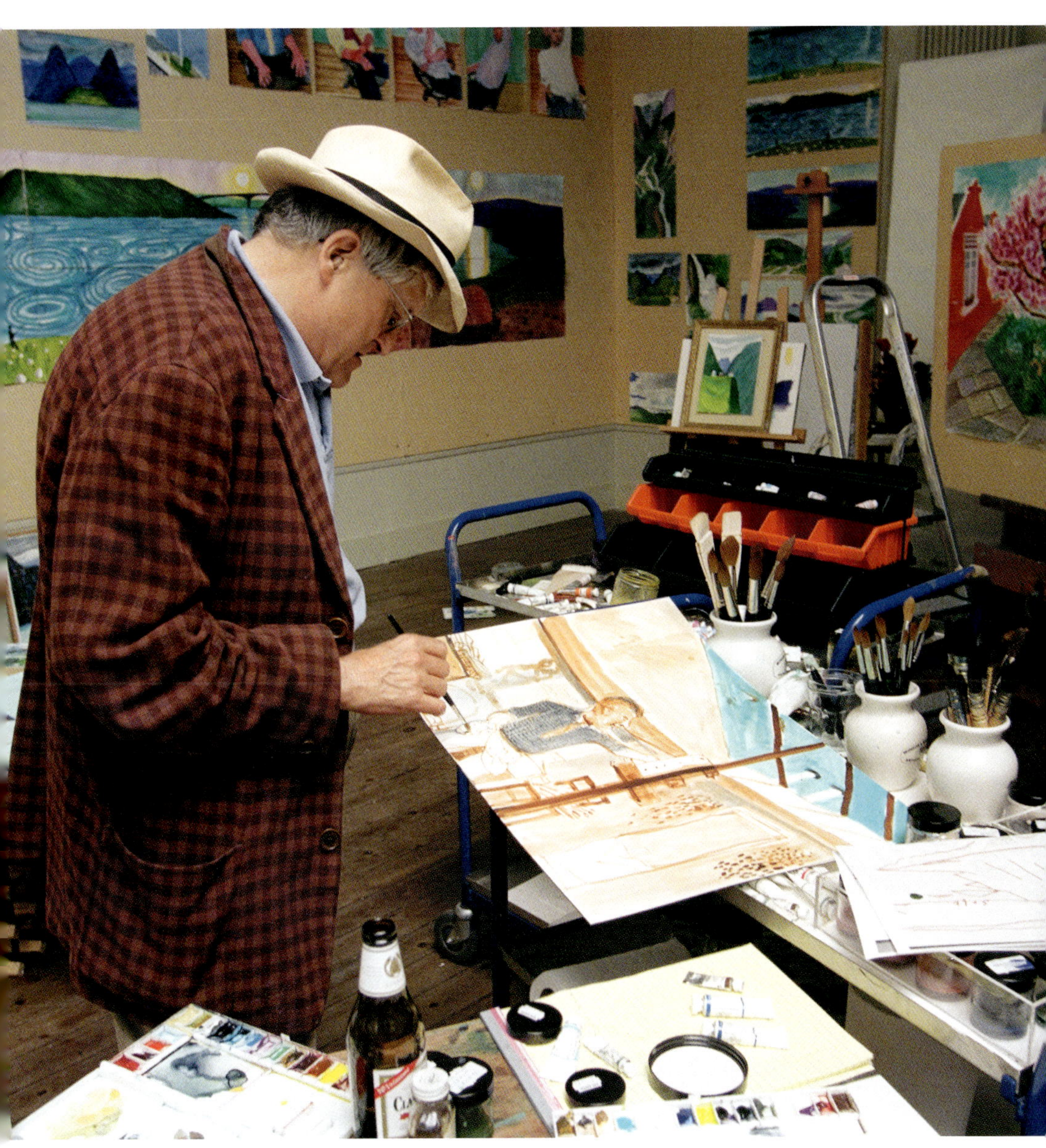

David Hockney drawing *Lucian Looks Youthful Painting*, London 2002.
Photo: Jim McHugh

Unusually, Hockney also paints a religious motif, *Expulsion from the Garden of Eden* (pp. 388/389). He takes the figures of Adam and Eve from the famous painting of the same subject by Renaissance artist Masaccio (one of the early proponents of one-point perspective), while paradise looks like a jungle of almost abstract marks: "The American painter Thomas Cole made a version of this subject in 1827, which I saw in the *American Sublime* show at the Tate Gallery. It was bombastic, even operatic, with the figures very small. What did the Garden of Eden look like? That seemed to me an interesting visual problem. The subject is, of course, the only real subject. Here Adam and Eve are leaving Paradise, where there is no perspective, no shadows, and no measurements."

Solo: *Egyptian Journeys,* Palace of the Arts, Cairo (Jan 16–Feb 16); catalog with a text by Marco Livingstone, Cairo: American University in Cairo Press. *Words and Pictures,* Couvent des Cordeliers, Forcalquier (Jul 11–Aug 18); touring exhibition organized by the British Council, London; travels to Istituto Nazionale per la Grafica, Rome; Pinacoteca nazionale di Bologna; Museum of Modern Art, Bogota; Museo Nacional de Bellas Artes, Santiago; Benaki Museum, Athens, and many others (through 2016); catalog *David Hockney: Prints from the British Council Collection* with a text by Richard Riley. *Prints 1973–1998,* Nishimura Gallery, Tokyo (Feb 12–Mar 16). *Stage Works,* Richard Gray Gallery, New York (Feb 19–Mar 30); travels to Richard Gray Gallery, Chicago (May 4–Jun 29).

Group: *Transition: The London Art Scene in the Fifties,* Barbican Art Gallery, London (Jan 31–Apr 14); catalog. *Head On: Art with the Brain in Mind,* Science Museum, London (Mar 14–Jul 28); catalog. *Das zweite Gesicht: Metamorphosen des fotografischen Porträts,* Deutsches Museum, Munich (May 8–Aug 11); catalog. *Summer Exhibition,* Royal Academy of Arts, London (Jun 7–Aug 19). *New: Recent Acquisitions of Contemporary British Art,* Scottish National Gallery of Modern Art, Edinburgh (Jul 6–Nov 17); catalog. *Blast to Freeze: Britische Kunst im 20. Jahrhundert,* Kunstmuseum Wolfsburg (Sep 14, 2002–Jan 19, 2003); travels to Les Abattoirs, Toulouse; catalog. *The Art of Collaboration: The Big Americans,* National Gallery of Australia, Canberra (Oct 4, 2002–Jan 27, 2003); catalog.

Film: *David Hockney: Secret Knowledge,* GB, 75 min., dir. by Randall Wright, starring David Hockney.

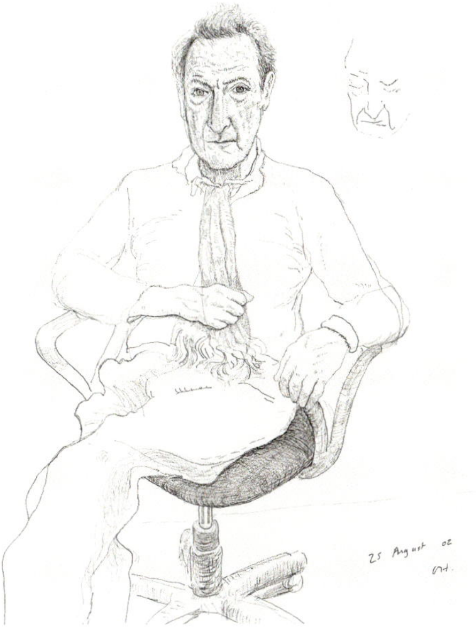

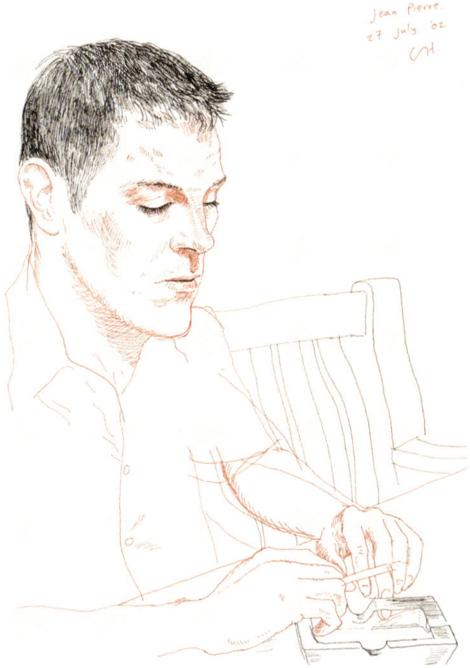

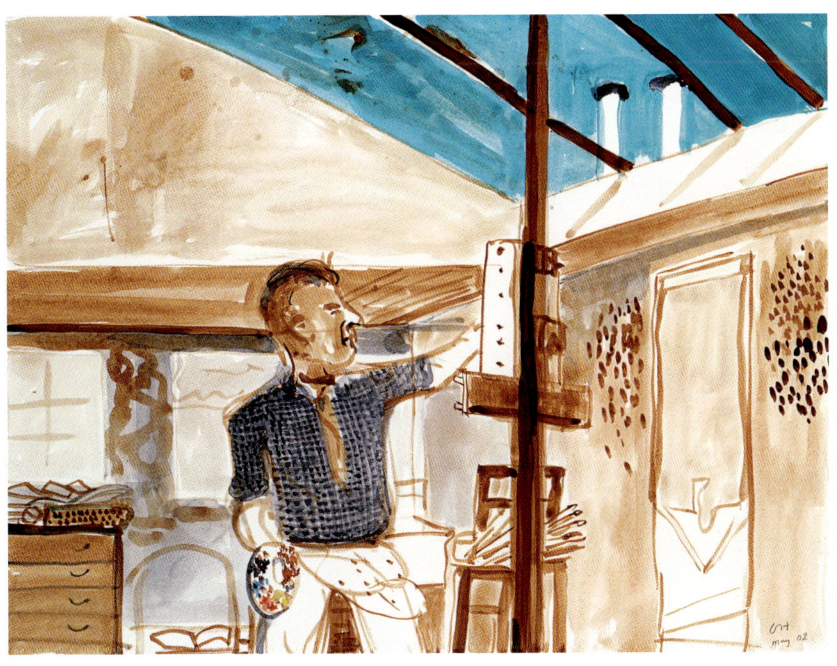

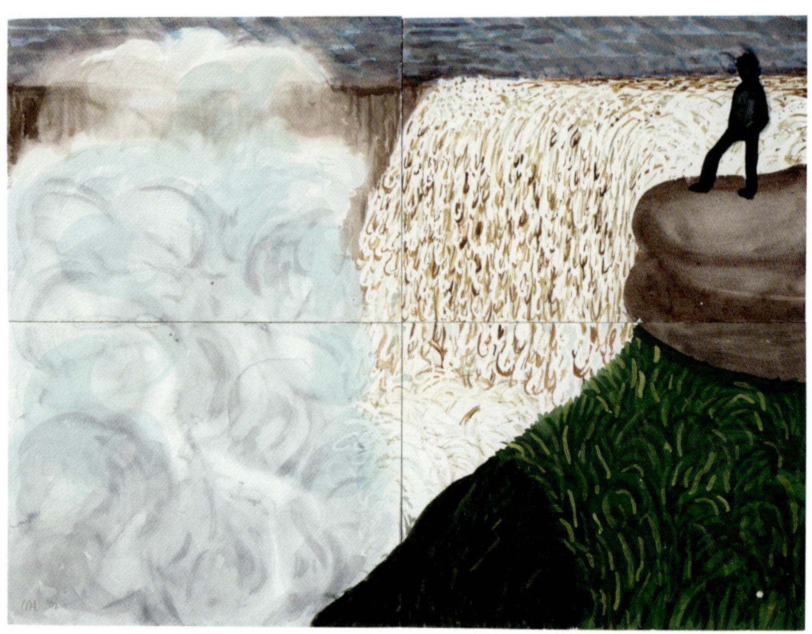

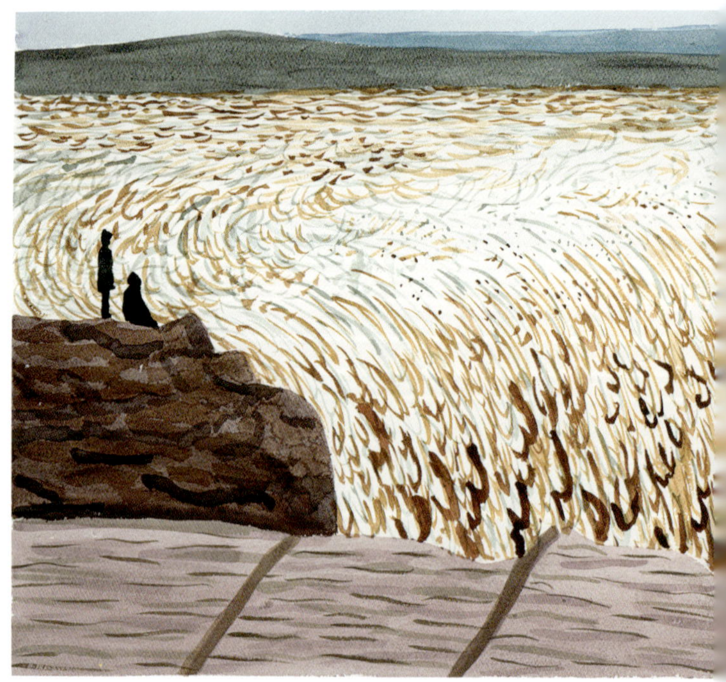

Dettifoss from the Other Side,
2002, watercolor on 4 sheets
of paper, 36 1/4 x 48 in. /
92.1 x 121.9 cm

Dettifoss, 2002, watercolor on
2 sheets of paper, 18 x 48 in. /
45.7 x 121.9 cm

Dettifoss with 2 Figures, 2002,
watercolor on 2 sheets of paper,
18 x 48 in. / 45.7 x 121.9 cm

Page 383: *Lucian Freud,* 2002,
ink on paper, 24 x 18 1/8 in. /
61 x 46 cm

Jean-Pierre de Lima II, 2002,
ink on paper, 14 1/4 x 10 1/4 in. /
36.2 x 26 cm

Lucian Looks Youthful Painting,
2002, watercolor on paper,
18 x 24 in. / 45.7 x 61 cm

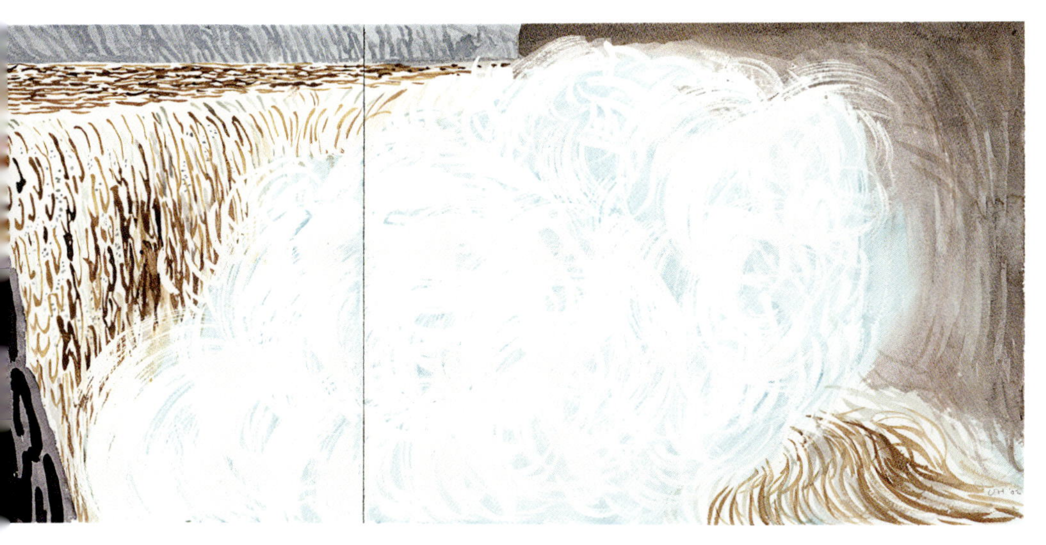

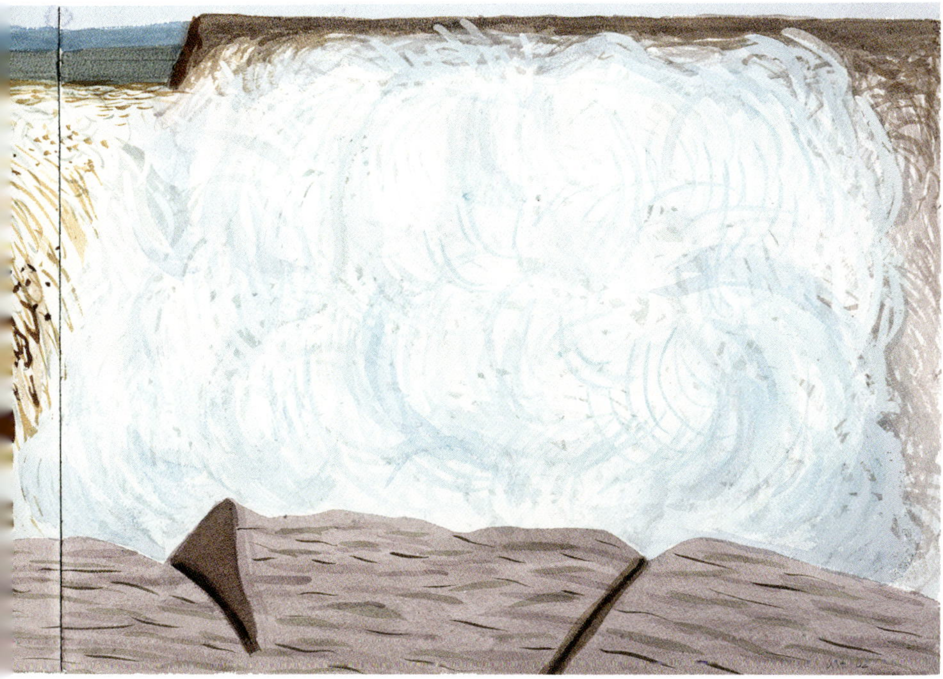

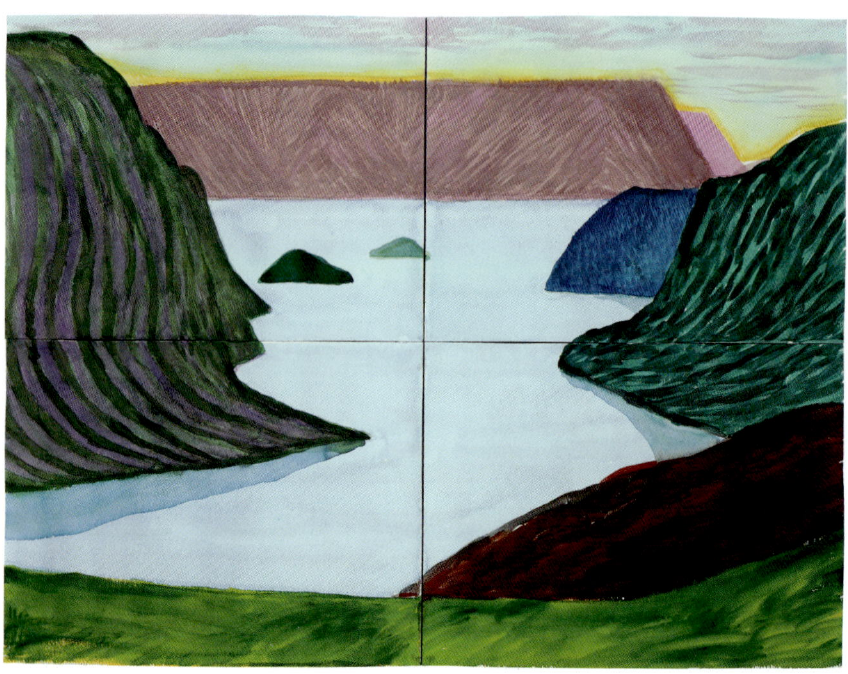
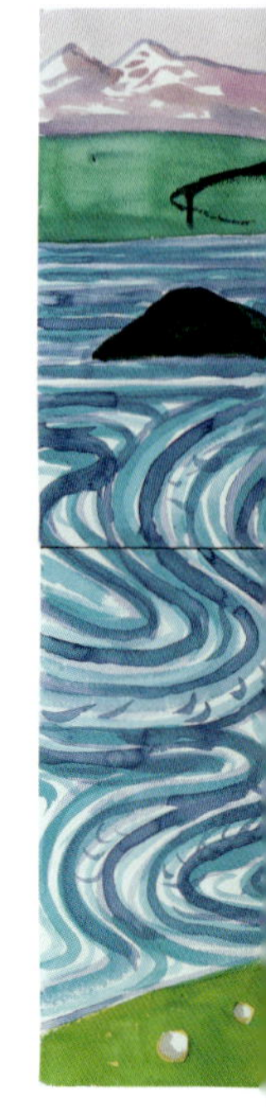
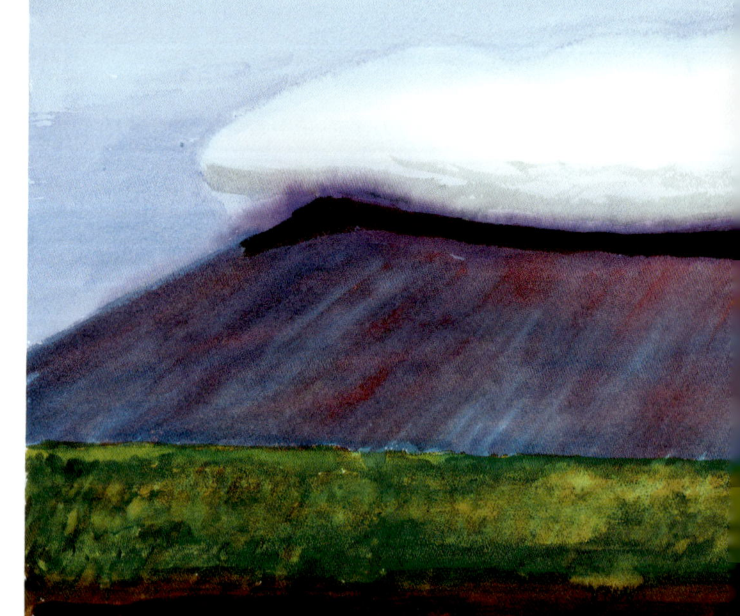

Fjord Kamoyvaer, 2002,
watercolor on 4 sheets of paper,
36 x 48 in. / 91.4 x 121.9 cm

The Maelstrom, Bodo, 2002,
watercolor on 6 sheets of paper,
36 x 72 in. / 91.4 x 182.9 cm

Mountain & Cloud, Iceland, 2002,
watercolor on 2 sheets of paper,
18 x 48 in. / 45.7 x 121.9 cm

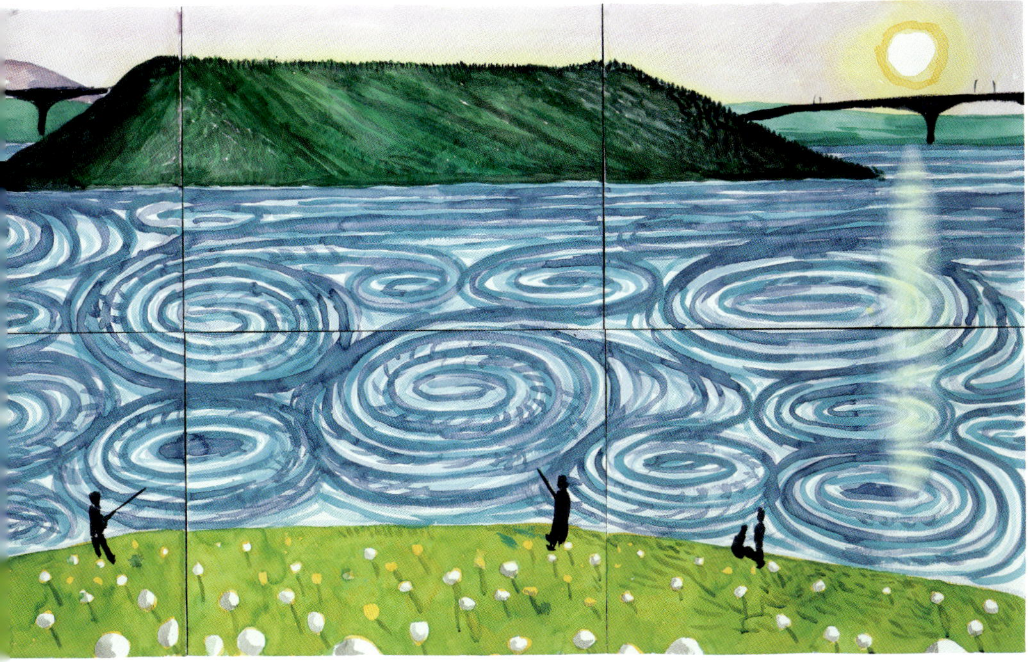

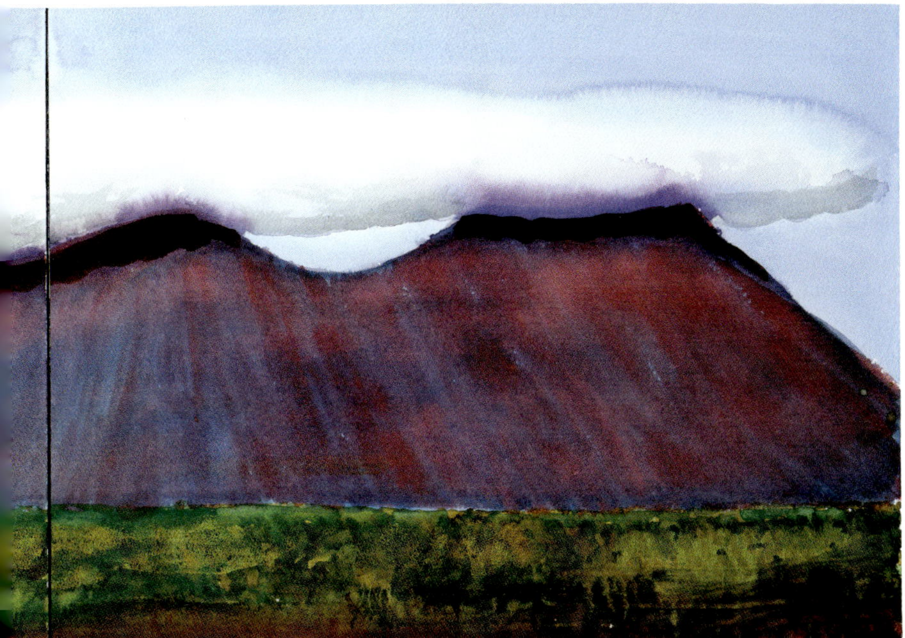

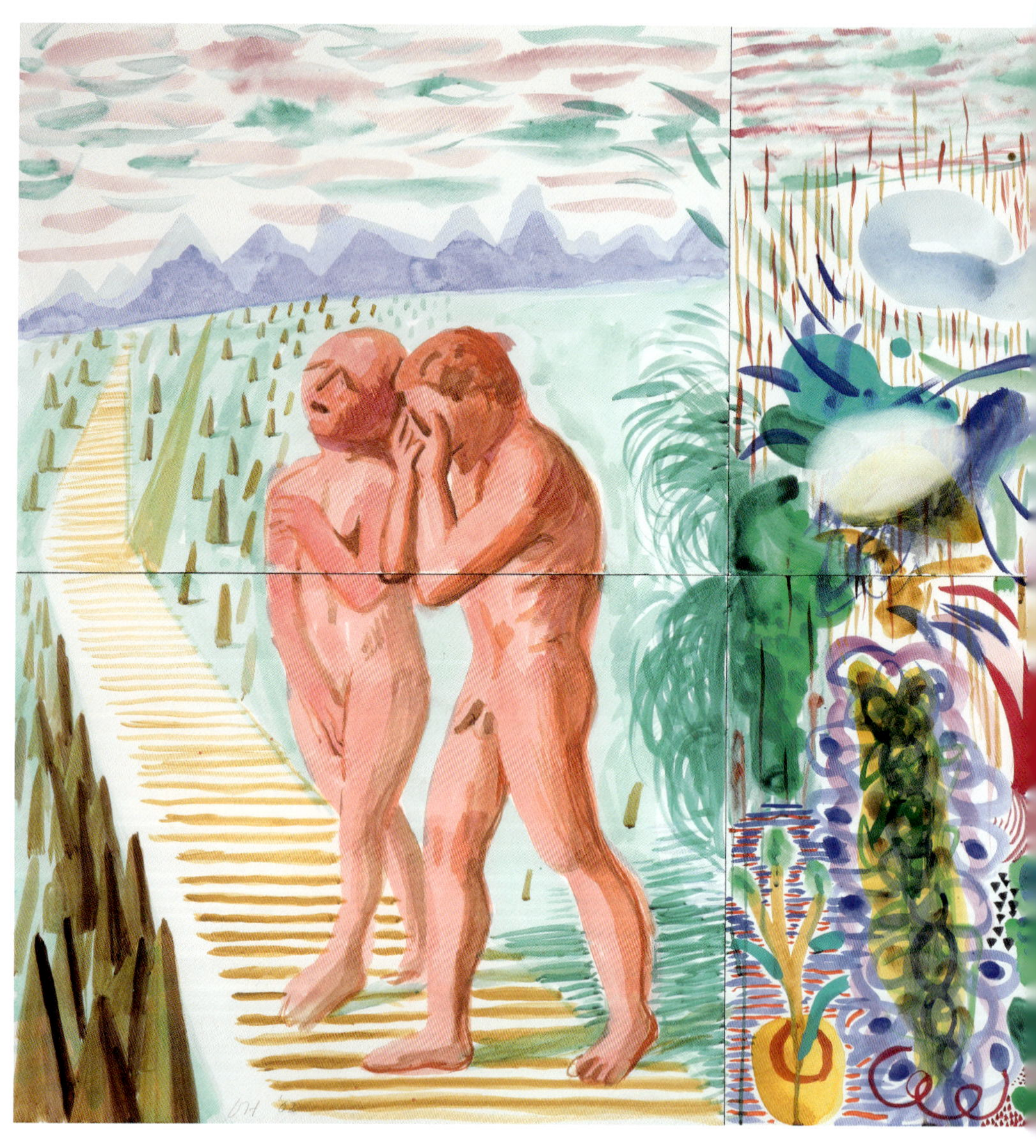

The Expulsion from the Garden of Eden, 2002, watercolor on 6 sheets of paper, 36 ¼ x 72 ⅛ in. / 92.1 x 183.1 cm

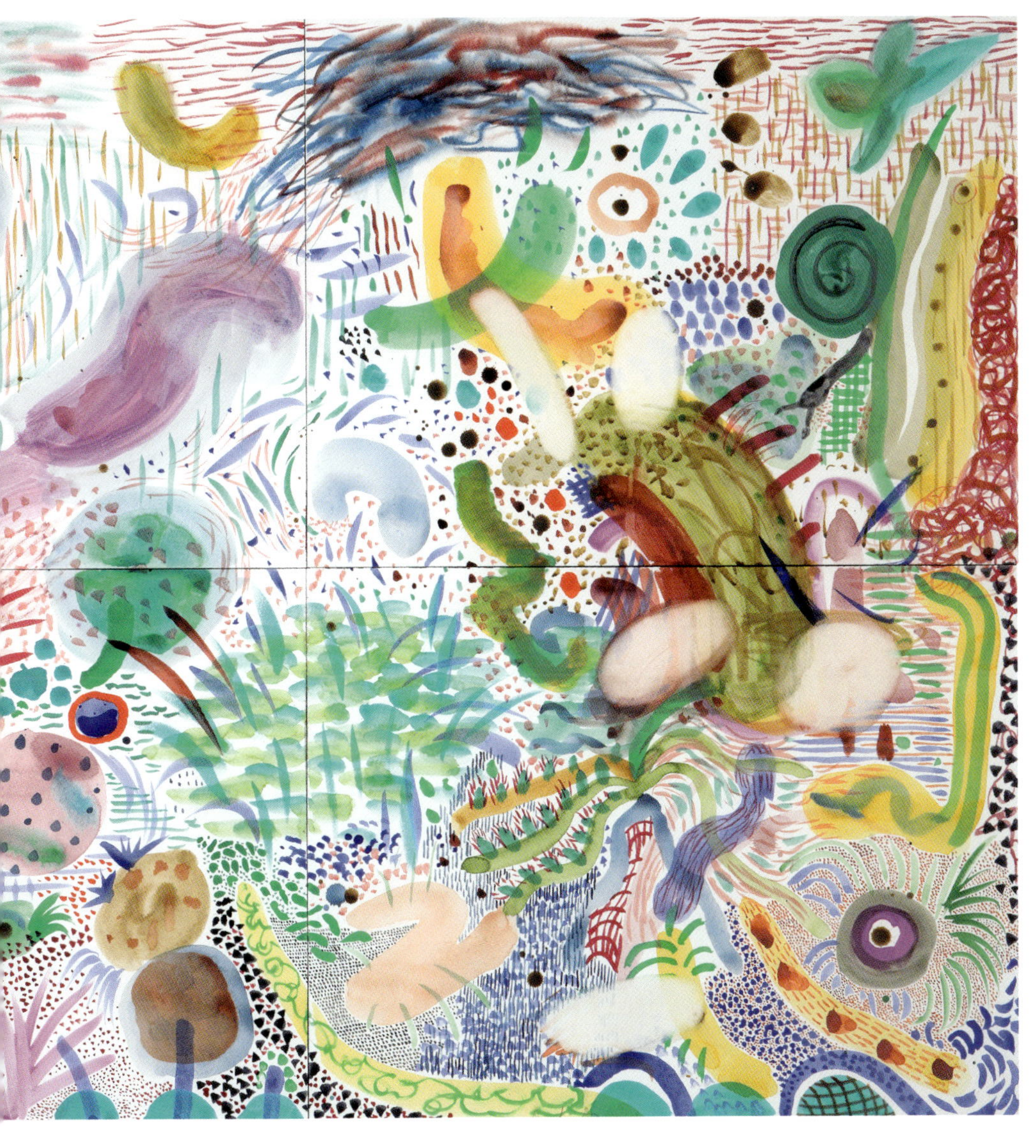

Pages 390/391: Lucian Freud
and David Hockney at Freud's
studio, London 2002. Photo:
David Dawson

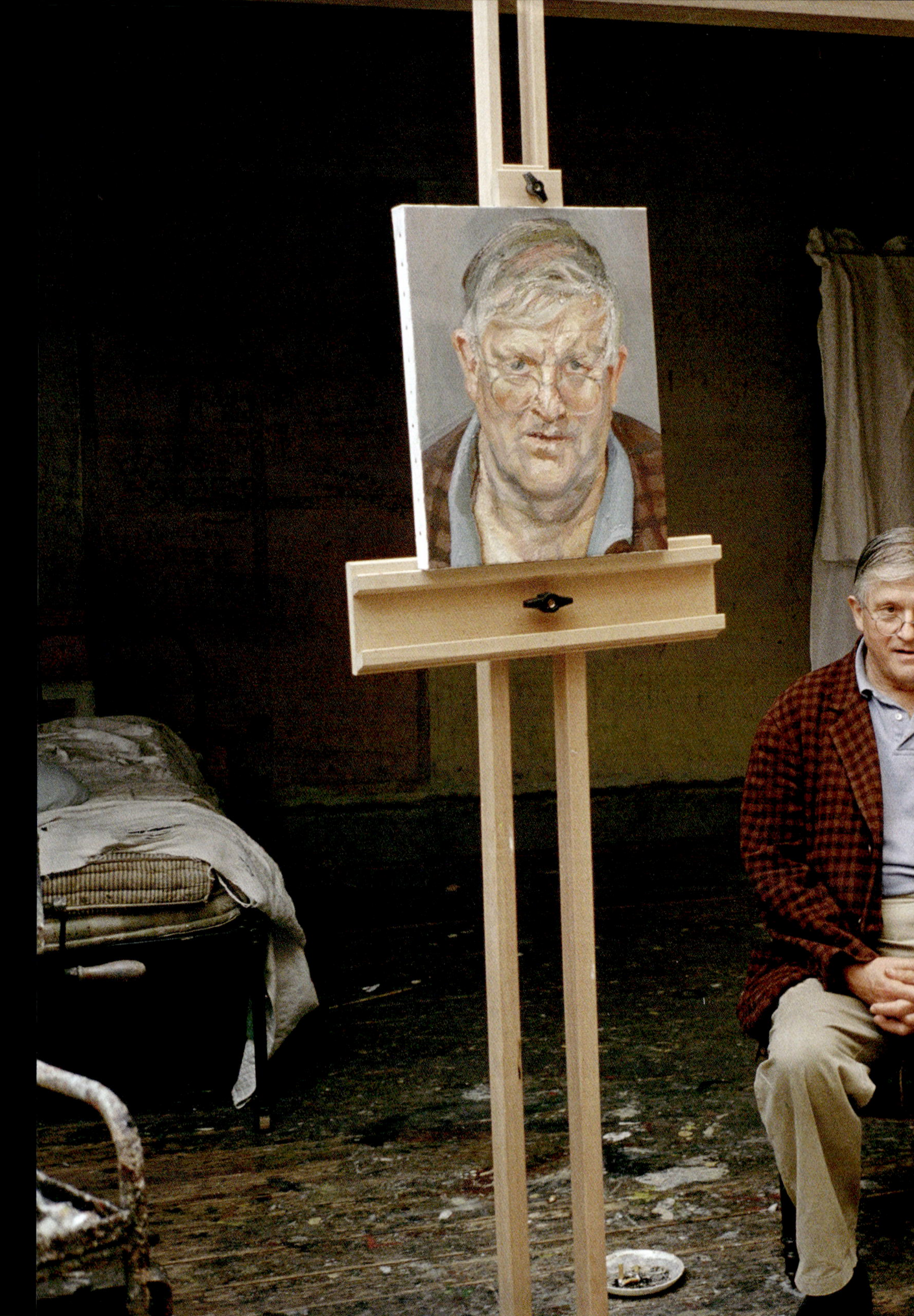

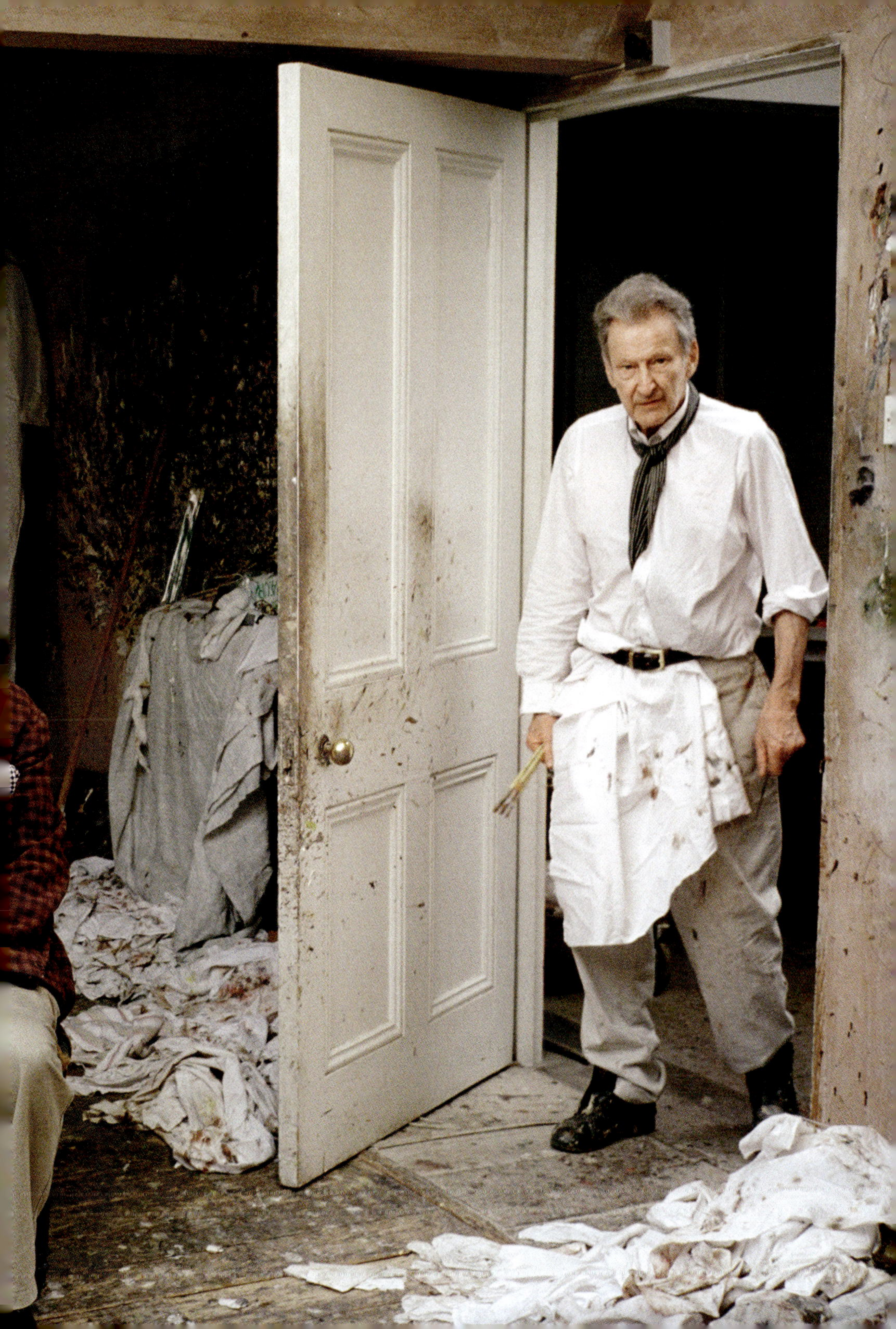

2003

At the start of the year, Andrew Marr reports in the *Guardian* that Hockney "has returned to drawing and painting. More controversially, to that version of drawing and painting that has been derided for a century as the refuge of the weekend painter, the timid stippler: watercolours." And indeed, when the artist's watercolor portraits and landscapes are shown a few weeks later at the National Portrait Gallery and simultaneously at Annely Juda Fine Art in London, reviews are mostly mixed. Adrian Searle in the *Guardian* dislikes the portraits (p. 395): "The set-up for the portraits is always the same: in the foreground, two figures sitting on modern office chairs. Bare floorboards parallel to the picture plane trudge away to an undifferentiated pale green wall. The subjects don't inhabit a space so much as they inhabit themselves, and that is what Hockney tries to give us. Each painting is executed on four sheets of paper, which quarter the composition. This stops us paying too much attention to the overall composition, and makes us go from part to part, head to torso, hands to shoes, without really encountering their interconnectedness in any interesting way." He likes the landscapes much better, though: "Here is full, saturated colour, a greater freedom and playfulness (mountains and fjords and weather can't complain about likeness)—and so much more invention. These paintings are not afraid of their own joyful decorativeness… Hockney is great at rocks and black glaciers, Iceland with its examples of weather, the Naples yellow horizon light at Nordkapp, and the white sun indistinguishable from the moon. Under the northern light, Hockney almost finds himself as a visionary."

Hockney returns to Los Angeles still early in the year, continuing his work in watercolor, painting his studio and garden, portraits and figure studies. The seven-panel *The Massacre and the Problems of Depiction* (pp. 396/397) quotes Picasso's *Massacre in Korea* from 1951, incongruously adding a photographer with an old-fashioned camera recording the scene. The painting is shown at Richard Gray Gallery and appears on the cover of the *Times Literary Supplement*. Hockney accompanies it with a note, describing how Picasso's painting "was generally dismissed as propaganda and compared very unfavorably with *Guernica*, and was rarely discussed again. Years later, on seeing it in the Picasso show at MoMA, I was struck by it. It stayed with me, and I began to see another interpretation. In 1950, images from the Second World War were still vivid and shocking; recovery from the war was just under way, when news of a new conflict

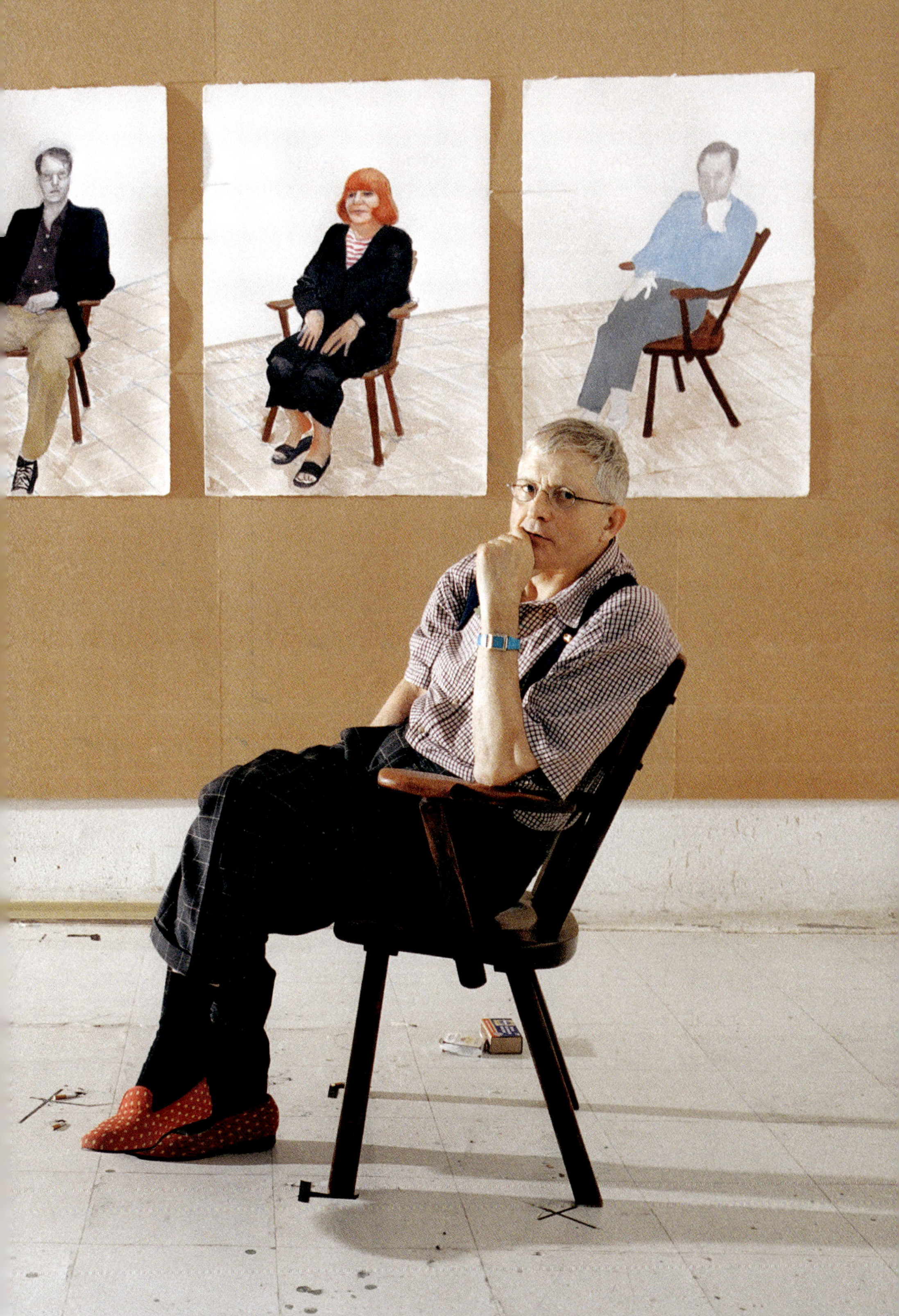

far away from Paris arrived…My point is that his image is a universal one, yet Picasso realized that the photographs were after the event, indeed in a way not telling us of the terrible brutal activity of the camps but of the survivors—the few as against the terrible number of deaths. So his subject is perhaps a painter's response to the limitations of photography, limitations that are still with us, and need some debate today."

While his work goes well, Hockney no longer feels at home in Los Angeles as he once did—he cannot even smoke in public any more—and after his close friend John Fitzherbert has been sent back to Britain by customs on a technicality, Hockney goes to England himself, to set up his headquarters in his London studio near Holland Park.

Solo: *David Hockney,* National Portrait Gallery, London (Jan 16–Jun 29). *David Hockney,* Kunstverein Ulm (Jul 20–Aug 3). *Painting on Paper,* Annely Juda Fine Art, London (Jan 17–Mar 1); catalog. *David Hockney,* Leslie Sacks Fine Art, Los Angeles (Feb 1–22). *Gravures et lithographies,* Galerie Lelong, Paris (Nov 5–Dec 23).

Group: *Focus on the Figure,* Palm Springs Desert Museum (Jan 23–Feb 16). *Splendid Pages: The Molly and Walter Bareiss Collection of Modern Illustrated Books,* Toledo Museum of Art, Toledo, OH (Feb 14–May 11); catalog. *Editions Alecto: A Fury for Prints. Artist's Prints and Multiples 1960–1981,* Whitworth Art Gallery, Manchester (May 14–Aug 14); travels to London and Edinburgh. *Looking at Photographs: 125 Masterpieces from the Museum of Modern Art,* The State Hermitage Museum, St. Petersburg (Jun 21–Aug 31); travels to State Pushkin Museum of Fine Arts, Moscow. *Reverie: Works from the Collection of Douglas S. Cramer,* Speed Art Museum, Louisville (Jul 22–Oct 5); catalog. *A Bigger Splash: British Art from Tate, 1960–2003,* Pavilhão Lucas Nogueira Garcez (Aug 4–Oct 26) and Instituto Tomie Ohtake (Aug 5–Sep 21), São Paulo; catalog. *Made in California: Selections from the Frederick R. Weisman Art Foundation Collection,* Todd Madigan Gallery, California State University, Bakersfield (Sep 12–Nov 15); catalog.

Publication: *Hockney's Portraits and People,* with texts by Marco Livingstone and Kay Heymer, London: Thames and Hudson.

Film: *David Hockney: Double Portrait,* GB, 49 min., dir. by Bruno Wollheim and Christopher Swayne.

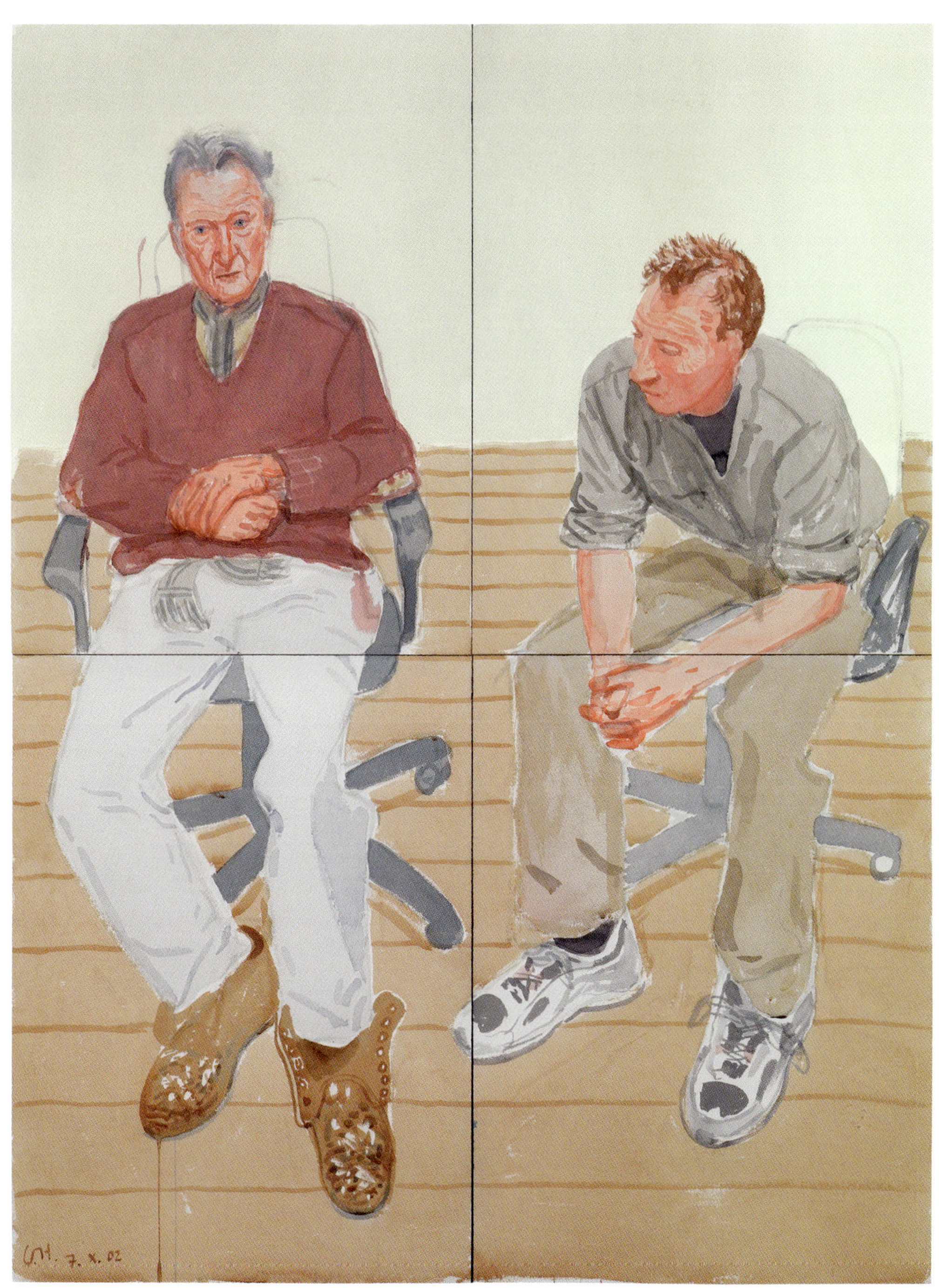

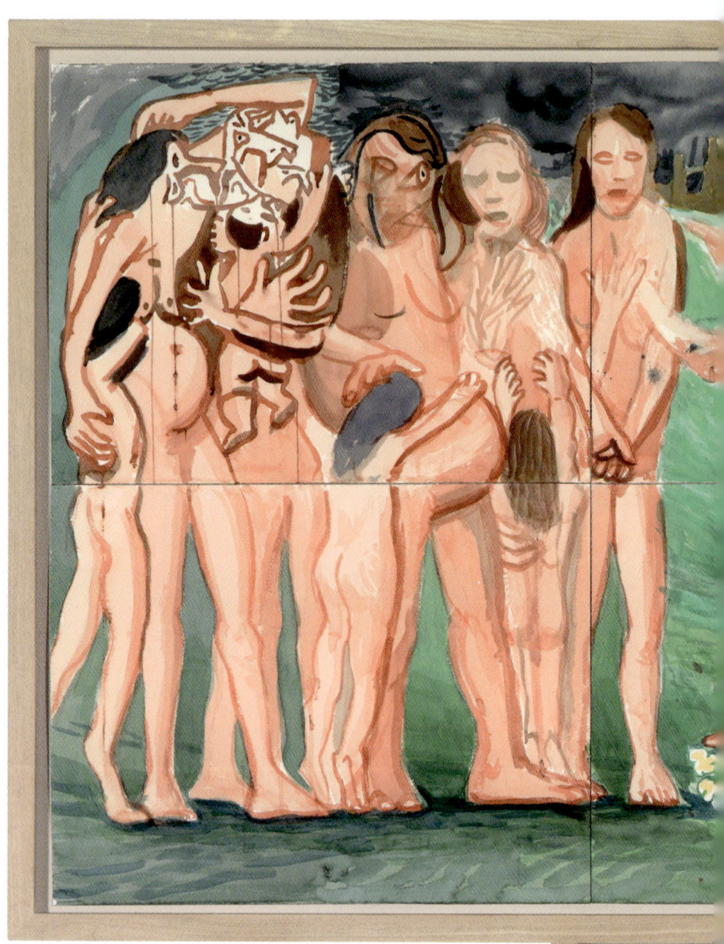

The Massacre and the Problems of Depiction, after Picasso, 2003, watercolor on 7 sheets of paper, 56 ¹/₂ x 72 ¹/₄ in. / 143.6 x 183.5 cm

Page 393: David Hockney in his studio, Los Angeles 2003. Photo: Susanna Howe

Page 395: *Lucian Freud and David Dawson,* 2002, watercolor on 4 sheets of paper, 48 x 36 in. / 121.9 x 91.4 cm

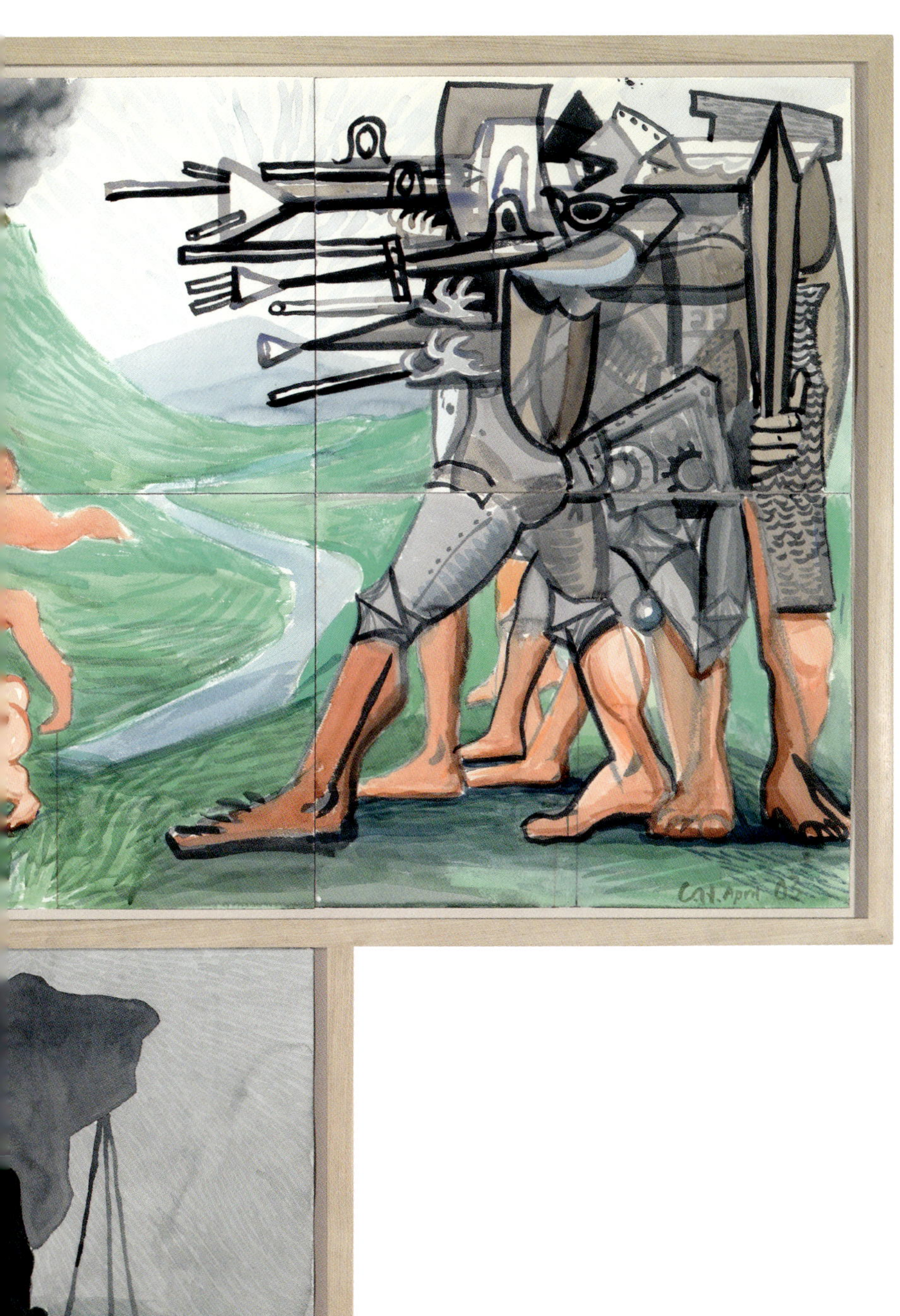

2004 Early in the year, Hockney travels through Spain and France, painting watercolors of the landscape and architectural sites wherever he goes (pp. 402–403). He spends Easter at Lake Como, where writer Jeremy Lewis witnesses him at work: "Despite the rain, David Hockney painted every day on the terrace, perched under an umbrella, the occasional raindrop adding verisimilitude to his watercolors. He smoked incessantly, was deaf as a post, talked wonderfully well about every subject known to man and wore flamboyant check suits with huge pockets in the lining from which he withdrew brushes, paints, a sketchbook, and a collapsible canvas bucket."

Hockney shows a selection of Spanish watercolors at the Royal Academy summer exhibition he curates with Allen Jones, whom he first met at the Royal College of Art in their student days. They focus the exhibition on drawings, and discuss their very open concept in the *Guardian*: "DH: All engineers before photography could draw quite well. If you think about it—to draw something that somebody could then make. AJ: Norman Rosenthal [exhibitions secretary of the Royal Academy] said: 'Where do you draw the line? Everything has to have been drawn originally. Any invention. It has to have been drawn.' I decided that anyone whose drawings are a part of the final manifestation—like a car designer—wouldn't count. I was interested in drawing as near to the creative impulse as possible. There's stuff by poets, sportsmen, composers—Brian Eno's notebooks are something to behold. DH: Last time I saw Eno he told me he'd made a record where he'd collected all the slow movements of Haydn string quartets and put them together. I thought, what a brilliant idea."

Hockney spends the summer with his sister Margaret in Bridlington painting the East Yorkshire landscape. He is accompanied by his new assistant, Jean-Pierre Gonçalves de Lima, who starts taking sequential digital photographs of the artist at work, keeping a detailed record of how each work evolves (p. 401). Among many other sheets, Hockney produces the 36 watercolors of the series *Midsummer: East Yorkshire* (pp. 404–407).

During that time, Lawrence Weschler visits the artist in his studio: "Hockney got up and shambled over to a side drawer, riffled about for a moment, and pulled out a moleskin sketchbook. 'I was able to procure one of these Japanese-style sketchbooks, whose pages are attached and folded in one upon the other in such a way that—see?—they can accordion out into one long scroll. And I set

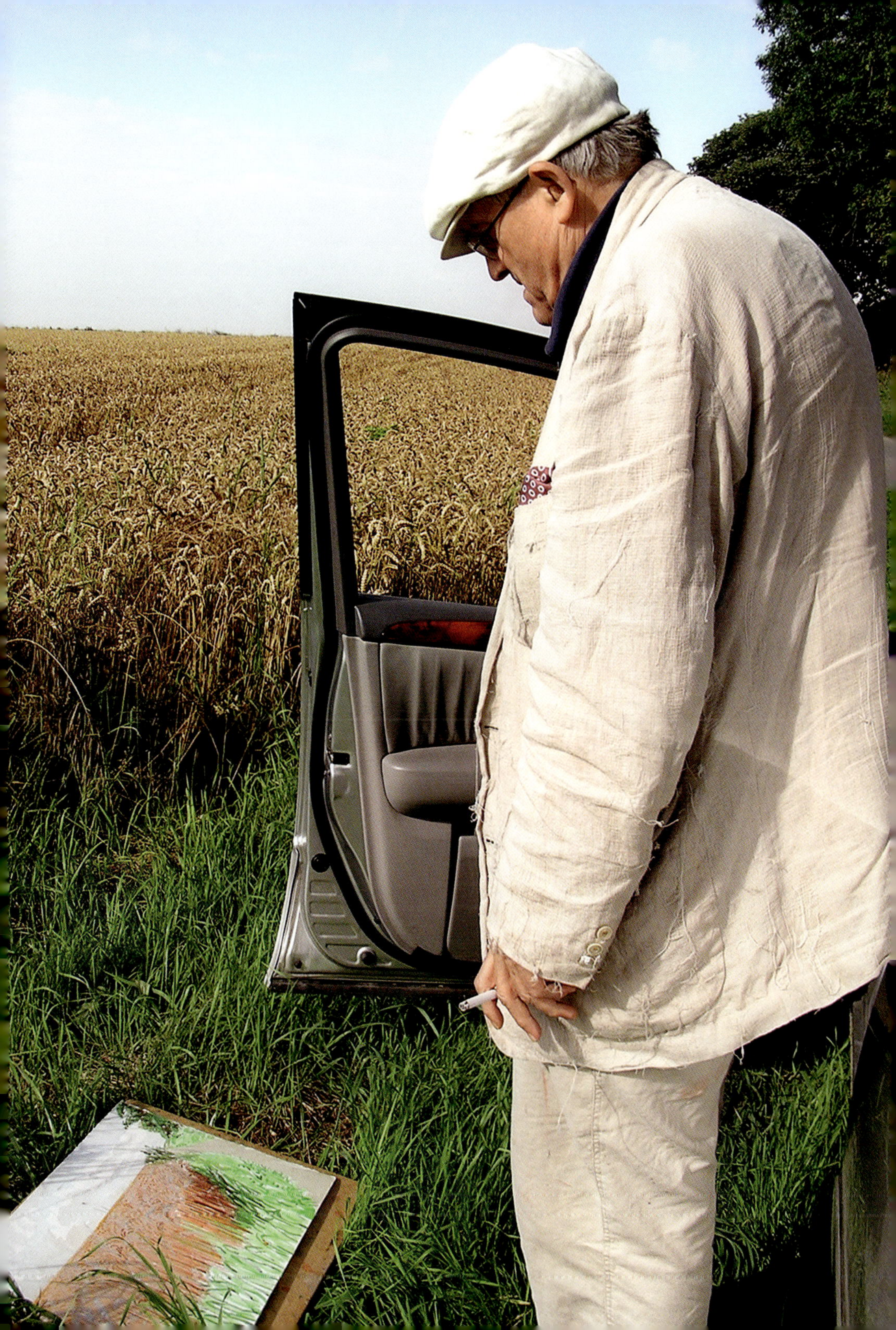

out one day with my friend Jean-Pierre driving. I was sitting in the passenger seat, and every few yards I'd have him pull over and stop so that I could sketch a particular stalk of grass or weed in the low roadside hedge. See? Each one quite distinct, quite different. The point being, the more you draw, the more you see and then you start seeing everywhere, order emerging out of chaos, an order you can draw on the next time you take on the subject of an entire foreground hedge.'"

Solo: *An Intimate Eye,* Richard Gray Gallery, New York (Mar 6–Apr 16); catalog with a text by Marco Livingstone. *Hockney Graphics,* Leslie Sacks Fine Art, Los Angeles (May 15–Jun 19).

Group: *Modernism in American Contemporary Art,* Hokkaido Obihiro Museum, Obihiro (Feb 6–Mar 24). *Whitney Biennial,* Whitney Museum of American Art, New York (Mar 11–May 30); catalog. *Gems of Twentieth Century Printmaking: From Picasso and Matisse to Warhol,* Museum of Modern Art, Gunma (Apr 17–Jun 13). *Pop Art UK: British Pop Art 1956–1972,* Galleria Civica di Modena (Apr 18–Jul 4); catalog. *Summer Exhibition,* Royal Academy of Arts, London (Jun 8–Aug 16); catalog. *British Art and the Sixties,* Tate Britain, London (Jun 30–Oct 3); travels to Birmingham, Melbourne, and Auckland; catalog. *Water Level of Image: Transformation and Reflection of Narcissus,* Toyota Municipal Museum of Art, Toyota (Jul 6–Sep 5). *Co-Conspirators: Artist and Collector,* Orlando Museum of Art, Orlando (Jul 24–Oct 31); catalog. *The Flower as Image,* Louisiana Museum for Moderne Kunst, Humlebæk (Sep 10, 2004–Jan 16, 2005); travels as *Blumenmythos: Von Vincent van Gogh bis Jeff Koons,* Fondation Beyeler, Basel; catalog.

Publication: *Hockney's Pictures: The Definitive Retrospective,* compiled and with commentary by David Hockney, London: Thames and Hudson; New York: Bulfinch.

Film: *David Hockney: The Colors of Music,* Canada, 52 min., dir. by Maryte Kavaliauskas and Seth Schneidman, starring David Hockney, Gwyneth Jones, Ken Silver, and others.

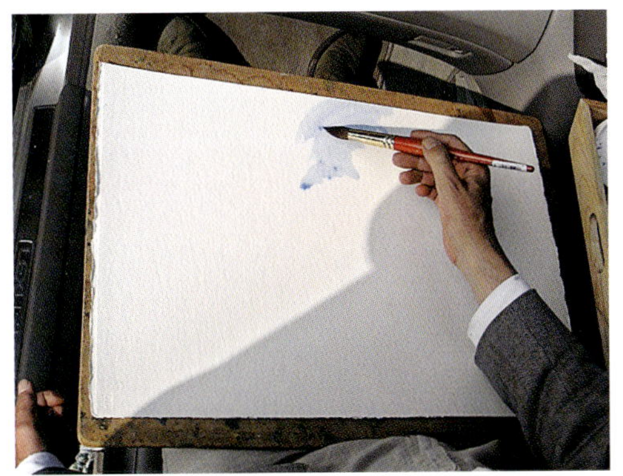
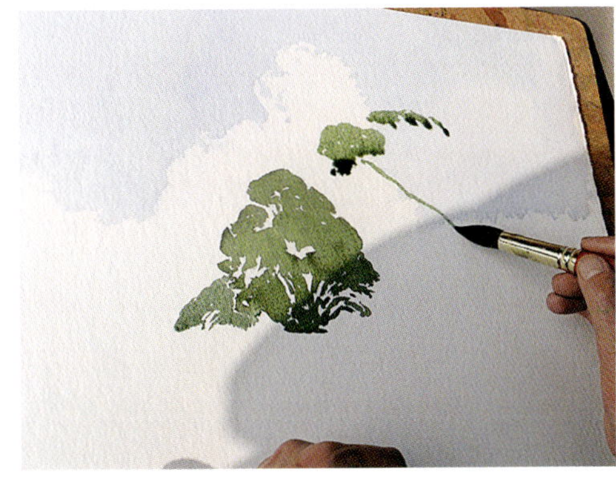
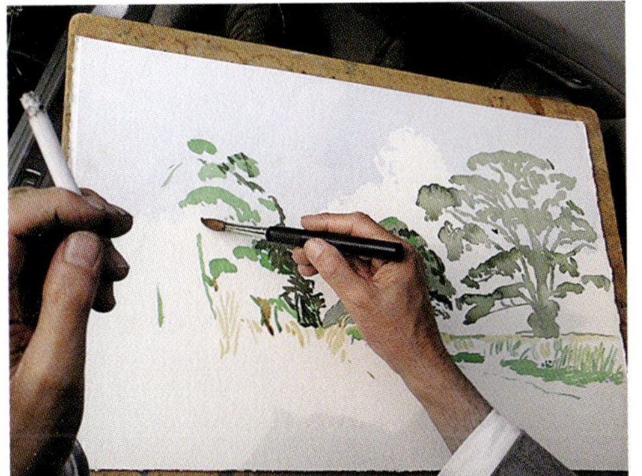
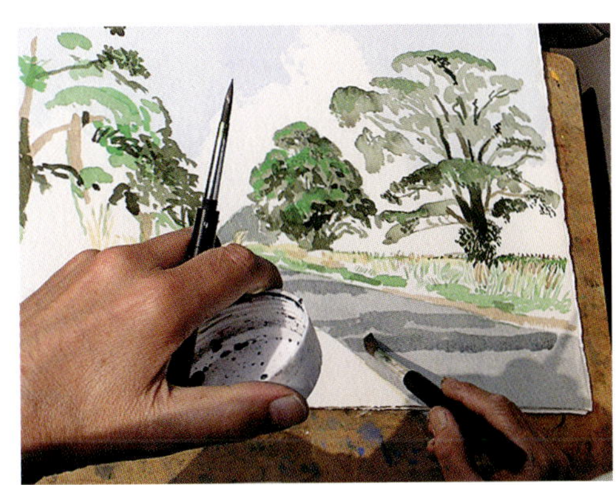
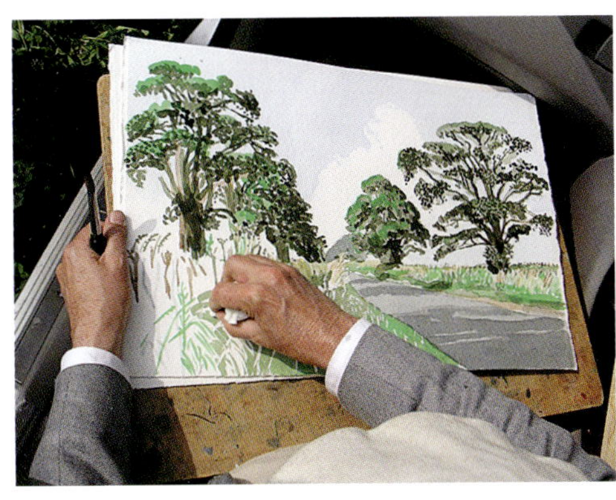
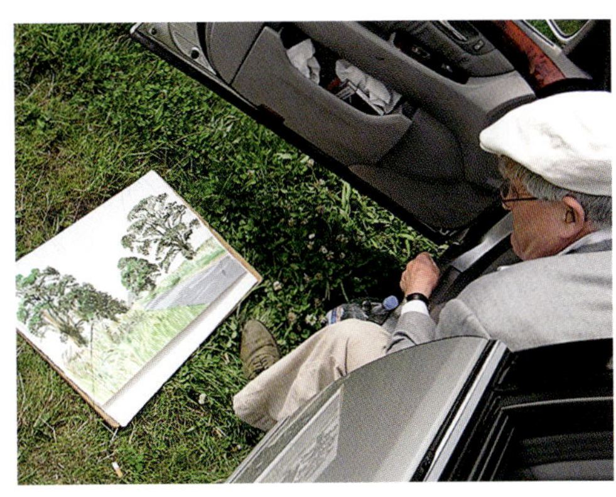

David Hockney painting *Trees near Rudston* from *Midsummer: East Yorkshire*, August 2004. Photos: Jean-Pierre Gonçalves de Lima

Page 399: David Hockney studying *Ripe Corn on the Roman Road. East Yorkshire* from *Midsummer: East Yorkshire*, August 2004. Photo: Jean-Pierre Gonçalves de Lima

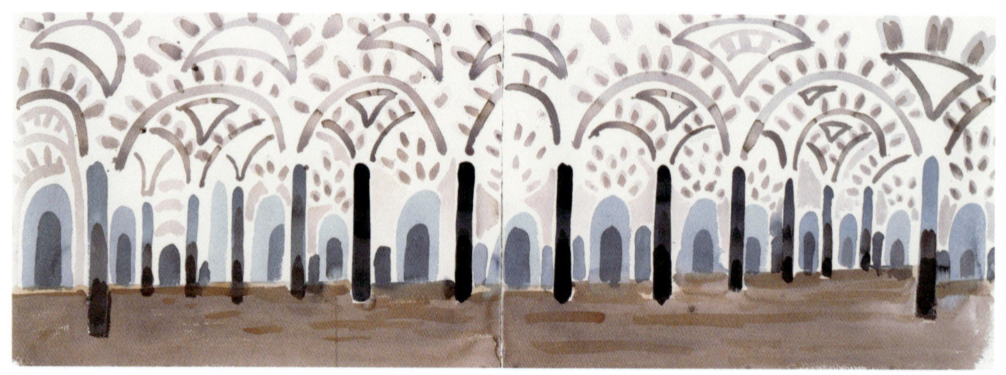

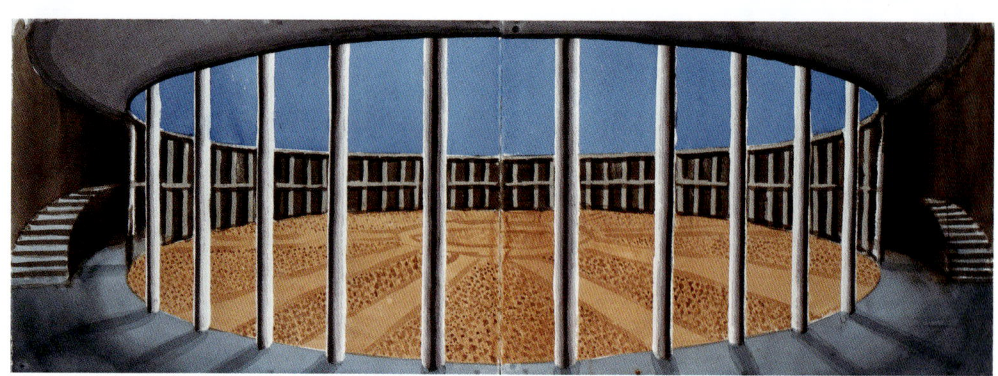

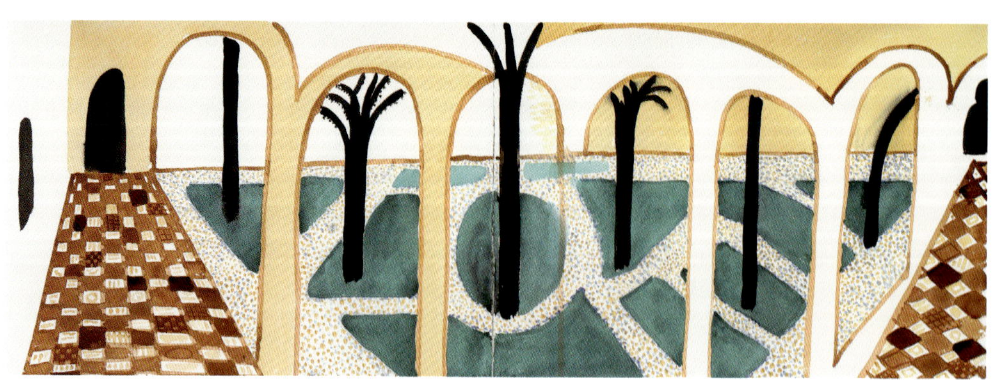

Andalucia. Mosque, Cordova, 2004, watercolor on 2 sheets of paper, 29 ¹/₂ x 83 in. / 74.9 x 210.8 cm

Courtyard, Palace of Carlos V, Alhambra, Granada (Second Version), 2004, watercolor on 2 sheets of paper, 29 ¹/₂ x 83 in. / 74.9 x 210.8 cm

Andalucia. Courtyard, Seville, 2004, watercolor on 2 sheets of paper, 29 ¹/₂ x 83 in. / 74.9 x 210.8 cm

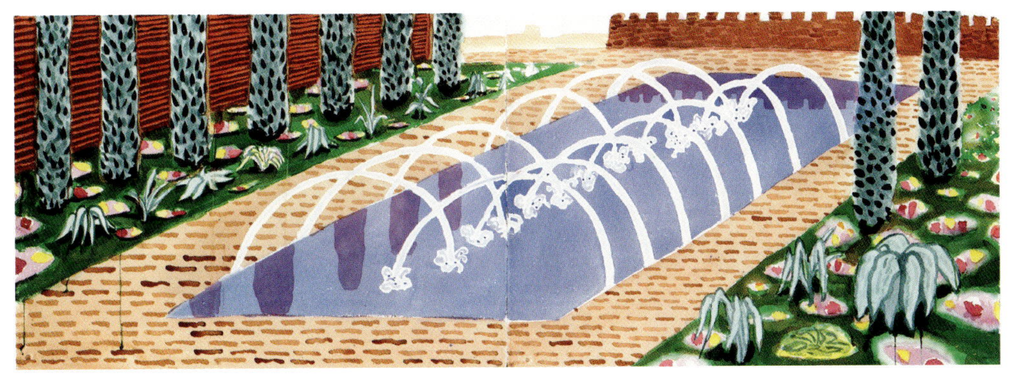

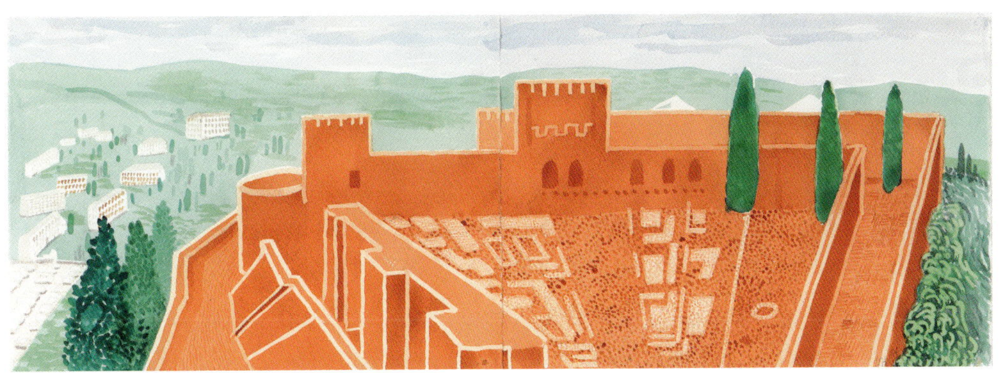

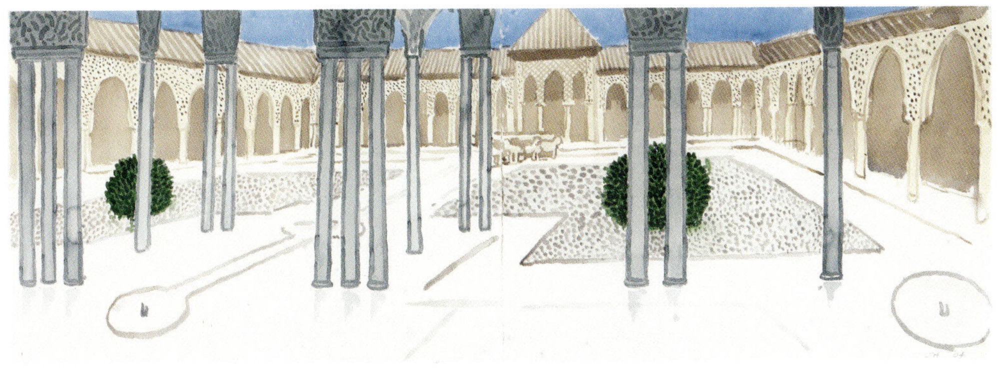

Andalucia. Fountains, Cordova, 2004, watercolor on 2 sheets of paper, 29 ¹/₂ x 83 in. / 74.9 x 210.8 cm

Andalucia. Alcazaba, Granada, 2004, watercolor on 2 sheets of paper, 29 ¹/₂ x 83 in. / 74.9 x 210.8 cm

Andalucia. Courtyard, Alhambra, 2004, watercolor on 2 sheets of paper, 29 ¹/₂ x 83 in. / 74.9 x 210.8 cm

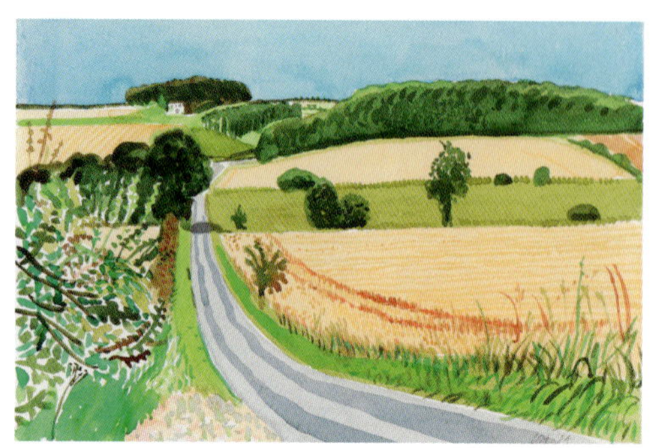
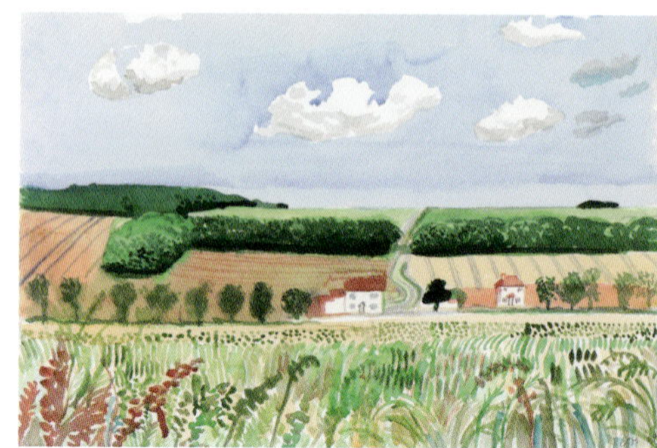
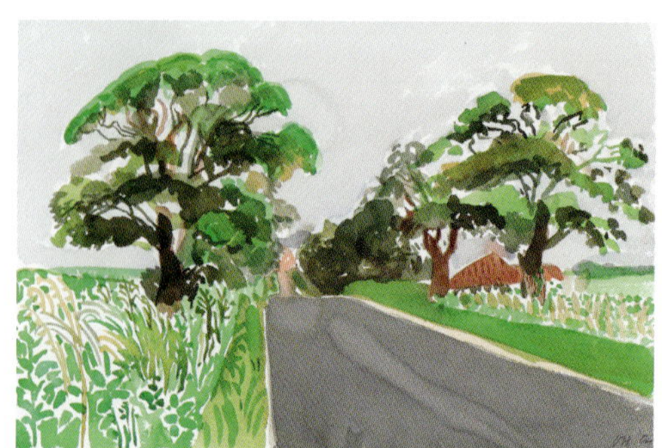
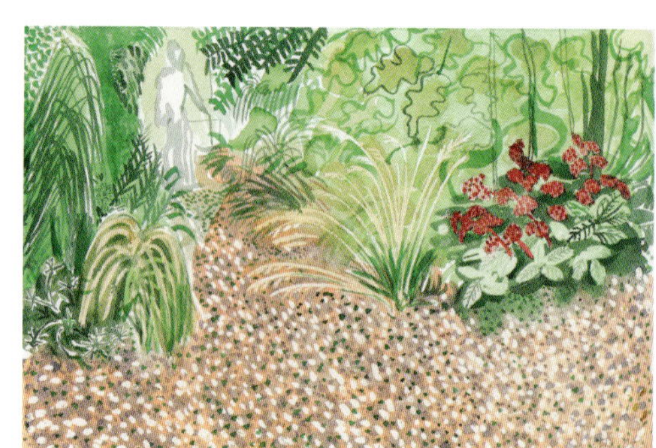
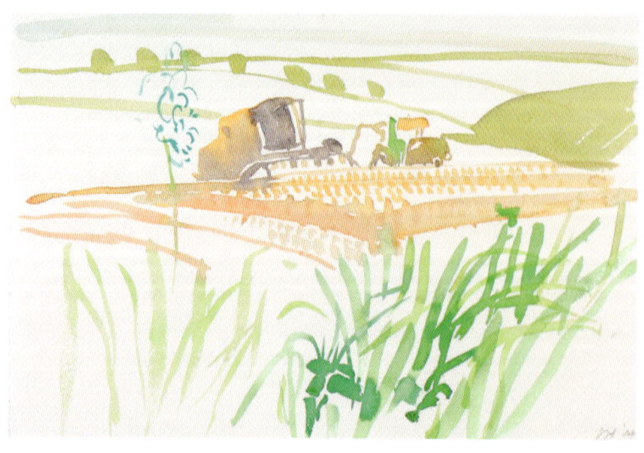
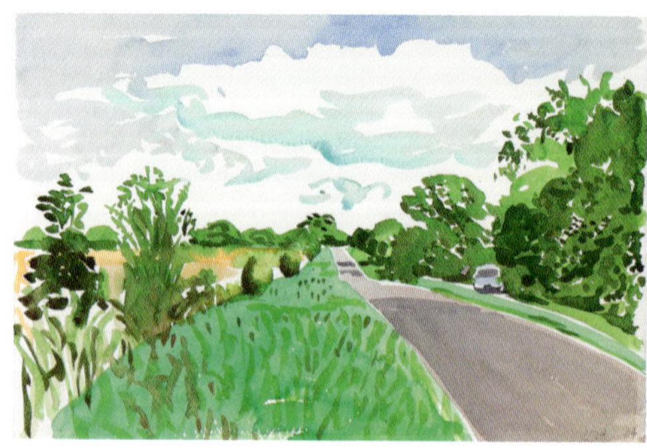

Midsummer: East Yorkshire, 2004,
36 watercolors on paper, each
15 x 22 ¹⁄₂ in. / 38 x 57.2 cm

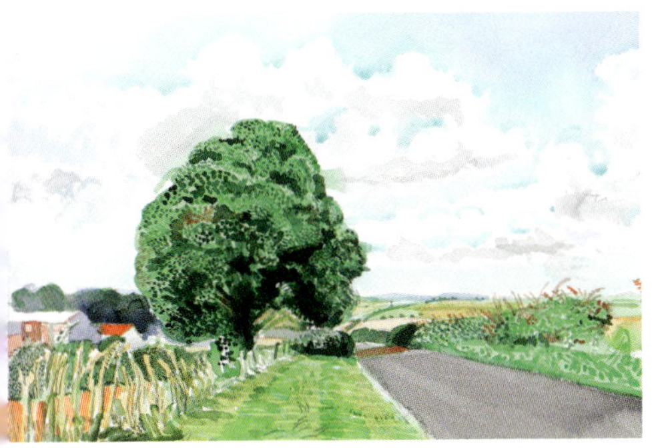
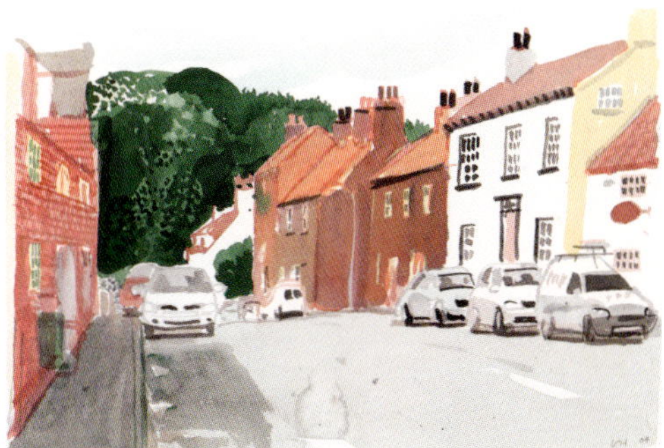
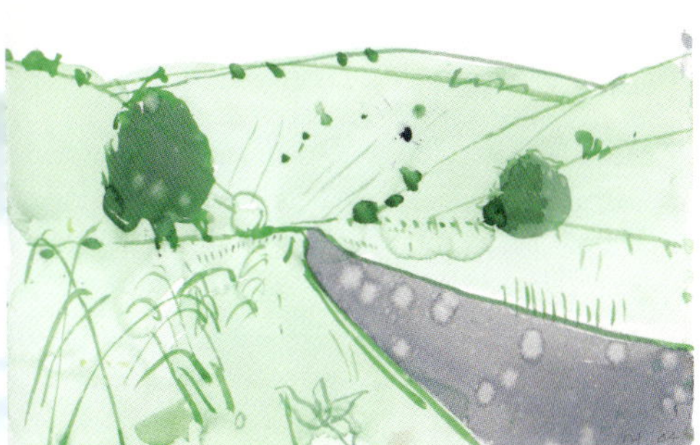
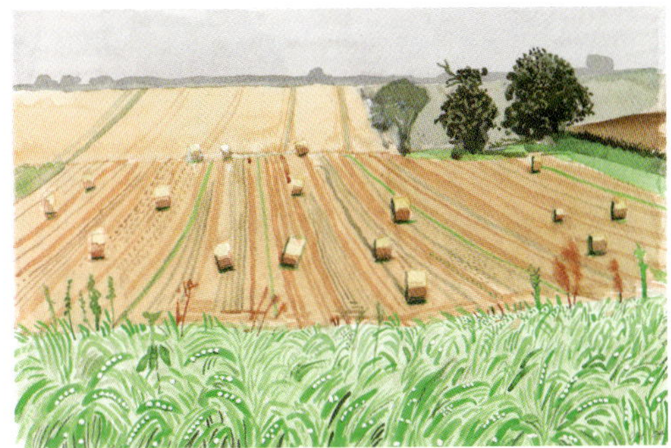
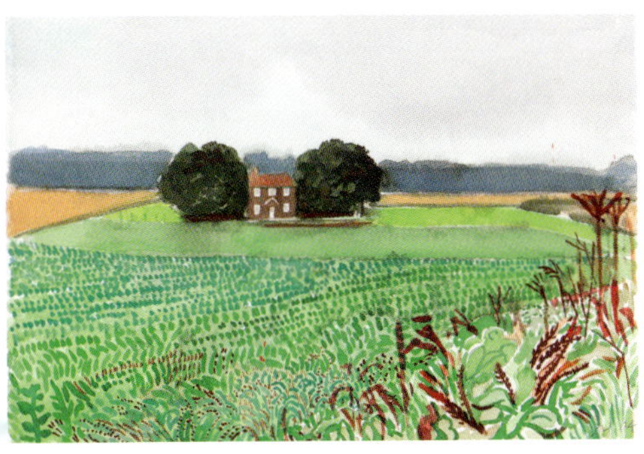
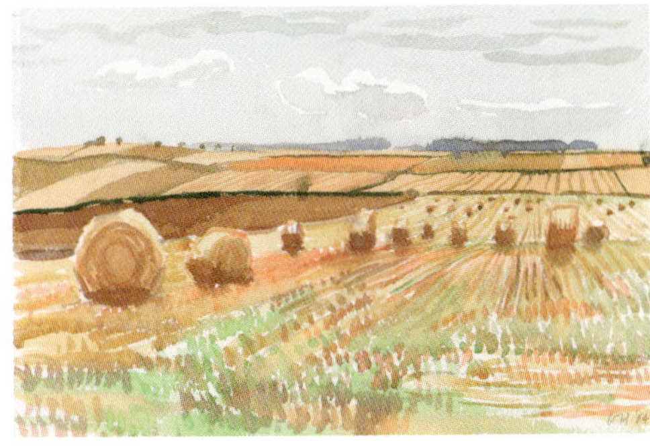

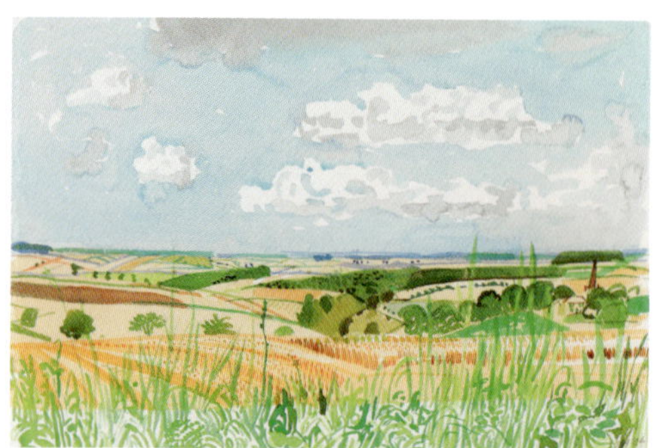
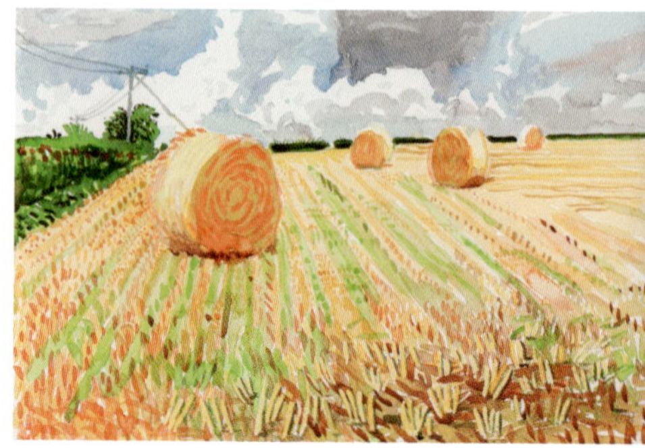
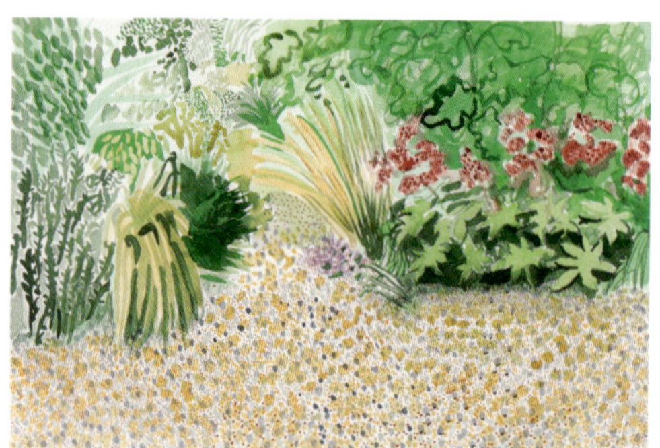
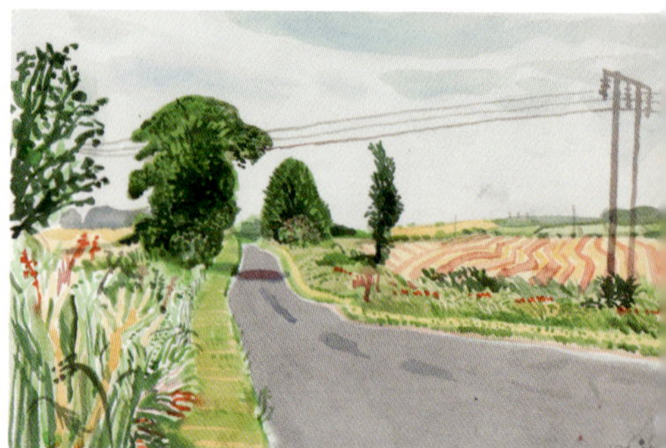
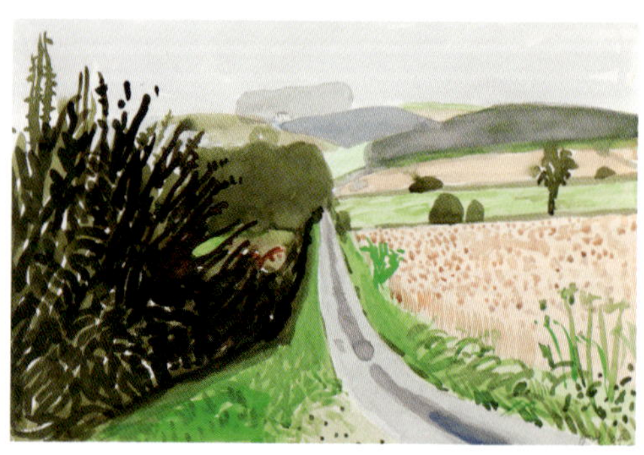
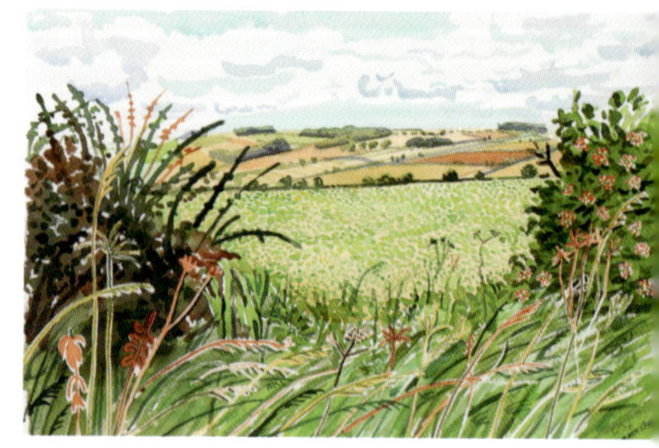

Midsummer: East Yorkshire, 2004,
36 watercolors on paper, each
15 x 22 ¹/₂ in. / 38 x 57.2 cm

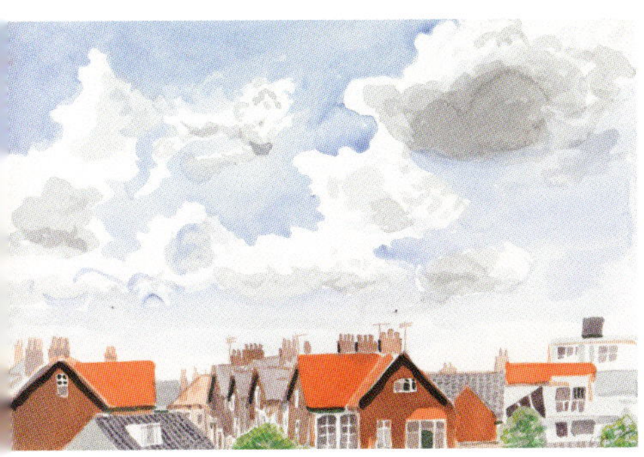
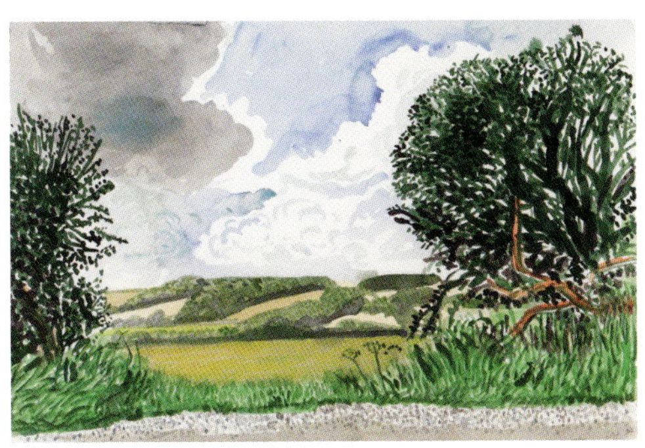

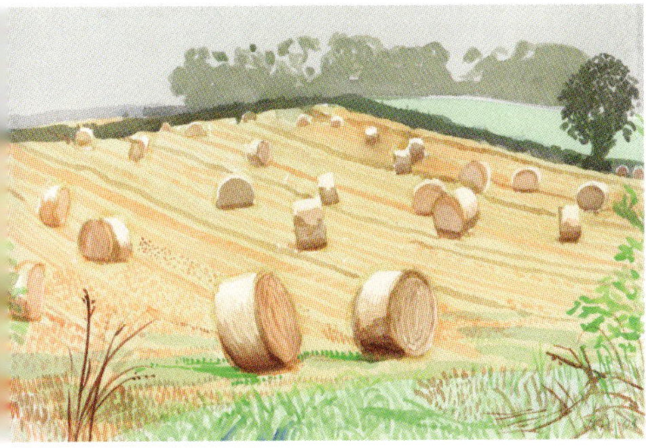
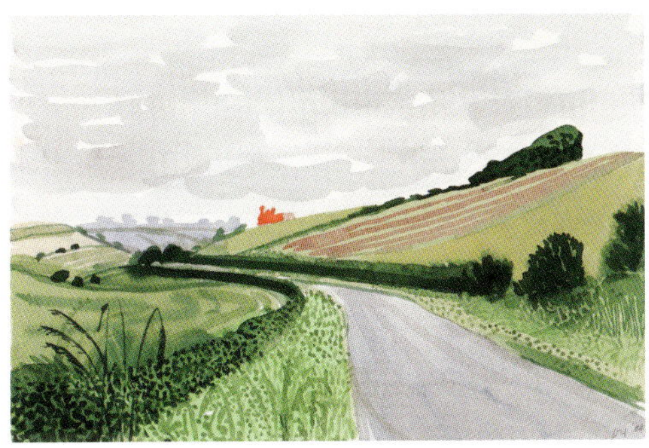

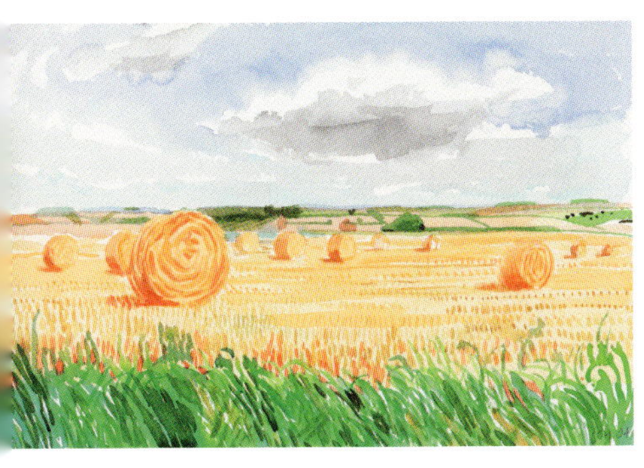
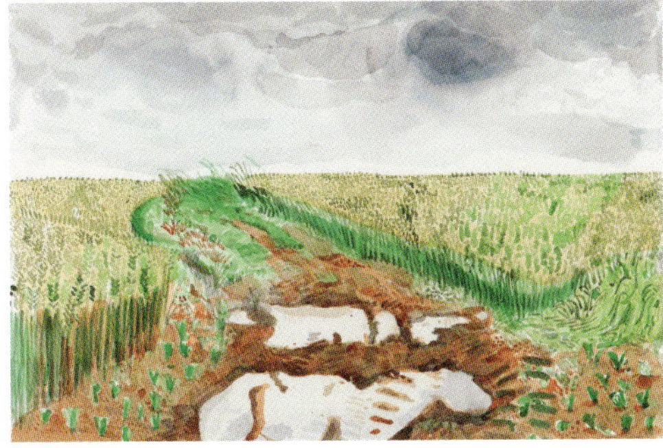

2005 During a stay in Los Angeles, Hockney begins a new series of almost life-size single and double portraits, painting with oils directly onto canvas with no previous drawing (pp. 409, 411–413): "When you've been doing watercolors, oil paint is like a luxury medium. You can do what you want with it. I mean with watercolor, you have to work from light to dark. With oil paint you can do whatever you want, so going back to it was rather thrilling."

In February, the exhibition *Hand, Eye, Heart* at L.A. Louver presents Hockney's Yorkshire watercolors of the previous year. David Pagel in the *Los Angeles Times*: "You don't have to know much about David Hockney or watercolor painting to see that the artist's 55 new works are amazing documents of rambling drives through the English countryside. Each casually exquisite picture of leafless trees, golden fields, puddled lanes, blossoming flowers, distant farmhouses, rolling hillsides, and quiet towns is an astutely observed moment that would never make it to a postcard but is all the more lovely for being ordinary. In these enlivening images glimpsed through car windows, Hockney doesn't take your breath away so much as he gets you to breathe deeply, soaking in every detail of the fleeting scenes." In the show's catalog, Hockney explains the advantages of painting his homeland to Lawrence Weschler: "These were hardly my first forays into landscape painting. By contrast, though, in Norway, for example, or Iceland, or earlier, during my travels across the American West, I was always painting views, I was sightseeing. Whereas there, around Bridlington, I was painting the land, land that I myself had worked. I had dwelt in those fields, so that out there, seeing, for me, necessarily came steeped in memory."

Hockney permanently returns to Bridlington in July and spends the summer painting East Yorkshire landscapes, this time in oil, setting up his easel out in the open air (pp. 414–417). He explores the area, finding spots that he will return to again and again, such as the old Roman road at Woldgate or the small alleyway he dubs the Tunnel: "I realized it was quite a good place to work. You were left alone. You could work 24 hours a day. You could keep things in your head; you didn't have to change in the evening and think of something else…The subject is more than just the landscape. There's a perverse side of me that of course loves the idea of 'Oh, you can't paint the landscape now,' and that says, 'Yes you can, and I'll show you how to do it exciting, new.'" John Fitzherbert and Jean-Pierre

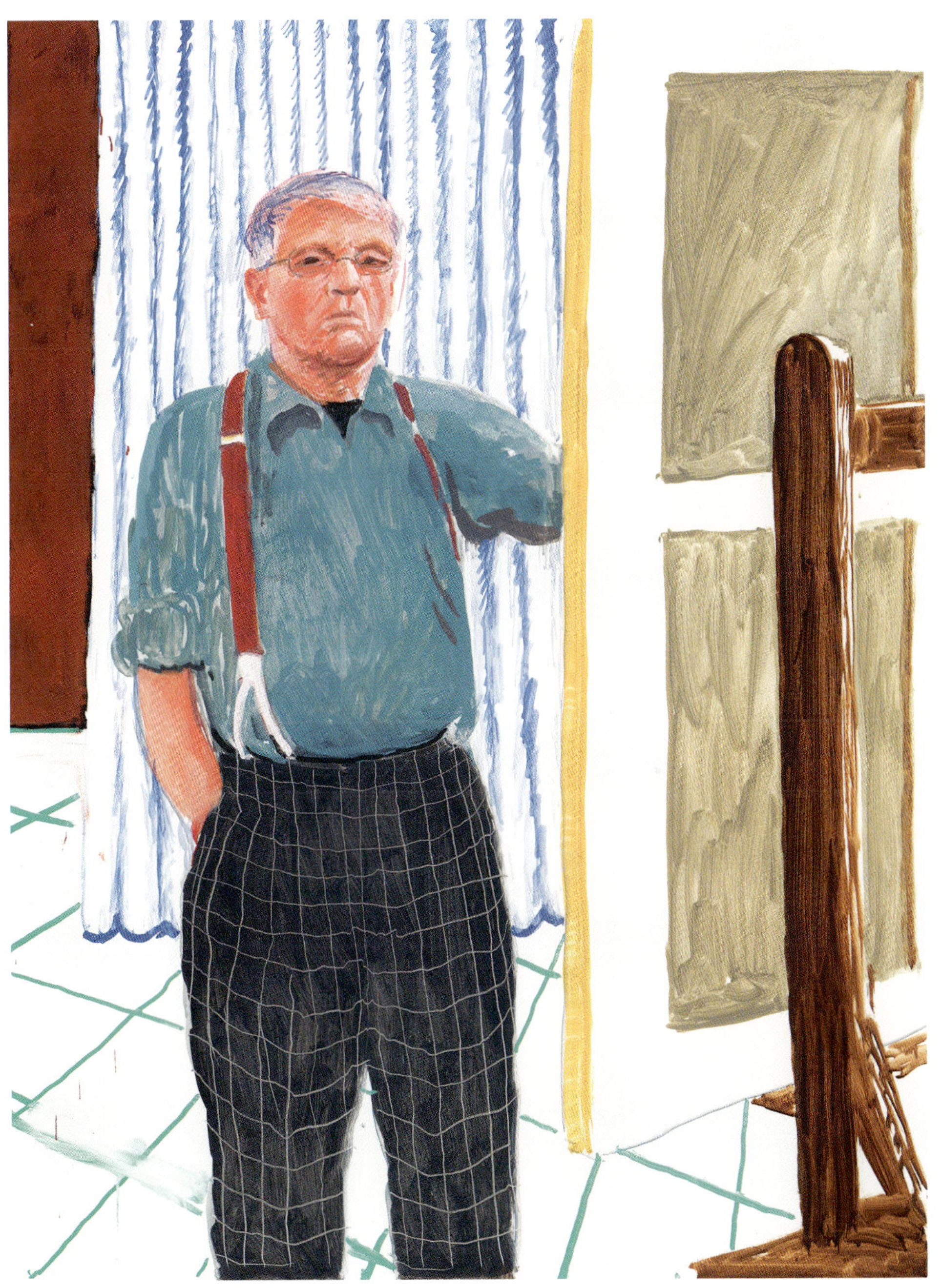

Gonçalves de Lima also move to Bridlington to help Hockney run the house and studio.

Outside of art, Hockney raises his voice against a new British legislation drawn up to prohibit all smoking in public spaces. He speaks at the Labour Party Conference, as the BBC reports: "Mr. Hockney, speaking for the smokers' lobby group Forest, told delegates that the proposals were 'a step too far…death awaits you whether you smoke or not. Pubs are not health clubs. People go to drown their sorrows.'" In autumn, Hockney visits Germany, then returns to Bridlington to continue with his Yorkshire landscapes through December. He also paints portraits in oil in preparation for a big traveling exhibition in the following year.

Solo: *Hand, Eye, Heart,* L.A. Louver, Venice, CA (Feb 26–Apr 2); catalog with a text by Lawrence Weschler. *David Hockney,* 1853 Gallery, Saltaire (Jun 4–Sep 30).

Group: *Drawing from the Modern, 1945–1975,* Museum of Modern Art, New York (Mar 30–Aug 29); catalog. *Art Struck: The William D. Merwin Collection,* St. Louis University Museum of Art, St. Louis (Apr 8–Jul 17). *Summer Exhibition,* Royal Academy of Arts, London (Jun 7–Aug 15); catalog. *Metamorphosis: British Art of the Sixties,* Museum of Modern Art, Basil & Elise Goulandris Foundation, Andros (Jun 26–Sep 25); catalog. *British Pop,* Museo de Bellas Artes de Bilbao (Oct 17, 2005–Feb 12, 2006); catalog.

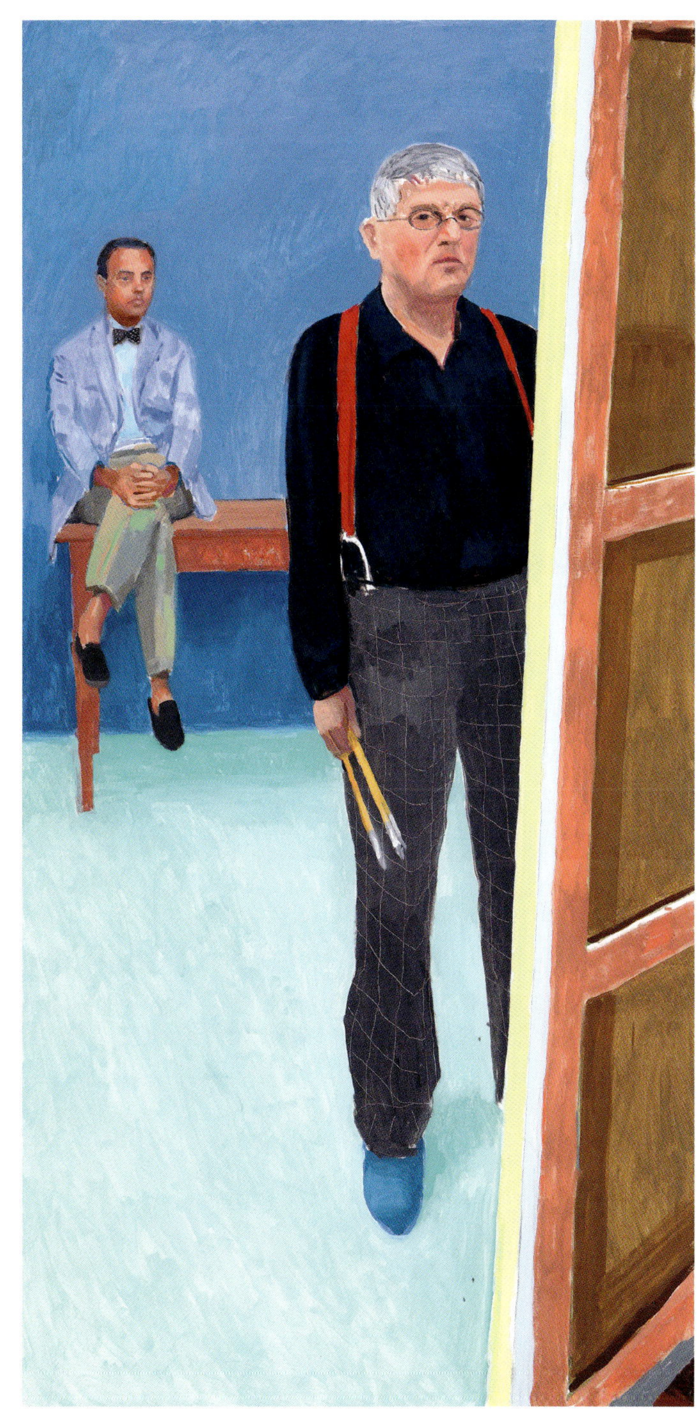

Self Portrait with Charlie, 2005,
oil on canvas, 72 x 36 in. /
182.9 x 91.4 cm

Page 409: *Self Portrait
Standing with Red Braces,* 2005,
oil on canvas, 48 x 36 in. /
121.9 x 91.4 cm

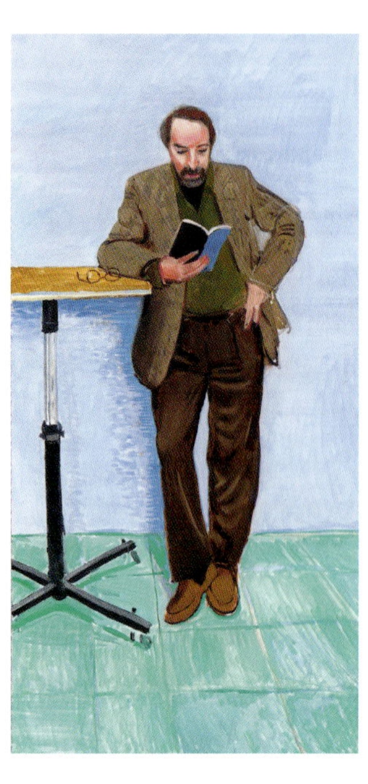

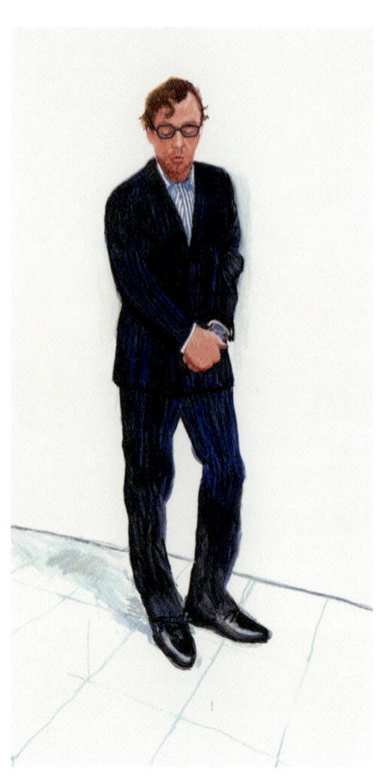

Lawrence Weschler, 2005, oil on canvas, 72 x 36 in. / 182.9 x 91.4 cm

Gregory Evans, 2005, oil on canvas, 72 x 36 in. / 182.9 x 91.4 cm

Arthur Lambert, 2005, oil on canvas, 72 x 36 in. / 182.9 x 91.4 cm

Charlie Scheips, 2005, oil on canvas, 72 x 36 in. / 182.9 x 91.4 cm

Richard Schmidt, 2005, oil on canvas, 72 x 36 in. / 182.9 x 91.4 cm

Right page: *The Photographer and His Daughter,* 2005, oil on canvas, 56 x 76 in. / 142.2 x 193 cm

Ann and David, Los Angeles, March 10, 2005, oil on canvas, 56 x 76 in. / 142.2 x 193 cm

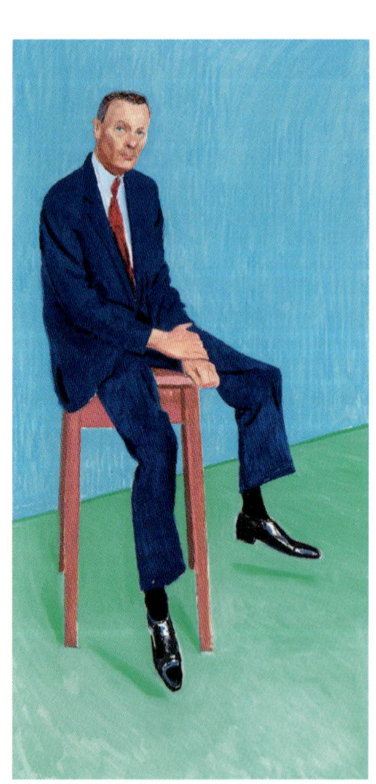

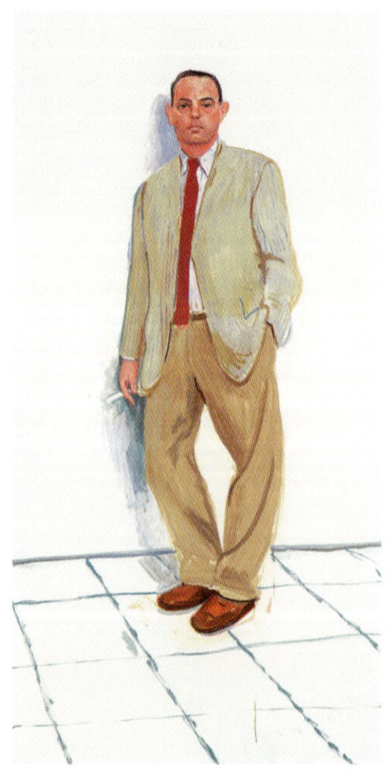

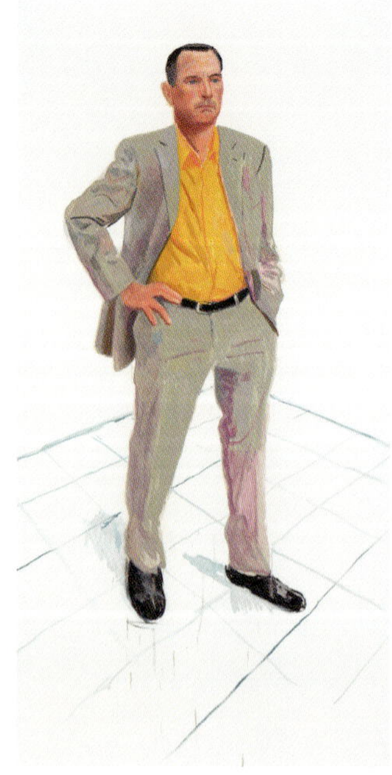

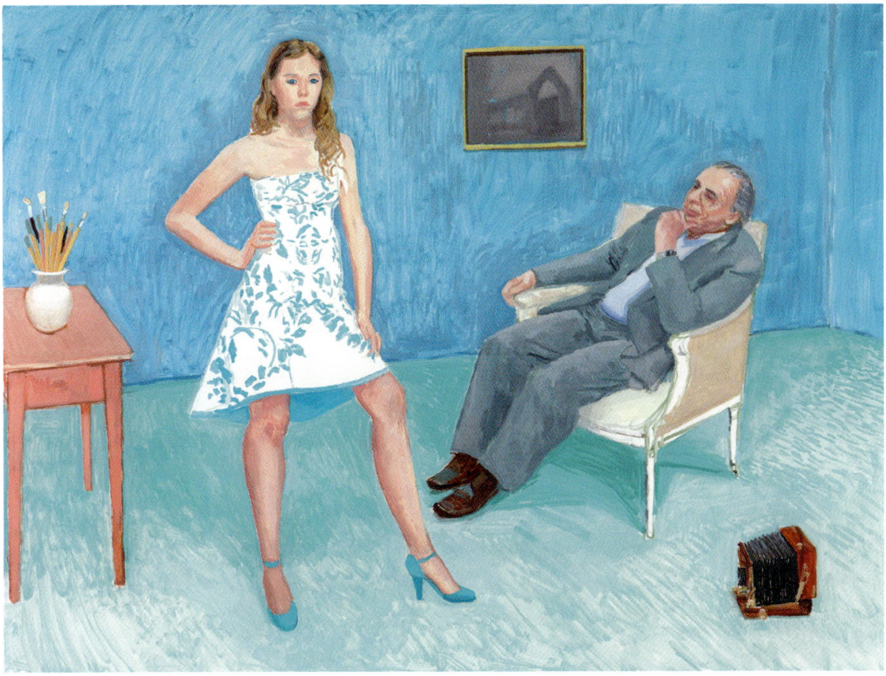

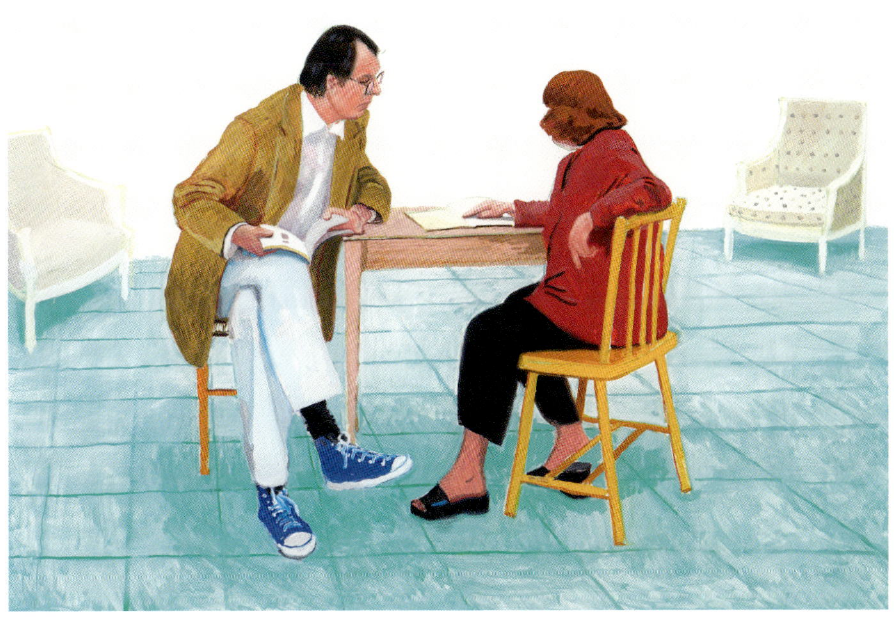

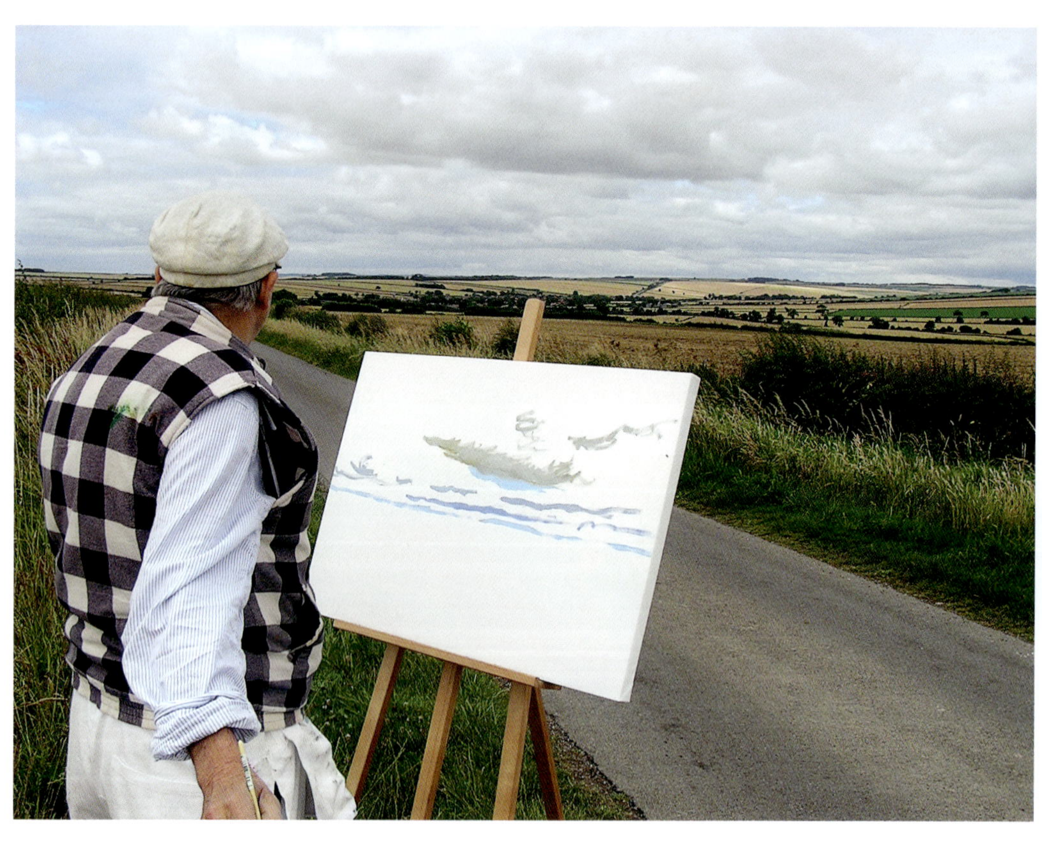

David Hockney painting *Kilham to Langtoft*, 25 July 2005

Right page: David Hockney painting *The Tunnel Early Autumn, October,* 2005

Hockney in Woldgate, November 2005. All photos: Jean-Pierre Gonçalves de Lima

Page 416: *Wheat Field near Friday-thorpe, August 2005,* oil on canvas, 36 x 48 in. / 91.4 x 121.9 cm

Path through Wheat Field, July, 2005, oil on canvas, 24 x 36 in. / 61 x 91.4 cm

Page 417: *Tree Tunnel, August,* 2005, oil on canvas, 24 x 36 in. / 61 x 91.4 cm

Woldgate, 24 November 2005, oil on canvas, 36 x 48 in. / 91.4 x 121.9 cm

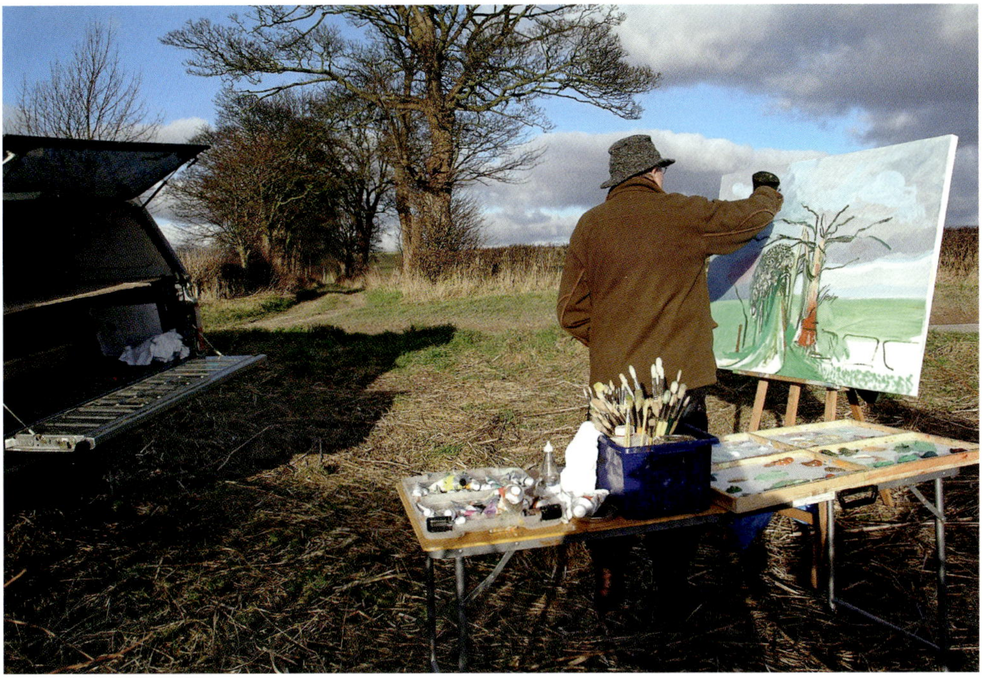

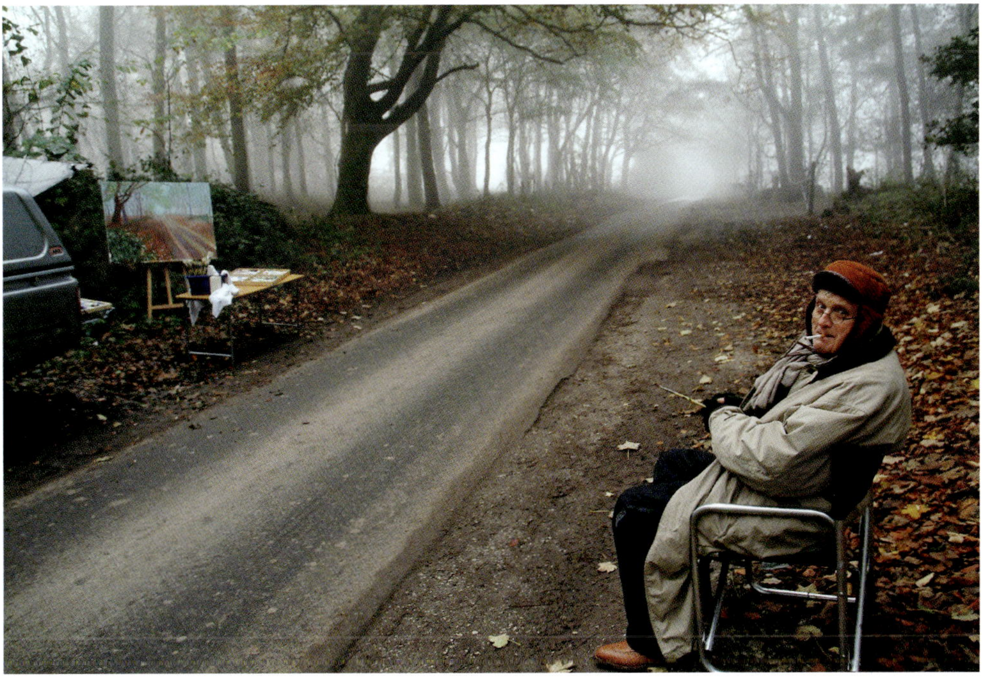

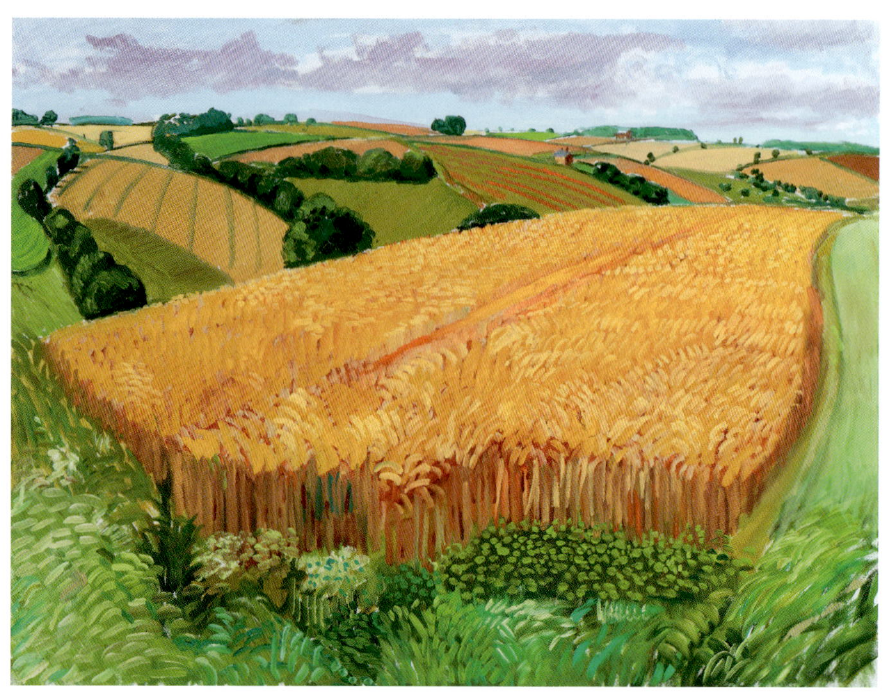

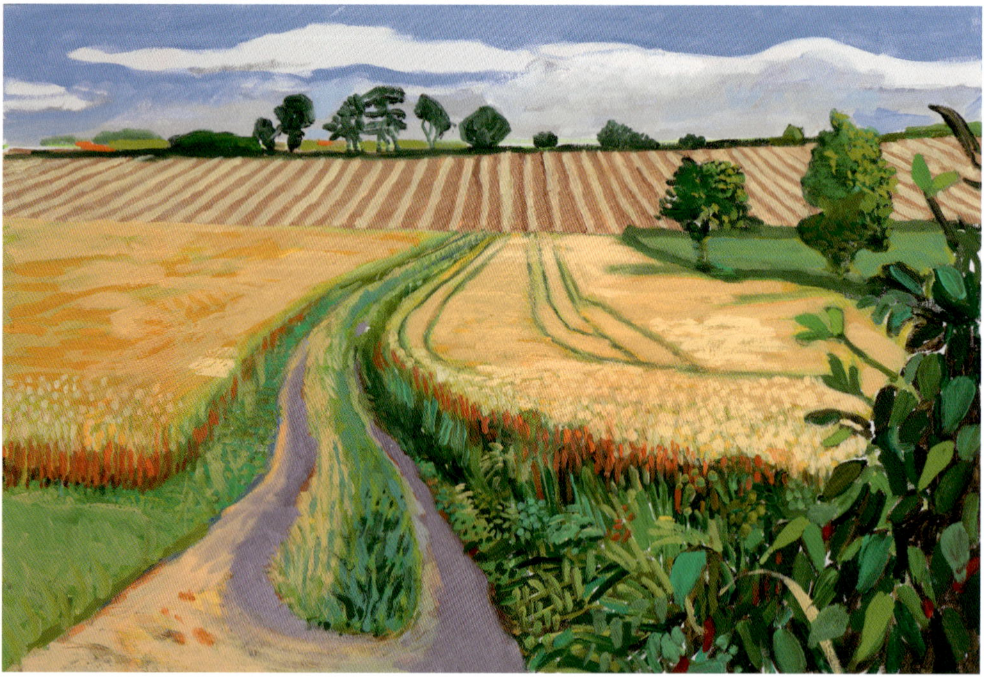

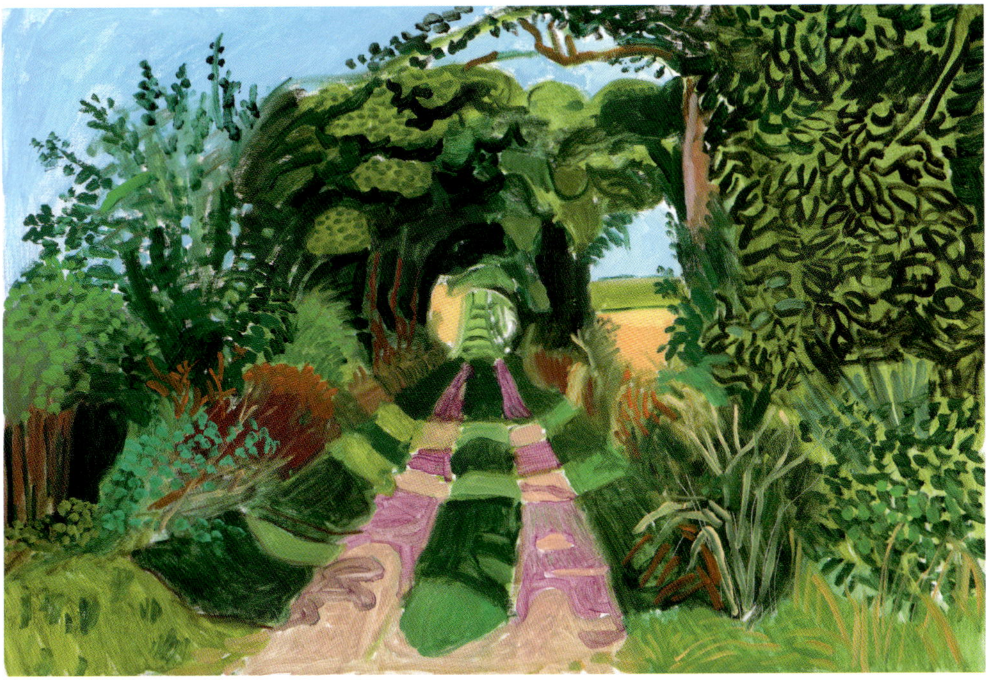

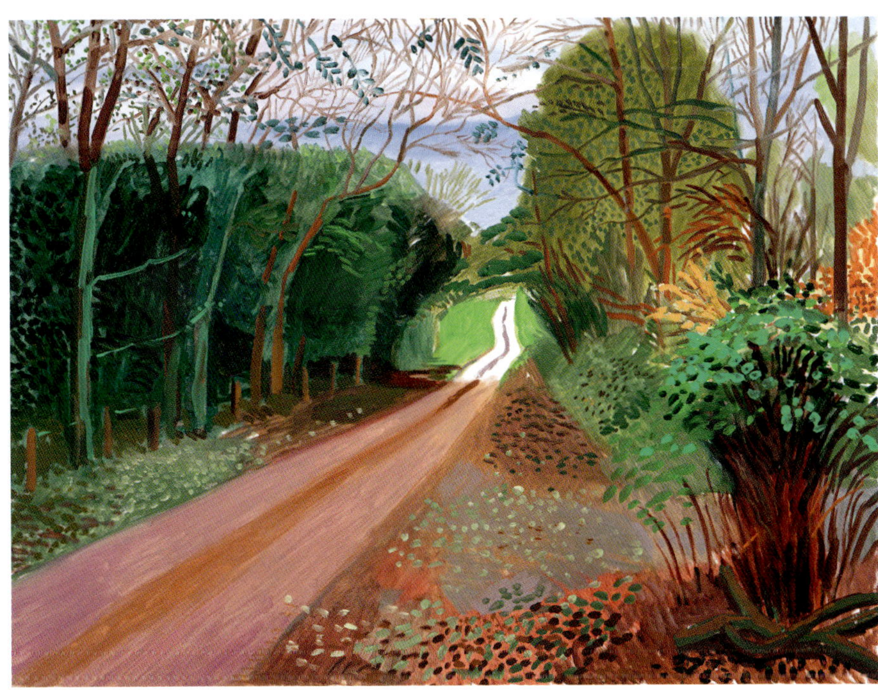

2006

Hockney continues painting the East Yorkshire landscape outdoors in front of his motif. He increases the scale by joining several canvases to form one large picture, painting them separately, or two side by side on one easel. For his first painting of the *Woldgate Woods* (pp. 422/423) he starts using six panels, a favorite format that causes some practical problems, until he buys a more suitable vehicle: "At first we had to go out with several cars so that returning, we could lay out the wet canvases on the back seats without smudging them. Eventually we built a sort of rack in the back of the truck with six shelves, so we could transport all six canvases at once, even if all of them were wet. It's like I always say: You've really got to prepare if you're going to try to be spontaneous." In the new, larger format, the paintings appear much more engaging: "Once I moved to the bigger scale, I realized that this was better. The watercolors were painted essentially with the wrist. The small oil paintings are painted with your elbow, and when you get to the bigger ones you're painting with your shoulder, and when you get to put a few together you're painting with your whole body, and that got more and more exciting. You get bolder. But as I then got more confident I was drawing with bigger brushes, so you're responding directly to the space you're in and that's what gives the pictures that feeling that people think they're in the landscape. They're closer to it."

Hockney becomes a familiar sight in the area, scouting out motifs and immersing himself in the landscape. He tells the *Times*: "To do landscapes, you've got to know the place rather well. You've got to love it actually. You've got to know where the sun will be. In the summer I should be out at six in the morning, because if it's sunny the light from six till nine is magic. Of course to paint in the winter, you've got to prepare yourself. You need thick clothing and things. I mean we often looked like Michelin Men. The first winter I spent here I began to see how beautiful the winters were. There was far more color than I expected. Occasionally a farmer would come and talk to me. They didn't think I'd exaggerated color. They thought my paintings were very accurate, and talking to them I noticed that they knew just how beautiful it is here."

Through most of the year, a large exhibition of Hockney's *Portraits* (pp. 424–425) travels, starting at the Museum of Fine Arts in Boston in March over to the Los Angeles County Museum of Art, to the National Portrait Gallery in London in autumn. There are several festivities plus a concurrent show at Annely

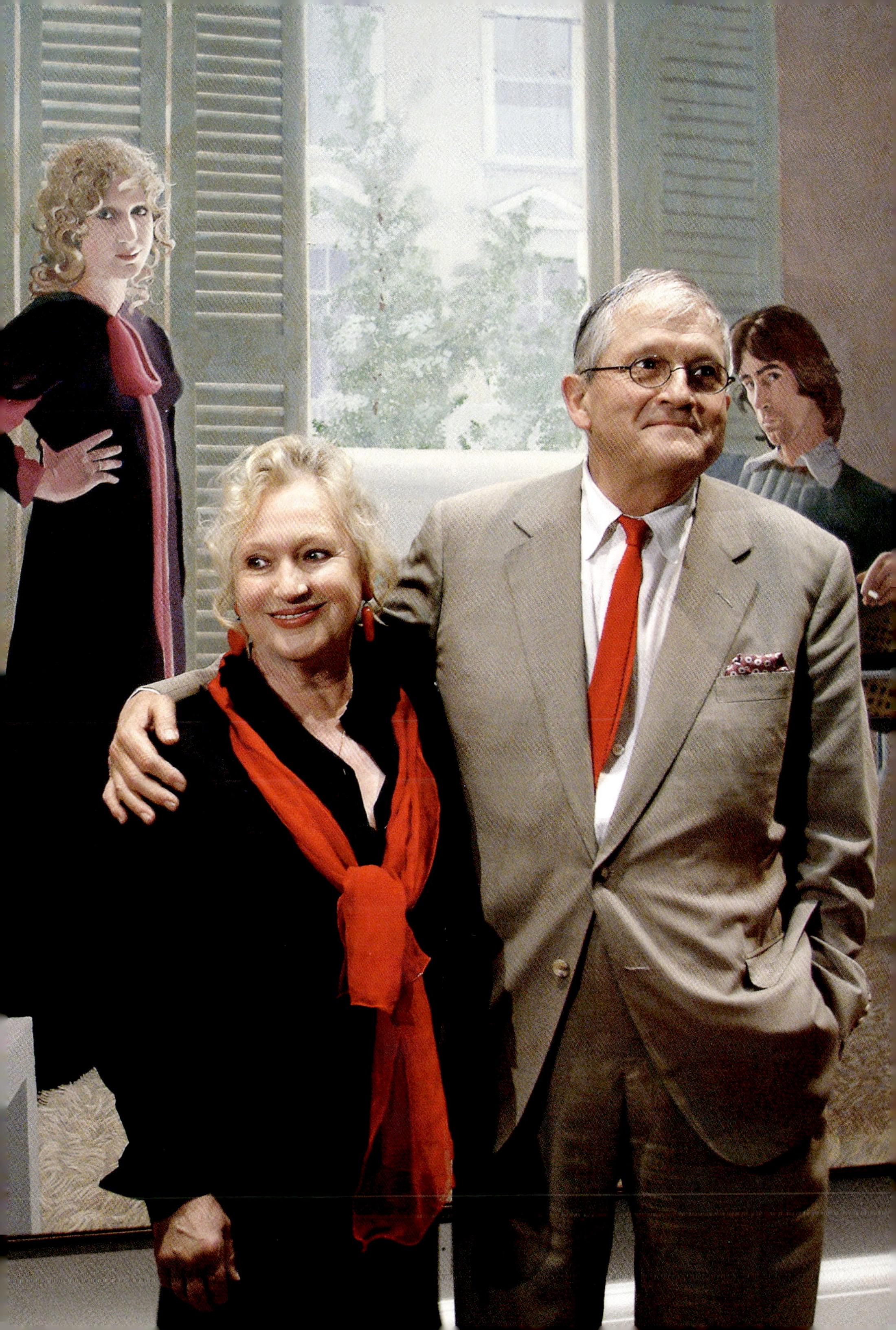

Juda Fine Art. Sarah Howgate for the *Times*: "The NPG's retrospective of half a century of his portraiture shows a depth and a breadth that is hard to match in any artist working today. There are perhaps rather too many of the very recent portraits—more rigorous selection would have made viewing easier—but there is no slackening off in quality. Annely Juda's show of the new landscapes indicates that, if anything, David Hockney is having yet another late flowering. In a long career, he has frequently seemed to have reached a peak, only to dart off at a tangent and, in another style, another medium, surpass himself. His most recent work shows a serene, soaring mastery."

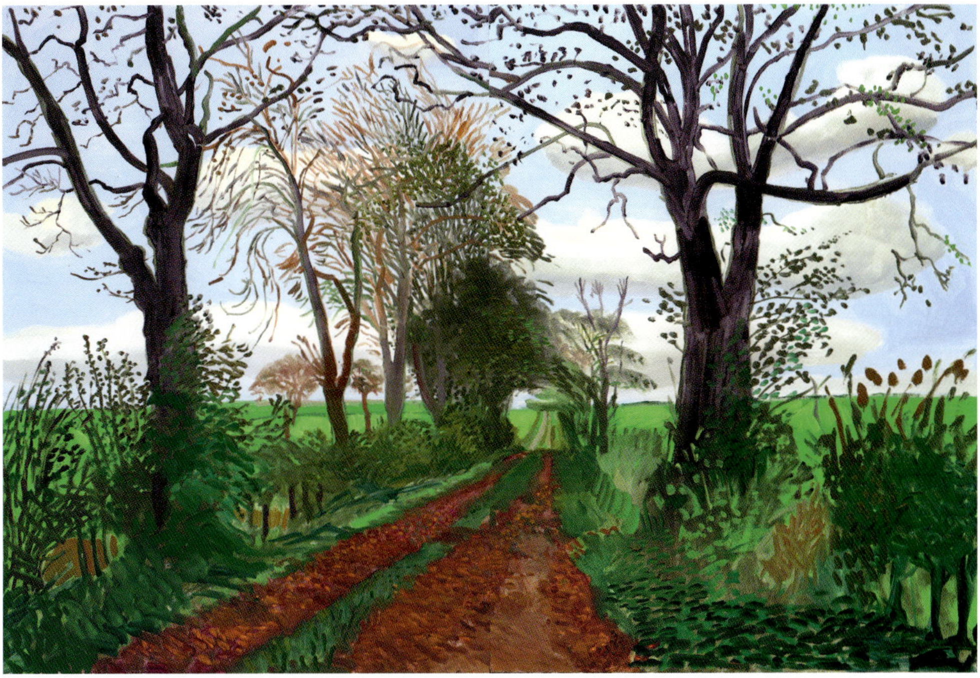

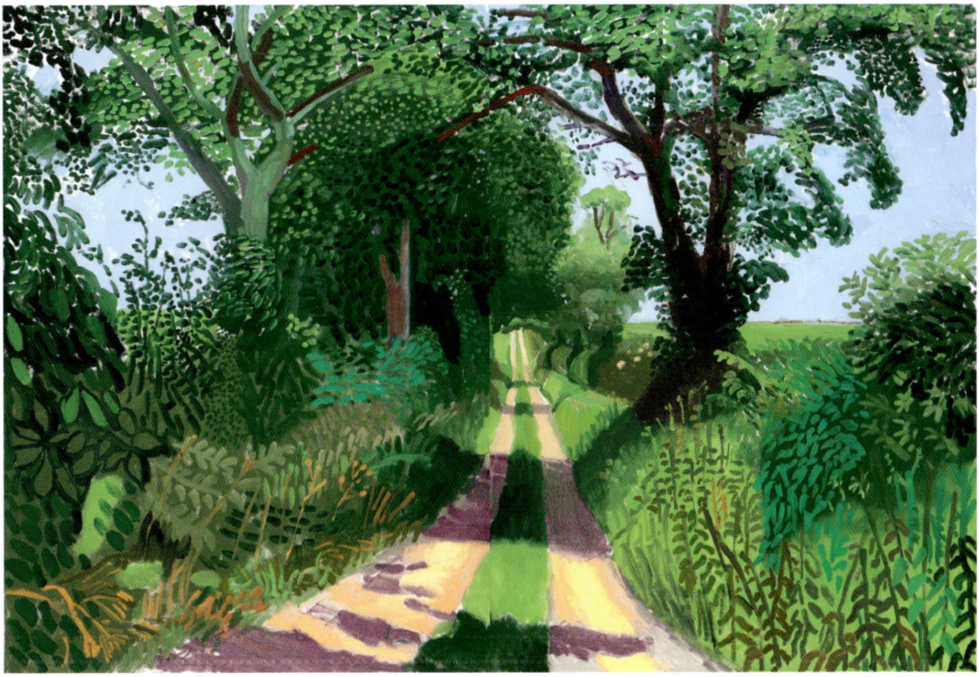

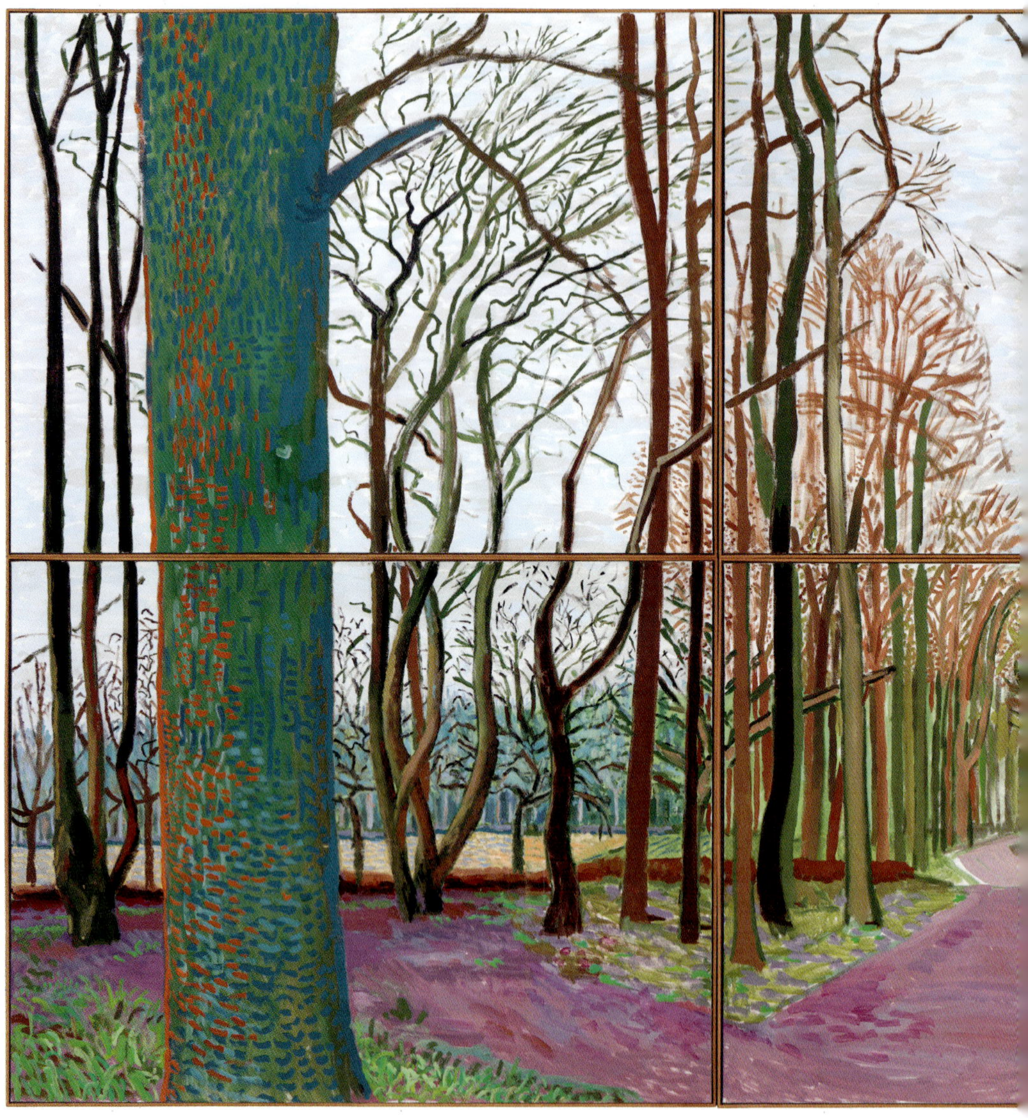

Woldgate Woods, 30 March–21 April 2006, oil on 6 canvases, 72 x 144 in. / 182.9 x 365.8 cm

Page 419: Celia Birtwell and David Hockney in front of *Mr. and Mrs. Clark and Percy* (1970–1971), National Portrait Gallery, London 2006. Photo: Jim McHugh

Page 421: *Mid November Tunnel,* 2006, oil on 2 canvases, 48 x 72 in. / 121.9 x 182.9 cm

Early July Tunnel, 2006, oil on 2 canvases, 48 x 72 in. / 121.9 x 182.9 cm

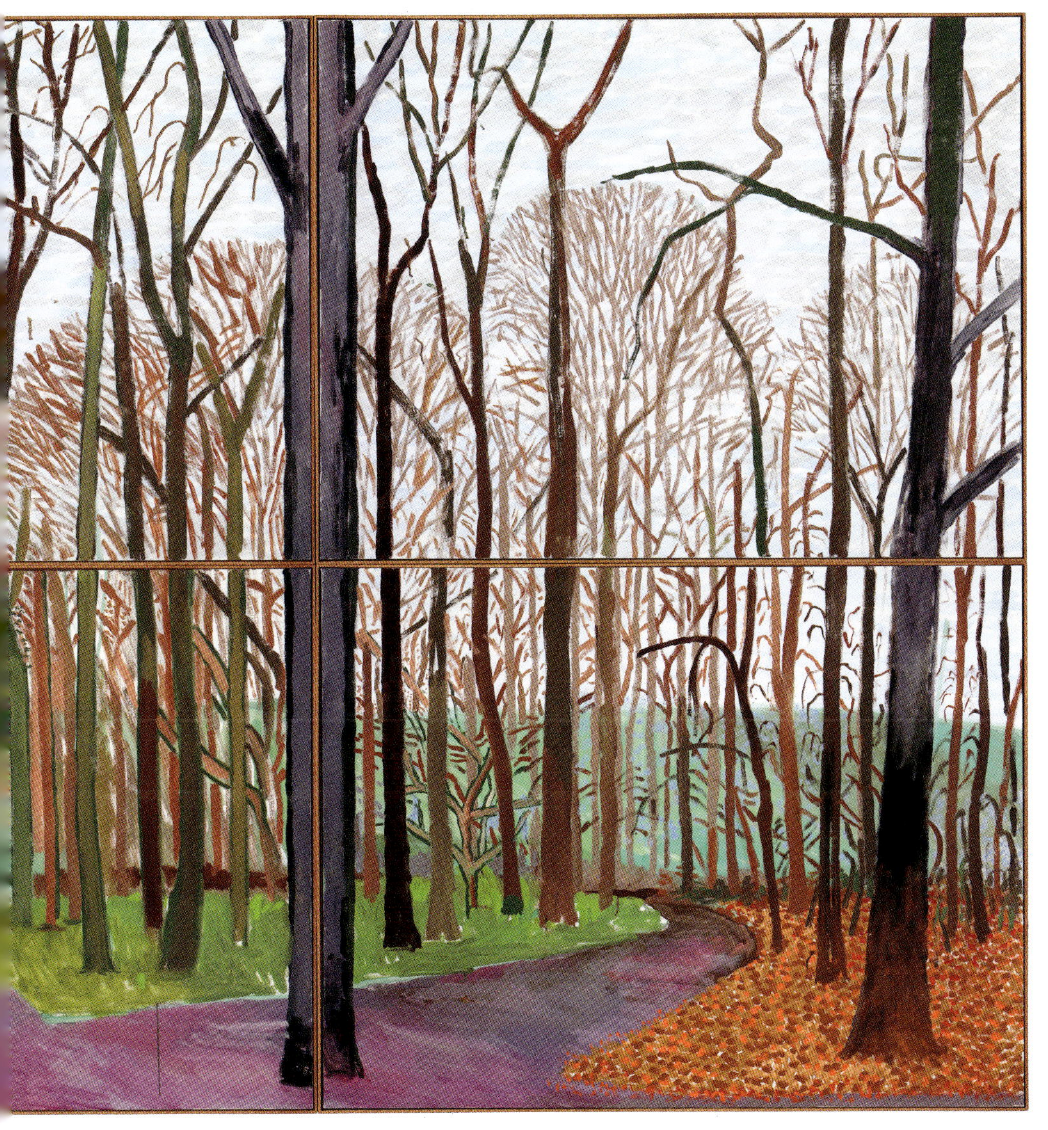

Page 424: *David Hockney: Portraits,* exhibition views, National Portrait Gallery, London 2006

Page 425: *David Hockney: Portraits,* exhibition views, LA County Museum of Art, Los Angeles 2006

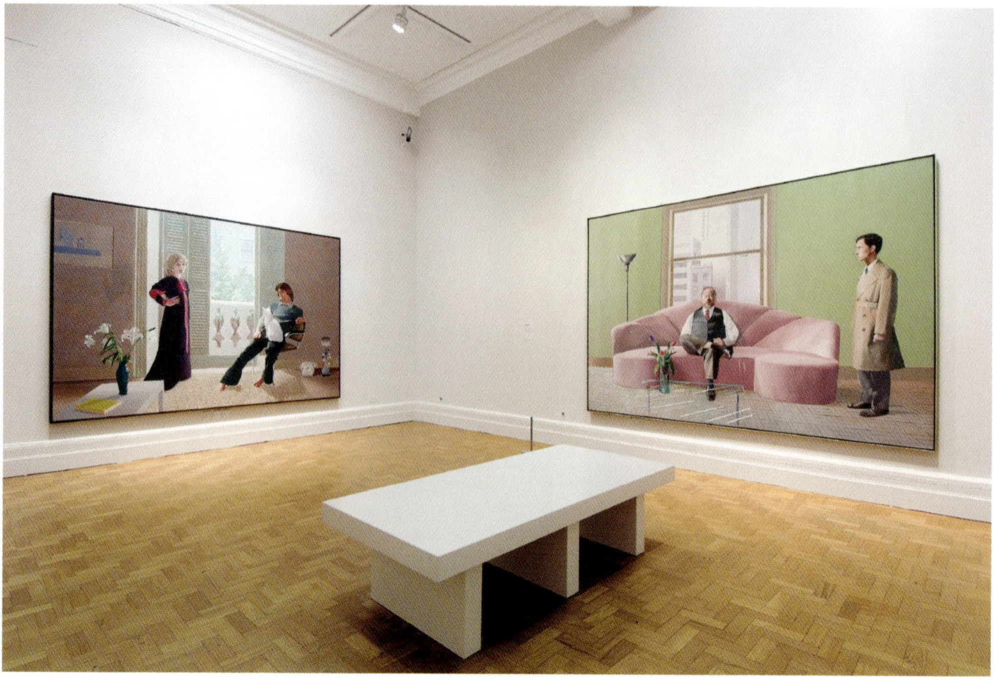

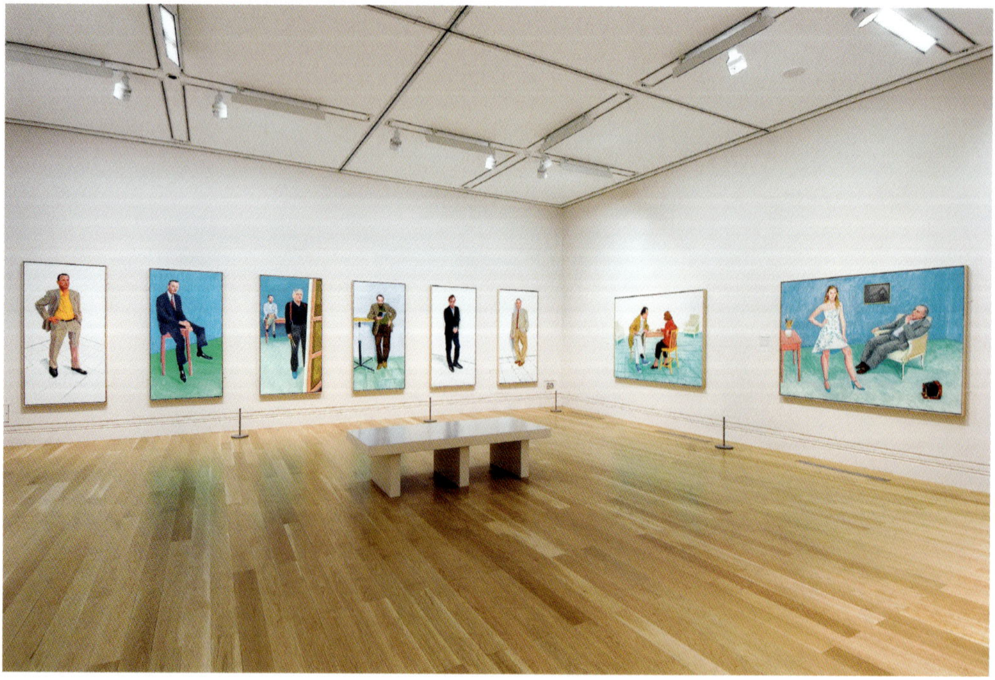

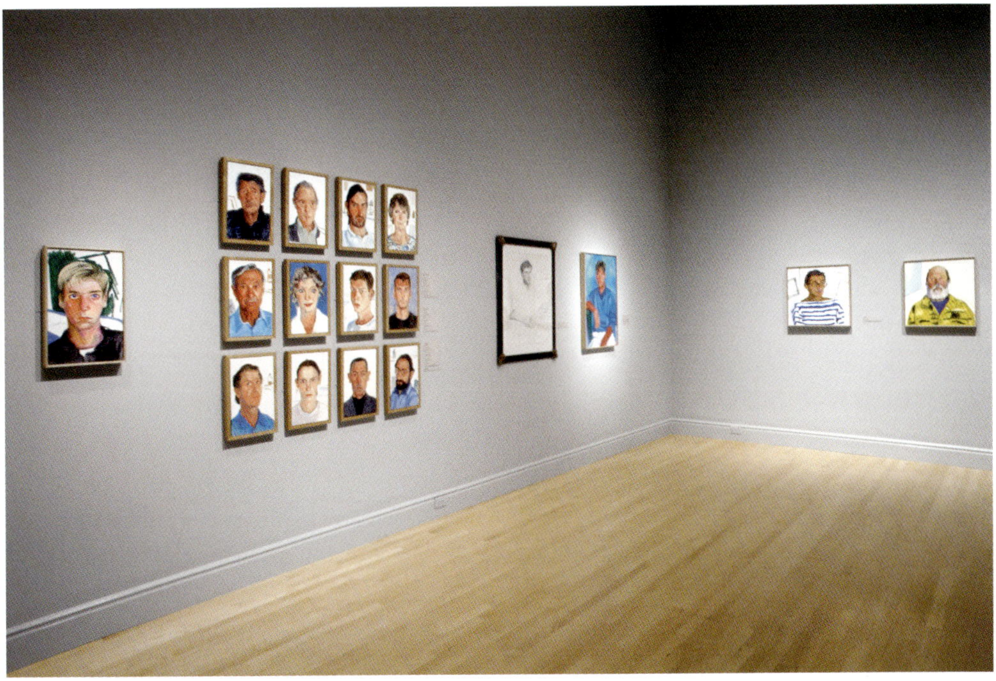

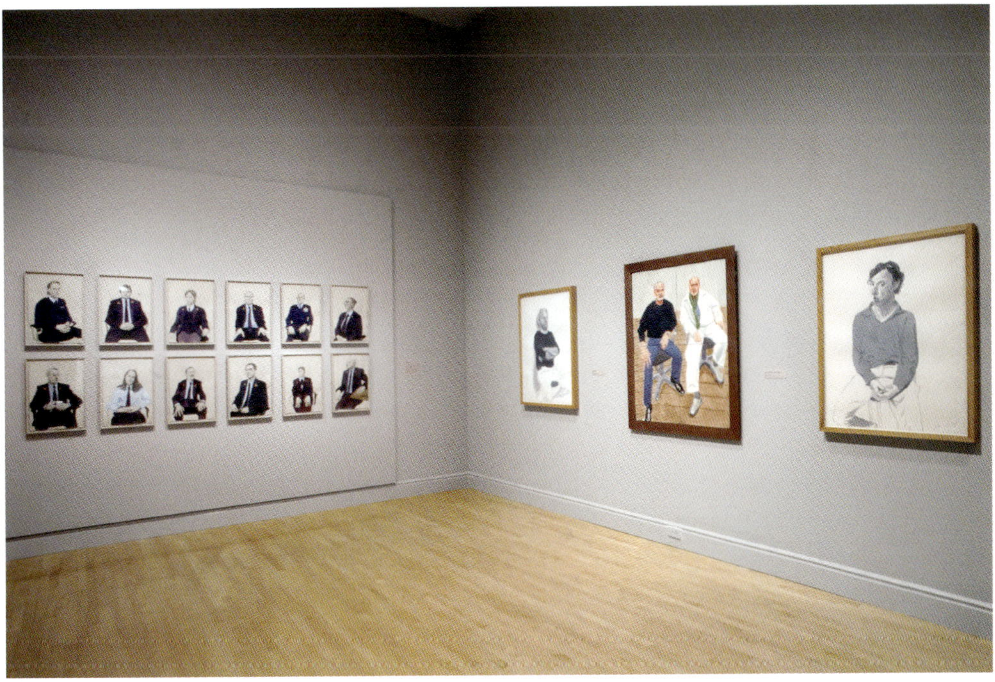

2007

Studying reproductions of several of his six-panel landscape paintings side by side, Hockney sees the possibilities of a similar picture in huge dimensions. Before he even starts painting, he manages to secure an exhibition space: a complete wall at the greatest gallery of Burlington House at the upcoming Royal Academy summer exhibition. This allows him to create a painting measuring 15 by 40 feet, which he divides into 50 canvases. For a motif, he chooses a grove of trees near the village of Warter: "I'd go and sit there for three hours at a time just looking at the branches, lying down practically so I looked up. Then I began drawings, which weren't detailed, because I didn't want to make a drawing that I just then blew up. They were to guide me about where each canvas was in the composition. The painting had essentially to be done in one go—meaning, once you started, you had to carry on until you finished it. It needed a hell of a lot of planning, but we did it rather quickly. The deadline wasn't the summer exhibition. The deadline was the arrival of spring, which changes things."

Hockney paints mostly outdoors, making digital photos of each new state of every panel and combining them on a computer matrix to check the overall progress and keep the complete composition before his eyes. He has the pickup truck fitted with more racks and buys an additional van to carry the canvases. As the picture is too big for his studio, the artist rents a warehouse near Bridlington for assembly. He describes his own impressions: "It's not a painting that makes you think, 'I want to step into it.' Your mind already is in it. The picture engulfs you. That's how I hope people will experience it. It is an enormous painting. There are not many paintings this big." Indeed, *Bigger Trees near Warter or/ou Peinture sur le motif pour le Nouvel Age Post-Photographique* (pp. 430/431) is the biggest painting ever on show in the Royal Academy, and probably the biggest picture ever painted *en plein air*. Reviews are mostly enthusiastic. Critic Bryan Appleyard visits the exhibition with artist Michael Craig-Martin for the *Sunday Times*: "Craig-Martin and I agree that the giant Hockney is one of his best ever. It is a triumphant vindication of his obsessive pursuit of the perfect expression of what painting alone can do. Even the splashes from his brush are challenges to the capabilities of the camera." Martin Gayford in the *Telegraph*: "The subject is about as unsensational as you could get—an ordinary corner of English countryside. There is a little copse in the centre, with one spreading tree to the fore, a

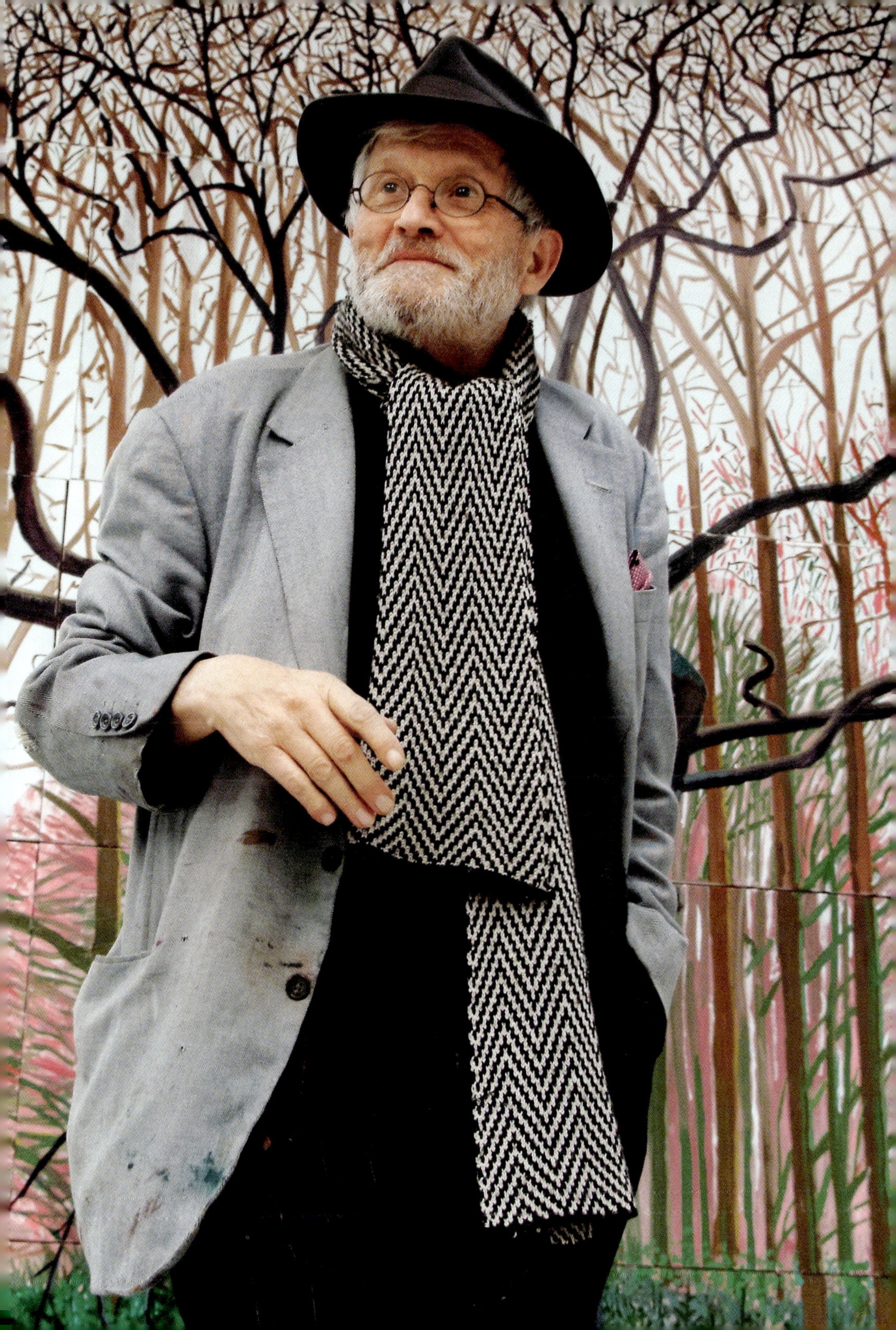

couple of buildings to one side and a curving road. But the effect is completely extraordinary. It's like standing in front of a real tree. This is the culmination of an obsession with painting the landscape of East Yorkshire that has gripped Hockney for the past two and a half years." And Norman Rosenthal reportedly says: "It's fucking good. Great proportions."

On occasion of his 70th birthday, Tate Britain invites Hockney to curate the largest exhibition of Turner watercolors to date, titled *Hockney on Turner Watercolours*. This is accompanied by a separate show of five of Hockney's latest six-part Yorkshire landscapes and a huge birthday party, which includes the previously unheard-of permission for Hockney to smoke a cigarette in the rooms.

Solo: *David Hockney,* Shoalhaven City Arts Centre, Nowra (Apr 29–Aug). *Hockney on Turner Watercolours,* Tate Britain, London (Jun 11, 2007–Jan 21, 2008); catalog ed. by Simon Grant, text by David Hockney. *The East Yorkshire Landscape,* L.A. Louver, Venice, CA (Feb 9–Mar 24); catalog with a text by Peter Goulds.

Group: *The Mirror and the Mask: Portraiture in the Age of Picasso,* Museo Thyssen-Bornemisza and Fundación Caja, Madrid (Feb 6–May 20); travels to Kimbell Art Museum, Fort Worth; catalog. *Variations on America: Masterworks from American Art Forum Collections,* Smithsonian American Art Museum, Washington, D.C. (Apr 13–Jul 29); catalog. *The Naked Portrait 1900–2007,* Scottish National Portrait Gallery, Edinburgh (Jun 6–Sep 2); travels to Compton Verney; catalog. *Summer Exhibition,* Royal Academy of Arts, London (Jun 11–Aug 19); catalog. *The Painting of Modern Life: 1960s to Now,* Hayward Gallery, London (Oct 4–Dec 30); travels to Castello di Rivoli, Turin; catalog. *Pop Art Portraits,* National Portrait Gallery, London (Oct 11, 2007–Jan 20, 2008); travels to Staatsgalerie Stuttgart; catalog.

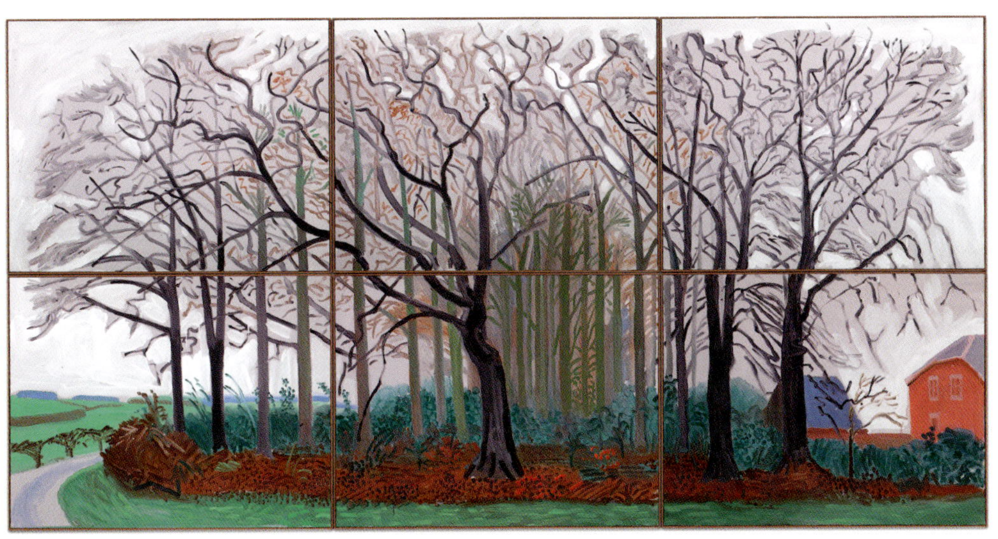

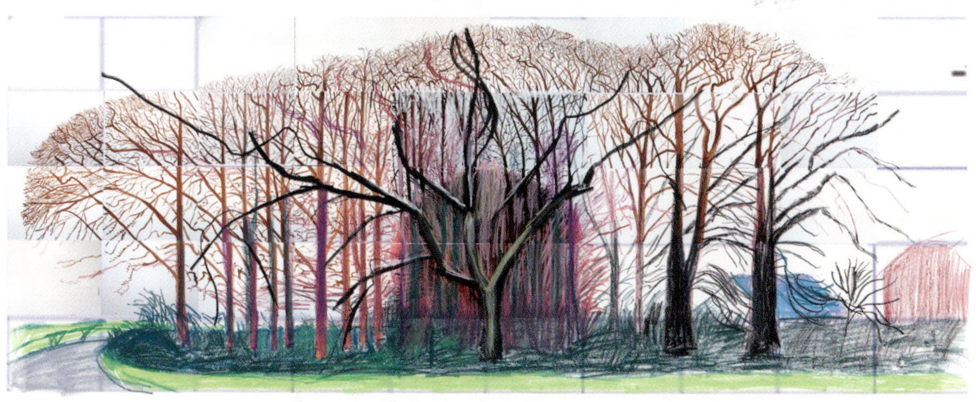

Six Part Study for Bigger Trees, 2007, oil on 6 canvases, 72 x 144 in. / 182.9 x 365.8 cm

Drawing of *Bigger Trees near Warter or/ou Peinture sur le motif pour le Nouvel Age Post-Photographique,* version X, 2007, crayon on inkjet, mounted on foam core, 22 ¼ x 43 in. / 56.5 x 109.2 cm

Page 427: David Hockney in front of *Bigger Trees near Warter,* 2007. Photo: Jean-Pierre Gonçalves de Lima

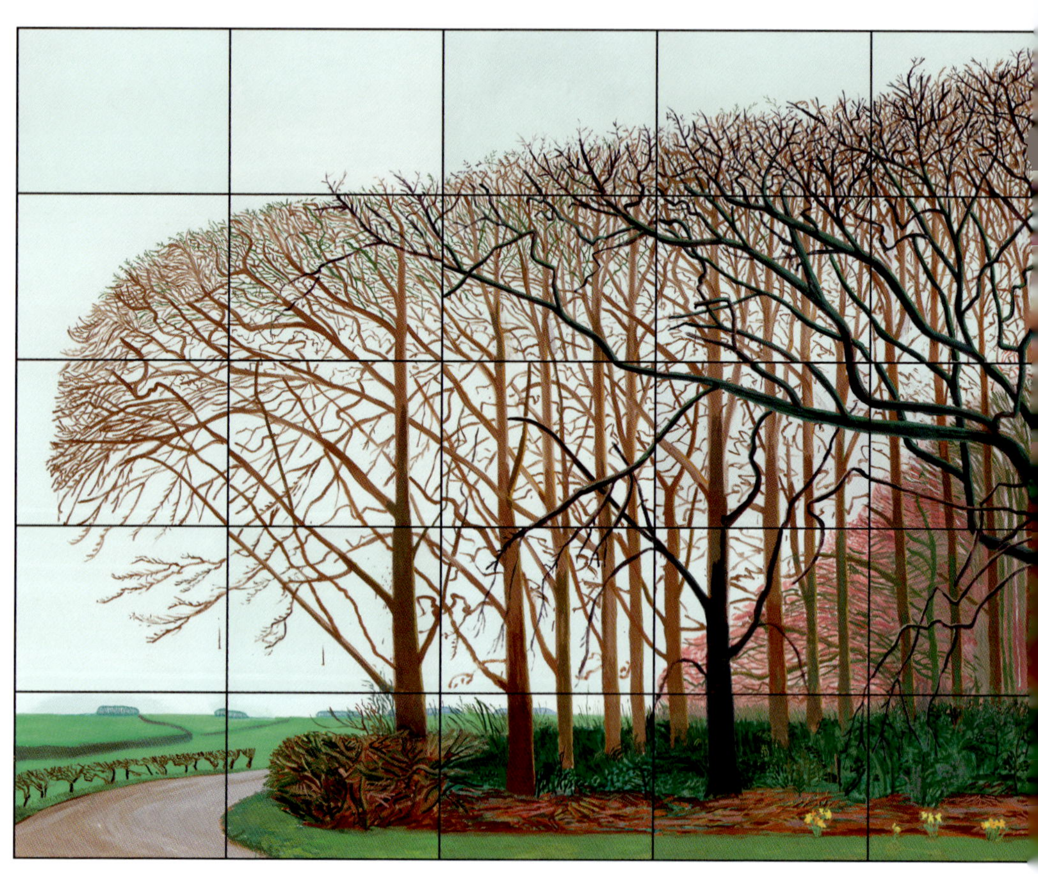

*Bigger Trees near Warter or/ou Peinture
sur le motif pour le Nouvel Age Post-
Photographique*, 2007, oil on 50 canvases,
180 x 480 in. / 457.2 x 1219.2 cm

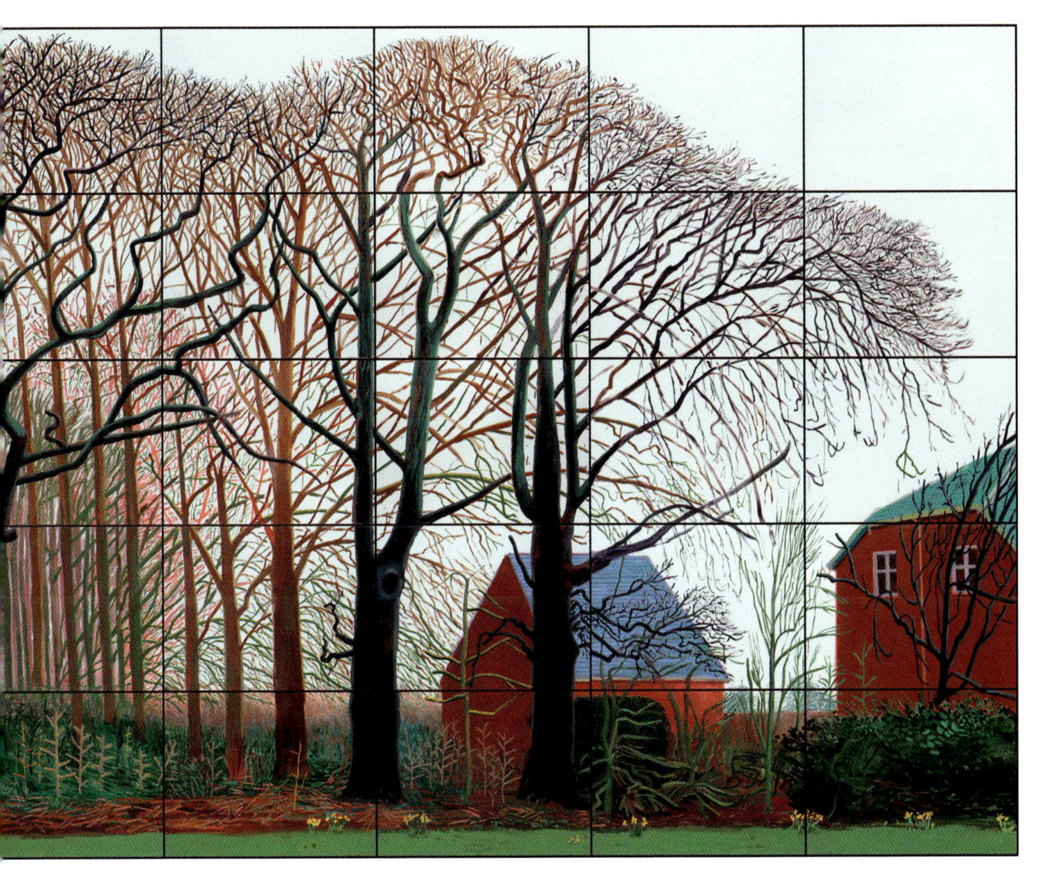

Pages 432/433: David Hockney painting *Three Trees near Thixendale, Autumn 2008,* Bridlington 2008. Photo: Jean-Pierre Gonçalves de Lima

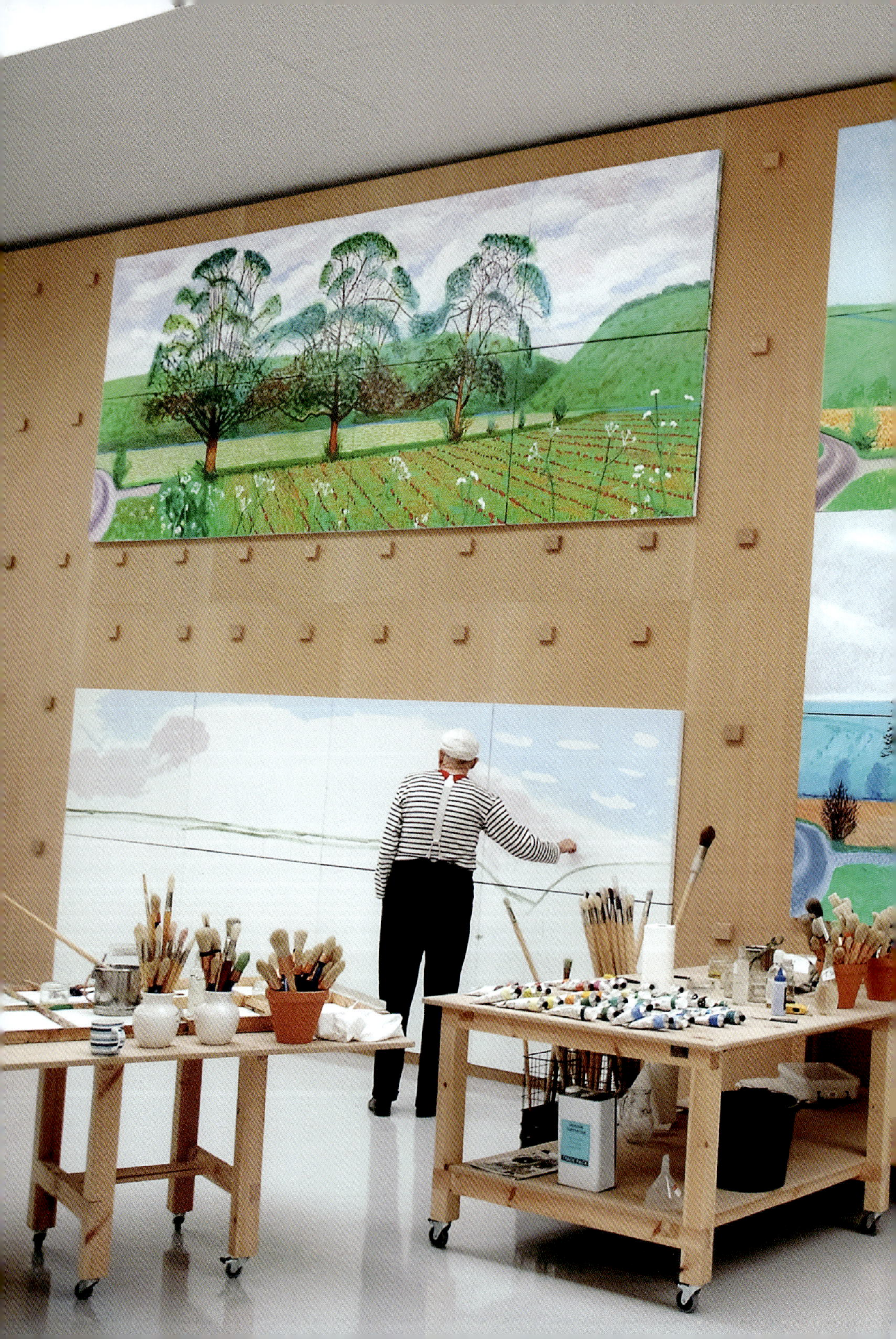

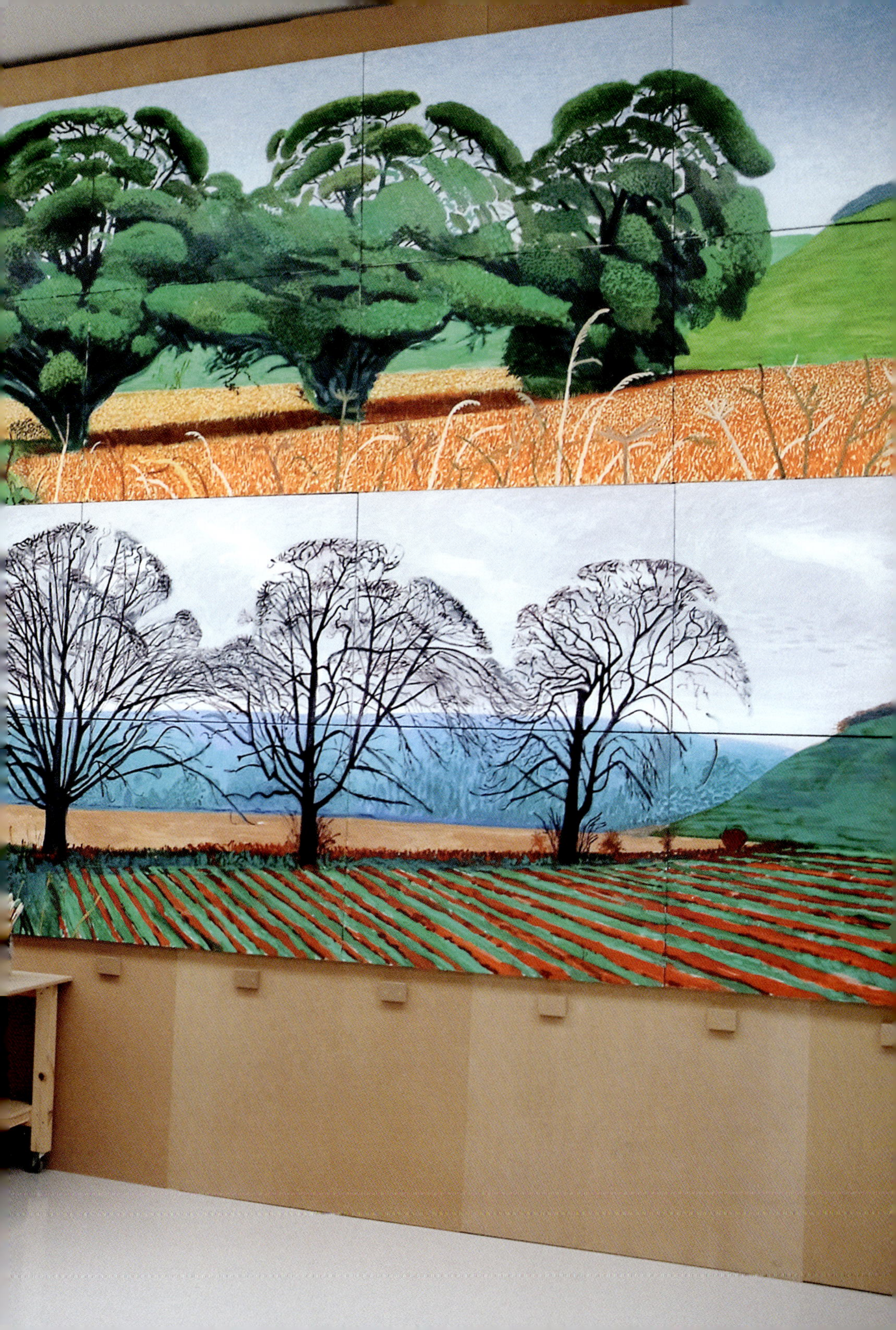

2008

Hockney donates *Bigger Trees near Warter,* his giant 50-panel painting of the previous year, to the Tate. Most of his canvases now have a larger format: "Perhaps today to make big statements with paintings, you have to paint them big. The size is a bit overwhelming, even for me. It's quite a problem drawing on that scale, but I am doing it. I would never have expected to be painting with such ambition at this age. I seem to have more energy than I did a decade ago." A large exhibition of his landscape paintings is scheduled at the Royal Academy for 2012, so Hockney leases an industrial warehouse to accommodate the new formats, a space of 10,000 square feet, lit through skylights in the ceiling. "I've just rented a very, very large warehouse in Bridlington," Hockney tells Martin Gayford. "When I signed the lease for five years, I felt twenty years younger. I stopped feeling frail and started feeling energetic." Soon the walls fill with canvases.

Among these are four views across all seasons of *Three Trees near Thixendale* (pp. 438–441), begun in the previous year: "I thought I'd do them in August because the trees looked majestic to me. I realized they were about 200 years old each. In the winter you wouldn't notice them as much…In the summer it's just the largeness, the weight it seems to have; the branches are bending down because of the weight of the foliage. In December they are reaching for the light. So once you've done the second one, you think, 'Well, when spring comes along, and it's changing, I'll do another.' So I did. The spring was quite hard, because spring happens very quickly here. We call it 'action week.'" Hockney no longer paints most of the canvases out in the open: "Now for autumn, I have recorded some changes in the last week through drawings and through computer drawings, and I will do some more later this week…I began to work in the studio because I wanted to use memory, you see. I felt I had done enough outside. I had done a lot of hard looking. I was beginning to get a vocabulary."

Hockney starts a series of large charcoal drawings (p. 437), mostly of cut timber lying on the forest floor. Medium and motif go hand in hand: "A stick of charcoal is a piece of wood, a piece of a tree. You can get a very good range of grays from the charcoal, and you can get rich blacks from it." He also creates computer drawings that he prints out on an inkjet printer with the help of his new technology assistant Jonathan Wilkinson: "Photoshop is a computer tool for picture-making," Hockney describes the possibilities. "It allows you to draw di-

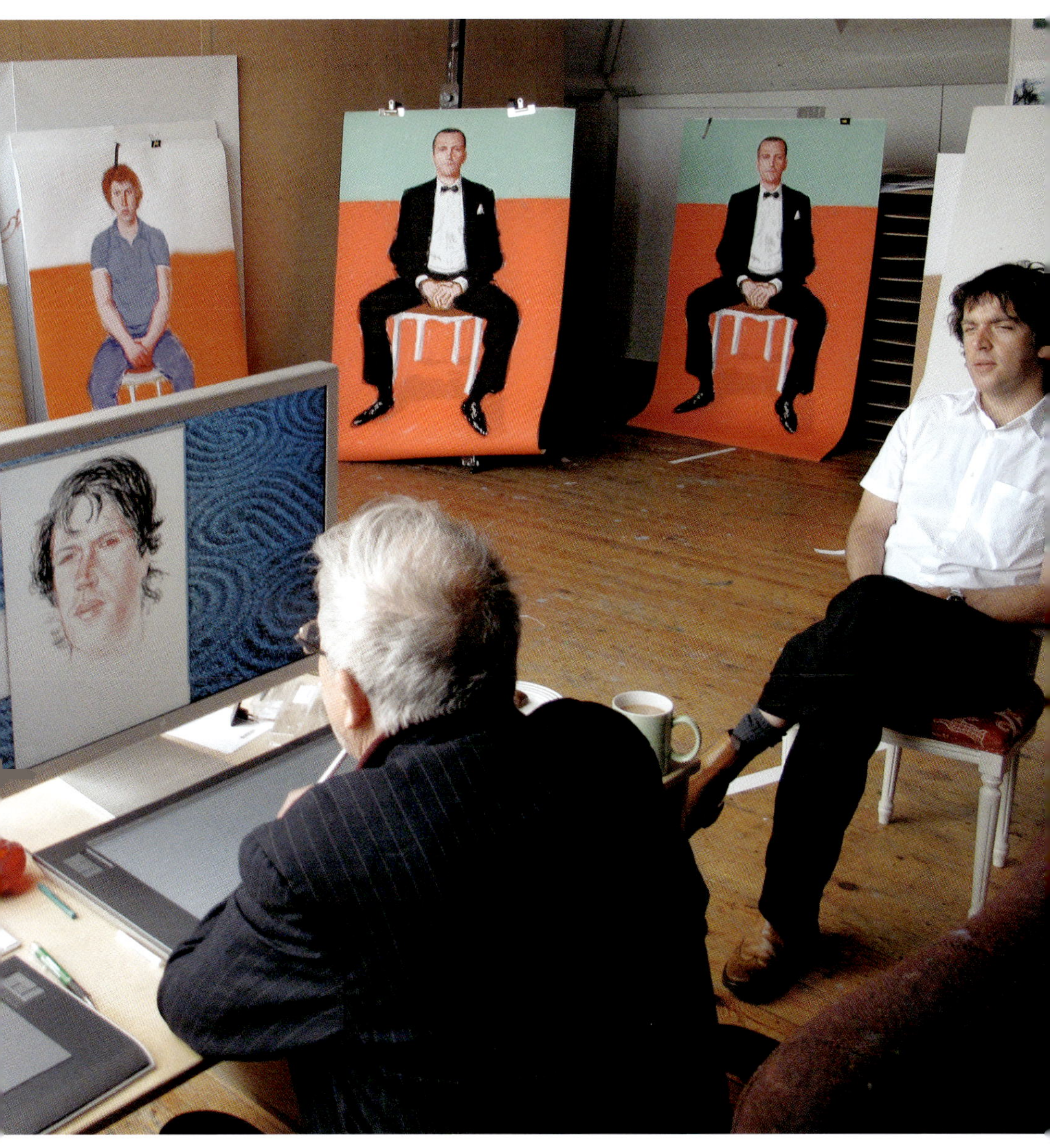

David Hockney drawing Jonathan
Wilkinson, 2008. Photo: Jean-Pierre
Gonçalves de Lima

rectly in a printing machine. One draws with the colors the printing machine has, and the printing machine is one anyone can have…I used to think the computer was too slow for a draftsman. You had finished a line and the computer was 15 seconds later, an absurd position for someone drawing. But things have improved, and it now enables one to draw freely and fast with color." With these new series and his new studio, he is more prolific than ever: "If you knew what you were going to do six months from now and were planning it, you almost wouldn't be doing it," he reflects. His work is more unpredictable: "You don't know what it will really look like, you don't know where it will lead. That's the excitement for me, especially at my age."

Solo: *Looking at Woldgate Woods,* The Arts Club of Chicago (Apr 25–Jul 18); catalog with a text by Lawrence Weschler.

Group: *Love,* City Museum and Art Gallery, Bristol (Jan 19–Apr 6); travels to Newcastle upon Tyne and London; catalog. *Europop,* Kunsthaus Zürich (Feb 15–May 12); catalog. *Twelve Travels: British Art in Sensibility and Experience,* Tochigi Prefectural Museum of Fine Arts, Utsunomiya (Apr 27–Jun 22); travels to Shizuoka, Toyama, and Tokyo; catalog. *Time & Place: Los Angeles 1958–1968,* Moderna Museet, Stockholm (Oct 4, 2008–Jan 6, 2009); travels to Kunsthaus Zürich; catalog.

Publication: Lawrence Weschler, *True to Life: Twenty-Five Years of Conversations with David Hockney,* Berkeley and Los Angeles: University of California Press.

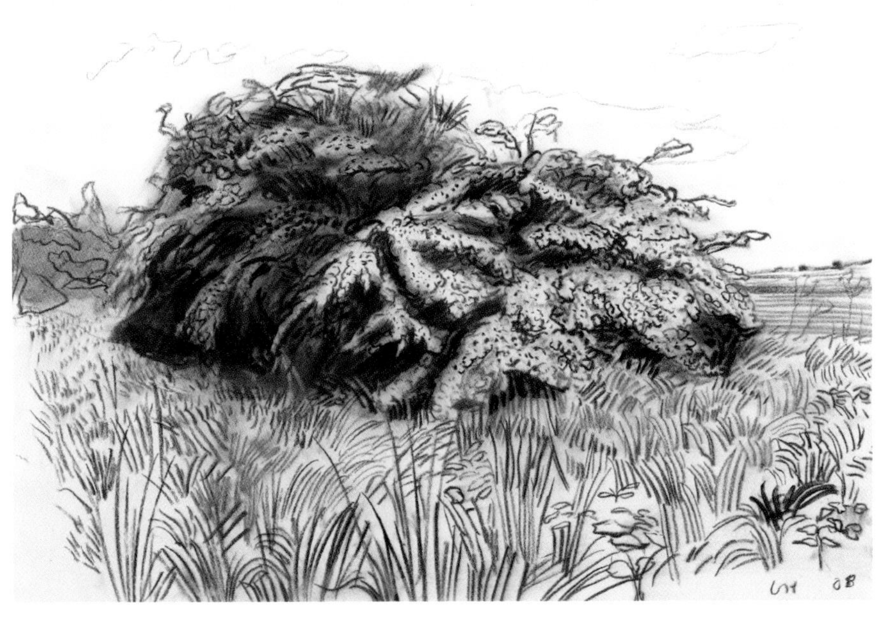

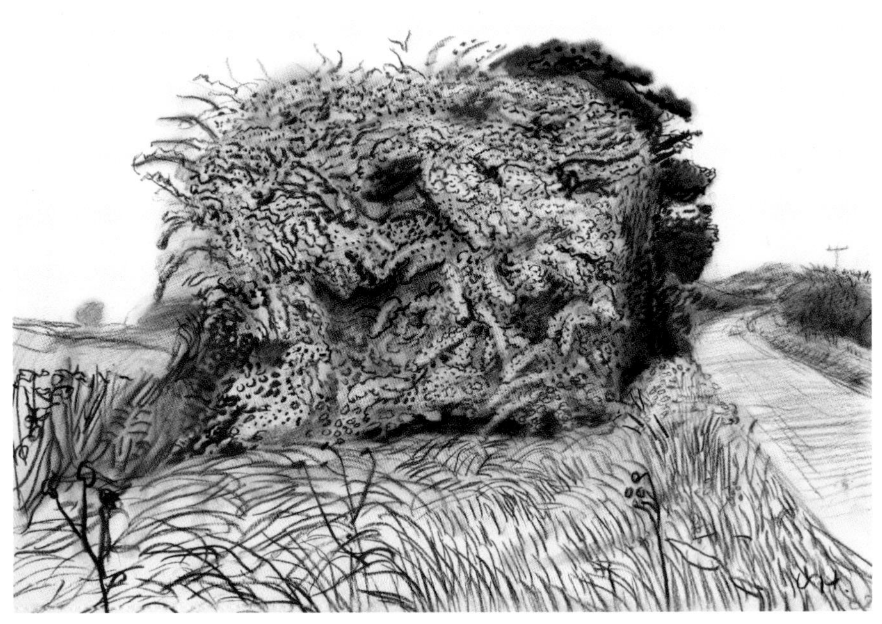

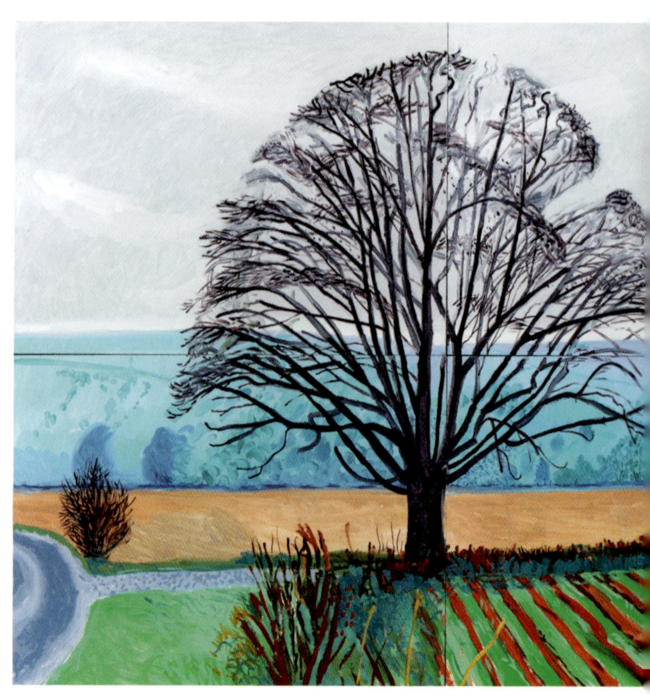

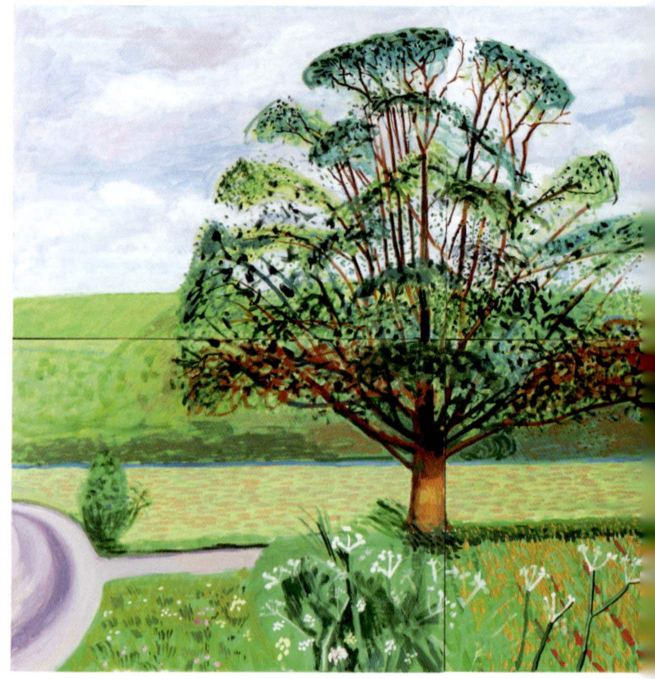

Three Trees near Thixendale, Winter 2007, oil on 8 canvases, 72 x 192 in. / 182.9 x 487.7 cm

Three Trees near Thixendale, Spring 2008, oil on 8 canvases, 72 x 192 in. / 182.9 x 487.7 cm

Page 437: *Hawthorn Bush near Kilham,* 2008, charcoal on paper, 18 x 24 in. / 45.7 x 61 cm

The Big Hawthorn, 2008, charcoal on paper, 18 x 24 in. / 45.7 x 61 cm

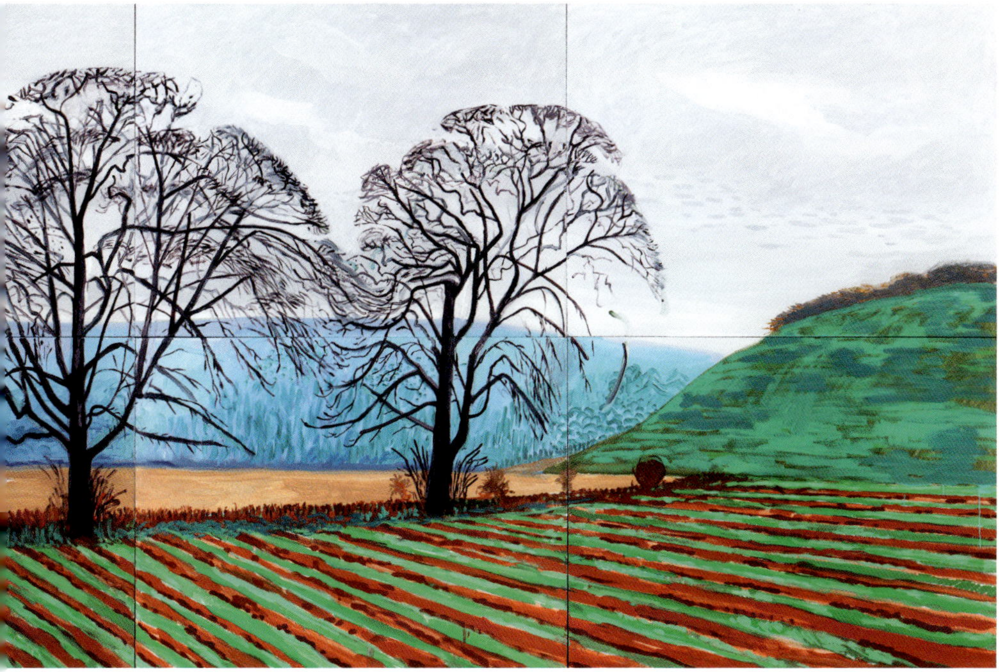

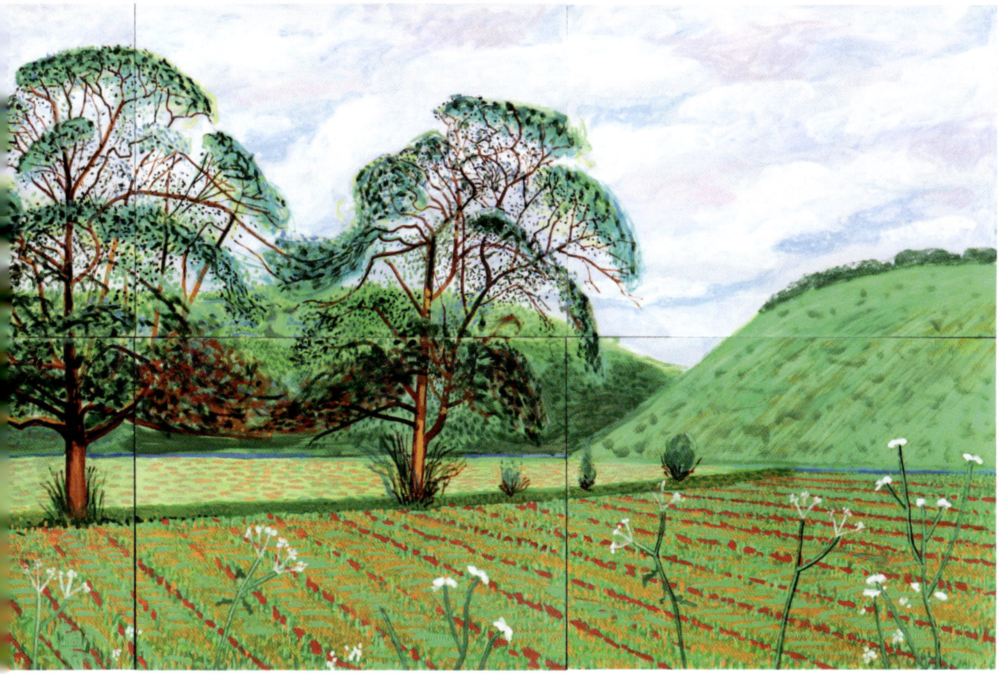

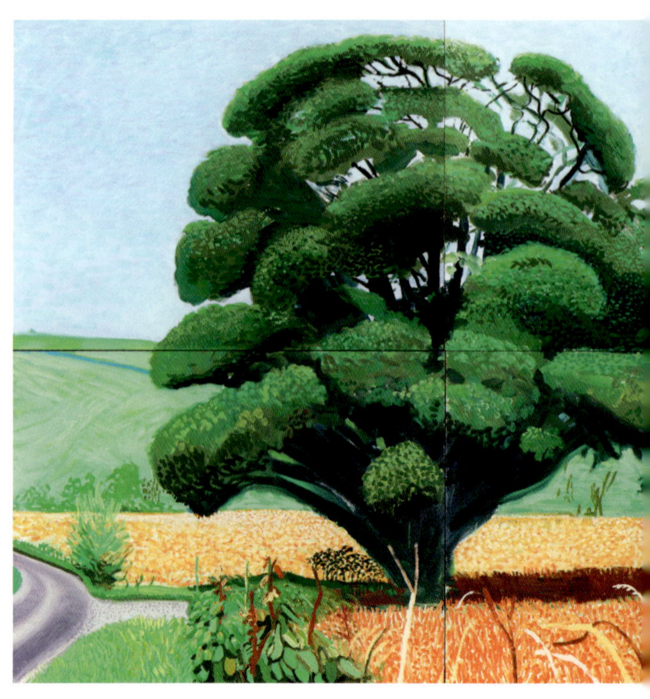

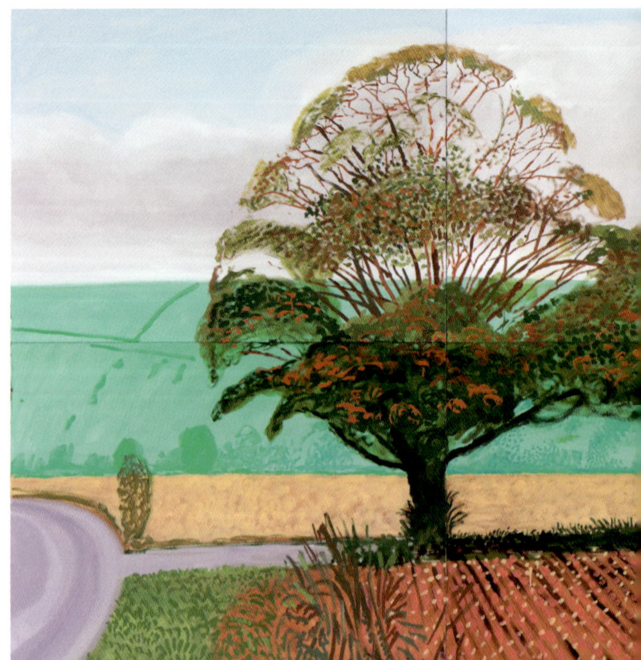

Three Trees near Thixendale, Summer 2007, oil on 8 canvases, 72 x 192 in. / 182.9 x 487.7 cm

Three Trees near Thixendale, Autumn 2008, oil on 8 canvases, 72 x 192 in. / 182.9 x 487.7 cm

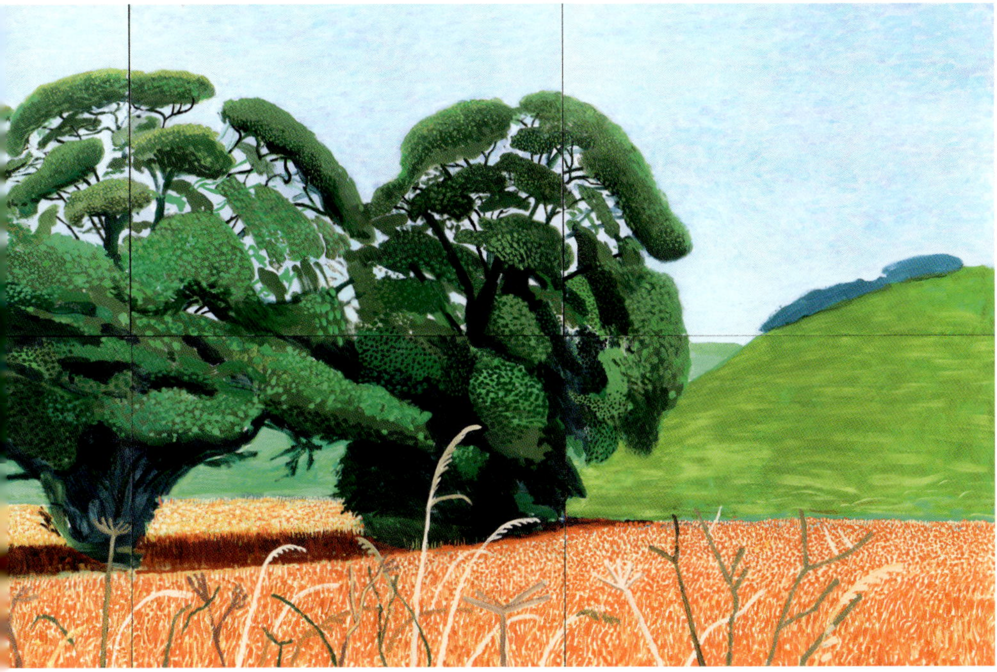

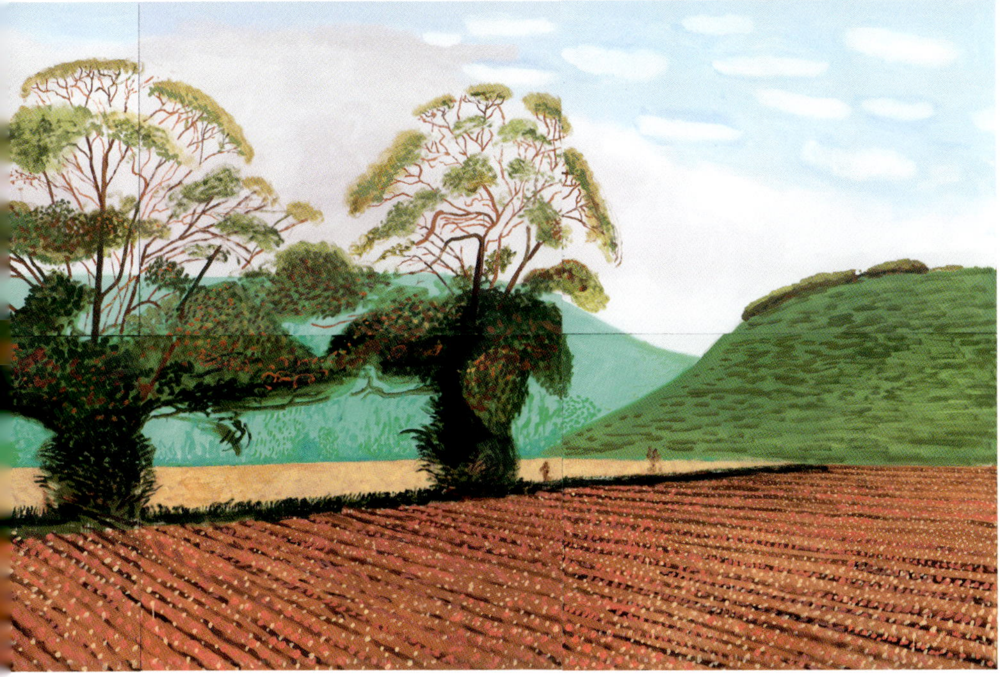

2009 Hockney adds a new tool to his painting arsenal: the iPhone, on which he paints with the Brushes app (p. 445). Geordie Greig reports in the *London Evening Standard*: "'Who would ever have thought that the telephone would bring back drawing,' says David Hockney, who has been using an iPhone to make some of his new pictures. He has swapped paint for pixels to extend the scope of his ever-changing art. He has only had an iPhone for four months but is an evangelical convert." It takes Hockney some time to master the technique, but from the outset he sees a host of possibilities: "I was aware immediately when I started drawing on the iPhone that it was a new medium—and not only a new medium, but also a very new way to distribute pictures…One quickly realizes that it is a luminous medium and very good for luminous subjects. I began to draw the sunrise seen from my bed on the east coast of England. The iPhone was by my bed; it contained everything you needed…I wouldn't have drawn the sunrise with just a pencil and a piece of paper." He sends these new works to friends as soon as they are finished.

He also continues work in his huge Bridlington studio, now dubbed the Atelier, painting portraits and especially landscapes, with more complex compositions and brighter colors. Carol Kino visits him for the *New York Times* and accompanies him on the hunt for motifs: "It was a brilliantly sunny autumn day in East Yorkshire, and the artist David Hockney was taking me for a drive through the countryside. 'What it is I'm going to show you is an alleyway of trees,' he said in his gruff Yorkshire burr as he turned his open-topped Audi roadster off the one-lane road into an even narrower byway bordered by swaying beech, sycamore and ash trees…Then he slowed down so we had time to appreciate each tree individually, and began issuing orders about how to look. 'Watch!' he called out. 'The ash tree now comes in—look at the shape of it! And now then on the right, another tree. There's a point where each one stands on its own. There. Now. It's surrounded by sky. Now the next one, and it stands on its own. You see?' It was as though he were giving director's notes. Eventually the trees grew small behind us, and Mr. Hockney's clear blue eyes, shielded by a white linen cap, turned back to the road. Although he had filmed and photographed the alleyway on many occasions, and studied it from every direction, he still hadn't managed to make 'a marvelous painting of my experience,' he said. 'I haven't quite figured out yet, simply because it's not one viewpoint. But I will.'"

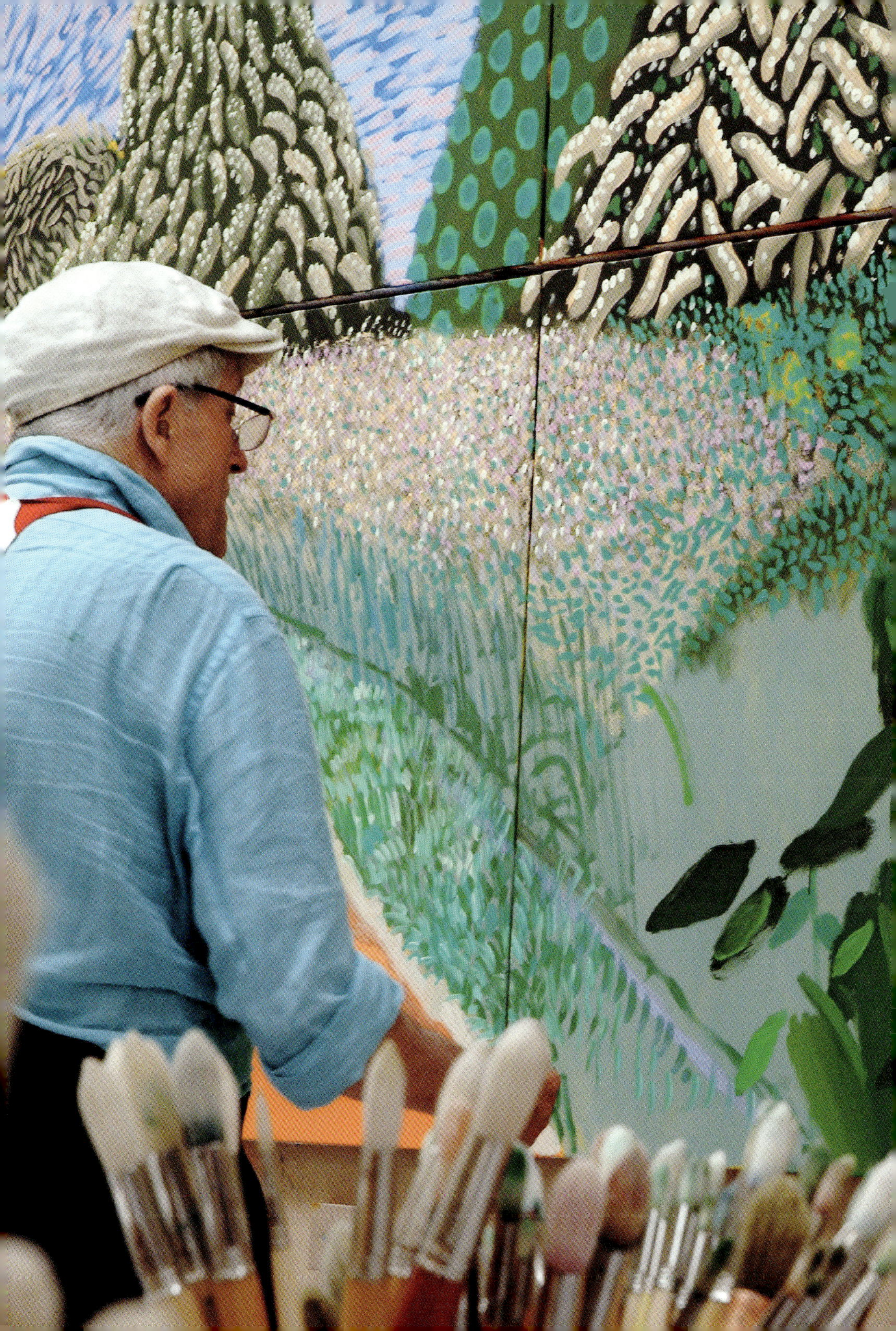

In October, Hockney exhibits his recent landscape paintings at two venues of Pace Wildenstein, his first major show in New York in over 12 years. Stephen Mueller in *Art in America*: "The shows included large and small oils of woods, felled timber along country roads, blossoming hawthorn and panoramic views of hills. Color ranges from fanciful to outrageous—red shadows, lavender trail, turquoise tree trunk. The liberties Hockney takes may owe as much to Photoshop as to van Gogh: after painting outdoors, Hockney works things out on a computer back in the studio…It's good to see Hockney turn to a fairly straightforward evocation of nature. He seems to be enjoying himself immensely, and we share the pleasure."

Solo: *Nur Natur / Just Nature,* Kunsthalle Würth, Schwäbisch Hall (Apr 26–Sep 27); catalog with texts by Gregory Evans, Christoph Becker, Marco Livingstone, Richard Cork, and Ian Barker. *Drawing in a Printing Machine,* L.A. Louver, Venice, CA (Feb 26–Mar 28). *Classic Graphics,* Leslie Sacks Fine Art, Los Angeles (Apr 4–May 11). *Drawing in a Printing Machine,* Annely Juda Fine Art, London (May 1–Jul 11); catalog. *Portraits,* Pace Prints, New York (Oct 23–Nov 28). *Paintings 2006–2009,* Pace Wildenstein, East 57th Street (Oct 23–Dec 24) and Pace Wildenstein, West 25th Street (Oct 29–Dec 24), New York; catalog with a text by Lawrence Weschler. *1960–1968: A Marriage of Styles,* Nottingham Contemporary, Nottingham (Nov 14, 2009–Jan 24, 2010); catalog ed. by Alex Farquharson, Fiona Parry, Abi Spinks, and Jim Waters.

Group: *Ingres et les modernes,* Musée national des beaux-arts du Québec (Feb 5–May 31); travels to Musée Ingres, Montauban. *Fotografie trifft Malerei: Die Sammlung Wilde,* Sprengel Museum, Hanover (Feb 15–Aug 30). *Stage Pictures: Drawing for Performance,* Museum of Modern Art, New York (Mar 11–Sep 7). *Reflections / Refractions: Self-Portraiture in the Twentieth Century,* Smithsonian National Portrait Gallery, Washington, D.C. (Apr 10–Aug 16); catalog.

Film: *David Hockney: A Bigger Picture,* GB, 60 min., dir. by Bruno Wollheim.

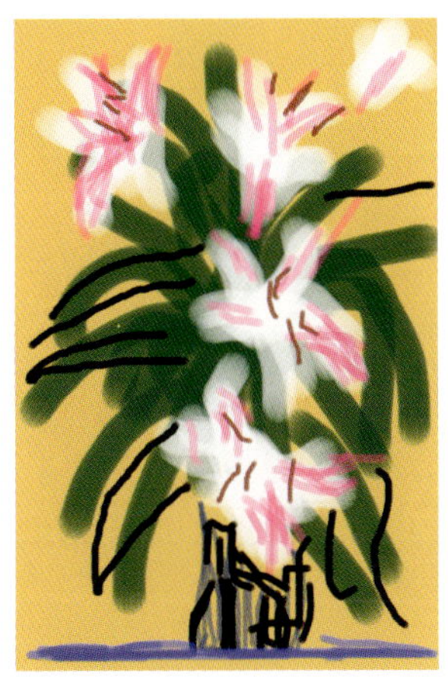 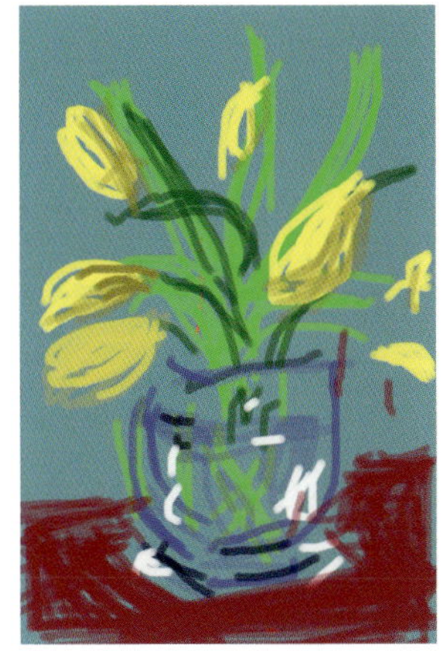 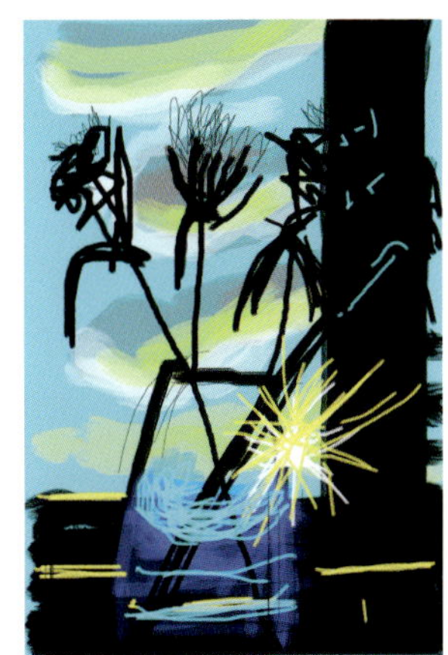

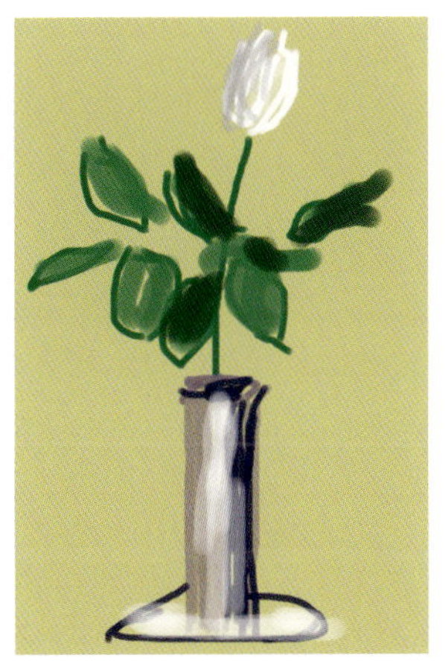 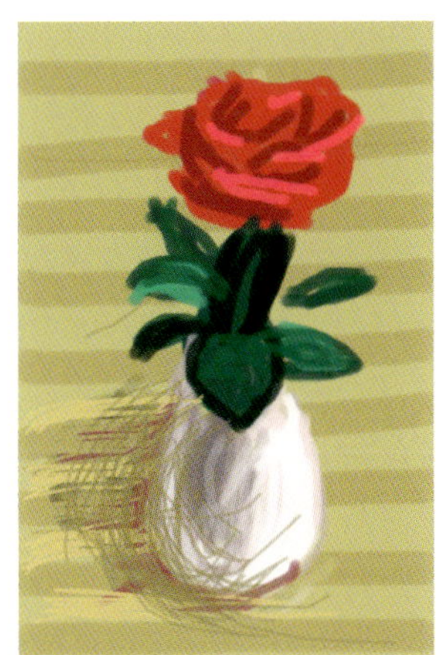 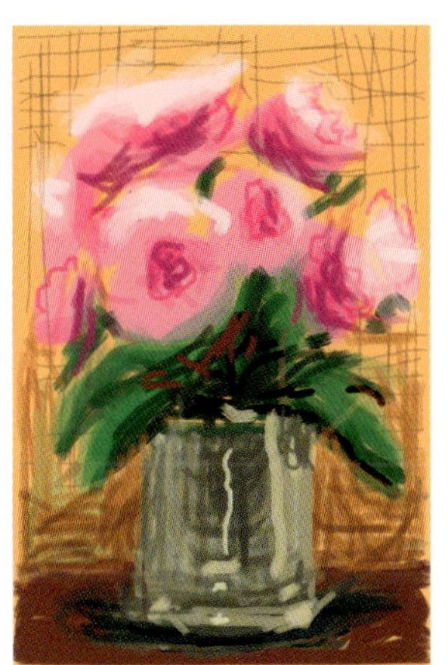

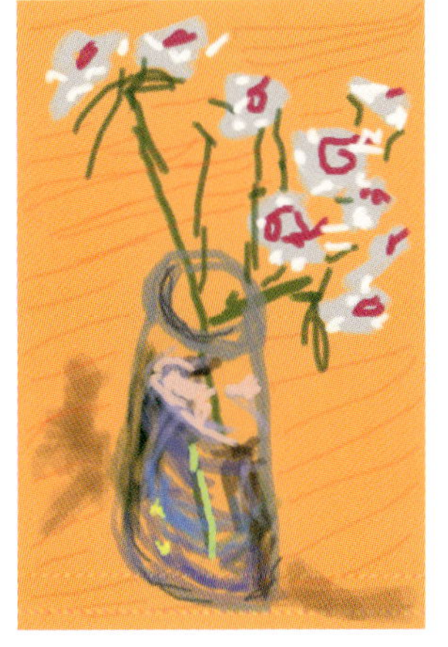 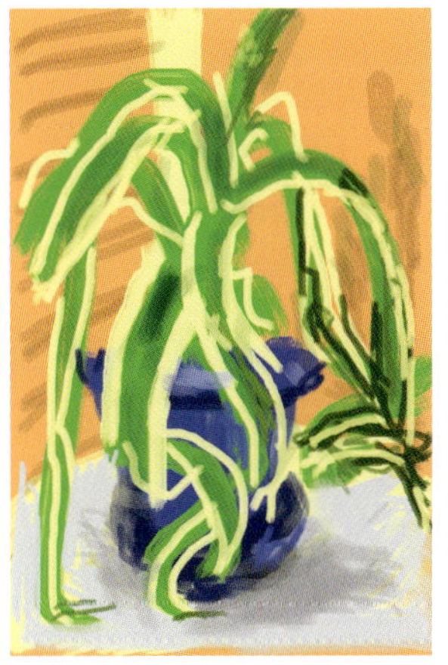 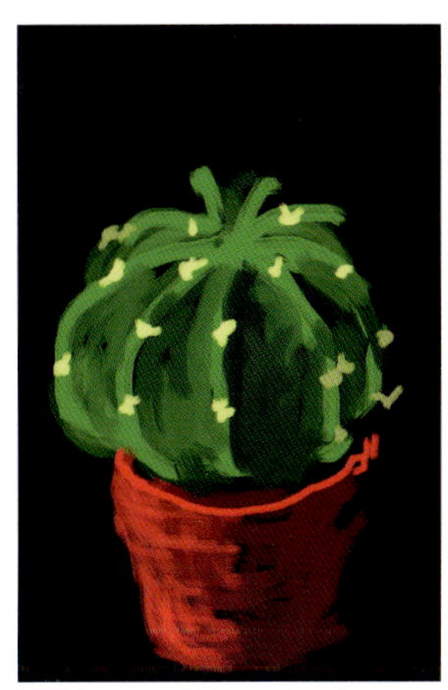

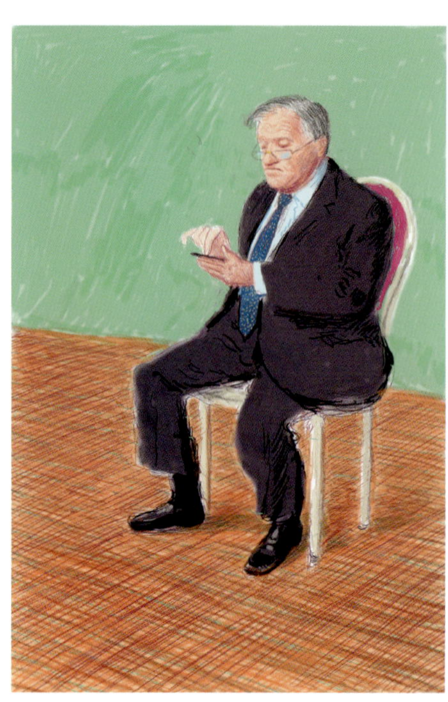

Paul Hockney 2, 2009, inkjet printed computer drawing on paper, edition of 12, 49 x 33 ½ in. / 124.5 x 85.1 cm

Paul and Margaret Hockney, 2009, inkjet printed computer drawing on paper, edition of 12, 49 x 33 ½ in. / 124.5 x 85.1 cm

Page 443: David Hockney painting *May Blossom on the Roman Road,* summer 2009. Photo: Jean-Pierre Gonçalves de Lima

Page 445: iPhone drawings, 2009

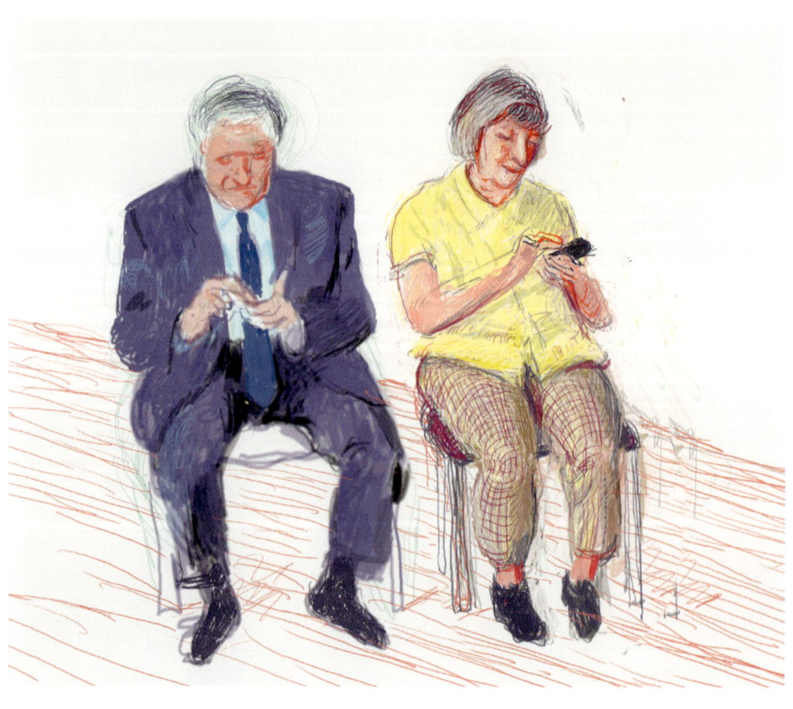

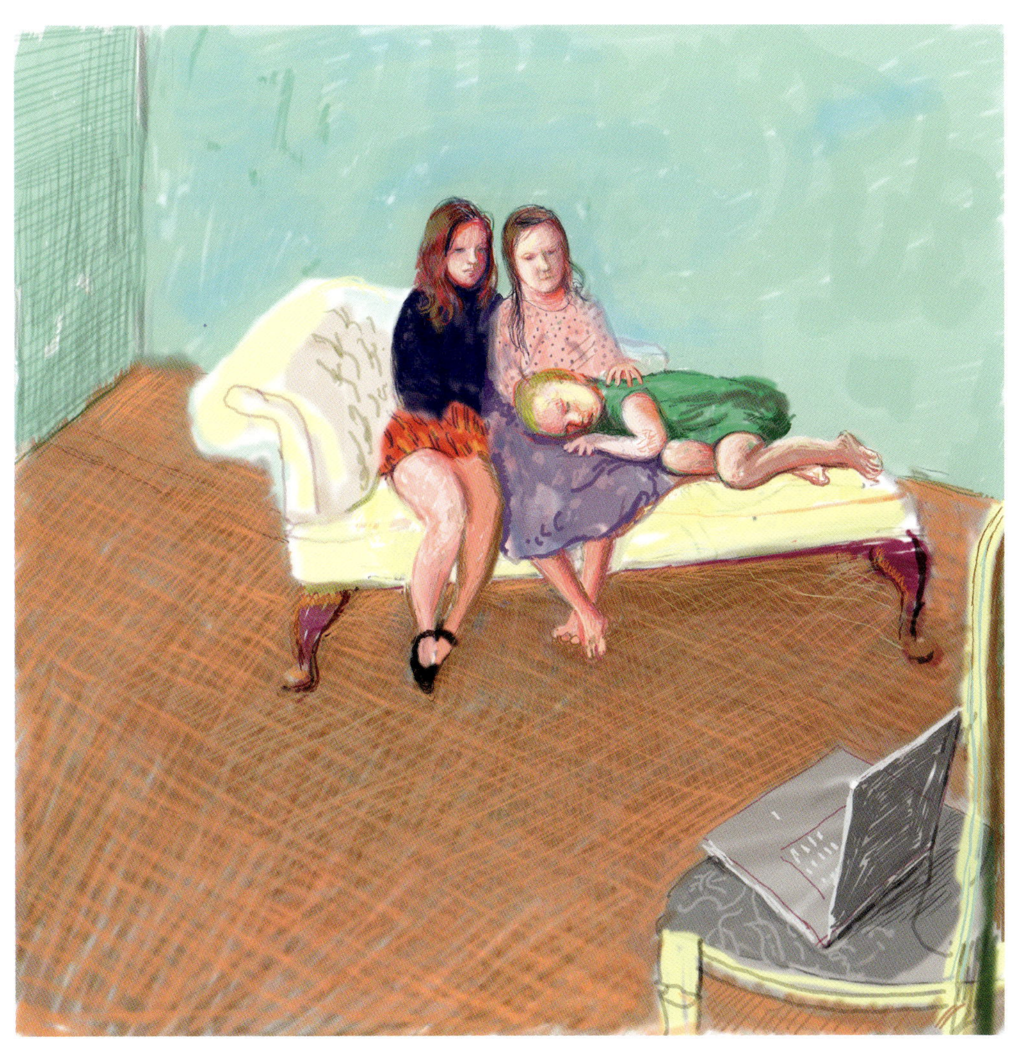

Isabella, Matilda and Lola Clark, 2009,
inkjet printed computer drawing on
paper, 36 ³/₄ x 37 in. / 93.3 x 94 cm

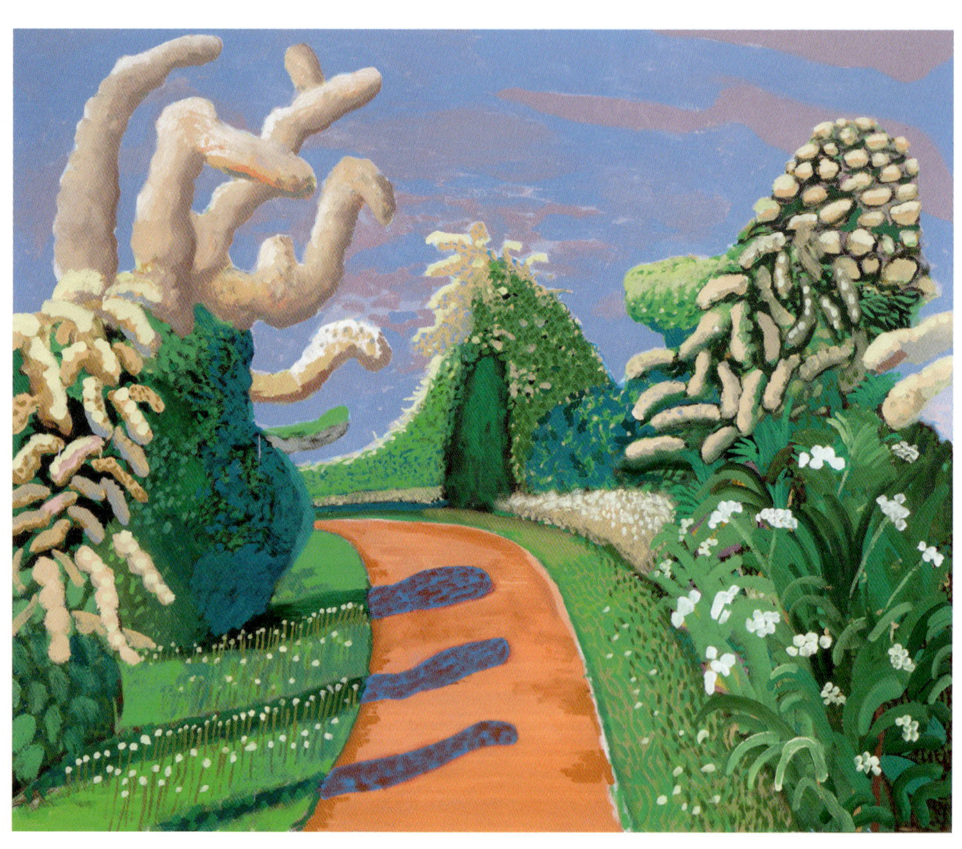

Hawthorn Blossom, Woldgate No. 5,
2009, oil on canvas, 60 x 72 in. /
152.4 x 182.9 cm

Right page: *Hawthorn Blossom,*
Woldgate No. 2, 2009, oil on canvas,
36 x 48 in. / 91.4 x 121.9 cm

Hawthorn Blossom, Woldgate No. 3,
2009, oil on canvas, 36 x 48 in. /
91.4 x 121.9 cm

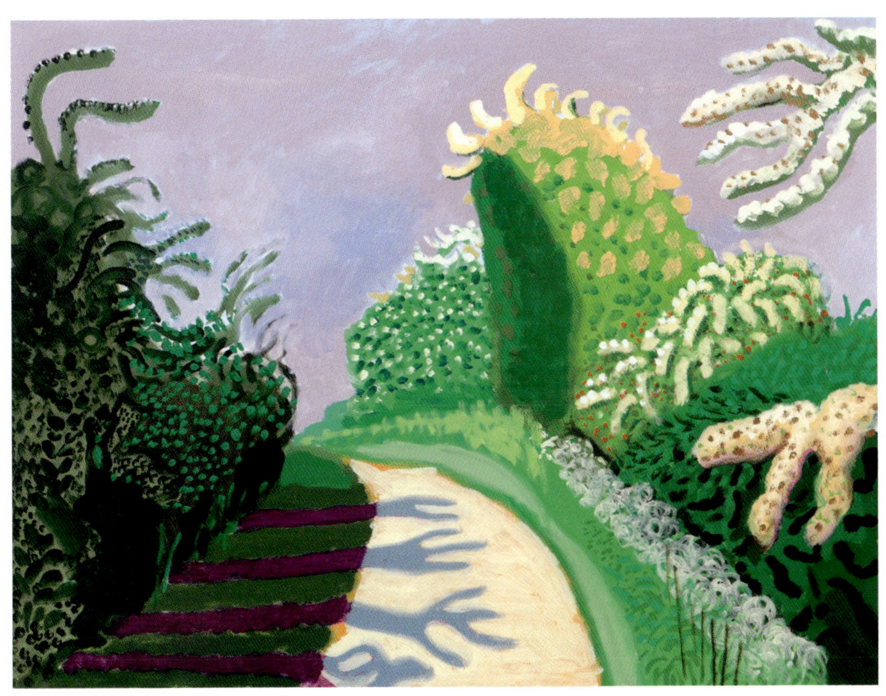

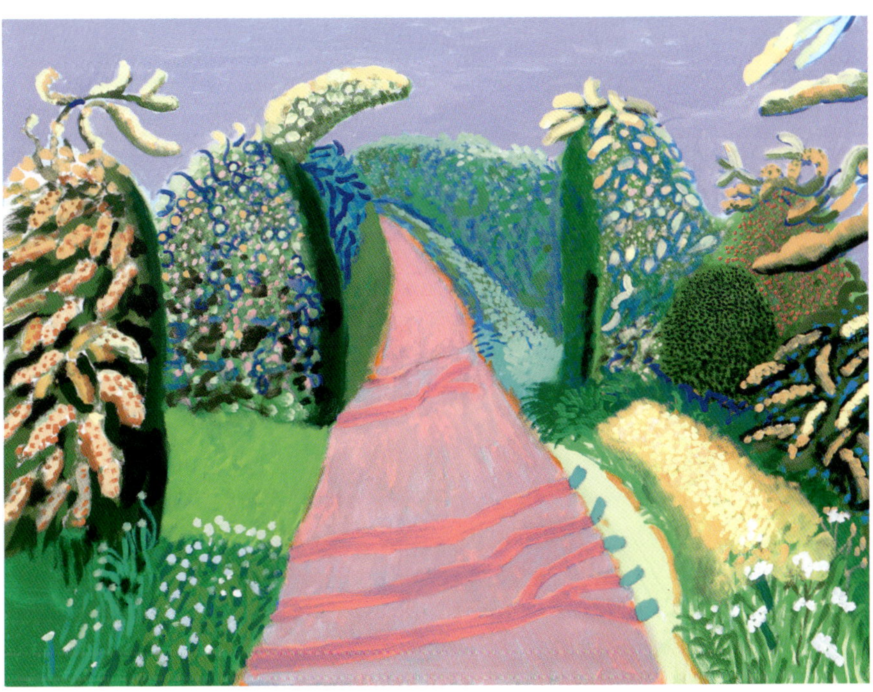

2010 In April, Hockney buys one of the first iPads immediately upon its release, since it offers a bigger screen than the phone: "I assumed the drawings could be more complicated. I suggested to friends that they get one and I would send them the drawings…It took me some months to learn the techniques, but by then I knew how to get anything I wanted, almost. It's a superb medium for some things. Turner would have loved it. You can be very, very subtle with transparent layers. The light changes quickly here so you have to choose how you want to depict it. I realized how fast I can capture it with the iPad, a lot faster than watercolors for example." He makes series of flower still lifes, quick sketches of furniture details, and landscapes (pp. 453–455). When the Fondation Pierre Bergé – Yves Saint Laurent in Paris exhibits *Fleurs fraîches* in October, Hockney sends fresh flower images by email and the foundation presents them in their original scale and luminosity on iPhones and iPads lining the walls.

Visiting the Frick Collection in New York, Hockney is fascinated by a Claude Lorrain painting from 1656: "It was mostly the space in the picture that attracted me. I knew it was called *The Sermon on the Mount,* but if you just see the painting, its subject is not that obvious. It's very dark, you don't see the figures clearly. What you do see is something that appears to be like an island rising out of the land." He asks for a high-resolution image from the museum and starts cleaning it up on the computer: "I did it quite thoroughly, not covering anything up but revealing more and more. I followed his brushstrokes…" Hockney then repaints the cleaned image in his own style on 30 canvases. The painting is called *A Bigger Message* (pp. 456/457) and its size befits the subject: "It is a picture about looking up, which rather fascinated me…The people in the painting are gazing at someone giving a sermon on a hill. You've got the focus of interest halfway up in the sky."

Meanwhile in Bridlington, Hockney creates video works on the same familiar Yorkshire paths where he finds his motifs for landscape paintings (pp. 458/459). The idea is to record nine videos in one movement from a driving car, and show them synchronized on nine monitors as a single picture. Hockney explains the process to Gregory Evans: "We built a frame to hold the cameras on the front of a jeep, and all the wire from them fed into the monitors I was looking at. We drove as slow as possible, JP got very good at it, almost keeping a steady five

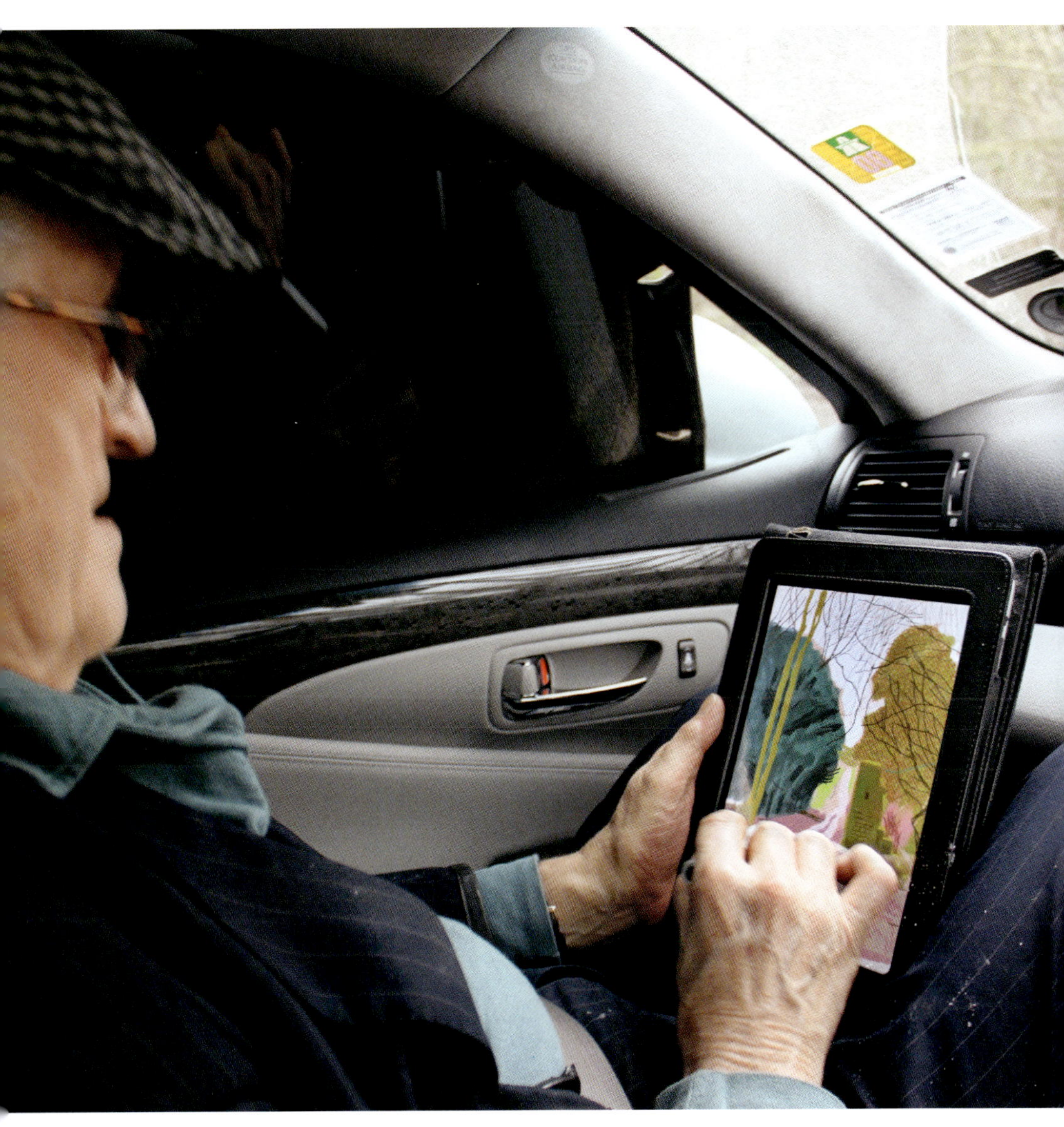

David Hockney drawing *The Arrival of Spring in Woldgate, East Yorkshire in 2011 (twenty eleven) – 29 January* on his iPad. Photo: Jean-Pierre Gonçalves de Lima

Page 453: *Untitled, 643,* 2011; *Untitled, 245,* 2010; *Untitled, 655,* 2011; *Untitled, 852,* 2011; iPad drawings

Pages 454/455: *The Yosemite Suite Nos. 1, 2, 8, 10, 12, 20, 22, 23,* 2010, series of 24 iPad drawings printed on paper, edition of 25, each 37 x 28 in. / 94 x 71.1 cm

miles an hour for an hour or so. We knew the optimum lighting conditions for every nearby road and any direction." For Hockney, using video is not essentially different from using a pen: "There's a drawing base to this. It's a matter of making a coherent space. These cameras are all pointing in different directions, some upwards. But you've got to think of all the images relating on a flat surface. After a while, I realized that with this technique you could not only draw in space, you could draw in *time*…because it's a different time in this corner and that, when you look from one to the other you look through time. I think we see that way anyway—we do see in bits, and link one bit with another bit and another bit. The time makes the space somehow."

Solo: *Fleurs fraîches – Dessins sur iPhone et iPad,* Fondation Pierre Bergé – Yves Saint Laurent, Paris (Oct 20, 2010–Jan 30, 2011). *More Drawing in a Printing Machine,* L.A. Louver, Venice, CA (Apr 8–May 8).

Group: *Colour in Art,* Louisiana Museum for Moderne Kunst, Humlebæk (Feb 5–Jun 13). *Calder to Warhol: Introducing the Fisher Collection,* San Francisco Museum of Modern Art, San Francisco (Jun 25–Sep 19); catalog. *Hide/Seek: Difference and Desire in American Portraiture,* Smithsonian National Portrait Gallery, Washington, D.C. (Oct 30, 2010–Feb 13, 2011); travels to Brooklyn Museum, New York; catalog.

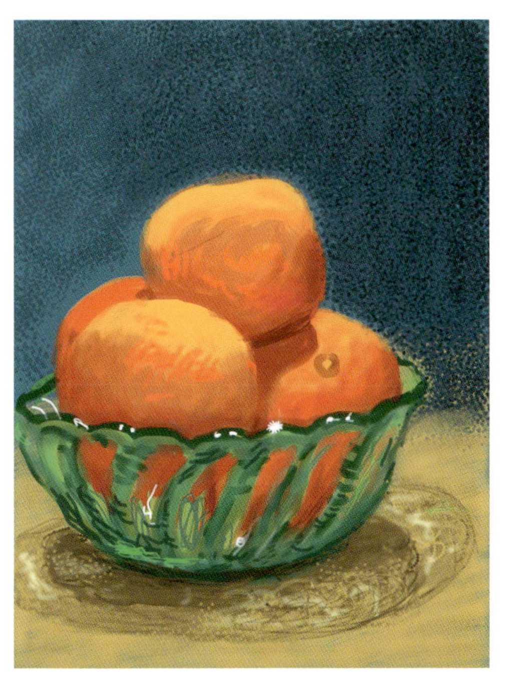
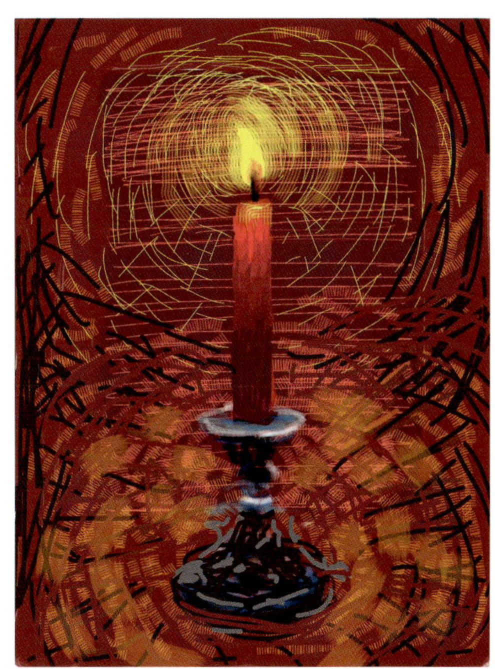
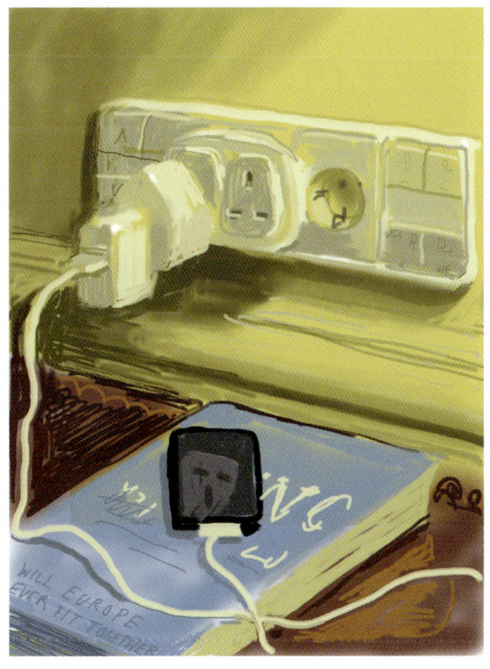

WILL EUROPE
EVER FIT TOGETHER

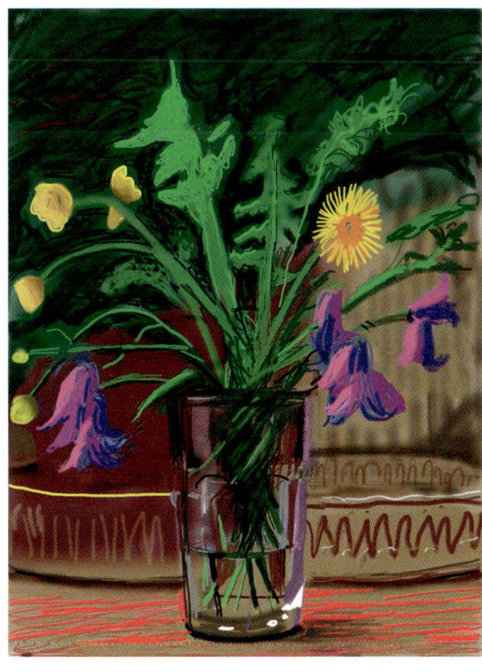

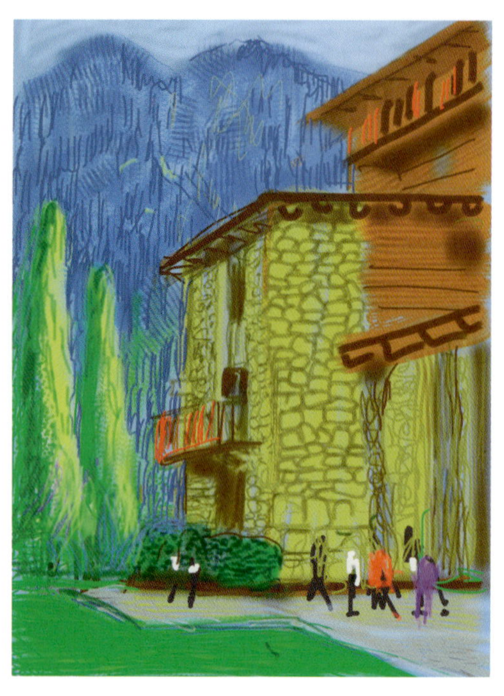

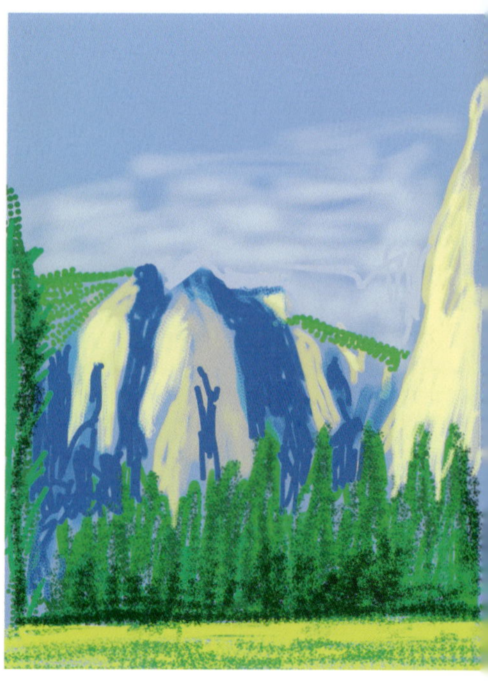

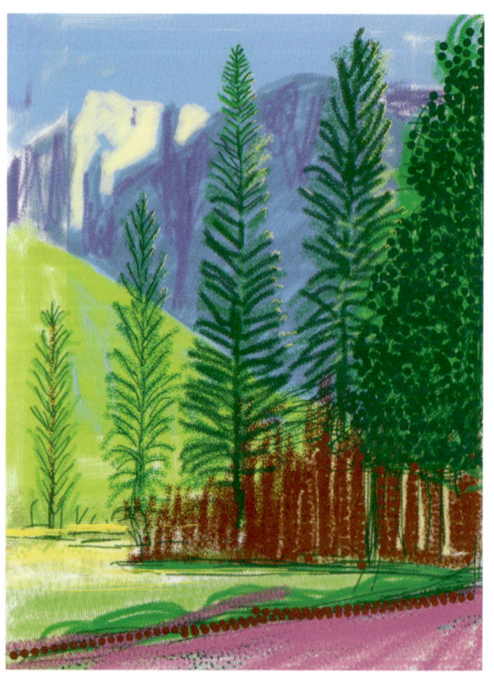

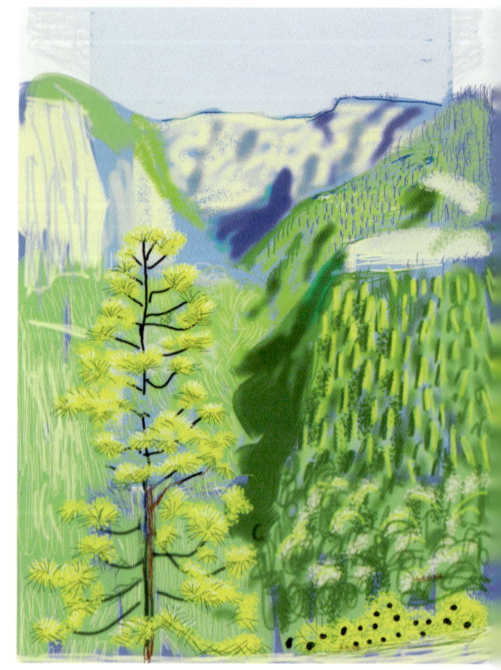

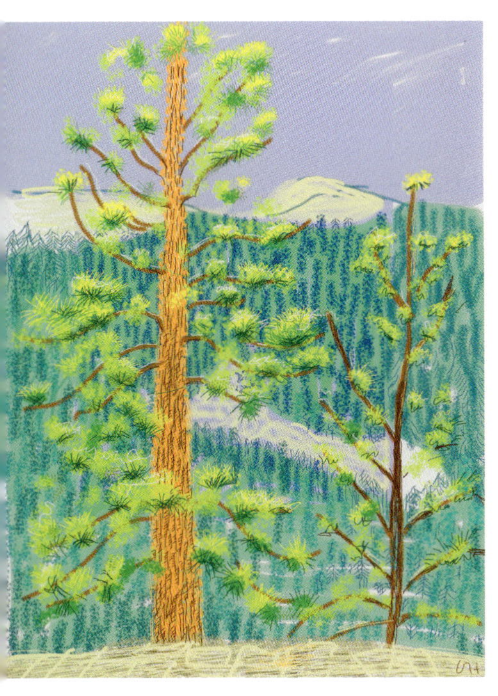
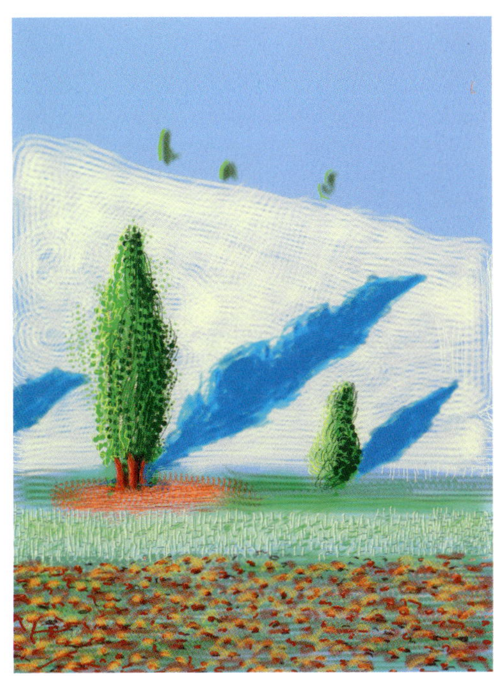
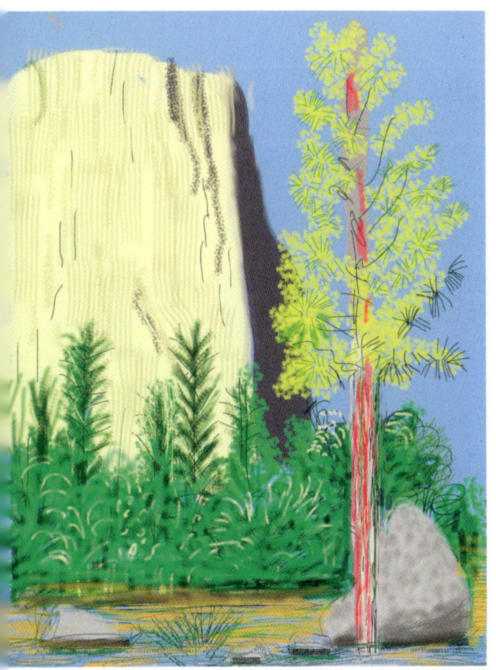
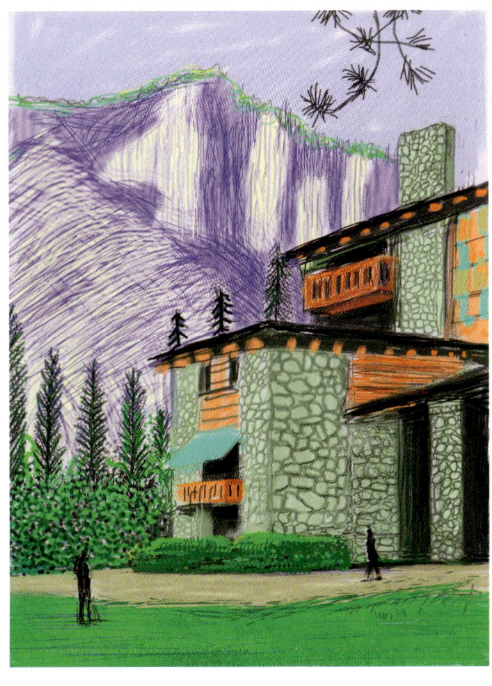

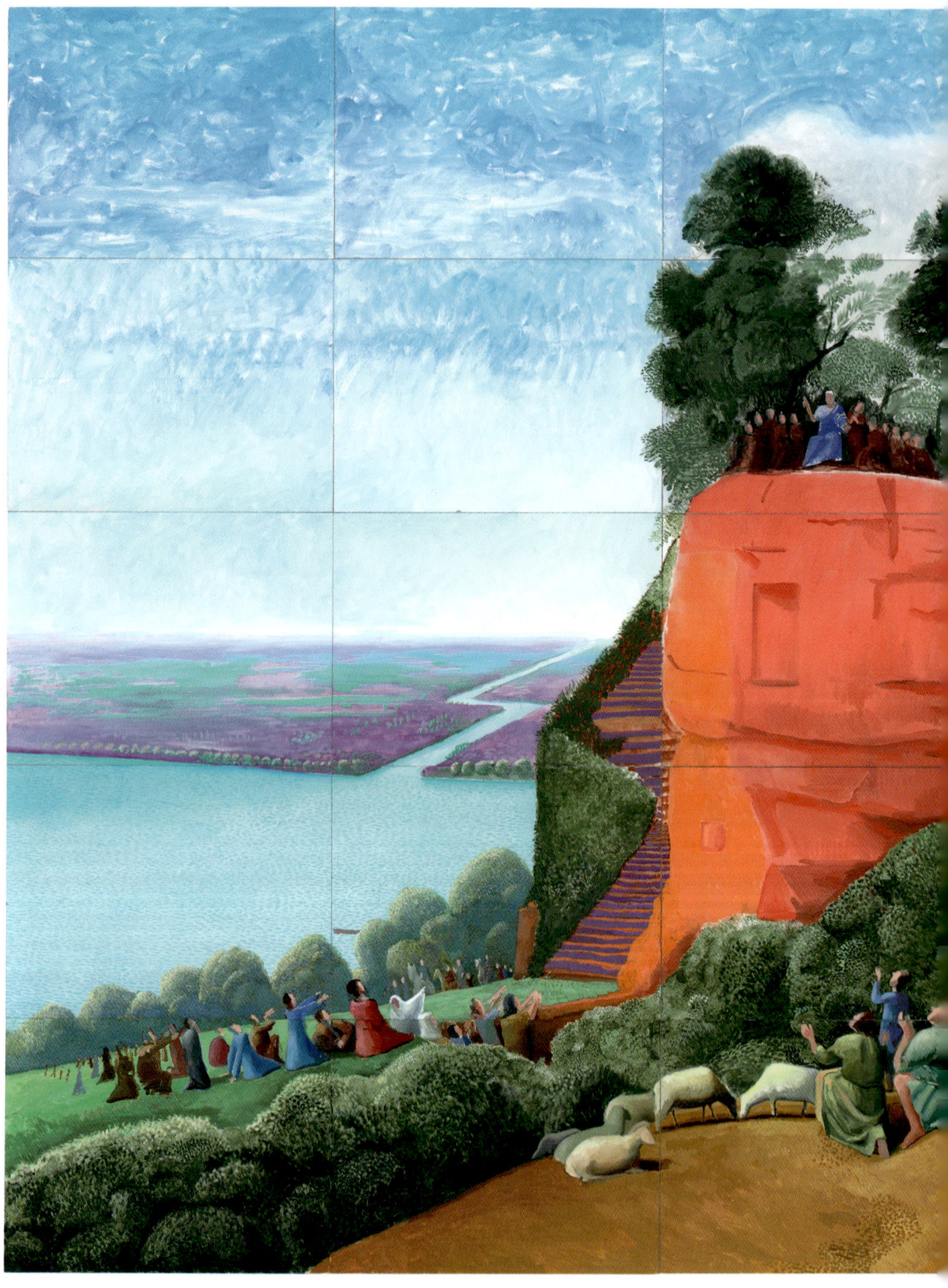

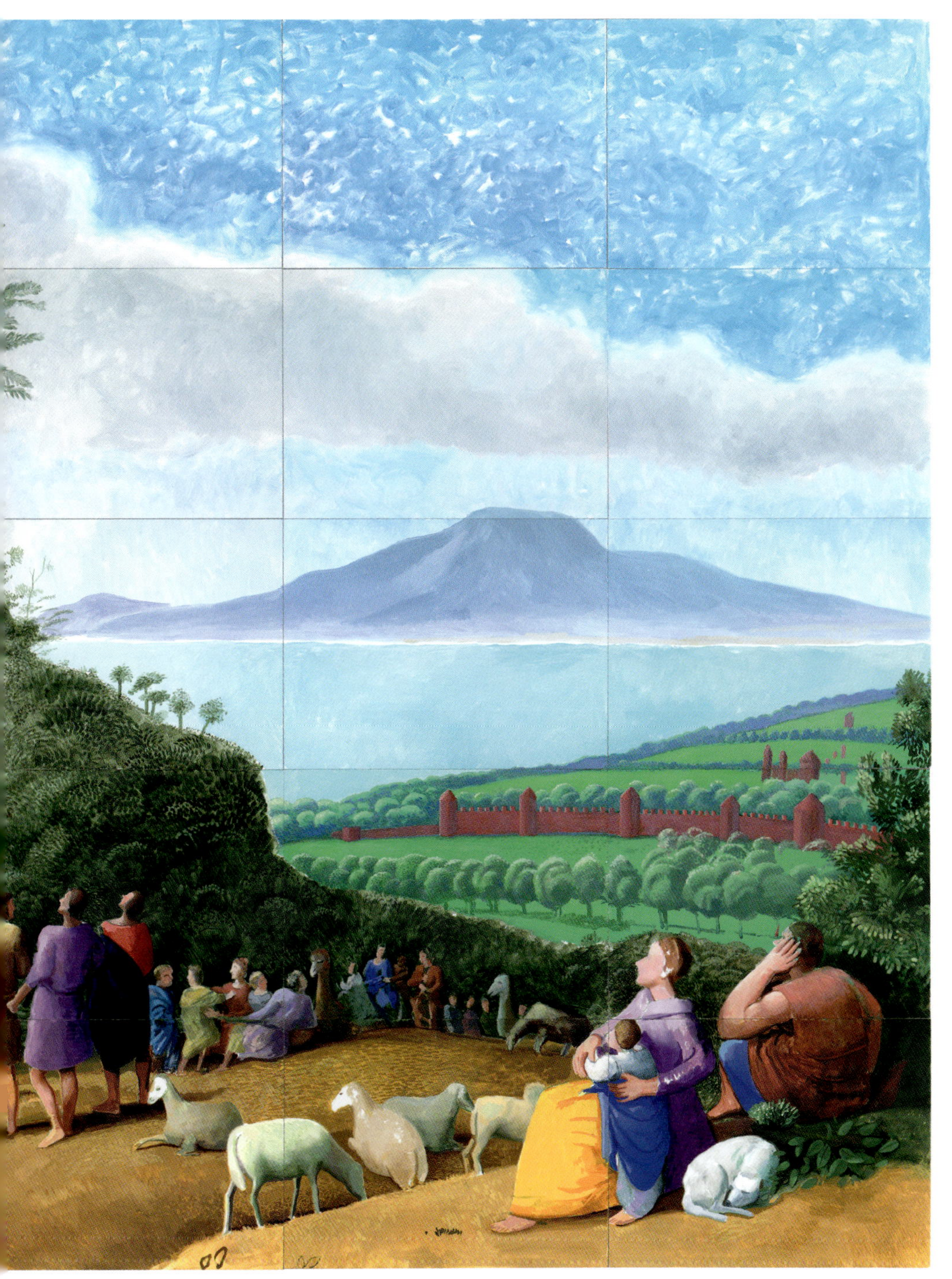

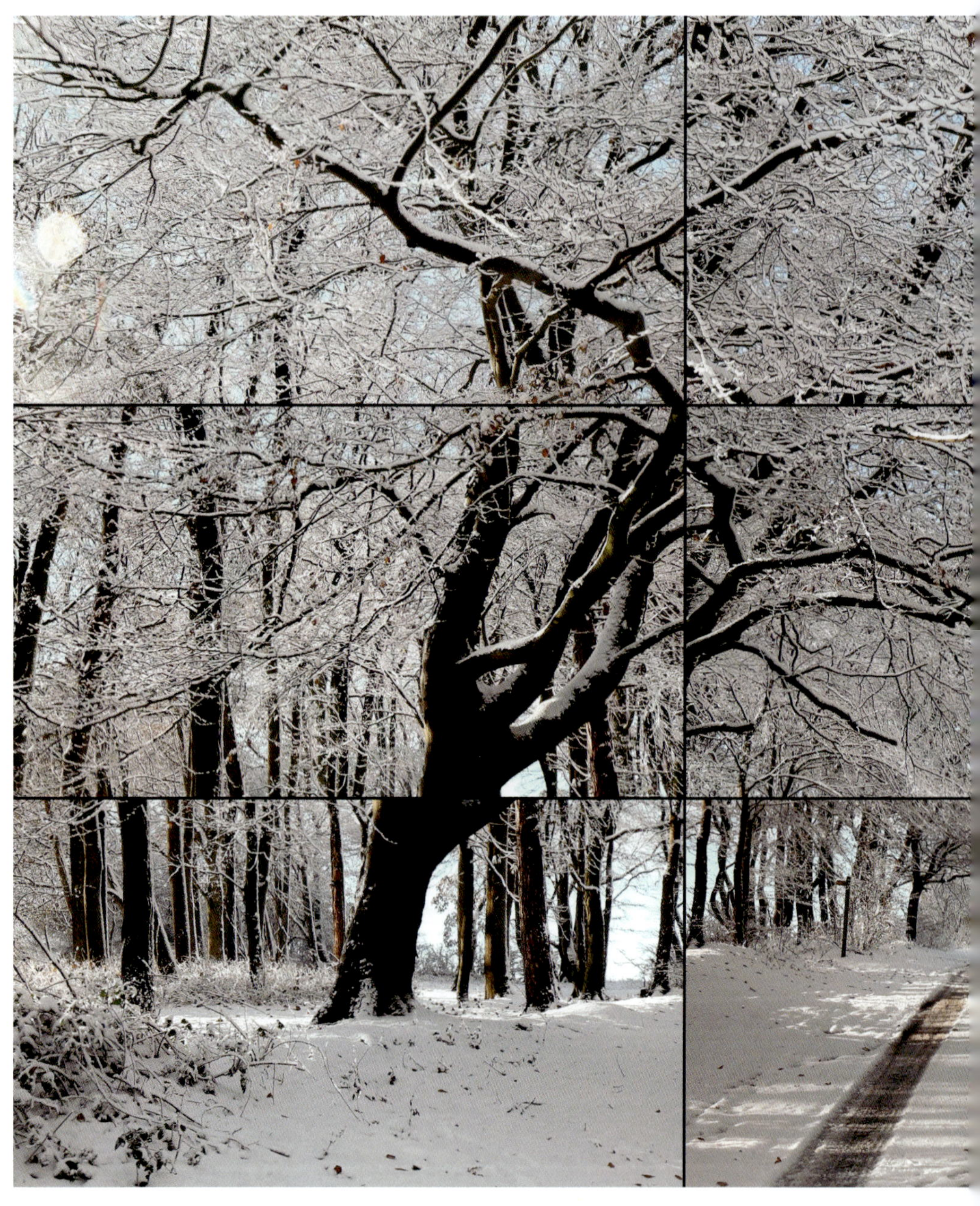

Woldgate Woods, Winter 2010,
9 digital videos synchronized and
presented on 9 55-inch monitors
to comprise a single artwork, edition
of 10 with 2 APs, 81 x 142 ½ in. /
205.7 x 362 cm, 49:00 min.

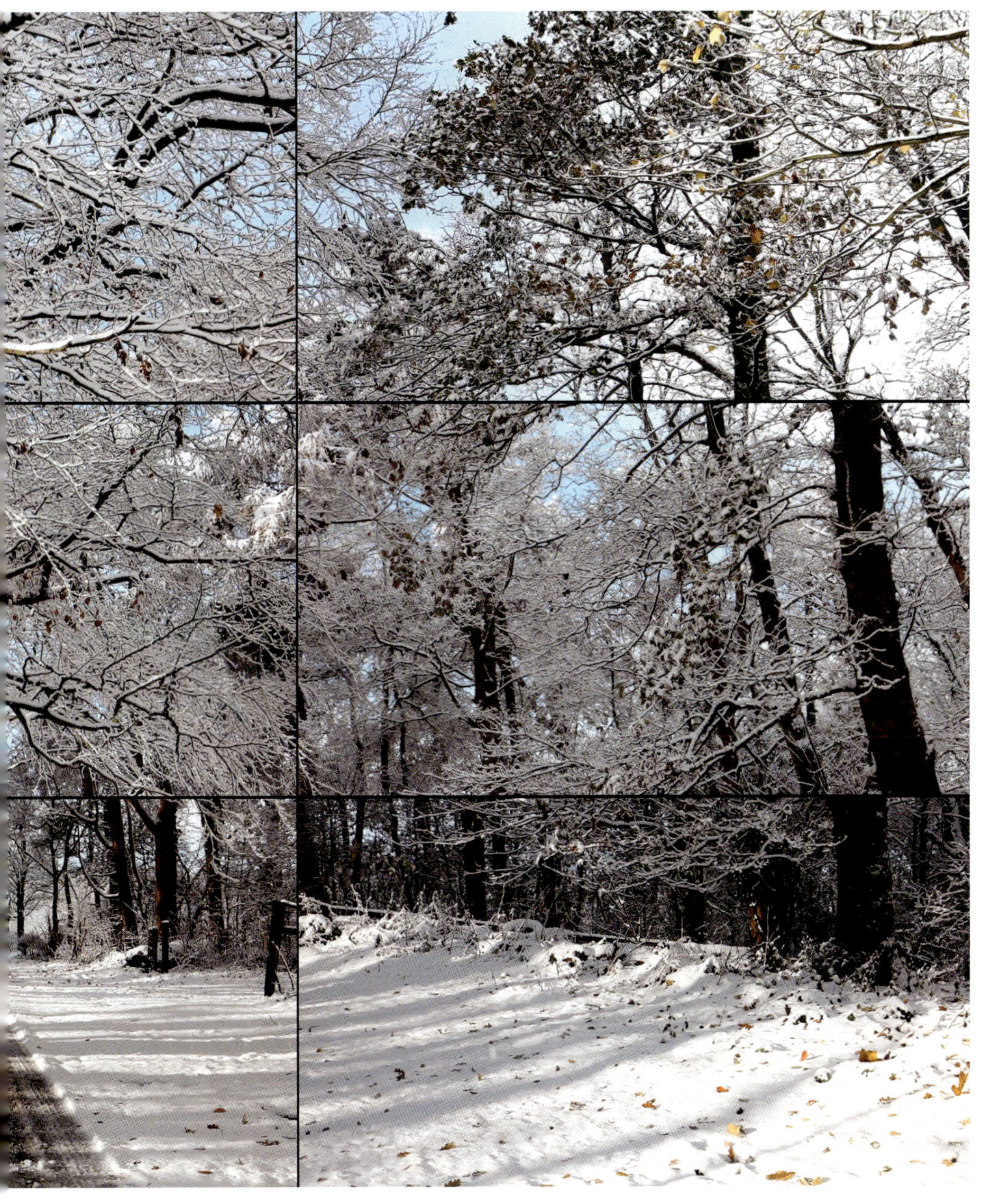

Pages **456/457:** *A Bigger Message,*
2010, oil on 30 canvases,
180 x 288 in. / 457.2 x 731.5 cm

2011 During the first months of the year, Hockney produces a multipart work for his 2012 exhibition at the Royal Academy in London, consisting of 51 iPad drawings and one huge painting on 32 canvases, together titled *The Arrival of Spring in Woldgate* (pp. 463–467). While previously the files of the iPad drawings have proven too lossy for enlargement, and would best be shown on the type of gadget they were created on, now they can be printed out up to 7.5 feet high, and editioned.

Martin Gayford, whose book of conversations with the artist has just been published, visits Hockney once more to follow up on his video work (pp. 468/469). He reports for the *MIT Technology Review*: "We are watching 18 screens showing high-definition images captured by nine cameras. Each camera was set at a different angle, and many were set at different exposures. In some cases, the images were filmed a few seconds apart, so the viewer is looking, simultaneously, at two different points in time. The result is a moving collage, a sight that has never quite been seen before. But what the cameras are pointing at is so ordinary that most of us would drive past it with scarcely a glance. At the moment, the 18 screens are showing a slow progression along a country road. We are looking at grasses, wildflowers, and plants at very close quarters… 'A lot of people have told me,' Hockney remarks, 'that before they see these films they can't imagine what nine cameras could do that one can't. When they see them, they understand. It's showing a lot more; there's simply a lot more to see. It seems you can see almost more on these screens than if you were really there. Everything is in focus, so you're looking at something very complicated but with incredible clarity.'" A quite different work for 18 video screens is shot in the vast studio spaces of the Atelier in Bridlington: a ballet choreographed by Wayne Sleep which is titled *A Bigger Space for Dancing* (pp. 468/469).

The Yorkshire tourist board has long wanted to establish a Hockney trail stopping at the sites of his landscape paintings, and the artist now gives his blessing. Rebecca Rose follows the trail for the *Financial Times*: "Without a tip-off from two of the artist's friends who live locally, I wouldn't have found the spot where he painted *Bigger Trees near Warter*—let alone some of the more obscure rural scenes, partly thanks to the creeping November mist…But there is another reason why these spots aren't instantly recognizable: Hockney is no slave to nature. While *Bigger Trees* is just about identifiable because of the road and the

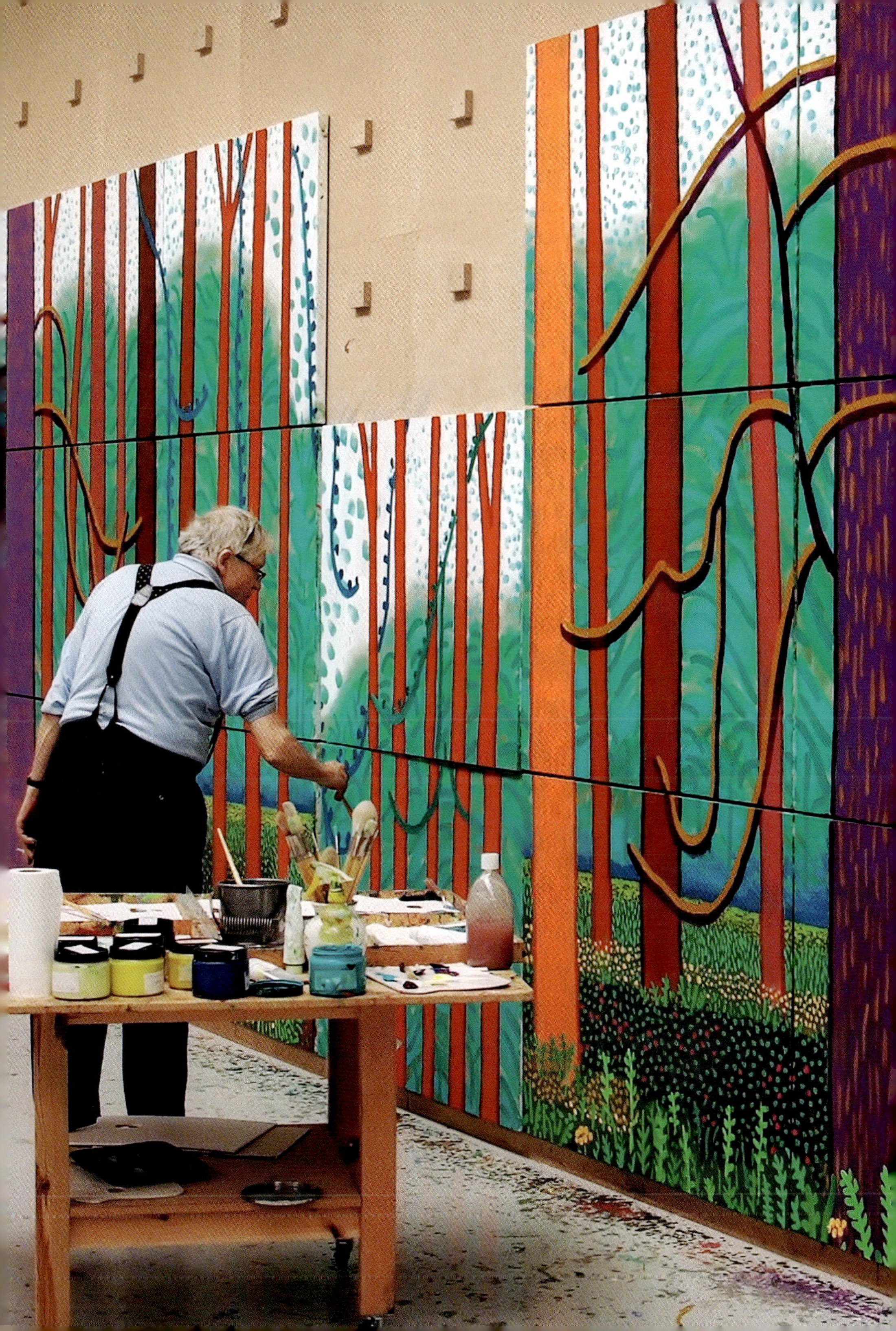

red-brick house, the actual painting makes the wooded area seem much broader and more panoramic. This deliberate distortion is the result of Hockney's concern with capturing the actual way we see, made up of multiple viewpoints and composite images, as opposed to the restrictive single viewpoint of a camera. Next was Woldgate Woods, an area not far from Bridlington that Hockney has painted again and again over the past few years. We drove along the long road that cuts through the middle, past the halfway tree stump that Hockney calls 'The Totem,' and which I recognized from his various paintings, even though in reality it is mossy brown, rather than vivid violet." The *Bigger Trees near Warter* themselves are traveling to several Yorkshire venues throughout the year.

Solo: *Bigger Trees near Warter or/ou Peinture sur le Motif pour le Nouvel Age Post-Photographique,* York Art Gallery, York (Feb 12–Jun 12); travels to Ferens Art Gallery, East Yorkshire (Jun 25–Sep 18); Cartwright Hall Art Gallery, Bradford (Oct 1, 2011–Mar 4, 2012). *Me Draw on iPad,* Louisiana Museum for Moderne Kunst, Humlebæk (Apr 8–Aug 28). *David Hockney's Fresh Flowers: Drawings on iPhones and iPads,* Royal Ontario Museum, Toronto (Oct 8, 2011–Jan 1, 2012).

Group: *A Sense of Place: Landscapes from Monet to Hockney,* Bellagio Gallery of Fine Art, Las Vegas (Apr 16–Jul 31); catalog. *Collection in Focus: Plates, Blocks and Stones: Five Centuries of International Prints,* Art Gallery of Western Australia, Perth (Jul 30–Nov 28). *Pacific Standard Time: Crosscurrents in L.A. Painting and Sculpture, 1950–1970,* J. Paul Getty Museum, Los Angeles (Oct 1, 2011–Feb 5, 2012); travels to Martin-Gropius-Bau, Berlin; catalog. *Proof: The Rise of Printmaking in Southern California,* Norton Simon Museum, Pasadena (Oct 1, 2011–Apr 2, 2012); catalog.

Publications: *David Hockney: My Yorkshire,* interviews by Marco Livingstone, London: Enitharmon Editions. Martin Gayford, *A Bigger Message: Conversations with David Hockney,* London and New York: Thames and Hudson, 2011. Christopher Simon Sykes, *David Hockney: The Biography, 1937–1975. A Rake's Progress,* New York: Doubleday; London: Century.

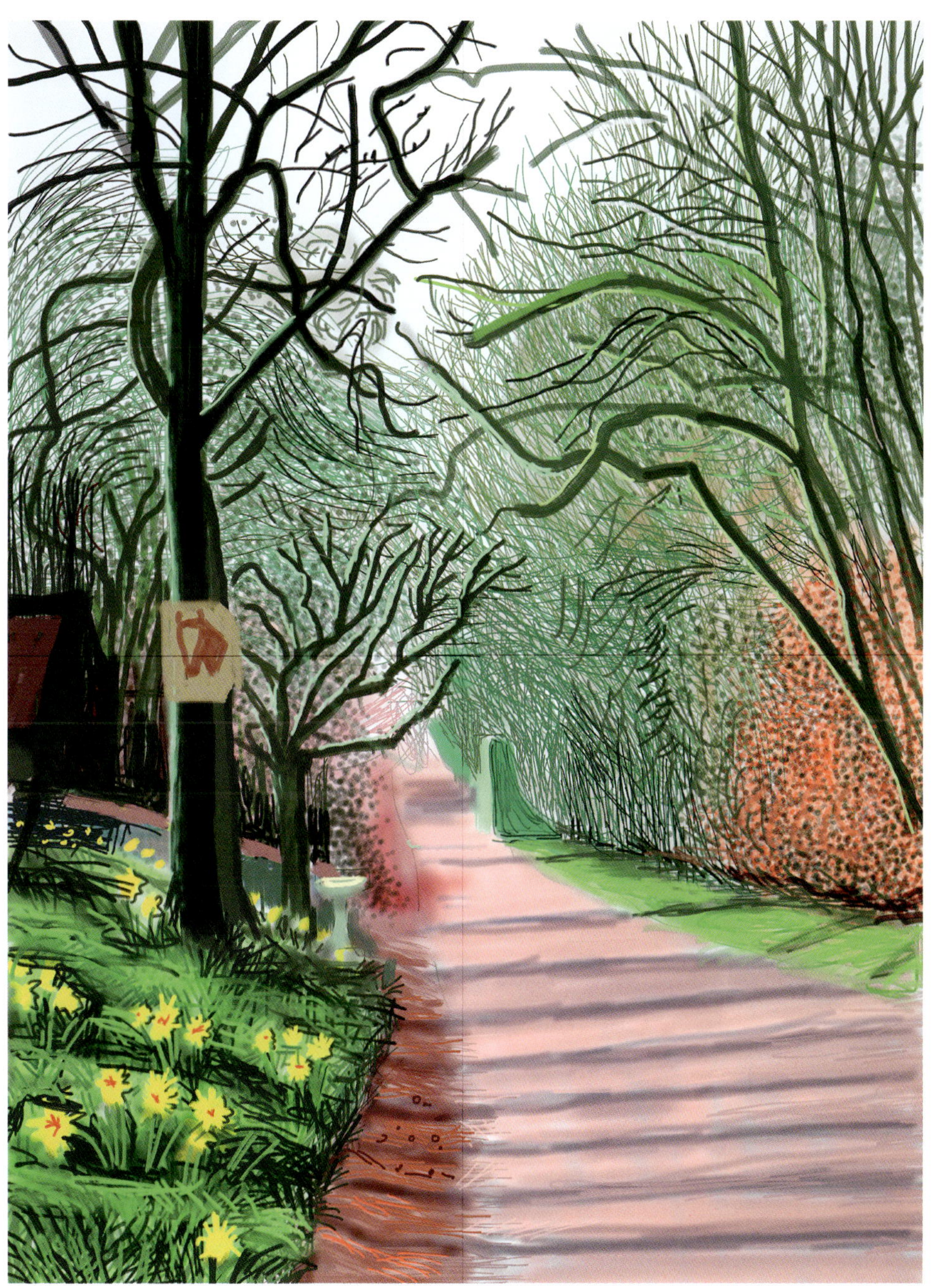

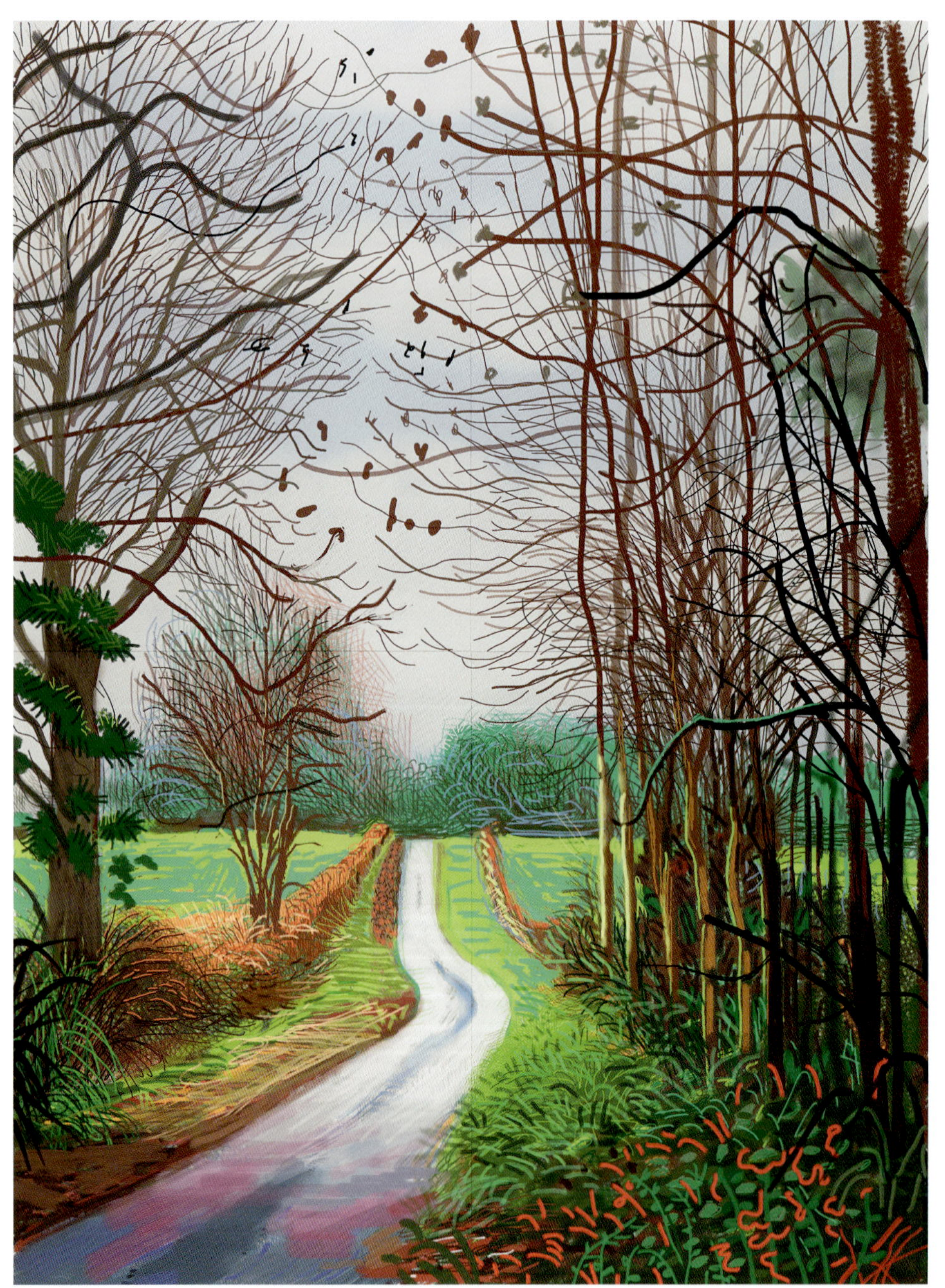

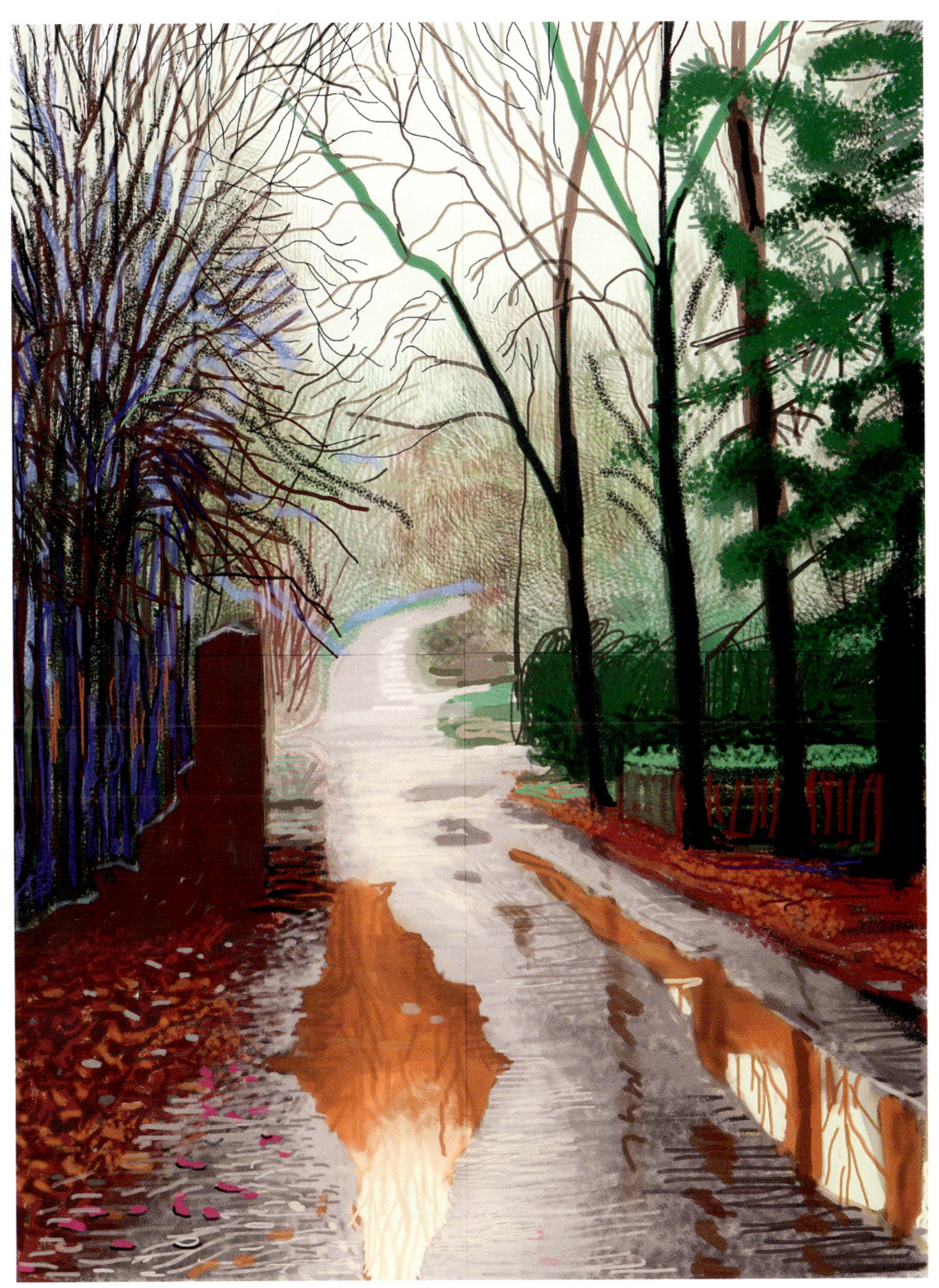

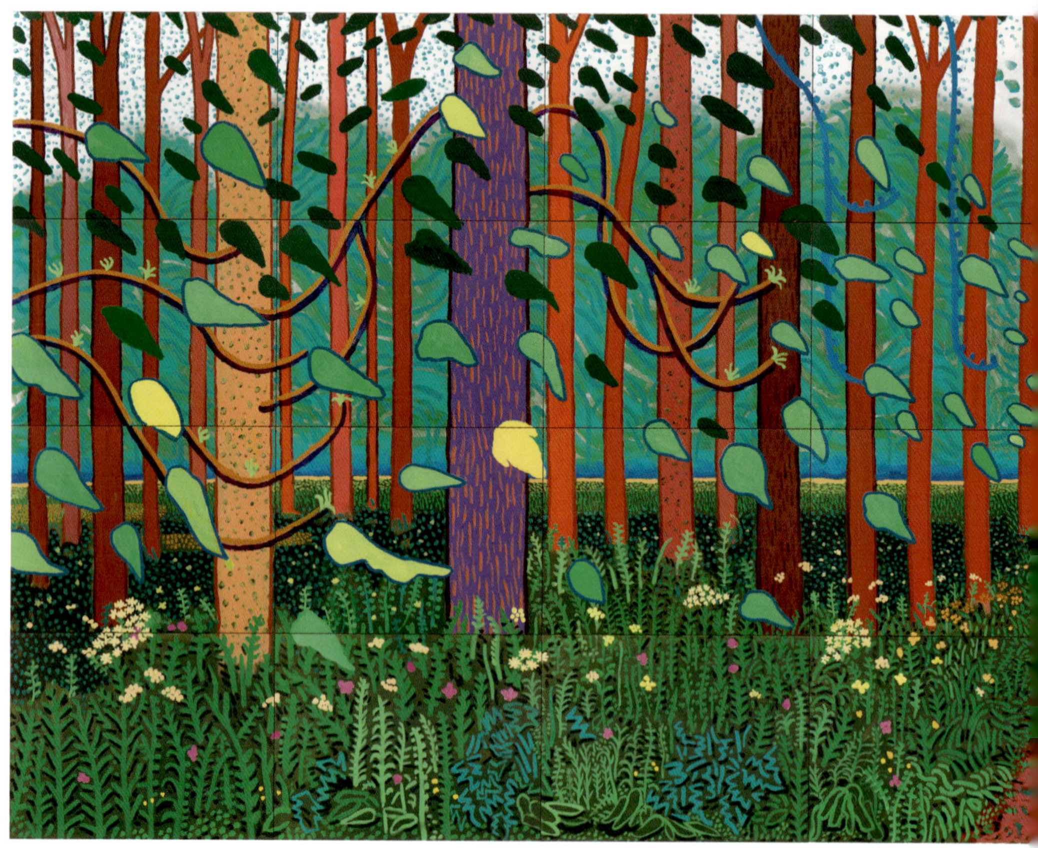

*The Arrival of Spring in Woldgate,
East Yorkshire in 2011 (twenty
eleven),* oil on 32 canvases,
144 x 384 in. / 365.7 x 975.4 cm

Page 461: David Hockney painting
*The Arrival of Spring in Woldgate,
East Yorkshire in 2011 (twenty
eleven).* Photo: Jean-Pierre
Gonçalves de Lima

Page 463: *The Arrival of Spring
in Woldgate, East Yorkshire in 2011
(twenty eleven) – 25 March,* iPad
drawing printed on 4 sheets of paper,
mounted on 4 sheets of Dibond,
edition of 10, 93 x 70 in. /
236.2 x 177.8 cm

Page 464: *The Arrival of Spring
in Woldgate, East Yorkshire in 2011
(twenty eleven) – 29 December,
No. 1,* iPad drawing printed on
4 sheets of paper, mounted on
4 sheets of Dibond, edition of 10,
93 x 70 in. / 236.2 x 177.8 cm

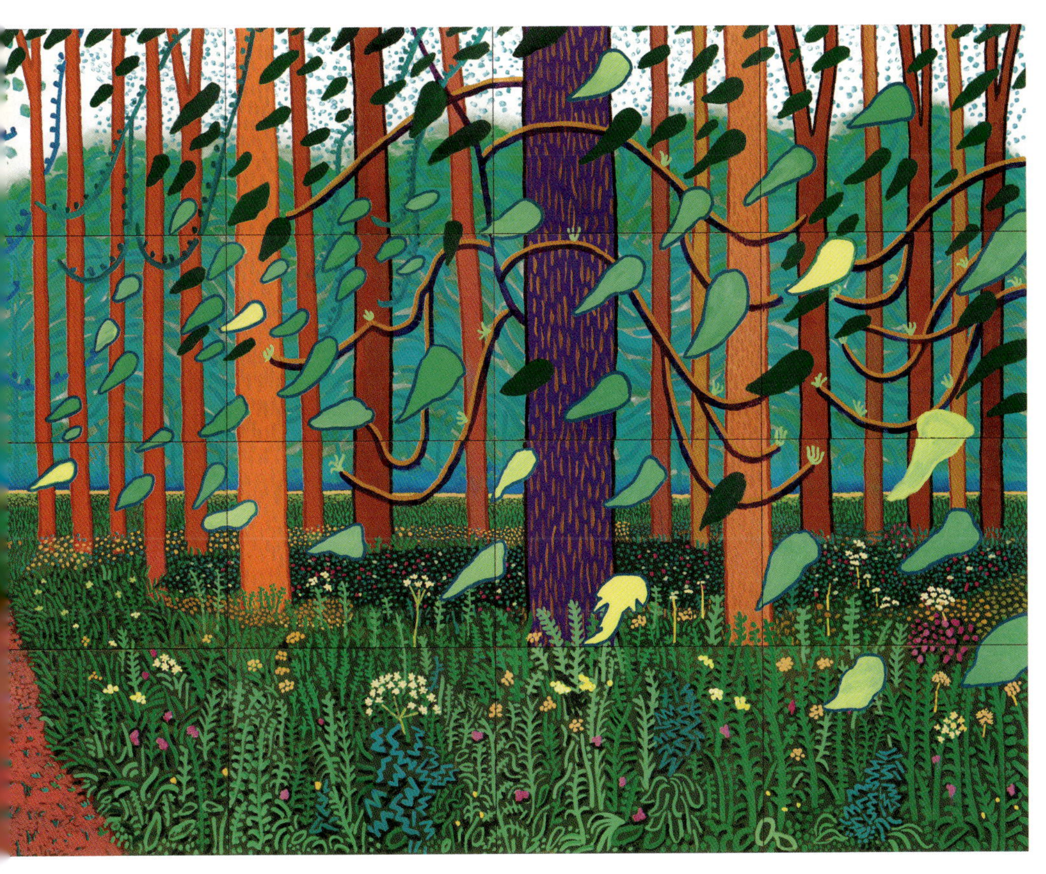

Page 465: *The Arrival of Spring in Woldgate, East Yorkshire in 2011 (twenty eleven) – 29 December, No. 2,* iPad drawing printed on 4 sheets of paper, mounted on 4 sheets of Dibond, edition of 10, 93 x 70 in. / 236.2 x 177.8 cm

Pages 468/469: *Seven Yorkshire Landscapes, 2011,* 18 digital videos synchronized and presented on 18 55-inch monitors to comprise a single artwork, edition of 10 with 2 APs, 81 x 287 in. / 205.7 x 729 cm, 12:39 min.

Sept. 4th 2011, The Atelier, 11:30 am: A Bigger Space for Dancing, 18 digital videos synchronized and presented on 18 55-inch monitors to comprise a single artwork, 81 x 287 in. / 205.7 x 729 cm, 12:39 min.

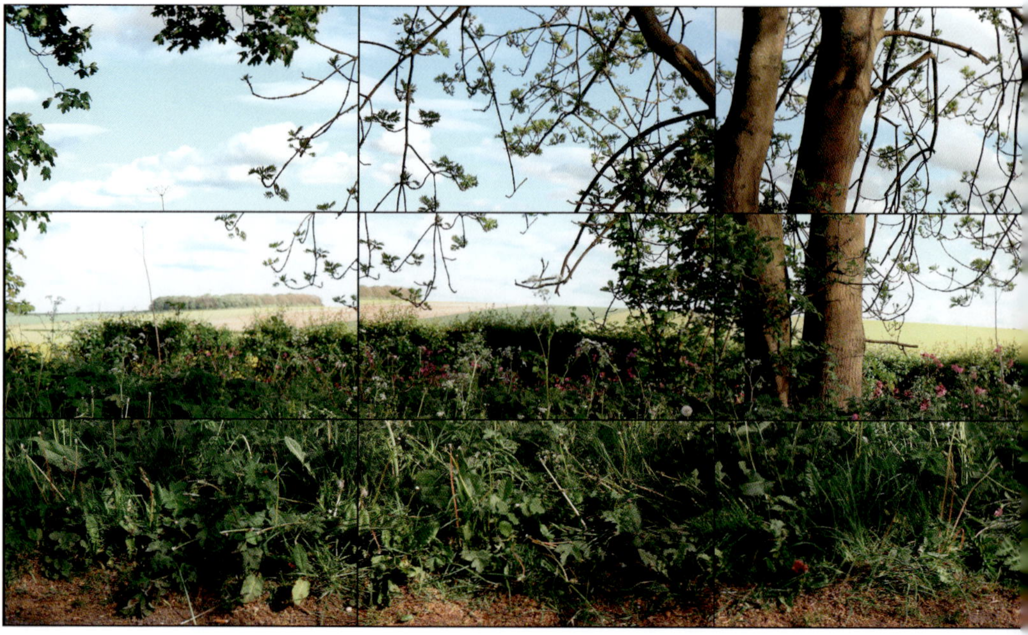

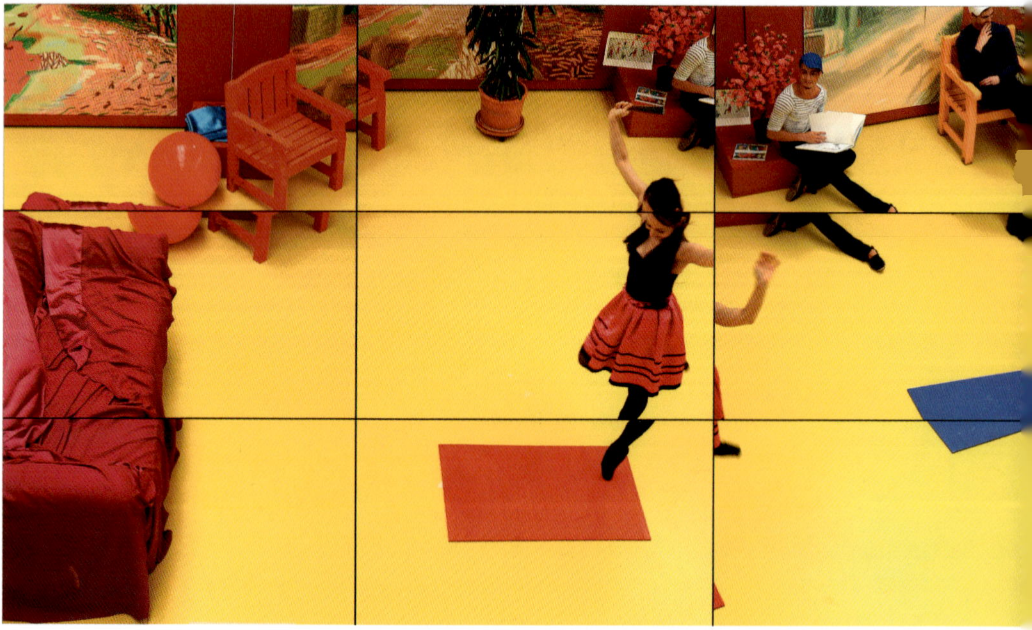

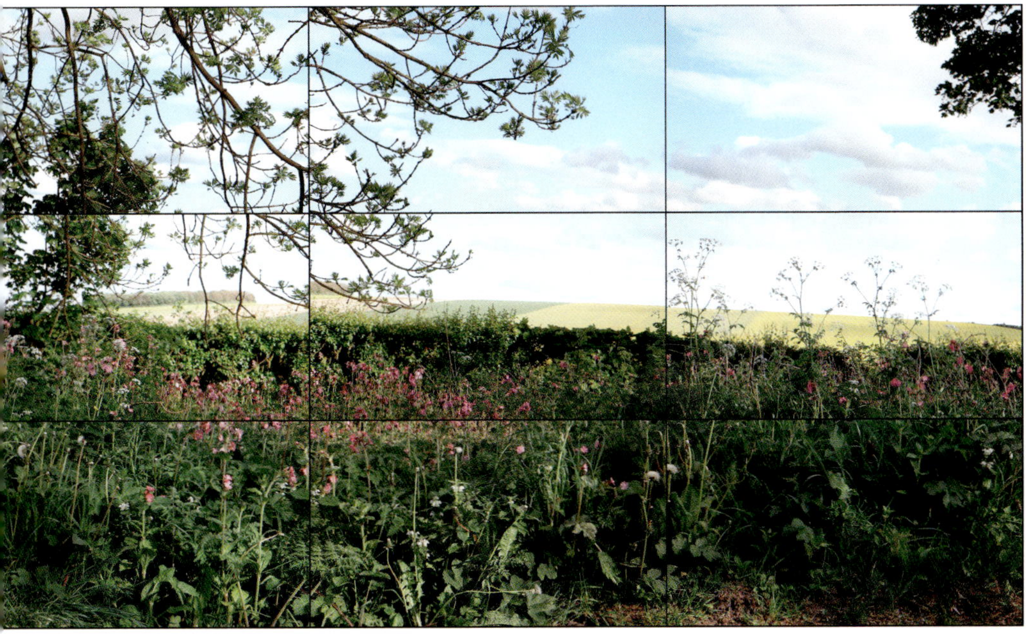

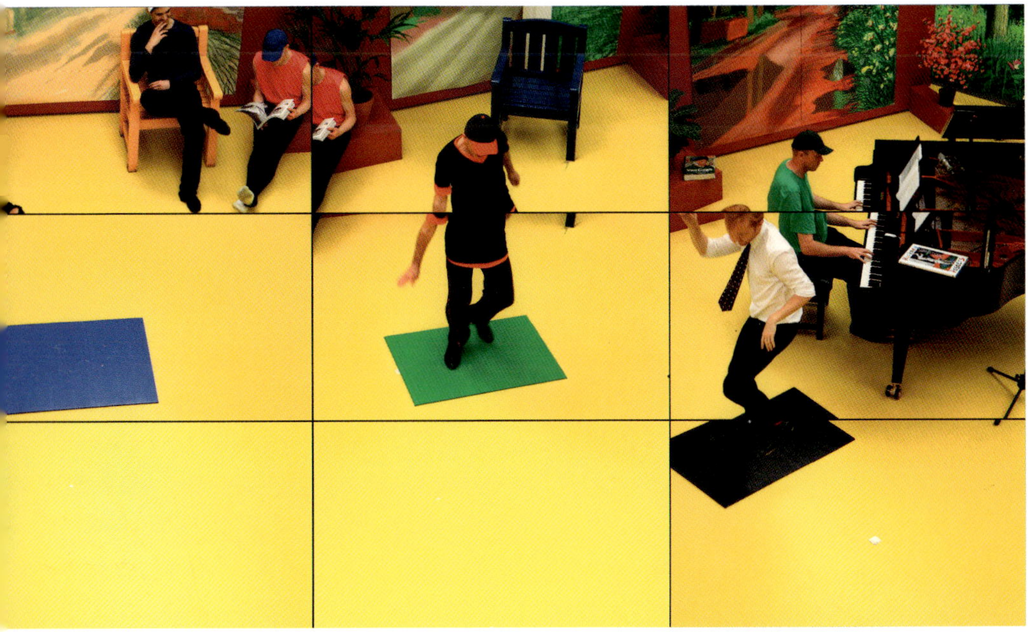

2012

At the Royal Academy in January, Hockney opens the exhibition *A Bigger Picture* (pp. 478–479), which later travels to Bilbao and Cologne. It is the year he will turn 75, among other honors he receives the Order of Merit—and yet he does not plan a retrospective. Instead he presents a themed exhibition of 150 paintings of the Yorkshire landscape, most of them done over the last eight years. The artist does not feel like looking back, as he remarks in the show's catalog: "I'm still too excited about what I will do tomorrow. You don't retire doing this. You just do it till you fall over. It's an interesting life. My mind is occupied. That's what you want at my age, but I always wanted it. In fact I'm greedy for it."

Reviewers are overwhelmed, most by the painter's fertility, some by the number of works on display. Rachel Campbell-Johnston in the *Times*: "Colour is a giddy delight. Purple roads wind through woods of lush green. Ripe corn glows a rich orange. Blossom pours over hedgerows in luscious dollops of yellow cream. The Sunday painter's joy in the landscape about him meets an almost visionary imagination in paintings that, constructed with the skill of a superlative draughtsman, capture an eerie sense of the world's incandescent space. These works are not the retreat of a celebrated painter into mellow nostalgia. They trumpet perceptions that remain as passionate as those of youth. They bear vivid testimony to a still unfinished quest." And Martin Kettle in the *Guardian*: "Hockney's trumpeted and garlanded landscape show at the Royal Academy is more than just the must-see art exhibition of the new year, though it is certainly that too. It is also a bold assertion about the place of skill, craftsmanship, and beauty in the making of art…This is a show about a man, his craft, and the land. It is a statement about the primacy of skilled drawing and painting in the visual arts and about the challenge of doing them with originality in the 21st century."

On the occasion of physicist Stephen Hawking's 70th birthday, the Science Museum in London organizes an exhibition and invites Hockney to create a portrait, and he brings his iPad to a sitting in the museum's office (p. 473). The work is displayed as an iPad movie in which viewers can follow the act of drawing.

Toward the end of the year, health problems slow Hockney down: "I had had a very minor stroke that had kept me in London, and the first drawing afterwards took me two days to do (the days are a lot shorter in November). The stroke only manifested itself in my speech. I found I couldn't finish sentences, and al-

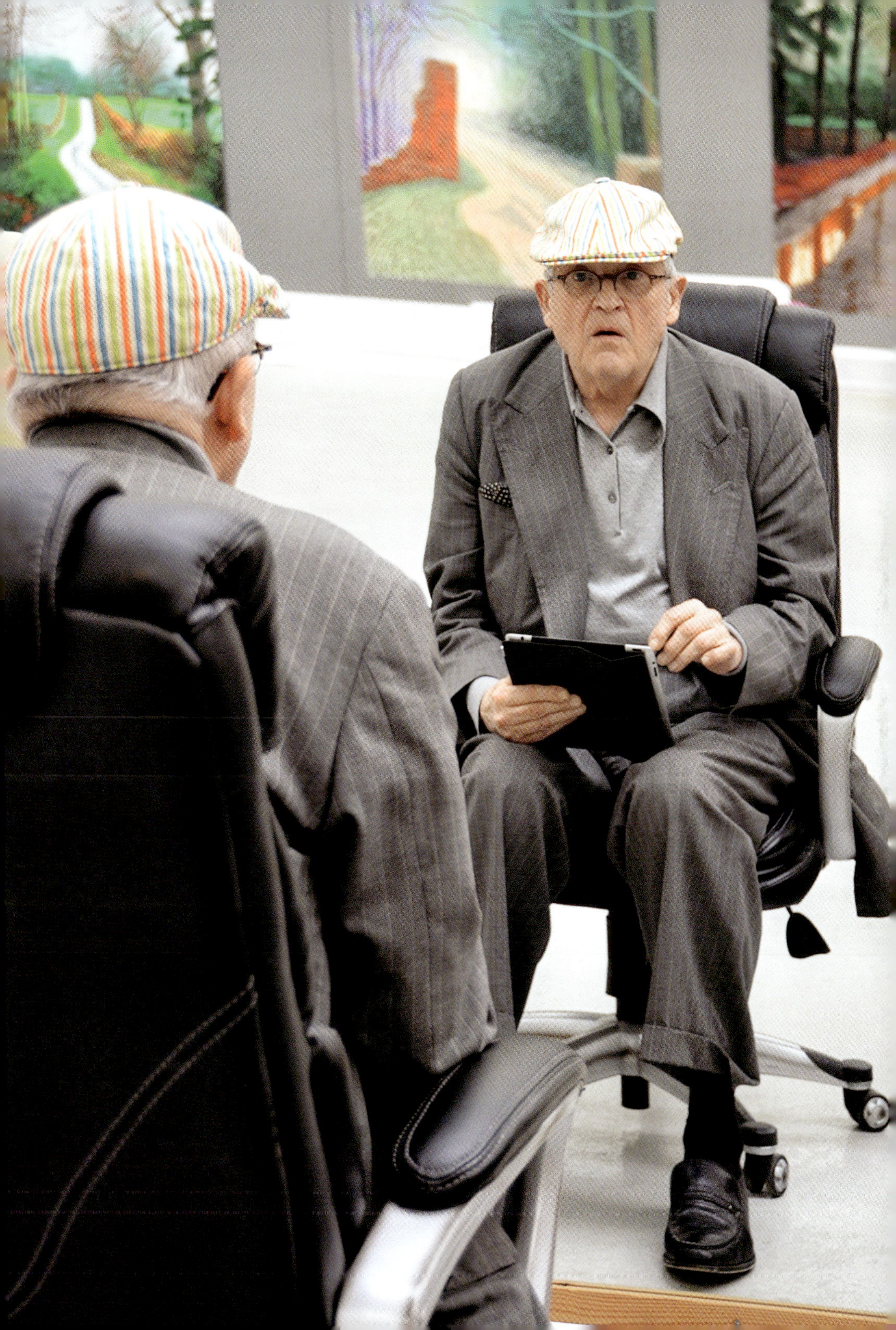

though it came back after about a month I find now I talk a lot less." He makes large drawings in charcoal of a tree trunk he calls the Totem, which often appears in earlier paintings (pp. 476–477): "I drove out on Woldgate and noticed the Totem had been deliberately sawn through. A bit before this I was sent photographs of graffiti that had been painted on it. Annoying, but I thought the winter would take them away. I was at first very sad and went to bed for two days a bit depressed by the vandalism. Then I decided to draw it." He also makes regular charcoal studies of his own face (p. 475). While a series of iPad self-portraits earlier in the year (p. 474) had shown a wide range of expressions bordering on the caricaturesque, now the drawings present a more somber look.

Solo: *A Bigger Picture,* Royal Academy of Arts, London (Jan 21–Apr 9); travels to Guggenheim Bilbao (May 15–Sep 30) and Museum Ludwig, Cologne (Oct 27, 2012–Feb 3, 2013); catalog with texts by Marco Livingstone, Margaret Drabble, Tim Barringer, Xavier F. Salomon, Martin Gayford, and David Hockney, London: Thames and Hudson. *Northern Landscapes,* Nordnorsk Kunstmuseum, Tromosø (Jun 16–Sep 30).

Group: *Self-Portrait,* Louisiana Museum for Moderne Kunst, Humlebæk (Sep 14, 2012–Jan 13, 2013); catalog. *Regarding Warhol: Sixty Artists, Fifty Years,* The Metropolitan Museum of Art, New York (Sep 18–Dec 31); travels to The Andy Warhol Museum, Pittsburgh; catalog. *Encounter: The Royal Academy in Asia,* Institute of Contemporary Arts, Singapore (Sep 19–Oct 24). *Treasure Island: British Art from Holbein to Hockney,* Fundación Juan March, Madrid (Oct 5, 2012–Jan 20, 2013); catalog.

Publication: *David Hockney: A Yorkshire Sketchbook,* London: Royal Academy of Arts.

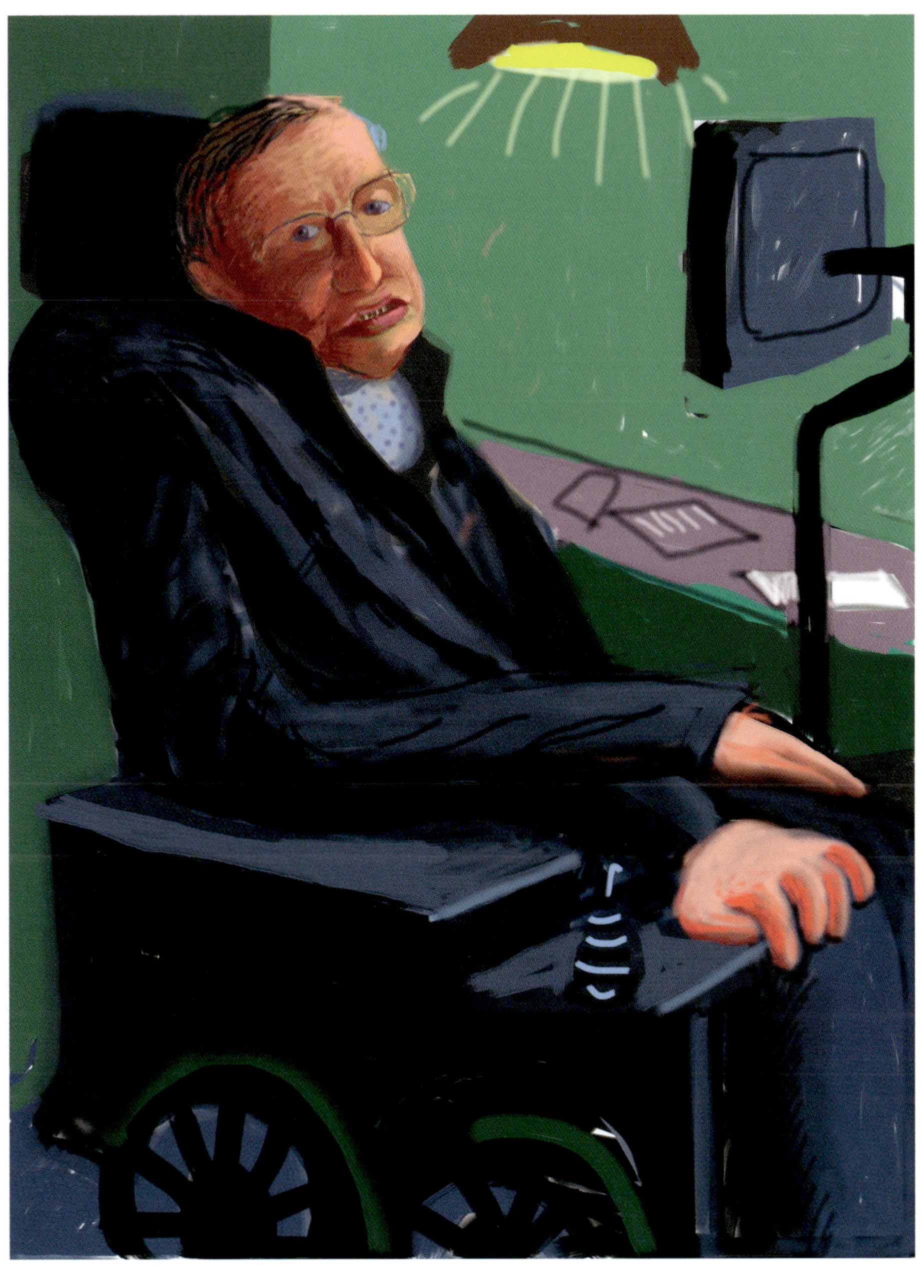

Stephen Hawking, 2012, iPad drawing printed on paper, 22 x 17 in. / 55.9 x 43.2 cm

Page 471: David Hockney drawing a self-portrait on his iPad, April 2012. Photo: Jean-Pierre Gonçalves de Lima

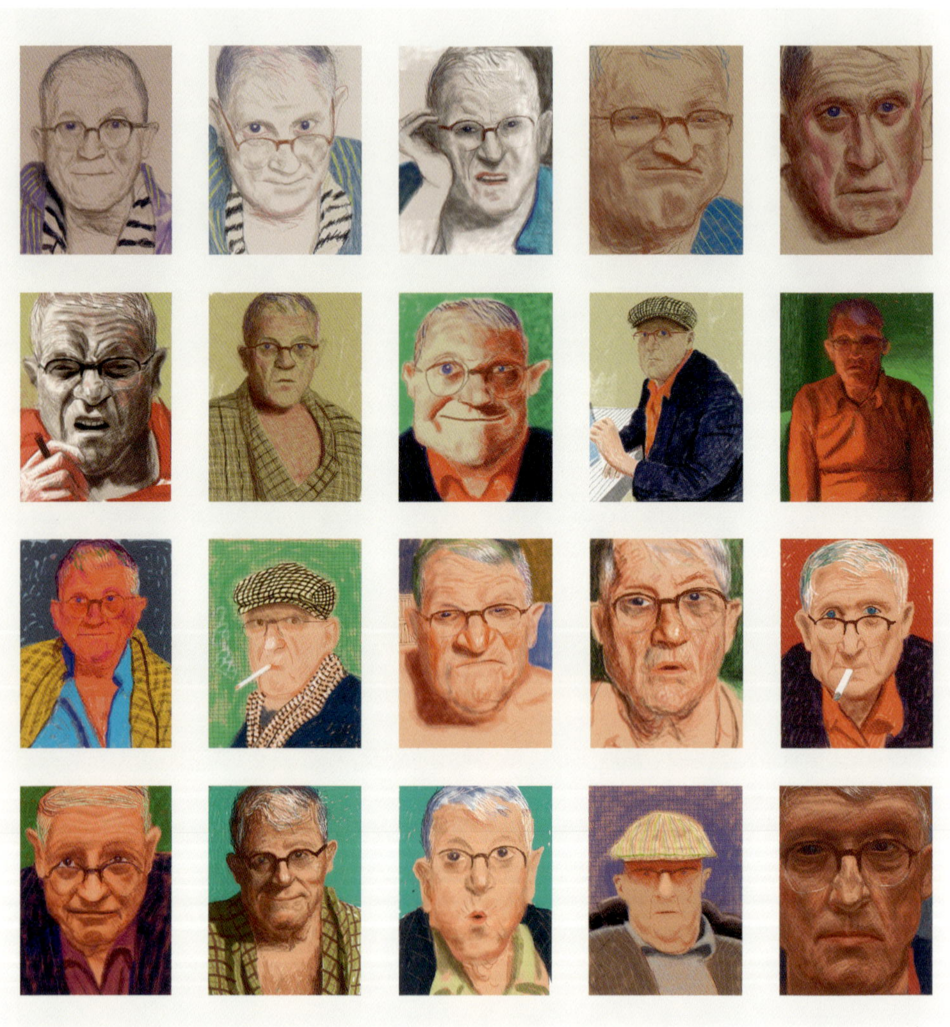

Twenty Self Portraits, 2012, iPad
drawings printed on 2 sheets of paper,
75 x 76 ¹/₂ in. / 190.5 x 194.3 cm

Right page: *Self Portrait,
17 December 2012,* charcoal on paper,
30 ¹/₄ x 22 ⁵/₈ in. / 76.8 x 57.5 cm

Pages 476–477: *Vandalized Totem,
16–17 November 2012; Vandalized
Totem, 19–20 November 2012;
Vandalized Totem, 25 November 2012;
Vandalized Totem, 22 November 2012;*
charcoal on paper, each
22 ⁵/₈ x 30 ¹/₄ in. / 57.4 x 77 cm

Pages 478–479: *David Hockney:
A Bigger Picture,* exhibition views,
Royal Academy of Arts, London 2012

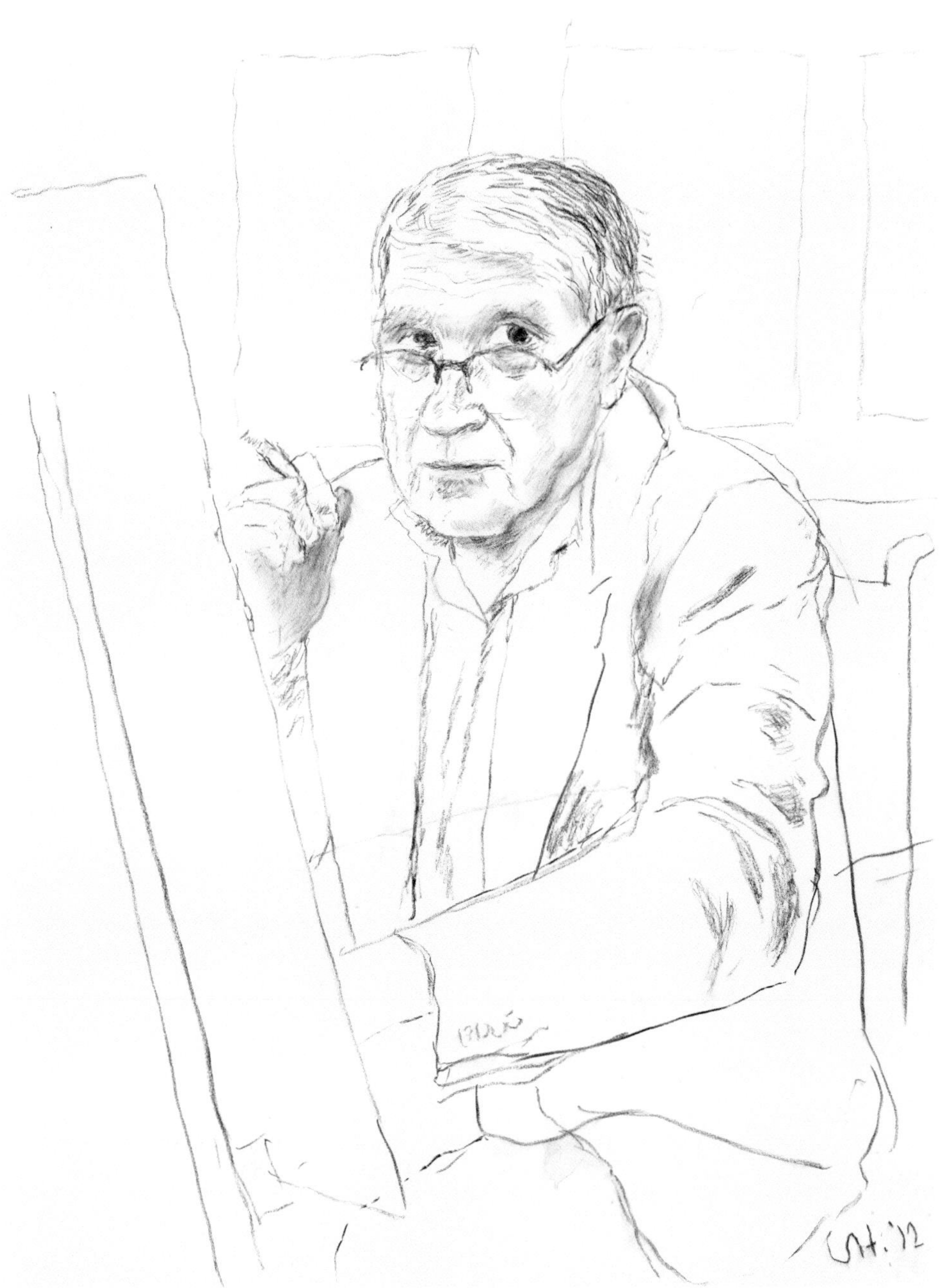

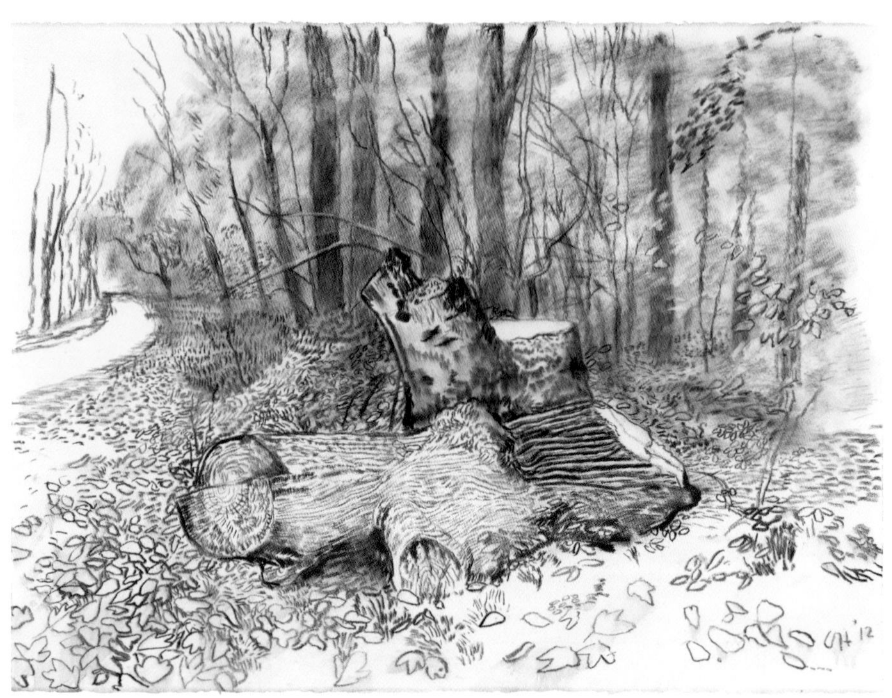

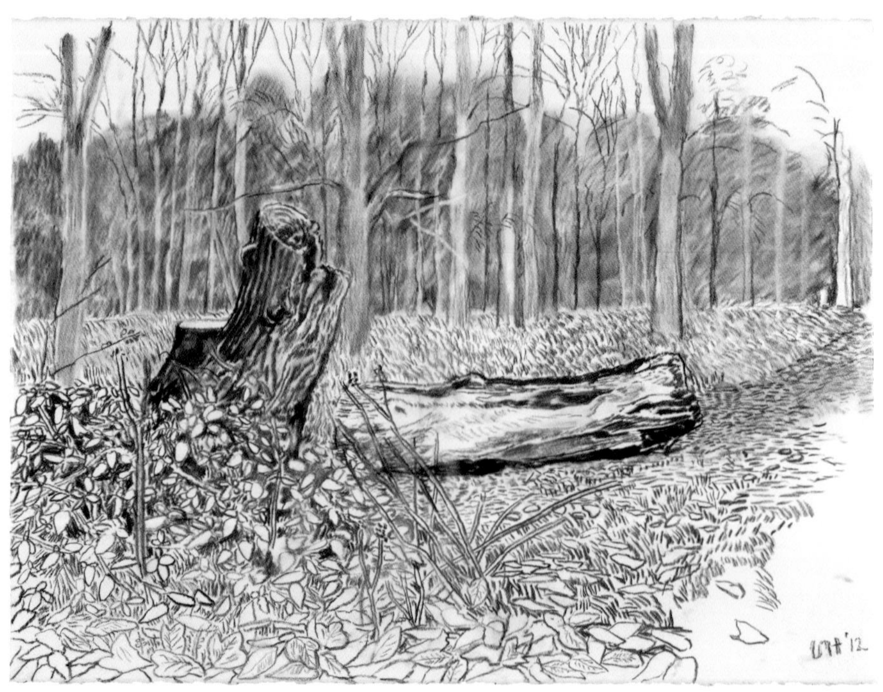

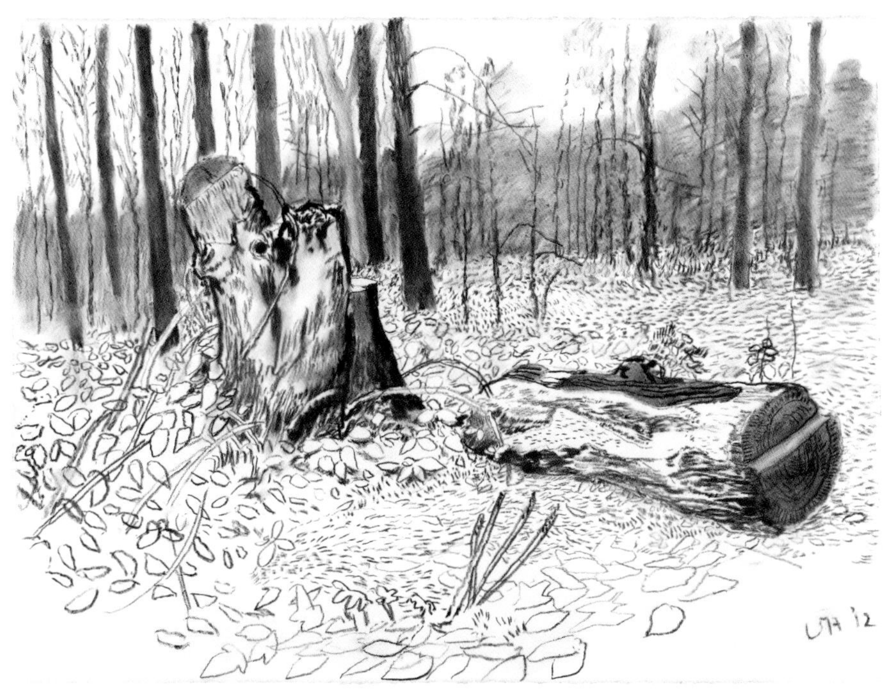

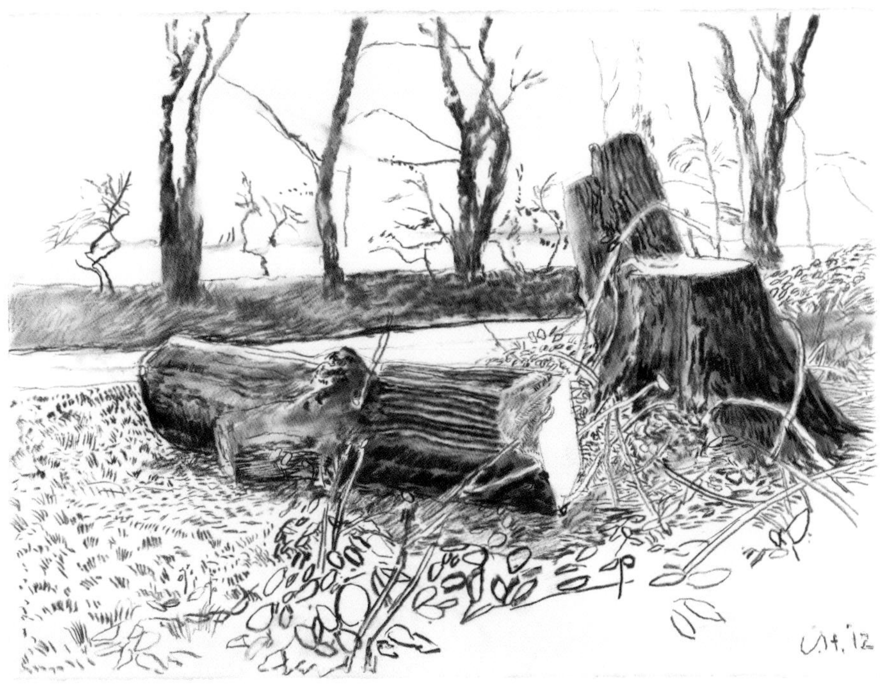

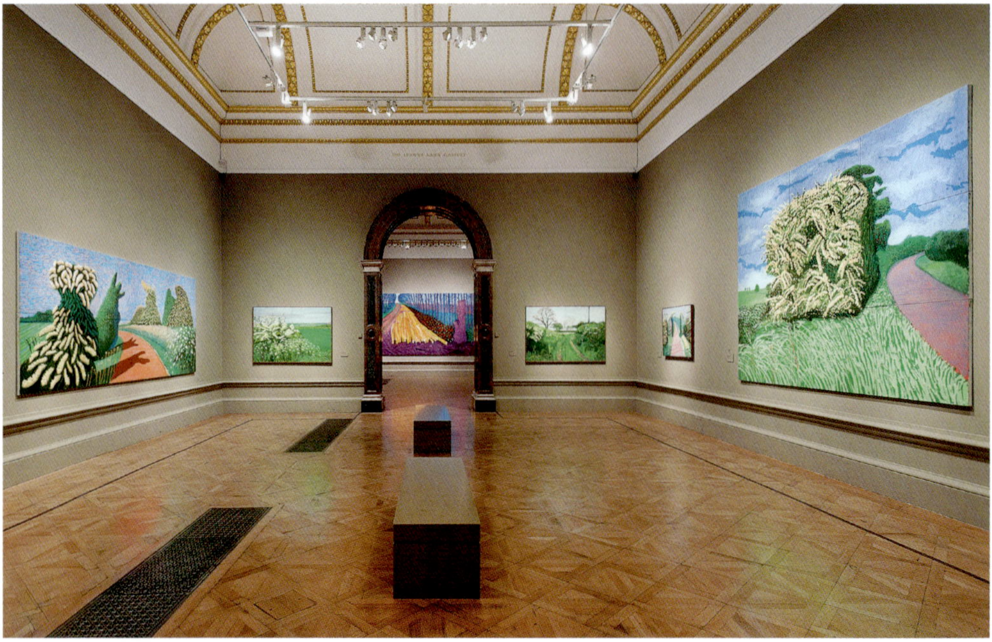

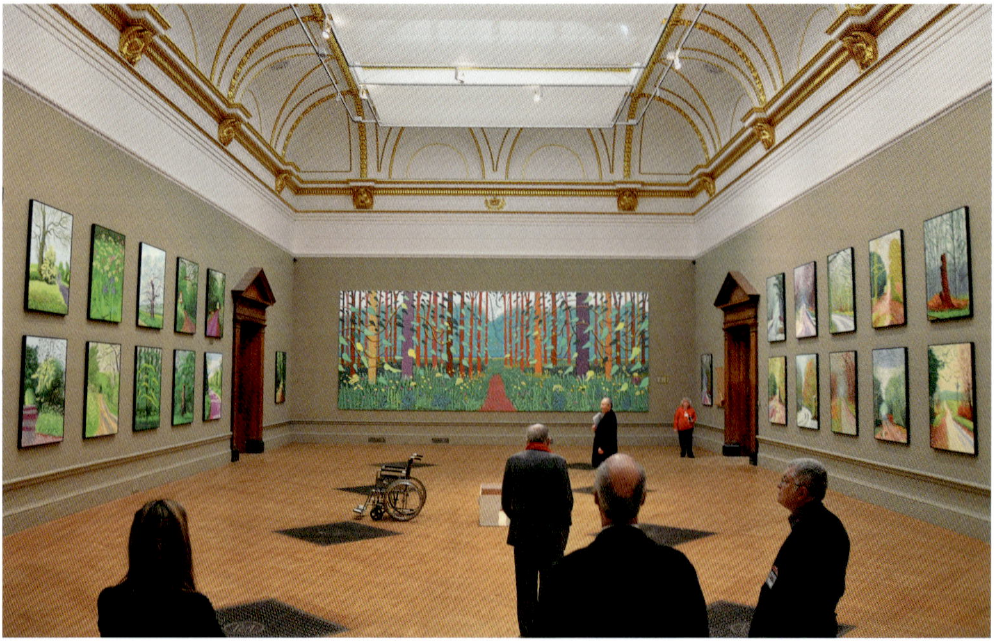

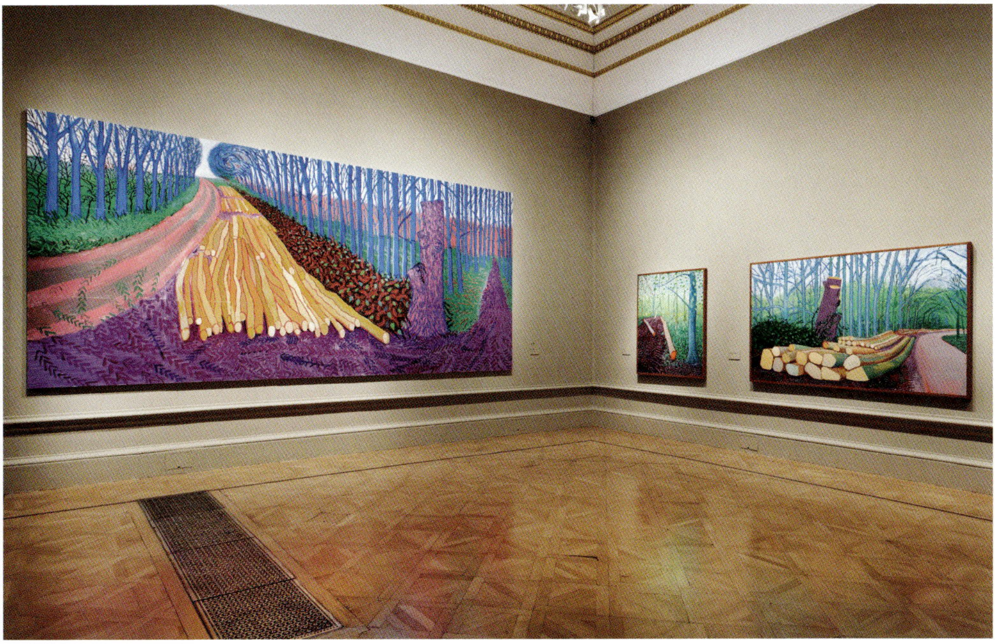

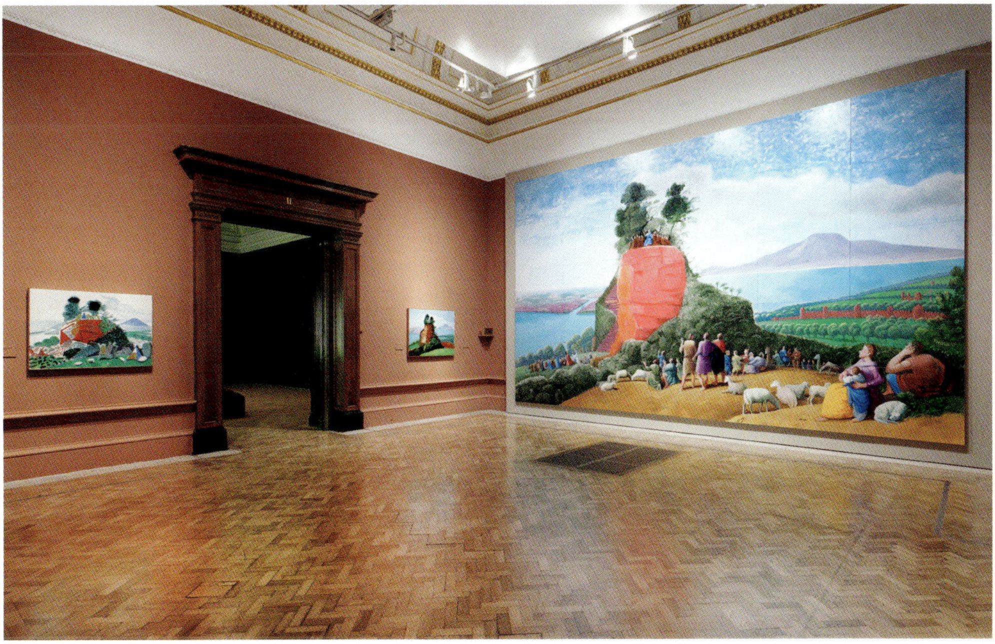

2013 As he has done in previous years, Hockney observes and draws *The Arrival of Spring* (pp. 486/487), this time in charcoal, which makes it more difficult to record the fresh colors the season brings. "The Chinese say black and white contains color, and so it can," Hockney says. "There are five separate views of Woldgate, and with each one I had to wait for the changes to happen. Some were too close to the previous ones and I realized I was being impatient. I had to wait for a bigger change." But in March the undertaking is interrupted by the death of a young assistant. "The intention was to go back whenever the spring occurred. But then Dominic died. It was an awful time and I was very upset. I thought I might not do it at all this year. I thought I might go back to LA for a bit. I didn't quite know what to do." He still finishes the series in Yorkshire, but moves to Los Angeles in July.

In the Hollywood Hills, Hockney begins painting portraits of his friends sitting on a chair in front of a blue background. The first is Jean-Pierre Gonçalves de Lima, holding his head in his hands in a pose inspired by van Gogh's *At Eternity's Gate* (p. 483). "We were all feeling a bit like that," Hockney tells Caroline Daniel of the *Financial Times,* who visits the studio. She reports: "The real surprise is the new portraits, done in just the past few weeks, in strong LA colors—swimming-pool aquamarines and turquoise blues…The change from Yorkshire has clearly been energizing. 'I feel I couldn't have done them in England,' Hockney says, fondly scrutinizing the portraits, which are in the acrylic paint he first used when he came to LA more than 40 years ago. 'And these grew. I didn't plan them, really. I mean I did once I'd got three done, three or four, but they just grew and that's what happens to me sometimes.'"

In October, a huge solo exhibition opens at the de Young Museum in San Francisco. Roberta Smith in the *New York Times*: "At 76, David Hockney is in one of his primes, and apparently he knows it. Not for nothing is his exuberant, immersive survey at the de Young Museum here cheekily titled *David Hockney: A Bigger Exhibition* (pp. 484–485). This sprawling romp through more than 300 works in several mediums and technologies fills 10 often large galleries and yet primarily covers work from the last decade of Mr. Hockney's 60-year career. It is dominated by radiant landscapes—some the size of murals—of the fields and woods in different seasons of East Yorkshire in Britain, near where Mr. Hockney was born and grew up…Synthesizing aspects of Munch, Klimt,

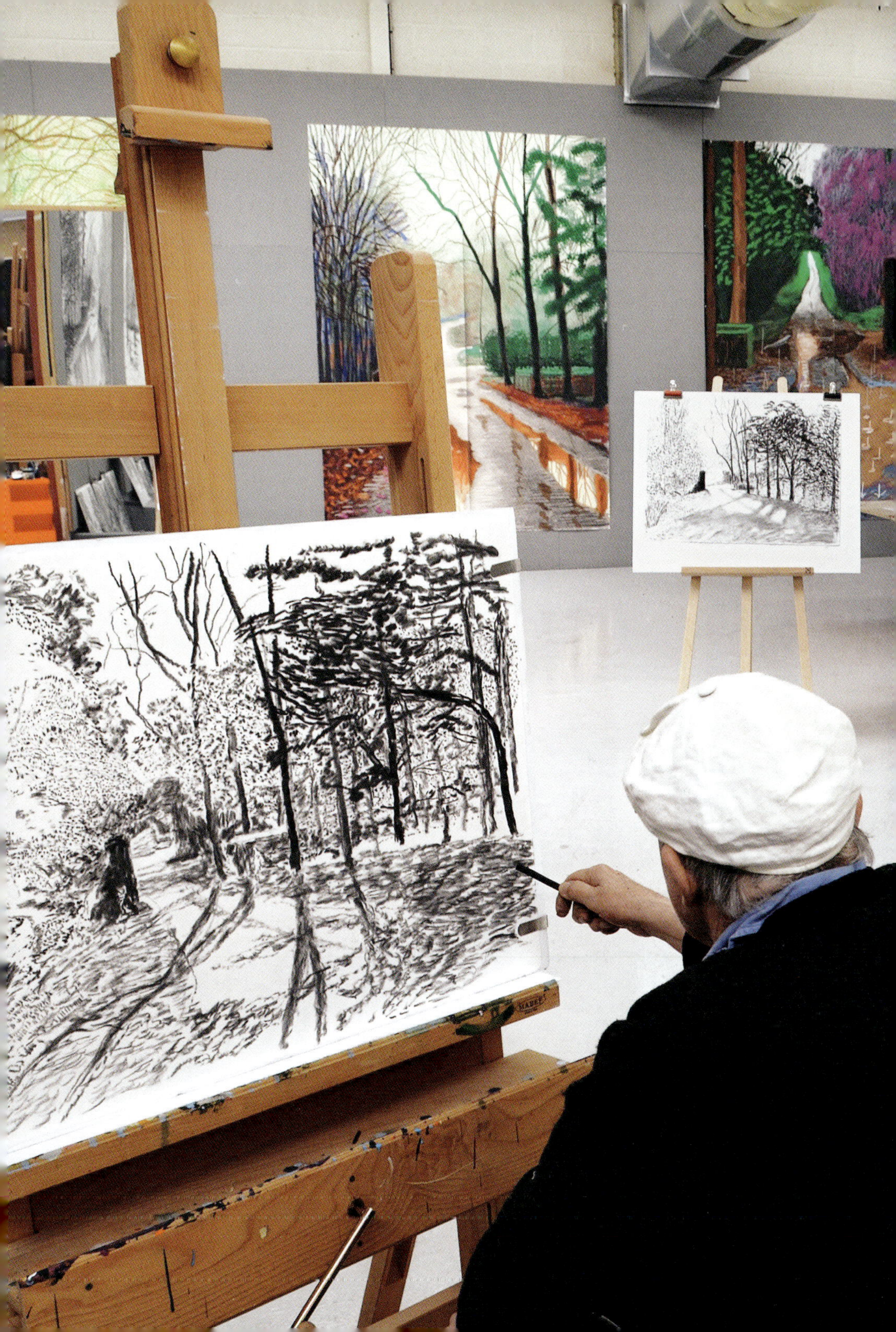

Derain, Cézanne, van Gogh, and late Bonnard, these works are alluringly modern for their startling colors—roads of light magenta, tree trunks of purple or orange, along with quantities of different greens and yellows—their notably nonprecious, dashed-off tactility of surface, their welcoming spaciousness and bold internal scale, and their often Abstract Expressionist size. With an emphasis on bucolic farmland that seems very British, they nonetheless convey the grandeur of nature, still the mother of us all, and of all art. And they also confirm Mr. Hockney's theory that representational painting can tell you more about reality and perception than either photography or the human eye, which is one reason it can still thrill."

Solo: *The Jugglers,* Whitney Museum of American Art, New York (May 23–Sep 1). *Early Reflections,* Walker Art Gallery, Liverpool (Oct 11, 2013–Mar 16, 2014). *A Bigger Exhibition,* de Young Museum, San Francisco (Oct 26, 2013–Jan 20, 2014); catalog with texts by Richard Benefield, Lawrence Weschler, Sarah Howgate, and David Hockney. *Seven Yorkshire Landscape Videos, 2011,* LA County Museum of Art, Los Angeles (Nov 3, 2013–Jan 26, 2014). *Drawing in a Printing Machine,* Galerie Lelong, Paris (Jan 17–Mar 2). *The Thrill Is Spatial,* Richard Gray Gallery, Chicago (Nov 21, 2013–Jan 11, 2014).

Group: *The Polaroid Years: Instant Photography and Experimentation,* Frances Lehman Loeb Art Center, Poughkeepsie (Apr 12–Jun 30); travels to Leigh Block Museum of Art, Evanston; catalog. *Moving: Norman Foster on Art,* Carré d'Art – Musée d'art contemporain, Nîmes (May 3–Sep 15); catalog. *Davant l'horitzó,* Fundació Joan Miró, Barcelona (Oct 24, 2013–Feb 16, 2014); catalog.

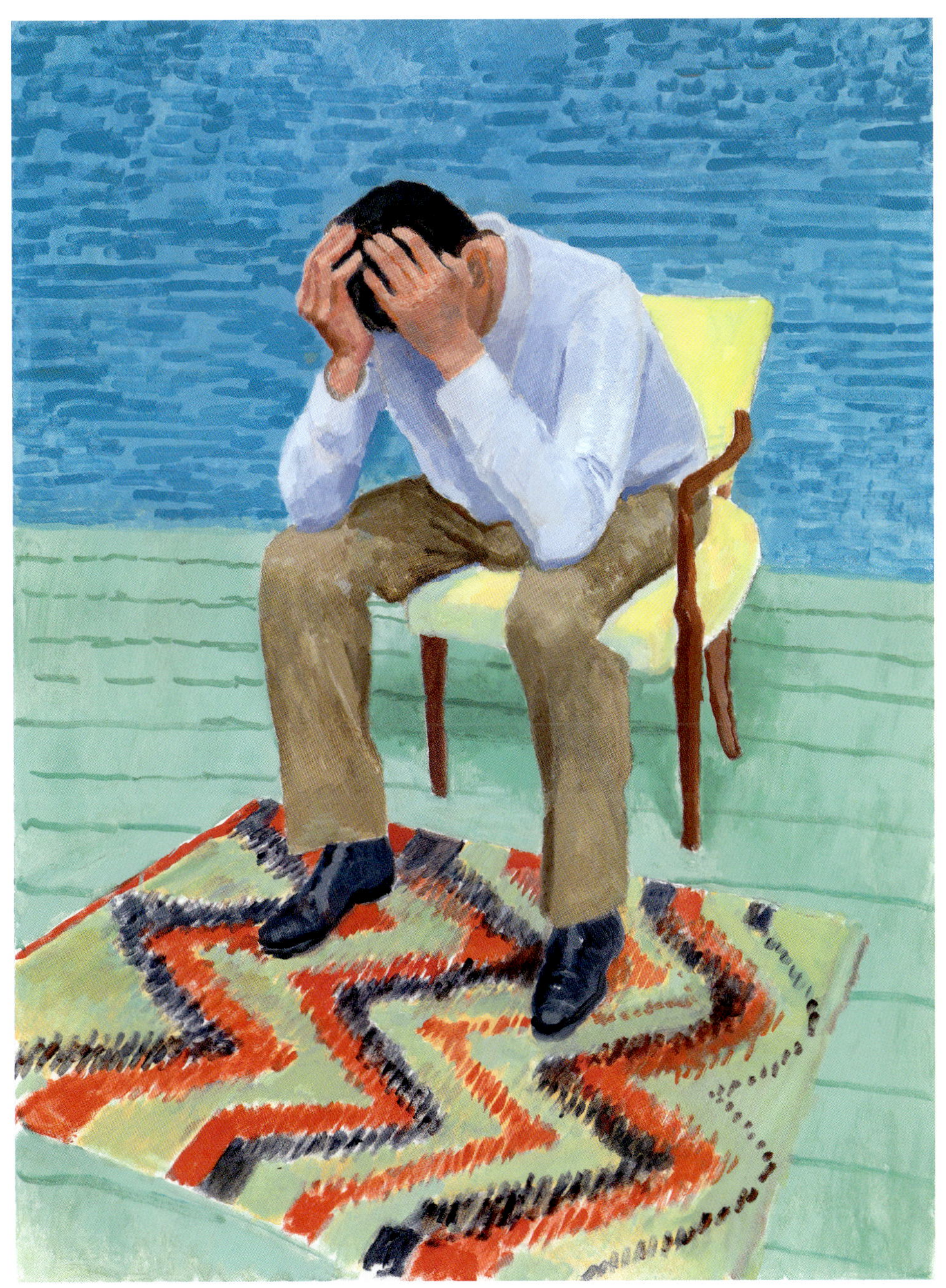

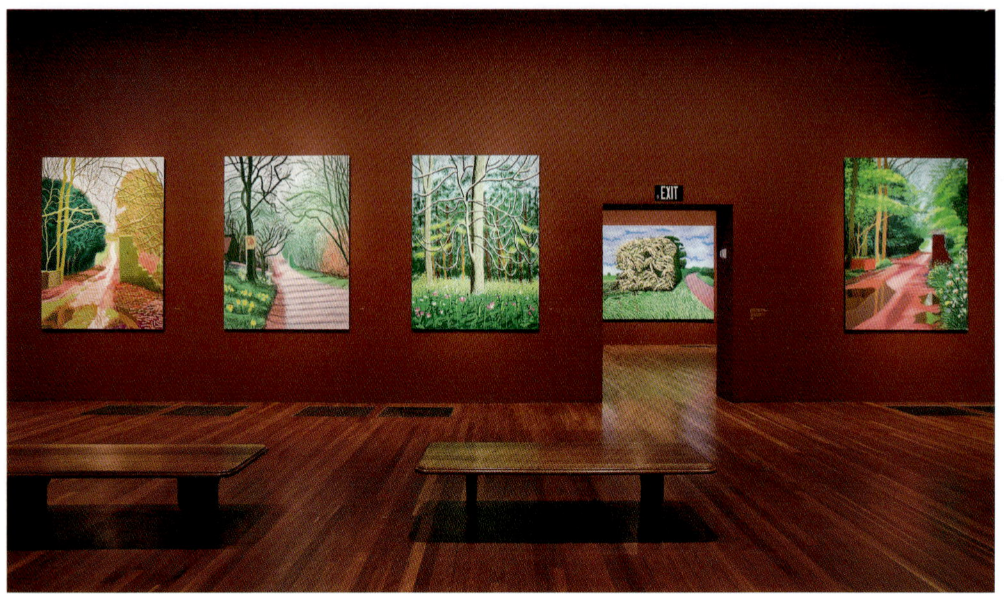

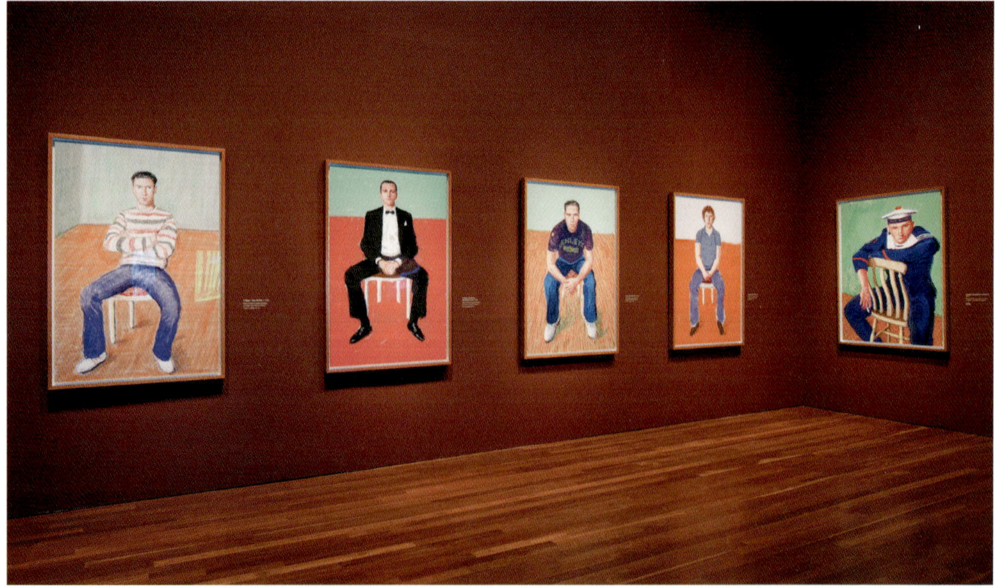

David Hockney: A Bigger Exhibition,
exhibition views, de Young Museum,
San Francisco 2013

Page 481: David Hockney drawing
Woldgate, 27 May from *The Arrival of
Spring in 2013 (twenty thirteen)*. Photo:
Jean-Pierre Gonçalves de Lima

Page 483: *J-P Gonçalves de Lima,
11th, 12th, 13th July 2013,* acrylic on
canvas, 48 x 36 in. / 121.9 x 91.4 cm

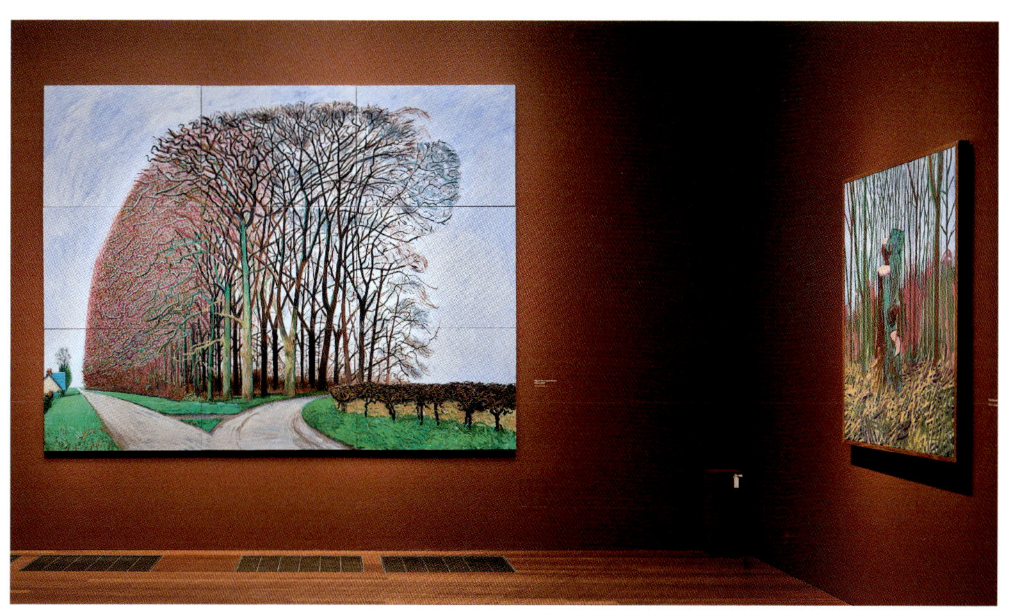

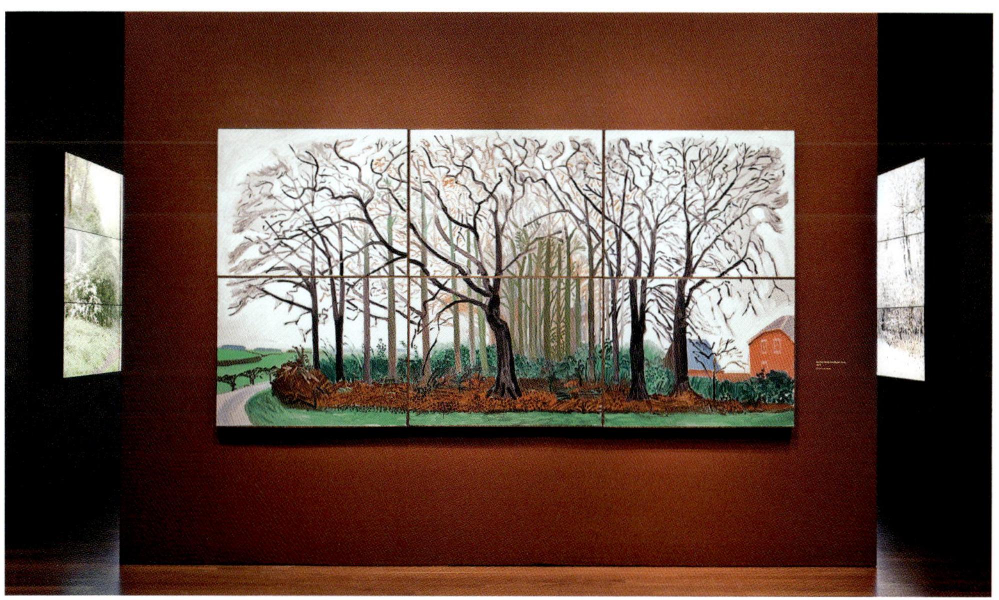

Pages 486/487: *The Arrival of Spring in 2013 (twenty thirteen),* 25 charcoal drawings on paper, each 22 ⁵⁄₈ x 30 ¹⁄₄ in. / 57.4 x 77 cm

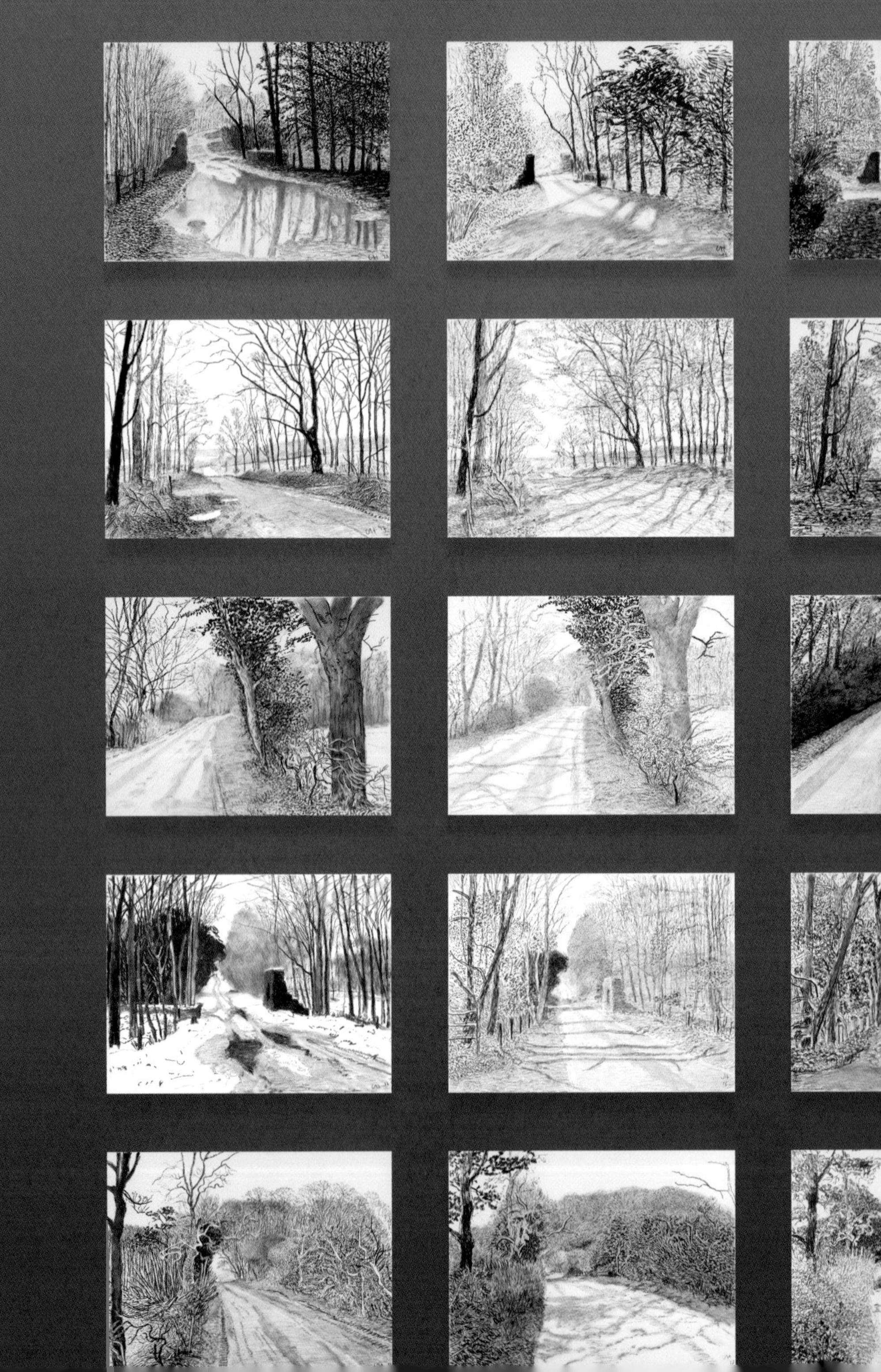

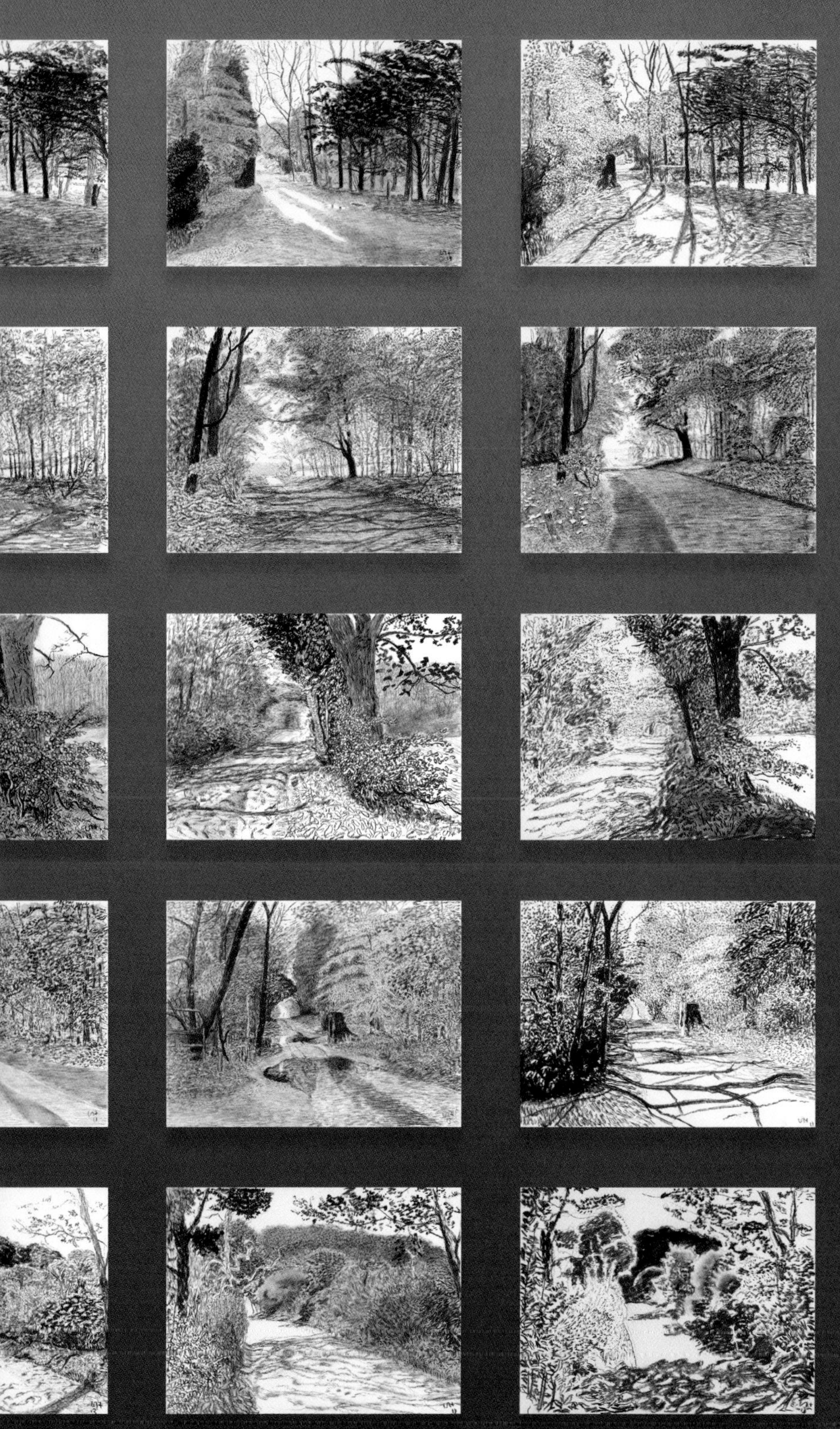

2014

Throughout the first half of the year, Hockney paints more portraits of friends and visitors, all sat on a chair in front of a blue background, gazing out at the viewer in poses of their own choice, some relaxed, some self-conscious. The painter is usually taking three sessions of six or seven hours to finish what he calls a 20-hour exposure of his subject.

He also starts painting groups of people moving around his studio (p. 491), looking at pictures, discussing something, using one of the many pieces of furniture. They first pose as a group, which makes their interaction more complex: "There's a weird spatial thing going on which seems to me to be about the center of the picture, not the edges. In these groups, there's a general perspective for the room but also for each person, because I'm looking at them. In fact, they may have several. If a figure is close to me, I am seeing his face head-on, but also looking down at his feet. So you are moving in to view just that one individual. Then, you have to turn to look at another person…You make space through time, I think. And the space between where you end and I begin is the most interesting space of all." In later pictures of the same studio scene (pp. 492–493), Hockney collages up to 200 digital photographs together, creating a complex array of multiple viewpoints and timelines suggested by several appearances of the same figure in the final image.

Whereas these group pictures portray friends and acquaintances, Hockney invites a professional troupe for *The Dancers* (pp. 494/495). Martin Gayford witnesses them at work: "In the morning, a group of five young dancers assembled in Hockney's Los Angeles studio. When everybody was there Hockney stood, charcoal in hand, at the easel and gave his first instruction: 'Hold hands, spread out a bit, start going round.' And they began to rotate with slow, graceful steps. For a short while, Hockney just watched. Then he told them to stop and drew one of the dancers. The position in which this young man was frozen—poised with one leg on tiptoe—looked extremely hard to hold, but he remained amazingly steady while Hockney captured his outline." Hockney describes the development of the series: "The very first picture of the dancers was of them stood in a circle, it was ok, but they weren't moving, they weren't dancing. I got them to go round in a circle, then I would say stop, and draw one and I slowly built it up. Now I've moved out of the room and put them in a landscape—on top of the world, really." With the more abstract background, the pictures show a marked reference to Matisse's *Dance*.

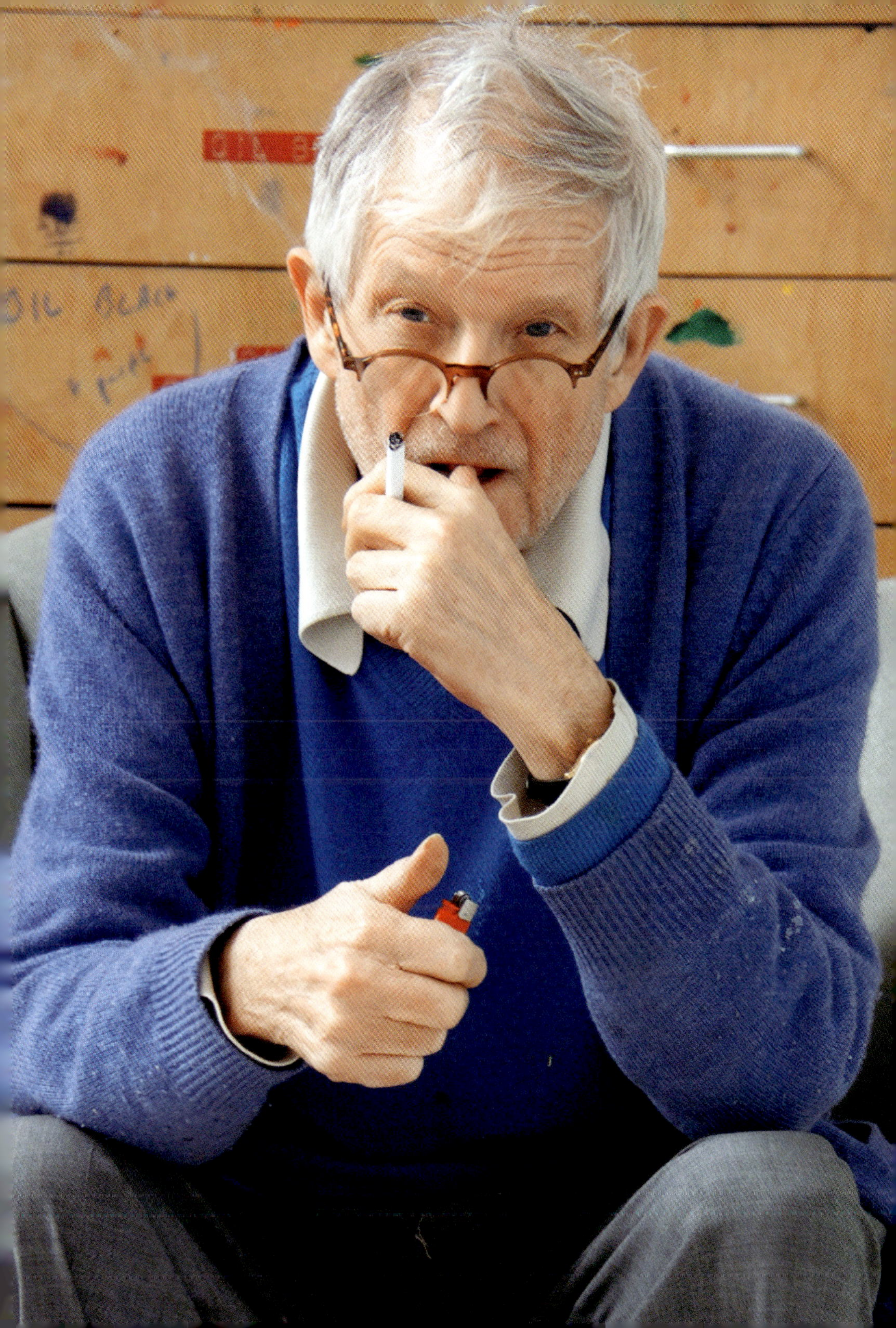

The new work is exhibited at Pace Gallery in New York in November. Ryan Steadman in the *Observer* singles out the portraits: "Hockney has always been a master of the beautifully removed character study, and his latest speedy blocks and zags of colour are no exception. They are also some of the best works in the show…The variety makes the show feel more 'hit or miss' than a single series would have. Yet it's inspiring to witness an older artist still feverishly working through new visual ideas. It gives you the rich sense that art making is as involuntary as breathing to Mr. Hockney, and everything he does—the people he's with, the places he goes—is in deference to it."

Solo: *The Jugglers,* LA County Museum of Art, Los Angeles (Feb 1–Apr 20). *Hockney, Printmaker,* Dulwich Picture Gallery, London (Feb 5–May 11); catalog with a text by Richard Lloyd. *The Arrival of Spring,* Annely Juda Fine Art, London (May 8–Jul 12); catalog with a text by David Hockney. *The Arrival of Spring,* L.A. Louver, Venice, CA (Jul 10–Aug 29). *The Arrival of Spring,* Pace Gallery, New York (Sep 5–Nov 1); catalog with a text by David Hockney. *Some New Painting (and Photography),* Pace Gallery, New York (Nov 8, 2014–Jan 10, 2015); catalog with a text by Martin Gayford.

Group: *Keywords: Art, Culture and Society in 1980s Britain,* Tate Liverpool (Feb 28–May 11). *Art and Yorkshire: From Turner to Hockney,* Mercer Art Gallery, Harrogate (Apr 12–Oct 12). *Face Value: Portraiture in the Age of Abstraction,* The National Portrait Gallery, Washington, D.C. (Apr 18, 2014–Jan 11, 2015); catalog. *Visual Deception II: Into the Future,* The Bunkamura Museum of Art, Tokyo (Aug 9–Oct 5); travels to Kobe and Nagoya.

Publication: Christopher Simon Sykes, *Hockney: The Biography Volume 2, 1975–2012. A Pilgrim's Progress,* New York: Doubleday; London: Century.

Film: *Hockney,* GB, 113 min., dir. by Randall Wright.

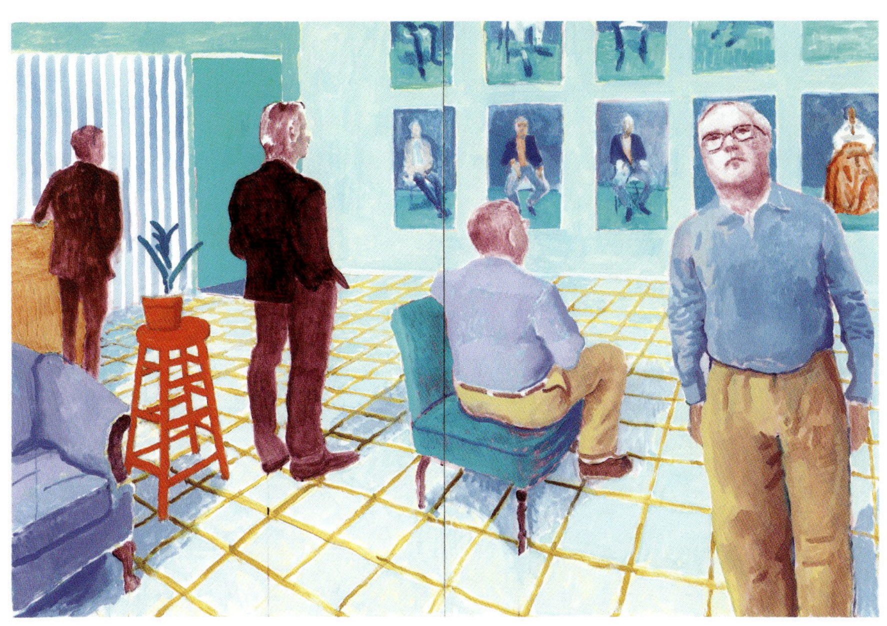

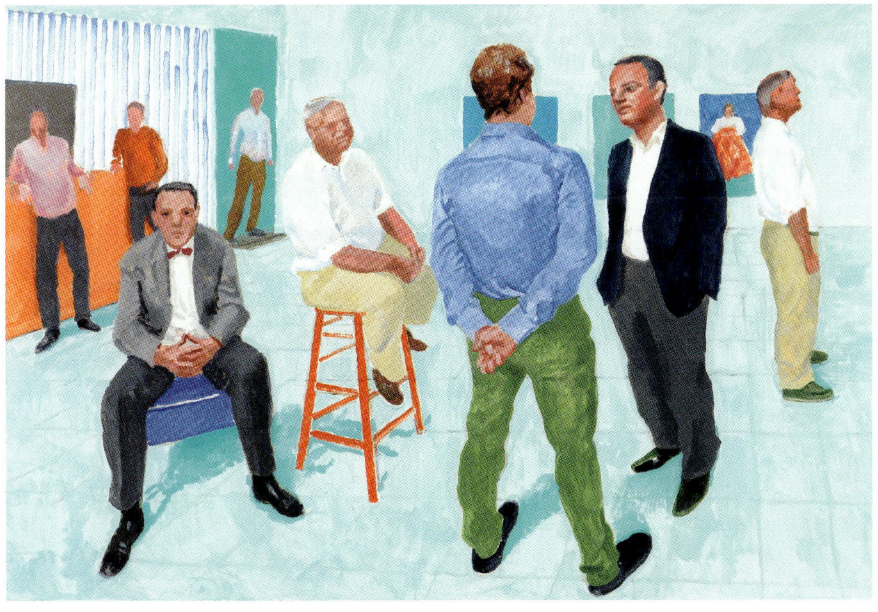

The Group I, 31 March–11 April 2014, acrylic on 2 canvases, 48 x 72 in. / 121.9 x 182.9 cm

The Group V, 6–11 May 2014, acrylic on canvas, 48 x 72 in. / 121.9 x 182.9 cm

Page 489: David Hockney, 2014. Photo: Jean-Pierre Gonçalves de Lima

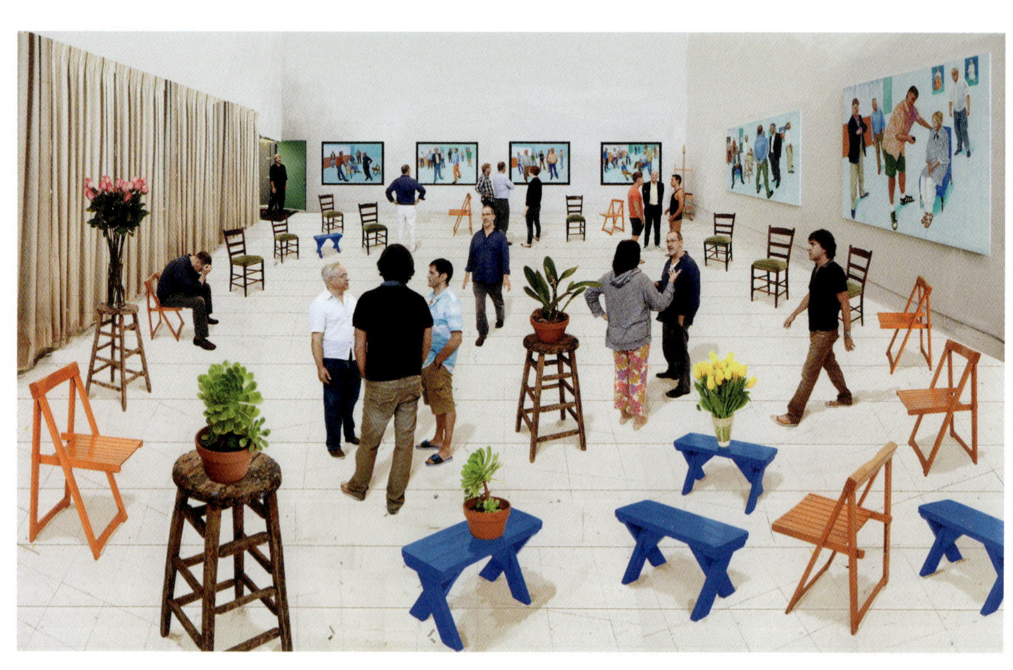

4 Blue Stools, 2014, photographic
drawing printed on paper,
mounted on Dibond, edition of 25,
42 $\frac{1}{2}$ x 69 $\frac{1}{2}$ in. / 108 x 176.6 cm

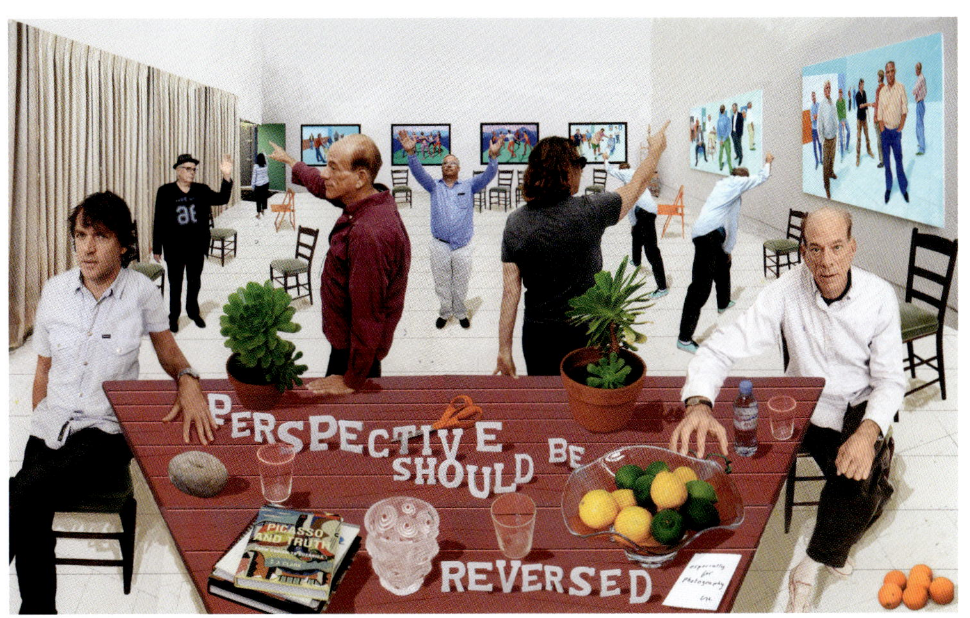

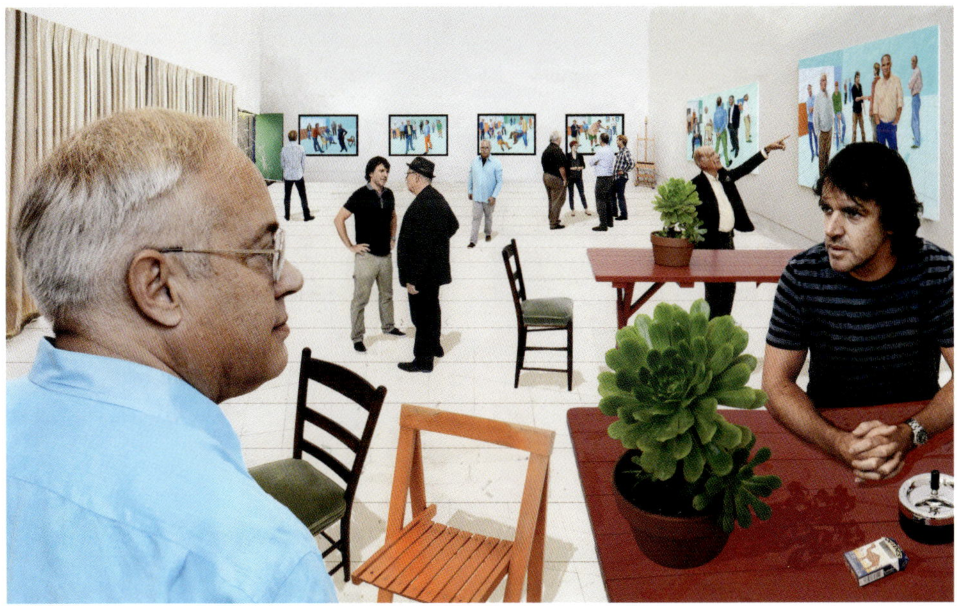

Perspective Should Be Reversed, 2014, photographic drawing printed on paper, mounted on Dibond, edition of 25, 42 ¹/₂ x 69 ¹/₂ in. / 108 x 176.6 cm

The Red Table, 2014, photographic drawing printed on paper, mounted on Dibond, edition of 25, 42 ¹/₂ x 69 ¹/₂ in. / 108 x 176.6 cm

Pages 494/495: *The Dancers III,* 13 August–8 September 2014, acrylic on canvas, 48 x 72 in. / 121.9 x 182.9 cm

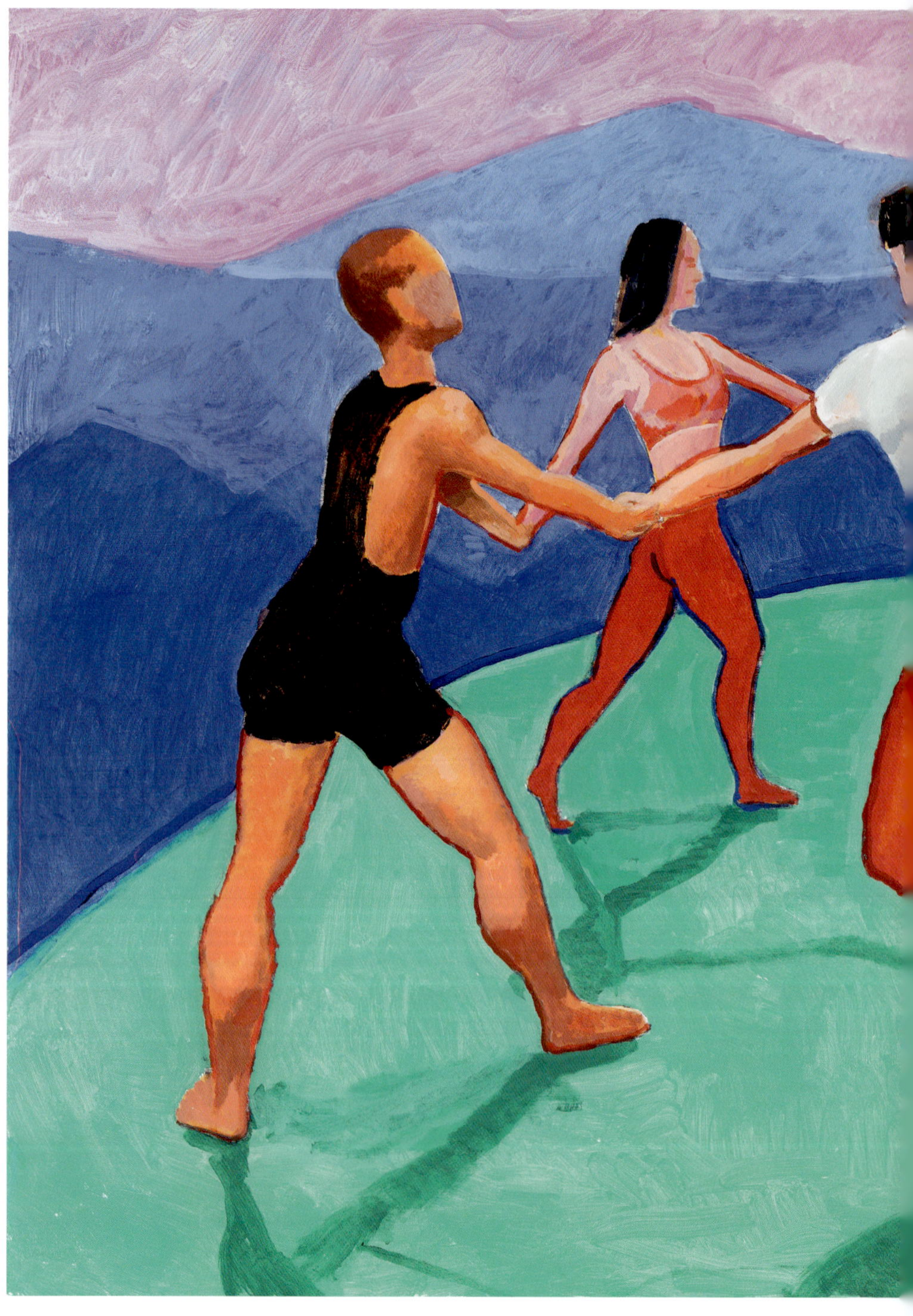

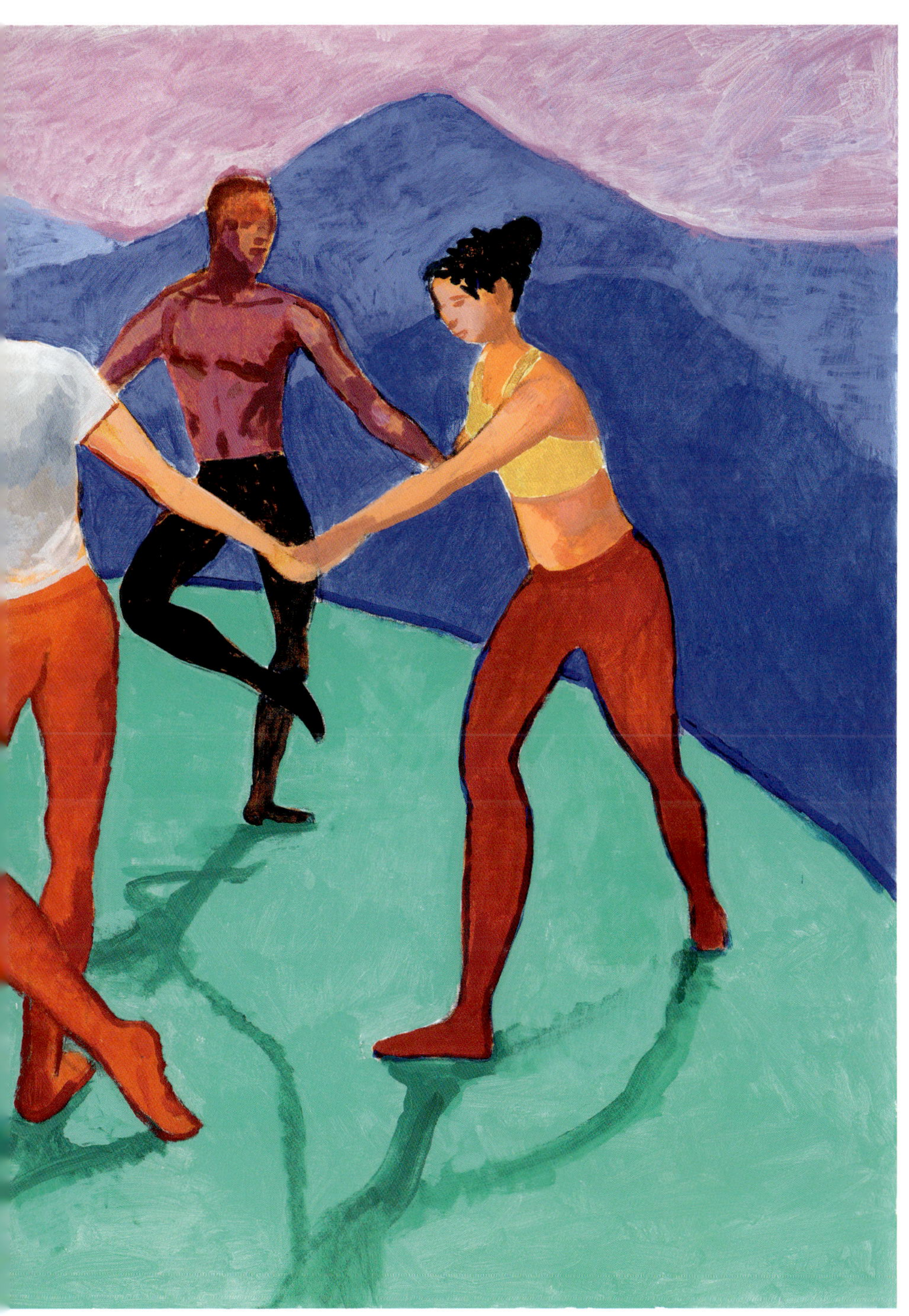

2015–2016

In several works that combine digital photography with computer-painted elements (p. 501), Hockney shows card players sitting at a (reverse-perspective) table, inspired by Cézanne's version of the motif. The images reflect all his interest in composite images with multiple viewpoints, and along with paintings from his portrait series they are exhibited at Annely Juda Fine Art. Francis Hodgson in the *Financial Times*: "Hockney isn't trying to kid us: he leaves the traces of his multiple-angled gaze fully visible. A face is perfectly sharp, seen from close. But so is the carpet four or five feet lower. The lines on a floor move in several different directions, as they really do as you move over them. In life, we move our eyes to acquire the information that the brain processes into a 'view.' That's what Hockney has done."

In July 2016 the exhibition *82 Portraits and 1 Still Life* opens at the Royal Academy to present the complete series Hockney has created since 2013 (pp. 497, 499), plus a still life of fruit and vegetables on a bench painted when a sitter had to cancel at the last minute. Rachel Campbell-Johnston in the *Times*: "The first impression may be that Hockney knows lots of middle-aged white men with paunches. Then the choice of clothing starts to fascinate. Shoes begin to work almost like emblems: akin to the identifying mascots of medieval saints. And the eye moves onwards and inwards, past sartorial accoutrements. Through postures and expressions, the arrangement of hands or the placing of legs, through knees crossed or splayed, feet tipped, turned or planted, each sitter conveys his character, disposition and temperament…This show requires us to study our intrinsic human nature. That's about as deeply traditional and yet as utterly individual as the work of an artist can get."

In autumn, two books appear: a SUMO-sized visual survey of Hockney's work published by Taschen and curated by the artist himself, and a *History of Pictures* written together with Martin Gayford, which broadens Hockney's ideas about the use of optics in art into a personal philosophy of picture-making: "What makes a work of art? I don't know…I'd prefer to say I'm making pictures—depictions. We've had a great many histories of art, what we need now is a history of pictures." Hockney's outlook is always directed toward the future: "Pictures will go on changing, as they always have in the past. In the 23rd century they won't look back at 21st-century television, and think: Well, this was reality, as it looked then!

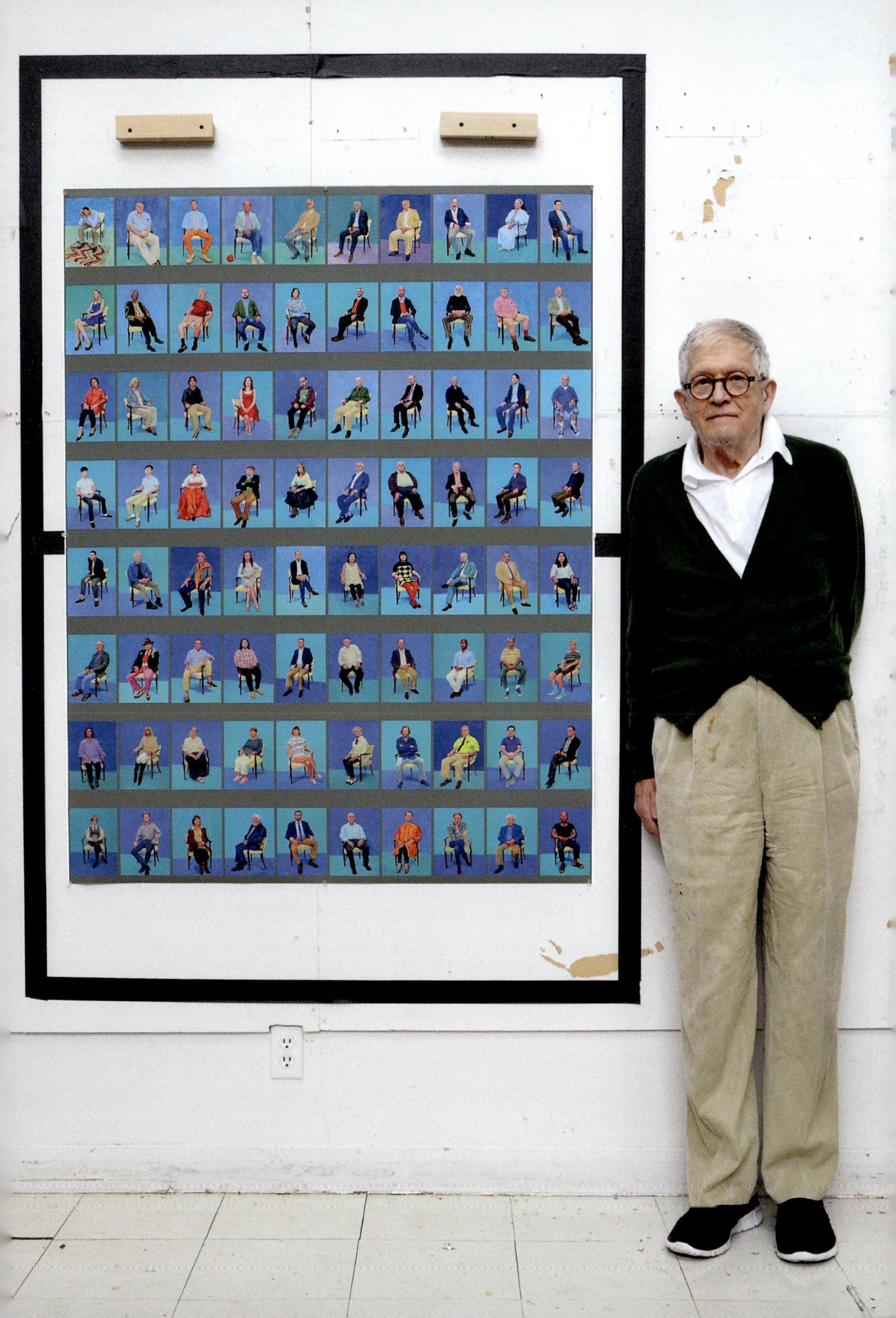

They'll regard it as some old-fashioned method of depiction…One thing that is not going to be destroyed, though, is drawing. There are many handmade images in the digital world. For example, video games are drawn pictures. And a lot of them are rather good, actually. Now you can live in a virtual world if you want to, and perhaps that's where most people are going to finish up—in a world of pictures."

Hockney himself, close to his 80th birthday, remains as prolific as always, and keen on new adventures. "Are you as happy as you've ever been?" he is asked by Jon Snow for *Channel 4 News.* "Yes, really," Hockney answers. "I mean, I like painting, I like making pictures, I now see there's new ways to make pictures. And I find that very exciting."

Solo: *Louisiana on Paper: David Hockney,* Louisiana Museum for Moderne Kunst, Humlebæk (Mar 19–Jun 21, 2015). *A Rake's Progress,* Portland Art Museum, Portland (Apr 18–Aug 2, 2015); brochure with a text by Mary Weaver Chapin. *82 Portraits and 1 Still Life,* Royal Academy of Arts, London (Jul 2–Oct 2, 2016); catalog with texts by Tim Barringer, Edith Devaney, and David Hockney. *Draw, I Do,* Metropolitan Arts Centre, Belfast (Aug 19–Oct 16, 2016). *L'Arrivée du printemps,* Fondation Vincent Van Gogh, Arles (Oct 11, 2015–Jan 17, 2016); catalog with a text by Bice Curiger, interview by Martin Bailey. *David Hockney,* National Gallery of Victoria, Melbourne (Nov 11, 2016–Mar 13, 2017). *The Arrival of Spring,* 1853 Gallery, Saltaire (opens Feb 18, 2015). *The Arrival of Spring,* Pace Beijing (Apr 18–Jun 6, 2015). *Painting and Photography,* Annely Juda Fine Art, London (May 15–Jun 27, 2015); travels to L.A. Louver, Venice, CA (Jul 15–Sep 19, 2015); catalog. *The Arrival of Spring,* Galerie Lelong, Paris (May 21–Jul 24, 2015). *The Arrival of Spring,* Annely Juda Fine Art, London (Jul 9–Aug 29, 2015). *Early Drawings,* Paul Kasmin Gallery, New York (Nov 3–Dec 1, 2015). *The Yosemite Suite,* Pace Gallery, New York (Apr 29–Jun 18, 2016); postcard book; travels to Annely Juda Fine Art, London (Jun 28–Aug 19, 2016); L.A. Louver, Venice, CA (Jul 13–Oct 1, 2016); and Nishimura Gallery, Tokyo (Oct 1–Nov 26, 2016).

Publications: David Hockney and Martin Gayford, *A History of Pictures: From the Cave to the Computer Screen,* London: Thames and Hudson; New York: Harry N. Abrams. *David Hockney: A Bigger Book,* ed. by David Hockney and Hans Werner Holzwarth, Cologne: Taschen.

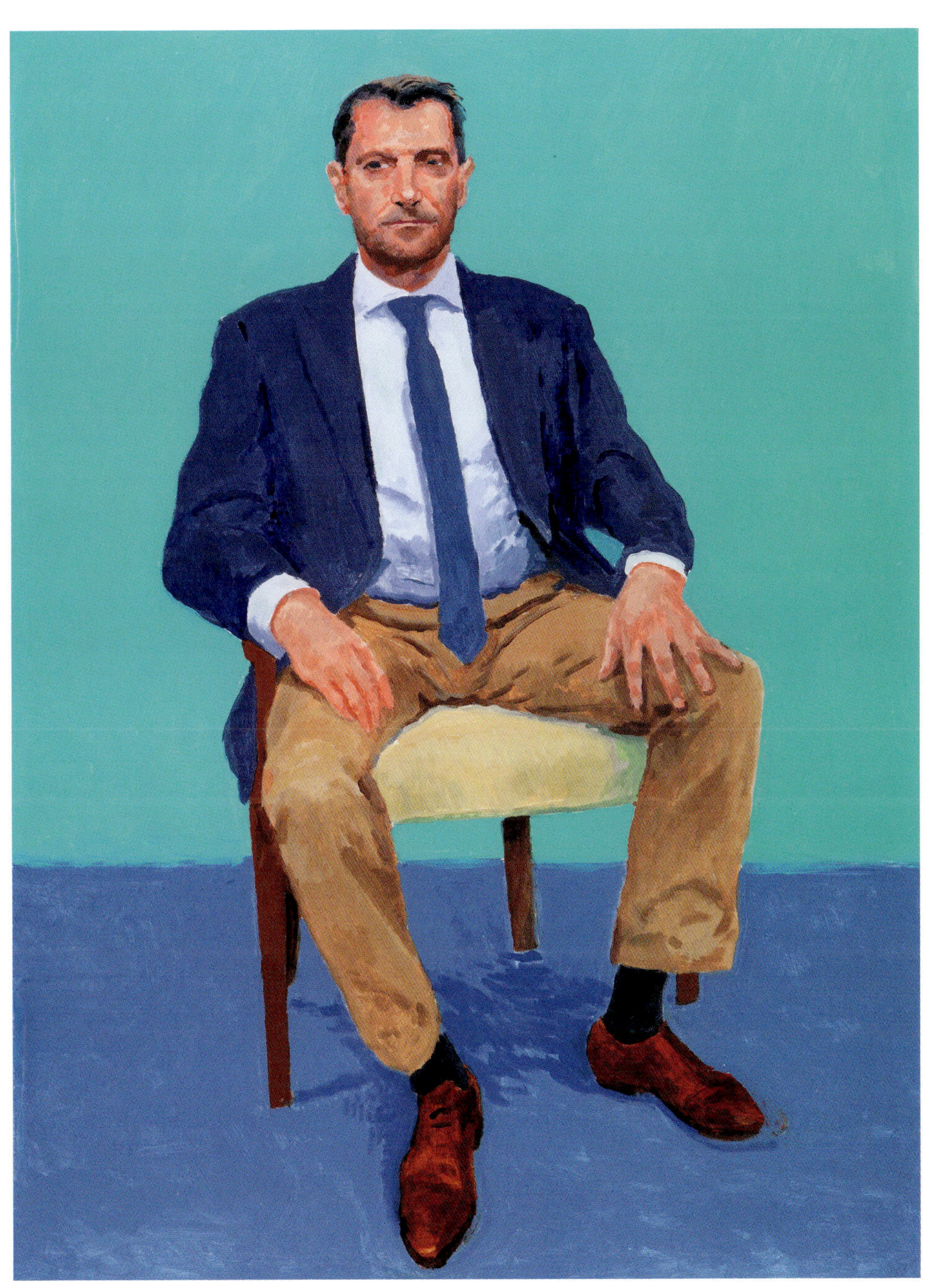

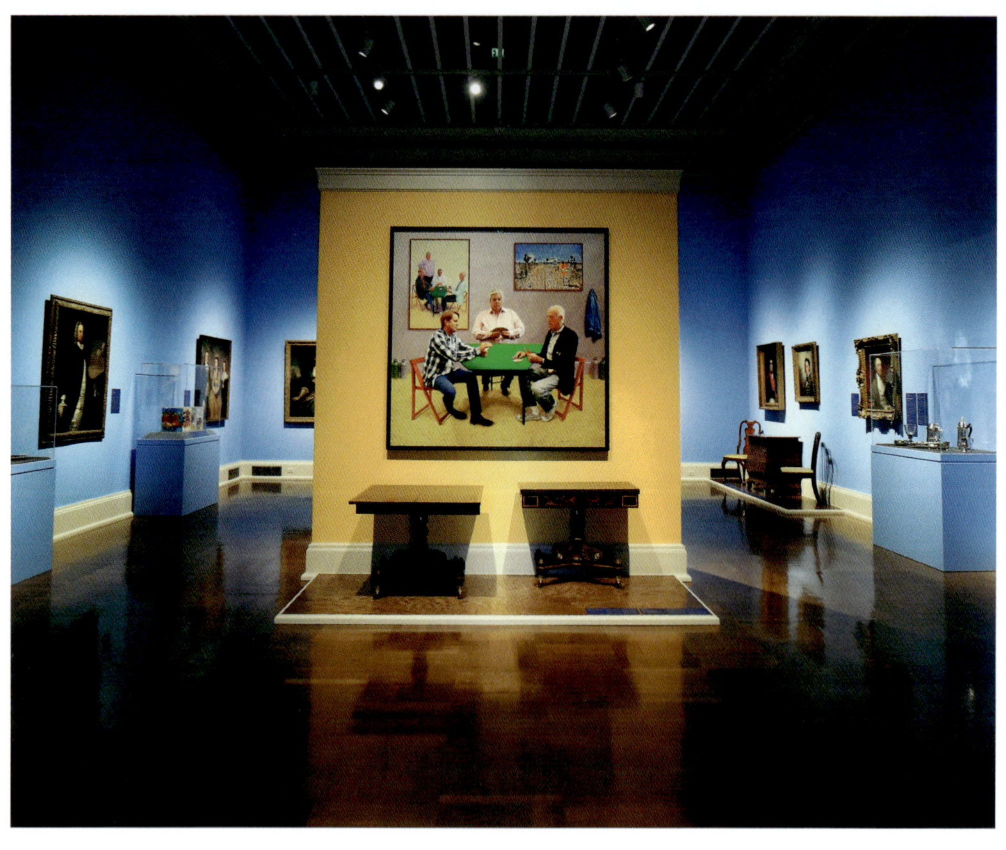

A Bigger Card Players, 2015, photographic drawing printed on paper,
mounted on aluminum, edition of 12,
69 ¾ x 69 ¾ in. / 177.2 x 177.2 cm,
installation view, Toledo Museum of Art,
Toledo, Ohio

Page 497: David Hockney with
80 portraits, May 2016. Photo:
Jean-Pierre Gonçalves de Lima

Page 499: *J-P Gonçalves de Lima,
15th, 16th, 17th January 2016,*
acrylic on canvas, 48 x 36 in. /
121.9 x 91.4 cm

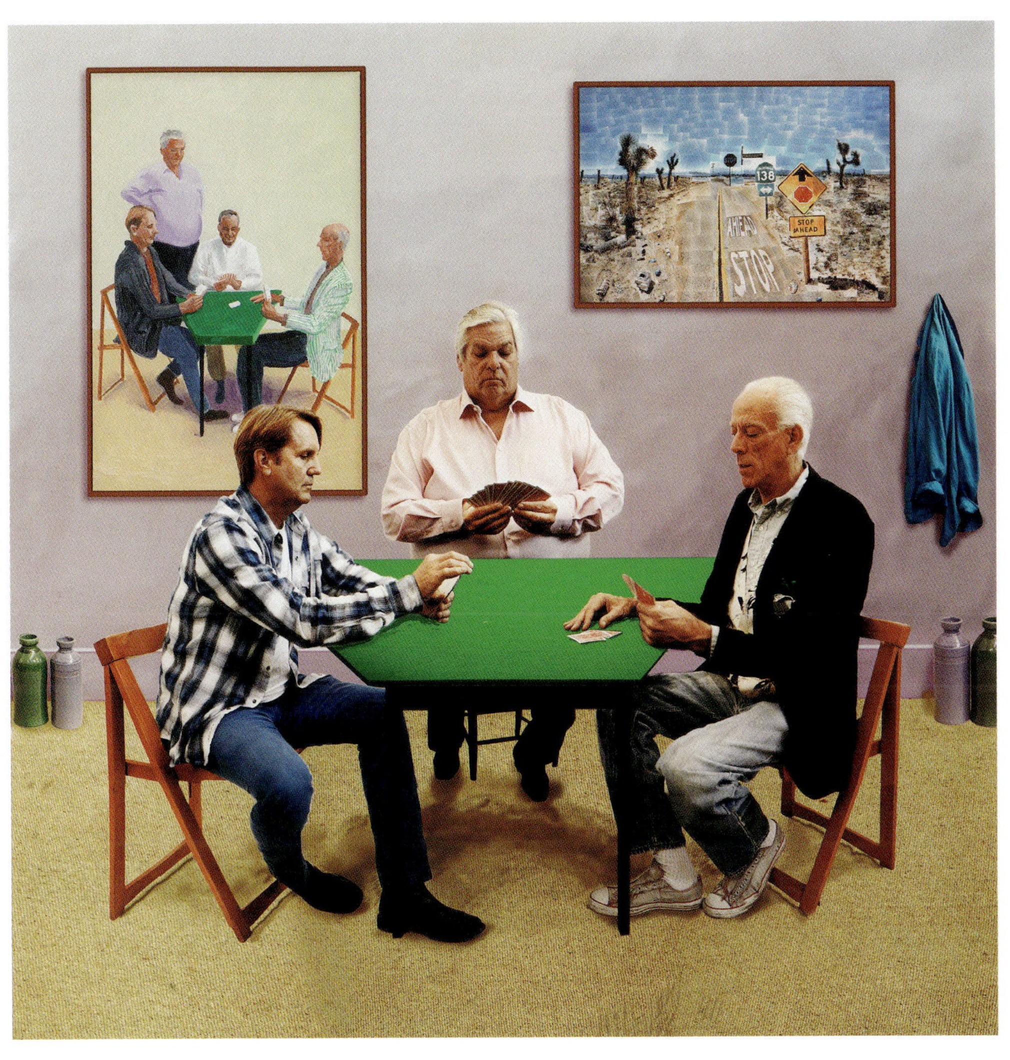

The Card Players, 2015, photographic
drawing printed on paper, mounted on
Dibond, edition of 25, 42 ¼ x 42 ¼ in. /
107.3 x 107.3 cm

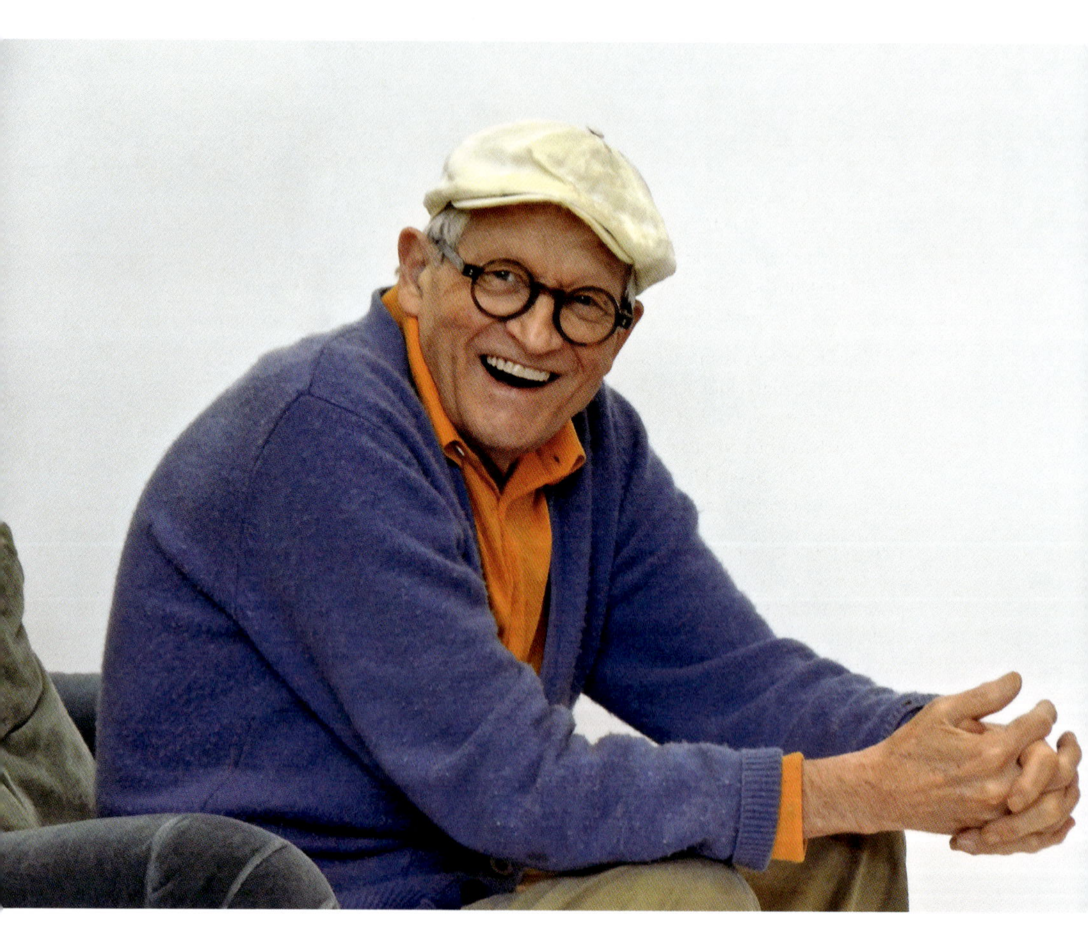

David Hockney, Los Angeles 2016.
Photo: Jean-Pierre Gonçalves
de Lima

Jean-Pierre Gonçalves de Lima, Hans Werner Holzwarth, and myself spent a year making the large SUMO and then the Chronology book published together in 2016. It was the first time I reflected back on what I had done in the last 60 years. Painters live in the "Now," or I thought I did. The book you hold in your hand grew out of these, and now the complete story is in one place.

I would like to first thank JP, who has been my right hand for 20 years. I love him, he has a marvelous sense of humor that first attracted me to him. We still have a laugh every day. He has a very good eye which I value enormously and now, at 83, I rely on him for almost everything. We are at the moment in Normandy, living in a small Seven Dwarfs house in the middle of a four-acre field, where I'm painting the changing seasons.

Hans Werner Holzwarth also has a good sense of humor, which meant that we all got on splendidly. I listened to what both of them had to say, but in the end it had to be my choices that made the books what they are, so I think I must take most of the blame for their content. The text, which struck me as very clear and precise, was written by Lutz Eitel, who at first I thought was English as the clarity was so fine. We have met only once but I would like to thank him for it. And last but not least my thanks to Benedikt Taschen for harassing me for years to do these books.

—DAVID HOCKNEY, NORMANDY, SEPTEMBER 2020

TEXT SOURCES

1937–1952: David Hockney, *That's the Way I See It*, London: Thames and Hudson, 1993, p. 11f. *David Hockney by David Hockney: My Early Years*, London: Thames and Hudson, 1976, p. 28. Ibid., p. 28f. Ibid., p. 27.

1953–1958: *My Early Years*, p. 34. Hockney in Christopher Simon Sykes, *David Hockney: The Biography, 1937–1975*, New York: Doubleday, 2011, p. 40. *My Early Years*, p. 38. Ibid., p. 39. Ibid., p. 34. Ibid., p. 38.

1959–1960: *My Early Years*, p. 40. R. B. Kitaj in *David Hockney: A Retrospective*, Los Angeles: LA County Museum of Art, 1988, p. 3. *My Early Years*, p. 40. Ibid., p. 41. Ibid. "London Group 1960," *Times*, Jan 15, 1960, p. 16. *My Early Years*, p. 62f. Ibid. Ibid, p. 44. Ibid. Ibid., p. 63.

1961: *My Early Years*, p. 42. "Promising Art by Students," *Times*, Feb 13, 1961, p. 6. *My Early Years*, p. 62. Ibid., p. 64. Ibid., p. 65. Ibid., p. 66. Ibid., p. 87.

1962: *My Early Years*, p. 66. "The Serious Side of Pop Art," *Times*, Jul 27, 1962, p. 15. *My Early Years*, p. 88. Emma Yorke in *Town Magazine*, Sep 1962, after Sykes, *The Biography, 1937–1975*, p. 110. *My Early Years*, p. 61. *Image in Progress*, exhibition catalog Grabowski Gallery, 1962, after *David Hockney: Paintings, Prints and Drawings*, London: Whitechapel Art Gallery, 1970, p. 25.

1963: *My Early Years*, p. 90. Ibid., p. 93. Ibid., p. 92. Nigel Gosling, "Top of the Hips," *Observer*, Dec 15, 1963, p. 26. Bryan Robertson, "The New Generation: Opportunities and Pitfalls," *Times*, Dec 17, 1963, p. 11.

1964: *My Early Years*, p. 97. Ibid., p. 98. Stewart Preston, "A Square World," *New York Times*, Oct 4, 1964 (online).

1965: *My Early Years*, p. 100. Ibid., p. 101. Ibid. "David Hockney Stimulated by Trip to California," *Times*, Dec 9, 1965, p. 13.

1966: Paul Overy in the *Listener*, Aug 4, 1966, after Whitechapel 1970, p. 85. *My Early Years*, p. 103. David Thompson, "David Hockney: A Natural Dandy and 'Ubu Roi,'" *New York Times*, Aug 14, 1966 (online). *My Early Years*, p. 151.

1967: *My Early Years*, p. 151. Ibid., p. 124f. Ibid., p. 124. Ibid. p. 149.

1968: Guy Brett, "California through Hockney's Eyes," *Times*, Jan 26, 1968, p. 7. *My Early Years*, p. 152. Ibid. Ibid., p. 157f. Ibid., p. 193.

1969: Hilton Kramer, "Comedies of Manners," *New York Times*, May 11, 1969 (online). *My Early Years*, p. 195. Nigel Gosling, "Hockney and Grimm," *Observer*, Dec 7, 1969, p. 40.

1970: *My Early Years*, p. 202. Ibid. Ibid., p. 203. Norbert Lynton, "Hockney Retrospective," *Guardian*, Apr 2, 1970, p. 10. James Burr in *Apollo*, Apr 1970 after Sykes, *The Biography, 1937–1975*, p. 234. Hockney in Whitechapel 1970, p. 9. *My Early Years*, p. 203f.

1971: Peter Quennell, "Art in London: Portraiture? Why, It's a 'Snap!'" *New York Times*, March 28, 1971 (online). *My Early Years*, p. 204. Ibid., p. 240. Ibid., p. 241. Ibid., p. 250.

1972: *My Early Years*, p. 247. Ibid., p. 248. James Mellow, "Hockney: From Pop to Parody," *New York Times*, May 28, 1972 (online). Hockney in Lawrence Weschler, *True to Life: Twenty-five Years of Conversations with David Hockney*, Berkeley: University of California Press, 2008, ebook, p. 136. *My Early Years*, p. 250.

1973: *That's the Way I See It*, p. 16f. Ibid., p. 17. Sykes, *The Biography, 1937–1975*, p. 296.

1974: Pierre Restany and David Hockney, "A Conversation in Paris," in *David Hockney: Tableaux et dessins,* Paris: Musée des Arts Décoratifs, 1974, p. 21f. Ibid., p. 23. *My Early Years,* p. 286. Ibid., p. 285. Ibid., p. 248. David Robertson, "First Fruits of Cannes," *Times,* May 22, 1974, p. 11. *My Early Years,* p. 286. Ibid. *That's the Way I See It,* p. 22.

1975: *That's the Way I See It,* p. 23. William Mann, "More Hockney than Hogarth," *Times,* June 23, 1975, p. 8. *My Early Years,* p. 294. *That's the Way I See It,* p. 32.

1976: Billy Wilder in Peter Webb, *Portrait of David Hockney* (1988), London: Paladin, 1990, p. 219. Hockney in Charles Ingham, *Words in Pictures,* University of Essex 1986, after Christopher Simon Sykes, *Hockney: The Biography, Vol. 2 1975–2012,* London: Century, 2014, p. 18. Ibid., p. 37. Sykes, *The Biography, Vol. 2,* p. 40. Grace Glueck, "Art People," *New York Times,* Dec 3, 1976 (online).

1977: Hockney in the *Times Literary Supplement,* Jan 21, 1977, after Sykes, *The Biography, Vol. 2,* p. 37. R. B. Kitaj and David Hockney, "In Conversation," *New Review,* Jan/Feb 1977, p. 76. William Feaver in the *Observer,* Jul 24, 1977, after Sykes, *The Biography, Vol. 2,* p. 57f. Peter Fuller, "An Interview with David Hockney," *Art Monthly,* 1977, online at *laurencefuller.squarespace.com,* Sep 11, 2015. Hilton Kramer, "The Fun of David Hockney," *New York Times,* Nov 4, 1977 (online).

1978: Gillian Widdicombe, "Filling the Flute with Triangles," *Observer,* May 28, 1978, p. 27. Desmond Shawe-Taylor in the *Sunday Times,* Jun 1, 1978, after Sykes, *The Biography, Vol. 2,* p. 71. *That's the Way I See It,* p. 47. Ibid., p. 52.

1979: William Feaver, "Hockney's Hybrids," *Observer,* Feb 11, 1979, p. 16. David Hockney, "No Joy at the Tate," *Observer,* Mar 4, 1979, p. 33. *That's the Way I See It,* p. 53.

1980: *That's the Way I See It,* p. 57f. Hockney in a letter to R. B. Kitaj from Aug 19, 1980, after Sykes, *The Biography, Vol. 2,* p. 122. *That's the Way I See It,* p. 67. Hockney in *David Hockney,* ed. by Marco Livingstone, London: Thames and Hudson, 1996, after Sykes, *The Biography, Vol. 2,* p. 133. Weschler, *True to Life,* p. 165.

1981: Donal Henahan, "Met's 'Parade,' Captivating Triple Bill," *New York Times,* Feb 22, 1981 (online). Theodore W. Libbey Jr., "Dexter and Hockney Team for Stravinsky Triple Bill," *New York Times,* Nov 29, 1981 (online). *That's the Way I See It,* p. 78. Ibid., p. 82f. David Hockney, *Looking at Pictures in a Book,* London: National Gallery, 1981, p. 8. Ibid. Anna Kisselgoff, "Reviving Diaghilev's Avant-Garde," *New York Times,* Dec 20, 1981 (online).

1982: Weschler, *True to Life,* p. 45. *Hockney on Art: Conversations with Paul Joyce,* London: Little, Brown, 1999, p. 19. Andy Grundberg, "Photography View: A New Chapter for Hockney," *New York Times,* Jun 13, 1982 (online). *David Hockney: Photographs,* London: Petersburg Press, 1982, p. 26.

1983: *That's the Way I See It,* p. 98. Ibid., p. 100. George Rowley, *The Principles of Chinese Paintings,* Princeton University Press, 1947, p. 61, after *A Retrospective,* p. 91. Hockney in Lawrence Weschler, "A Visit with David and Stanley," in *A Retrospective,* p. 90. Friedman in Paul Froiland, "A New Stage," *Horizon,* Nov/Dec 1983, after Sykes, *The Biography, Vol. 2,* p. 203. John Russell Taylor in the *Times,* Aug 6, 1985, after Sykes, *The Biography, Vol. 2,* p. 204. "Hockney on Hockney: David Hockney's Faces," *Los Angeles Times,* Jan 18, 1987 (online). David Hockney, *On Photography* (1983), reprint Bradford: National Museum of Photography, Film and Television, 1985, p. 19. Ibid., p. 10f. Ibid., p. 28f.

1984: Weschler, *True to Life*, p. 75. Ibid., p. 184. Tyler 2012 in Sykes, *The Biography, Vol. 2*, p. 211. Hockney 1984 in an interview for the Smithsonian Institute, after Webb, *Portrait of David Hockney*, p. 291.

1985: Hockney in a letter to R.B. Kitaj from May 21, 1985, after Sykes, *The Biography, Vol. 2*, p. 209. Ibid., p. 216. "Vogue par David Hockney," *Vogue*, Dec 1985, p. 257.

1986: Weschler, *True to Life*, p. 139. *Painting with Light: David Hockney*, GB 1986, dir. by David Goldsmith. *That's the Way I See It*, p. 112. Andy Grundberg, "From Hockney, New Perspectives in Photography," *New York Times*, Sep 12, 1986 (online).

1987: *Telegraph and Argus*, Feb 24, 1987, p. 1. Waldemar Januszczak, "Hockney at 50," *Guardian*, May 21, 1987, p. 12. John Russell, "Hockney's Design for 'Tristan und Isolde' in Los Angeles," *New York Times*, Dec 8, 1987 (online).

1988: Henry Geldzahler, "Hockney: Young and Older," in *A Retrospective*, p. 13. John Russell, "David Hockney's Serious Playfulness, at the Met," *New York Times*, Jun 17, 1988 (online). Julian Spalding, "Exhibition Reviews: London, Tate Gallery, David Hockney," *Burlington Magazine*, Jan 1989, p. 53. Joyce, *Hockney on Art*, p. 178. *That's the Way I See It*, p. 190f. Joyce, *Hockney on Art*, p. 183.

1989: *That's the Way I See It*, p. 198. Ibid., p. 204. Martin Wainwright, "True Fax Revealed about Hockney Art," *Guardian*, Nov 11, 1989, p. 5.

1990: Weschler 1996 in *True to Life*, p. 210. *That's the Way I See It*, p. 206. Barbara Isenberg, "David Hockney's New Toys," *Los Angeles Times*, Sep 16, 1990 (online).

1991: Geordie Greig, "Colourful Court of King David," *Sunday Times*, May 5, 1991, p. 10. Eamonn McCabe, "On the Lighter Side in Bradford," *Guardian*, Jun 6, 1991, p. 25. *That's the Way I See It*, p. 221f.

1992: John von Rhein, "'Turandot' a Dazzler," *Chicago Tribune*, Jan 13, 1992 (online). Joyce, *Hockney on Art*, p. 189. Anthony Peatty, "A Colourful Double Act," *Independent*, Oct 31, 1992 (online). *That's the Way I See It*, p. 240.

1993: Roberta Smith, "Art in Review," *New York Times*, Jan 22, 1993 (online). Richard Cork, "Postcards from His Private World," *Times*, summer 1993 (clipping from the artist's archive). Trip Gabriel, "At Home with David Hockney; Acquainted with the Light," *New York Times*, Jan 21, 1993 (online).

1994: Dalya Alberge, "Hockney Exhibits New Drawings," *Independent*, Jun 27, 1994 (online). Jonathan Silver, "What it's like to be drawn by David Hockney," exhibition notes, 1853 Gallery, Salts Mill, 1994, after Sykes, *The Biography, Vol. 2*, p. 315f. Paul Goldberger, "Henry Geldzahler, 59, Critic, Public Official and Contemporary Art's Champion, Is Dead," *New York Times*, Aug 17, 1994 (online). Michael Church, "Hockney's Best Friends," *Sunday Telegraph*, Jun 12, p. 5.

1995: "Hockney's Pedigree Portraits," *You*, Nov 5, 1995, p. 45. Joyce, *Hockney on Art*, p. 194. William Wilson, "Hockney Puts a Different Angle on Abstract Cubism," *Los Angeles Times*, Apr 15, 1995 (online). Edouard Beaucamp, "Der sprunghafte Liebhaber," *Frankfurter Allgemeine Zeitung*, Aug 29, 1995, p. 27. William Feaver, "Still Making a Splash," *Observer*, Nov 12, 1995, p. D10. Joyce, *Hockney on Art*, p. 203f.

1996: Joyce, *Hockney on Art*, p. 206. Hockney 1998 to Weschler after Sykes, *The Biography, Vol. 2*, p. 322f. Andrew Graham-Dixon, "No One Home," *Independent*, Nov 26, 1996 (online). John Russell Taylor, "Hockney's

Flowering Power," *Times,* Nov 23, 1996 (clipping from the artist's archives).

1997: Martin Gayford, "Has Hockney Become Hackneyed?" *Telegraph,* May 10, 1997 (online). Joyce, *Hockney on Art,* p. 231. Ibid., p. 232.

1998: Alfred Hickling, "California Dreaming," *Guardian,* Jan 3, 1998, p. A7. Joyce, *Hockney on Art,* p. 231. William Wilson, "Landscape: A Panoramic Look at Hockney's Use of Space," *Los Angeles Times,* Sep 22, 1998 (online). David Hockney, "A Wider View," *Modern Painters,* spring 1998, p. 74. Tim Adams, "Hockney's Final Frontier," *Observer,* May 30, 1999, p. 83.

1999: Weschler, *True to Life,* p. 271. David Hockney, *Secret Knowledge,* new and expanded edition, London: Thames and Hudson, 2006, p. 12f. Weschler, *True to Life,* p. 288.

2000: Weschler, *True to Life,* p. 336. Andrew Marr, "Portrait of the Artist as a Cheat," *Observer,* Feb 6, 2000, p. 19.

2001: Peter Robb, "Candid Camera," *Guardian,* Oct 20, 2001 (online). Sarah Boxer, "Paintings too Perfect?" *New York Times,* Dec 4, 2001 (online). Weschler, *True to Life,* p. 404. Marco Livingstone, "Exhibition Reviews: Bonn, David Hockney," *Burlington Magazine,* Sep 2001, p. 587.

2002: Weschler, *True to Life,* p. 418f. Nigel Farndale, "The Talented Mr. Hockney," *Sunday Telegraph Magazine,* Nov 16, 2003, p. 17. Hockney in *Painting on Paper,* London: Annely Juda Fine Art, 2003. David Hockney, "Some Pages for Tatler," *Tatler,* Jan 2003, p. 98f.

2003: Andrew Marr, "A Brush with the Hawk," *Guardian,* Jan 6, 2003, p. B2. Adrian Searle, "Watercolour Challenge," *Guardian,* Jan 21, 2003, p. A12. Ibid. David Hockney, "The Massacre and the Problems of Depiction," *Times Literary Supplement* May 2, 2003, p. 36.

2004: Jeremy Lewis, *Grub Street Irregular,* 2008, after Sykes, *The Biography, Vol. 2,* p. 359. David Hockney and Allen Jones, "Top Drawers," *Guardian,* May 26, 2004 (online). Weschler, *True to Life,* p. 426.

2005: Hockney 2006 in Sykes, *The Biography, Vol. 2,* p. 362. David Pagel, "Rustic Rides with David Hockney," *Los Angeles Times,* Mar 11, 2005 (online). Weschler, *True to Life,* p. 420. *David Hockney: My Yorkshire,* interviews by Marco Livingstone, London: Enitharmon Editions, p. 13f. "Hockney Leads Smoking Ban Protest," *BBC News,* Sep 28, 2005 (online).

2006: Weschler, *True to Life,* p. 447. Hockney in Sykes, *The Biography, Vol. 2,* p. 365. Hockney in the *Times,* Sep 2, 2006, after Sykes, *The Biography, Vol. 2,* p. 363. Sarah Howgate, "The Three David Hockneys," *Times,* Oct 25, 2006 (online).

2007: Martin Gayford, *A Bigger Message: Conversations with David Hockney,* London: Thames and Hudson, 2011, p. 70f. Ibid., p. 65. Bryan Appleyard, "Royal Academy Summer Exhibition," *Sunday Times,* Jun 10, 2007, retrieved from bryanappleyard.com. Martin Gayford, "A Rare Case Where Bigger May Be Better," *Telegraph,* May 26, 2007 (online). Norman Rosenthal in *David Hockney: A Bigger Picture,* London: Royal Academy of the Arts, 2012, after Sykes, *The Biography, Vol. 2,* p. 368.

2008: Gayford, *A Bigger Message,* p. 81. Ibid., p. 76. Livingstone, *My Yorkshire,* p. 28f. Ibid., p. 29. Ibid., p. 39. Hockney Nov 2008, published in the press release for *Drawing in a Printing Machine,* L.A. Louver, Venice, CA, Feb 2009 (online). Livingstone, *My Yorkshire,* p. 39.

2009: Geordie Greig, "David Hockney, iPriest of Art," *London Evening Standard,* Apr 30, 2009 (online). Hockney in the press release for *David Hockney's Fresh Flowers: Drawings on iPhones and iPads,* Royal Ontario Museum, Toronto 2011 (online). Carol Kino, "David Hockney's Long Road Home," *New York Times,* Oct 15, 2009 (online). Stephen Mueller, "David Hockney: New York City, at Pace Wildenstein," *Art in America,* Jan 15, 2010 (online).

2010: Exhibition brochure for *David Hockney's Fresh Flowers,* Royal Ontario Museum, Toronto 2011, p. 8. Gayford, *A Bigger Message,* p. 148. Ibid., p. 149. Ibid., p. 153. Hockney Jul 2011 to Gregory Evans, after Sykes, *The Biography, Vol. 2,* p. 384. Gayford, *A Bigger Message,* p. 233f.

2011: Martin Gayford, "The Mind's Eye," *MIT Technology Review,* Aug 23, 2011 (online). Rebecca Rose, "On the Hockney Trail," *Financial Times,* Dec 9, 2011 (online).

2012: Hockney in *A Bigger Picture,* after Sykes, *The Biography, Vol. 2,* p. 390. Rachel Campbell-Johnston, "David Hockney: A Bigger Picture at the Royal Academy," *Times,* Jan 16, 2012 (online). Martin Kettle, "David Hockney Is Still an Artist Who Genuinely Matters," *Guardian,* Jan 18, 2012 (online). "David Hockney's Yorkshire Spring Drawings," *Guardian,* Apr 18, 2014 (online). Ibid.

2013: "Yorkshire Spring Drawings," ibid. Nicholas Wroe, "David Hockney on Assistant's Death," *Guardian,* May 24, 2013 (online). Caroline Daniel, "David Hockney Returns to LA," *Financial Times,* Oct 11, 2013 (online). Roberta Smith, "Returning Home, But Always Going Forward," *New York Times,* Dec 23, 2013 (online).

2014: Martin Gayford, "David Hockney Reveals What Life Is Like in His Los Angeles Studio," *It's Nice That,* May 3, 2016 (online). Ibid. Ibid. Ryan Steadman, "Motherwell and Hockney, Two 20th Century Titans, Star in Major Chelsea Shows," *Observer,* Nov 12, 2014 (online).

2015–2016: Francis Hodgson, "David Hockney: Painting and Photography," *Financial Times,* May 22, 2015 (online). Rachel Campbell-Johnston, "Visual Art: David Hockney, Royal Academy," *Times,* Jun 28, 2016 (online). David Hockney and Martin Gayford, *A History of Pictures,* London: Thames and Hudson, 2016, p. 10. Ibid., p. 334. "David Hockney: 'When I Paint, I Feel I'm 30,'" *Channel 4 News,* posted on YouTube, May 14, 2015.

PHOTO CREDITS

All photographs © David Hockney, 2020
(photo Richard Schmidt on cover, pp. 5, 9,
10, 11, 13, 17, 37 bottom right, 38 bottom,
60 bottom, 61, 72, 74–75, 90–91, 98–99,
119 bottom, 129, 151, 158, 159, 166,
174–175, 179, 181, 182 bottom, 188–189,
190, 192–193, 201 bottom, 207, 209–213,
219 top, 220, 221 bottom, 225, 229 top left,
236 top, 245, 248–249, 252–253, 258–259,
267 top, 275–277, 284–285, 286–287, 293,
300 bottom, 302–303, 307 bottom left,
316 top, 317 top left, 317 top right,
325 bottom, 328–329, 333, 336–337, 339,
341, 347, 350 top, 350 bottom, 352–353,
357, 358, 359, 360 bottom, 361, 368–371,
376, 377, 402 bottom, 403 center and bottom,
409, 412–413, 421, 429, 437, 454–455, 474,
475, 494–495; photo Boab Tryckeri on p.
228/229 below; photo Jean-Pierre Gonçalves
de Lima on pp. 399, 401, 414, 415, 427,
432–433, 435, 443, 451, 461, 471, 478
bottom, 481, 489, 497, 502; photo Jonathan
Wilkinson on pp. 448, 449, 466–467)

Except photographs pp. 15, 20, 25, 39, 51, 53,
79, 106–107, 163: © Tate, London 2020
pp. 19, 21 photo Paul Oszvald
p. 23: Private Collection, photo © Geoffrey
Reeve / Bridgeman Images
p. 27 bottom: © P&O Heritage Collection
pp. 28 top, 30/31, 49, 62–63, 81 top, 147,
187, 383 top right, 383 bottom, 384–385,
402 top and center, 403 top: Prudence
Cuming Associates
p. 33: Sotheby's, London
p. 35 top left: Pinakothek der Moderne,
Munich
p. 35 top right: The Ferens Art Gallery, Hull,
England
p. 37 top: Museu Coleção Berardo, photo
© Jos. Manuel Costa Alves
pp. 41, 85: Private Collection, photo © The

Lewinski Archive at Chatsworth / Bridgeman
Images
pp. 44, 52 bottom left, 82 top, 88 bottom:
Christie's
pp. 52 bottom right, 156 top: Frank J. Thomas
pp. 54–55: Adam Reich
pp. 57: © Cecil Beaton Studio Archive at
Sotheby's
pp. 64–65, 89: Getty Research Institute,
Los Angeles (2001.M.1)
p. 67: Jane Bown © Guardian News & Media
Ltd 2016
p. 69 bottom: Museum of Modern Art / Art
Resources, NY
p. 73: Rheinisches Bildarchiv Köln
p. 77: Tony Evans / Getty Images
p. 80: Peter Mallet
pp. 60 top, 82 bottom, 148 bottom,
307 bottom right: Sotheby's
p. 87 top: National Portrait Gallery, London
p. 87 bottom: © Tate, London 2020, photo
Dave Lambert
p. 93: Picture Press / Camera Press / Cecil
Beaton
p. 101: Jack Garofalo / Paris Match via
Getty Images
p. 103 top: © Devonshire Collection,
Chatsworth, reproduced by permission of
Chatsworth Settlement Trustees
pp. 103 bottom, 112 bottom: Arts Council,
Southbank Centre, London
p. 105: Courtesy Whitechapel Gallery /
Whitechapel Gallery Archive
p. 109: Michael Ward / Getty Images
p. 113 top: The Art Institute of Chicago,
restricted gift of Mr. and Mrs. Solomon B.
Smith, photo © The Art Institute of Chicago
p. 117: © Estate of Bob Collins / National
Portrait Gallery, London
p. 120 top: Louisiana Museum of Modern
Art / Finn Brødum
p. 123: Metropolitan Museum of Art
pp. 124–125: Art Gallery of New South Wales,
The Lewis Collection, photo AGNSW

ADDITIONAL THANKS TO

Rob Berg
Alex Calderon
James Comer
Patty Choxon
Juan Carlos Elizondo
Sidney B. Felsen
Peter Goulds
Julie Green
Jill Iredale
David Juda
Shannan Kelly
Jim McHugh
Jonathan Mills
Greg Rose
Carol Savoie
Richard Schmidt
Robin Silver
George Snyder
Chris Stephens
David Thompson
Paul Thompson
Jonathan Wilkinson
Linda Wilkinson
Elise Wille

—DH and HWH

David Hockney – A Chronology
Edited by David Hockney and Hans Werner Holzwarth
with Jean-Pierre Gonçalves de Lima
Text by Lutz Eitel

Design: Hans Werner Holzwarth
Editorial assistance: Lutz Eitel, Julia Schneider, Matthias Zschaler

© 2025 TASCHEN GmbH
Hohenzollernring 53, D-50672 Köln,
www.taschen.com

Printed in Bosnia-Herzegovina
ISBN 978-3-8365-8249-0